CCNA®

Certificatio

Study Guid

Volume 1

Exam 200-301 v1.1

Second Edition

CCNA®

Certification

Study Guide

Volume 1

Exam 200-301 v1.1

Second Edition

Todd Lammle

Donald Robb

SYBEX

A Wiley Brand

Published by John Wiley & Sons, Inc., Hoboken, New Jersey.
Published simultaneously in Canada and the United Kingdom.

ISBNs: 9781394213016 (paperback), 9781394213030 (ePDF), 9781394213023 (ePub)

For general information on our other products and services, please contact our Customer Care Department within the United States at (800) 762-2974, outside the United States at (317) 572- 3993. For product technical support, you can find answers to frequently asked questions or reach us via live chat at https://sybexsupport.wiley.com.

Wiley also publishes its books in a variety of electronic formats. Some content that appears in print may not be available in electronic formats. For more information about Wiley products, visit our website at www.wiley.com.

Library of Congress Control Number: 2024948040

Cover image: © Getty Images Inc./Jeremy Woodhouse
Cover design: Wiley

SKY10087853_101524

Acknowledgments

Many people helped us build the new CCNA books in 2024 and 2025. First, Kenyon Brown helped me put together the book direction and managed the internal editing at Wiley. Thank you, Ken, for working diligently for many months to keep these books moving along.

Thanks also to Kim Wimpsett, my most excellent and highly dependable development editor at Wiley for well over a decade. She always does an excellent job, and I refuse to work on a book without her now!

We'd also like to thank John Sleeva and Tiffany Tayler for their hard work and edits in books one and two, respectively. They really helped us create fine-tuned books.

In this book, I enjoyed collaborating with Donald Robb from Canada. He played a crucial role in crafting the new table of contents and was instrumental in writing, editing, and thoroughly addressing the latest exam topics across various chapters. His expertise is unparalleled, and he worked tirelessly alongside me daily to bring this book to life. I'm confident you'll appreciate his contributions as much as I do. You can connect with Donald through his well-known blog at `https://the-packet-thrower.com`. He also serves as a leading moderator and contributor on Reddit: `https://www.reddit.com/r/ccna`.

About the Authors

Todd Lammle is widely regarded as one of the foremost authorities on Cisco certification and internetworking, holding certifications across nearly every Cisco certification category. With a career spanning more than three decades, Todd has established himself as a globally recognized author, speaker, trainer, and consultant. His expertise extends across a broad range of technologies, including LANs, WANs, and large-scale enterprise wireless networks, both licensed and unlicensed. In recent years, he has specialized in implementing extensive Cisco security networks, particularly using Firepower/FTD and ISE.

What sets Todd apart is his deep, hands-on experience, which is evident in his writing and training materials. He's not just an author; he's a seasoned networking engineer with practical knowledge gained from working on some of the largest and most complex networks in the world. His experience includes significant contributions to companies such as Xerox, Hughes Aircraft, Texaco, AAA, Cisco, and Toshiba, among many others. This real-world experience allows Todd to bring a unique, practical perspective to his work, making his books and training sessions invaluable resources for IT professionals at all levels.

Todd has authored more than 120 books, solidifying his reputation as a leading voice in the industry. Some of his most popular titles include the *CCNA: Cisco Certified Network Associate Study Guide*, *CCNA Wireless Study Guide*, *CCNA Data Center Study Guide*, *CCNP SNCF (Firepower)*, and *CCNP Security*. All of these works are published by Sybex, a respected name in technical publishing.

In addition to his writing and speaking engagements, Todd runs an international consulting and training company based in Idaho. His company provides expert guidance and training to organizations around the world, helping them to navigate the complexities of modern networking technologies. Despite his busy professional life, Todd still finds time to enjoy the natural beauty of Idaho, often spending his free time at the lake in the mountains, where he enjoys the outdoors with his beloved golden retrievers.

For those looking to dive deeper into Todd Lammle's work, you can find his extensive range of books at `https://www.lammle.com/order-our-books`. Additionally, Todd is accessible to his readers and clients through his website at `www.lammle.com`, where you can find more resources, updates, and ways to connect with him directly.

Donald Robb, widely recognized online as "The Packet Thrower," brings over two decades of experience in the IT industry. His career has spanned a diverse array of roles, beginning with help desk support and evolving into a position as one of the most respected consultants in the field. Donald has honed expert-level skills across various IT domains, including networking, security, collaboration, data center management, wireless technologies, and service providers. His depth of knowledge and technical expertise have made him a sought-after professional in the industry.

Currently, Donald is a principal network architect for Walt Disney Studios. In this role, he serves as a subject matter expert on various technologies, playing a critical role in shaping the company's network architecture and ensuring its reliability and performance. His work involves leading the design and implementation of complex networks and guiding teams and stakeholders through the technical intricacies of modern IT infrastructures.

Over the years, Donald has collaborated with major industry vendors and smaller, specialized companies, earning many advanced certifications along the way. His achievements include becoming a double JNCIE and obtaining most of Cisco's professional-level certifications, demonstrating his deep technical proficiency and commitment to continuous learning. His expertise has also been recognized through his selection as a Cisco Champion for four consecutive years, an honor awarded to top influencers in the networking community.

In addition to his hands-on work in the field, Donald has made significant contributions to IT education. He has had the privilege of working alongside Todd Lammle, a legendary figure in the IT world, coauthoring several books and developing courses that have helped countless professionals advance their careers. Through his extensive experience, certifications, and educational efforts, Donald Robb has solidified his reputation as a leading authority in the IT industry.

Contents at a Glance

Contents

Introduction

Welcome to the exciting world of Cisco certification! If you've picked up this book because you want to improve yourself and your life with a better, more satisfying, and secure job, you've done the right thing. Whether your plan is to enter the thriving, dynamic IT sector or to enhance your skill set and advance your position within it, being Cisco certified can seriously stack the odds in your favor to help you attain your goals.

Cisco certifications are powerful instruments of success that also just happen to improve your grasp of all things internetworking. As you progress through this book, you'll gain a complete understanding of networking that reaches far beyond Cisco devices. By the end of this book, you'll comprehensively know how disparate network topologies and technologies work together to form the fully operational networks that are vital to today's very way of life in the developed world. The knowledge and expertise you'll gain here are essential for and relevant to every networking job. It's why Cisco certifications are in such high demand—even at companies with few Cisco devices!

NOTE For up-to-the-minute updates covering additions or modifications to the Cisco certification exams, as well as additional study tools, review questions, videos, and bonus materials, be sure to visit the Todd Lammle website and forum at `www.lammle.com/ccna`.

Cisco's Network Certifications

Way back in 1998, obtaining the Cisco Certified Network Associate (CCNA) certification was the first pitch in the Cisco certification climb. It was also the official prerequisite to each of the more advanced levels. But that changed in 2007, when Cisco announced the Cisco Certified Entry Network Technician (CCENT) certification. Then again, in May 2016, Cisco announced new updates to the CCENT and CCNA Routing and Switching (R/S) tests. Today, things have changed dramatically again.

In July 2019, Cisco switched up the certification process more than they have in the last 20 years! They announced all-new certifications that started in February 2020, and then again, an update and revision in the summer of 2024, which is probably why you're reading this book!

So what's changed? For starters, the CCENT course and exam (ICND1 and ICND2) no longer exist, nor do the terms Routing & Switching (rebranded to Enterprise). On top of that, the CCNA is no longer a prerequisite for any of the higher certifications at all, meaning that you'll be able to jump straight to CCNP without having to take the new CCNA exam if you have already achieved the CCNA or have enough background to skip the CCNA.

The new Cisco certification process will look like this:

FIGURE I.1 The Cisco certification path

Entry	Associate	Professional	Expert
Starting point for individuals interested in starting a career as a networking professional.	Master the essentials needed to launch a rewarding career and expand your job possibilities with the latest technologies.	Select core technology track and a focused concentration exam to customize your professional-level certification.	This certification is accepted worldwide as the most prestigious certification in the technology industry.
Cisco Certified Support Technician (CCST)	CCNA	CCNP Enterprise	CCIE Enterprise Infrastructure

First, the CCST entry-level certification was added, and you can find the Wiley Study Guide for the CCST Network book authored by Todd Lammle and Donald Robb, as well as this CCNA Study Guide, at `https://www.lammle.com/order-our-books`.

If you have an entry-level network background, you will want to head directly to CCNA, using this book and the abundant resources on `www.lammle.com/ccna`, of course!

The Todd Lammle CCNA program, beginning with this book, is a powerful tool to get you started in your CCNA studies, and it's vital to understand the material found in this book and at `www.lammle.com/ccna` before you go on to conquer any other certifications!

What Does This Book Cover?

This first book in the CCNA series covers everything you need to know regarding internetworking, Ethernet, switching, and routing. Volume II starts right where this first book in the series leaves off.

But regardless of which Cisco certification path you choose, as I've said, taking plenty of time to study and practice with routers or a router simulator is the real key to success.

You will learn the following information in this book:

Chapter 1: Network Fundamentals In Chapter 1, you will learn the basics of network fundamentals, the Cisco three-layer model, and wide area networks. Ethernet cabling including, fiber-optic, is discussed. The chapter ends with an overview of PoE. Review questions await you at the end to test your understanding of the material.

Chapter 2: Ethernet Networking Chapter 2 provides you with the Ethernet foundation you need in order to pass both the CCST and CCNA exams. Data encapsulation is discussed in detail in this chapter as well. As with the other chapters, this chapter includes written labs and review questions to help you.

Chapter 3: TCP/IP Chapter 3 covers the protocols of TCP/IP. I'll begin by exploring the DoD's version of TCP/IP, then compare that version and its protocols with the OSI reference model. Lastly, I'll dive into the world of IP addressing and the different classes of IP addresses used in networks today. Review questions are included at the end of the chapter to test your understanding of the material.

Chapter 4: Easy Subnetting Chapter 4 picks up right where we left off in the last chapter and continues to explore the world of IP addressing. The chapter opens by showing you how to subnet an IP network. Prepare yourself because being able to subnet quickly and accurately is pretty challenging. Use the review questions to test your ability to understand subnetting. You can also use the bonus tools found at www.lammle.com/ccna.

Chapter 5: Troubleshooting IP Addressing Chapter 5 covers IP address troubleshooting while focusing on the steps Cisco recommends following when troubleshooting an IP network. Working through this chapter will hone your knowledge of IP addressing and networking while refining the essential skills you've attained so far.

Chapter 6: Cisco's Internetworking Operating System (IOS) Chapter 6 introduces you to the Cisco Internetworking Operating System (IOS) and command-line interface (CLI). You'll learn how to turn on a router and configure the basics of the IOS, including setting passwords, banners, and more. Be sure to complete the written lab and review questions.

Chapter 7: Managing a Cisco Internetwork Chapter 7 covers the finer points of layer 2 switching to ensure that you know exactly how it works. You should already know that we rely on switching to break up large collision domains into smaller ones and that a collision domain is a network segment with two or more devices sharing the same bandwidth. Switches have changed the way networks are designed and implemented. If a pure switched design is implemented well, the result will be a clean, cost-effective, and resilient internetwork.

Chapter 8: Managing Cisco Devices Chapter 8 describes the boot process of Cisco routers, the configuration register, and how to manage Cisco IOS files. The chapter finishes with a section on Cisco's new licensing strategy for IOS. The written labs and review questions will help you build a strong foundation for the objectives covered in this chapter.

Chapter 9: IP Routing Chapter 9 focuses on the core topic of the ubiquitous IP routing process. It's integral to networking because it pertains to all routers and configurations that use it—easily the lion's share. IP routing is basically the process of moving packets from one network to another network using routers, and this chapter covers IP routing in depth.

Chapter 10: Open Shortest Path First Chapter 10 discusses Open Shortest Path First (OSPF), which is by far the most popular and important routing protocol in use today—so important that I'm devoting an entire chapter to it! The chapter begins with the basics by completely familiarizing you with key OSPF terminology.

Chapter 11: Enhanced IGRP Chapter 11 covers Enhanced IGRP (EIGRP), which is a Cisco-proprietary routing protocol that has been available for other companies to add to their router operating systems for a few years now. This advanced distance-vector routing protocol is covered in depth, including exam essentials, a written lab, and review questions.

Chapter 12: Layer 2 Switching Chapter 12 provides the solid background you need on layer two switching, how switches perform address learning, and how to make forwarding and filtering decisions. In addition, switch port security with MAC addresses is covered in detail. As always, go through the hands-on labs, written lab, and review questions to make sure you've really got layer two switching down!

Chapter 13: VLANs and Inter-VLAN Routing Chapter 13 discusses how we break up broadcast domains in a pure switched internetwork. We do this by creating virtual local area networks (VLANs). We'll also guide you through troubleshooting techniques in this all-important chapter. The written lab and review questions reinforce the VLAN material.

Chapter 14: Cloud and Virtual Private Networks Chapter 14 provides in-depth coverage of VPNs. You'll learn some smart solutions that will help you meet your company's off-site network access needs and dive deep into how these networks utilize IP security to provide secure communications over a public network via the Internet using VPNs with IPsec. This VPN section wraps up by demonstrating how to create a tunnel using GRE (Generic Routing Encapsulation). We'll then dive into on-premises and cloud technologies. "Private cloud" is simply a fancy term for hosting resources inside your physical environment, usually in a data center. You might have heard the saying that "cloud is just using someone else's data center," but this time, we are referring to yours! Generally speaking, the terms "private cloud" and "on-premises" are used interchangeably.

Chapter 15: Introduction to Artificial Intelligence and Machine Learning Chapter 15 dives into the new and exciting world of machine learning and generative AI. By the end of the chapter, you will understand how they work and why they are beneficial to understand as a networking professional. We will even get into practical examples!

Appendix A: Answers to the Written Labs This appendix provides the answers to the end-of-chapter written labs.

Appendix B: Answers to the Review Questions This appendix provides the answers to the end-of-chapter review questions.

Interactive Online Learning Environment and Test Bank

The interactive online learning environment that accompanies the *CCNA Certification Study Guide* provides a test bank with study tools to help you prepare for the certification exams and increase your chances of passing them the first time! The test bank includes the following elements:

Sample Tests All of the questions in this book are provided in the test bank, including the assessment test, which you'll find at the end of this introduction, and the review questions at the end of each chapter. In addition, you'll find a bonus exam. Use these questions to test your knowledge of the study guide material. The online test bank runs on multiple devices.

Electronic Flashcards The flashcards are included for quick reference and are great tools for learning quick facts. You can even consider these as additional simple practice questions, which is essentially what they are.

PDF of Glossary of Terms There is a glossary included that covers the key terms used in this book.

NOTE The Sybex Interactive Online Test Bank, flashcards, and glossary can be accessed at `http://www.wiley.com/go/Sybextestprep`.

Todd Lammle Bonus Material and Labs Be sure to check `www.lammle.com/ccna` for directions on how to download all the latest bonus material created specifically to help you study for your CCNA exam.

Todd Lammle Videos I have created a full CCNA series of videos that can be purchased at `www.lammle.com/ccna`.

NOTE Like all exams, the CCNA certification is updated periodically and may eventually be retired or replaced. At some point after Cisco is no longer offering this exam, the old editions of our books and online tools will be retired. If you have purchased this book after the exam was retired, or you are attempting to register in the Sybex online learning environment after the exam was retired, please know that we make no guarantees that this exam's online Sybex tools will be available once the exam is no longer available.

CCNA Exam Overview

Cisco has designed the new CCNA program to prepare you for today's associate-level job roles in IT technologies. The CCNA now includes security and automation and programmability, and there is even a new CCNA DevNet certification. The new CCNA program has one certification that covers a broad range of fundamentals for IT careers.

The new CCNA certification covers a huge number of topics, including:

- Network fundamentals
- Network access
- IP connectivity
- IP services

- Security fundamentals
- Wireless
- Automation and programmability

Are There Any Prerequisites for Taking the CCNA Exam?

Not really, but having experience is really helpful. Cisco has no formal prerequisites for CCNA certification, but you should understand the exam topics before taking the exam.

CCNA candidates often also have:

- One or more years of experience implementing and administering Cisco solutions
- Knowledge of basic IP addressing
- A good understanding of network fundamentals

How to Use This Book

If you want a solid foundation for the serious effort of preparing for the new CCNA exam, then look no further. I've spent hundreds of hours putting together this book with the sole intention of helping you pass the Cisco exams, as well as really learning how to correctly configure Cisco routers and switches!

This book is loaded with valuable information, and you will get the most out of your study time if you understand the way in which the book is organized.

To maximize your benefit from this book, I recommend the following study method:

1. Take the assessment test that's provided at the end of this introduction. (The answers are at the end of the test.) It's okay if you don't know any of the answers; that's why you bought this book! Carefully read over the explanations for any questions you get wrong and note the chapters where the relevant material relevant is covered. This information should help you plan your study strategy.
2. Study each chapter carefully, making sure you fully understand the information and the test objectives listed at the beginning of each one. Pay extra-close attention to any chapter that includes material covered in questions you missed.
3. Answer all of the review questions related to each chapter. (The answers appear in Appendix A.) Note the questions that confuse you and study the topics they cover again until the concepts are crystal clear. And again—do not just skim these questions! Make sure you fully comprehend the reason for each correct answer. Remember, these will not be the exact questions you will find on the exam, but they're written to help you understand the chapter material and ultimately pass the exam!
4. Try your hand at the practice questions that are exclusive to this book. The questions can be found only at `http://www.wiley.com/go/sybextestprep`. Don't forget to

check out `www.lammle.com/ccna` for the most up-to-date Cisco exam prep questions, videos, hands-on labs, and Todd Lammle boot camps.

5. Test yourself using the flashcards, which are also found on the download link listed in step 4. These are brand-new and updated flashcards to help you prepare for the CCNA exam and a wonderful study tool!

To learn every bit of the material covered in this book, you'll have to apply yourself regularly and with discipline. Try to set aside the same time period every day to study, and select a comfortable and quiet place to do so. I'm confident that if you work hard, you'll be surprised at how quickly you will learn this material!

You can download bonus material and hands-on labs from `www.Lammle.com/ccna`, and by *doing hands-on labs every single day* in addition to using the review questions, the practice exams, the optional Todd Lammle video sections on `Lammle.com`, the electronic flashcards, and the written labs included with this book—it would actually be hard to fail the Cisco exams.

But understand that studying for the Cisco exams is a lot like getting in shape—if you do not go to the gym every day, it's not going to happen!

Where Do You Take the Exam?

You can take the CCNA Composite or any Cisco exam at any of the Pearson VUE authorized testing centers. For information, check `www.vue.com` or call 877-404-EXAM (3926).

To register for a Cisco exam, follow these steps:

1. Determine the number of the exam you want to take. (The CCNA exam number is 200-301.)
2. Register with the nearest Pearson VUE testing center. At this point, you will be asked to pay for the exam in advance. You can schedule exams up to six weeks in advance or as late as the day you want to take it—but if you fail a Cisco exam, you must wait five days before you will be allowed to retake it. If you need to cancel or reschedule your exam appointment, contact Pearson VUE at least 24 hours in advance.
3. When you schedule the exam, you'll get instructions regarding all appointment and cancellation procedures, the ID requirements, and information about the testing-center location.

Tips for Taking Your Cisco Exams

The Cisco exams contain approximately 50 questions and must be completed in about 90 minutes. It's difficult to provide exact details, as they frequently change. Typically, you need a score of around 85 percent to pass, but this can vary depending on the exam.

Many questions on the exam have answer choices that at first glance look identical—especially the syntax questions! So, remember to read through the choices carefully because close just doesn't cut it. If you get commands in the wrong order or forget one measly character, you'll get the question wrong.

Also, never forget that the right answer is the Cisco answer. In many cases, more than one appropriate answer is presented, but the *correct* answer is the one that Cisco recommends. On the exam, you will always be told to pick one, two, or three options, never "choose all that apply." The Cisco exam may include the following test formats:

- Multiple-choice single answer
- Multiple-choice multiple answer
- Drag-and-drop
- Router simulations

Cisco proctored exams will not show the steps to follow in completing a router interface configuration, but they do allow partial command responses. For example, `show run`, `sho running`, or `sh running-config` would all be acceptable.

Here are some general tips for exam success:

- Arrive early at the exam center so you can relax and review your study materials.
- Read the questions *carefully*. Don't jump to conclusions. Make sure you're clear about *exactly* what each question asks. I always tell my students, "Read twice, answer once."
- When answering multiple-choice questions that you're not sure about, use the process of elimination to get rid of the obviously incorrect answers first. Doing this greatly improves your odds if you need to make an educated guess.
- You can no longer move forward and backward through the Cisco exams, so double-check your answer before clicking Next, as you can't change your mind.

After you complete an exam, you'll get immediate online notification of your pass or fail status, along with a printed examination score report detailing your results by section. (The test administrator will provide the printed score report.)

Test scores are automatically forwarded to Cisco within 5 working days after you take the test, so you don't need to send your score to them. If you pass the exam, you'll receive confirmation from Cisco, typically within 2–4 weeks, though sometimes a bit longer.

CCNA Certification Exam 200-301 Objectives

This table shows where each exam is covered in this book series.

Objective	Volume, Chapter
1.0 Network Fundamentals	**Volume 1, Chapters 1/3/4/12/14** **Volume 2, Chapters 3/4/10/13/14**
1.1 Explain the role and function of network components	Volume 1, Chapter 1
• 1.1.a Routers	• Volume 1, Chapter 1
• 1.1.b Layer 2 and Layer 3 switches	• Volume 1, Chapter 1
• 1.1.c Next-generation firewalls and IPS	• Volume 1, Chapter 1
• 1.1.d Access points	• Volume 2, Chapter 10
• 1.1.e Controllers	• Volume 2, Chapter 10
• 1.1.f Endpoints	• Volume 1, Chapter 5
• 1.1.g Servers	• Volume 1, Chapter 5
• 1.1.h PoE	• Volume 1, Chapter 2
1.2 Describe characteristics of network topology architectures	Volume 1, Chapter 1
• 1.2.a Two-tier	• Volume 1, Chapter 1
• 1.2.b Three-tier	• Volume 1, Chapter 1 • Volume 2, Chapter 14
• 1.2.c Spine-leaf	• Volume 1, Chapter 1
• 1.2.d WAN	• Volume 1, Chapter 1
• 1.2.e Small office/home office (SOHO)	• Volume 1, Chapter 1
• 1.2.f On-premises and cloud	• Volume 1, Chapter 14
• 1.3 Compare physical interface and cabling types	• Volume 1, Chapter 2
• 1.3.a Single-mode fiber, multimode fiber, copper	• Volume 1, Chapter 2
• 1.3.b Connections (Ethernet shared media and point-to-point)	• Volume 1, Chapter 2
1.4 Identify interface and cable issues (collisions, errors, mismatch duplex, and/or speed)	Volume 1, Chapter 2
1.5 Compare TCP to UDP	Volume 1, Chapter 3

Objective	Volume, Chapter
1.6 Configure and verify IPv4 addressing and subnetting	Volume 1, Chapter 3/4/5 Volume 2, Chapter 4
1.7 Describe private IPv4 addressing	Volume 1, Chapter 3
1.8 Configure and verify IPv6 addressing and prefix	Volume 2, Chapter 3 Volume 2, Chapter 4
1.9 Describe IPv6 address types	Volume 2, Chapter 3
• 1.9.a Unicast (global, unique local, and link local)	• Volume 2, Chapter 3
• 1.9.b Anycast	• Volume 2, Chapter 3
• 1.9.c Multicast	• Volume 2, Chapter 3
• 1.9.d Modified EUI 64	• Volume 2, Chapter 3
1.10 Verify IP parameters for Client OS (Windows, Mac OS, Linux)	Volume 1, Chapter 5 Volume 2, Chapter 4
1.11 Describe wireless principles	Volume 2, Chapter 10
• 1.11.a Nonoverlapping Wi-Fi channels	• Volume 2, Chapter 10
• 1.11.b SSID	• Volume 2, Chapter 10
• 1.11.c RF	• Volume 2, Chapter 10
• 1.11.d Encryption	• Volume 2, Chapter 10
1.12 Explain virtualization fundamentals (server virtualization, containers, and VRFs)	Volume 2, Chapter 13
1.13 Describe switching concepts	Volume 1, Chapter 12
• 1.13.a MAC learning and aging	• Volume 1, Chapter 12
• 1.13.b Frame switching	• Volume 1, Chapter 12
• 1.13.c Frame flooding	• Volume 1, Chapter 12
• 1.13.d MAC address table	• Volume 1, Chapter 12
2.0 Network Access	**Volume 1, Chapter 1/8** **Volume 2, Chapter 1/6/12**
2.1 Configure and verify VLANs (normal range) spanning multiple switches	Volume 1, Chapter 13
• 2.1.a Access ports (data and voice)	• Volume 1, Chapter 13
• 2.1.b Default VLAN	• Volume 1, Chapter 13

Objective	Volume, Chapter
• 2.1.c InterVLAN connectivity	• Volume 1, Chapter 13
2.2 Configure and verify interswitch connectivity	Volume 1, Chapter 13
• 2.2.a Trunk ports	• Volume 1, Chapter 13
• 2.2.b 802.1Q	• Volume 1, Chapter 13
• 2.2.c Native VLAN	• Volume 1, Chapter 13
2.3 Configure and verify Layer 2 discovery protocols (Cisco Discovery Protocol and LLDP)	Volume 1, Chapter 8 Volume 2, Chapter 6
2.4 Configure and verify (Layer 2/Layer 3) EtherChannel (LACP)	Volume 2, Chapter 1
2.5 Interpret basic operations of Rapid PVST+ Spanning Tree Protocol	Volume 2, Chapter 1
• 2.5.a Root port, root bridge (primary/secondary), and other port names	• Volume 2, Chapter 1
• 2.5.b Port states and roles	• Volume 2, Chapter 1
• 2.5.c PortFast	• Volume 2, Chapter 1
• 2.5.d Root guard, loop guard, BPDU filter, and BPDU guard	• Volume 2, Chapter 1
2.6 Describe Cisco Wireless Architectures and AP modes	Volume 2, Chapter 11/12
2.7 Describe physical infrastructure connections of WLAN components (AP, WLC, access/trunk ports, and LAG)	Volume 2, Chapter 11/12
2.8 Describe network device management access (Telnet, SSH, HTTP, HTTPS, console, TACACS+/RADIUS, and cloud managed)	Volume 1, Chapter 8
2.9 Interpret the wireless LAN GUI configuration for client connectivity, such as WLAN creation, security settings, QoS profiles, and advanced settings	Volume 2, Chapter 11/12
3.0 IP Connectivity	**Volume 1, Chapter 9** **Volume 2, Chapter 4/8**
3.1 Interpret the components of routing table	Volume 1, Chapter 9 Volume 2, Chapter 4
• 3.1.a Routing protocol code	• Volume 1, Chapter 9
• 3.1.b Prefix	• Volume 1, Chapter 9

Objective	Volume, Chapter
• 3.1.c Network mask	• Volume 1, Chapter 9
• 3.1.d Next hop	• Volume 1, Chapter 9
• 3.1.e Administrative distance	• Volume 1, Chapter 9
• 3.1.f Metric	• Volume 1, Chapter 9
• 3.1.g Gateway of last resort	• Volume 1, Chapter 9
3.2 Determine how a router makes a forwarding decision by default	Volume 1, Chapter 9
• 3.2.a Longest prefix match	• Volume 1, Chapter 9
• 3.2.b Administrative distance	• Volume 1, Chapter 9
• 3.2.c Routing protocol metric	• Volume 1, Chapter 9
3.3 Configure and verify IPv4 and IPv6 static routing	Volume 1, Chapter 9 Volume 2, Chapter 3/4
• 3.3.a Default route	• Volume 1, Chapter 9
• 3.3.b Network route	• Volume 1, Chapter 9
• 3.3.c Host route	• Volume 1, Chapter 9
• 3.3.d Floating static	• Volume 1, Chapter 9
3.4 Configure and verify single area OSPFv2	Volume 1, Chapter 10
• 3.4.a Neighbor adjacencies	• Volume 1, Chapter 10
• 3.4.b Point-to-point	• Volume 1, Chapter 10
• 3.4.c Broadcast (DR/BDR selection)	• Volume 1, Chapter 10
• 3.4.d Router ID	• Volume 1, Chapter 10
3.5 Describe the purpose, functions, and concepts of first hop redundancy protocols	Volume 2, Chapter 8
4.0 IP Services	**Volume 1, Chapter 3/9** **Volume 2, Chapter 5/6/9**
4.1 Configure and verify inside source NAT using static and pools	Volume 2, Chapter 5
4.2 Configure and verify NTP operating in a client and server mode	Volume 2, Chapter 6

Objective	Volume, Chapter
4.3 Explain the role of DHCP and DNS within the network	Volume 1, Chapter 3/9
4.4 Explain the function of SNMP in network operations	Volume 1, Chapter 3 Volume 2, Chapter 6
4.5 Describe the use of syslog features, including facilities and severity levels	Volume 2, Chapter 6
4.6 Configure and verify DHCP client and relay	Volume 1, Chapter 9
4.7 Explain the forwarding per-hop behavior (PHB) for QoS such as classification, marking, queuing, congestion, policing, and shaping	Volume 2, Chapter 9
4.8 Configure network devices for remote access using SSH	Volume 2, Chapter 6
4.9 Describe the capabilities and functions of TFTP/FTP in the network	Volume 1, Chapter 3
5.0 Security Fundamentals	**Volume 1, Chapter 15** **Volume 2, Chapter 2/7/10/11/12/14**
5.1 Define key security concepts (threats, vulnerabilities, exploits, and mitigation techniques)	Volume 2, Chapter 7
5.2 Describe security program elements (user awareness, training, and physical access control)	Volume 2, Chapter 7
5.3 Configure and verify device access control using local passwords	Volume 2, Chapter 7
5.4 Describe security password policy elements, such as management, complexity, and password alternatives (multifactor authentication, certificates, and biometrics)	Volume 2, Chapter 7
5.5 Describe IPsec remote access and site-to-site VPNs	Volume 1, Chapter 14
5.6 Configure and verify access control lists	Volume 2, Chapter 2
5.7 Configure and verify Layer 2 security features (DHCP snooping, dynamic ARP inspection, and port security)	Volume 2, Chapter 7
5.8 Compare authentication, authorization, and accounting concepts	Volume 2, Chapter 7

Objective	Volume, Chapter
5.9 Describe wireless security protocols (WPA, WPA2, and WPA3)	Volume 2, Chapter 10
5.10 Configure and verify WLAN within the GUI using WPA2 PSK	Volume 2, Chapter 11/12
6.0 Automation and Programmability	**Volume 1, Chapter 15** **Volume 2, Chapters 14/15/16**
6.1 Explain how automation impacts network management	Volume 2, Chapter 14
6.2 Compare traditional networks with controller-based networking	Volume 2, Chapter 14
6.3 Describe controller-based, software defined architecture (overlay, underlay, and fabric)	Volume 2, Chapter 14
• 6.3.a Separation of control plane and data plane	• Volume 2, Chapter 14
• 6.3.b Northbound and Southbound APIs	• Volume 2, Chapter 14
6.4 Explain AI (generative and predictive) and machine learning in network operations	Volume 1, Chapter 15
6.5 Describe characteristics of REST-based APIs (authentication types, CRUD, HTTP verbs, and data encoding)	Volume 2, Chapter 15
6.6 Recognize the capabilities of configuration management mechanisms such as Ansible and Terraform	Volume 2, Chapter 16
6.7 Recognize components of JSON-encoded data	Volume 2, Chapter 15

How to Contact the Publisher

If you believe you have found a mistake in this book, please bring it to our attention. At John Wiley & Sons, we understand how important it is to provide our customers with accurate content, but even with our best efforts an error may occur.

In order to submit your possible errata, please email it to our Customer Service Team at `wileysupport@wiley.com` with the subject line "Possible Book Errata Submission."

Assessment Test

1. What is a network appliance that checks the state of a packet to determine whether the packet is legitimate?
   - A. Layer 2 switch
   - B. Load balancer
   - C. Firewall
   - D. LAN controller
2. Which type of organization should use a collapsed core architecture?
   - A. A large organization that requires a flexible and scalable network design
   - B. A large organization that must minimize downtime when hardware fails
   - C. A small company that needs to reduce networking costs
   - D. A small company that is expected to grow dramatically in the near future
3. Which WAN topology provides a combination of simplicity, quality, and availability?
   - A. Partial mesh
   - B. Full mesh
   - C. Point-to-point
   - D. Hub-and-spoke
4. What is the name of the layer in the Cisco borderless switched network design that is considered to be the backbone used for high-speed connectivity and fault isolation?
   - A. Data link
   - B. Access
   - C. Core
   - D. Network
   - E. Network access
5. What are two similarities between UTP Cat 5e and Cat 6a cabling? (Choose two.)
   - A. They both operate at a frequency of 500 MHz.
   - B. They both support runs of up to 55 meters.
   - C. They both support runs of up to 100 meters.
   - D. They both support speeds of at least 1 Gbps.
   - E. They both support speeds of up to 10 Gigabits.

6. Which three actions are taken in the operation of CSMA/CD when a collision occurs?
   A. A jam signal informs all devices that a collision occurred.
   B. The collision invokes a random backoff algorithm on the system involved in the collision.
   C. Each device on the Ethernet segment stops transmitting for a short time until its backoff timer expires.
   D. All hosts have equal priority to transmit after the timers have expired.
7. Which protocol does an IPv4 host use to obtain a dynamically assigned IP address?
   A. ARP
   B. DHCP
   C. CDP
   D. DNS
8. What is the authoritative source for an address lookup?
   A. A recursive DNS search
   B. The operating system cache
   C. The ISP local cache
   D. The browser cache
9. How is RFC 1918 addressing used in a network?
   A. It is used to access the Internet from the internal network without conversion.
   B. It is used in place of public addresses for Increased security.
   C. It is used with NAT to preserve public IPv4 addresses.
   D. It is used by Internet Service Providers to route over the Internet.
10. What is the capability of FTP in network management operations?
    A. It encrypts data before sending it between resources.
    B. Devices are directly connected and use UDP to pass file information.
    C. It uses separate control and data connections to move files between servers and clients.
    D. It offers proprietary support at the Session layer when transferring data.
11. Which of the following is the valid host range for the subnet on which the IP address 192.168.168.188 255.255.255.192 resides?
    A. 192.168.168.129–190
    B. 192.168.168.129–191
    C. 192.168.168.128–190
    D. 192.168.168.128–192

12. Which class of IP address provides 15 bits for subnetting?
    A. A
    B. B
    C. C
    D. D
13. Which of the following statements describe the IP address 10.16.3.65/23? (Choose two.)
    A. The subnet address is 10.16.3.0 255.255.254.0.
    B. The lowest host address in the subnet is 10.16.2.1 255.255.254.0.
    C. The last valid host address in the subnet is 10.16.2.254 255.255.254.0.
    D. The broadcast address of the subnet is 10.16.3.255 255.255.254.0.
    E. The network is not subnetted.
14. Traffic that is flowing over interface TenGigabitEthernet0/0 experiences slow transfer speeds. What is the reason for the issue?
    A. Heavy traffic congestion
    B. A duplex incompatibility
    C. A speed conflict
    D. Queuing drops
15. What is the best way to verify that a host has a path to other hosts in different networks?
    A. Ping the loopback address.
    B. Ping the remote network.
    C. Ping the local interface address.
    D. Ping the default gateway.
16. While you were troubleshooting a connection issue, a ping from one VLAN to another VLAN on the same switch failed. Which command verifies that IP routing is enabled on interfaces and that the local VLANs are up?
    A. `show ip route`
    B. `show ip interface brief`
    C. `show ip statistics`
    D. `show ip nat statistics`
17. You save the configuration on a router with the `copy running-config startup-config` command and reboot the router. The router, however, comes up with a blank configuration. What could be the problem?
    A. You didn't boot the router with the correct command.
    B. NVRAM is corrupted.
    C. The configuration register setting is incorrect.
    D. The newly upgraded IOS is not compatible with the hardware of the router.
    E. The configuration you saved is not compatible with the hardware.

18. Which command will install a right-to-use license so you can use an evaluation version of a feature?
    - A. `install right-to-use license feature` *`feature`*
    - B. `install temporary feature` *`feature`*
    - C. `license install feature`
    - D. `license boot module`

19. What is the AD of IS-IS and BGP Internal routes?
    - A. 120 and 200
    - B. 10 and 20
    - C. 15 and 20
    - D. 115 and 200

20. What of the following are drawbacks of implementing a link-state routing protocol? (Choose two.)
    - A. The large size of the topology table listing all advertised routes in the converged network
    - B. The requirement for a hierarchical IP addressing scheme for optimal functionality
    - C. The high demand on router resources to run the link-state routing algorithm
    - D. The sequencing and acknowledgment of link-state packets
    - E. The high volume of link-state advertisements in a converged network

21. You have two OSPF directly configured routers that are not forming an adjacency. What of the following should you check? (Choose three.)
    - A. Process ID
    - B. Hello and Dead timers
    - C. Link cost
    - D. Area
    - E. IP address/subnet mask

22. When do two adjacent routers enter the 2-way state?
    - A. After both routers have received Hello information
    - B. After they have exchanged topology databases
    - C. When they connect only to a DR or BDR
    - D. When they need to exchange RID information

23. Which of the following commands will place network 10.2.3.0/24 into area 0? (Choose two.)
    - A. `router eigrp 10`
    - B. `router ospf 10`

C. `router rip`

D. `network 10.0.0.0`

E. `network 10.2.3.0 255.255.255.0 area 0`

F. `network 10.2.3.0 0.0.0.255 area0`

G. `network 10.2.3.0 0.0.0.255 area 0`

24. How does STP prevent forwarding loops at OSI layer 2?

    A. TTL

    B. MAC address forwarding

    C. Collision avoidance

    D. Port blocking

25. An engineer must configure inter-switch VLAN communication between a Cisco switch and a third-party switch. Which action should be taken?

    A. Configure IEEE 802.1p

    B. Configure IEEE 802.1q

    C. Configure ISL

    D. Configure DSCP

26. Which encryption mode is used when a packet is sent from a site-to-site VPN connection where the source and destination IP address portion of a packet are unencrypted?

    A. PPTP

    B. Secure Shell

    C. Transport

    D. PPPoE

27. Which of the following are characteristics of a public cloud implementation? (Choose two.)

    A. It is owned and maintained by one party, but it is shared among multiple organizations.

    B. It enables an organization to fully customize how it deploys network resources.

    C. It provides services that are accessed over the Internet.

    D. It is a data center on the public Internet that maintains cloud services for only one company.

    E. It supports network resources from a centralized third-party provider and privately owned virtual resources.

28. Which AI subset is primarily concerned with enabling machines to interpret and understand visual data, such as images and videos?

    A. DNA Authoritative zones

    B. DNS Authoritative zones

    C. Computer vision

    D. Network Resolution Protocol

29. What is the primary benefit of using AIOps in network management?
    - A. It enhances automation and enables proactive monitoring and issue resolution.
    - B. Computer vision.
    - C. Network Resolution Protocol.
    - D. AIOps Helps determine network issues faster.

Answers to Assessment Test

1. C. Next-generation firewalls (NGFWs) perform deep packet inspection (DPI). See Chapter 1 for more information.

2. C. The collapsed core architecture, a simplified version of the three-tire model, is ideal for small- to medium-sized companies. Smaller institutions gain the advantage of using a collapsed core network while retaining the same benefits of a three-tier model. Small organizations, which often need help to afford the hardware and human resources to run a network, can benefit greatly from the collapsed core model, as it requires less oversight and reduces cost; in a traditional three-tier campus network, the core layer is typically a complex and expensive piece of hardware. The collapse core architecture eliminates this layer, reducing both cost and complexity. See Chapter 1 for more information.

3. C. Simplicity: Point-to-point communication links require minimal expertise to install and maintain. Quality: Point-to-point communication links usually offer high quality service, if they have adequate bandwidth. The dedicated capacity removes latency or jitter between the endpoints. Availability: Constant availability is essential for some applications, such as e-commerce. Point-to-point communication links provide permanent, dedicated capacity, which is required for VoIP or Video over IP. See Chapter 1 for more information.

4. C. The core layer in the Cisco borderless switched network design is the key to this implementation. See Chapter 1 for more information.

5. C, D. The following are the differences:

   Cat 5:

   Frequency: Up to 100 MHz

   Bandwidth: 100 Mbps (Fast Ethernet)

   Max Distance: 100 meters (328 feet)

   Cat 5e:

   Frequency: Up to 100 MHz

   Bandwidth: 1 Gbps (Gigabit Ethernet)

   Max Distance: 100 meters (328 feet)

   Cat 6:

   Frequency: Up to 250 MHz

   Bandwidth: 10 Gbps (10 Gigabit Ethernet)

   Max Distance: 55 meters (180 feet) for 10 Gbps; 100 meters (328 feet) for 1 Gbps

   Cat 6a:

   Frequency: Up to 500 MHz

   Bandwidth: 10 Gbps (10 Gigabit Ethernet)

   Max Distance: 100 meters (328 feet)

Cat 7:

Frequency: Up to 600 MHz

Bandwidth: 10 Gbps (10 Gigabit Ethernet)

Max Distance: 100 meters (328 feet)

Cat 8:

Frequency: Up to 2 GHz

Bandwidth: 25/40 Gbps (25/40 Gigabit Ethernet)

Max Distance: 30 meters (98 feet)

See Chapter 2 for more information.

6. A, C, D. The collision will invoke a backoff algorithm on all systems, not just those involved. See Chapter 2 for more information.

7. B. Dynamic Host Configuration Protocol (DHCP) provides IP configuration to hosts. See Chapter 3 for more information.

8. A. Technically, a recursive DNS search is the authoritative source for an address lookup for the exam. However, it is not the authoritative source but rather a middleman communicating with authoritative DNS servers to find an IP address. See Chapter 3 for more information.

9. C. The allocation of RFC 1918 permits full Network layer connectivity among all hosts inside an enterprise and among all public hosts. There is little cost of using private Internet address space. See Chapter 3 for more information.

10. C. The control connection uses very simple rules for communication. Through a control connection, we can transfer a line of a command or a line of a response at a time. The control connection is made between the control processes. The control connection remains connected during the entire interactive FTP session.

    The data connection uses very complex rules, as data types can vary. The data connection is made between data transfer processes. The data connection opens when a command is issued to transfer files and closes when the files are transferred. See chapter 3 for more information.

11. A. 256 – 192 = 64, so 64 is our block size. Just count in increments of 64 to find our subnet: 64 + 64 = 128. 128 + 64 = 192. The subnet is 128, the broadcast address is 191, and the valid host range is the numbers in between, or 129–190. See Chapter 4 for more information.

12. A. Class A addressing provides 22 bits for host subnetting. Class B provides 16 bits, but only 14 are available for subnetting. Class C provides only 6 bits for subnetting. See Chapter 4 for more information.

13. B, D. The mask 255.255.254.0 (/23) used with a Class A address means that there are 15 subnet bits and 9 host bits. The block size in the third octet is 2 (256–254), so this makes the subnets in the interesting octet 0, 2, 4, 6, etc., all the way to 254. The host 10.16.3.65 is in the 2.0 subnet. The next subnet is 4.0, so the broadcast address for the 2.0 subnet is 3.255. The valid host addresses are 2.1 through 3.254. See Chapter 4 for more information.

14. B. For the CCNA objectives, whenever you see congestion or slow speeds on an Ethernet interface, it typically is a duplex issue. See Chapter 5 for more information.

15. B. If you can ping a remote network, that is the best test for routing. See Chapter 5 for more information.

16. B. The best answer is `show ip interface brief`, which shows the interfaces, VLANs (if used), and IP addresses and their layer 1 and 2 status. See Chapter 5 for more information.

17. C. If you save a configuration and reload the router and it comes up either in setup mode or as a blank configuration, chances are the configuration register setting is incorrect. See Chapter 8 for more information.

18. D. The `license boot module` command installs a right-to-use license feature on a router. See Chapter 8 for more information.

19. D. IS-IS has a single administrative distance (trustworthiness), and BGP uses 20 for external routes and 200 for internal routes. See Chapter 9 for more information.

20. B, C. Link state uses more routing processing and memory but less bandwidth than distance vector. Also, link state must have a good network design to function and converge. See Chapter 9 for more information.

21. B, D, E. In order for two OSPF routers to create an adjacency, the Hello and Dead timers must match, be configured into the same area, and be in the same subnet. See Chapter 10 for more information.

22. A. The process starts by sending out Hello packets. Every listening router will then add the originating router to the neighbor database. The responding routers will reply with all of their Hello information so that the originating router can add them to its own neighbor table. At this point, the routers will have reached the 2-way state. Note that only certain routers will advance to this. See Chapter 10 for more information.

23. B, G. To enable OSPF, you must first start OSPF using a process ID. The number is irrelevant; choose a number from 1 to 65,535, and you're good to go. After starting the OSPF process, you must configure interfaces on which to activate OSPF using the `network` command with wildcards and an area specification. Option F is wrong because there must be a space after the parameter area and before you list the area number. See Chapter 10 for more information.

24. D. Port blocking prevents traffic from getting stuck going in circles between other ports on a layer 2 switched network. See Chapter 12 for more information.

25. B. VLAN trunking offers two options: ISL and 802.1Q. ISL is Cisco-proprietary and rarely used today, while 802.1Q is standards-based and supported by multiple vendors. See Chapter 13 for more information.

26. C. In the context of VPNs (virtual private networks), when the source and destination IP address portion of a packet is unencrypted while the actual payload of the packet is encrypted, it is using transport mode encryption. Transport mode encrypts only the data portion (payload) of the IP packet, leaving the header (which includes the source and destination

IP addresses) unencrypted. This is often used in site-to-site VPNs where the devices at the ends of the VPN tunnel are responsible for the IP header information. See Chapter 14 for more information.

27. A, C. A public cloud is a type of computing where resources are offered by a third-party provider via the internet and shared by organizations and individuals who want to use or purchase them. It is owned and maintained by one party, but it is shared among multiple organizations. Option E is incorrect because it describes a hybrid cloud model, not a public cloud model. A hybrid cloud is a type of cloud computing that combines on-premises, private cloud, and third-party public cloud services with orchestration between the platforms. This allows data and applications to be shared between them. Therefore, although a hybrid cloud includes aspects of a public cloud, it also includes private, on-premises infrastructure, which is not a characteristic of a public cloud. See Chapter 14 for more information.

28. C. Computer vision is a specialized subset of AI that focuses on enabling machines to "see" and interpret visual information from the world around them. It involves analyzing and understanding images, videos, and other visual inputs to perform tasks such as object detection, facial recognition, and image classification. This capability is crucial in applications like autonomous vehicles, security systems, and image-based diagnostics in healthcare. See Chapter 15 for more information.

29. A. AIOps, or artificial intelligence for IT operations, is a key application of AI in network management that enhances automation and allows for proactive monitoring and resolution of network issues. AIOps can analyze large amounts of data in real time, identify potential problems before they escalate, and automatically take corrective actions, thereby improving network reliability and reducing downtime. Unlike traditional reactive approaches, AIOps is designed to be proactive, helping to prevent issues rather than just responding to them. See Chapter 15 for more information.

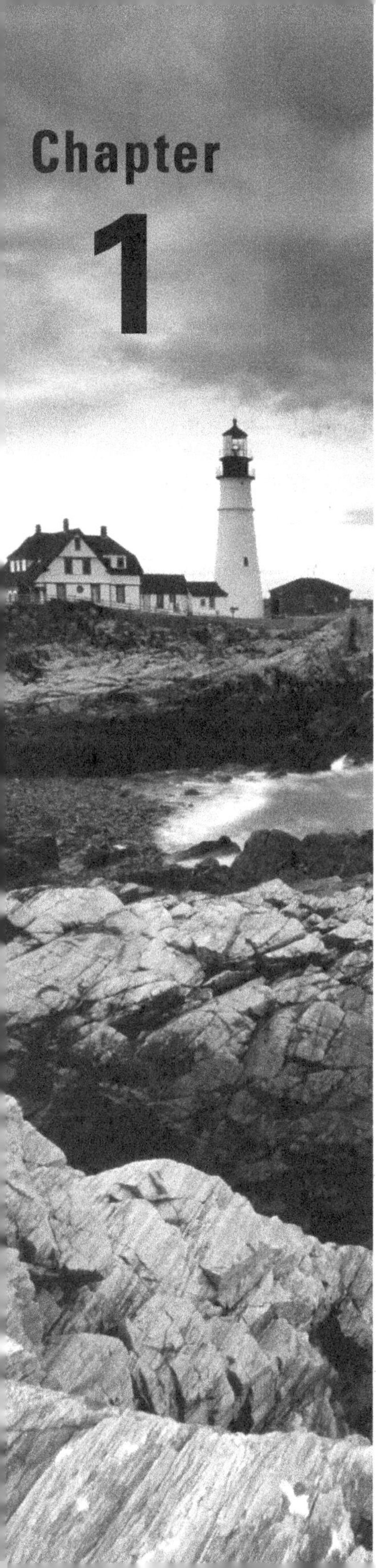

Chapter 1

Network Fundamentals

THE FOLLOWING CCNA EXAM TOPICS ARE COVERED IN THIS CHAPTER:

✓ ***1.0 Network Fundamentals***

- 1.1 Explain the role and function of network components
  - 1.1.a Routers
  - 1.1.b L2 and L3 switches
  - 1.1.c Next-generation firewalls and IPS
- 1.2 Describe characteristics of network topology architectures
  - 1.2.a Two-tier
  - 1.2.b Three-tier
  - 1.2.c Spine-leaf
  - 1.2.d WAN
  - 1.2.e Small office/home office (SOHO)

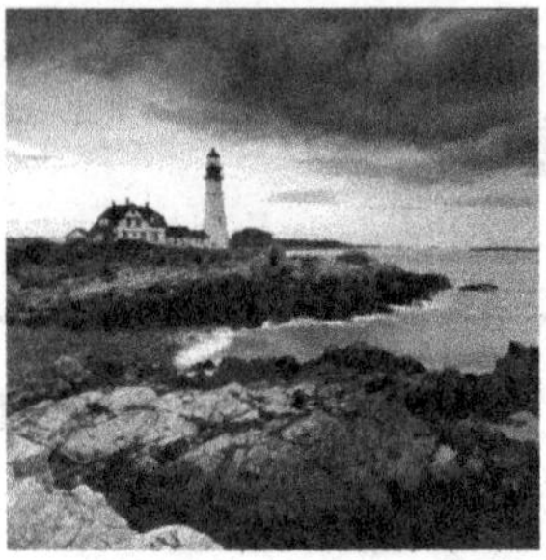

This chapter is really an internetworking review, focusing on how to connect networks together using Cisco routers and switches. As a heads-up, I've written it with the assumption that you have a bit of basic networking knowledge.

That said, there isn't a whole lot of new material here, but even if you're a seasoned network professional, you should still read through *all* the chapters to make sure you get how the objectives are currently covered.

To make sure we're all on the same page, let's define exactly what an internetwork is: you create an internetwork when you connect two or more networks via a router and configure a logical network addressing scheme with protocols like IP or IPv6.

The chapter starts by defining local area and small office/home office networks, and then covers network components like routers and switches. Next, I'll touch on next-generation firewalls and finish the chapter by talking about topology architectures and wide area networks.

> **NOTE** To find bonus material, as well as Todd Lammle videos, practice questions, and hands-on labs, please see `www.lammle.com/ccna`.

Network Components

So, why is it so important to learn Cisco internetworking, anyway?

Networks and networking have grown exponentially over the past 20 years, and understandably so. They've had to evolve at light speed to keep up with huge increases in basic mission-critical user needs, from simply sharing data and printers to bigger burdens like multimedia remote presentations, conferencing, and the like. Unless everyone who needs to share network resources is located in the same office space, the challenge is to connect relevant networks so that all users can share the wealth of whatever services and resources they need, on-site or remotely.

LANs and SOHOs

Figure 1.1 shows a basic *local area network (LAN)* connected via a *hub*, which is basically an antiquated device that connects wires together and is typically used in small office/home office (SOHO) networks.

FIGURE 1.1 A very basic SOHO network

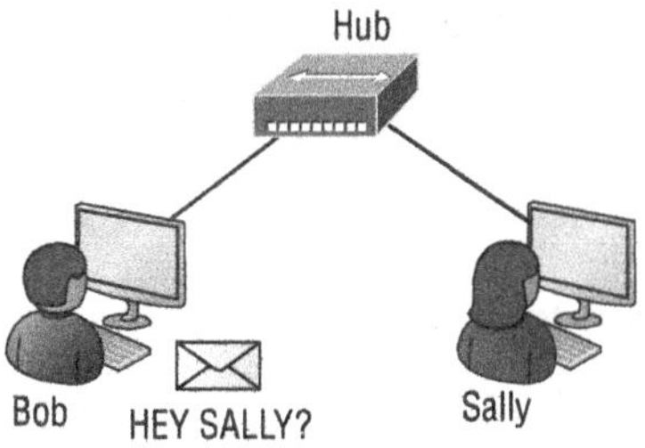

Keep in mind that a simple SOHO network like this one would be considered one collision domain and one broadcast domain.

Things really can't get much simpler than this. And yes, though you can still find this configuration in some SOHO networks, even many of those, as well as the smallest business networks are more complicated today.

Routers and Switches

Figure 1.2 shows a network that's been segmented with a switch, making each network segment that connects to the switch its own separate collision domain. Doing this results in a lot less chaos!

FIGURE 1.2 A switch can break up collision domains.

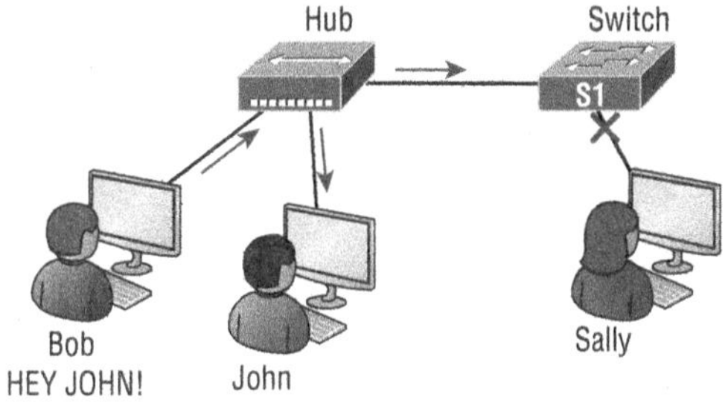

This is a great start, but I really want you to note that this network is still just one single broadcast domain. This means that we've really only reduced our PC's chaos, not eliminated it.

For example, if there's some sort of vital announcement that everyone in our network neighborhood needs to hear about, it will definitely still get loud! You can see that the hub used in Figure 1.2 just extended the one collision domain from the switch port. The result is that John received the data from Bob, but, happily, Sally did not, which is good because Bob intended to talk with John directly. If he had needed to send a broadcast instead, everyone, including Sally, would have received it, causing unnecessary congestion.

Here's a list of some of the things that commonly cause LAN traffic congestion:

- Too many hosts in a collision or broadcast domain
- Broadcast storms
- Too much multicast traffic
- Low bandwidth
- Adding hubs for connectivity to the network
- A bunch of ARP broadcasts

Take another look at Figure 1.2, and make sure you see that I extended the main hub from Figure 1.1 to a switch in Figure 1.2. I did that because hubs don't segment a network; they just connect network segments. Basically, it's an inexpensive way to connect a couple of PCs, which can work for really simple home use and troubleshooting, but that's about it!

As our community grows, we'll need to add more streets along with traffic control and even some basic security. We'll get this done by adding routers because these convenient devices are used to connect networks and route packets of data from one network to another. Cisco became the de facto standard for routers because of its unparalleled selection of high-quality router products and fantastic service. Never forget that, by default, routers are basically employed to efficiently break up a *broadcast domain*—the set of all devices on a network segment that are allowed to "hear" all broadcasts sent out on that specific segment.

Figure 1.3 depicts a router in our growing network, creating an internetwork and breaking up broadcast domains.

FIGURE 1.3 Routers create an internetwork.

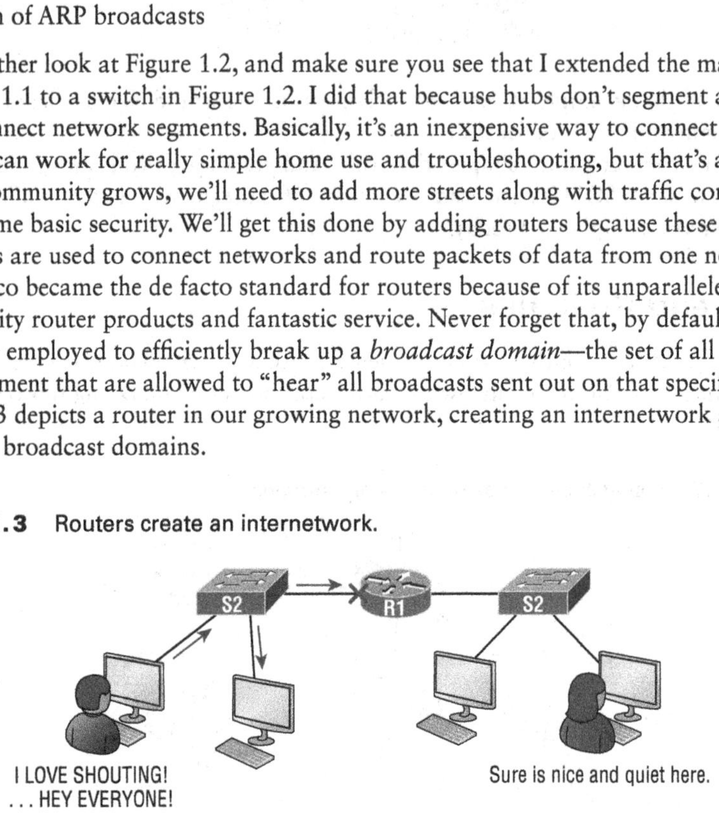
S2
R1
S2
I LOVE SHOUTING!
. . . HEY EVERYONE!
Sure is nice and quiet here.

The network in Figure 1.3 is actually a pretty cool little network. Each host is connected to its own collision domain because of the switch, and the router has created two broadcast domains. So, now Sally is happily living in peace in a completely different neighborhood, no longer subjected to Bob's incessant shouting! If Bob wants to talk with Sally, he has to send a packet with a destination address using her IP address—he cannot broadcast for her!

But there's more. Routers provide connections to wide area network services as well as via a serial interface for WAN connections—specifically, a V.35 physical interface on a Cisco router.

Let me make sure you understand why breaking up a broadcast domain is so important. When a host or server sends a network broadcast, every device on the network must read and process that broadcast—unless you have a router. When the router's interface receives this broadcast, it can respond by basically saying, "No, thanks," and discard the broadcast without forwarding it to other networks. Even though routers are known for breaking up broadcast domains by default, it's important to remember that they break up collision domains as well.

There are two advantages to using routers in your network:

- They don't forward broadcasts by default.
- They can filter the network based on layer 3 (Network layer) information such as an IP address.

Conversely, we don't use layer 2 switches to create internetworks because they don't break up broadcast domains by default; instead, they're employed to add functionality to a network LAN. The main purpose of these switches is to make a LAN work better—to optimize its performance—providing more bandwidth for the LAN's users. Also, these switches don't forward packets to other networks like routers do; instead, they only switch frames from one port to another within the switched network. And don't worry—even though you're probably thinking, "Wait—what are frames and packets?" I promise to completely fill you in later in this chapter. For now, think of a packet as a package containing data.

So, by default, switches break up collision domains, but what are these things? A *collision domain* is an Ethernet term used to describe a network scenario in which one device sends a packet out on a network segment and every other device on that same segment is forced to pay attention to it, no matter what. This isn't efficient because if a different device tries to transmit at the same time, a collision will occur, requiring both devices to retransmit one at a time—not good! And this happens a lot in a hub environment, where each host segment connects to a hub that represents only one collision domain and a single broadcast domain. By contrast, each and every port on a switch represents its own collision domain, allowing network traffic to flow much more smoothly.

Layer 2 switching is considered hardware-based bridging because it uses specialized hardware called an *application-specific integrated circuit (ASIC)*. ASICs can run up to high gigabit speeds with very low latency rates.

NOTE *Latency* is the time measured from when a frame enters a port to when it exits a port.

Switches read each frame as it passes through the network. The layer 2 device then puts the source hardware address in a filter table and keeps track of which port the frame was received on. This information—logged in the bridge's or switch's filter table—is what helps the machine determine the location of the specific sending device.

Figure 1.4 shows a switch in an internetwork and how John is sending packets to the Internet. Sally doesn't hear his frames because she's in a different collision domain. The destination frame goes directly to the default gateway router, so Sally doesn't even see John's traffic.

FIGURE 1.4 Switches work at layer 2.

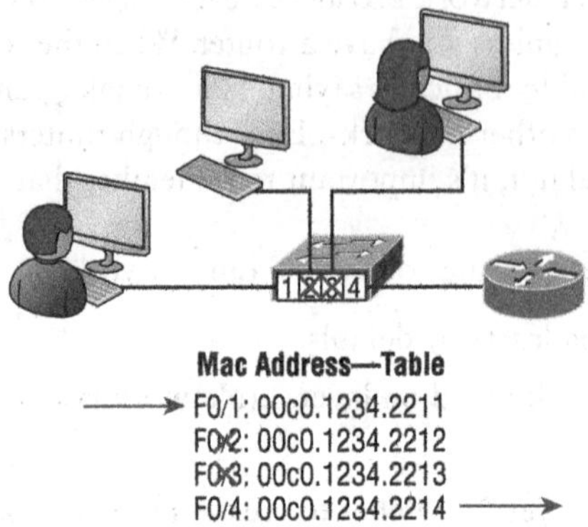

The real estate business is all about location, location, location, and it's the same way for layer 2 and layer 3 devices. Although both need to be able to negotiate the network, it's crucial to remember that they're concerned with very different parts of it. Primarily, layer 3 machines, like routers, need to locate specific networks, whereas layer 2 machines like switches and bridges need to eventually locate specific devices. So, networks are to routers as individual devices are to switches and bridges. And routing tables that "map" the internetwork are for routers as filter tables that "map" individual devices are for switches and bridges.

After a filter table is built on the layer 2 device, it will forward frames only to the segment where the destination hardware address is located. If the destination device is on the same segment as the source host, the layer 2 device will block the frame from going to any other segments. If the destination is on a different segment, the frame can be transmitted only to that segment. This is called *transparent bridging*.

When a switch interface receives a frame with a destination hardware address that isn't found in the device's filter table, it will forward the frame to all connected segments. If the unknown device that was sent the "mystery frame" replies to this forwarding action, the switch updates its filter table regarding that device's location. However, in the event that the destination address of the transmitting frame is a broadcast address, the switch will forward all broadcasts to every connected segment by default.

All devices that the broadcast is forwarded to are considered to be in the same broadcast domain. This can be a problem because layer 2 devices propagate layer 2 broadcast storms, which can seriously choke performance, and the only way to stop a broadcast storm from propagating through an internetwork is with a layer 3 device—a router!

Next-Generation Firewalls and IPS

Today's networks definitely need security, and as our network grows, we'll need to increase protection for it. Just like we'd add locks to our doors and windows, then maybe a fence, and then even a bigger fence—with a locked gate and even some barbed wire to top it off. We can go on and on here, but you get the picture.

There are new devices that are actually seriously solid firewalls. I'll mention next-generation firewalls (NGFWs) providing full layer 7 inspection, as though it's just a bump in the wire (meaning little delay), which is mostly true. However, it's totally true that every company, including Cisco, markets their devices like this.

Figure 1.5 illustrates devices in a small network and how a basic firewall or NGFW can be placed to provide security in a network.

FIGURE 1.5 The physical components of a network

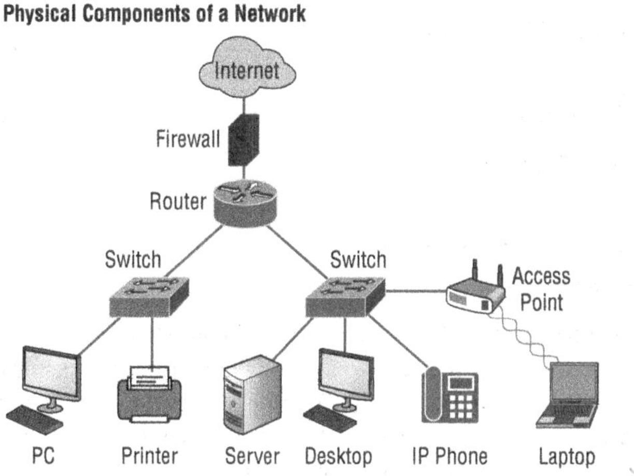

Firewall and NGFW design can be pretty complicated, but we don't need to get into the weeds here. Since this is a Cisco book, we're going to stick with Cisco technologies for our firewall. Cisco has an NGFW called Firepower, which they acquired from a company called Sourcefire in 2013.

> **NOTE** Note that this is going to be a brief introduction to NGFWs and intrusion prevention systems. Why? Because I have a two-book series, also by Sybex, on CCNP Security Securing Cisco Network Firewalls (SCNF) that covers this topic in depth with well over 1,500 pages of information! That's a lot of firewall info. We'll just get our feet wet for now.

Let's start by defining an NGFW and what it has to do with intrusion prevention systems (IPSs). NGFWs are considered third-generation firewall technology that provides full packet reassembly and deep-packet inspection up to and through layer 7.

NGFWs are popular because they permit Application Visibility and Control (AVC) as well as offer IPS policies, which help us look for attacks on known client vulnerabilities.

And no one said this technology is cheap. For example, the newer firewalls can provide SSL decryption, which sounds simple, but there's a catch: in order to be able provide that kind of shield at close to wire speed, you've got to have hardware encryption acceleration capability, which will cost you plenty!

The NGFWs today have everything but the kitchen sink in their code just to stay competitive, and this causes all sorts of issues for manufacturers when struggling to keep up with the market.

Here's a taste: all NGFWs must, at a minimum, include the following:

- Be router and switch compatible (L2/L3)
- Include packet filtering with IPS and malware inspection capability
- Provide Network Address Translation (NAT)
- Permit stateful inspection
- Permit virtual private networks (VPNs)
- Provide URL and application filtering
- Implement QoS
- Support third-party integration
- Support REST API

That's not a short list, and the items in it are all absolutely required because NGFWs must pack a powerful security punch in order to lock our modern networks down tight!

Figure 1.6 shows a Cisco Firepower NGFW blocking an attacker trying to exploit a vulnerability on my network, which IPS stopped dead. The red line on top indicates all the attacks, and the blue line is for the data. Wow—that's a lot of attacks!

Now, let's dig into those attacks. We'll see how the Cisco Firepower NGFW came to the rescue by blocking all those attacks via my IPS policy, as shown in Figure 1.6. Figure 1.7 displays some of the events that were caught by Cisco Firepower.

FIGURE 1.6 NGFW can stop attacks in real time.

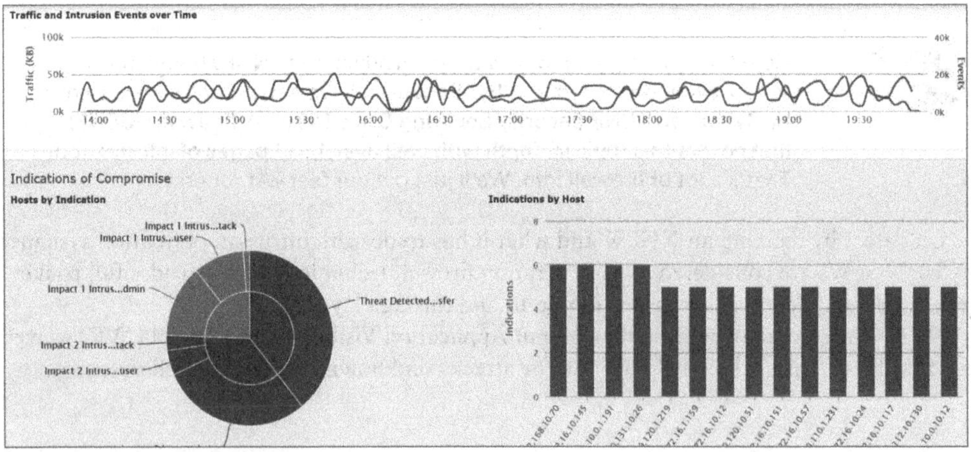

FIGURE 1.7 Cisco IPS policy to the rescue!

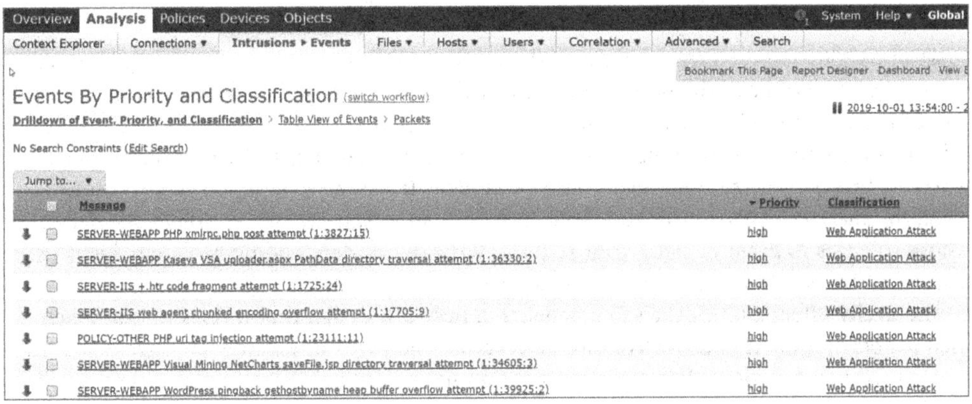

And, just so you know, some of those attacks shown in Figure 1.7 were some really serious ones! Figure 1.8 displays all the actual packets that were dropped.

FIGURE 1.8 Cisco Firepower IPS policy dropped the bad guys' packets!

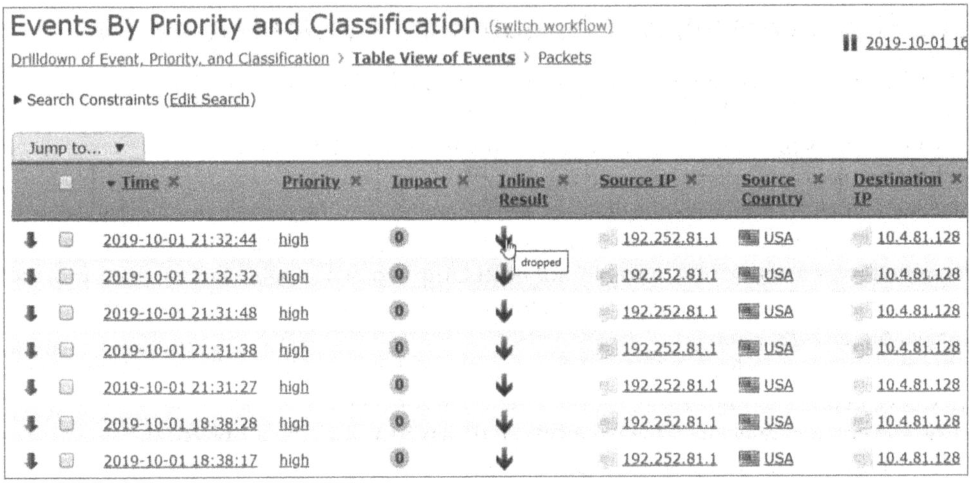

NGFWs perform a deeper inspection compared to your traditional firewall. For instance, the stateful ASA that Cisco is moving away from is being replaced with new Firepower Threat Defense (FTD) devices, which are true NGFW devices.

Network Topology Architectures

Most of us were exposed to hierarchy early in life, and anyone with older siblings learned what it was like to be at the bottom of it. Regardless of where you first discovered the concept of hierarchy, most of us experience it in many aspects of our lives. Its *hierarchy* that helps us understand where things belong, how things fit together, and what functions go where. It brings order to otherwise complex models. If you want a pay raise, for instance, hierarchy dictates that you ask your boss, not your subordinate, because that's the person whose role it is to grant or deny your request. Basically, understanding hierarchy helps us discern where we should go to get what we need.

Hierarchy offers a lot of the same benefits in network design that it does in life. When used properly, it makes networks more predictable and helps us define which areas should perform certain functions. For example, you can use tools like access lists at certain levels within hierarchical networks and avoid them at others.

Large networks can be extremely complicated, involving multiple protocols, detailed configurations, and diverse technologies. Hierarchy helps us summarize a complex collection of details into an understandable model, bringing order from the chaos. Then, as specific configurations are needed, the model dictates the correct way to apply them.

The Cisco Three-Layer Hierarchical Model (Three-Tier)

The Cisco hierarchical model can help you design, implement, and maintain a scalable, reliable, and cost-effective hierarchical internetwork.

Cisco defines three layers of hierarchy, each with specific functions, and it's referred to as a *three-tier network architecture* (see Figure 1.9).

Each layer has specific responsibilities. Keep in mind that the three layers are logical, so they aren't necessarily physical devices. Consider the OSI model, another logical hierarchy. Its seven layers describe functions but not necessarily protocols, right? Sometimes a protocol maps to more than one layer of the OSI model, and sometimes multiple protocols communicate within a single layer.

In the same way, when we build physical implementations of hierarchical networks, we may have many devices in a single layer, or there may be a single device performing functions at two layers. Just remember, the definition of the layers is logical, not physical!

Let's take a closer look at each of the layers.

Core Layer

The *core layer* is literally the core of the network. At the top of the hierarchy, this layer is responsible for transporting large amounts of traffic both reliably and quickly. The prime purpose of the network's core layer is to switch traffic as fast as possible. The traffic transported across the core is common to the majority of users, but user data is processed at the distribution layer, which forwards the requests to the core, if needed.

FIGURE 1.9 The Cisco hierarchical model

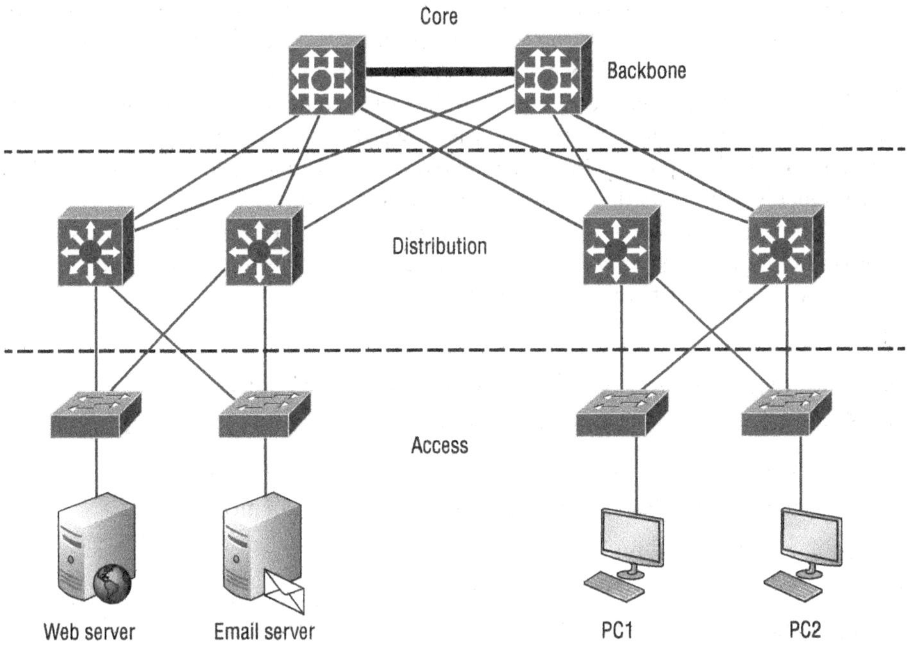

If there's a failure in the core, *every single user* can be affected! This is why fault tolerance at this layer is so important. The core is likely to see large volumes of traffic, so speed and latency are driving concerns here. Given the function of the core, some vital design specifics come into view. Let's start with things we don't want to happen here:

- Never do anything to slow down traffic. This includes making sure you don't use access lists, perform routing between virtual local area networks (VLANS), or implement packet filtering.
- Don't support workgroup access at this layer.
- Avoid expanding the core—e.g., adding routers as the internetwork grows. If performance becomes an issue in the core, go with upgrades over expansion.

Here's a list of goals we want to achieve as we design the core:

- Design the core for high reliability. Consider data-link technologies that facilitate both speed and redundancy, like 10, 40 and 100G speeds are most common in the core with redundant links or even 100 Gigabit Ethernet.
- Design with speed in mind. The core should have very little latency.
- Select routing protocols with lower convergence times. Fast and redundant data-link connectivity is no help if your routing tables are shot!

Distribution Layer

The *distribution layer*, sometimes referred to as the *workgroup layer*, is the communication point between the access layer and the core. The primary functions of the distribution layer provide routing, filtering, and WAN access and determine how packets can access the core, if needed. The distribution layer must determine the fastest way that network service requests are handled—for instance, how a file request is forwarded to a server. After the distribution layer determines the best path, it forwards the request to the core layer, if necessary. The core layer then quickly transports the request to the correct service.

The distribution layer is where we implement policies for the network because we have a lot of flexibility in defining network operation here. There are several things that should generally be handled at the distribution layer:

- Routing
- Implementing tools (like access lists), packet filtering, and queuing
- Implementing security and network policies, including address translation and firewalls
- Redistributing between routing protocols, including static routing
- Routing between VLANs and other workgroup support functions
- Defining broadcast and multicast domains

At the distribution layer, it's key to avoid anything limited to functions exclusively belonging to one of the other layers!

Access Layer

The *access layer* controls user and workgroup access to internetwork resources and is sometimes referred to as the *desktop layer*. The network resources most users need are available locally because the distribution layer handles any traffic for remote services.

Here are some of the tasks the access layer carries out:

- Continued (from distribution layer) use of access control and policies
- Creation of separate collision domains (microsegmentation/switches)
- Workgroup connectivity into the distribution layer
- Device connectivity
- Resiliency and security services
- Advanced technology capabilities (voice/video, etc.)

Technologies like Gigabit or Fast Ethernet switching are frequently seen in the access layer as well.

I can't stress this enough—just because there are three separate layers does not imply three separate devices! There could be fewer, or there could be more. After all, this is a *layered* approach.

Collapsed Core (Two-Tier)

The collapsed core design is also referred to as two-tier because it's only two layers. But in concept, it's like the three-tier only less expensive and geared for smaller companies. The design is meant to maximize performance and user availability to the network, while still allowing for design scalability over time.

In a two-tier design, the distribution is merged with the core layer, as shown in Figure 1.10.

FIGURE 1.10 Real-life collapsed core (two-tier) image

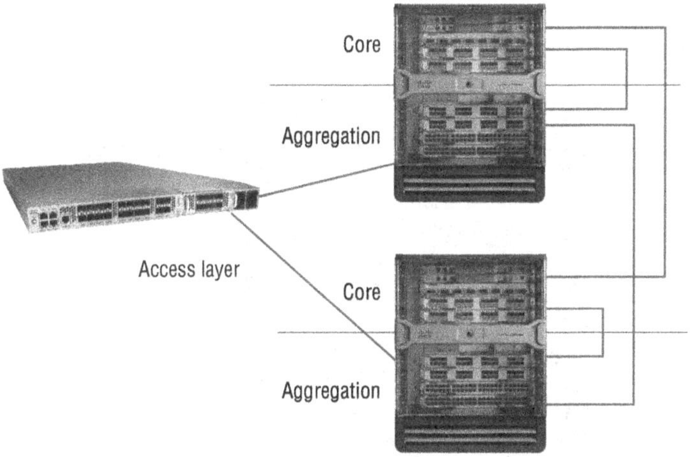

Here you see the core layer and distribution layer (also called *aggregation*) are both running on the same large enterprise switch. The access layer switches connect into the enterprise switch, only in the defined aggregation ports.

This design is much more economical, and it's still very functional in a campus environment, where your network may not grow significantly larger over time. It's known as a *collapsed core* and refers to a design in which a single device implements the distribution layer and core layer functions.

The collapsed core model is a reduced version of the three-tier model. The deduction was made to create a network for small and medium-sized campuses. This way smaller institutions can get the advantage of using a collapsed core network while still gaining the same benefits they would if they were using a three-tier model.

Small organizations often need help to afford the hardware and human resources to run the network can benefit greatly with less oversight necessary. And reduces costs: In a traditional three-tier campus network, the core layer is typically a complex and expensive piece of hardware. Collapsing core architecture eliminates this layer, reducing both cost and complexity.

Spine-Leaf

I've been writing about Cisco's three-tier network design for a really long time, and I just did again. But today's data centers demand a new design, and one was finally created that works really well called a *leaf-and-spine* topology. This design is still pretty old as of this writing; it's just not decades old!

Here's how it works: Your typical data center has racks filled with servers. In the leaf-and-spine design, there are switches found at the top of each rack that connect to these servers, with a server connecting into each switch for redundancy.

People refer to this as a *top-of-rack* (ToR) design because the switches physically reside at the top of a rack. Figure 1.11 shows a ToR network design.

FIGURE 1.11 Top-of-rack network design

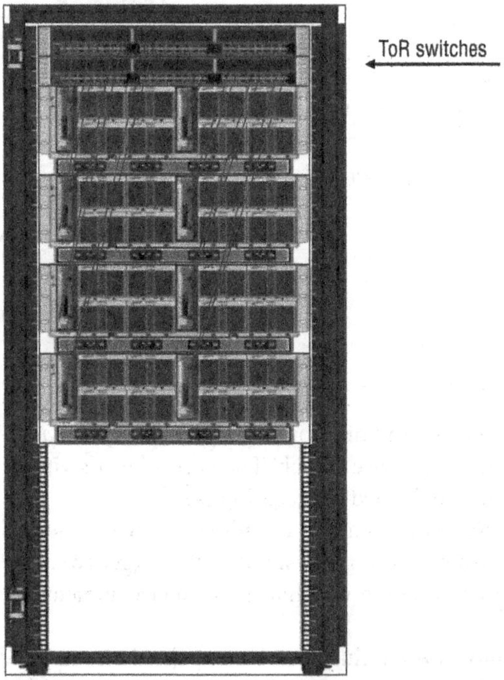

These ToR switches act as the leaves within the leaf-and-spine topology. The ports in the leaf switches connect to a node—e.g., a server in the rack, a firewall, a load-balancing appliance, or a router leaving the data center, as well as to the spine switch. Check out Figure 1.12.

You can see each leaf switch connecting to every spine switch, which is great because it means that we no longer need a gazillion connections between switches. Keep in mind that the spine only connects to leaf devices, not to servers or end devices.

FIGURE 1.12 Spine-leaf design

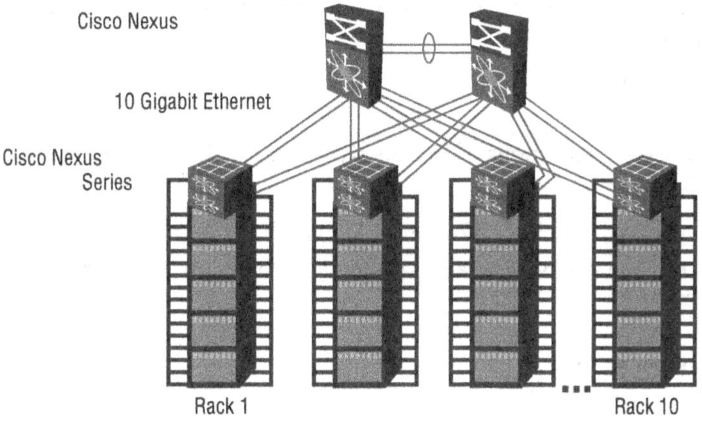

And, interestingly enough, when you connect your ToR data center switches in a leaf-and-spine topology, all of your switches are the same distance away from one another (single switch hop).

Wide Area Networks

Let's begin WAN basics by asking, what's the difference between a wide area network (WAN) and a local area network? Clearly, there's the distance factor, but modern wireless LANs can cover some serious turf, so there's more to it than that. What about bandwidth? Here again, really big pipes can be had for a price in many places, so that's not it either. So, what's the answer we're looking for?

A major distinction between a WAN and a LAN is that while you generally own a LAN infrastructure, you usually lease a WAN infrastructure from a service provider. Modern technologies sometimes blur this characteristic somewhat, but this factor still fits neatly into the context of Cisco's exam objectives.

There are several reasons why WANs are necessary in corporate environments today. LAN technologies provide pretty solid speeds—10/25/40/100 Gbps is now common—and they're definitely pricey. The thing is, these solutions really only work well in relatively small geographic areas. We still need WANs in a communications environment because some business needs require connections to remote sites for many reasons:

- People in the regional or branch offices of an organization need to be able to communicate and share data.
- Organizations often want to share information with other organizations across large distances.
- Employees who travel on company business frequently need to access information that resides on their corporate networks.

Here are three major characteristics of WANs:

- WANs generally connect devices that are separated by a broader geographic area than a LAN can serve.
- WANs use the services of carriers like telcos, cable companies, satellite systems, and network providers.
- WANs use serial connections of various types to provide access to bandwidth over large geographic areas.

The first key to understanding WAN technologies is to be familiar with the different WAN topologies, terms, and connection types commonly used by service providers to join our LANs together.

Defining WAN Terms

Before you run out and order a WAN service type from a provider, you really need to understand the following terms that service providers typically use. Figure 1.13 shows how they work together.

FIGURE 1.13 WAN terms

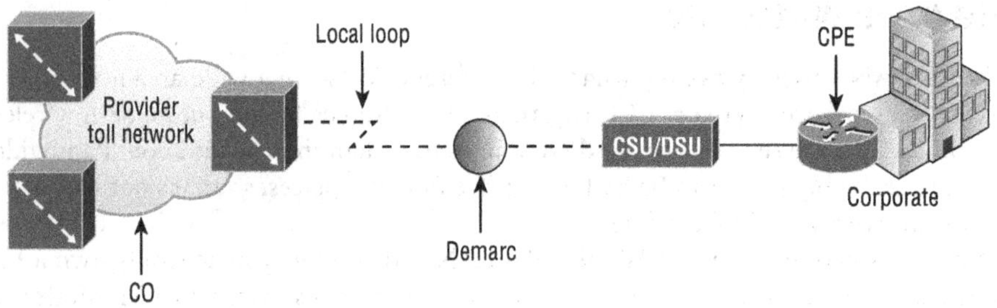

Customer Premises Equipment *Customer premises equipment (CPE)* is equipment that's typically owned by the subscriber and located on the subscriber's premises.

CSU/DSU A channel service unit/data service unit (CSU/DSU) is a device that's used to connect data termination equipment (DTE) to a digital circuit like a T1/T3 line. A device is considered DTE if it's either a source or destination for digital data—for example, PCs, servers, and routers. In Figure 1.13, the router is considered DTE because it's passing data to the CSU/DSU, which will forward the data to the service provider. Although the CSU/DSU connects to the service provider's infrastructure using a telephone or coaxial cable like a T1 or E1 line, it connects to the router with a serial cable. The most important aspect to remember for the CCNA objectives is that the CSU/DSU provides clocking of the line to the router.

Demarcation Point The *demarcation point* (demarc, for short) is the precise spot where the service provider's responsibility ends and the CPE begins. It's generally a device in a telecommunications closet owned and installed by the telecommunications company (telco). It's your responsibility to cable (extended demarc) from this box to the CPE, which is usually a connection to a CSU/DSU.

Local Loop The *local loop* connects the demarc to the closest switching office, referred to as the central office.

Central Office This point connects the customer's network to the provider's switching network. Make a mental note that a *central office (CO)* is sometimes also referred to as a *point of presence (POP)*.

Toll Network The *toll network* is a trunk line inside a WAN provider's network. This network is a collection of switches and facilities owned by the Internet service provider (ISP).

Optical Fiber Converters Even though this device is not deployed in Figure 1.13, optical fiber converters are used where a fiber-optic link terminates to convert optical signals into electrical signals and vice versa. You can also implement the converter as a router or switch module.

Ensure that you're comfortable with these terms, what they represent, and where they're located, as shown in Figure 1.13, because they're key to understanding WAN technologies.

WAN Connection Bandwidth

Next, I want you to know these basic but very important bandwidth terms used when referring to WAN connections:

Digital Signal 0 (DS0) This is the basic digital signaling rate of 64 Kbps, equivalent to one channel. Europe uses the E0, and Japan uses the J0 to reference the same channel speed. Typical to T-carrier transmission, this is the generic term used by several multiplexed digital carrier systems and is also the smallest-capacity digital circuit. 1 DS0 = 1 voice/data line.

T1 Also referred to as a DS1, a T1 line comprises 24 DS0 circuits bundled together for a total bandwidth of 1.544 Mbps.

E1 This is the European equivalent of a T1 line and comprises 30 DS0 circuits bundled together for a bandwidth of 2.048 Mbps.

T3 Referred to as a DS3, a T3 line comprises 28 DS1s bundled together, or 672 DS0s, for a bandwidth of 44.736 Mbps.

OC-3 Optical Carrier (OC) 3 uses fiber and is made up of three DS3s bundled together. It's made up of 2,016 DS0s and avails a total bandwidth of 155.52 Mbps.

OC-12 Optical Carrier 12 is made up of four OC-3s bundled together and contains 8,064 DS0s for a total bandwidth of 622.08 Mbps.

OC-48 Optical Carrier 48 is made up of four OC-12s bundled together and contains 32,256 DS0s for a total bandwidth of 2,488.32 Mbps.

Summary

I started this chapter by defining an internetwork, which is when you connect two or more networks via a router and configure a logical network addressing scheme with protocols like IP or IPv6.

I then moved on to covering network components such as routers and switches and defining what exactly creates a small office/home office network.

After that, I touched on next-generation firewalls and Cisco's design architecture of three-tier, two-tier, and spine-leaf.

Finally, I concluded the chapter with a thorough overview of wide area networks.

Exam Essentials

Differentiate between a switch and a router. Switches operate at layer 2 of the OSI model and only read frame hardware addresses in a frame to make a switching decision. Routers read to layer 3 and use routed (logical) addresses to make forwarding decisions on a packet.

Understand the term SOHO. SOHO, which stands for small office/home office, is small network connecting a user or small handful of users to the Internet and office resources such as servers and printers. A SOHO usually comprises just one router and a switch or two, plus a firewall.

Define three-tier architecture. The Cisco hierarchical model can help you design, implement, and maintain a scalable, reliable, and cost-effective hierarchical internetwork. Cisco defines three layers of hierarchy, the core, distribution, and access, each with specific functions. It's referred to as a three-tier network architecture.

Define two-tier architecture. Two-tier architecture is also referred to as the collapsed core design because it's only two layers. But in concept, it's like the three-tier only less expensive and geared for smaller companies. The design is meant to maximize performance and user availability to the network, while still allowing for design scalability over time. In a two-tier, the distribution layer is merged with the core layer.

Define spine-leaf. Also referred to as leaf-and-spine topology, in the leaf-and-spine design, there are switches found at the top of each rack that connect to the servers in the rack, with a server connecting into each switch for redundancy. People refer to this as a top-of-rack (TOR) design because the switches physically reside at the top of a rack.

Understand wide area networks (WANs). Remember the WAN terms and definitions for CPE, CSU/DSU, demarcation point, local loop, central office, toll network, and optical fiber converters.

Written Lab

You can find the answers to this lab in Appendix A, "Answers to the Written Labs."

1. What is the basic digital signaling rate of a DS0?
2. What is the total bandwidth of a T1 line?
3. What is the total bandwidth of an E1 line?
4. What is the total bandwidth of a T3 line?
5. What is the total bandwidth of an OC-3?
6. What is the total bandwidth of an OC-12?
7. What is the total bandwidth of an OC-48?

Review Questions

You can find the answers to these questions in Appendix B, "Answers to the Review Questions."

NOTE

The following questions are designed to test your understanding of this chapter's material. For more information on how to get additional questions, please see `www.lammle.com/ccna`.

1. Which one of the following is true about the Cisco core layer in the three-tier design?
   A. Never do anything to slow down traffic. This includes making sure you don't use access lists, perform routing between virtual local area networks, or implement packet filtering.
   B. It's best to support workgroup access here.
   C. Expanding the core, e.g., adding routers as the internetwork grows, is highly recommended as a first step in expansion.
   D. All cables from the core must connect to the TOR.

2. Which one of the following best describes a SOHO network?
   A. It uses ff:ff:ff:ff:ff:ff as a layer 2 unicast address, which makes it more efficient in a small network.
   B. It uses UDP as the Transport layer protocol exclusively, which saves bandwidth in a small network.
   C. It comprises a single or small group of users connecting to a switch, with a router providing a connection to the Internet.
   D. SOHO is the network cabling used from the access layer to the TOR.

3. Which two of the following describe the access layer in the three-tier network design?
   A. Microsegmentation
   B. Broadcast control
   C. PoE
   D. Connections to TOR

4. Switches break up ________ domains, and routers break up ________ domains.
   A. broadcast, broadcast
   B. collision, collision
   C. collision, broadcast
   D. broadcast, collision

5. What is the speed of a T3 line?
   A. 1.544 Mbps
   B. 2.0 Mbps
   C. 100 Mbps
   D. 44.763 Mbps
6. Which of the following is *not* provided by today's NGFWs?
   A. IPS inspection
   B. Layer 2 deep packet inspection
   C. Application Visibility and Control (AVC)
   D. Network Address Translation (NAT)
7. What is the function of a firewall?
   A. To automatically handle the configuration of wireless access points
   B. To allow wireless devices to connect to a wired network
   C. To monitor and control the incoming and outgoing network traffic
   D. To connect networks and intelligently choose the best paths between networks
8. Which of the following defines a two-tier design?
   A. The access layer connects to the distribution layer, and the two-tiers then connect to the core layer.
   B. In a two-tier design, the distribution layer is merged with the core layer.
   C. It's best to support workgroup access in the two-tier layer.
   D. All cables from the core must connect to the two-tier TOR.
9. A __________ is an example of a device that operates only at the physical layer.
   A. Hub
   B. Switch
   C. Router
   D. Bridge
10. In a spine-leaf design, which is true?
   A. The switches are found at the top of each rack that connect to the servers in the rack.
   B. The distribution layer is merged with the core layer.
   C. The access layer connects to the distribution layer, and the two-tiers then connect to the core layer.
   D. All cables from the core layer must connect to the spine, which connects to the leaf device.

Chapter 2

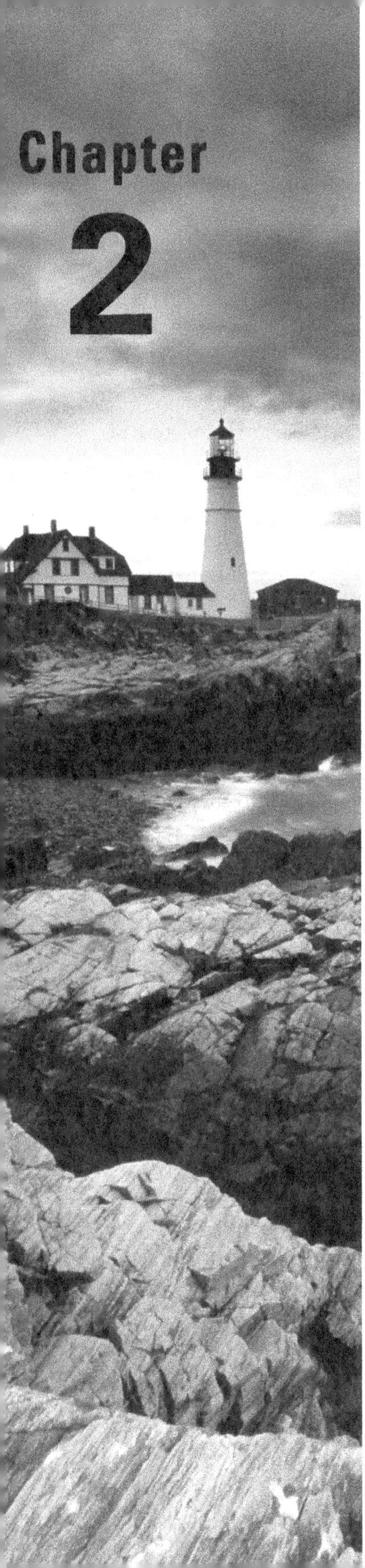

Ethernet Networking

THE FOLLOWING CCNA EXAM TOPICS ARE COVERED IN THIS CHAPTER:

✓ ***1.0 Network Fundamentals***

1.1.h PoE

1.3 Compare physical interface and cabling types

1.3.a Single-mode fiber, multimode fiber, copper

1.3.b Connections (Ethernet shared media and point-to-point)

1.4 Identify interface and cable issues (collisions, errors, mismatch duplex, and/or speed)

Before exploring a set of key foundational topics like the TCP/IP DoD model, IP addressing, subnetting, and routing in the upcoming chapters, I really want you to grasp the big picture of LANs conceptually.

The role Ethernet plays in today's networks as well as what Media Access Control (MAC) addresses are and how they are used are two more critical networking basics you'll want a solid understanding of as well.

We'll cover these important subjects and more in this chapter, beginning with Ethernet basics and the way MAC addresses are used on an Ethernet LAN, and then we'll focus on the actual protocols used with Ethernet at the Data Link layer. To round out this discussion, you'll also learn about some very important Ethernet specifications.

You know by now that there are a whole bunch of different devices specified at the various layers of the OSI model and that it's essential to be really familiar with the many types of cables and connectors employed to hook them up to the network correctly.

In this chapter, I'll review the types of cabling used with Cisco devices, including fiber optic, demonstrate how to connect to a router or switch, plus show you how to connect a router or switch via a console connection.

NOTE To find bonus material, as well as Todd Lammle videos, practice questions, and hands-on labs, please see `www.lammle.com/ccna`.

Ethernet Networks in Review

Ethernet is a contention-based media access method that allows all hosts on a network to share the same link's bandwidth. Some reasons it's so popular are that Ethernet is pretty simple to implement and it makes troubleshooting fairly straightforward. Ethernet is also readily scalable, meaning that it eases the process of integrating new technologies into an existing network infrastructure, like upgrading from Fast Ethernet to Gigabit Ethernet.

Ethernet uses both Data Link and Physical layer specifications, so you'll be presented with information relative to both layers, which you'll need to effectively implement, troubleshoot, and maintain an Ethernet network.

Collision Domain

In Chapter 1, "Network Fundamentals," you learned that the Ethernet term *collision domain* refers to a network scenario in which one device sends a frame out on a physical network segment, forcing every other device on the same segment to pay attention to it. This is bad because if two devices on a single physical segment just happen to transmit simultaneously, it will cause a collision and require these devices to retransmit. Think of a collision event as a situation where each device's digital signals totally interfere with one another on the wire. Figure 2.1 shows an old, legacy network that's a single collision domain where only one host can transmit at a time.

FIGURE 2.1 A legacy collision domain design

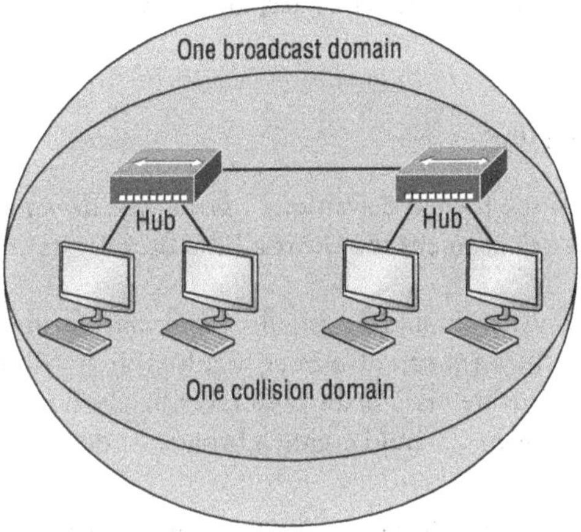

The hosts connected to each hub are in the same collision domain, so if one of them transmits, all the others must take the time to listen for and read the digital signal. It is easy to see how collisions can be a serious drag on network performance, so I'll show you how to strategically avoid them soon!

Take another look at the network pictured in Figure 2.1. True, it has only one collision domain, but worse, it's also a single broadcast domain—what a mess! Let's check out an example, in Figure 2.2, of a typical network design still used today and see if it's any better.

FIGURE 2.2 A typical network you'd see today

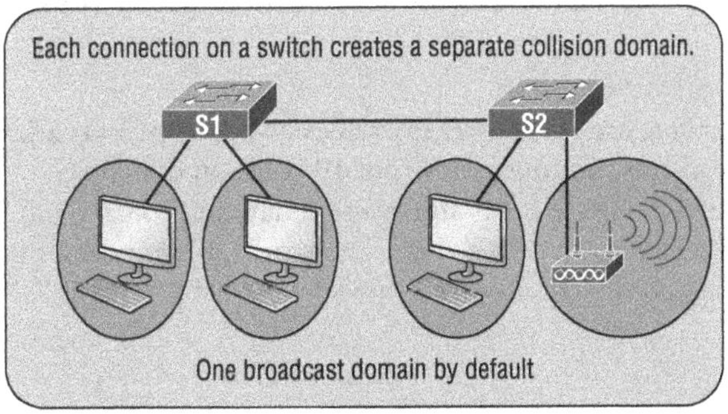

Because each port off a switch is a single collision domain, we gain more bandwidth for users, which is a great start. But switches don't break up broadcast domains by default, so this is still only one broadcast domain, which is not so good. This can work in a really small network, but to expand it at all, we would need to break up the network into smaller broadcast domains; otherwise, our users wouldn't get enough bandwidth.

You're probably wondering about that device in the lower-right corner, right? That's a *wireless access point*, sometimes referred to as an AP, which stands for access point. It's a wireless device that allows hosts to connect wirelessly using the IEEE 802.11 specification. I added it to the figure to demonstrate how these devices can be used to extend a collision domain. But still, understand that APs don't actually segment the network; they only extend it, meaning our LAN just got a lot bigger, with an unknown number of hosts that are all still part of one measly broadcast domain! This clearly demonstrates why it's so important to understand exactly what broadcast domains are, and now is a great time to talk about them in detail.

Broadcast Domains

Let me start by giving you the formal definition: a *broadcast domain* refers to a group of devices on a specific network segment that hear all the broadcasts sent out on that specific network segment.

But even though a broadcast domain is usually a boundary delimited by physical media like switches and routers, the term can also refer to a logical division of a network segment, where all hosts can communicate via a Data Link layer hardware address broadcast.

Figure 2.3 shows how a router would create a broadcast domain boundary.

FIGURE 2.3 A router creates broadcast domain boundaries

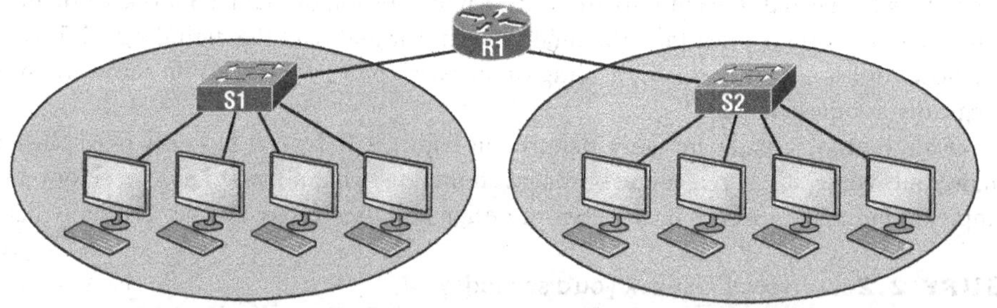

Two broadcast domains. How many collision domains do you see?

Here you can see there are two router interfaces giving us two broadcast domains, and I count 10 switch segments, meaning we've got 10 collision domains.

The design depicted in Figure 2.3 is still in use today, and routers will be around for a long time, but in the latest, modern switched networks, it's important to create small broadcast domains. We achieve this by building virtual LANs (VLANs) within our switched networks, which I'll demonstrate shortly. Without employing VLANs in today's switched environments, there wouldn't be much bandwidth available to individual users. Switches break up collision domains with each port, which is awesome, but they're still only one broadcast domain by default. It's also one more reason why it's extremely important to design networks very carefully.

And key to carefully planning your network design is to never to allow broadcast domains to grow too large and get out of control. Both collision and broadcast domains can easily be controlled with routers and VLANs, so there's just no excuse to allow user bandwidth to slow to a pitiful crawl when there are plenty of tools in your arsenal to prevent the suffering.

An important reason for this book's existence is to ensure that you really get the foundational basics of Cisco networks nailed down so you can effectively design, implement, configure, troubleshoot, and even dazzle colleagues and superiors with elegant designs that lavish your users with all the bandwidth their hearts could possibly desire.

To make it to the top of that mountain, you need more than just the basic story, so let's move on to explore the collision detection mechanism used in half-duplex Ethernet.

CSMA/CD

Ethernet networking uses a protocol called *Carrier Sense Multiple Access with Collision Detection (CSMA/CD)*, which helps devices share the bandwidth evenly while preventing two devices from transmitting simultaneously on the same network medium. CSMA/CD was actually created to overcome the problem of the collisions that occur when packets are transmitted from different nodes at the same time. And trust me—good collision management is crucial, because when a node transmits in a CSMA/CD network, all the other nodes on the network receive and examine that transmission. Only switches and routers can effectively prevent a transmission from propagating throughout the entire network!

So, how does the CSMA/CD protocol work? Let's start by taking a look at Figure 2.4.

When a host wants to transmit over the network, it first checks for the presence of a digital signal on the wire. If all is clear and no other host is transmitting, the host will then proceed with its transmission.

But it doesn't stop there. The transmitting host constantly monitors the wire to make sure no other hosts begin transmitting. If the host detects another signal on the wire, it sends out an extended jam signal that causes all nodes on the segment to stop sending data—think busy signal.

The nodes respond to that jam signal by waiting a bit before attempting to transmit again. Backoff algorithms determine when the colliding stations can retransmit. If collisions keep occurring after 15 tries, the nodes attempting to transmit will then time out. Half-duplex can be pretty messy!

When a collision occurs on an Ethernet LAN, the following happens:

1. A jam signal informs all devices that a collision occurred.
2. The collision invokes a random backoff algorithm.

3. Each device on the Ethernet segment stops transmitting for a short time until its backoff timer expires.
4. All hosts have equal priority to transmit after the timers have expired.

FIGURE 2.4 CSMA/CD

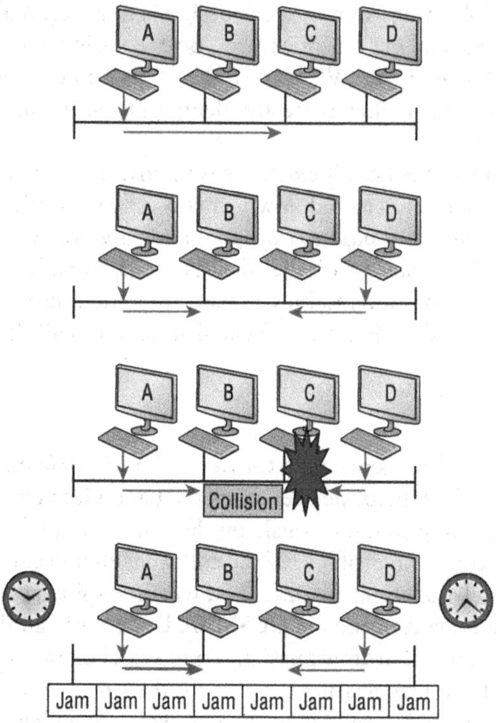

The ugly effects of having a CSMA/CD network sustain heavy collisions are delay, low throughput, and congestion.

> **NOTE** Backoff on an Ethernet network is the retransmission delay that's enforced when a collision occurs. When that happens, a host will resume transmission only after the forced time delay has expired. Keep in mind that after the backoff has elapsed, all stations have equal priority to transmit data.

At this point, let's take a minute to talk about Ethernet in detail at both the Data Link layer (layer 2) and the Physical layer (layer 1).

Half- and Full-Duplex Ethernet

Half-duplex Ethernet is defined in the original IEEE 802.3 Ethernet specification, which differs a bit from how Cisco describes things. Cisco says Ethernet uses only one wire pair with a digital signal running in both directions on the wire. Even though the IEEE specifications discuss the half-duplex process somewhat differently, it's not actually a full-blown technical disagreement. Cisco is really just talking about a general sense of what's happening with Ethernet.

Half-duplex also uses the CSMA/CD protocol I just discussed to help prevent collisions and to permit retransmitting if one occurs. If a hub is attached to a switch, it must operate in half-duplex mode because the end stations must be able to detect collisions. Figure 2.5 shows a network with four hosts connected to a hub.

FIGURE 2.5 Half-duplex example

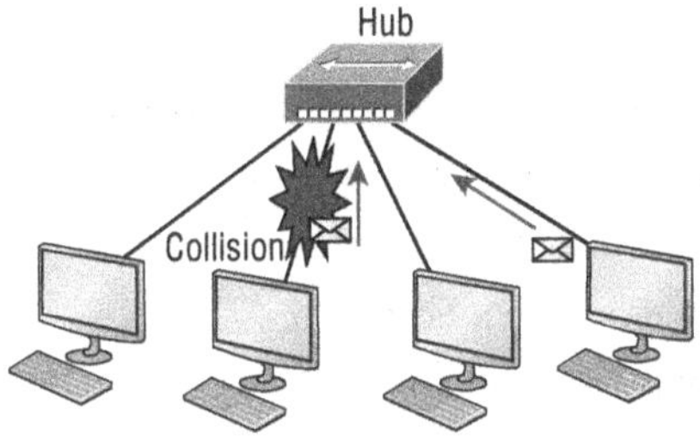

The problem here is that we can only run half-duplex, so if two hosts communicate at the same time, there will be a collision. Also, half-duplex Ethernet is only about 30 to 40 percent efficient because a large 100Base-T network will usually only give you 30 to 40 Mbps, at most, due to overhead.

But full-duplex Ethernet uses two pairs of wires at the same time instead of a single wire pair like half-duplex. And full-duplex uses a point-to-point connection between the transmitter of the transmitting device and the receiver of the receiving device. This means that full-duplex data transfers happen a lot faster compared to half-duplex transfers. Also, because the transmitted data is sent on a different set of wires than the received data, collisions won't happen.

Figure 2.6 shows four hosts connected to a switch, plus a hub. Definitely avoid using hubs, so this is just as an example to differentiate them from a switch.

Theoretically, all hosts connected to the switch in Figure 2.6 can communicate at the same time because they can run full-duplex. Just keep in mind that the switch port connecting to the hub, as well as the hosts connecting to that hub, must run at half-duplex.

The reason you don't need to worry about collisions is because now it's like a freeway with multiple lanes instead of the single-lane road provided by half-duplex. Full-duplex Ethernet is supposed to offer 100 percent efficiency in both directions—for example, you can get 20 Mbps with a 10 Mbps Ethernet running full-duplex, or 200 Mbps for Fast Ethernet. But this rate is known as an aggregate rate, which translates as "you're supposed to get" 100 percent efficiency. No guarantees—in networking as in life!

FIGURE 2.6 Full-duplex example

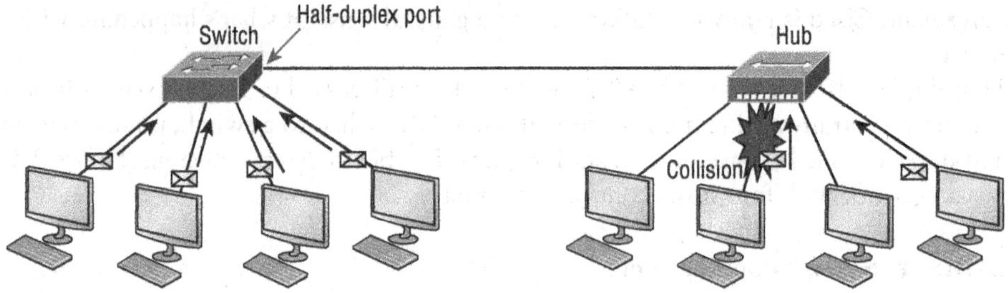

You can use full-duplex Ethernet in at least the following six situations:

- With a connection from a switch to a host
- With a connection from a switch to a switch
- With a connection from a host to a host
- With a connection from a switch to a router
- With a connection from a router to a router
- With a connection from a router to a host

NOTE Full-duplex Ethernet requires a point-to-point connection when only two nodes are present. You can run full-duplex with just about any device except a hub.

Now, this may be a little confusing because if it's capable of all that speed, why wouldn't it actually deliver? Well, when a full-duplex Ethernet port is powered on, it first connects to the remote end and then negotiates with the other end of the Fast Ethernet link. This is called an *auto-detect mechanism*. This mechanism first decides on the exchange capability, which means it checks to see if it can run at 10, 100, or even 1,000 Mbps or more. It then checks to see if it can run full-duplex, and if it can't, it will run half-duplex.

NOTE Remember that half-duplex Ethernet shares a collision domain and provides a lower effective throughput than full-duplex Ethernet, which typically has a private per-port collision domain plus a higher effective throughput.

Lastly, remember these important points:

- There are no collisions in full-duplex mode.
- A dedicated switch port is required for each full-duplex node.
- The host network card and the switch port must be capable of operating in full-duplex mode.
- The default behavior of 10Base-T and 100Base-T hosts is 10 Mbps half-duplex if the autodetect mechanism fails, so it is always good practice to set the speed and duplex of each port on a switch if you can.

Now let's take a look at how Ethernet works at the Data Link layer.

Ethernet at the Data Link Layer

Ethernet at the Data Link layer is responsible for Ethernet addressing, commonly referred to as MAC or hardware addressing. Ethernet is also responsible for framing packets received from the Network layer and preparing them for transmission on the local network through the Ethernet contention-based media access method.

Ethernet Addressing

Here's where we get into how Ethernet addressing works. It uses the *Media Access Control (MAC)* address burned into each and every Ethernet network interface card (NIC). The MAC, or hardware, address is a 48-bit (6-byte) address written in a hexadecimal format.

Figure 2.7 shows the 48-bit MAC addresses and how the bits are divided.

FIGURE 2.7 Ethernet addressing using MAC addresses

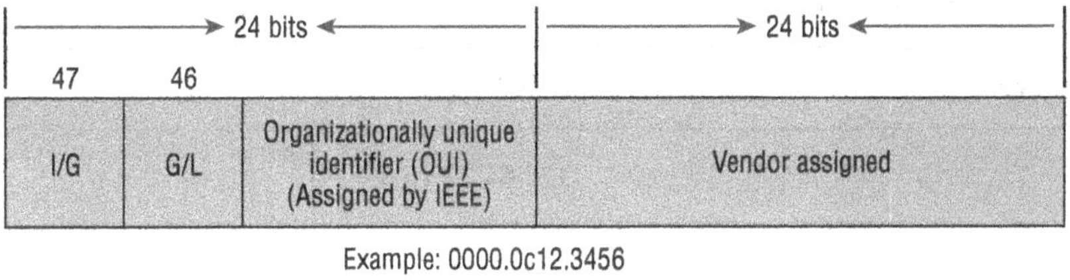

The *organizationally unique identifier (OUI)* is assigned by the IEEE to an organization. It's composed of 24 bits, or 3 bytes, and, in turn, it assigns a globally administered address also made up of 24 bits, or 3 bytes, that's supposedly unique to each and every adapter an organization manufactures. (Surprisingly, there's no guarantee when it comes to that unique claim!) Okay, now look closely at Figure 2.7. The high-order bit is the Individual/Group (I/G) bit. When it has a value of 0, we can assume that the address is the MAC address of a device and that it may well appear in the source portion of the MAC header. When it's a 1, we can assume that the address represents either a broadcast or multicast address in Ethernet.

The next bit is the Global/Local bit, sometimes called the G/L bit or U/L bit, where *U* means *universal*. When set to 0, this bit represents a globally administered address, as assigned by the IEEE, but when it's a 1, it represents a locally governed and administered address. The low-order 24 bits of an Ethernet address represent a locally administered or manufacturer-assigned code. This portion commonly starts with 24 0s for the first card made and continues in order until there are 24 1s for the last (16,777,216th) card made. You'll find that many manufacturers use these same six hex digits as the last six characters of their serial number on the same card.

Let's stop for a minute and go over some addressing schemes important in the Ethernet world.

Binary to Decimal and Hexadecimal Conversion

Before we get into working with the TCP/IP protocol and IP addressing, which we'll do in Chapter 3, "TCP/IP," it's really important for you to understand the differences between binary, decimal, and hexadecimal numbers and how to convert one format into the other.

We'll start with binary numbering, which is really pretty simple. The digits used are limited to either a 1 or a 0, and each digit is called a *bit*, which is short for *binary digit*. Typically, you group either 4 or 8 bits together, with these being referred to as a *nibble* and a *byte*, respectively.

The interesting thing about binary numbering is how the value is represented in a decimal format—the typical decimal format being the base-10 number scheme that we've all used since kindergarten. The binary numbers are placed in a value spot, starting at the right and moving left, with each spot having double the value of the previous spot.

Table 2.1 shows the decimal values of each bit location in a nibble and a byte. Remember, a nibble is 4 bits and a byte is 8 bits.

TABLE 2.1 Binary values

Nibble Values	Byte Values
8 4 2 1	128 64 32 16 8 4 2 1

What all this means is that if a one digit (1) is placed in a value spot, then the nibble or byte takes on that decimal value and adds it to any other value spots that have a 1. If a zero (0) is placed in a bit spot, you don't count that value.

Let me clarify this a little. If we have a 1 placed in each spot of our nibble, we would then add up 8 + 4 + 2 + 1 to give us a maximum value of 15. Another example for our nibble values would be 1001, meaning that the 8 bit and the 1 bit are turned on, which equals a decimal value of 9. If we have a nibble binary value of 0110, then our decimal value would be 6 because the 4 and 2 bits are turned on.

But the *byte* decimal values can add up to a number that's significantly higher than 15. This is how: if we counted every bit as a one (1), then the byte binary value would look like the following example because, remember, 8 bits equal a byte:

11111111

We would then count up every bit spot because each is turned on. It would look like this, which demonstrates the maximum value of a byte:

128 + 64 + 32 + 16 + 8 + 4 + 2 + 1 = 255

There are plenty of other decimal values that a binary number can equal. Let's work through a few examples:

10010110

Which bits are on? The 128, 16, 4, and 2 bits are on, so we'll just add them up: 128 + 16 + 4 + 2 = 150.

01101100

Which bits are on? The 64, 32, 8, and 4 bits are on, so we just need to add them up: 64 + 32 + 8 + 4 = 108.

11101000

Which bits are on? The 128, 64, 32, and 8 bits are on, so just add the values up: 128 + 64 + 32 + 8 = 232.

I highly recommend you memorize Table 2.2 before you start studying subnetting in Chapter 4, "Easy Subnetting."

TABLE 2.2 Binary to decimal memorization chart

Binary Value	Decimal Value
10000000	128
11000000	192
11100000	224
11110000	240
11111000	248
11111100	252
11111110	254
11111111	255

Hexadecimal addressing is completely different from binary or decimal—it's converted by reading nibbles, not bytes. By using a nibble, we can convert these bits to hex pretty simply. First, understand that the hexadecimal addressing scheme uses only the characters 0 through 9. Because the numbers 10, 11, 12, and so on can't be used (because they are two-digit numbers), the letters *A*, *B*, *C*, *D*, *E*, and *F* are used instead to represent 10, 11, 12, 13, 14, and 15, respectively.

NOTE *Hex* is short for *hexadecimal*, which is a numbering system that uses the first six letters of the alphabet, *A* through *F*, to extend beyond the available 10 characters in the decimal system. These values are not case sensitive.

Table 2.3 shows both the binary value and the decimal value for each hexadecimal digit.

TABLE 2.3 Hex to binary to decimal chart

Hexadecimal Value	Binary Value	Decimal Value
0	0000	0
1	0001	1
2	0010	2
3	0011	3
4	0100	4
5	0101	5
6	0110	6
7	0111	7
8	1000	8
9	1001	9
A	1010	10
B	1011	11
C	1100	12
D	1101	13
E	1110	14
F	1111	15

Did you notice that the first 10 hexadecimal digits (0–9) are the same value as the decimal values? If not, look again because this handy fact makes those values super easy to convert!

Now, suppose you have something like this: 0x6A. This is important because sometimes Cisco likes to put *0x* in front of characters so you know they are a hex value. It doesn't have any other special meaning. So, what are the binary and decimal values? All you have to remember is that each hex character is one nibble and that two hex characters joined together make a byte. To figure out the binary value, put the hex characters into two nibbles and then join them together into a byte. Six equals 0110, and A, which is 10 in hex, equals 1010, so the complete byte would be 01101010.

To convert from binary to hex, just take the byte and break it into nibbles. Let me clarify this.

Say you have the binary number 01010101. First, break it into nibbles—0101 and 0101—with the value of each nibble being 5 since the 1 and 4 bits are on. This makes the hex answer 0x55. And in decimal format, the binary number is 01010101, which converts to 64 + 16 + 4 + 1 = 85.

Here's another binary number:

11001100

Your answer would be 1100 = 12 and 1100 = 12; therefore, it's converted to CC in hex. The decimal conversion answer would be 128 + 64 + 8 + 4 = 204.

One more example, and then we need to get working on the Physical layer. Suppose you had the following binary number:

10110101

The hex answer would be 0xB5, since 1011 converts to B and 0101 converts to 5 in hex value. The decimal equivalent is 128 + 32 + 16 + 4 + 1 = 181.

Ethernet Frames

The Data Link layer is responsible for combining bits into bytes and bytes into frames. Frames are used at the Data Link layer to encapsulate packets handed down from the Network layer for transmission on a type of media access.

The function of Ethernet stations is to pass data frames between each other using a group of bits known as a MAC frame format. This provides error detection from a *cyclic redundancy check (CRC)*. But remember—this is error detection, not error correction. An example of a typical Ethernet frame used today is shown in Figure 2.8:

FIGURE 2.8 Typical Ethernet frame format

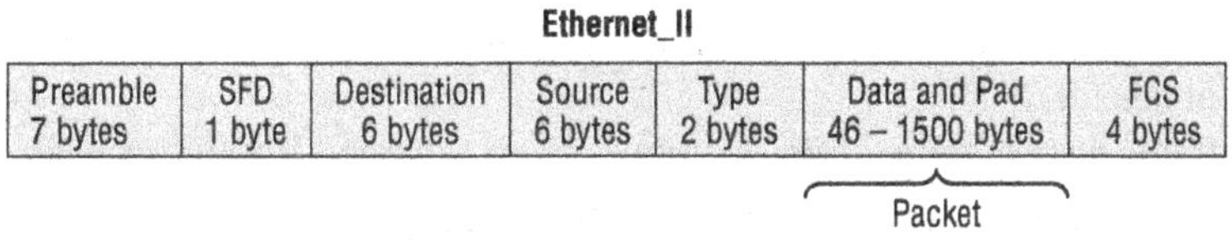

NOTE

Encapsulating a frame within a different type of frame is called *tunneling*.

Following are the details of the various fields in the typical Ethernet frame type:

Preamble An alternating 1,0 pattern provides a clock at the start of each packet, which allows the receiving devices to lock the incoming bit stream.

Start Frame Delimiter (SFD)/Synch The preamble is seven octets, and the SFD is one octet (synch). The SFD is 10101011, where the last pair of 1s allows the receiver to come into the alternating 1,0 pattern somewhere in the middle and still sync up to detect the beginning of the data.

Destination Address (DA) This transmits a 48-bit value using the least significant bit (LSB) first. The DA is used by receiving stations to determine if an incoming packet is addressed to a particular node. The destination address can be an individual address or a broadcast or multicast MAC address. Remember, a broadcast is all 1s—all *F*s in hex—and is sent to all devices. A multicast is sent only to a similar subset of nodes on a network.

Source Address (SA) The SA is a 48-bit MAC address used to identify the transmitting device, and it uses the least significant bit first. Broadcast and multicast address formats are illegal within the SA field.

Length or Type 802.3 uses a Length field, but the Ethernet_II frame uses a Type field to identify the Network layer protocol. The old, original 802.3 cannot identify the upper-layer protocol and must be used with a proprietary LAN—IPX, for example.

Data This is a packet sent down to the Data Link layer from the Network layer. The size can vary from 46 to 1,500 bytes.

Frame Check Sequence (FCS) FCS is a field at the end of the frame that's used to store the cyclic redundancy check (CRC) answer. The CRC is a mathematical algorithm that's run when each frame is built based on the data in the frame. When a receiving host receives the frame and runs the CRC, the answer should be the same. If not, the frame is discarded, assuming errors have occurred.

Let's pause here for a minute and take a look at some frames caught on my trusty network analyzer. You can see that the following frame has only three fields: Destination, Source, and Type, which is shown as Protocol Type on this particular analyzer:

```
Destination: 00:60:f5:00:1f:27
Source: 00:60:f5:00:1f:2c
Protocol Type: 08-00 IP
```

This is an Ethernet_II frame. Notice that the Type field is IP, or 08-00, mostly just referred to as 0x800 in hexadecimal.

The next frame has the same fields, so it must be an Ethernet_II frame as well:

```
Destination: ff:ff:ff:ff:ff:ff Ethernet Broadcast
Source: 02:07:01:22:de:a4
Protocol Type: 08-00 IP
```

Did you notice that this frame was a broadcast? You can tell because the destination hardware address is all 1s in binary, or all *F*s in hexadecimal.

Let's take a look at one more Ethernet_II frame. I'll talk about this next example again when we use IPv6 in Volume 2's Chapter 3, "Internet Protocol Version 6 (IPv6)," but you can see that the Ethernet frame is the same Ethernet_II frame used with the IPv4 routed protocol. The Type field has 0x86dd when the frame is carrying IPv6 data, and when we have IPv4 data, the frame uses 0x0800 in the protocol field:

```
Destination: IPv6-Neighbor-Discovery_00:01:00:03 (33:33:00:01:00:03)
Source: Aopen_3e:7f:dd (00:01:80:3e:7f:dd)
Type: IPv6 (0x86dd)
```

This is the beauty of the Ethernet_II frame. Because of the Type field, we can run any Network layer routed protocol, and the frame will carry the data because it can identify the Network layer protocol.

Ethernet at the Physical Layer

Ethernet was first implemented by a group called DIX, which stands for Digital, Intel, and Xerox. They created and implemented the first Ethernet LAN specification, which the IEEE used to create the IEEE 802.3 committee. This was a 10 Mbps network that ran on coax and then eventually twisted-pair and fiber physical media.

The IEEE extended the 802.3 committee to three new committees known as 802.3u (Fast Ethernet), 802.3ab (Gigabit Ethernet on Category 5), and finally one more, 802.3ae (10 Gbps over fiber and coax). There are more standards evolving almost daily, such as 100 Gbps Ethernet (802.3ba).

When designing your LAN, it's really important to understand the different types of Ethernet media available to you. Sure, it would be great to run Gigabit Ethernet to each desktop and 10 Gbps between switches, but, well, you would definitely need to figure out how to justify the cost of that network! However, if you mix and match the different types of Ethernet media methods currently available, you can come up with a cost-effective network solution that still works really great.

The *EIA/TIA* (Electronic Industries Alliance and the newer Telecommunications Industry Association) is the standards body that creates the Physical layer specifications for Ethernet. The EIA/TIA specifies that Ethernet use a *registered jack (RJ) connector* on *unshielded twisted-pair (UTP)* cabling (RJ-45). But the industry is moving toward simply calling this an 8-pin modular connector.

Every Ethernet cable type that's specified by the EIA/TIA has inherent attenuation, which is defined as the loss of signal strength as it travels the length of a cable and is measured in decibels (dB). The cabling used in corporate and home markets is measured in categories. A higher-quality cable will have a higher-rated category and lower attenuation. For example, Category 5 is better than Category 3 because Category 5 cables have more wire twists per foot and, therefore less crosstalk. Crosstalk is the unwanted signal interference from adjacent pairs in the cable.

Here is a list of some of the most common IEEE Ethernet standards, starting with 10 Mbps Ethernet:

10Base-T (IEEE 802.3) 10 Mbps using Category 3 unshielded twisted pair (UTP) wiring for runs up to 100 meters. Unlike with the 10Base-2 and 10Base-5 networks, each device must connect into a hub or switch, and you can have only one host per segment or wire. It uses an RJ-45 connector (8-pin modular connector) with a physical star topology and a logical bus.

100Base-TX (IEEE 802.3u) 100Base-TX, most commonly known as Fast Ethernet, uses EIA/TIA Category 5, 5E, or 6 UTP two-pair wiring. One user per segment; up to 100 meters long. It uses an RJ-45 connector with a physical star topology and a logical bus.

100Base-FX (IEEE 802.3u) 100Base-FX uses 62.5/125-micron multimode fiber cabling. Point-to-point topology; up to 412 meters long. It uses ST and SC connectors, which are media-interface connectors.

1000Base-CX (IEEE 802.3z) Copper twisted-pair, called twinax, is a balanced coaxial pair that can run only up to 25 meters and uses a special 9-pin connector known as the High-Speed Serial Data Connector (HSSDC). This is used in Cisco's Data Center technologies.

1000Base-T (IEEE 802.3ab) Category 5, four-pair UTP wiring up to 100 meters long and up to 1 Gbps.

1000Base-SX (IEEE 802.3z) The implementation of 1 Gigabit Ethernet runs over multimode fiber-optic cable instead of copper twisted-pair cable, using short wavelength laser and LEDs. Multimode fiber (MMF) using 62.5- and 50-micron core; uses an 850 nanometer (nm) laser and can go up to 220 meters with 62.5-micron, 550 meters with a 50-micron core.

1000Base-LX (IEEE 802.3z) Single-mode fiber that uses a 9-micron core and 1,300 nm laser and can go from 3 kilometers up to 10 kilometers.

1000Base-ZX (Cisco standard) 1000BaseZX, or 1000Base-ZX, is a Cisco-specified standard for Gigabit Ethernet communication. 1000BaseZX operates on ordinary single-mode fiber-optic links with spans up to 43.5 miles (70 km).

10GBase-T (802.3an) 10GBase-T is a standard proposed by the IEEE 802.3an committee to provide 10 Gbps connections over conventional UTP cables, (Category 5e, 6, or 7 cables). 10GBase-T allows the conventional RJ-45 connector used for Ethernet LANs and can support signal transmission at the full 100-meter distance specified for LAN wiring.

TIP

If you want to implement a network medium that is not susceptible to electromagnetic interference (EMI), fiber-optic cable provides a more secure, long-distance cable that is not susceptible to EMI at high speeds.

Armed with the basics covered so far in this chapter, you're equipped to go to the next level and put Ethernet to work using various Ethernet cabling.

Interference or Host Distance Issue?

Quite a few years ago, I was consulting at a very large aerospace company in the Los Angeles area. In the very busy warehouse, they had hundreds of hosts providing many different services to the various departments working in that area.

However, a small group of hosts had been experiencing intermittent outages that no one could explain since most hosts in the same area had no problems whatsoever. So, I decided to take a crack at this problem and see what I could find.

First, I traced the backbone connection from the main switch to multiple switches in the warehouse area. Assuming that the hosts with the issues were connected to the same switch, I traced each cable, and, much to my surprise, they were connected to various switches! My interest really peaked because the simplest issue had been eliminated right off the bat. It wasn't a simple switch problem!

I continued to trace each cable one by one, and this is what I found:

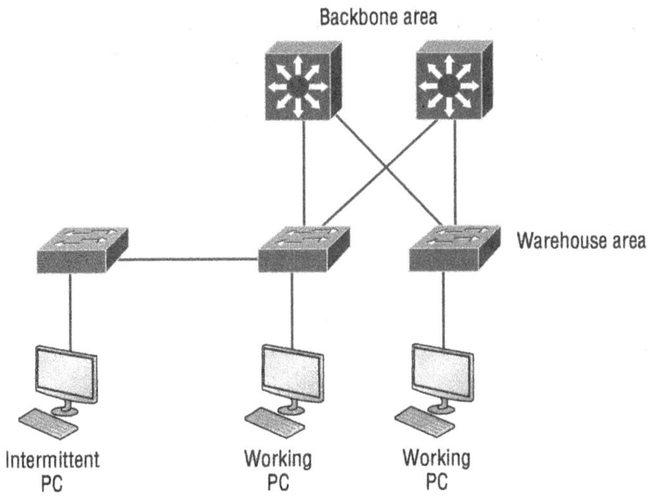

As I drew out this network, I noticed that it had many repeaters in place, which isn't a cause for immediate suspicion since bandwidth was not their biggest requirement here. So, I looked deeper still. At this point, I decided to measure the distance of one of the intermittent hosts connecting to their hub/repeater.

This is what I measured. Can you see the problem?

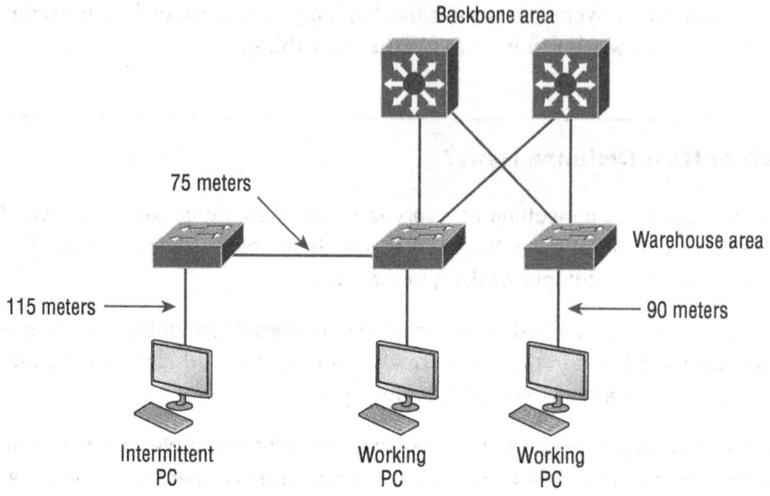

Having a hub or repeater in your network isn't a problem, unless you need better bandwidth (which they didn't in this case), but the distance sure was! It's not always easy to tell how far away a host is from its connection in an extremely large area, so these hosts ended up having a connection past the 100-meter Ethernet specification, which created a problem for the hosts not cabled correctly. Understand that this didn't stop the hosts from completely working, but the workers felt the hosts stopped working when they were at their most stressful point of the day. Sure, that makes sense, because whenever my host stops working, that becomes my most stressful part of the day!

Ethernet Cabling

A discussion about Ethernet cabling is an important one, especially if you are planning to take the Cisco exams. You need to really understand the following three types of cables:

- Straight-through cable
- Crossover cable
- Rolled cable

We will look at each in the following sections, but first, let's take a look at the most common Ethernet cable used today, the Category 5 Enhanced Unshielded Twisted-Pair (UTP), shown in Figure 2.9.

The Category 5 Enhanced UTP cable can handle speeds up to a gigabit with a distance of up to 100 meters. Typically, we'd use this cable for 100 Mbps and Category 6 for a gigabit, but the Category 5 Enhanced is rated for gigabit speeds and Category 6 is rated for 10 Gbps!

FIGURE 2.9 Category 5 Enhanced UTP cable

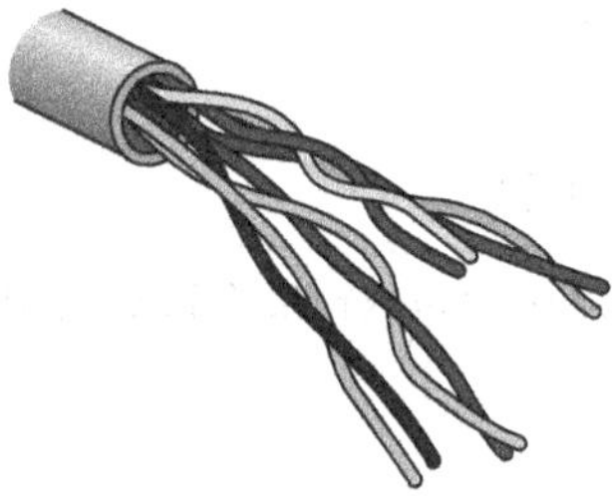

Categories of Ethernet Cables

I want to summarize the various categories of Ethernet cables for you here:

Cat 5

Frequency: Up to 100 MHz

Bandwidth: 100 Mbps (Fast Ethernet)

Max Distance: 100 meters (328 feet)

Cat 5e

Frequency: Up to 100 MHz

Bandwidth: 1 Gbps (Gigabit Ethernet)

Max Distance: 100 meters (328 feet)

Cat 6

Frequency: Up to 250 MHz

Bandwidth: 10 Gbps (10 Gigabit Ethernet)

Max Distance: 55 meters (180 feet) for 10 Gbps; 100 meters (328 feet) for 1 Gbps

Cat 6a

Frequency: Up to 500 MHz

Bandwidth: 10 Gbps (10 Gigabit Ethernet)

Max Distance: 100 meters (328 feet)

Cat 7

Frequency: Up to 600 MHz

Bandwidth: 10 Gbps (10 Gigabit Ethernet)

Max Distance: 100 meters (328 feet)

Cat 8

Frequency: Up to 2 GHz

Bandwidth: 25/40 Gbps (25/40 Gigabit Ethernet)

Max Distance: 30 meters (98 feet)

Straight-Through Cable

The *straight-through cable* is used to connect the following devices:

- Host to switch or hub
- Router to switch or hub

Four wires are used in straight-through cable to connect Ethernet devices. It's relatively simple to create this type. Figure 2.10 shows the four wires used in a straight-through Ethernet cable.

FIGURE 2.10 Straight-through Ethernet cable

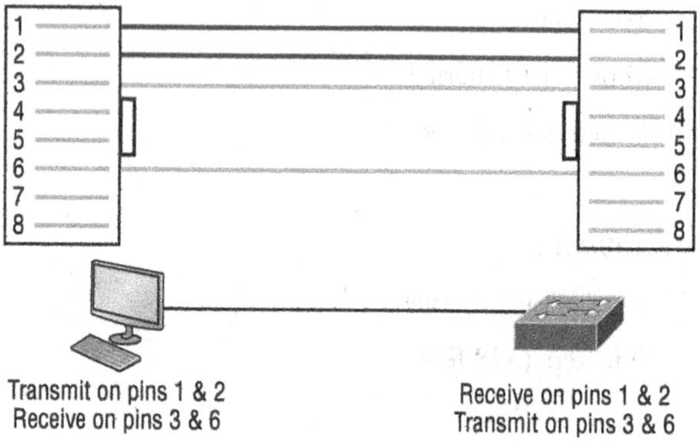

Notice that only pins 1, 2, 3, and 6 are used. Just connect 1 to 1, 2 to 2, 3 to 3, and 6 to 6, and you'll be up and networking in no time. However, remember that this would be a 10/100 Mbps Ethernet-only cable and wouldn't work with gigabit, voice, or other LAN or WAN technology.

Crossover Cable

The *crossover cable* can be used to connect the following devices:

- Switch to switch
- Hub to hub
- Host to host
- Hub to switch
- Router direct to host
- Router to router

The same four wires used in the straight-through cable are used in this cable—we connect different pins together. Figure 2.11 shows how the four wires are used in a crossover Ethernet cable.

FIGURE 2.11 Crossover Ethernet cable

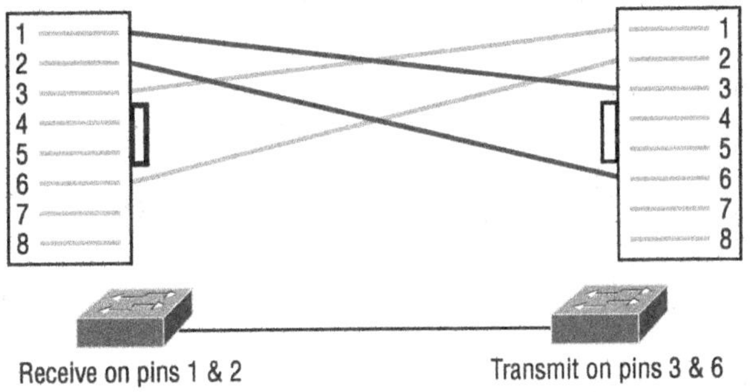

Notice that instead of connecting 1 to 1, 2 to 2, and so on, here we connect pins 1 to 3 and 2 to 6 on each side of the cable. Figure 2.12 shows some typical uses of straight-through and crossover cables:

FIGURE 2.12 Typical uses for straight-through and cross-over Ethernet cables

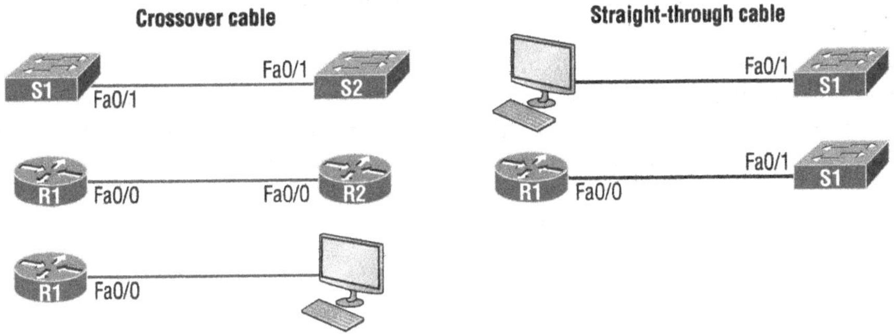

The crossover examples in Figure 2.12 are switch port to switch port, router Ethernet port to router Ethernet port, and router Ethernet port to PC Ethernet port. For the straight-through examples, I used PC Ethernet to switch port and router Ethernet port to switch port.

TIP It's very possible to connect a straight-through cable between two switches, and it will start working because of autodetect mechanisms called *auto-mdix*. But be advised that the CCNA objectives do not typically consider autodetect mechanisms valid between devices!

UTP Gigabit Wiring (1000Base-T)

In the previous examples of 10Base-T and 100Base-T UTP wiring, only two wire pairs were used, but that is not good enough for Gigabit UTP transmission.

1000Base-T UTP wiring (Figure 2.13) requires four wire pairs and uses more advanced electronics so that each and every pair in the cable can transmit simultaneously. Even so, gigabit wiring is almost identical to my earlier 10/100 example, except that we'll use the other two pairs in the cable.

FIGURE 2.13 UTP Gigabit crossover Ethernet cable

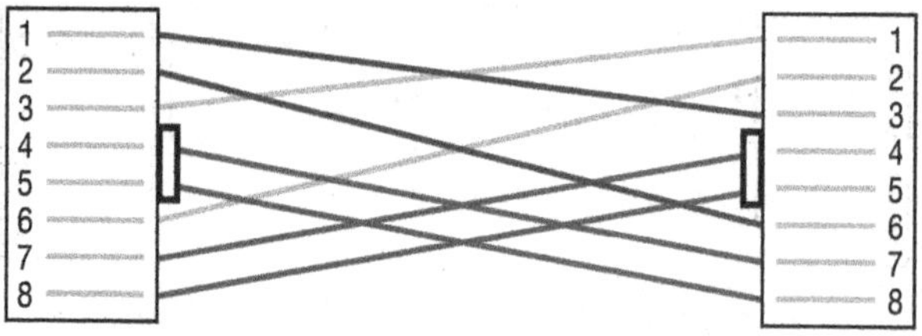

For a straight-through cable, it's still 1 to 1, 2 to 2, and so on, up to pin 8. And in creating the gigabit crossover cable, you'd still cross 1 to 3 and 2 to 6, but you would add 4 to 7 and 5 to 8—pretty straightforward!

Rolled Cable

Although *rolled cable* isn't used to connect any Ethernet connections, you can use a rolled Ethernet cable to connect a host EIA-TIA 232 interface to a router console serial communication (COM) port.

If you have a Cisco router or switch, you would use this cable to connect your PC, Mac, or a device like an iPad to the Cisco hardware. Eight wires are used in this cable to connect serial devices, although not all eight are used to send information, just as in Ethernet networking. Figure 2.14 shows the eight wires used in a rolled cable:

FIGURE 2.14 Rolled Ethernet cable

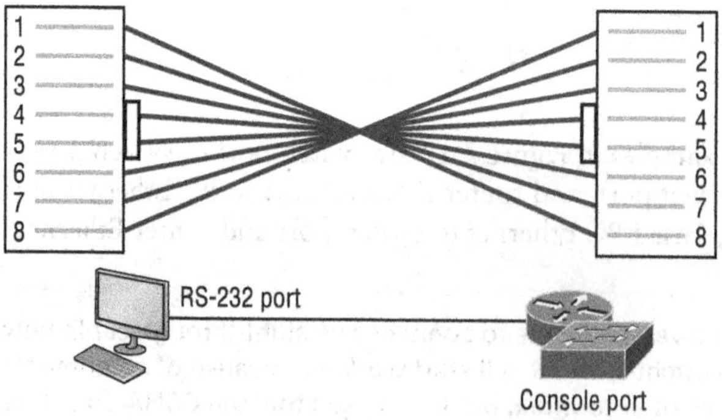

These are probably the easiest cables to make because you just cut the end off on one side of a straight-through cable, turn it over, and put it back on—with a new connector, of course!

Okay, once you have the correct cable connected from your PC to the Cisco router or switch console port, you can start your emulation program such as PuTTY or SecureCRT to create a console connection and configure the device. To find your com port in Windows, go to Device Manager. Set the configuration as shown in Figure 2.15:

FIGURE 2.15 Configuring your console emulation program

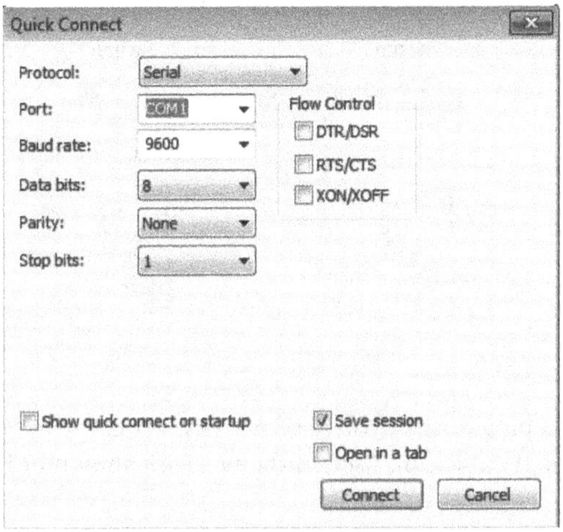

Notice that Baud Rate is set to 9600, Data Bits to 8, Parity to None, and no Flow Control options are set. At this point, you can click Connect and press the Enter key, and you should be connected to your Cisco device console port.

Figure 2.16 shows a nice 2960 switch with two console ports:

FIGURE 2.16 A Cisco 2960 console connection

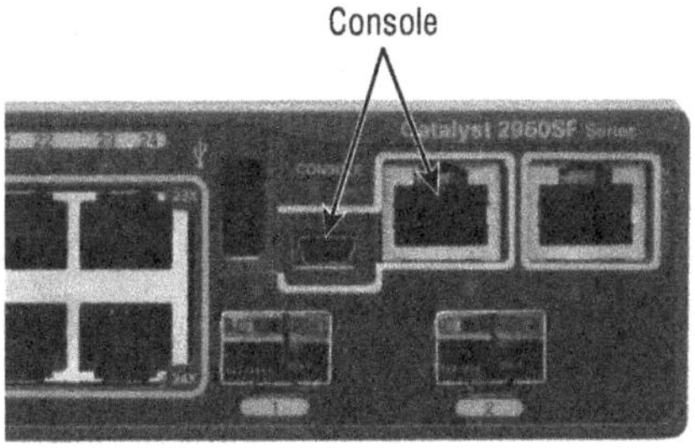

Notice there are two console connections on this new switch: a typical original RJ-45 connection and the newer mini type-B USB console. Remember, the new USB port supersedes the RJ-45 port if you just happen to plug into both at the same time, and the USB port can have speeds up to 115,200 Kbps, which is awesome if you have to use Xmodem to update an IOS. I've even seen some cables that work on iPhones and iPads and allow them to connect to these mini USB ports!

Now that you've seen the various RJ-45 UTP cables, what type of cable is used between the switches in Figure 2.17?

FIGURE 2.17 RJ-45 UTP cable question #1

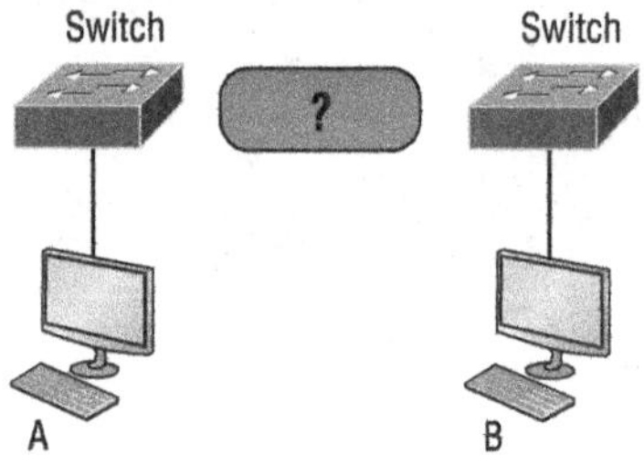

In order for host A to ping host B, you need a crossover cable to connect the two switches together. But what types of cables are used in the network shown in Figure 2.18?

FIGURE 2.18 RJ-45 UTP cable question #2

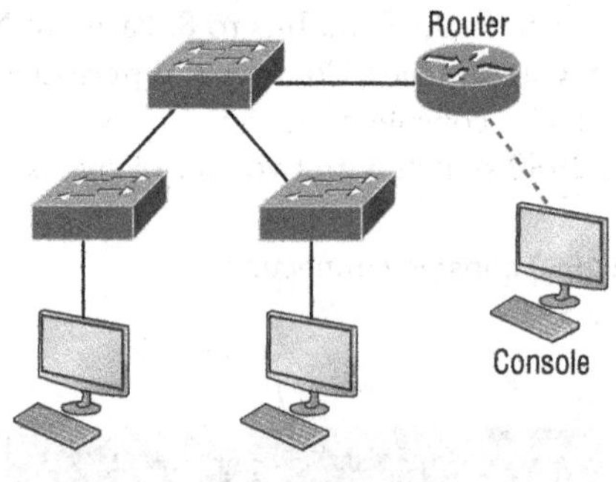

In Figure 2.18, there's a whole menu of cables in use. For the connection between the switches, we'd obviously use a crossover cable like we saw in Figure 2.13. The trouble is that you must understand that we have a console connection that uses a rolled cable. Plus, the connection from the router to the switch is a straight-through cable, as is true for the hosts to the switches. Keep in mind that if we had a serial connection, which we don't, we would use a V.35 connector to connect us to a WAN.

Fiber-Optic

Fiber-optic cabling has been around for a long time and has some solid standards. The cable allows for very fast transmission of data, is made of glass (or even plastic), is very thin, and works as a waveguide to transmit light between two ends of the fiber. Fiber-optic cabling has been used to go very long distances, as in intercontinental connections, but it is becoming more and more popular in Ethernet LAN networks due to the fast speeds available and because, unlike UTP, it's immune to interference like cross-talk.

Some main components of this cable are the core and the cladding. The core will hold the light, and the cladding confines the light in the core. The tighter the cladding, the smaller the core, and when the core is small, less light will be sent, but it can go faster and farther.

In Figure 2.19 you can see that there is a 9-micron core, which is very small and can be measured against a human hair, (50 microns.)

FIGURE 2.19 Typical fiber cable dimensions are in um (10^{-6} meters). Not to scale.

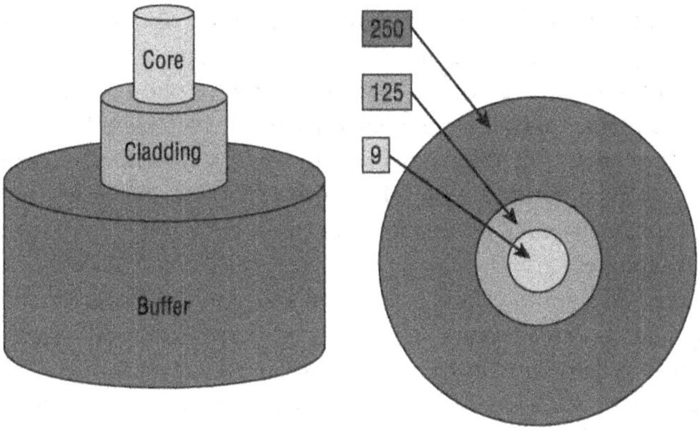

The cladding is 125 microns, which is actually a fiber standard that allows manufacturers to make connectors for all fiber cables. The last piece of this cable is the buffer, which is there to protect the delicate glass.

There are two major types of fiber optics: single-mode and multimode. Figure 2.20 shows the differences between multimode and single-mode fibers.

Single-mode is more expensive, has a tighter cladding, and can go much farther distances than multimode. The difference comes in the tightness of the cladding, which makes a smaller core, meaning that only one mode of light will propagate down the fiber. Multimode is looser and has a larger core, so it allows multiple light particles to travel down the glass. These particles have to be put back together at the receiving end, so distance is less than that with single-mode fiber, which allows only very few light particles to travel down the fiber.

There are about 70 different connectors for fiber, and Cisco uses a few different types. Looking back at Figure 2.16, the two bottom ports are referred to as Small Form-Factor Pluggables, or SFPs.

FIGURE 2.20 Multimode and single-mode fibers

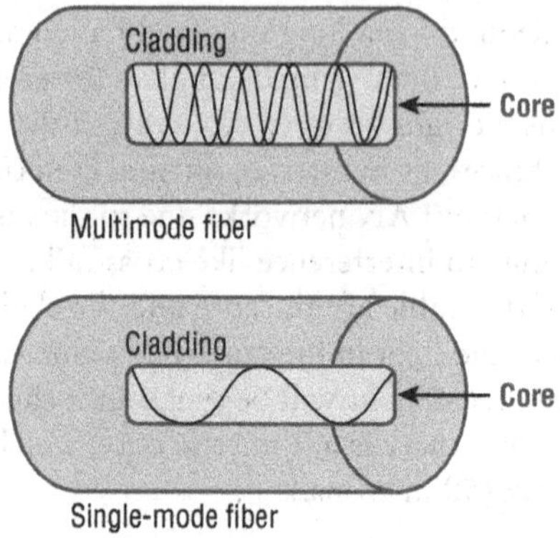

Power over Ethernet (802.3af, 802.3at)

Power over Ethernet (PoE and PoE+) technology describes a system for transmitting electrical power, along with data, to remote devices over standard twisted-pair cable in an Ethernet network. This technology is useful for powering IP phones (Voice over IP, or VoIP), wireless LAN access points, network cameras, remote network switches, embedded computers, and other appliances. These are all situations where it would be inconvenient, expensive, and possibly not even feasible to supply power separately. A big reason for this is that the main wiring must be installed by qualified, licensed electricians in order to meet legal and/or insurance mandates.

The IEEE has created a standard for PoE called 802.3af. For PoE+, it's referred to as 802.3at. These standards describe precisely how a powered device is detected and also defines two methods of delivering Power over Ethernet to a given powered device. Keep in mind that PoE+ standard, 802.3at, delivers more power than 802.3af, which is compatible with Gigabit Ethernet with four-wire pairs at 30w.

This process happens one of two ways: either by receiving the power from an Ethernet port on a switch (or other capable device) or via a power injector. And you can't use both approaches to get the job done. And be careful here because doing this wrong can lead to serious trouble! Be sure before connecting.

Remember, if you don't have a switch with PoE, you can use a power injector.

WARNING: Be really careful when using an external power injector! Take your time and make darn sure the power injector provides the voltage level for which your device was manufactured.

Summary

In this chapter, you learned the fundamentals of Ethernet networking and how hosts communicate on a network. You discovered how CSMA/CD works in an Ethernet half-duplex network.

I also talked about the differences between half- and full-duplex modes and discussed the collision detection mechanism called CSMA/CD.

I also described the common Ethernet cable types used in today's networks. You'd be wise to study that section really well!

Exam Essentials

Describe the operation of Carrier Sense Multiple Access with Collision Detection (CSMA/CD). CSMA/CD is a protocol that helps devices share the bandwidth evenly without having two devices transmit at the same time on the network medium. Although it does not eliminate collisions, it helps to greatly reduce them, which reduces retransmissions, resulting in a more efficient transmission of data for all devices.

Differentiate half-duplex and full-duplex communication and define the requirements to utilize each method. Full-duplex Ethernet uses two pairs of wires at the same time instead of one wire pair like half-duplex. Full-duplex allows for sending and receiving at the same time, using different wires to eliminate collisions, whereas half-duplex can send or receive but not at the same time and still can suffer collisions. To use full-duplex, the devices at both ends of the cable must be capable of and configured to perform full-duplex.

Describe the sections of a MAC address and the information contained in each section. The MAC, or hardware, address is a 48-bit (6-byte) address written in a hexadecimal format. The first 24 bits, or 3 bytes, are called the organizationally unique identifier (OUI), which is assigned by the IEEE to the manufacturer of the NIC. The balance of the number uniquely identifies the NIC.

Identify the binary and hexadecimal equivalent of a decimal number. Any number expressed in one format can also be expressed in the other two. The ability to perform this conversion is critical to understanding IP addressing and subnetting. Be sure to go through the written labs covering binary to decimal to hexadecimal conversion.

Identify the fields in the Data Link portion of an Ethernet frame. The fields in the Data Link portion of a frame include the preamble, Start Frame Delimiter, destination MAC address, source MAC address, Length or Type, Data, and Frame Check Sequence.

Identify the IEEE physical standards for Ethernet cabling. These standards describe the capabilities and physical characteristics of various cable types and include, but are not limited to, 10Base-2, 10Base-5, and 10Base-T.

Differentiate types of Ethernet cabling and identify their proper application. The three types of cables that can be created from an Ethernet cable are straight-through (to connect a PC's or router's Ethernet interface to a hub or switch), crossover (to connect hub to hub, hub to switch, switch to switch, or PC to PC), and rolled (for a console connection from a PC to a router or switch).

Describe the data encapsulation process and the role it plays in packet creation. Data encapsulation is a process whereby information is added to the frame from each layer of the OSI model. This is also called *packet creation*. Each layer communicates only with its peer layer on the receiving device.

Understand how to connect a console cable from a PC to a router and switch. Take a rolled cable and connect it from the COM port of the host to the console port of a router. Start your emulation program, such as PuTTy or SecureCRT, and set the bits per second to 9600 and flow control to None.

Written Labs

You can find the answers to these labs in Appendix A, "Answers to the Written Labs."

In this section, you'll complete the following labs to make sure you've got the information and concepts contained within them fully dialed in:

Lab 2.1: Binary/Decimal/Hexadecimal Conversion

Lab 2.2: CSMA/CD Operations

Lab 2.3: Cabling

Written Lab 2.1: Binary/Decimal/Hexadecimal Conversion

1. Convert from decimal IP address to binary format.

   Complete the following table to express 192.168.10.15 in binary format:

128	64	32	16	8	4	2	1	Binary

Complete the following table to express 172.16.20.55 in binary format:

128	64	32	16	8	4	2	1	Binary

Complete the following table to express 10.11.12.99 in binary format:

128	64	32	16	8	4	2	1	Binary

2. Convert the following from binary format to decimal IP address.

Complete the following table to express 11001100.00110011.10101010.01010101 in decimal IP address format:

128	64	32	16	8	4	2	1	Decimal

128	64	32	16	8	4	2	1	Decimal

Complete the following table to express 11000110.11010011.00111001.11010001 in decimal IP address format:

128	64	32	16	8	4	2	1	Decimal

Complete the following table to express 10000100.11010010.10111000.10100110 in decimal IP address format:

128	64	32	16	8	4	2	1	Decimal

3. Convert the following from binary format to hexadecimal.

Complete the following table to express 11011000.00011011.00111101.01110110 in hexadecimal:

128	64	32	16	8	4	2	1	Hexadecimal

Complete the following table to express 11001010.11110101.10000011.11101011 in hexadecimal:

128	64	32	16	8	4	2	1	Hexadecimal

Complete the following table to express 10000100.11010010.01000011.10110011 in hexadecimal:

128	64	32	16	8	4	2	1	Hexadecimal

128	64	32	16	8	4	2	1	Hexadecimal

Written Lab 2.2: CSMA/CD Operations

Carrier Sense Multiple Access with Collision Detection (CSMA/CD) helps to minimize collisions in the network, thereby increasing data transmission efficiency. Place the following steps of its operation in the order in which they occur after a collision.

- All hosts have equal priority to transmit after the timers have expired.
- Each device on the Ethernet segment stops transmitting for a short time until the timers expire.
- The collision invokes a random backoff algorithm.
- A jam signal informs all devices that a collision occurred.

Written Lab 2.3: Cabling

For each of the following situations, determine whether a straight-through, crossover, or rolled cable would be used.

1. Host to host
2. Host to switch or hub
3. Router direct to host
4. Switch to switch
5. Router to switch or hub
6. Hub to hub
7. Hub to switch
8. Host to a router console serial communication (COM) port

Review Questions

You can find the answers to these questions in Appendix B, "Answers to the Review Questions."

NOTE The following questions are designed to test your understanding of this chapter's material. For more information on how to get additional questions, please see www.lammle.com/ccna.

1. Which of the following three options are not similar between UTP Cat 5e and Cat 6a cabling? (Choose three.)
   A. Both operate at a frequency of 500 MHz.
   B. Both support runs of up to 55 meters.
   C. Both support runs of up to 100 meters.
   D. Both support speeds of at least 1 Gigabit.
   E. Both support speeds of up to 10 Gigabit.
2. ________ on an Ethernet network is the retransmission delay that's enforced when a collision occurs.
   A. Backoff
   B. Carrier sense
   C. Forward delay
   D. Jamming
3. On which type of device could the situation shown in the diagram occur?

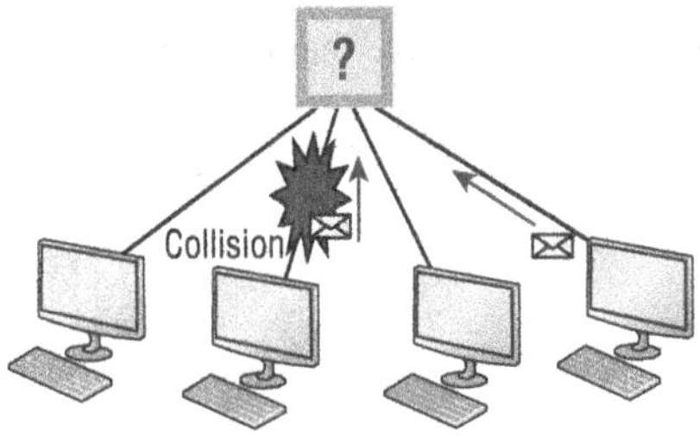

   A. Hub
   B. Switch
   C. Router
   D. Bridge

4. In the Ethernet II frame shown here, what is the function of the section labeled "FCS"?

Ethernet_II

Preamble 7 bytes	SFD 1 byte	Destination 6 bytes	Source 6 bytes	Type 2 bytes	Data and Pad 46 – 1500 bytes	FCS 4 bytes

   A. Allows the receiving devices to lock the incoming bit stream
   B. Error detection
   C. Identifies the upper-layer protocol
   D. Identifies the transmitting device

5. A network interface port has collision detection and carrier sensing enabled on a shared twisted-pair network. From this statement, what is known about the network interface port?
   A. This is a 10 Mbps switch port.
   B. This is a 100 Mb/s switch port.
   C. This is an Ethernet port operating at half-duplex.
   D. This is an Ethernet port operating at full-duplex.
   E. This is a port on a network interface card in a PC.

6. For what purposes does the Ethernet protocol use physical addresses? (Choose two.)
   A. To uniquely identify devices at layer 2
   B. To allow communication with devices on a different network
   C. To differentiate a layer 2 frame from a layer 3 packet
   D. To establish a priority system to determine which device gets to transmit first
   E. To allow communication between different devices on the same physical LAN network
   F. To allow detection of a remote device when its physical address is unknown

7. Between which systems could you use a cable that uses the pinout pattern shown here?

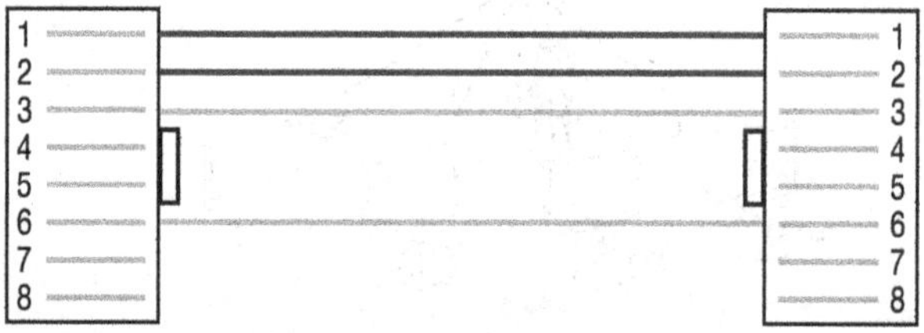

   A. With a connection from a switch to a switch
   B. With a connection from a router to a router
   C. With a connection from a host to a host
   D. With a connection from a host to a switch

8. In an Ethernet network, under what two scenarios can devices transmit? (Choose two.)
   - **A.** When they receive a special token
   - **B.** When there is a carrier
   - **C.** When they detect that no other devices are sending
   - **D.** When the medium is idle
   - **E.** When the server grants access

9. What type of cable uses the pinout shown here?

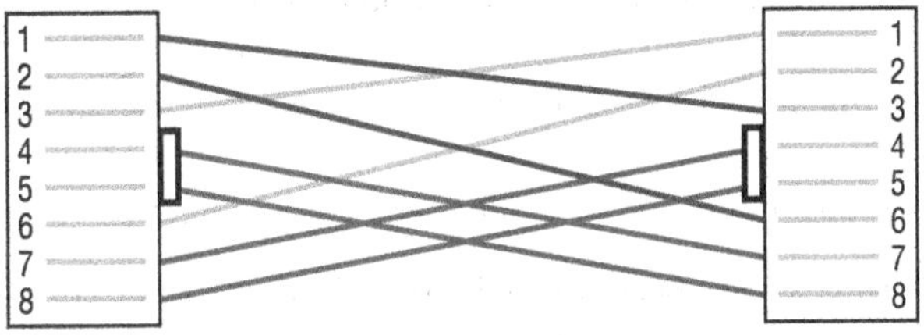

   - **A.** Fiber-optic
   - **B.** Crossover Gigabit Ethernet cable
   - **C.** Straight-through Fast Ethernet
   - **D.** Coaxial

10. When configuring a terminal emulation program, which of the following is an incorrect setting?
    - **A.** Bit rate: 9600
    - **B.** Parity: None
    - **C.** Flow control: None
    - **D.** Data bits: 1

11. Which part of a MAC address indicates whether the address is a locally or globally administered address?
    - **A.** FCS
    - **B.** I/G bit
    - **C.** OUI
    - **D.** U/L bit

12. What cable type uses the pinout arrangement shown here?

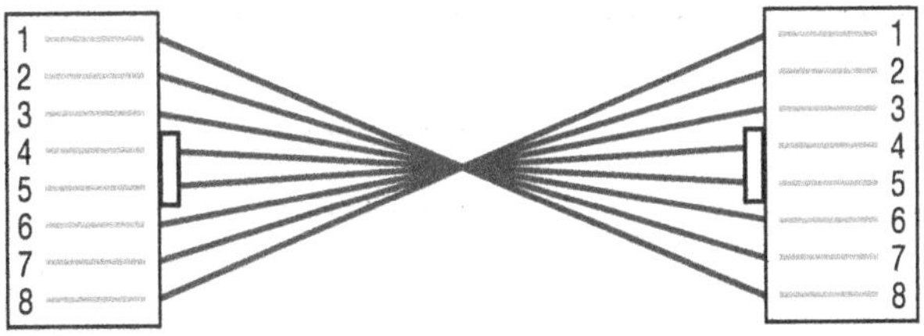

A. Fiber-optic

B. Rolled

C. Straight-through

D. Crossover

13. Which of the following is *not* one of the actions taken in the operation of CSMA/CD when a collision occurs?

A. A jam signal informs all devices that a collision occurred.

B. The collision invokes a random backoff algorithm on the systems involved in the collision.

C. Each device on the Ethernet segment stops transmitting for a short time until its backoff timer expires.

D. All hosts have equal priority to transmit after the timers have expired.

14. Which of the following statements is *false* with regard to Ethernet?

A. There are very few collisions in full-duplex mode.

B. A dedicated switch port is required for each full-duplex node.

C. The host network card and the switch port must be capable of operating in full-duplex mode to use full-duplex.

D. The default behavior of 10Base-T and 100Base-T hosts is 10 Mbps half-duplex if the autodetect mechanism fails.

15. In the following diagram, identify the cable types required for connections A and B.

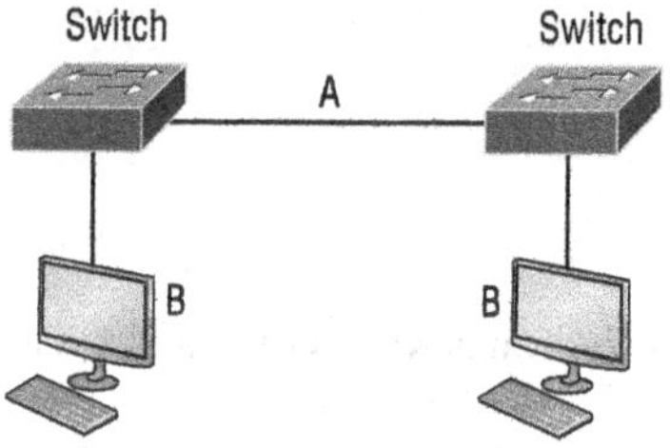

A. A= crossover, B= crossover

B. A= crossover, B= straight-through

C. A= straight-through, B= straight-through

D. A= straight-through, B= crossover

16. In the following image, match the cable type to the standard with which it goes.

IEEE 802.3u	100Base-Tx
IEEE 802.3	10Base-T

IEEE 802.3ab	1000Base-T
IEEE 802.3z	1000Base-SX

17. The cable used to connect to the console port on a router or switch is called a __________ cable.
    - **A.** Crossover
    - **B.** Rolled
    - **C.** Straight-through
    - **D.** Full-duplex
18. Which of the following items does a socket comprise?
    - **A.** IP address and MAC address
    - **B.** IP address and port number
    - **C.** Port number and MAC address
    - **D.** MAC address and DLCI
19. Which of the following hexadecimal numbers converts to 28 in decimal?
    - **A.** 1c
    - **B.** 12
    - **C.** 15
    - **D.** ab
20. What cable type is shown in the following graphic?

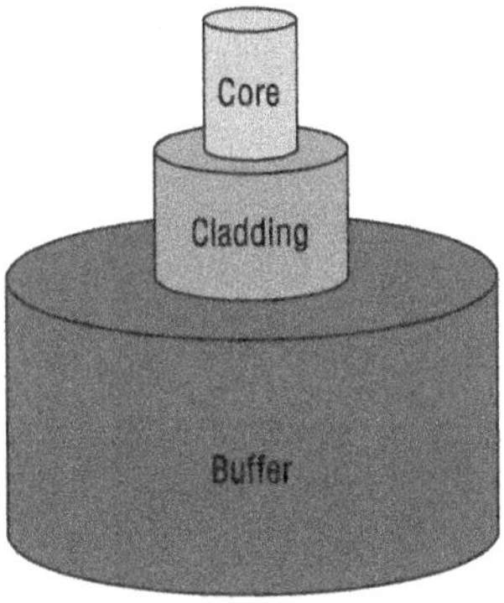

- **A.** Fiber optic
- **B.** Rolled
- **C.** Coaxial
- **D.** Full-duplex

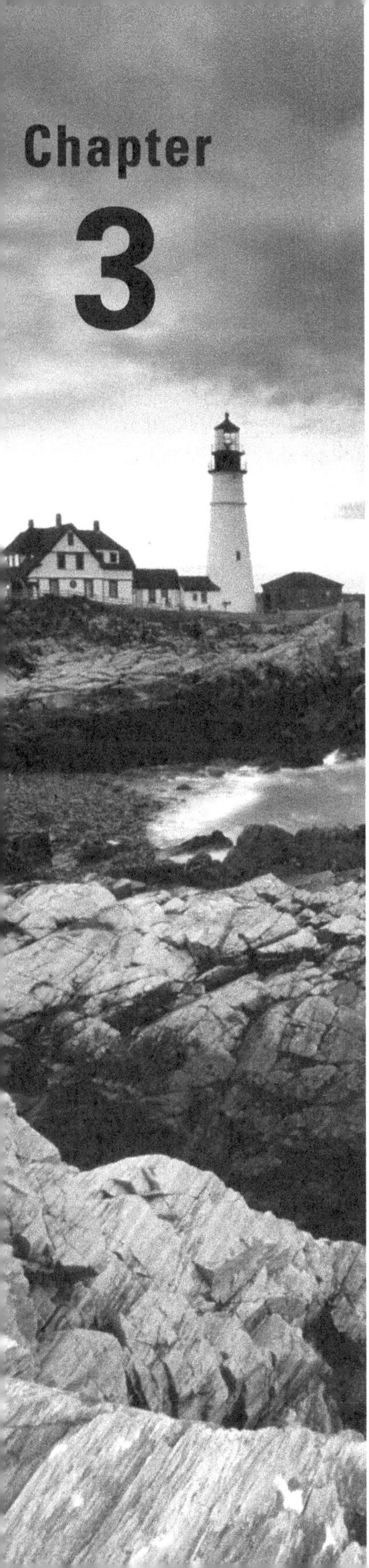

Chapter 3

TCP/IP

THE CCNA EXAM TOPICS COVERED IN THIS CHAPTER INCLUDE THE FOLLOWING:

✓ ***1.0 Network Fundamentals***

- 1.5 Compare TCP to UDP
- 1.6 Configure and verify IPv4 addressing and subnetting
- 1.7 Describe private IPv4 addressing

✓ ***4.0 IP Services***

- 4.3 Explain the role of DHCP and DNS within the network
- 4.4 Explain the function of SNMP in network operations
- 4.9 Describe the capabilities and function of TFTP/FTP in the network

The *Transmission Control Protocol/Internet Protocol (TCP/IP)* suite was designed and implemented by the Department of Defense (DoD) to ensure and preserve data integrity as well as maintain communications in the event of catastrophic war. So, it follows that if designed and implemented correctly, a TCP/IP network can be secure, dependable, and resilient.

In this chapter, I'll cover the protocols of TCP/IP, and throughout this book, you'll learn how to create a solid TCP/IP network with Cisco routers and switches.

We'll begin by exploring the DoD's version of TCP/IP, and then compare that version and its protocols with the OSI reference model that we discussed earlier.

Once you understand the protocols and processes used at the various levels of the DoD model, we'll take the next logical step by delving into the world of IP addressing and the different classes of IP addresses used in networks today.

Because having a good grasp of the various IPv4 address types is critical to understanding IP addressing and subnetting, we'll go into these key topics in detail. I'll close this chapter by discussing the various types of IPv4 addresses you'll need to have down before moving on to the rest of the book.

NOTE To find bonus material, as well as Todd Lammle videos, practice questions, and hands-on labs, please see `www.lammle.com/ccna`.

Introducing TCP/IP

TCP/IP is at the very core of all things networking, so I really want to make sure you have a comprehensive and functional command of it. I'll start by giving you the whole TCP/IP backstory, including its inception, and then move on to describe the important technical goals as defined by its original architects. And, of course, I'll include how TCP/IP compares to the theoretical OSI model.

A Brief History of TCP/IP

TCP first came on the scene way back in 1973, and in 1978, it was divided into two distinct protocols: TCP and IP. Later, in 1983, TCP/IP replaced the Network Control Protocol (NCP) and was authorized as the official means of data transport for anything connecting to ARPAnet, the Internet's ancestor. The DoD's Advanced Research Projects Agency (ARPA) created this ancient network way back in 1957 in a Cold War reaction to the Soviet launch of *Sputnik*. Also in 1983, ARPA was renamed DARPA and divided into ARPAnet and MILNET until both were finally dissolved in 1990.

It may be counterintuitive, but most of the development work on TCP/IP happened at UC Berkeley in Northern California, where a group of scientists were simultaneously working on the Berkeley version of UNIX, which soon became known as the Berkeley Software Distribution (BSD) series of UNIX versions. Of course, because TCP/IP worked so well, it was packaged into subsequent releases of BSD Unix and offered to other universities and institutions if they bought the distribution tape. So, basically, BSD Unix bundled with TCP/IP began as shareware in the world of academia. As a result, it became the foundation for the tremendous success and unprecedented growth of today's Internet as well as smaller, private and corporate intranets.

As usual, what started as a small group of TCP/IP aficionados evolved, and as it did, the US government created a program to test any new published standards and make sure they passed certain criteria. This was to protect TCP/IP's integrity and ensure that no developer changed anything too dramatically or added any proprietary features. It's this very quality—this open-systems approach to the TCP/IP family of protocols—that sealed its popularity because it guarantees a solid connection between myriad hardware and software platforms with no strings attached.

TCP/IP and the DoD Model

The DoD model is basically a condensed version of the OSI model that comprises four instead of seven layers:

- Process/Application layer
- Host-to-Host layer or Transport layer
- Internet layer
- Network Access layer or Link layer

Figure 3.1 offers a comparison of the DoD model and the OSI reference model. As you can see, the two are similar in concept, but each has a different number of layers with different names. Cisco may at times use different names for the same layer, such as Host-to-Host and Transport at the layer above the Internet layer, as well as Network Access and Link to describe the bottom layer.

A vast array of protocols join forces at the DoD model's *Process/Application layer*. These processes integrate the various activities and duties spanning the focus of the OSI's corresponding top three layers (Application, Presentation, and Session). We'll focus on a few of the most important applications found in the CCNA objectives. In short, the Process/Application layer defines protocols for node-to-node application communication and controls user-interface specifications.

FIGURE 3.1 The DoD and OSI models

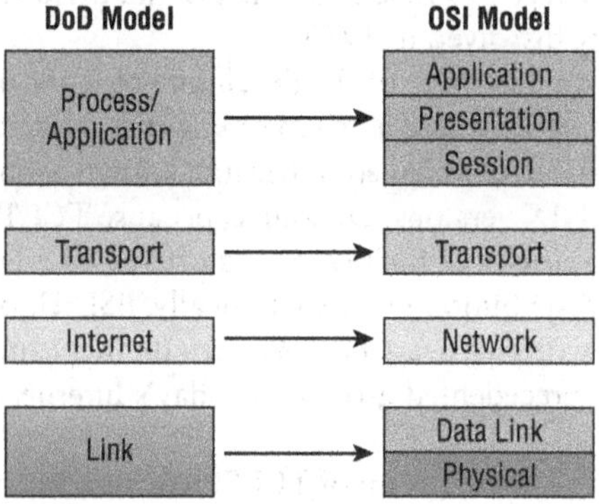

The *Host-to-Host layer or Transport layer* parallels the functions of the OSI's Transport layer, defining protocols for setting up the level of transmission service for applications. It tackles issues like creating reliable end-to-end communication and ensuring the error-free delivery of data. It handles packet sequencing and maintains data integrity.

The *Internet layer* corresponds to the OSI's Network layer, designating the protocols relating to the logical transmission of packets over the entire network. It takes care of the addressing of hosts by giving them an IP (Internet Protocol) address and handles the routing of packets among multiple networks.

At the bottom of the DoD model, the *Network Access layer or Link layer* implements the data exchange between the host and the network. The equivalent of the Data Link and Physical layers of the OSI model, the Network Access layer oversees hardware addressing and defines protocols for the physical transmission of data. Again, the reason TCP/IP became so popular is because there were no set physical layer specifications, meaning that it could run on any existing or future physical network!

The DoD and OSI models are alike in design and concept and have similar functions in similar layers. Figure 3.2 shows the TCP/IP protocol suite and how its protocols relate to the DoD model layers.

FIGURE 3.2 The TCP/IP protocol suite

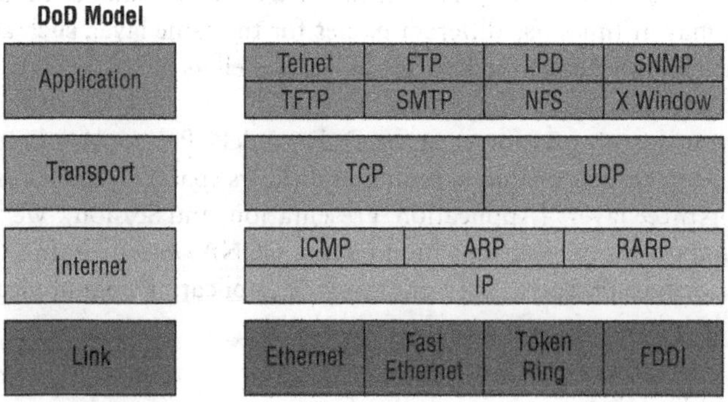

Next, we'll look at the different protocols in more detail, beginning with those found at the Process/Application layer.

The Process/Application Layer Protocols

In this section, I'll describe the different applications and services typically used in IP networks. Although there are many more protocols than defined here, we'll focus on the protocols most relevant to the CCNA objectives. Here's a list of the protocols and applications we'll cover in this section:

- Telnet
- SSH
- FTP
- TFTP
- SNMP
- HTTP
- HTTPS
- NTP
- DNS
- DHCP/BootP
- APIPA

Telnet

Telnet was one of the first Internet standards. It was developed in 1969, and is the chameleon of protocols—its specialty is terminal emulation. It allows a user on a remote client machine, called the Telnet client, to access the resources of another machine, the Telnet server, in order to access a command-line interface. Telnet achieves this by pulling a fast one on the Telnet server and making the client machine appear as though it were a terminal directly attached to the local network. This projection is actually a software image—a virtual terminal that can interact with the chosen remote host. A major drawback is that there are no encryption techniques available within the Telnet protocol, so everything must be sent in cleartext—including passwords! Figure 3.3 shows an example of a Telnet client trying to connect to a Telnet server.

These emulated terminals are of the text-mode type and can execute defined procedures such as displaying menus that give users the opportunity to choose options and access the applications on the duped server. Users begin a Telnet session by running the Telnet client software and then logging into the Telnet server. Telnet uses an 8-bit, byte-oriented data connection over TCP, which makes it very thorough. It's still in use today because it is so simple and easy to use, with very low overhead—but again, as with everything sent in cleartext, it's not recommended in production.

FIGURE 3.3 Telnet

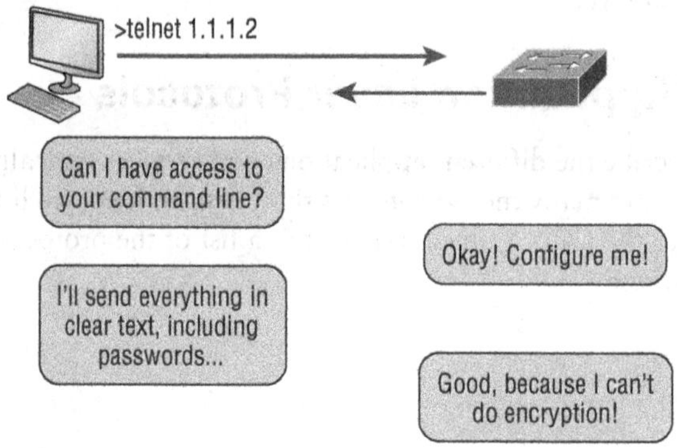

Secure Shell (SSH)

Secure Shell (SSH) sets up a secure session that's similar to Telnet over a standard TCP/IP connection. It's used for doing things like logging into systems, running programs on remote systems, and moving files from one system to another—and it does all of this while maintaining an encrypted connection. Figure 3.4 shows a SSH client trying to connect to a SSH server. The client must send the data encrypted.

FIGURE 3.4 Secure Shell

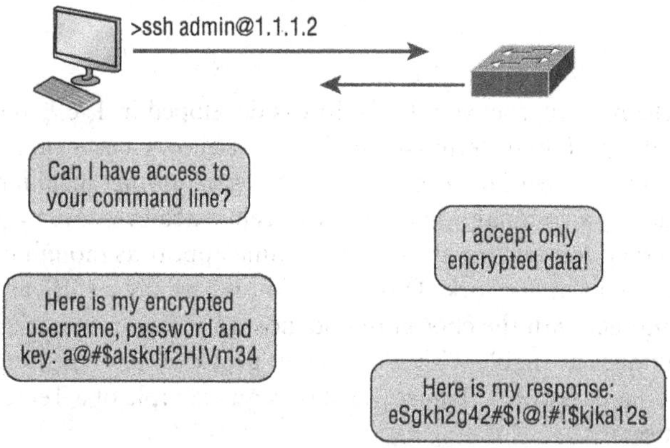

You can think of SSH as the new-generation protocol used in place of the antiquated and very unused *rsh* and *rlogin*—even Telnet.

File Transfer Protocol (FTP)

File Transfer Protocol (FTP) actually lets us transfer files, and it can accomplish this between any two machines using it. But FTP isn't just a protocol; it's also a program. Operating as a protocol, FTP is used by applications. As a program, it's employed by users to perform file tasks by hand. FTP also allows for access to both directories and files and can accomplish certain types of directory operations, such as relocating into different ones (Figure 3.5).

FIGURE 3.5 FTP

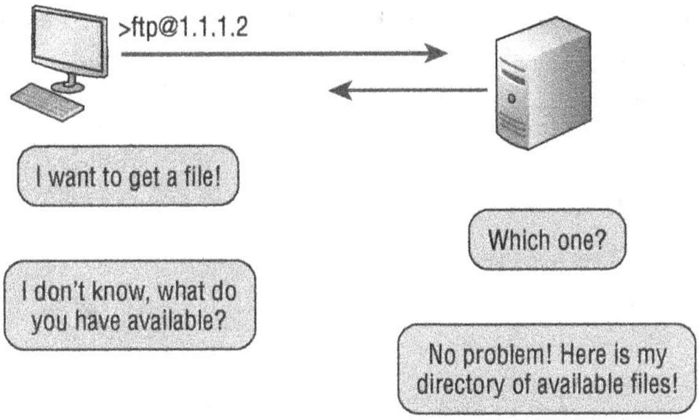

But accessing a host through FTP is only the first step. Users must then be subjected to an authentication login that's usually secured with usernames and passwords implemented by system administrators to restrict access. You can get around this somewhat by adopting the username *anonymous*, but you'll be limited in what you'll be able to access.

Even when employed by users manually as a program, FTP's functions are limited to listing and manipulating directories, typing file contents, and copying files between hosts. It can't execute remote files as programs.

Trivial File Transfer Protocol (TFTP)

Trivial File Transfer Protocol (TFTP) is the stripped-down, stock version of FTP. It's the protocol of choice if you know exactly what you want and where to find it because it's so fast and easy to use.

But TFTP doesn't offer the abundance of functions that FTP does because it has no directory-browsing abilities, meaning that it can only send and receive files, (Figure 3.6). Still, it's heavily used for managing file systems on Cisco devices.

This compact little protocol also skimps in the data department, sending much smaller blocks of data than FTP. Also, there's no authentication as with FTP, so it's even more insecure. Few sites support it because of the inherent security risks.

Real World Scenario

When Should You Use FTP?

Let's say everyone at your San Francisco office needs a 50 GB file emailed to them right away. What do you do? Many email servers would reject that email due to size limits because many ISPs don't allow files larger than 10 MB to be emailed. Even if there are no size limits on the server, it would still take a while to send this huge file. FTP to the rescue!

If you need to send someone a large file or you need to get a large file from someone, FTP is a nice choice. To use FTP, you would need to set up an FTP server on the Internet so that the files can be shared.

Besides resolving size issues, FTP is faster than email. In addition, because it uses TCP and is connection-oriented, if the session dies, FTP can sometimes start up where it left off. Try that with your email client!

FIGURE 3.6 TFTP

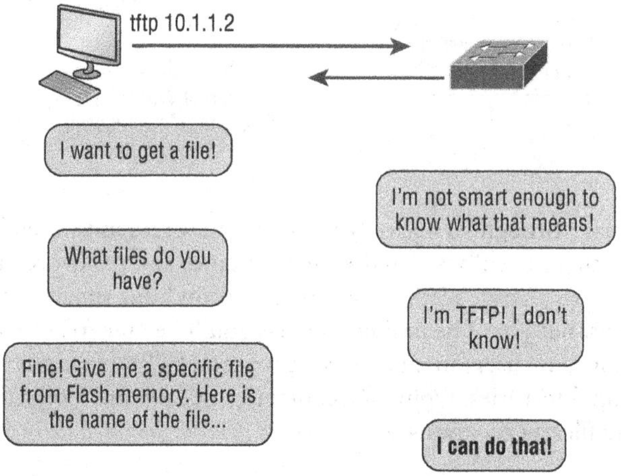

Simple Network Management Protocol (SNMP)

Simple Network Management Protocol (SNMP) collects and manipulates valuable network information, as you can see in Figure 3.7. It gathers data by polling the devices on the network from a network management station (NMS) at fixed or random intervals, requiring them to disclose certain information, or even asking for certain information from the device. In addition, network devices can inform the NMS station about problems as they occur so the network administrator is alerted.

FIGURE 3.7 SNMP

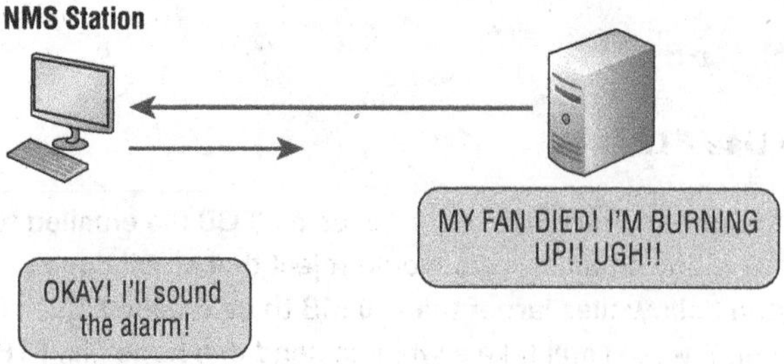

When all is well, SNMP receives something called a *baseline*—a report delimiting the operational traits of a healthy network. This protocol can also stand as a watchdog over the network, quickly notifying managers of any sudden turn of events. These network watchdogs are called *agents*, and when aberrations occur, agents send an alert called a *trap* to the management station.

SNMP Versions 1, 2, and 3

SNMP versions 1 and 2 are pretty much obsolete. This doesn't mean you won't see them in a network now and then, but you'll only come across v1 rarely, if ever. SNMPv2 provided improvements, especially in performance. But one of the best additions was called GETBULK, which allowed a host to retrieve a large amount of data at once. Even so, v2 never really caught on in the networking world, and SNMPv3 is now the standard. Unlike v1, which used only UDP, v3 uses both TCP and UDP and added even more security, message integrity, authentication, and encryption.

Hypertext Transfer Protocol (HTTP)

All those snappy websites comprising a mélange of graphics, text, links, ads, and so on rely on the *Hypertext Transfer Protocol (HTTP)* to make it all possible (Figure 3.8). It's used to manage communications between web browsers and web servers and opens the right resource when you click a link, wherever that resource may actually reside.

FIGURE 3.8 HTTP

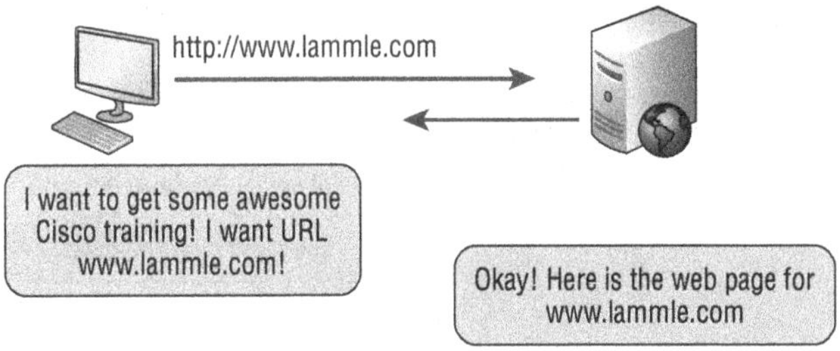

In order for a browser to display a web page, it must first find the exact server that has the right web page, plus the exact details that identify the information requested. This information must then be sent back to the browser. Nowadays, it's highly doubtful that a web server would have only one page to display!

Your browser can understand what you need when you enter a Uniform Resource Locator (URL), which we usually refer to as a web address, such as `www.lammle.com/ccna` and `www.lammle.com/blog`.

So, basically, each URL defines the protocol used to transfer data, the name of the server, and the particular web page on that server.

Hypertext Transfer Protocol Secure (HTTPS)

Hypertext Transfer Protocol Secure (HTTPS) is also known as Secure Hypertext Transfer Protocol. It uses Secure Sockets Layer (SSL). Sometimes, you'll see it referred to as SHTTP or S-HTTP, which were slightly different protocols, but since Microsoft supported HTTPS, it became the de facto standard for securing web communication. As indicated, it's a secure version of HTTP that arms you with a whole bunch of security tools for keeping transactions secure between a web browser and a server.

It's what your browser needs to fill out forms, sign in, authenticate, and encrypt an HTTP message when you do things online like make a reservation, access your bank, or buy something.

Network Time Protocol (NTP)

Cheers to Professor David Mills of the University of Delaware for coming up with this handy protocol that's used to synchronize the clocks on our computers to one standard time source (typically, an atomic clock). *Network Time Protocol (NTP)* works by synchronizing devices to ensure that all computers on a given network agree on the time (Figure 3.9).

FIGURE 3.9 NTP

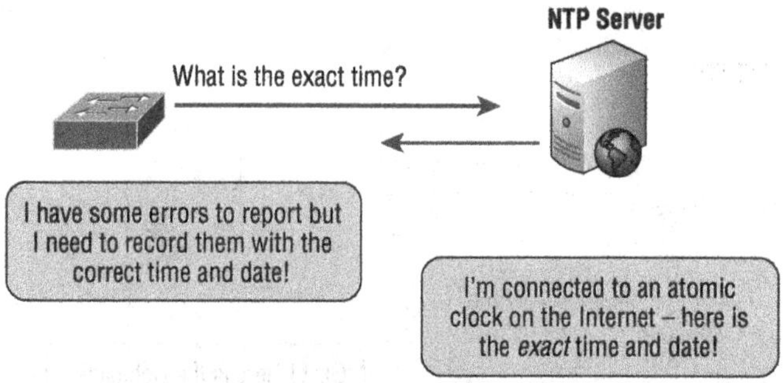
NTP Server
What is the exact time?
I have some errors to report but I need to record them with the correct time and date!
I'm connected to an atomic clock on the Internet – here is the *exact* time and date!

This may sound pretty simple, but it's very important because so many of the transactions done today are time and date stamped. Think about databases—a server can get messed up pretty badly and crash if it's out of sync with the machines connected to it even by mere seconds. You just can't have a transaction entered by a machine at, say, 1:50 a.m. when the server records that transaction as having occurred at 1:45 a.m. So basically, NTP works to prevent a "back to the future" scenario from bringing down the network—very important indeed!

Domain Name Service (DNS)

Domain Name Service (DNS) resolves hostnames—specifically, Internet names, such as `www.lammle.com`. But you don't have to actually use DNS. You just type in the IP address of any device you want to communicate with and find the IP address of a URL by using the Ping program. For example, `>ping www.cisco.com` will return the IP address resolved by DNS.

An IP address identifies hosts on a network and the Internet as well, but DNS was designed to make our lives easier. Think about this: What would happen if you wanted to move your web page to a different service provider? The IP address would change, and no one would know what the new one is. DNS allows you to use a domain name to specify an IP address. You can change the IP address as often as you want, and no one will know the difference.

To resolve a DNS address from a host, you'd typically type in the URL from your favorite browser, which would hand the data to the Application layer interface to be transmitted on the network. The application would look up the DNS address and send a UDP request to your DNS server to resolve the name (Figure 3.10).

FIGURE 3.10 DNS

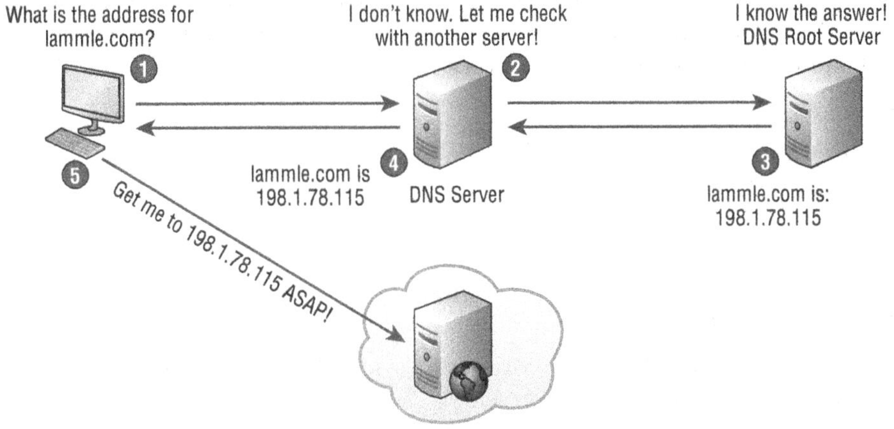

If your first DNS server doesn't know the answer to the query, then the DNS server forwards a TCP request to its root DNS server. Once the query is resolved, the answer is transmitted back to the originating host, which means the host can now request the information from the correct web server.

DNS is used to resolve a *fully qualified domain name (FQDN)*—for example, `www.lammle.com` or `todd.lammle.com`. An FQDN is a hierarchy that can logically locate a system based on its domain identifier.

If you want to resolve the name *todd*, you either must type in the FQDN of `todd.lammle.com` or have a device such as a PC or router add the suffix for you. For example, on a Cisco router, you can use the command `ip domain-name lammle.com` to append each request with the `lammle.com` domain. If you don't do that, you'll have to type in the FQDN to get DNS to resolve the name.

TIP An important thing to remember about DNS is that if you can ping a device with an IP address but cannot use its FQDN, then you might have some type of DNS configuration failure.

Dynamic Host Configuration Protocol (DHCP)/Bootstrap Protocol (BootP)

Dynamic Host Configuration Protocol (DHCP) assigns IP addresses to hosts. It allows for easier administration and works well in small to very large network environments. Many types of hardware can be used as a DHCP server, including a Cisco router.

DHCP differs from BootP in that BootP assigns an IP address to a host but the host's hardware address must be entered manually in a BootP table. You can think of DHCP as a dynamic BootP, but remember that BootP is also used to send an operating system that a host can boot from. DHCP can't do that.

Even so, there's still a lot of information a DHCP server can provide to a host when the host is requesting an IP address from the DHCP server. Here's a list of the most common types of information a DHCP server can provide:

- IP address
- Subnet mask
- Domain name
- Default gateway (routers)
- DNS server address
- WINS server address

A client that sends out a DHCP Discover message in order to receive an IP address sends out a broadcast at both layer 2 and layer 3.

- The layer 2 broadcast is all *F*s in hex, which looks like this: ff:ff:ff:ff:ff:ff.
- The layer 3 broadcast is 255.255.255.255, which means all networks and all hosts.

DHCP is connectionless, which means it uses User Datagram Protocol (UDP) at the Transport layer. The Transport layer is also known as the Host-to-Host layer. We'll talk about this a bit later.

Seeing is believing, so here's an example of output from my analyzer showing the layer 2 and layer 3 broadcasts:

```
Ethernet II, Src: 0.0.0.0 (00:0b:db:99:d3:5e),Dst:
Broadcast(ff:ff:ff:ff:ff:ff)
Internet Protocol, Src: 0.0.0.0 (0.0.0.0),Dst: 255.255.255.255(255.255.255.255)
```

The Data Link and Network layers are both sending out "all hands" broadcasts saying, "Help—I don't know my IP address!"

Figure 3.11 shows the process of a client/server relationship using a DHCP connection.

FIGURE 3.11 DHCP client four-step process (DORA)

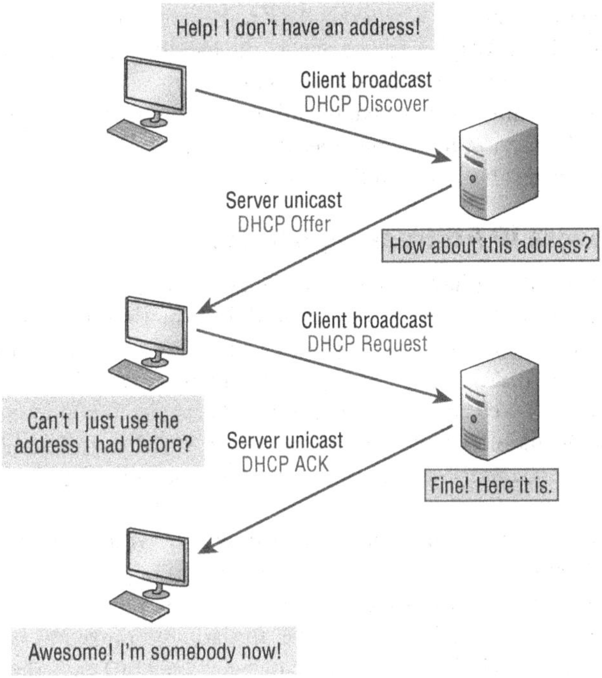

This is the four-step process a client takes to receive an IP address from a DHCP server using what we call DORA, or Discover, Offer, Request, Acknowledgement:

1. The DHCP client broadcasts a DHCP **Discover** message looking for a DHCP server (port 67).
2. The DHCP server that received the DHCP Discover message sends a layer 2 unicast DHCP **Offer** message back to the host.
3. The client then broadcasts to the server a DHCP **Request** message asking for the offered IP address and possibly other information.
4. The server finalizes the exchange with a unicast DHCP **Acknowledgment** message.

DHCP Conflicts

A DHCP address conflict occurs when two hosts use the same IP address. This sounds bad, and it is. (We won't have to discuss this problem once we get to the chapter on IPv6!)

So, during IP address assignment, a DHCP server checks for conflicts using the Ping program to test the availability of the address before it's assigned from the pool. If no host replies, then the DHCP server assumes that the IP address is not already allocated. This helps the server know that it's providing a good address, but what about the host? To provide extra protection against that ugly IP conflict issue, the host can broadcast for its own address.

A host uses something called a *gratuitous ARP* to help avoid a possible duplicate address. The DHCP client sends an ARP broadcast out on the local LAN or VLAN using its newly assigned address to solve conflicts before they occur.

So, if an IP address conflict is detected, the address is removed from the DHCP pool (scope). And it's really important to remember that the address will not be assigned to a host until the administrator resolves the conflict by hand!

Automatic Private IP Addressing (APIPA)

Okay, so what happens if you have a few hosts connected together with a switch or hub and you don't have a DHCP server? You can add IP information by hand, known as *static IP addressing*, but later Windows operating systems provide a feature called Automatic Private IP Addressing (APIPA). With APIPA, clients can automatically self-configure an IP address and subnet mask—basic IP information that hosts use to communicate—when a DHCP server isn't available. The IP address range for APIPA is 169.254.0.1 through 169.254.255.254. The client also configures itself with a default Class B subnet mask of 255.255.0.0.

But when you're in your corporate network working and you have a DHCP server running, and your host shows that it's using this IP address range, it means that either your DHCP client on the host is not working or the server is down or can't be reached due to some network issue. No one who's seen a host in this address range has been happy about it!

Now, let's take a look at the Transport layer, or what the DoD calls the Host-to-Host layer.

The Host-to-Host or Transport Layer Protocols

The main purpose of the Host-to-Host layer is to shield the upper-layer applications from the complexities of the network. This layer says to the upper layer, "Just give me your data stream, with any instructions, and I'll begin the process of getting your information ready to send."

Next, I'll introduce you to the two protocols at this layer:

- Transmission Control Protocol (TCP)
- User Datagram Protocol (UDP)

In addition, we'll look at some of the key host-to-host protocol concepts, as well as the port numbers.

> **NOTE** Remember, this is still considered layer 4, and Cisco really likes the way layer 4 can use acknowledgments, sequencing, and flow control.

Transmission Control Protocol (TCP)

Transmission Control Protocol (TCP) takes large blocks of information from an application and breaks them into segments. It numbers and sequences each segment so that the destination's TCP stack can put the segments back into the order the application intended. After these segments are sent on the transmitting host, TCP waits for an acknowledgment of the receiving end's TCP virtual circuit session, retransmitting any segments that aren't acknowledged.

Before a transmitting host starts to send segments down the model, the sender's TCP stack contacts the destination's TCP stack to establish a connection. This creates a *virtual circuit*, and this type of communication is known as *connection-oriented*. During this initial handshake, the two TCP layers also agree on the amount of information that's going to be sent before the recipient's TCP sends back an acknowledgment. With everything agreed upon in advance, the path is paved for reliable communication to take place.

TCP is a full-duplex, connection-oriented, reliable, and accurate protocol, but establishing all these terms and conditions, in addition to error checking, is no small task. TCP is very complicated, and so not surprisingly, it's costly in terms of network overhead. And since today's networks are much more reliable than those of yore, this added reliability is often unnecessary. Most programmers use TCP because it removes a lot of programming work, but for real-time video and VoIP, *User Datagram Protocol (UDP)* is often better because using it results in less overhead.

TCP Segment Format

Since the upper layers just send a data stream to the protocols in the Transport layers, I'll use Figure 3.12 to demonstrate how TCP segments a data stream and prepares it for the Internet layer. When the Internet layer receives the data stream, it routes the segments as packets through an internetwork. The segments are handed to the receiving host's Host-to-Host layer protocol, which rebuilds the data stream for the upper-layer applications or protocols.

FIGURE 3.12 TCP segment format

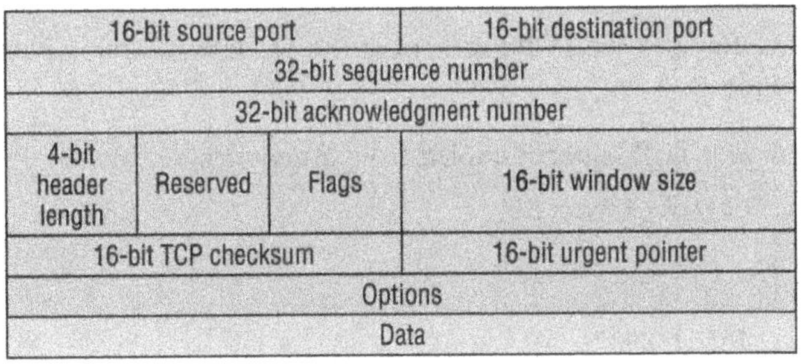

16-bit source port
16-bit destination port
32-bit sequence number
32-bit acknowledgment number
4-bit header length
Reserved
Flags
16-bit window size
16-bit TCP checksum
16-bit urgent pointer
Options
Data

Figure 3.12 shows the TCP segment format and the different fields within the TCP header. This isn't important to memorize for the Cisco exam objectives, but you need to understand it well because it's really good foundational information.

The TCP header is 20 bytes long, or up to 24 bytes with options. Again, it's good to understand what each field in the TCP segment is in order to build a strong educational foundation:

Source Port This is the port number of the application on the host sending the data, which I'll talk about more thoroughly a little later in this chapter.

Destination Port This is the port number of the application requested on the destination host.

Sequence Number A number used by TCP that puts the data back in the correct order or retransmits missing or damaged data during a process called sequencing.

Acknowledgment Number The value is the TCP octet that is expected next.

Header Length The number of 32-bit words in the TCP header, which indicates where the data begins. The TCP header (even one including options) is an integral number of 32 bits in length.

Reserved Always set to zero.

Code Bits/Flags Controls functions used to set up and terminate a session.

Window The window size the sender is willing to accept, in octets.

Checksum The cyclic redundancy check (CRC), used because TCP doesn't trust the lower layers and checks everything. The CRC checks the header and data fields.

Urgent A valid field only if the Urgent pointer in the code bits is set. If so, this value indicates the offset from the current sequence number, in octets, where the segment of non-urgent data begins.

Options May be 0, meaning that no options have to be present, or a multiple of 32 bits. However, if any options are used that do not cause the option field to total a multiple of 32 bits, a padding of 0s must be used to make sure the data begins on a 32-bit boundary. These boundaries are known as words.

Data Handed down to the TCP protocol at the Transport layer, which includes the upper-layer headers.

Let's take a look at a TCP segment copied from a network analyzer:

```
TCP - Transport Control Protocol
Source Port: 5973
Destination Port: 23
Sequence Number: 1456389907
Ack Number: 1242056456
Offset: 5
Reserved: %000000
Code: %011000
```

```
Ack is valid
Push Request
Window: 61320
Checksum: 0x61a6
Urgent Pointer: 0
No TCP Options
TCP Data Area:
vL.5.+.5.+.5.+.5 76 4c 19 35 11 2b 19 35 11 2b 19 35 11
2b 19 35 +. 11 2b 19
Frame Check Sequence: 0x0d00000f
```

Did you notice that everything I talked about earlier is in the segment? As you can see from the number of fields in the header, TCP creates a lot of overhead. Again, this is why application developers may opt for efficiency over reliability to save overhead and go with UDP instead. It's also defined at the Transport layer as an alternative to TCP.

User Datagram Protocol (UDP)

User Datagram Protocol (UDP) is basically the scaled-down economy model of TCP, which is why UDP is sometimes referred to as a thin protocol. Like a thin person on a park bench, a thin protocol doesn't take up a lot of room—or in this case, require much bandwidth on a network.

UDP doesn't offer all the bells and whistles of TCP, but it does a fabulous job of transporting information that doesn't require reliable delivery, using far less network resources. (UDP is covered thoroughly in Request for Comments [RFC] 768.)

So clearly, there are times that it's wise for developers to opt for UDP rather than TCP, one of them being when reliability is already taken care of at the Process/Application layer. Network File System (NFS) handles its own reliability issues, making the use of TCP both impractical and redundant. Ultimately, however, it's up to the application developer to opt for using UDP or TCP, not the user who wants to transfer data faster!

UDP does *not* sequence the segments and does not care about the order in which the segments arrive at the destination. It just sends the segments off and forgets about them. It doesn't follow through, check up on them, or even allow for an acknowledgment of safe arrival—complete abandonment! Because of this, it's referred to as an unreliable protocol. This does not mean that UDP is ineffective, only that it doesn't deal with reliability issues at all.

Furthermore, UDP doesn't create a virtual circuit, nor does it contact the destination before delivering information to it. Because of this, it's also considered a *connectionless* protocol. Since UDP assumes that the application will use its own reliability method, it doesn't use any itself. This presents an application developer with a choice when running the Internet Protocol stack: TCP for reliability or UDP for faster transfers.

It's important to know how this process works because if the segments arrive out of order, which is commonplace in IP networks, they'll simply be passed up to the next layer in whatever order they were received. This can result in some seriously garbled data! On the other hand, TCP sequences the segments so they get put back together in exactly the right order—something UDP just can't do.

UDP Segment Format

Figure 3.13 clearly illustrates UDP's markedly lean overhead as compared to TCP's hungry requirements. Look at the figure carefully—can you see that UDP doesn't use windowing or provide for acknowledgments in the UDP header?

FIGURE 3.13 UDP segment

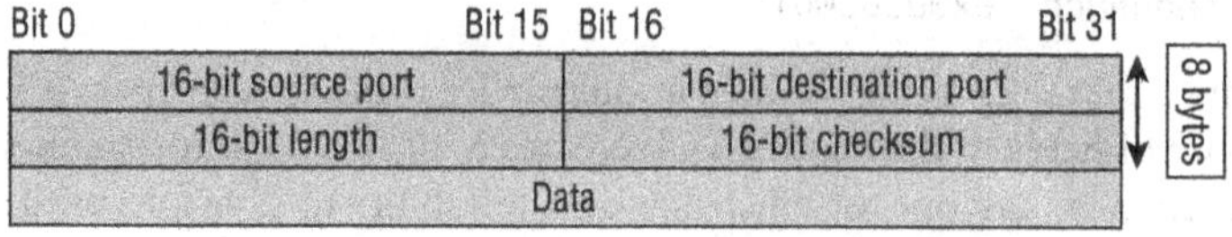

It's important for you to understand what each field in the UDP segment is:

Source Port Port number of the application on the host sending the data

Destination Port Port number of the application requested on the destination host

Length Length of UDP header and UDP data

Checksum Checksum of both the UDP header and UDP data fields

Data Upper-layer data

Like TCP, UDP doesn't trust the lower layers and runs its own CRC. Remember, the Frame Check Sequence (FCS) is the field that houses the CRC, which is why you can see the FCS information.

The following shows a UDP segment caught on a network analyzer:

```
UDP - User Datagram Protocol
Source Port: 1085
Destination Port: 5136
Length: 41
Checksum: 0x7a3c
UDP Data Area:
..Z......00 01 5a 96 00 01 00 00 00 00 00 11 0000 00
...C..2._C._C 2e 03 00 43 02 1e 32 0a 00 0a 00 80 43 00 80
Frame Check Sequence: 0x00000000
```

Notice that low overhead! Try to find the sequence number, ack number, and window size in the UDP segment. You can't, because they just aren't there!

Key Concepts of Host-to-Host Protocols

Since you've now seen both a connection-oriented (TCP) and connectionless (UDP) protocol in action, it's a good time to summarize the two here. Table 3.1 highlights some of the key concepts about these two protocols for you to memorize.

TABLE 3.1 Key features of TCP and UDP

TCP	UDP
Sequenced	Unsequenced
Reliable	Unreliable
Connection-oriented	Connectionless
Virtual circuit	Low overhead
Acknowledgments	No acknowledgment
Windowing flow control	No windowing or flow control of any type

Just in case all of this isn't quite clear yet, a telephone analogy will really help you understand how TCP works. Most of us know that before you speak to someone on a phone, you must first establish a connection with that other person no matter where they are. This is akin to establishing a virtual circuit with the TCP protocol. If you were giving someone important information during your conversation, you might say something like, "Did you get that?" Saying things like that is a lot like a TCP acknowledgment—it's designed to get you verification. From time to time, especially on mobile phones, people ask, "Are you still there?" And people end their conversations with a "goodbye" of some kind, putting closure on the phone call, which you can think of as tearing down the virtual circuit that was created for your communication session. TCP performs these types of functions.

Conversely, using UDP is more like sending a postcard. To do that, you don't need to contact the other party first; you simply write your message, address the postcard, and send it off. This is analogous to UDP's connectionless orientation. Since the message on the postcard is probably not vitally important, you don't need an acknowledgment of its receipt. Similarly, UDP does not involve acknowledgments.

Take a look at Figure 3.14, which includes TCP, UDP, and the applications associated to each protocol. We'll talk about all of this in the next section.

FIGURE 3.14 Port numbers for TCP and UDP

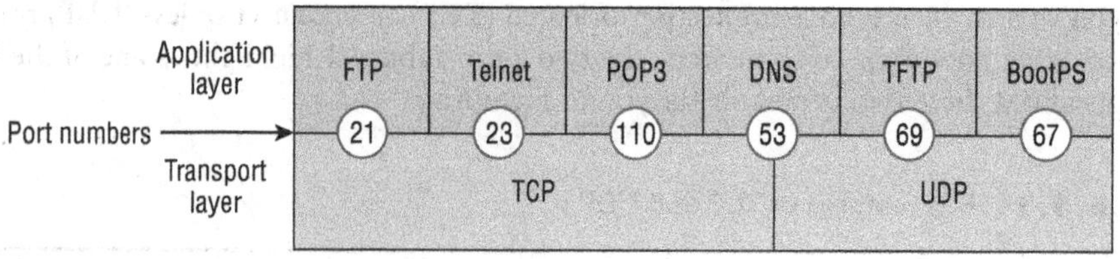

Port Numbers

TCP and UDP must use *port numbers* to communicate with the upper layers because these are what keep track of different conversations crossing the network simultaneously. Originating-source port numbers are dynamically assigned by the source host and will equal some number starting at 1024. Port numbers 1023 and below are defined in RFC 3232 (or just see `www.iana.org`), which discusses what we call well-known port numbers.

Virtual circuits that don't use an application with a well-known port number are assigned port numbers randomly from a specific range instead. These port numbers identify the source and destination application or process in the TCP segment.

NOTE

The Requests for Comments (RFCs) form a series of notes about the Internet (originally the ARPAnet) started in 1969. These notes discuss many aspects of computer communication, focusing on networking protocols, procedures, programs and concepts. They also include meeting notes, opinions, and sometimes, even humor. You can find the RFCs by visiting `www.iana.org`.

Figure 3.14 illustrates how both TCP and UDP use port numbers. I'll cover the different port numbers that can be used next:

- Numbers below 1024 are considered well-known port numbers and are defined in RFC 3232.
- Numbers 1024 and above are used by the upper layers to set up sessions with other hosts and by TCP and UDP to use as source and destination addresses in the segment.

TCP Session: Source Port

Let's take a minute to check out analyzer output showing a TCP session I captured with my analyzer software session:

```
TCP - Transport Control Protocol
Source Port: 5973
Destination Port: 23
Sequence Number: 1456389907
Ack Number: 1242056456
Offset: 5
```

```
Reserved: %000000
Code: %011000
Ack is valid
Push Request
Window: 61320
Checksum: 0x61a6
Urgent Pointer: 0
No TCP Options
TCP Data Area:
vL.5.+.5.+.5.+.5 76 4c 19 35 11 2b 19 35 11 2b 19 35 11
2b 19 35 +. 11 2b 19
Frame Check Sequence: 0x0d00000f
```

Notice that the source host makes up the source port, which in this case is 5973. The destination port is 23, which is used to tell the receiving host the purpose of the intended connection (Telnet).

By looking at this session, you can see that the source host makes up the source port by using numbers from 1024 to 65535. But why does the source make up a port number? The source does that to differentiate between sessions with different hosts because how would a server know where information is coming from if it didn't have a different number from a sending host? TCP and the upper layers don't use hardware and logical addresses to understand the sending host's address, like the Data Link and Network layer protocols do. They use port numbers instead.

TCP Session: Destination Port

You'll sometimes look at an analyzer and see that only the source port is above 1024 and the destination port is a well-known port, as shown in the following trace:

```
TCP - Transport Control Protocol
Source Port: 1144
Destination Port: 80 World Wide Web HTTP
Sequence Number: 9356570
Ack Number: 0
Offset: 7
Reserved: %000000
Code: %000010
Synch Sequence
Window: 8192
Checksum: 0x57E7
Urgent Pointer: 0
TCP Options:
Option Type: 2 Maximum Segment Size
Length: 4
```

```
MSS: 536
Option Type: 1 No Operation
Option Type: 1 No Operation
Option Type: 4
Length: 2
Opt Value:
No More HTTP Data
Frame Check Sequence: 0x43697363
```

Sure enough—the source port is over 1024, but the destination port is 80, indicating an HTTP service. The server, or receiving host, will change the destination port if it needs to.

In the preceding trace, a "SYN" packet (listed as Synch Sequence in this analysis) is sent to the destination device. This Synch Sequence, as shown in the output, is what's used to inform the remote destination device that it wants to create a session.

TCP Session: Syn Packet Acknowledgment

The next trace shows an acknowledgment to the SYN packet:

```
TCP - Transport Control Protocol
Source Port: 80 World Wide Web HTTP
Destination Port: 1144
Sequence Number: 2873580788
Ack Number: 9356571
Offset: 6
Reserved: %000000
Code: %010010
Ack is valid
Synch Sequence
Window: 8576
Checksum: 0x5F85
Urgent Pointer: 0
TCP Options:
Option Type: 2 Maximum Segment Size
Length: 4
MSS: 1460
No More HTTP Data
Frame Check Sequence: 0x6E203132
```

Notice the `Ack is valid`, which means that the source port was accepted and the device agreed to create a virtual circuit with the originating host.

So, here again, you can see the response from the server shows that the source is 80 and the destination is the 1144 sent from the originating host—all's well!

Table 3.2 lists the typical applications used in the TCP/IP suite by showing their well-known port numbers and the Transport layer protocols used by each application or process. It's a really good idea to memorize this table:

TABLE 3.2 Key protocols that use TCP and UDP

TCP	UDP
Telnet 23	SNMP 161
SMTP 25	TFTP 69
HTTP 80	DNS 53
FTP 20, 21	BootP/DHCP 67
DNS 53	NTP 123
HTTPS 443	
SSH 22	
POP3 110	
IMAP4 143	

Notice that DNS uses both TCP and UDP. Whether it opts for one or the other depends on what it's trying to do. Even though it's not the only application that can use both protocols, it's certainly one that you should make sure to remember.

NOTE: What makes TCP reliable is sequencing, acknowledgments, and flow control (windowing). Remember: no reliability with UDP!

I want to discuss one more item before we move down to the Internet layer—session multiplexing. Session multiplexing is used by both TCP and UDP and basically allows a single computer, with a single IP address, to have multiple sessions occurring simultaneously. Say you go to `www.lammle.com`, begin browsing, and click a link to another page. Doing this opens another session to your host. Now you go to `www.lammle.com/ccna` from another window, and that site opens a window as well. Now you have three sessions open using one IP address because the Session layer is sorting the separate requests based on the Transport layer port number. This is the job of the Session layer: to keep Application layer data separate!

The Internet Layer Protocols

In the DoD model, there are two main reasons for the Internet layer's existence: routing and providing a single network interface to the upper layers.

None of the other upper- or lower-layer protocols have any functions relating to routing—that complex and important task belongs entirely to the Internet layer. The Internet layer's second duty is to provide a single network interface to the upper-layer protocols. Without this layer, application programmers would need to write "hooks" into every one of their applications for each different Network Access layer protocol. This would not only be a pain in the neck, but it would lead to different versions of each application—one for Ethernet, another one for wireless, and so on. To prevent this, IP provides one single network interface for the upper-layer protocols. With that mission accomplished, it's then the job of IP and the various Network Access layer protocols to get along and work together.

All network roads don't lead to Rome—they lead to IP. And all the other protocols at this layer, as well as all those at the upper layers, use it. Never forget that. All paths through the DoD model go through IP. Here's a list of the important protocols at the Internet layer, which I'll cover individually in detail coming up:

- Internet Protocol (IP)
- Internet Control Message Protocol (ICMP)
- Address Resolution Protocol (ARP)

Internet Protocol (IP)

Internet Protocol (IP) essentially is the Internet layer. The other protocols found here merely exist to support it. IP holds the big picture and could be said to "see all" because it's aware of all the interconnected networks. It can do this because all the machines on the network have a software or logical address called an IP address. We'll explore this more thoroughly later in this chapter.

For now, understand that IP looks at each packet's destination address. Then, using a routing table, it decides where a packet is to be sent next, choosing the best path to send it upon. The protocols of the Network Access layer at the bottom of the DoD model don't possess IP's enlightened scope of the entire network; they deal only with physical links (local networks).

Identifying devices on networks requires answering these two questions: Which network is it on? And what is its ID on that network? The first answer is the *software address*, or *logical address*. You can think of this as the part of the address that specifies the correct street. The second answer is the hardware address, which goes a step further to specify the correct mailbox. All hosts on a network have a logical ID called an IP address. This is the software, or logical, address and contains valuable encoded information, greatly simplifying the complex task of routing. (IP is discussed in RFC 791.)

IP receives segments from the Host-to-Host layer and fragments them into datagrams (packets) if necessary. IP then reassembles datagrams back into segments on the receiving side. Each datagram is assigned the IP address of the sender and that of the recipient. Each router or switch (layer 3 device) that receives a datagram makes routing decisions based on the packet's destination IP address.

Figure 3.15 shows an IP header. This will give you a picture of what the IP protocol has to go through every time user data that's destined for a remote network is sent from the upper layers.

FIGURE 3.15 IP header

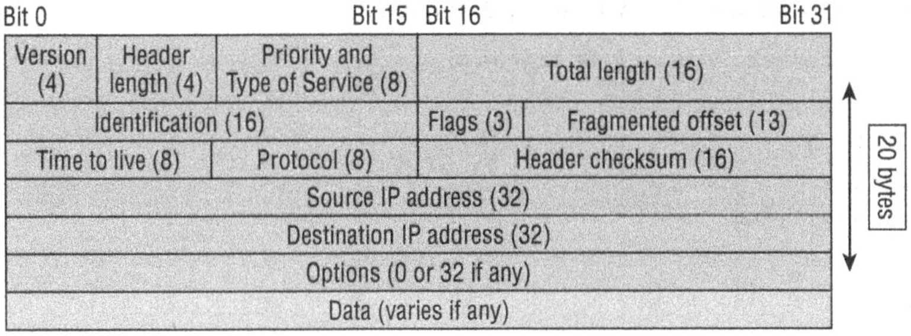

The following fields make up the IP header:

Version IP version number.

Header Length Header length (HLEN) in 32-bit words.

Priority and Type of Service Type of Service tells how the datagram should be handled. The first 3 bits are the priority bits, now called the differentiated services bits.

Total Length Length of the packet, including header and data.

Identification Unique IP-packet value used to differentiate fragmented packets from different datagrams.

Flags Specifies whether fragmentation should occur.

Fragment Offset Provides fragmentation and reassembly if the packet is too large to put in a frame. It also allows different maximum transmission units (MTUs) on the Internet.

Time To Live The time to live (TTL) is set into a packet when it's originally generated. If it doesn't get to where it's supposed to go before the TTL expires, boom—it's gone. This stops IP packets from continuously circling the network looking for a home.

Protocol The port of the upper-layer protocols; for example, TCP is port 6, and UDP is port 17. Also supports Network layer protocols (not ports), like ARP and ICMP, and can be referred to as the Type field in some analyzers. We'll talk about this field more in a minute.

Header Checksum Cyclic redundancy check (CRC) on header only.

Source IP Address 32-bit IP address of sending station.

Destination IP Address 32-bit IP address of the station this packet is destined for.

Options Used for network testing, debugging, security, and more.

Data After the IP option field, will be the upper-layer data.

Here's a snapshot of an IP packet caught on a network analyzer. Notice that all the header information discussed previously appears here:

```
IP Header - Internet Protocol Datagram
Version: 4
Header Length: 5
Precedence: 0
Type of Service: %000
Unused: %00
Total Length: 187
Identifier: 22486
Fragmentation Flags: %010 Do Not Fragment
Fragment Offset: 0
Time To Live: 60
IP Type: 0x06 TCP
Header Checksum: 0xd031
Source IP Address: 10.7.1.30
Dest. IP Address: 10.7.1.10
No Internet Datagram Options
```

The IP Type field is typically a Protocol field, but this analyzer sees it as an IP Type field. This is important: if the header didn't carry the protocol information for the next layer, IP wouldn't know what to do with the data carried in the packet. The preceding example clearly tells IP to hand the segment to TCP.

Figure 3.16 demonstrates how the Network layer sees the protocols at the Transport layer when it needs to hand a packet up to the upper-layer protocols.

FIGURE 3.16 The Protocol field in an IP header

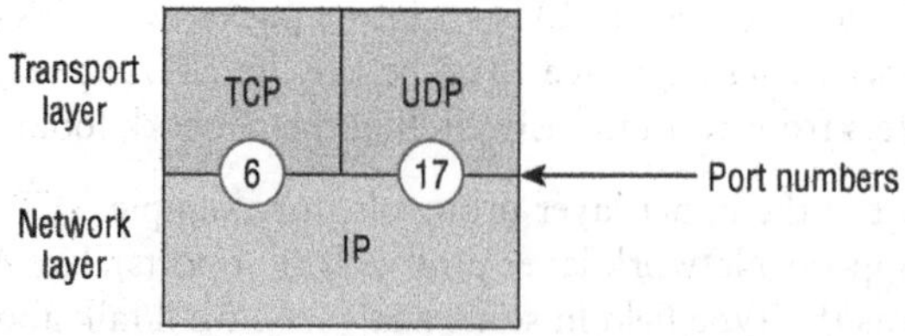

In this example, the Protocol field tells IP to send the data to either TCP 6h or UDP 17h. It will be UDP or TCP only if the data is part of a data stream headed for an upper-layer service or application. It could just as easily be destined for Internet Control Message Protocol (ICMP), Address Resolution Protocol (ARP), or some other type of Network layer protocol.

Table 3.3 lists some other popular protocols that can be specified in the Protocol field.

TABLE 3.3 Possible protocols found in the Protocol field of an IP header

Protocol	Protocol Number
ICMP	1
IP in IP (tunneling)	4
TCP	6
UDP	17
EIGRP	88
OSPF	89
IPv6	41
GRE	47
Layer 2 Tunnel (L2TP)	115

NOTE: You can find a complete list of Protocol field numbers at `www.iana.org/assignments/protocol-numbers`.

Internet Control Message Protocol (ICMP)

Internet Control Message Protocol (ICMP) works at the Network layer and is used by IP for many different services. ICMP is basically a management protocol and messaging service provider for IP. Its messages are carried as IP datagrams. RFC 1256 is an annex to ICMP, which gives hosts extended capability in discovering routes to gateways.

ICMP packets have the following characteristics:

- They can provide hosts with information about network problems.
- They are encapsulated within IP datagrams.

The following are some common events and messages that ICMP relates to:

Destination Unreachable If a router can't send an IP datagram any further, it uses ICMP to send a message back to the sender, advising it of the situation.

For example, take a look at Figure 3.17, which shows that interface e0 of the Lab_B router is down.

FIGURE 3.17 An ICMP error message is sent to the sending host from the remote router.

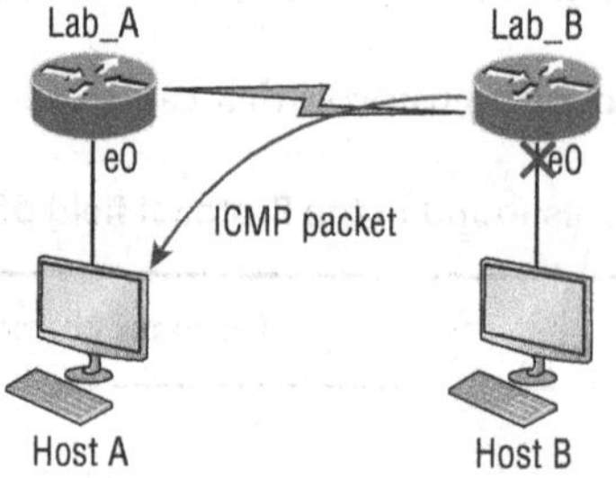

When Host A sends a packet destined for Host B, the Lab_B router will send an ICMP destination unreachable message back to the sending device—Host A in this example.

Buffer Full/Source Quench If a router's memory buffer for receiving incoming datagrams is full, it will use ICMP to send out this message alert until the congestion abates.

Hops/Time Exceeded Each IP datagram is allotted a certain number of routers, called *hops*, to pass through. If it reaches its limit of hops before arriving at its destination, the last router to receive that datagram deletes it. The executioner router then uses ICMP to send an obituary message, informing the sending machine of the demise of its datagram.

Ping Packet Internet Groper (Ping) uses ICMP echo request and reply messages to check the physical and logical connectivity of machines on an internetwork.

Traceroute Using ICMP time-outs, Traceroute is used to discover the path a packet takes as it traverses an internetwork.

NOTE Traceroute is usually just called trace. Microsoft Windows uses tracert to allow you to verify address configurations in your internetwork.

The following data is from a network analyzer catching an ICMP echo request:

```
Flags: 0x00
Status: 0x00
Packet Length: 78
Timestamp: 14:04:25.967000 12/20/03
Ethernet Header
Destination: 00:a0:24:6e:0f:a8
Source: 00:80:c7:a8:f0:3d
Ether-Type: 08-00 IP
IP Header - Internet Protocol Datagram
Version: 4
Header Length: 5
```

```
Precedence: 0
Type of Service: %000
Unused: %00
Total Length: 60
Identifier: 56325
Fragmentation Flags: %000
Fragment Offset: 0
Time To Live: 32
IP Type: 0x01 ICMP
Header Checksum: 0x2df0
Source IP Address: 100.100.100.2
Dest. IP Address: 100.100.100.1
No Internet Datagram Options
ICMP - Internet Control Messages Protocol
ICMP Type: 8 Echo Request
Code: 0
Checksum: 0x395c
Identifier: 0x0300
Sequence Number: 4352
ICMP Data Area:
abcdefghijklmnop 61 62 63 64 65 66 67 68 69 6a 6b 6c 6d 6e 6f 70
qrstuvwabcdefghi 71 72 73 74 75 76 77 61 62 63 64 65 66 67 68 69
Frame Check Sequence: 0x00000000
```

Notice anything unusual? Did you catch the fact that even though ICMP works at the Internet (Network) layer, it still uses IP to do the Ping request? The IP Type field in the IP header is 0x01, which specifies that the data we're carrying is owned by the ICMP protocol. Remember, all segments or data *must* go through IP!

NOTE The Ping program uses the alphabet in the data portion of the packet as a payload, typically around 100 bytes by default, unless, of course, you are pinging from a Windows device, which thinks the alphabet stops at the letter *W* (and doesn't include *X*, *Y*, or *Z*) and then starts at *A* again. Go figure!

If you remember reading about the Data Link layer and the different frame types in your CCNA pre-foundation studies, you should be able to look at the preceding trace and tell what type of Ethernet frame this is. The only fields are destination hardware address, source hardware address, and Ether-Type. The only frame that uses an Ether-Type field exclusively is an Ethernet_II frame.

We'll move on soon, but before we get into the ARP protocol, let's take another look at ICMP in action. Figure 3.18 shows an internetwork—it has a router, so it's an internetwork, right?

FIGURE 3.18 ICMP in action

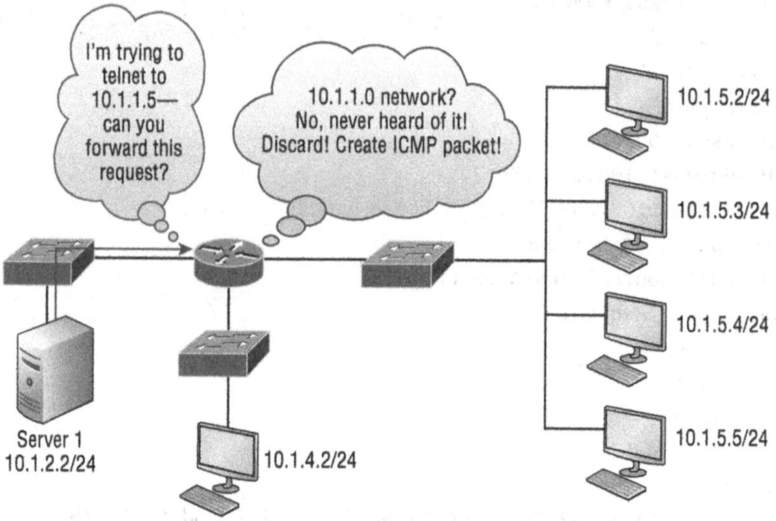

Server 1 (10.1.2.2) Telnets to 10.1.1.5 from a DOS prompt. What do you think Server 1 will receive as a response? Server 1 will send the Telnet data to the default gateway, which is the router, and the router will drop the packet because there isn't a network 10.1.1.0 in the routing table. Because of this, Server 1 will receive an ICMP network unreachable message back from the router.

Address Resolution Protocol (ARP)

Address Resolution Protocol (ARP) finds the hardware address of a host from a known IP address. Here's how it works: When IP has a datagram to send, it must inform a Network Access protocol, such as Ethernet or wireless, of the destination's hardware address on the local network. Remember that it has already been informed by upper-layer protocols of the destination's IP address. If IP doesn't find the destination host's hardware address in the ARP cache, it uses ARP to find this information.

As IP's detective, ARP interrogates the local network by sending out a broadcast asking the machine with the specified IP address to reply with its hardware address. Basically, ARP translates the software (IP) address into a hardware address—for example, the destination machine's Ethernet adapter address—and from it, deduces its whereabouts on the LAN by broadcasting for this address.

Figure 3.19 shows how an ARP broadcast looks to a local network.

FIGURE 3.19 Local ARP broadcast

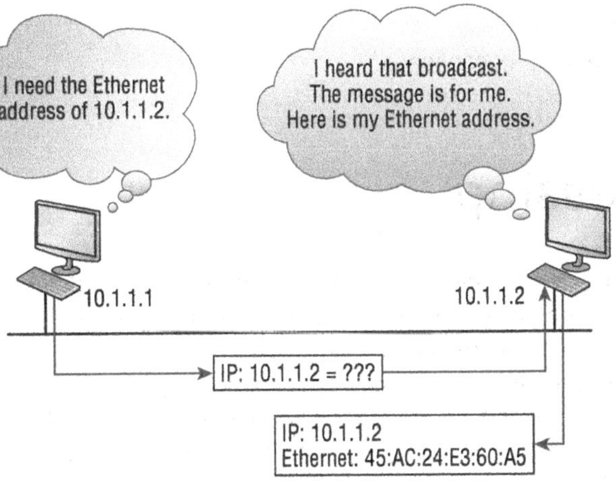

NOTE

ARP resolves IP addresses to Ethernet (MAC) addresses.

The following trace shows an ARP broadcast—notice that the destination hardware address is unknown and is all *F*s in hex (all 1s in binary)—and is a hardware address broadcast:

```
Flags: 0x00
Status: 0x00
Packet Length: 64
Timestamp: 09:17:29.574000 12/06/03
Ethernet Header
Destination: FF:FF:FF:FF:FF:FF Ethernet Broadcast
Source: 00:A0:24:48:60:A5
Protocol Type: 0x0806 IP ARP
ARP - Address Resolution Protocol
Hardware: 1 Ethernet (10Mb)
Protocol: 0x0800 IP
Hardware Address Length: 6
Protocol Address Length: 4
Operation: 1 ARP Request
Sender Hardware Address: 00:A0:24:48:60:A5
Sender Internet Address: 172.16.10.3
Target Hardware Address: 00:00:00:00:00:00 (ignored)
Target Internet Address: 172.16.10.10
```

```
Extra bytes (Padding):
................ 0A 0A 0A 0A 0A 0A 0A 0A 0A 0A 0A 0A 0A
0A 0A 0A 0A 0A
Frame Check Sequence: 0x00000000
```

IP Addressing

One of the most important topics in any discussion of TCP/IP is IP addressing. An *IP address* is a numeric identifier assigned to each machine on an IP network. It designates the specific location of a device on the network.

An IP address is a software address, not a hardware address—the latter is hard-coded on a network interface card (NIC) and used for finding hosts on a local network. IP addressing was designed to allow hosts on one network to communicate with a host on a different network regardless of the type of LANs the hosts are participating in.

Before we get into the more complicated aspects of IP addressing, you need to understand some of the basics. First, I'm going to explain some of the fundamentals of IP addressing and its terminology, and then I'll discuss the hierarchical IP addressing scheme and private IP addresses.

IP Terminology

Throughout this chapter, you're being introduced to several important terms that are vital to understanding the Internet Protocol. Here are a few to get you started:

Bit A bit is one digit, either a 1 or a 0.

Byte A byte is 7 or 8 bits, depending on whether parity is used. For the rest of this chapter, always assume a byte is 8 bits.

Octet An octet, made up of 8 bits, is just an ordinary 8-bit binary number. In this chapter, the terms *byte* and *octet* are completely interchangeable.

Network Address This is the designation used in routing to send packets to a remote network—for example, 10.0.0.0, 172.16.0.0, and 192.168.10.0.

Broadcast Address The address used by applications and hosts to send information to all nodes on a network is called the broadcast address. Examples of layer 3 broadcasts include 255.255.255.255, which is any network, all nodes; 172.16.255.255, which is all subnets and hosts on network 172.16.0.0; and 10.255.255.255, which broadcasts to all subnets and hosts on network 10.0.0.0.

The Hierarchical IP Addressing Scheme

An IP address consists of 32 bits of information. These bits are divided into four sections, referred to as octets or bytes, with each containing 1 byte (8 bits). You can depict an IP address using one of three methods:

- Dotted-decimal, as in 172.16.30.56
- Binary, as in 10101100.00010000.00011110.00111000
- Hexadecimal, as in AC.10.1E.38

All these examples represent the same IP address. Pertaining to IP addressing, hexadecimal isn't used as often as dotted-decimal or binary, but you still might find an IP address stored in hexadecimal in some programs.

The 32-bit IP address is a structured, or hierarchical address, as opposed to a flat, or nonhierarchical, address. Although either type of addressing scheme could have been used, *hierarchical addressing* was chosen for a good reason. The advantage of this scheme is that it can handle a large number of addresses, namely 4.3 billion (a 32-bit address space with two possible values for each position—either 0 or 1—gives you 2^{32}, or 4,294,967,296). The disadvantage of the flat addressing scheme, and the reason it's not used for IP addressing, relates to routing. If every address were unique, all routers on the Internet would need to store the address of each and every machine on the Internet. This would make efficient routing impossible, even if only a fraction of the possible addresses were used!

The solution to this problem is to use a two- or three-level hierarchical addressing scheme that is structured by network and host or by network, subnet, and host.

This two- or three-level scheme can also be compared to a telephone number. The first section, the area code, designates a very large area. The second section, the prefix, narrows the scope to a local calling area. The final segment, the customer number, zooms in on the specific connection. IP addresses use the same type of layered structure. Rather than all 32 bits being treated as a unique identifier as in flat addressing, a part of the address is designated as the network address, and the other part is designated as either the subnet and host address or just the node address.

Next, we'll cover IP network addressing and the different classes of addresses we can use to address our networks.

Network Addressing

The *network address* (which can also be called the *network number*) uniquely identifies each network. Every machine on the same network shares that network address as part of its IP address. For example, in the IP address 172.16.30.56, 172.16 represents the network address.

The *node address* is assigned to—and uniquely identifies—each machine on a network. This part of the address must be unique because it identifies a particular machine—an individual—as opposed to a network, which is a group. This number can also be referred to as a *host address*. In the sample IP address 172.16.30.56, the 30.56 represents the node address.

The designers of the Internet decided to create classes of networks based on network size. For the small number of networks possessing a very large number of nodes, they created the rank *Class A network*. At the other extreme is the *Class C network*, which is reserved for the numerous networks with a small number of nodes. The class distinction for networks between very large and very small is predictably called the *Class B network*.

Subdividing an IP address into a network and node address is determined by the class designation of one's network. Figure 3.20 summarizes the three classes of networks used to address hosts—a subject I'll explain in much greater detail throughout this chapter.

FIGURE 3.20 Summary of the three classes of networks

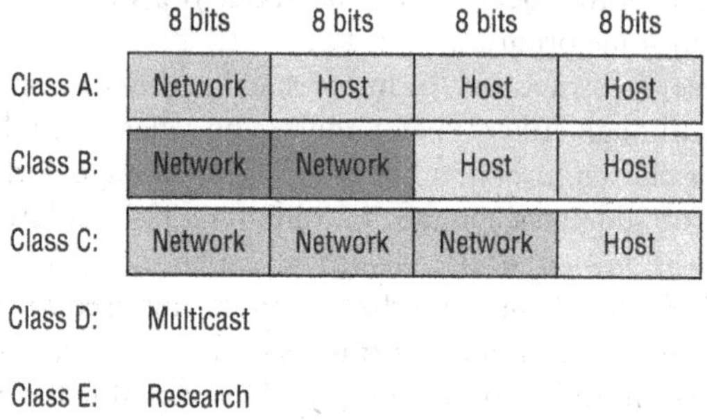

To ensure efficient routing, Internet designers defined a mandate for the leading-bits section of the address for each different network class. For example, since a router knows that a Class A network address always starts with a 0, the router might be able to speed a packet on its way after reading only the first bit of its address. This is where the address schemes define the difference between a Class A, a Class B, and a Class C address. Coming up, I'll discuss the differences between these three classes, followed by a discussion of the Class D and Class E addresses. Classes A, B, and C are the only ranges used to address hosts in our networks.

Network Address Range: Class A

The designers of the IP address scheme decided that the first bit of the first byte in a Class A network address must always be off, or 0. This means a Class A address must be between 0 and 127 in the first byte, inclusive.

Consider the following network address:

```
0xxxxxxx
```

If we turn the other 7 bits all off and then turn them all on, we find the Class A range of network addresses:

```
00000000 = 0
01111111 = 127
```

So, a Class A network is defined in the first octet between 0 and 127, and it can't be less or more. Understand that 0 and 127 are not valid in a Class A network because they're reserved addresses—something I'll go over soon.

Network Address Range: Class B

In a Class B network, the RFCs state that the first bit of the first byte must always be turned on, but the second bit must always be turned off (10). If you turn the other 6 bits all off and then all on, you find the range for a Class B network:

```
10000000 = 128
10111111 = 191
```

As you can see, a Class B network is defined when the first byte is configured from 128 to 191.

Network Address Range: Class C

For Class C networks, the RFCs define the first two bits of the first octet as always turned on, but the third bit can never be on. Following the same process as the previous classes, convert from binary to decimal to find the range. Here's the range for a Class C network:

```
11000000 = 192
11011111 = 223
```

So, if you see an IP address that starts at 192 and goes to 223, you'll know it is a Class C IP address.

Network Address Ranges: Classes D and E

The addresses between 224 to 255 are reserved for Class D and E networks. Class D (224–239) is used for multicast addresses, and Class E (240–255) for scientific purposes. I'm not going into these types of addresses because they are beyond the scope of knowledge you need to gain from this book.

Network Addresses: Special Purpose

Some IP addresses are reserved for special purposes, so network administrators can't ever assign these addresses to nodes. Table 3.4 lists the members of this exclusive little club and the reasons why they're included in it.

TABLE 3.4 Reserved IP addresses

Address	Function
Network address of all 0s	Interpreted to mean "this network or segment."
Network address of all 1s	Interpreted to mean "all networks."
Network 127.0.0.1	Reserved for loopback tests. Designates the local node and allows that node to send a test packet to itself without generating network traffic.

TABLE 3.4 Reserved IP addresses *(continued)*

Address	Function
Node address of all 0s	Interpreted to mean "network address" or any host on a specified network.
Node address of all 1s	Interpreted to mean "all nodes" on the specified network; for example, 128.2.255.255 means "all nodes" on network 128.2 (Class B address).
Entire IP address set to all 0s	Used by Cisco routers to designate the default route. Could also mean "any network."
Entire IP address set to all 1s (same as 255.255.255.255)	Broadcast to all nodes on the current network; sometimes called an "all 1s broadcast" or local broadcast.

Class A Addresses

In a Class A network address, the first byte is assigned to the network address, and the three remaining bytes are used for the node addresses. The Class A format is as follows:

`network.node.node.node`

For example, in the IP address 49.22.102.70, the 49 is the network address and 22.102.70 is the node address. Every machine on this particular network would have the distinctive network address of 49.

Class A network addresses are 1 byte long, with the first bit of that byte reserved and the remaining 7 bits available for manipulation (addressing). As a result, the maximum number of Class A networks that can be created is 128. Why? Because each of the 7 bit positions can be either a 0 or a 1, thus, 2^7, or 128.

To complicate matters further, the network address of all 0s (0000 0000) is reserved to designate the default route (see Table 2.4 in the previous section). Additionally, the address 127, which is reserved for diagnostics, can't be used either, which means that you can really only use the numbers 1 to 126 to designate Class A network addresses. This means the actual number of usable Class A network addresses is 128 minus 2, or 126.

NOTE The IP address 127.0.0.1 is used to test the IP stack on an individual node and cannot be used as a valid host address. However, the loopback address creates a shortcut method for TCP/IP applications and services that run on the same device to communicate with each other.

Each Class A address has 3 bytes (24-bit positions) for the node address of a machine. This means there are 2^{24}—or 16,777,216—unique combinations and, therefore, precisely that many possible unique node addresses for each Class A network. Because node addresses with the two patterns of all 0s and all 1s are reserved, the actual maximum usable number of nodes for a Class A network is 2^{24} minus 2, which equals 16,777,214. Either way, that's a huge number of hosts on a single network segment!

Class A Valid Host IDs

Here's an example of how to figure out the valid host IDs in a Class A network address:

- All host bits off is the network address: 10.0.0.0.
- All host bits on is the broadcast address: 10.255.255.255.

The valid hosts are the numbers in between the network address and the broadcast address: 10.0.0.1 through 10.255.255.254. Notice that 0s and 255s can be valid host IDs. All you need to remember when trying to find valid host addresses is that the host bits can't all be turned off or on at the same time.

Class B Addresses

In a Class B network address, the first 2 bytes are assigned to the network address, and the remaining 2 bytes are used for node addresses. The format is as follows:

```
network.network.node.node
```

For example, in the IP address 172.16.30.56, the network address is 172.16, and the node address is 30.56.

With a network address being 2 bytes (8 bits each), you get 2^{16} unique combinations. The Internet designers decided that all Class B network addresses should start with the binary digit 1, then 0. This leaves 14 bit positions to manipulate: therefore, 16,384, or 2^{14} unique Class B network addresses.

A Class B address uses 2 bytes for node addresses. This is 2^{16} minus the two reserved patterns of all 0s and all 1s, for a total of 65,534 possible node addresses for each Class B network.

Class B Valid Host IDs

Here's an example of how to find the valid hosts in a Class B network:

- All host bits turned off is the network address: 172.16.0.0.
- All host bits turned on is the broadcast address: 172.16.255.255.

The valid hosts would be the numbers in between the network address and the broadcast address: 172.16.0.1 through 172.16.255.254.

Class C Addresses

The first 3 bytes of a Class C network address are dedicated to the network portion of the address, with only 1 measly byte remaining for the node address. Here's the format:

```
network.network.network.node
```

Using the example IP address 192.168.100.102, the network address is 192.168.100, and the node address is 102.

In a Class C network address, the first three-bit positions are always the binary 110. The calculation is as follows: 3 bytes, or 24 bits, minus 3 reserved positions leaves 21 positions. Hence, there are 2^{21}, or 2,097,152, possible Class C networks.

Each unique Class C network has 1 byte to use for node addresses. This leads to 2^8, or 256, minus the two reserved patterns of all 0s and all 1s, for a total of 254 node addresses for each Class C network.

Class C Valid Host IDs

Here's an example of how to find a valid host ID in a Class C network:

- All host bits turned off is the network ID: 192.168.100.0.
- All host bits turned on is the broadcast address: 192.168.100.255.

The valid hosts would be the numbers in between the network address and the broadcast address: 192.168.100.1 through 192.168.100.254.

Private IP Addresses (RFC 1918)

The people who created the IP addressing scheme also created private IP addresses. These addresses can be used on a private network, but they're not routable through the Internet. This is designed for the purpose of creating a measure of well-needed security, but it also conveniently saves valuable IP address space.

If every host on every network were required to have real routable IP addresses, we would have run out of IP addresses years ago. But by using private IP addresses, ISPs, corporations, and home users only need a relatively tiny group of bona fide IP addresses to connect their networks to the Internet. This is economical because they can use private IP addresses on their inside networks and get along just fine.

To accomplish this task, the ISP and the corporation—the end users, no matter who they are—need to use something called *Network Address Translation (NAT)*. NAT basically takes a private IP address and converts it for use on the Internet. Chapter 3 of book two in this series, "Network Address Translation (NAT)," covers NAT.

Many people can use the same real IP address to transmit out onto the Internet. Doing things this way saves tons of address space—good for us all!

The reserved private addresses are listed in Table 3.5.

TABLE 3.5 Reserved IP address space

Address Class	Reserved Address Space
Class A	10.0.0.0 through 10.255.255.255
Class B	172.16.0.0 through 172.31.255.255
Class C	192.168.0.0 through 192.168.255.255

Which Private IP Address Should I Use?

That's a really great question: should you use Class A, Class B, or even Class C private addressing when setting up your network? Let's take Acme Corporation in SF as an example. This company is moving into a new building and needs a whole new network. It has 14 departments, with about 70 users in each. You could probably squeeze one or two Class C addresses to use, or maybe you could use a Class B or even a Class A address just for fun.

The rule of thumb in the consulting world is, when you're setting up a corporate network—regardless of how small it is—you should use a Class A network address because it gives you the most flexibility and growth options. For example, if you used the 10.0.0.0 network address with a /24 mask, then you'd have 65,536 networks, each with 254 hosts—a lot of room for growth with that network!

But if you're setting up a home network, you'd opt for a Class C address because it is the easiest for people to understand and configure. Using the default Class C mask gives you one network with 254 hosts—plenty for a home network.

With the Acme Corporation, a nice 10.1.x.0 with a /24 mask (the x is the subnet for each department) makes this easy to design, install, and troubleshoot.

IPv4 Address Types

Most people use the term *broadcast* as a generic term, and most of the time, we understand what they mean—but not always! For example, you might say, "The host broadcasted through a router to a DHCP server," but, well, it's pretty unlikely that this would ever really happen. What you probably mean—using the correct technical jargon—is, "The DHCP client broadcasted for an IP address, and a router then forwarded this as a unicast packet to the DHCP server." Oh, and remember that with IPv4, broadcasts are pretty important, but with IPv6, there aren't any broadcasts sent at all!

So, I've referred to IP addresses throughout this chapter, and even showed you some examples, but I really haven't gone into the different terms and uses associated with them yet, and it's about time I did. Here are the address types that I'd like to define for you:

Loopback (Localhost) Used to test the IP stack on the local computer. Can be any address from 127.0.0.1 through 127.255.255.254.

Layer 2 Broadcasts These are sent to all nodes on a LAN.

Broadcasts (Layer 3) These are sent to all nodes on the network.

Unicast This is an address for a single interface and are used to send packets to a single destination host.

Multicast These are packets sent from a single source and transmitted to many devices on different networks. Referred to as "one-to-many."

Layer 2 Broadcasts

First, understand that layer 2 broadcasts are also known as hardware broadcasts. They only go out on a LAN, and they don't go past the LAN boundary (router).

The typical hardware address is 6 bytes (48 bits) and looks something like 45:AC:24:E3:60:A5. The broadcast would be all 1s in binary, which would be all *F*s in hexadecimal, as in ff:ff:ff:ff:ff:ff, as shown in Figure 3.21.

FIGURE 3.21 Local layer 2 broadcasts

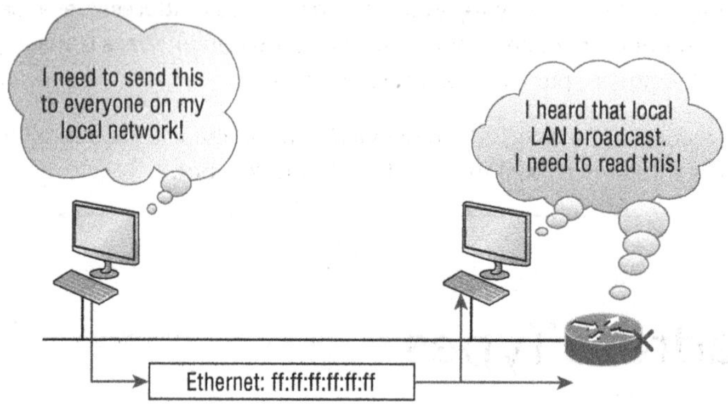

Every network interface card (NIC) will receive and read the frame, including the router, (since this was a layer 2 broadcast), but the router would never, ever forward this!

Layer 3 Broadcasts

Then there are the plain old broadcast addresses at layer 3. Broadcast messages are meant to reach all hosts on a broadcast domain. These are the network broadcasts that have all host bits on.

Here's an example that you're already familiar with: the network address of 172.16.0.0 255.255.0.0 would have a broadcast address of 172.16.255.255—all host bits on. Broadcasts can also be "any network and all hosts," as indicated by 255.255.255.255 and shown in Figure 3.22.

FIGURE 3.22 Layer 3 broadcasts

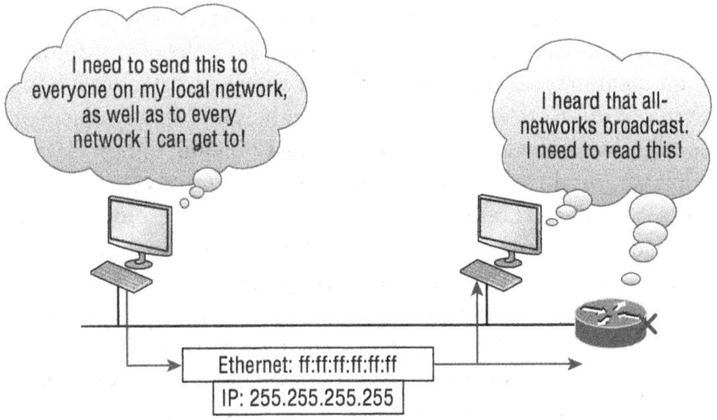

In Figure 3.22, all hosts on the LAN will get this broadcast on their NIC, including the router, but by default, the router would never forward this packet.

Unicast Address

A unicast address is defined as a single IP address that's assigned to a network interface card and is the destination IP address in a packet—in other words, it's used for directing packets to a specific host.

In Figure 3.23, both the MAC address and the destination IP address are for a single NIC on the network. All hosts on the broadcast domain would receive this frame and accept it. Only the destination NIC of 10.1.1.2 would accept the packet; the other NICs would discard the packet.

FIGURE 3.23 Unicast address

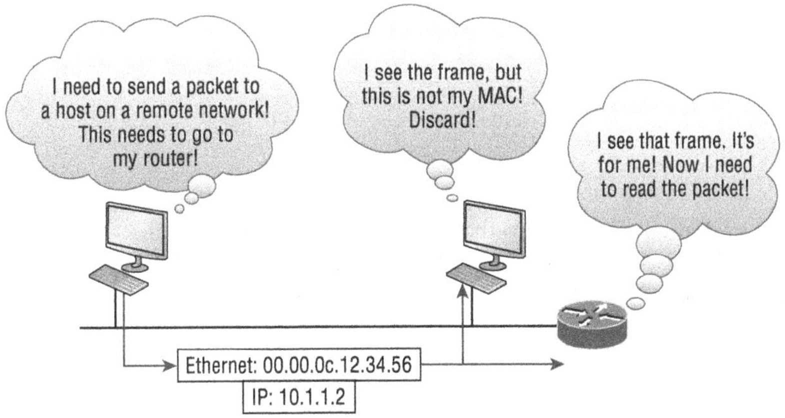

Multicast Address

Multicast addresses are a different beast entirely. At first glance, it appears to be a hybrid of unicast and broadcast communication, but that isn't quite the case. Multicast does allow point-to-multipoint communication, which is similar to broadcasts, but it happens in a different way. The crux of *multicast* address is that it enables multiple recipients to receive messages without flooding them to all hosts on a broadcast domain. Still, this isn't the default behavior—it's what we *can* do with multicasting if it's configured correctly.

Multicast works by sending messages or data to IP *multicast group* addresses. Unlike with broadcasts, which aren't forwarded, routers then forward copies of the packet out to every interface that has hosts *subscribed* to that group address. This is where multicast differs from broadcast messages—with multicast communication, copies of packets, in theory, are sent only to subscribed hosts. For example, when I say in theory, I mean that the hosts will receive a multicast packet destined for 224.0.0.10. This is an EIGRP packet, and only a router running the EIGRP protocol will read these. All hosts on the broadcast LAN, and Ethernet is a broadcast multiaccess LAN technology, will pick up the frame, read the destination address, then immediately discard the frame unless they're in the multicast group. This saves PC processing, not LAN bandwidth. So be warned: multicasting can cause some serious LAN congestion if it's not implemented carefully! Figure 3.24 shows a Cisco router sending an EIGRP multicast packet on the local LAN, with only the other Cisco router accepting and reading the packet.

FIGURE 3.24 EIGRP multicast example

There are several different groups that users or applications can subscribe to. The range of multicast addresses starts with 224.0.0.0 and goes through 239.255.255.255. As you can see, this range of addresses falls within IP Class D address space based on classful IP assignment.

Summary

If you made it this far and understood everything the first time through, fantastic! This chapter covered a lot of ground. If you don't think you completely got it, no worries—it really wouldn't hurt anyone to read this chapter more than once. That's because understanding the information in this chapter is absolutely vital to being able to navigate well through the rest of this book.

There is still a lot of ground to cover, so just make sure you've got this material nailed down to avoid pain later. What we're doing up to this point is building a solid foundation to build upon as you advance.

With that in mind, after you learned about the DoD model, the layers, and associated protocols, you found out about the oh-so-important topic of IP addressing. I discussed in detail the difference between each address class, how to find a network address and broadcast address, and what denotes a valid host address range. And not nagging but, I can't stress enough how important it is for you to have this chapter's critical information clearly and completely down before moving on to Chapter 4.

Exam Essentials

Differentiate between the DoD and the OSI network models. The DoD model is a condensed version of the OSI model, composed of four layers instead of seven, but is nonetheless like the OSI model in that it can be used to describe packet creation and devices and protocols can be mapped to its layers.

Identify Host-to-Host layer protocols. Transmission Control Protocol (TCP) is a connection-oriented protocol that provides reliable network service by using acknowledgments and flow control. User Datagram Protocol (UDP) is a connectionless protocol that provides low overhead and is considered unreliable.

Identify Internet layer protocols. Internet Protocol (IP) is a connectionless protocol that provides network addresses and routing through an internetwork. Address Resolution Protocol (ARP) finds a hardware address from a known IP address. Reverse ARP (RARP) finds an IP address from a known hardware address. Internet Control Message Protocol (ICMP) provides diagnostics and destination unreachable messages.

Describe the functions of DNS and DHCP in the network. Dynamic Host Configuration Protocol (DHCP) provides network configuration information (including IP addresses) to hosts, eliminating the need to perform the configurations manually. Domain Name Service (DNS) resolves hostnames—both Internet names such as `www.lammle.com` and device names such as Workstation 2—to IP addresses, eliminating the need to know the IP address of a device for connection purposes.

Identify what is contained in the TCP header of a connection-oriented transmission. The fields in the TCP header include the source port, destination port, sequence number, acknowledgment number, header length, a field reserved for future use, code bits, window size, checksum, urgent pointer, options field, and, finally, the data field.

Identify what is contained in the UDP header of a connectionless transmission. The fields in the UDP header include only the source port, destination port, length, checksum, and data. The smaller number of fields as compared to the TCP header comes at the expense of providing none of the more advanced functions of the TCP frame.

Identify what is contained in the IP header. The fields of an IP header include version, header length, priority or type of service, total length, identification, flags, fragment offset, time to live, protocol, header checksum, source IP address, destination IP address, options, and, finally, data.

Compare and contrast UDP and TCP characteristics and features. TCP is connection-oriented, acknowledged, and sequenced and has flow and error control, whereas UDP is connectionless, unacknowledged, and not sequenced and provides no error or flow control.

Understand the role of port numbers. Port numbers are used to identify the protocol or service that is to be used in the transmission.

Identify the role of ICMP. Internet Control Message Protocol (ICMP) works at the Network layer and is used by IP for many different services. ICMP is a management protocol and messaging service provider for IP.

Define the Class A IP address range. The IP range for a Class A network is 1–126. This provides 8 bits of network addressing and 24 bits of host addressing by default.

Define the Class B IP address range. The IP range for a Class B network is 128–191. Class B addressing provides 16 bits of network addressing and 16 bits of host addressing by default.

Define the Class C IP address range. The IP range for a Class C network is 192 through 223. Class C addressing provides 24 bits of network addressing and 8 bits of host addressing by default.

Identify the private IP ranges. The Class A private address range is 10.0.0.0 through 10.255.255.255. The Class B private address range is 172.16.0.0 through 172.31.255.255. The Class C private address range is 192.168.0.0 through 192.168.255.255.

Understand the difference between a broadcast, unicast, and multicast address. A broadcast address is to all devices in a subnet; a unicast address is to one device; and a multicast address is to some but not all devices.

Written Labs

You can find the answers to these labs in Appendix A, "Answers to the Written Labs."

In this section, you'll complete the following labs to make sure you've got the information and concepts contained within them fully dialed in:

Lab 3.1: TCP/IP

Lab 3.2: Mapping Applications to the DoD Model

Written Lab 3.1: TCP/IP

Answer the following questions about TCP/IP:

1. What is the Class C address range in decimal and in binary?
2. Which layer of the DoD model is equivalent to the Transport layer of the OSI model?
3. What is the valid range of a Class A network address?
4. What is the 127.0.0.1 address used for?
5. How do you find the network address from a listed IP address?
6. How do you find the broadcast address from a listed IP address?
7. What is the Class A private IP address space?
8. What is the Class B private IP address space?
9. What is the Class C private IP address space?
10. What are all the available characters you can use in hexadecimal addressing?

Written Lab 3.2: Mapping Applications to the DoD Model

The four layers of the DoD model are Process/Application, Host-to-Host, Internet, and Network Access. Identify the layer of the DoD model on which each of the following protocols operates:

1. Internet Protocol (IP)
2. Telnet
3. FTP
4. SNMP
5. DNS
6. Address Resolution Protocol (ARP)
7. DHCP/BootP
8. Transmission Control Protocol (TCP)

9. User Datagram Protocol (UDP)
10. Internet Control Message Protocol (ICMP)
11. TFTP
12. SMTP

Review Questions

You can find the answers to these questions in Appendix B, "Answers to the Review Questions."

NOTE The following questions are designed to test your understanding of this chapter's material. For more information on how to get additional questions, please see `www.lammle.com/ccna`.

1. What must happen if a DHCP IP conflict occurs?
   - **A.** Proxy ARP will fix the issue.
   - **B.** The client uses a gratuitous ARP to fix the issue.
   - **C.** The administrator must fix the conflict by hand at the DHCP server.
   - **D.** The DHCP server will reassign new IP addresses to both computers.
2. Which of the following Application layer protocols sets up a secure session that's similar to Telnet?
   - **A.** FTP
   - **B.** SSH
   - **C.** DNS
   - **D.** DHCP
3. Which of the following mechanisms is used by the client to avoid a duplicate IP address during the DHCP process?
   - **A.** Ping
   - **B.** Traceroute
   - **C.** Gratuitous ARP
   - **D.** Pathping
4. Which of the following describe the DHCP Discover message? (Choose two.)
   - **A.** It uses ff:ff:ff:ff:ff:ff as a layer 2 broadcast.
   - **B.** It uses UDP as the Transport layer protocol.
   - **C.** It uses TCP as the Transport layer protocol.
   - **D.** It does not use a layer 2 destination address.
5. Which of the following services use TCP? (Choose three.)
   - **A.** DHCP
   - **B.** SMTP
   - **C.** SNMP
   - **D.** FTP

E. HTTP

F. TFTP

6. Which of the following is an example of a multicast address?

A. 10.6.9.1

B. 192.168.10.6

C. 224.0.0.10

D. 172.16.9.5

7. Which of the following are private IP addresses? (Choose two.)

A. 12.0.0.1

B. 168.172.19.39

C. 172.20.14.36

D. 172.33.194.30

E. 192.168.24.43

8. Which layer in the TCP/IP stack is equivalent to the Transport layer of the OSI model?

A. Application

B. Host-to-Host

C. Internet

D. Network Access

9. Which statements are true regarding ICMP packets? (Choose two.)

A. ICMP guarantees datagram delivery.

B. ICMP can provide hosts with information about network problems.

C. ICMP is encapsulated within IP datagrams.

D. ICMP is encapsulated within UDP datagrams.

10. What is the address range of a Class B network address in binary?

A. 01xxxxxx

B. 0xxxxxxx

C. 10xxxxxx

D. 110xxxxx

11. Which layer 4 protocol is used for a Telnet connection?

A. IP

B. TCP

C. TCP/IP

D. UDP

E. ICMP

12. Private IP addressing was specified in RFC ________.

13. The following illustration shows a data structure header. What protocol is this header from?

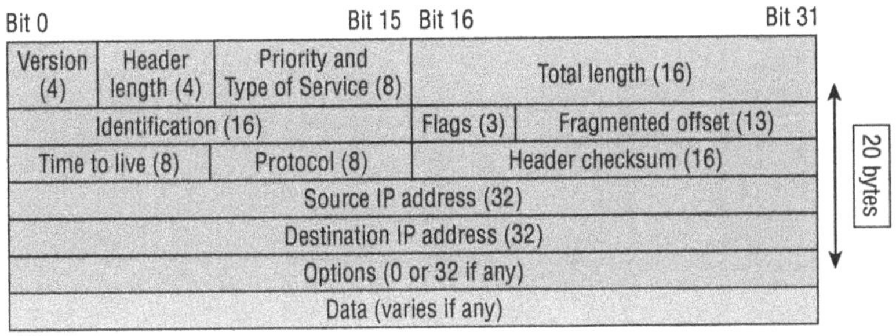

A. IP
B. ICMP
C. TCP
D. UDP
E. ARP
F. RARP

14. The DoD model (also called the TCP/IP stack) has four layers. Which layer of the DoD model is equivalent to the Network layer of the OSI model?

A. Application
B. Host-to-Host
C. Internet
D. Network Access

15. Drag the steps in the DHCP process and place them in the correct order on the right.

DHCPOffer	Drop Target A
DHCPDiscover	Drop Target B
DHCPAck	Drop Target C
DHCPRequest	Drop Target D

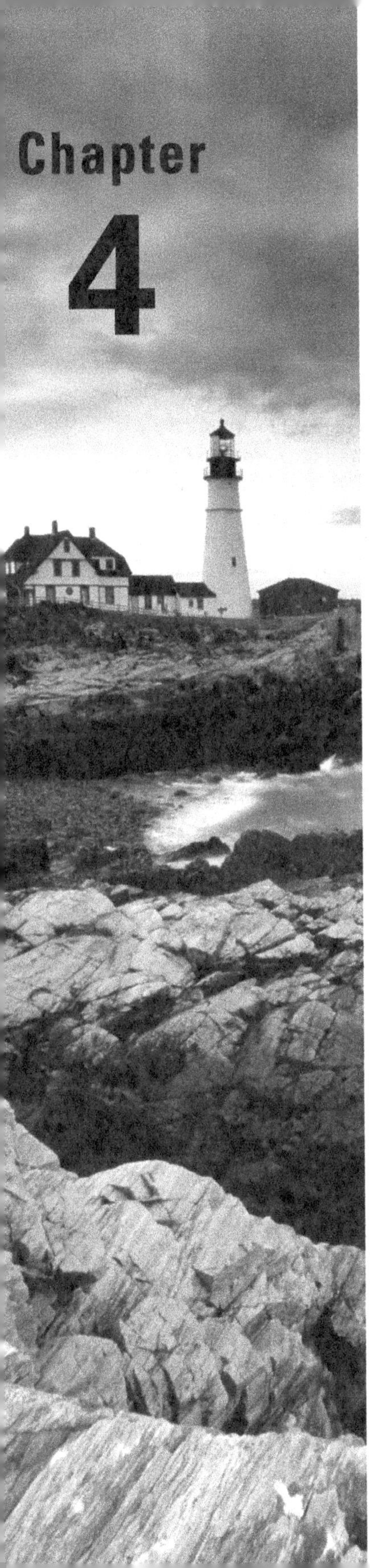

Easy Subnetting

THE CCNA EXAM TOPICS COVERED IN THIS CHAPTER INCLUDE THE FOLLOWING:

✓ ***1.0 Network Fundamentals***

- 1.6 Configure and verify IPv4 addressing and subnetting

We'll pick up right where we left off in the last chapter and continue to explore the world of IP addressing. The chapter opens by showing you how to subnet an IP network—an indispensable skill that's central to mastering networking in general. Forewarned is forearmed, so prepare yourself, because being able to subnet quickly and accurately is quite challenging. You'll definitely need time to practice what you learn to get good at it. So, be patient and don't give up on this key aspect of networking until your skills are seriously sharp!

What I'm about to say might sound weird to you, but you'll be much better off if you just try to forget everything you've already learned about subnetting before reading this chapter—especially if you've been to an official Cisco or Microsoft class! I think these forms of special torture often do more harm than good and sometimes even scare people away from networking completely. Those who survive and persevere usually at least question the sanity of continuing to study in this field. If this is you, relax and know that you'll find the way I tackle the issue of subnetting is relatively painless because I'm going to show you a whole new, much easier method to conquer this monster!

After working through this chapter, you'll be able to tame the IP addressing/subnetting beast—just don't give up! I promise you'll be really glad you didn't. It's one of those things that once you get it down, you'll wonder why you used to think it was so hard.

NOTE To find bonus material, as well as Todd Lammle videos, practice questions, and hands-on labs, please see `www.lammle.com/ccna`.

Subnetting Basics

In Chapter 3, "TCP/IP," you learned how to define and find the valid host ranges used in a Class A, Class B, and Class C network address by turning the host bits all off and then all on. This is very good, but here's the catch: you were defining only one network, as shown in Figure 4.1.

You probably know that having one large network is not a good thing, so how would you fix the out-of-control problem that Figure 4.1 illustrates? Wouldn't it be nice to be able to break up that one, huge network address and create more manageable networks from it? You bet it would, but to make that happen, you would need to apply the infamous trick of *subnetting* because it's the best way to break up a giant network into a bunch of smaller ones.

FIGURE 4.1 One network

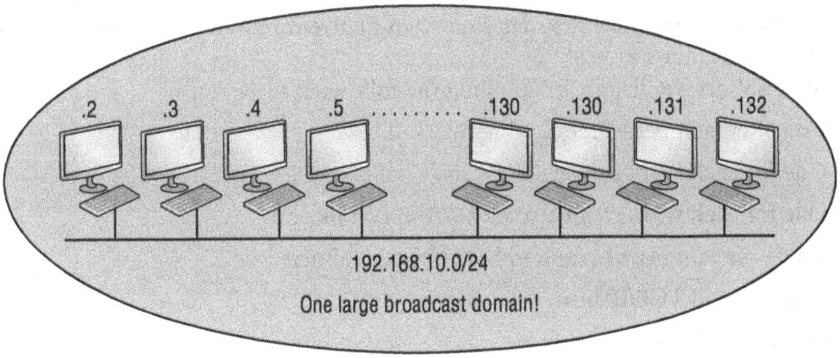

Check out Figure 4.2 to see how this might look.

FIGURE 4.2 Multiple networks connected together

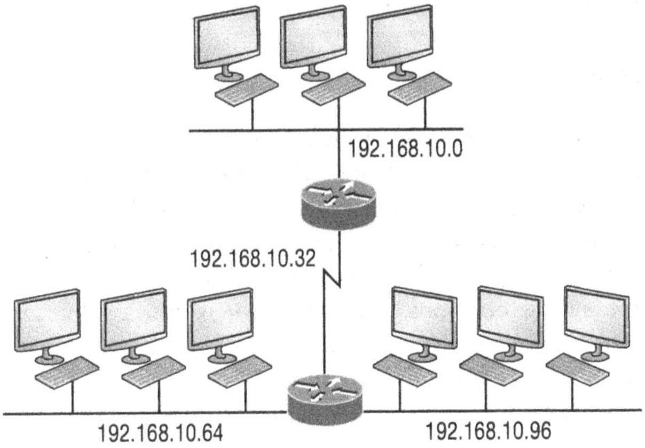

What are those 192.168.10.*x* addresses shown in the figure? Well, that is what this chapter will explain—how to make one network into many networks.

Let's take off from where we left in Chapter 2 and start working in the host section (host bits) of a network address, where we can borrow bits to create subnets.

How to Create Subnets

Creating subnetworks is essentially the act of taking bits from the host portion of the address and reserving them to define the subnet address instead. Clearly, this will result in fewer bits being available for defining your hosts, which is something you'll always want to keep in mind.

Later in this chapter, I'll guide you through the entire process of creating subnets, starting with Class C addresses. As always in networking, before you actually implement anything, including subnetting, you must first determine your current requirements and make sure to plan for future conditions as well.

To create a subnet, we'll start by fulfilling the following three steps:

1. Determine the number of required network IDs:
   - One for each LAN subnet
   - One for each wide area network (WAN) connection
2. Determine the number of required host IDs per subnet:
   - One for each TCP/IP host
   - One for each router interface
3. Based on the previous requirements, create the following:
   - A unique subnet mask for your entire network
   - A unique subnet ID for each physical segment
   - A range of host IDs for each subnet

Subnet Masks

In order for the subnet addressing scheme to work, every machine on the network must know which part of the host address will be used as the subnet address. This condition is met by assigning a *subnet mask* to each machine. A subnet mask is a 32-bit value that allows the device that's receiving IP packets to distinguish the network ID portion of the IP address from the host ID portion of the IP address. This 32-bit subnet mask is composed of 1s and 0s, where the 1s represent the positions that refer to the network subnet addresses.

Not all networks need subnets, and if not, it really means they're using the default subnet mask, which is basically the same as saying that a network doesn't have a subnet address. Table 4.1 shows the default subnet masks for Classes A, B, and C.

TABLE 4.1 Default subnet masks

Class	Format	Default Subnet Mask
A	*network.node.node.node*	255.0.0.0
B	*network.network.node.node*	255.255.0.0
C	*network.network.network.node*	255.255.255.0

Although you can use any mask in any way on an interface, typically it's not usually good to mess with the default masks. In other words, you don't want to make a Class B subnet mask read 255.0.0.0, and some hosts won't even let you type it in—although, these days, most devices will. For a Class A network, you wouldn't change the first byte in a subnet mask because it should read 255.0.0.0 at a minimum. Similarly, you wouldn't assign 255.255.255.255 because this is all 1s, which is a broadcast address. A Class B address starts with 255.255.0.0, and a Class C starts with 255.255.255.0. For the CCNA especially, there is no reason to change the defaults!

Understanding the Powers of 2

Powers of 2 are important to understand and memorize for use with IP subnetting. Reviewing powers of 2, remember that when you see a number noted with an exponent, it means you should multiply the number by itself as many times as the upper number specifies. For example, 2^3 is 2 x 2 x 2, which equals 8. Here's a list of powers of 2 to commit to memory:

$2^1 = 2$

$2^2 = 4$

$2^3 = 8$

$2^4 = 16$

$2^5 = 32$

$2^6 = 64$

$2^7 = 128$

$2^8 = 256$

$2^9 = 512$

$2^{10} = 1{,}024$

$2^{11} = 2{,}048$

$2^{12} = 4{,}096$

$2^{13} = 8{,}192$

$2^{14} = 16{,}384$

Memorizing these powers of 2 is a good idea, but it's not absolutely necessary. Just remember that since you're working with powers of 2, each successive power of 2 is double the previous one.

It works like this: all you have to do to remember the value of 2^9 is to first know that 2^8 = 256. Why? Because when you double 2 to the eighth power (256), you get 2^9 (or 512). To determine the value of 2^{10}, simply start at 2^8 = 256, and then double it twice.

You can go the other way as well. If you needed to know what 2^6 is, for example, you just cut 256 in half two times: once to reach 2^7 and then one more time to reach 2^6.

Classless Inter-Domain Routing (CIDR)

Another term you need to familiarize yourself with is *Classless Inter-Domain Routing (CIDR)*. It's basically the method that Internet service providers (ISPs) use to allocate a number of addresses to a company, a home—their customers. They provide addresses in a certain block size, something I'll talk about in greater detail soon.

When you receive a block of addresses from an ISP, what you get will look something like this: 192.168.10.32/28. This is telling you what your subnet mask is. The slash notation (/) means how many bits are turned on (1s). Obviously, the maximum could only be /32 because a byte is 8 bits, and there are 4 bytes in an IP address: (4 × 8 = 32). But keep in mind that regardless of the class of address, the largest subnet mask available relevant to the Cisco exam objectives can only be a /30 because you've got to keep at least 2 bits for host bits.

Take, for example, a Class A default subnet mask, which is 255.0.0.0. This tells us that the first byte of the subnet mask is all ones (1s), or 11111111. When referring to a slash notation, you need to count all the 1 bits to figure out your mask. The 255.0.0.0 is considered a /8 because it has 8 bits that are 1s—that is, 8 bits that are turned on.

A Class B default mask would be 255.255.0.0, which is a /16 because 16 bits are ones (1s): 11111111.11111111.00000000.00000000.

Table 4.2 has a listing of every available subnet mask and its equivalent CIDR slash notation.

TABLE 4.2 CIDR values

Subnet Mask	CIDR Value
255.0.0.0	/8
255.128.0.0	/9
255.192.0.0	/10
255.224.0.0	/11
255.240.0.0	/12
255.248.0.0	/13
255.252.0.0	/14
255.254.0.0	/15
255.255.0.0	/16
255.255.128.0	/17
255.255.192.0	/18

Subnet Mask	CIDR Value
255.255.224.0	/19
255.255.240.0	/20
255.255.248.0	/21
255.255.252.0	/22
255.255.254.0	/23
255.255.255.0	/24
255.255.255.128	/25
255.255.255.192	/26
255.255.255.224	/27
255.255.255.240	/28
255.255.255.248	/29
255.255.255.252	/30

The /8 through /15 can only be used with Class A network addresses; the /16 through /23 can be used by Class A and B network addresses; and the /24 through /30 can be used by Class A, B, and C network addresses. This is a big reason why most companies use Class A network addresses. Since they can use all subnet masks, they get the maximum flexibility in network design.

NOTE

No, you cannot configure a Cisco router using this slash format. But wouldn't that be nice? Nevertheless, it's *really* important for you to know subnet masks in the slash notation (CIDR).

IP Subnet-Zero

Even though `ip subnet-zero` is not a new command, Cisco courseware and Cisco exam objectives didn't used to cover it. They do now! This command allows you to use the first and last subnet in your network design. For instance, the Class C mask of 255.255.255.192 provides subnets 64 and 128, another facet of subnetting that I discuss more thoroughly later in this chapter. But with the `ip subnet-zero` command, you now get to use subnets 0, 64, 128, and 192. It may not seem like a lot, but this provides two more subnets for every subnet mask we use.

Even though I don't discuss the command-line interface (CLI) here, it's important for you to be at least a little familiar with this command at this point:

```
Router#sh running-config
Building configuration...
Current configuration : 827 bytes
!
hostname Pod1R1
!
ip subnet-zero
!
```

This router output shows that the command `ip subnet-zero` is enabled on the router. Cisco has turned this command on by default starting with Cisco IOS version 12.*x*, and now we're running 15.*x* code.

When taking your Cisco exams, make sure you read very carefully to see if Cisco is asking you *not* to use `ip subnet-zero`. There are actually instances where this may happen.

Subnetting Class C Addresses

There are many different ways to subnet a network. The right way is the way that works best for you. In a Class C address, only 8 bits are available for defining the hosts. Remember that subnet bits start at the left and move to the right, without skipping bits. This means that the only Class C subnet masks can be the following:

```
Binary Decimal CIDR
---------------------------------------------------------
00000000 = 255.255.255.0 /24
10000000 = 255.255.255.128 /25
11000000 = 255.255.255.192 /26
11100000 = 255.255.255.224 /27
11110000 = 255.255.255.240 /28
11111000 = 255.255.255.248 /29
11111100 = 255.255.255.252 /30
```

We can't use a /31 or /32 because, as I've said, we must have at least 2 host bits for assigning IP addresses to hosts. But this is only mostly true. We certainly can never use a /32 because that would mean zero host bits available, yet Cisco has various forms of the IOS, as well as the new Cisco Nexus switches' operating system that support the /31 mask. The /31 is beyond the scope of the CCNA objectives, so I won't be covering it in this book.

Coming up, I'm going to teach you that significantly less painful method of subnetting I promised you at the beginning of this chapter, which makes it ever so much easier to subnet larger numbers in a flash. Excited? Good! Because I'm not kidding when I tell you that you absolutely need to be able to subnet quickly and accurately to succeed in both the networking real world and on the exam.

Subnetting a Class C Address—The Fast Way!

When you've chosen a possible subnet mask for your network and need to determine the number of subnets, valid hosts, and the broadcast addresses of a subnet that mask will provide, all you need to do is answer five simple questions:

- How many subnets does the chosen subnet mask produce?
- How many valid hosts per subnet are available?
- What are the valid subnets?
- What's the broadcast address of each subnet?
- What are the valid hosts in each subnet?

This is where you'll be really glad you followed my advice and took the time to memorize your powers of 2. If you didn't, now would be a good time. Just refer back to the sidebar "Understanding the Powers of 2" earlier if you need to brush up.

Here's how you arrive at the answers to those five big questions:

- *How many subnets?* 2^x = number of subnets. x is the number of masked bits, or the 1s. For example, in 11000000, the number of 1s gives us 2^2 subnets. So, in this example, there are 4 subnets.
- *How many hosts per subnet?* $2^y - 2$ = number of hosts per subnet. y is the number of unmasked bits, or the 0s. For example, in 11000000, the number of 0s gives us $2^6 - 2$ hosts, or 62 hosts per subnet. You need to subtract 2 for the subnet address and the broadcast address, which are not valid hosts.
- *What are the valid subnets?* 256 – subnet mask = block size, or increment number. An example would be the 255.255.255.192 mask, where the interesting octet is the fourth octet (interesting because that is where our subnet numbers are). Just use this math: 256 – 192 = 64. The block size of a 192 mask is always 64. Start counting at zero in blocks of 64 until you reach the subnet mask value, and these are your subnets in the fourth octet: 0, 64, 128, 192. Easy, huh?
- *What's the broadcast address for each subnet?* Now, here's the really easy part. Since we counted our subnets in the last section as 0, 64, 128, and 192, the broadcast address is always the number right before the next subnet. For example, the 0 subnet has a broadcast address of 63 because the next subnet is 64. The 64 subnet has a broadcast address of 127 because the next subnet is 128, and so on. Remember, the broadcast address of the last subnet is always 255.
- *What are the valid hosts?* Valid hosts are the numbers between the subnets, omitting the all-0s and all-1s. For example, if 64 is the subnet number and 127 is the broadcast address, then 65–126 is the valid host range. Your valid range is *always* the group of numbers between the subnet address and the broadcast address.

If you're still confused, don't worry because it really isn't as hard as it seems at first—just hang in there! To help lift any mental fog, try a few of the practice examples next.

Subnetting Practice Examples: Class C Addresses

Here's your opportunity to practice subnetting Class C addresses using the method I just described. This is so cool. We're going to start with the first Class C subnet mask and work through every subnet we can, using a Class C address. When we're done, I'll show you how easy this is with Class A and B networks, too.

Practice Example #1C: 255.255.255.128 (/25)

Since 128 is 10000000 in binary, there is only 1 bit for subnetting and 7 bits for hosts. We're going to subnet the Class C network address 192.168.10.0.

192.168.10.0 = Network address

255.255.255.128 = Subnet mask

Now, let's answer our big five questions:

- *How many subnets?* Since 128 is 1 bit on (10000000), the answer would be $2^1 = 2$.
- *How many hosts per subnet?* We have 7 host bits off (10000000), so the equation would be $2^7 - 2 = 126$ hosts. Once you figure out the block size of a mask, the number of hosts is always the block size minus 2. No need to do extra math if you don't need to!
- *What are the valid subnets?* 256 – 128 = 128. Remember, we'll start at zero and count in our block size, so our subnets are 0, 128. By just counting your subnets when counting in your block size, you really don't need to do steps 1 and 2. We can see we have two subnets, and in the step before this one, just remember that the number of hosts is always the block size minus 2—in this example, that gives us 2 subnets, each with 126 hosts.
- *What's the broadcast address for each subnet?* The number right before the value of the next subnet is all host bits turned on and equals the broadcast address. For the zero subnet, the next subnet is 128, so the broadcast of the 0 subnet is 127.
- *What are the valid hosts?* These are the numbers between the subnet and broadcast address. The easiest way to find the hosts is to write out the subnet address and the broadcast address, which makes valid hosts completely obvious. The following table shows the 0 and 128 subnets, the valid host ranges of each, and the broadcast address of both subnets:

Subnet	0	**128**
First host	1	129
Last host	126	254
Broadcast	**127**	**255**

Looking at a Class C /25, it's pretty clear that there are two subnets. But so what—why is this significant? Well, actually, it's not, because that's not the right question. What you really want to know is what you would do with this information!

The key to understanding subnetting is to understand the very reason you need to do it, and I'm going to demonstrate this by going through the process of building a physical network.

Because we added that router shown in Figure 4.3, in order for the hosts on our internetwork to communicate, they must now have a logical network addressing scheme. We could use IPv6, but IPv4 is still the most popular for now. It's also what we're studying at the moment, so that's what we're going with.

FIGURE 4.3 Implementing a Class C /25 logical network

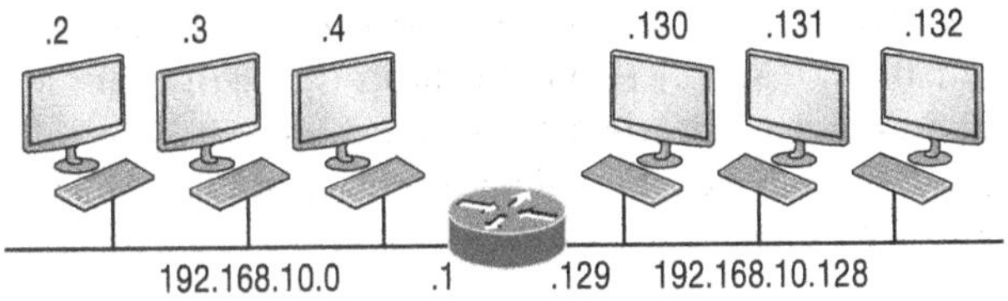


```
Router#show ip route
 [output cut]
C 192.168.10.0 is directly connected to Ethernet 0
C 192.168.10.128 is directly connected to Ethernet 1
```

Looking at Figure 4.3, you can see there are two physical networks, so we're going to implement a logical addressing scheme that allows for two logical networks. As always, it's a really good idea to look ahead and consider likely short- and long-term growth scenarios, but for this example in this book, a /25 gets it done.

Figure 4.3 shows us that both subnets have been assigned to a router interface, which creates our broadcast domains and assigns our subnets. Use the command `show ip route` to see the routing table on a router. Notice that instead of one large broadcast domain, there are now two smaller broadcast domains, providing for up to 126 hosts in each. The C in the router output translates to "directly connected network," and we can see we have two of those with two broadcast domains and that we created and implemented them. So congratulations—you did it! You have successfully subnetted a network and applied it to a network design. Nice! Let's do it again.

Practice Example #2C: 255.255.255.192 (/26)

This time, we're going to subnet the network address 192.168.10.0 using the subnet mask 255.255.255.192.

192.168.10.0 = Network address

255.255.255.192 = Subnet mask

Now, let's answer the big five:

- *How many subnets?* Since 192 is 2 bits on (11000000), the answer would be $2^2 = 4$ subnets.
- *How many hosts per subnet?* We have 6 host bits off (11000000), giving us $2^6 - 2 = 62$ hosts. The number of hosts is always the block size minus 2.
- *What are the valid subnets?* 256 – 192 = 64. Remember to start at zero and count in our block size. This means our subnets are 0, 64, 128, and 192. We can see we have a block size of 64, so we have 4 subnets, each with 62 hosts.
- *What's the broadcast address for each subnet?* The number right before the value of the next subnet is all host bits turned on and equals the broadcast address. For the zero subnet, the next subnet is 64, so the broadcast address for the zero subnet is 63.
- *What are the valid hosts?* These are the numbers between the subnet and broadcast address. As I said, the easiest way to find the hosts is to write out the subnet address and the broadcast address, which clearly delimits our valid hosts. The following table shows the 0, 64, 128, and 192 subnets, the valid host ranges of each, and the broadcast address of each subnet:

The subnets (do this first)	0	64	128	192
Our first host (perform host addressing last)	1	65	129	193
Our last host	62	126	190	254
The broadcast address (do this second)	63	127	191	255

Again, before getting into the next example, you can see that we can now subnet a /26 as long as we can count in increments of 64. And what are you going to do with this fascinating information? Implement it! We'll use Figure 4.4 to practice a /26 network implementation.

The /26 mask provides four subnetworks, and we need a subnet for each router interface. With this mask, in this example, we actually have room with a spare subnet to add to another router interface in the future. Again, always plan for growth if possible!

Practice Example #3C: 255.255.255.224 (/27)

This time, we'll subnet the network address 192.168.10.0 and subnet mask 255.255.255.224.

192.168.10.0 = Network address

255.255.255.224 = Subnet mask

- *How many subnets?* 224 is 11100000, so our equation would be $2^3 = 8$.
- *How many hosts?* $2^5 - 2 = 30$.
- *What are the valid subnets?* 256 – 224 = 32. We just start at zero and count to the subnet mask value in blocks (increments) of 32: 0, 32, 64, 96, 128, 160, 192, and 224.

- *What's the broadcast address for each subnet?* (Always the number right before the next subnet.)
- *What are the valid hosts?* (The numbers between the subnet number and the broadcast address.)

FIGURE 4.4 Implementing a class C /26 (with three networks)

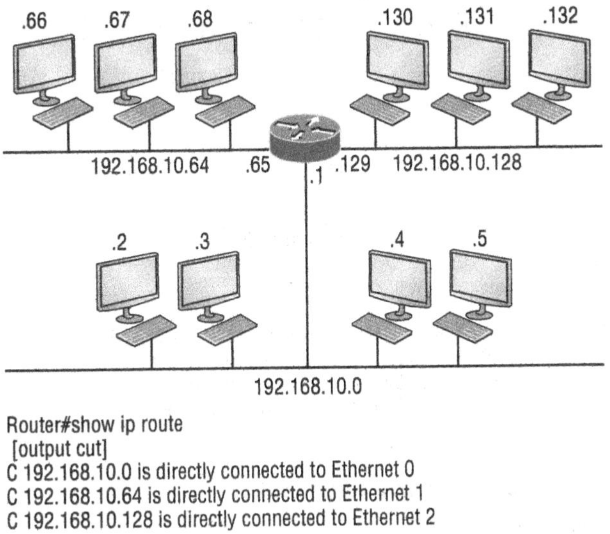
.66
.67
.68
.130
.131
.132
192.168.10.64
.65
.1
.129
192.168.10.128
.2
.3
.4
.5
192.168.10.0
Router#show ip route
[output cut]
C 192.168.10.0 is directly connected to Ethernet 0
C 192.168.10.64 is directly connected to Ethernet 1
C 192.168.10.128 is directly connected to Ethernet 2

To answer the last two questions, first just write out the subnets, then write out the broadcast addresses—the number right before the next subnet. Last, fill in the host addresses. The following table gives you all the subnets for the 255.255.255.224 Class C subnet mask:

The subnet address	**0**	**32**	**64**	**96**	**128**	**160**	**192**	**224**
The first valid host	1	33	65	97	129	161	193	225
The last valid host	30	62	94	126	158	190	222	254
The broadcast address	31	63	95	127	159	191	223	255

In practice example #3C, we're using a 255.255.255.224 (/27) network, which provides eight subnets, as shown previously. We can take these subnets and implement them as shown in Figure 4.5, using any of the subnets available.

Notice that this used six of the eight subnets available for my network design. The lightning bolt symbol in the figure represents a wide area network (WAN), which would be a connection through an ISP or telco. In other words, something you don't own, but it's still a subnet just like any LAN connection on a router. As usual, I used the first valid host in each subnet as the router's interface address. This is just a rule of thumb; you can use any address in the valid host range as long as you remember what address you configured so you can set the default gateways on your hosts to the router address.

FIGURE 4.5 Implementing a Class C /27 logical network

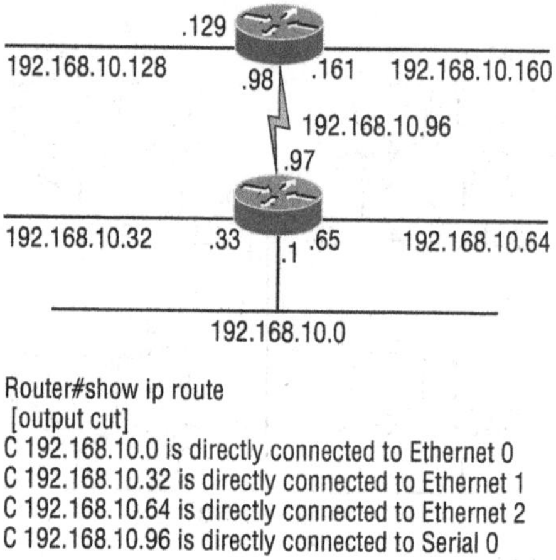
.129
192.168.10.128
.98
.161
192.168.10.160
192.168.10.96
.97
192.168.10.32
.33
.1
.65
192.168.10.64
192.168.10.0
Router#show ip route
[output cut]
C 192.168.10.0 is directly connected to Ethernet 0
C 192.168.10.32 is directly connected to Ethernet 1
C 192.168.10.64 is directly connected to Ethernet 2
C 192.168.10.96 is directly connected to Serial 0

Practice Example #4C: 255.255.255.240 (/28)

Let's practice another one:

192.168.10.0 = Network address

255.255.255.240 = Subnet mask

- *Subnets?* 240 is 11110000 in binary. $2^4 = 16$.
- *Hosts?* 4 host bits, or $2^4 - 2 = 14$.
- *Valid subnets?* 256 – 240 = 16. Start at 0: 0 + 16 = 16. 16 + 16 = 32. 32 + 16 = 48. 48 + 16 = 64. 64 + 16 = 80. 80 + 16 = 96. 96 + 16 = 112. 112 + 16 = 128. 128 + 16 = 144. 144 + 16 = 160. 160 + 16 = 176. 176 + 16 = 192. 192 + 16 = 208. 208 + 16 = 224. 224 + 16 = 240.
- *Broadcast address for each subnet?*
- *Valid hosts?*

To answer the last two questions, check out the following table. It gives you the subnets, valid hosts, and broadcast addresses for each subnet. First, find the address of each subnet using the block size (increment). Second, find the broadcast address of each subnet increment, which is always the number right before the next valid subnet, and then just fill in the host addresses.

The following table shows the available subnets, hosts, and broadcast addresses provided from a Class C 255.255.255.240 mask.

Subnet	0	16	32	48	64	80	96	112	128	144	160	176	192	208	224	240
First host	1	17	33	49	65	81	97	113	129	145	161	177	193	209	225	241
Last host	14	30	46	62	78	94	110	126	142	158	174	190	206	222	238	254
Broadcast	15	31	47	63	79	95	111	127	143	159	175	191	207	223	239	255

TIP

Cisco has figured out that most people cannot count in 16s and therefore, have a hard time finding valid subnets, hosts, and broadcast addresses with the Class C 255.255.255.240 mask. You'd be wise to study this mask.

Practice Example #5C: 255.255.255.248 (/29)

Let's keep practicing:

192.168.10.0 = Network address

255.255.255.248 = Subnet mask

- *Subnets?* 248 in binary = 11111000. $2^5 = 32$.
- *Hosts?* $2^3 - 2 = 6$.
- *Valid subnets?* 256 – 248 = 0, 8, 16, 24, 32, 40, 48, 56, 64, 72, 80, 88, 96, 104, 112, 120, 128, 136, 144, 152, 160, 168, 176, 184, 192, 200, 208, 216, 224, 232, 240, and 248.
- *Broadcast address for each subnet?*
- *Valid hosts?*

Take a look at the following table. It shows some of the subnets (first four and last four only), valid hosts, and broadcast addresses for the Class C 255.255.255.248 mask:

Subnet	0	8	16	24	...	224	232	240	248
First host	1	9	17	25	...	225	233	241	249
Last host	6	14	22	30	...	230	238	246	254
Broadcast	7	15	23	31	...	231	239	247	255

TIP

If you try to configure a router interface with the address 192.168.10.6 255.255.255.248 and receive the following error, this means that `ip subnet-zero` is not enabled:

```
Bad mask /29 for address 192.168.10.6
```

You must be able to subnet in order to see that the address used in this example is in the zero subnet.

Practice Example #6C: 255.255.255.252 (/30)

Okay—just one more:

192.168.10.0 = Network address

255.255.255.252 = Subnet mask

- *Subnets?* 64.
- *Hosts?* 2.
- *Valid subnets?* 0, 4, 8, 12, etc., all the way to 252.
- *Broadcast address for each subnet?* (Always the number right before the next subnet.)
- *Valid hosts?* (The numbers between the subnet number and the broadcast address.)

The following table shows the subnet, valid host, and broadcast address of the first four and last four subnets in the 255.255.255.252 Class C subnet:

Subnet	0	4	8	12	. . .	240	244	248	252
First host	1	5	9	13	. . .	241	245	249	253
Last host	2	6	10	14	. . .	242	246	250	254
Broadcast	3	7	11	15	. . .	243	247	251	255

Real World Scenario

Should We Really Use This Mask That Provides Only Two Hosts?

You are the network administrator for Acme Corporation with dozens of WAN links connecting to your corporate office. Right now, your network is a classful network, which means that the same subnet mask is on each host and router interface. You've read about classless routing, where you can have different-sized masks, but you don't know what to use on your point-to-point WAN links. Is the 255.255.255.252 (/30) a helpful mask in this situation?

Yes, this is a very helpful mask in WANs and, of course, with any type of point-to-point link!

If you were to use the 255.255.255.0 mask in this situation, then each network would have 254 hosts. But you use only 2 addresses with a WAN or point-to-point link, which is a waste of 252 hosts per subnet! If you use the 255.255.255.252 mask, then each subnet has only 2 hosts, and you don't want to waste precious addresses. This is a really important subject, one that we'll address in a lot more detail in the section on VLSM network design in the next chapter.

Subnetting in Your Head: Class C Addresses

Is it really possible to subnet in your head? Yes, and it's not all that hard either. Consider the following example:

192.168.10.50 = Node address

255.255.255.224 = Subnet mask

First, determine the subnet and broadcast address of the network in which the previous IP address resides. You can do this by answering question 3 of the big 5 questions: 256 – 224 = 32. 0, 32, 64, and so on. The address of 50 falls between the two subnets of 32 and 64 and must be part of the 192.168.10.32 subnet. The next subnet is 64, so the broadcast address of the 32 subnet is 63. Don't forget that the broadcast address of a subnet is always the number right before the next subnet. The valid host range equals the numbers between the subnet and broadcast address, or 33–62. Oh, this is just too easy!

Let's try another one. We'll subnet another Class C address:

192.168.10.50 = Node address

255.255.255.240 = Subnet mask

What is the subnet and broadcast address of the network of which the previous IP address is a member? 256 – 240 = 16. Now, just count by our increments of 16 until you pass the host address: 0, 16, 32, 48, 64. Bingo—the host address is between the 48 and 64 subnets. The subnet is 192.168.10.48, and the broadcast address is 63 because the next subnet is 64. The valid host range equals the numbers between the subnet number and the broadcast address, or 49–62.

Let's do a couple more to make sure you have this down.

You have a node address of 192.168.10.174 with a mask of 255.255.255.240. What is the valid host range?

The mask is 240, so you'd do a 256 – 240 = 16. This is your block size. Just keep adding 16 until you pass the host address of 174, starting at zero, of course: 0, 16, 32, 48, 64, 80, 96, 112, 128, 144, 160, 176. The host address of 174 is between 160 and 176, so the subnet is 160. The broadcast address is 175; the valid host range is 161–174. That was a tough one!

One more—just for fun. This one is the easiest of all Class C subnetting:

192.168.10.17 = Node address

255.255.255.252 = Subnet mask

What is the subnet address and broadcast address of the subnet in which the previous IP address resides? 256 – 252 = 0. (Always start at zero unless told otherwise.) 0, 4, 8, 12, 16, 20, etc. You've got it! The host address is between the 16 and 20 subnets. The subnet is 192.168.10.16, and the broadcast address is 19. The valid host range is 17–18.

Now that you're all over Class C subnetting, let's move on to Class B subnetting. But before we do, let's go through a quick review.

What Do We Know?

Okay, here's where you can really apply what you've learned so far and begin committing it all to memory. This is a very cool section that I've been using in my classes for years. It will really help you nail down subnetting for good!

When you see a subnet mask or slash notation (CIDR), you should know the following:

/25 What do we know about a /25?

- 128 mask
- 1 bit on and 7 bits off (10000000)
- Block size of 128
- Subnets 0 and 128
- 2 subnets, each with 126 hosts

/26 What do we know about a /26?

- 192 mask
- 2 bits on and 6 bits off (11000000)
- Block size of 64
- Subnets 0, 64, 128, 192
- 4 subnets, each with 62 hosts

/27 What do we know about a /27?

- 224 mask
- 3 bits on and 5 bits off (11100000)
- Block size of 32
- Subnets 0, 32, 64, 96, 128, 160, 192, 224
- 8 subnets, each with 30 hosts

/28 What do we know about a /28?

- 240 mask
- 4 bits on and 4 bits off
- Block size of 16
- Subnets 0, 16, 32, 48, 64, 80, 96, 112, 128, 144, 160, 176, 192, 208, 224, 240
- 16 subnets, each with 14 hosts

/29 What do we know about a /29?

- 248 mask
- 5 bits on and 3 bits off

- Block size of 8
- Subnets 0, 8, 16, 24, 32, 40, 48, etc.
- 32 subnets, each with 6 hosts

/30 What do we know about a /30?

- 252 mask
- 6 bits on and 2 bits off
- Block size of 4
- Subnets 0, 4, 8, 12, 16, 20, 24, etc.
- 64 subnets, each with 2 hosts

Table 4.3 puts all of the previous information into one compact little table. You should practice writing out this table, and if you can do it, write it down before you start your exam!

TABLE 4.3 What do you know?

CIDR Notation	Mask	Bits	Block Size	Subnets	Hosts
/25	128	1 bit on and 7 bits off	128	0 and 128	2 subnets, each with 126 hosts
/26	192	2 bits on and 6 bits off	64	0, 64, 128, 192	4 subnets, each with 62 hosts
/27	224	3 bits on and 5 bits off	32	0, 32, 64, 96, 128, 160, 192, 224	8 subnets, each with 30 hosts
/28	240	4 bits on and 4 bits off	16	0, 16, 32, 48, 64, 80, 96, 112, 128, 144, 160, 176, 192, 208, 224, 240	16 subnets, each with 14 hosts
/29	248	5 bits on and 3 bits off	8	0, 8, 16, 24, 32, 40, 48, etc.	32 subnets, each with 6 hosts
/30	252	6 bits on and 2 bits off	4	0, 4, 8, 12, 16, 20, 24, etc.	64 subnets, each with 2 hosts

Regardless of whether you have a Class A, Class B, or Class C address, the /30 mask will provide you with only two hosts, ever. As suggested by Cisco, this mask is suited almost exclusively for use on point-to-point links.

If you can memorize this "What Do We Know?" section, you'll be much better off in your day-to-day job and in your studies. Try saying it out loud, which helps you memorize things—yes, others nearby may think you've lost it, but they probably already do if you're in the networking field. And if you're not yet in the networking field but are studying all this to break into it, get used to it!

It's also helpful to write these on some type of flashcards and have people test your skill. You'd be amazed at how fast you can get subnetting down if you memorize block sizes as well as this "What Do We Know?" section.

Subnetting Class B Addresses

Before we dive into this, let's first look at all the possible Class B subnet masks. Notice that we have a lot more possible subnet masks than we do with a Class C network address:

```
255.255.0.0   (/16)
255.255.128.0 (/17) 255.255.255.0   (/24)
255.255.192.0 (/18) 255.255.255.128 (/25)
255.255.224.0 (/19) 255.255.255.192 (/26)
255.255.240.0 (/20) 255.255.255.224 (/27)
255.255.248.0 (/21) 255.255.255.240 (/28)
255.255.252.0 (/22) 255.255.255.248 (/29)
255.255.254.0 (/23) 255.255.255.252 (/30)
```

We know the Class B network address has 16 bits available for host addressing. This means we can use up to 14 bits for subnetting because we need to leave at least 2 bits for host addressing. Using a /16 means you are not subnetting with Class B, but it *is* a mask you can use.

NOTE

By the way, do you notice anything interesting about that list of subnet values—a pattern, maybe? Ah ha! That's exactly why I had you memorize the binary-to-decimal numbers earlier in Chapter 2, "Ethernet Networking." Since subnet mask bits start on the left and move to the right and bits can't be skipped, the numbers are always the same regardless of the class of address. If you haven't already, memorize this pattern!

The process of subnetting a Class B network is pretty much the same as it is for a Class C, except that you have more host bits and you start in the third octet.

Use the same subnet numbers for the third octet with Class B that you used for the fourth octet with Class C, but add a zero to the network portion and a 255 to the broadcast section in the fourth octet. The following table shows you an example host range of three subnets used in a Class B 240 (/20) subnet mask:

Subnet Address	16.0	32.0	48.0
Broadcast address	31.255	47.255	63.255

Just add the valid hosts between the numbers and you're set!

NOTE The preceding example is true only until you get up to /24. After that, it's numerically exactly like Class C.

Subnetting Practice Examples: Class B Addresses

Next, you'll get an opportunity to practice subnetting Class B addresses. Again, I have to mention that this is the same as subnetting with Class C, except we start in the third octet—with the exact same numbers.

Practice Example #1B: 255.255.128.0 (/17)

172.16.0.0 = Network address

255.255.128.0 = Subnet mask

- *Subnets?* $2^1 = 2$ (same amount as Class C).
- *Hosts?* $2^{15} - 2 = 32{,}766$ (7 bits in the third octet, and 8 in the fourth).
- *Valid subnets?* 256 – 128 = 128. 0, 128. Remember, subnetting is performed in the third octet, so the subnet numbers are really 0.0 and 128.0, as shown in the next table. These are the exact numbers we used with Class C; we use them in the third octet and add a 0 in the fourth octet for the network address.
- *Broadcast address for each subnet?*
- *Valid hosts?*

This table shows the two subnets available, the valid host range, and the broadcast address of each:

Subnet	0.0	**128.0**
First host	0.1	128.1
Last host	127.254	255.254
Broadcast	127.255	255.255

Okay, notice that we just added the fourth octet's lowest and highest values and came up with the answers. And again, it's done exactly the same way as for a Class C subnet. We just used the same numbers in the third octet and added 0 and 255 in the fourth octet. Pretty simple, huh? I really can't say this enough—it's just not that hard! The numbers never change; we just use them in different octets.

Question: Using the previous subnet mask, do you think 172.16.10.0 is a valid host address? What about 172.16.10.255? Can 0 and 255 in the fourth octet ever be a valid host address? The answer is absolutely, yes, those are valid hosts! Any number between the subnet number and the broadcast address is always a valid host.

Practice Example #2B: 255.255.192.0 (/18)

172.16.0.0 = Network address

255.255.192.0 = Subnet mask

- *Subnets?* $2^2 = 4$.
- *Hosts?* $2^{14} - 2 = 16,382$ (6 bits in the third octet, and 8 in the fourth).
- *Valid subnets?* 256 – 192 = 64. 0, 64, 128, 192. Remember, the subnetting is performed in the third octet, so the subnet numbers are really 0.0, 64.0, 128.0, and 192.0, as shown in the following table.
- *Broadcast address for each subnet?*
- *Valid hosts?*

The following table shows the four subnets available, the valid host range, and the broadcast address of each:

Subnet	0.0	64.0	128.0	192.0
First host	0.1	64.1	128.1	192.1
Last host	63.254	127.254	191.254	255.254
Broadcast	63.255	127.255	191.255	255.255

Again, it's pretty much the same as it is for a Class C subnet—we just added 0 and 255 in the fourth octet for each subnet in the third octet.

Practice Example #3B: 255.255.240.0 (/20)

172.16.0.0 = Network address

255.255.240.0 = Subnet mask

- *Subnets?* $2^4 = 16$.
- *Hosts?* $2^{12} - 2 = 4,094$.
- *Valid subnets?* 256 – 240 = 0, 16, 32, 48, etc., up to 240. Notice that these are the same numbers as a Class C 240 mask—we just put them in the third octet and add a 0 and 255 in the fourth octet.
- *Broadcast address for each subnet?*
- *Valid hosts?*

The following table shows the first four subnets, valid hosts, and broadcast addresses in a Class B 255.255.240.0 mask:

Subnet	0.0	16.0	32.0	48.0
First host	0.1	16.1	32.1	48.1
Last host	15.254	31.254	47.254	63.254
Broadcast	15.255	31.255	47.255	63.255

Practice Example #4B: 255.255.248.0 (/21)

172.16.0.0 = Network address

255.255.248.0 = Subnet mask

- *Subnets?* 2^5 = 32.
- *Hosts?* $2^{11} - 2$ = 2,046.
- *Valid subnets?* 256 – 248 = 0, 8, 16, 24, 32, etc., up to 248.
- *Broadcast address for each subnet?*
- *Valid hosts?*

The following table shows the first five subnets, valid hosts, and broadcast addresses in a Class B 255.255.248.0 mask:

Subnet	0.0	8.0	16.0	24.0	32.0
First host	0.1	8.1	16.1	24.1	32.1
Last host	7.254	15.254	23.254	31.254	39.254
Broadcast	7.255	15.255	23.255	31.255	39.255

Practice Example #5B: 255.255.252.0 (/22)

172.16.0.0 = Network address

255.255.252.0 = Subnet mask

- *Subnets?* 2^6 = 64.
- *Hosts?* $2^{10} - 2$ = 1,022.
- *Valid subnets?* 256 – 252 = 0, 4, 8, 12, 16, etc., up to 252.
- *Broadcast address for each subnet?*
- *Valid hosts?*

This table shows the first five subnets, valid hosts, and broadcast addresses in a Class B 255.255.252.0 mask:

Subnet	0.0	4.0	8.0	12.0	16.0
First host	0.1	4.1	8.1	12.1	16.1
Last host	3.254	7.254	11.254	15.254	19.254
Broadcast	3.255	7.255	11.255	15.255	19.255

Practice Example #6B: 255.255.254.0 (/23)

172.16.0.0 = Network address

255.255.254.0 = Subnet mask

- *Subnets?* $2^7 = 128$.
- *Hosts?* $2^9 - 2 = 510$.
- *Valid subnets?* 256 – 254 = 0, 2, 4, 6, 8, etc., up to 254.
- *Broadcast address for each subnet?*
- *Valid hosts?*

The following table shows the first five subnets, valid hosts, and broadcast addresses in a Class B 255.255.254.0 mask:

Subnet	0.0	2.0	4.0	6.0	8.0
First host	0.1	2.1	4.1	6.1	8.1
Last host	1.254	3.254	5.254	7.254	9.254
Broadcast	1.255	3.255	5.255	7.255	9.255

Practice Example #7B: 255.255.255.0 (/24)

Contrary to popular belief, 255.255.255.0 used with a Class B network address is not called a Class B network with a Class C subnet mask. It's amazing how many people see this mask used in a Class B network and think it's a Class C subnet mask. This is a Class B subnet mask with 8 bits of subnetting—it's logically different from a Class C mask. Subnetting this address is fairly simple:

172.16.0.0 = Network address

255.255.255.0 = Subnet mask

- *Subnets?* $2^8 = 256$.
- *Hosts?* $2^8 - 2 = 254$.

- *Valid subnets?* 256 – 255 = 1. 0, 1, 2, 3, etc., all the way to 255.
- *Broadcast address for each subnet?*
- *Valid hosts?*

The following table shows the first four and last two subnets, the valid hosts, and the broadcast addresses in a Class B 255.255.255.0 mask:

Subnet	0.0	1.0	2.0	3.0	...	254.0	255.0
First host	0.1	1.1	2.1	3.1	...	254.1	255.1
Last host	0.254	1.254	2.254	3.254	...	254.254	255.254
Broadcast	0.255	1.255	2.255	3.255	...	254.255	255.255

Practice Example #8B: 255.255.255.128 (/25)

This is actually one of the hardest subnet masks you can play with. And worse, it actually is a really good subnet to use in production because it creates over 500 subnets with 126 hosts for each subnet—a nice mixture. So, don't skip over it!

172.16.0.0 = Network address
255.255.255.128 = Subnet mask

- *Subnets?* 2^9 = 512.
- *Hosts?* $2^7 - 2$ = 126.
- *Valid subnets?* Now for the tricky part. 256 – 255 = 1. 0, 1, 2, 3, etc., for the third octet. But you can't forget the one subnet bit used in the fourth octet. Remember when I showed you how to figure one subnet bit with a Class C mask? You figure this the same way. You actually get two subnets for each third octet value, hence the 512 subnets. For example, if the third octet is showing subnet 3, the two subnets would actually be 3.0 and 3.128.
- *Broadcast address for each subnet?* The numbers right before the next subnet.
- *Valid hosts?* The numbers between the subnet numbers and the broadcast address.

The following graphic shows how you can create subnets, valid hosts, and broadcast addresses using the Class B 255.255.255.128 subnet mask. The first eight subnets are shown, followed by the last two subnets:

Subnet	0.0	0.128	1.0	1.128	2.0	2.128	3.0	3.128	...	255.0	255.128
First host	0.1	0.129	1.1	1.129	2.1	2.129	3.1	3.129	...	255.1	255.129
Last host	0.126	0.254	1.126	1.254	2.126	2.254	3.126	3.254	...	255.126	255.254
Broadcast	0.127	0.255	1.127	1.255	2.127	2.255	3.127	3.255	...	255.127	255.255

Practice Example #9B: 255.255.255.192 (/26)

Now, this is where Class B subnetting gets easy. Since the third octet has a 255 in the mask section, whatever number is listed in the third octet is a subnet number. And now that we have a subnet number in the fourth octet, we can subnet this octet just as we did with Class C subnetting. Let's try it out:

172.16.0.0 = Network address

255.255.255.192 = Subnet mask

- *Subnets?* 2^{10} = 1,024.
- *Hosts?* $2^6 - 2$ = 62.
- *Valid subnets?* 256 – 192 = 64. The subnets are shown in the following table. Do these numbers look familiar?
- *Broadcast address for each subnet?*
- *Valid hosts?*

The following table shows the first eight subnet ranges, valid hosts, and broadcast addresses:

Subnet	0.0	0.64	0.128	0.192	1.0	1.64	1.128	1.192
First host	0.1	0.65	0.129	0.193	1.1	1.65	1.129	1.193
Last host	0.62	0.126	0.190	0.254	1.62	1.126	1.190	1.254
Broadcast	0.63	0.127	0.191	0.255	1.63	1.127	1.191	1.255

Notice that for each subnet value in the third octet, you get subnets 0, 64, 128, and 192 in the fourth octet.

Practice Example #10B: 255.255.255.224 (/27)

This one is done the same way as the preceding subnet mask, except we just have more subnets and fewer hosts per subnet available.

172.16.0.0 = Network address

255.255.255.224 = Subnet mask

- *Subnets?* 2^{11} = 2,048.
- *Hosts?* $2^5 - 2$ = 30.
- *Valid subnets?* 256 – 224 = 32. 0, 32, 64, 96, 128, 160, 192, 224.
- *Broadcast address for each subnet?*
- *Valid hosts?*

The following table shows the first eight subnets:

Subnet	0.0	0.32	0.64	0.96	0.128	0.160	0.192	0.224
First host	0.1	0.33	0.65	0.97	0.129	0.161	0.193	0.225
Last host	0.30	0.62	0.94	0.126	0.158	0.190	0.222	0.254
Broadcast	0.31	0.63	0.95	0.127	0.159	0.191	0.223	0.255

And the following table shows the last eight subnets:

Subnet	**255.0**	**255.32**	**255.64**	**255.96**	**255.128**	**255.160**	**255.192**	**255.224**
First host	255.1	255.33	255.65	255.97	255.129	255.161	255.193	255.225
Last host	255.30	255.62	255.94	255.126	255.158	255.190	255.222	255.254
Broadcast	255.31	255.63	255.95	255.127	255.159	255.191	255.223	255.255

Subnetting in Your Head: Class B Addresses

Are you nuts? Subnet Class B addresses in our heads? It's actually easier than writing it out—I'm not kidding! Let me show you how:

Question: What is the subnet and broadcast address of the subnet in which 172.16.10.33 /27 resides?

Answer: The interesting octet is the fourth one. 256 – 224 = 32. 32 + 32 = 64. You've got it: 33 is between 32 and 64. But remember that the third octet is considered part of the subnet, so the answer would be the 10.32 subnet. The broadcast is 10.63, since 10.64 is the next subnet. That was a pretty easy one.

Question: What subnet and broadcast address is the IP address 172.16.66.10 255.255.192.0 (/18) a member of?

Answer: The interesting octet here is the third octet instead of the fourth one. 256 – 192 = 64. 0, 64, 128. The subnet is 172.16.64.0. The broadcast must be 172.16.127.255 since 128.0 is the next subnet.

Question: What subnet and broadcast address is the IP address 172.16.50.10 255.255.224.0 (/19) a member of?

Answer: 256 – 224 = 0, 32, 64. (Remember, we always start counting at 0.) The subnet is 172.16.32.0, and the broadcast must be 172.16.63.255 since 64.0 is the next subnet.

Question: What subnet and broadcast address is the IP address 172.16.46.255 255.255.240.0 (/20) a member of?

Answer: 256 – 240 = 16. The third octet is important here: 0, 16, 32, 48. This subnet address must be in the 172.16.32.0 subnet, and the broadcast must be 172.16.47.255 since 48.0 is the next subnet. So, yes, 172.16.46.255 is a valid host.

Question: What subnet and broadcast address is the IP address 172.16.45.14 255.255.255.252 (/30) a member of?

Answer: Where is our interesting octet? 256 – 252 = 0, 4, 8, 12, 16—the fourth. The subnet is 172.16.45.12, with a broadcast of 172.16.45.15 because the next subnet is 172.16.45.16.

Question: What is the subnet and broadcast address of the host 172.16.88.255/20?

Answer: What is a /20 written out in dotted decimal? If you can't answer this, you can't answer this question, can you? A /20 is 255.255.240.0, which gives us a block size of 16 in the third octet, and since no subnet bits are on in the fourth octet, the answer is always 0 and 255 in the fourth octet: 0, 16, 32, 48, 64, 80, 96. Because 88 is between 80 and 96, the subnet is 80.0, and the broadcast address is 95.255.

Question: A router receives a packet on an interface with a destination address of 172.16.46.191/26. What will the router do with this packet?

Answer: Discard it. Do you know why? 172.16.46.191/26 is a 255.255.255.192 mask, which gives us a block size of 64. Our subnets are then 0, 64, 128, and 192. 191 is the broadcast address of the 128 subnet, and by default, a router will discard any broadcast packets.

TIP To get more subnetting practice, head over to `www.lammle.com/ccna`.

Summary

Were Chapters 3 and 4 crystal clear to you on the first pass? If so, wonderful—congratulations! But you probably really did get lost a couple of times right? No worries—that's usually what happens.

Don't waste time feeling bad if you have to read each chapter more than once, or even 10 times, before you're truly good to go. If you read the chapters more than once, you'll be seriously better off in the long run even if you were pretty comfortable the first time through!

This chapter provided you with critical understanding of IP subnetting—the painless way! And when you've got the material I presented in this chapter completely down, you should be able to subnet IP addresses in your head.

This chapter is extremely essential to your Cisco certification process, so if you just skimmed it, please go back, read it thoroughly, and be sure to practice all the scenarios.

Exam Essentials

Identify the advantages of subnetting. Benefits of subnetting a physical network include reduced network traffic, optimized network performance, simplified management, and facilitated spanning of large geographical distances.

Describe the effect of the `ip subnet-zero` command. This command allows you to use the first and last subnet in your network design.

Identify the steps to subnet a classful network. Understand how IP addressing and subnetting work. First, determine your block size by using the 256-subnet mask math. Then count your subnets and determine the broadcast address of each subnet—it is always the number right before the next subnet. Your valid hosts are the numbers between the subnet address and the broadcast address.

Determine possible block sizes. This is an important part of understanding IP addressing and subnetting. The valid block sizes are always 2, 4, 8, 16, 32, 64, 128, etc. You can determine your block size by using the 256-subnet mask math.

Describe the role of a subnet mask in IP addressing. A subnet mask is a 32-bit value that allows the recipient of IP packets to distinguish the network ID portion of the IP address from the host ID portion of the IP address.

Written Labs

You can find the answers to these labs in Appendix A, "Answers to the Written Labs."

In this section, you'll complete the following labs to make sure you've got the information and concepts contained within them fully dialed in:

Lab 4.1: Written Subnet Practice #1

Lab 4.2: Written Subnet Practice #2

Lab 4.3: Written Subnet Practice #3

Written Lab 4.1: Written Subnet Practice #1

Write the subnet, broadcast address, and a valid host range for questions 1–6. Then answer the remaining questions.

1. 192.168.100.25/30
2. 192.168.100.37/28
3. 192.168.100.66/27
4. 192.168.100.17/29

5. 192.168.100.99/26
6. 192.168.100.99/25
7. You have a Class B network and need 29 subnets. What is your mask?
8. What is the broadcast address of 192.168.192.10/29?
9. How many hosts are available with a Class C /29 mask?
10. What is the subnet for host ID 10.16.3.65/23?

Written Lab 4.2: Written Subnet Practice #2

Given a Class B network and the net bits identified (CIDR), complete the following table to identify the subnet mask and the number of host addresses possible for each mask.

Classful Address	Subnet Mask	Number of Hosts per Subnet ($2x - 2$)
/16		
/17		
/18		
/19		
/20		
/21		
/22		
/23		
/24		
/25		
/26		
/27		
/28		
/29		
/30		

Written Lab 4.3: Written Subnet Practice #3

Complete the following based on the decimal IP address.

Decimal IP Address	Address Class	Number of Subnet and Host Bits	Number of Subnets (2*x*)	Number of Hosts (2*x* – 2)
10.25.66.154/23				
172.31.254.12/24				
192.168.20.123/28				
63.24.89.21/18				
128.1.1.254/20				
208.100.54.209/30				

Review Questions

You can find the answers to these questions in Appendix B, "Answers to the Review Questions."

NOTE The following questions are designed to test your understanding of this chapter's material. For more information on how to get additional questions, please see `www.lammle.com/ccna`.

1. What is the maximum number of IP addresses that can be assigned to hosts on a local subnet that uses the 255.255.255.224 subnet mask?
   - **A.** 14
   - **B.** 15
   - **C.** 16
   - **D.** 30
   - **E.** 31
   - **F.** 62

2. You have a network that needs 29 subnets while maximizing the number of host addresses available on each subnet. How many bits must you borrow from the host field to provide the correct subnet mask?
   - **A.** 2
   - **B.** 3
   - **C.** 4
   - **D.** 5
   - **E.** 6
   - **F.** 7

3. What is the subnetwork address for a host with the IP address 200.10.5.68/28?
   - **A.** 200.10.5.56
   - **B.** 200.10.5.32
   - **C.** 200.10.5.64
   - **D.** 200.10.5.0

4. The network address of 172.16.0.0/19 provides how many subnets and hosts?
   - **A.** 7 subnets, 30 hosts each
   - **B.** 7 subnets, 2,046 hosts each
   - **C.** 7 subnets, 8,190 hosts each
   - **D.** 8 subnets, 30 hosts each

E. 8 subnets, 2,046 hosts each

F. 8 subnets, 8,190 hosts each

5. Which of the following statements describe the IP address 10.16.3.65/23? (Choose two.)

 A. The subnet address is 10.16.3.0 255.255.254.0.

 B. The lowest host address in the subnet is 10.16.2.1 255.255.254.0.

 C. The last valid host address in the subnet is 10.16.2.254 255.255.254.0.

 D. The broadcast address of the subnet is 10.16.3.255 255.255.254.0.

 E. The network is not subnetted.

6. If a host on a network has the address 172.16.45.14/30, what subnetwork does this host belong to?

 A. 172.16.45.0

 B. 172.16.45.4

 C. 172.16.45.8

 D. 172.16.45.12

 E. 172.16.45.16

7. Which mask should you use on point-to-point links in order to reduce the waste of IP addresses?

 A. /27

 B. /28

 C. /29

 D. /30

 E. /31

8. What is the subnetwork number of a host with an IP address of 172.16.66.0/21?

 A. 172.16.36.0

 B. 172.16.48.0

 C. 172.16.64.0

 D. 172.16.0.0

9. You have an interface on a router with the IP address of 192.168.192.10/29. Including the router interface, how many hosts can have IP addresses on the LAN attached to the router interface?

 A. 6

 B. 8

 C. 30

 D. 62

 E. 126

10. You need to configure a server that is on the subnet 192.168.19.24/29. The router has the first available host address. Which of the following should you assign to the server?

  A. 192.168.19.0 255.255.255.0
  B. 192.168.19.33 255.255.255.240
  C. 192.168.19.26 255.255.255.248
  D. 192.168.19.31 255.255.255.248
  E. 192.168.19.34 255.255.255.240

11. You have an interface on a router with the IP address of 192.168.192.10/29. What is the broadcast address the hosts will use on this LAN?

  A. 192.168.192.15
  B. 192.168.192.31
  C. 192.168.192.63
  D. 192.168.192.127
  E. 192.168.192.255

12. You need to subnet a network that has 5 subnets, each with at least 16 hosts. Which classful subnet mask would you use?

  A. 255.255.255.192
  B. 255.255.255.224
  C. 255.255.255.240
  D. 255.255.255.248

13. You configure a router interface with the IP address 192.168.10.62 255.255.255.192 and receive the following error:

```
Bad mask /26 for address 192.168.10.62
```

Why did you receive this error?

  A. You typed this mask on a WAN link, and that is not allowed.
  B. This is not a valid host and subnet mask combination.
  C. `ip subnet-zero` is not enabled on the router.
  D. The router does not support IP.

14. If an Ethernet port on a router were assigned an IP address of 172.16.112.1/25, what would be the valid subnet address of this interface?

  A. 172.16.112.0
  B. 172.16.0.0
  C. 172.16.96.0
  D. 172.16.255.0
  E. 172.16.128.0

15. The network ID is 192.168.10.0/28. Using the eighth subnet, what would be the IP address of E0 if you were using the last available IP address in the range? The zero subnet should not be considered valid for this question.

A. 192.168.10.142

B. 192.168.10.66

C. 192.168.100.254

D. 192.168.10.143

E. 192.168.10.126

16. What would be the IP address of E0 of a router if you were using the first subnet? The network ID is 192.168.10.0/28, and you need to use the last available IP address in the range. Again, the zero subnet should not be considered valid for this question.

A. 192.168.10.24

B. 192.168.10.62

C. 192.168.10.30

D. 192.168.10.127

17. Which configuration command must be in effect to allow the use of 8 subnets if the Class C subnet mask is 255.255.255.224?

A. `Router(config)#`**`ip classless`**

B. `Router(config)#`**`ip version 6`**

C. `Router(config)#`**`no ip classful`**

D. `Router(config)#`**`ip unnumbered`**

E. `Router(config)#`**`ip subnet-zero`**

F. `Router(config)#`**`ip all-nets`**

18. You have a network with a subnet of 172.16.17.0/22. Which of the following is the valid host address?

A. 172.16.17.1 255.255.255.252

B. 172.16.0.1 255.255.240.0

C. 172.16.20.1 255.255.254.0

D. 172.16.16.1 255.255.255.240

E. 172.16.18.255 255.255.252.0

F. 172.16.0.1 255.255.255.0

19. Your router has the following IP address on Ethernet0: 172.16.2.1/23. Which of the following can be valid host IDs on the LAN interface attached to the router? (Choose two.)

A. 172.16.0.5

B. 172.16.1.100

C. 172.16.1.198

D. 172.16.2.255

E. 172.16.3.0

F. 172.16.3.255

20. To test the IP stack on your local host, which IP address would you ping?

A. 172.0.0.1

B. 1.0.0.127

C. 127.0.0.1

D. 127.255.255.255

E. 255.255.255.255

Chapter 5

Troubleshooting IP Addressing

THE CCNA EXAM TOPICS COVERED IN THIS CHAPTER INCLUDE THE FOLLOWING:

✓ ***1.0 Network Fundamentals***

- 1.1.f Endpoints
- 1.1.g Servers
- 1.6 Configure and verify IPv4 addressing and subnetting
- 1.10 Verify IP parameters for Client OS (Windows, Mac OS, Linux)

In this chapter, we'll cover IP address troubleshooting while focusing on the steps Cisco recommends following when troubleshooting an IP network.

The tools I'm going to share with you and the skills you'll gain after learning how to use them will give you a huge advantage when taking the exam. Even more importantly, they'll give you a serious edge in the professional real world! Working through this chapter will hone your knowledge of IP addressing and networking while refining the essential skills you've attained so far.

So let's get started!

> **NOTE** To find bonus material, as well as Todd Lammle videos, practice questions, and hands-on labs, please see `www.lammle.com/ccna`.

Endpoint Overview

Because this chapter is going to dive into some server technologies, it is a good idea to make sure you are clear about some of the endpoints we can find in the network. This will hopefully make things a bit more apparent when we dive into the abstract world of virtualization.

An endpoint is just something that connects to the network through a wired or wireless connection. Most vendors license based upon how many active endpoints on the network are using the service the product provides. I'll quickly cover some common endpoints now.

Desktops/Laptops

Desktops and laptops are by far the most prevalent endpoints in our networks because pretty much every employee has at least one assigned to them.

Most companies are either running Microsoft Windows 11 or are in the process of upgrading from Windows 7 or Windows 10. Some also have a few Apple Mac computers in the mix, but you usually won't find Linux on the end-user side of things.

And, of course, all computers can use wired or wireless connections interchangeably.

Mobile Phones/Tablets

It's also common for staff to be issued a mobile phone and/or a tablet that will often connect to an SSID provided by the office. Most companies also allow employees to use their own devices on the network, but access is usually restricted via security policies.

Typical mobile devices are Apple iPhones/iPads or some Android variants, which tend to use wireless connections exclusively.

Access Points

Even though these devices are there to provide wireless access to your endpoints, they also connect to the network, so they're also considered endpoints.

Access points typically use wired connections for power supply and to get on the network, but they can also use wireless connections in more advanced configurations.

IP Phones

Most companies either have a Voice over IP (VoIP) solution or are talking about it. Because phones hog many switch ports, office computers are often connected to the IP Phone's built-in switch to save on cabling requirements. That way, only the phone gets connected to the access switch.

IP phones typically use wired ethernet connections for power rather than plugging into the wall.

Internet of Things

With the genesis of the IoT, everything from light bulbs to fridges and alarm systems are now on the network, and they're all endpoints, too!

Servers

It's like your server at a restaurant—the server on the network delivers what you've ordered. Servers are basically higher-end computers used to provide infrastructure or application services to users, and they tend to come in the five forms, as described in the following sections:

Tower

Tower end servers are pretty much just standard computer towers that can provide a few more resources than a regular computer.

Rack Server

The most common type of server is a rack-mounted simple server that's usually one rack unit (RU) in size but can be bigger. People sometimes call rack servers pizza boxes because they're often large squares.

Blade Server

This is the most complex type of server, which is actually a blade that connects to a large chassis. These systems are designed to be very redundant and resilient.

Hypervisor

I'll discuss this role more in the next section when we get to virtualization, but for now, know that it allows us to run virtual machines.

Bare Metal

This is simply a term for running a server without any virtualization.

Server Roles

There are way too many different server roles out there for me to talk about all of them in this chapter, but here's a list of the most common kinds of servers found in a network:

Active Directory

Microsoft AD is the flagship role of the Windows Server for user and computer management, and almost every company uses it in some way!

DNS

Using the Internet in any kind of efficient way depends on DNS because, without it, we would all be surfing by memorizing IP addresses.

DHCP

Covered earlier, DHCP is how your endpoints dynamically learn their IP address to get on the network.

RADIUS

This role is largely used by wireless to authenticate connections into the network.

TACACS+

This role is used for device administration and can control what a user has access to when they log into a device.

Email

This server manages sending and receiving email messages.

File

File servers store many files for users to access.

Databases

These servers store data in mysterious tables run by crazy wizards known as database administrators (DBAs). Avoid DBAs at all costs!

Web

This type of server runs the web pages we browse on the Internet.

Now, let's dive into troubleshooting IP!

Cisco's Way of Troubleshooting IP

Because running into trouble now and then in networking is a given, being able to troubleshoot IP addressing is a vital skill. I'm not being negative here—just realistic. The positive here is that if you're the one equipped with the tools to diagnose and clear up inevitable trouble, you get to be the hero when you save the day. And the icing on the cake is you can usually fix an IP network regardless of whether you're on site or not!

We're going to focus on the "Cisco way" of troubleshooting IP addressing. Let's use Figure 5.1 as an example of some basic IP trouble. Poor Sally can't log in to the Windows server. Do you deal with this by calling the Microsoft team to tell them their server is a pile of junk and causing all your problems? Though tempting, a better approach is to first verify your network.

FIGURE 5.1 Basic IP troubleshooting

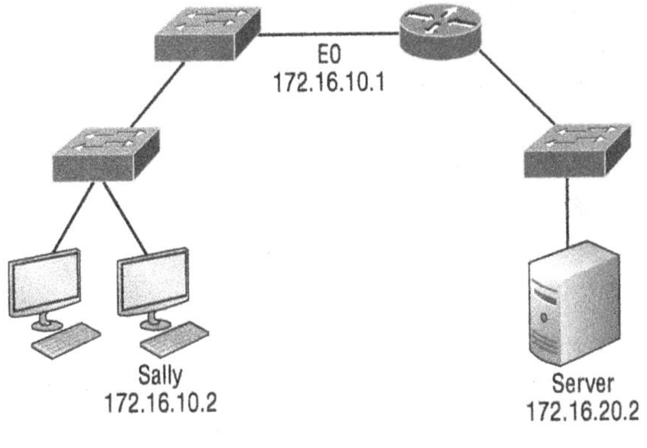

Let's walk through the Cisco approach to troubleshooting using a clear, step-by-step approach. These steps are pretty simple: start by imagining you/re at a customer host who's complaining they can't communicate to a server, which just happens to be on a remote network. In this scenario, here are the four troubleshooting steps Cisco recommends:

1. Open a Command window and ping 127.0.0.1. This is the diagnostic, or loopback, address, and if you get a successful ping, your IP stack is considered initialized. If it fails, then you have an IP stack failure and need to reinstall TCP/IP on the host:

```
C:\>ping 127.0.0.1
Pinging 127.0.0.1 with 32 bytes of data:
Reply from 127.0.0.1: bytes=32 time
Reply from 127.0.0.1: bytes=32 time
Reply from 127.0.0.1: bytes=32 time
Reply from 127.0.0.1: bytes=32 time
Ping statistics for 127.0.0.1:
Packets: Sent = 4, Received = 4, Lost = 0 (0% loss),
Approximate round trip times in milli-seconds:
Minimum = 0ms, Maximum = 0ms, Average = 0ms
```

2. From the Command window, ping the IP address of the local host. (We'll assume correct configuration here, but always check the IP configuration, too!). If that's successful, your network interface card (NIC) is functioning. If it fails, there is a problem with the NIC. Just so you know, success here doesn't necessarily mean that a cable is plugged into the NIC, only that the IP protocol stack on the host can communicate to the NIC via the LAN driver:

```
C:\>ping 172.16.10.2
Pinging 172.16.10.2 with 32 bytes of data:
Reply from 172.16.10.2: bytes=32 time
Reply from 172.16.10.2: bytes=32 time
Reply from 172.16.10.2: bytes=32 time
Reply from 172.16.10.2: bytes=32 time
Ping statistics for 172.16.10.2:
Packets: Sent = 4, Received = 4, Lost = 0 (0% loss),
Approximate round trip times in milli-seconds:
Minimum = 0ms, Maximum = 0ms, Average = 0ms
```

3. From the Command window, ping the default gateway (router). If the ping works, it means that the NIC is plugged into the network and can communicate on the local network. If it fails, you have a local physical network problem that could be anywhere from the NIC to the router:

```
C:\>ping 172.16.10.1
Pinging 172.16.10.1 with 32 bytes of data:
Reply from 172.16.10.1: bytes=32 time
Reply from 172.16.10.1: bytes=32 time
Reply from 172.16.10.1: bytes=32 time
Reply from 172.16.10.1: bytes=32 time
```

```
Ping statistics for 172.16.10.1:
Packets: Sent = 4, Received = 4, Lost = 0 (0% loss),
Approximate round trip times in milli-seconds:
Minimum = 0ms, Maximum = 0ms, Average = 0ms
```

4. If steps 1 through 3 were successful, try to ping the remote server. If that works, then you know you have IP communication between the local host and the remote server. You also know that the remote physical network is working:

```
C:\>ping 172.16.20.2
Pinging 172.16.20.2 with 32 bytes of data:
Reply from 172.16.20.2: bytes=32 time
Reply from 172.16.20.2: bytes=32 time
Reply from 172.16.20.2: bytes=32 time
Reply from 172.16.20.2: bytes=32 time
Ping statistics for 172.16.20.2:
Packets: Sent = 4, Received = 4, Lost = 0 (0% loss),
Approximate round trip times in milli-seconds:
Minimum = 0ms, Maximum = 0ms, Average = 0ms
```

If the user still can't communicate with the server after steps 1 through 4 have been completed successfully, you probably have some type of name resolution problem and need to check your Domain Name System (DNS) settings. But if the ping to the remote server fails, then you know you have some type of remote physical network problem and need to go to the server and work through steps 1 through 3 until you find the snag.

Verify IP Parameters for Operating Systems

Before moving on to determining IP address problems and how to fix them, I just want to mention some basic commands that you can use to troubleshoot your network from a Windows PC, Cisco devices, as well as MacOS and Linux hosts. Keep in mind that though these commands may do the same thing, they're implemented differently.

`ping` Uses ICMP echo request and replies to test if a node IP stack is initialized and alive on the network.

`traceroute` Displays the list of routers on a path to a network destination by using TTL time-outs and ICMP error messages. This command won't work from a command prompt.

`tracert` Same function as `traceroute`, but it's a Microsoft Windows command, and it won't work on a Cisco router.

`arp -a` Displays IP-to-MAC-address mappings on a Windows PC.

`show ip arp` Same function as `arp -a` but displays the ARP table on a Cisco router. Like the commands `traceroute` and `tracert`, `arp -a` and `show ip arp`, these aren't interchangeable through Windows and Cisco.

`ipconfig /all` Used only from a Windows command prompt; shows you the PC network configuration.

`ifconfig` Used by MacOS and Linux to get the IP address details of the local machine.

`ipconfig getifaddr en0` Used to find your IP address if you are connected to a wireless network or use en1 if you are connected to an Ethernet for MacOS or Linux.

`curl ifconfig.me` This command will display your global Internet IP address in Terminal for MacOS or Linux.

`curl ipecho.net/plain ; echo` This command will display your global Internet IP address in Terminal for MacOS or Linux.

Once you've gone through all these steps and, if necessary, used the appropriate commands, what do you do when you find a problem? How do you go about fixing an IP address configuration error? Time to cover the next step: determining and fixing the issue at hand!

Determining IP Address Problems

It's common for a host, router, or other network device to be configured with the wrong IP address, subnet mask, or default gateway. Because this happens way too often, you've got to know how to find and fix IP address configuration errors.

A good way to start is to draw out the network and IP addressing scheme. If that's already been done, consider yourself lucky because though sensible, it's rarely done. Even if it is, it's usually outdated or inaccurate anyway. So, either way, it's a good idea to bite the bullet and start from scratch.

Once you have your network accurately drawn out, including the IP addressing scheme, you need to verify each host's IP address, mask, and default gateway address to establish the problem. Of course, this assumes that you don't have a physical layer problem, or if you do, that you've already fixed it.

Check out the example illustrated in Figure 5.2.

A user in the sales department calls and tells you that they can't get to ServerA in the marketing department. You ask them they can get to ServerB in the marketing department, but they don't know because they don't have rights to log on to that server. What do you do?

First, guide your user through the four troubleshooting steps you learned in the preceding section. Let's say steps 1 through 3 work, but step 4 fails. By looking at the figure, can you determine the problem? Look for clues in the network drawing. First, the WAN link between the Lab A router and the Lab B router shows the mask as a /27. You should already know this mask is 255.255.255.224 and determine that all networks are using this mask. The network address is 192.168.1.0. What are your valid subnets and hosts? 256 – 224 = 32, so this makes our subnets 0, 32, 64, 96, 128, etc. So, by looking at the figure, you can see that subnet 32 is being used by the sales department; the WAN link is using subnet 96; and the marketing department is using subnet 64.

FIGURE 5.2 IP address problem 1

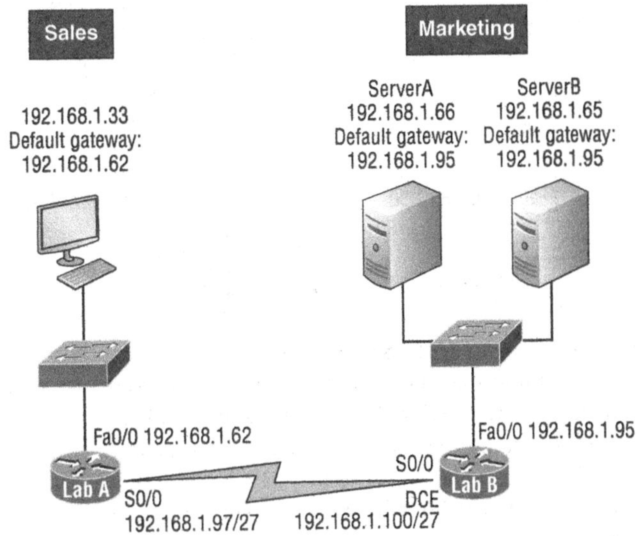

Next, you need to establish what the valid host ranges are for each subnet. From what you've learned already, you should now be able to easily determine the subnet address, broadcast addresses, and valid host ranges. The valid hosts for the Sales LAN are 33 through 62, and the broadcast address is 63 because the next subnet is 64, right? For the Marketing LAN, the valid hosts are 65 through 94 (broadcast 95), and for the WAN link, 97 through 126 (broadcast 127). By closely examining the figure, you can determine that the default gateway on the Lab B router is incorrect. That address is the broadcast address for subnet 64, so there's no way it could be a valid host!

TIP If you tried to configure that address on the Lab B router interface, you'd receive a bad mask error. Cisco routers don't let you type in subnet and broadcast addresses as valid hosts!

Did you get all that? Let's try another one to make sure. Figure 5.3 illustrates a network problem.

FIGURE 5.3 IP address problem 2

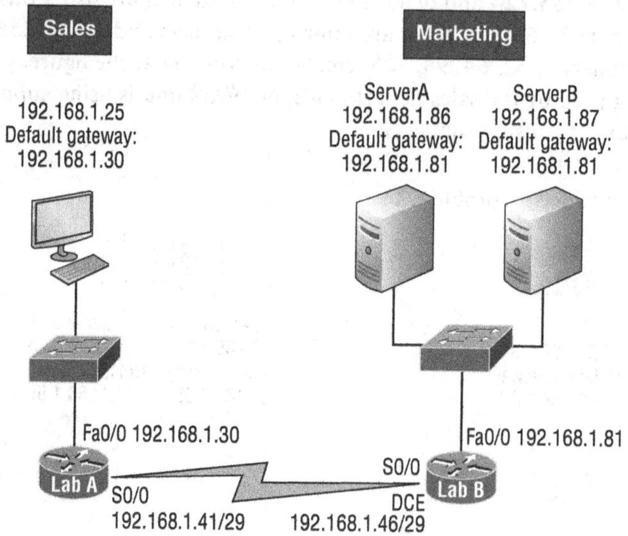

A user in the Sales LAN can't get to ServerB. You have the user run through the four basic troubleshooting steps and find that the host can communicate to the local network but not to the remote network. Find and define the IP addressing problem.

If you went through the same steps used to solve the last problem, you can see that the WAN link again provides the subnet mask to use: /29, or 255.255.255.248. Assuming classful addressing, you need to determine what the valid subnets, broadcast addresses, and valid host ranges are to solve this problem.

The 248 mask is a block size of 8 (256 – 248 = 8), so the subnets both start and increment in multiples of 8. By looking at the figure, you see that the Sales LAN is in the 24 subnet; the WAN is in the 40 subnet; and the Marketing LAN is in the 80 subnet. Can you see the problem yet? The valid host range for the Sales LAN is 25–30, and the configuration appears correct. The valid host range for the WAN link is 41–46, and this also appears correct. The valid host range for the 80 subnet is 81–86, with a broadcast address of 87 because the next subnet is 88. ServerB has been configured with the broadcast address of the subnet.

Okay, so now that you can figure out misconfigured IP addresses on hosts, what do you do if a host doesn't have an IP address and you need to assign one? You need to scrutinize the other hosts on the LAN and figure out the network, mask, and default gateway. Let's take a look at a couple of examples about how to find and apply valid IP addresses to hosts.

You need to assign a server and router IP addresses on a LAN. The subnet assigned on that segment is 192.168.20.24/29. The router needs to be assigned the first usable address, and the server needs the last valid host ID. What is the IP address, mask, and default gateway assigned to the server?

To answer this, you must know that a /29 is a 255.255.255.248 mask, which provides a block size of 8. The subnet is known as 24, and the next subnet in a block of 8 is 32, so the broadcast address of the 24 subnet is 31, and the valid host range is 25–30.

Server IP address: 192.168.20.30

Server mask: 255.255.255.248

Default gateway: 192.168.20.25 (the router's IP address)

Take a look at Figure 5.4 and solve this problem.

Look at the router's IP address on Ethernet0. What IP address, subnet mask, and valid host range could be assigned to the host?

FIGURE 5.4 Find the valid host #1

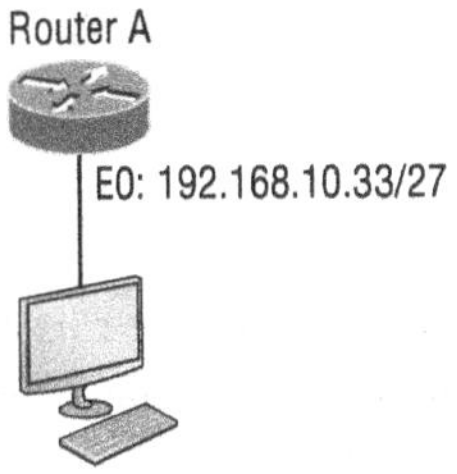

The IP address of the router's Ethernet0 is 192.168.10.33/27. As you already know, a /27 is a 224 mask with a block size of 32. The router's interface is in the 32 subnet. The next subnet is 64, so that makes the broadcast address of the 32 subnet 63 and the valid host range 33–62.

Host IP address: 192.168.10.34–62 (any address in the range except for 33, which is assigned to the router)

Mask: 255.255.255.224

Default gateway: 192.168.10.33

Figure 5.5 shows two routers with Ethernet configurations already assigned. What are the host addresses and subnet masks of HostA and HostB?

Router A has an IP address of 192.168.10.65/26, and Router B has an IP address of 192.168.10.33/28. What are the host configurations? Router A Ethernet0 is in the 192.168.10.64 subnet, and Router B Ethernet0 is in the 192.168.10.32 network.

Host A IP address: 192.168.10.66–126

Host A mask: 255.255.255.192

Host A default gateway: 192.168.10.65

Host B IP address: 192.168.10.34–46

Host B mask: 255.255.255.240

Host B default gateway: 192.168.10.33

FIGURE 5.5 Find the valid host #2

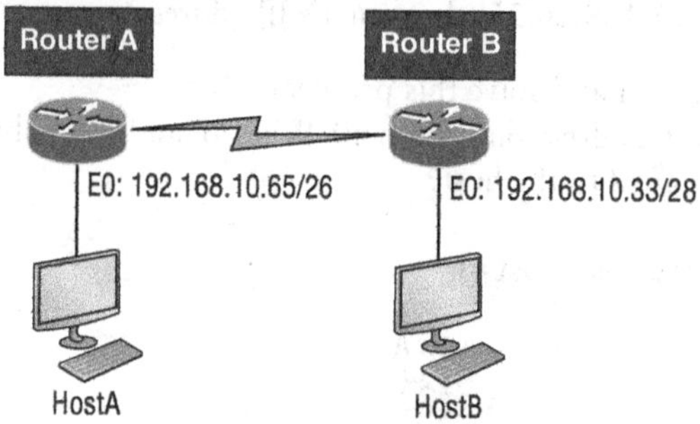

Just a couple more examples before you can put this chapter behind you—hang in there!

Figure 5.6 shows two routers. You need to configure the S0/0 interface on RouterA. The IP address assigned to the serial link on RouterA is 172.16.17.0/22 (No, that is not a subnet address, but a valid host IP address on that interface—most people miss this one.) Which IP address can be assigned to the router interface on RouterB?

FIGURE 5.6 Find the valid host address #3

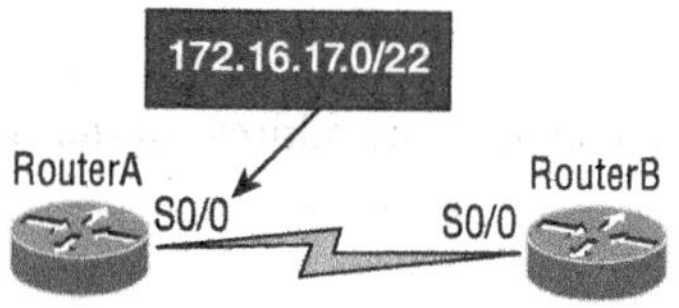

First, know that a /22 CIDR is 255.255.252.0, which makes a block size of 4 in the third octet. Since 17 is listed as the interface IP address, the available range is 16.1 through 19.254; so, in this example, the IP address S0/0 on RouterB could be 172.16.18.255 since that's within the range.

Okay, last one! You need to find a classful network address that has one Class C network ID, and you need to provide one usable subnet per city while allowing enough usable host addresses for each city specified in Figure 5.7. What is your mask?

Actually, this is probably the easiest thing you've done all day! I count 5 subnets needed, and the Wyoming office needs 16 users—always look for the network that needs the most hosts! What block size is needed for the Wyoming office? The answer is 32. You can't use a block size of 16 because you always have to subtract 2. What mask provides you with a block size of 32? 224 is the answer because this provides 8 subnets, each with 30 hosts.

FIGURE 5.7 Find the valid subnet mask

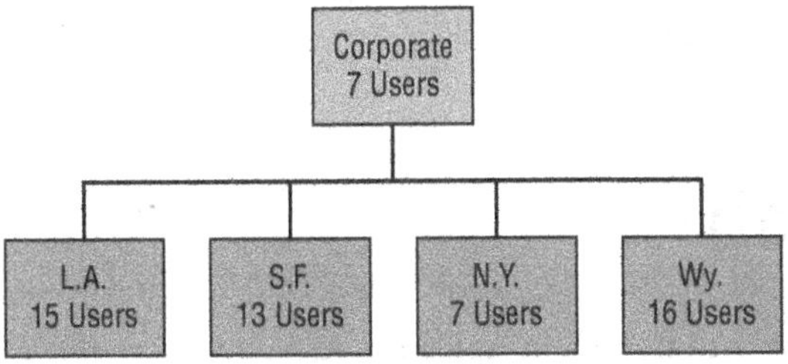

You're done—whew! Time to take a break, but skip the shot and the beer if that's what you had in mind because you need to keep going with your studies!

Summary

Again, if you got to this point without getting lost along the way a few times, you're awesome. If you did get lost, don't stress because most people do! Just be patient and go back over the material that tripped you up until it's all crystal clear. You'll get there!

And make sure you understand and memorize Cisco's troubleshooting methods. You must remember the four steps that Cisco recommends when trying to narrow down exactly where a network and/or IP addressing problem is and then know how to proceed systematically to fix it. In addition, you should be able to find valid IP addresses and subnet masks by looking at a network diagram.

Exam Essentials

Remember the four diagnostic steps. The four simple steps that Cisco recommends for troubleshooting are as follows: ping the loopback address, ping the NIC, ping the default gateway, and ping the remote device.

Identify and mitigate an IP addressing problem. Once you go through the four troubleshooting steps that Cisco recommends, you must be able to determine the IP addressing problem by drawing out the network and finding the valid and invalid hosts addressed in your network.

Understand the troubleshooting tools that you can use from your host and a Cisco router. The `ping 127.0.0.1` command tests your local IP stack, and `tracert` is a Windows command to track the path a packet takes through an internetwork to a destination. Cisco routers use the command `traceroute`, or just `trace` for short. Don't confuse the Windows and Cisco commands. Although they produce the same output, they don't work from the same prompts. The command `ipconfig /all` will display your PC network configuration from a DOS prompt, and `arp -a` (again from a DOS prompt) will display IP-to-MAC-address mapping on a Windows PC.

Written Lab

You can find the answers to this lab in Appendix A, "Answers to the Written Labs."

1. What are the four steps Cisco recommends when troubleshooting a host problem?
2. What IP address range will you ping to test an IP stack on a host?
3. Which two network protocols do the `ping` programs use at the Network layer?
4. You successfully ping a server with an IP address, but you cannot ping using the name. What could the problem be?
5. How does the `tracert` command work compared to the `ping` program?

Review Questions

You can find the answers to these questions in Appendix B, "Answers to the Review Questions."

NOTE The following questions are designed to test your understanding of this chapter's material. For more information on how to get additional questions, please see www.lammle.com/ccna.

1. If a host is configured with an incorrect default gateway and all the other computers and router are known to be configured correctly, which of the following statements is *true*?
   - A. Host A cannot communicate with the router.
   - B. Host A can communicate with other hosts in the same subnet.
   - C. With an incorrect gateway, Host A will not be able to communicate with the router or beyond the router but will be able to communicate within the subnet.
   - D. Host A can communicate with no other systems.
2. Which of the following troubleshooting steps, if completed successfully, also confirms that the other steps will succeed as well?
   - A. Ping a remote computer.
   - B. Ping the loopback address.
   - C. Ping the NIC.
   - D. Ping the default gateway.
3. When a ping to the local host IP address fails, what can you assume?
   - A. The IP address of the local host is incorrect.
   - B. The IP address of the remote host is incorrect.
   - C. The NIC is not functional.
   - D. The IP stack has failed to initialize.
4. When a ping to the local host IP address succeeds but a ping to the default gateway IP address fails, what can you rule out? (Choose all that apply.)
   - A. The IP address of the local host is incorrect.
   - B. The IP address of the gateway is incorrect.
   - C. The NIC is not functional.
   - D. The IP stack has failed to initialize.
5. What network service is the most likely problem if you can ping a computer by IP address but not by name?
   - A. DNS
   - B. DHCP
   - C. ARP
   - D. ICMP

6. When you issue the `ping` command, what protocol are you using?
   A. DNS
   B. DHCP
   C. ARP
   D. ICMP

7. Which of the following commands displays the networks traversed on a path to a network destination?
   A. `ping`
   B. `traceroute`
   C. `pingroute`
   D. `pathroute`

8. What command generated the following output?

```
Reply from 172.16.10.2: bytes=32 time
Reply from 172.16.10.2: bytes=32 time
Reply from 172.16.10.2: bytes=32 time
```

   A. `traceroute`
   B. `show ip route`
   C. `ping`
   D. `pathping`

9. What switch must be added to the `ipconfig` command on a PC to verify DNS configuration?
   A. `/dns`
   B. `-dns`
   C. `/all`
   D. `/Showall`

10. Which of the following commands can be used by MacOS and Linux to get the IP address details of the local machine?
   A. ifconfig
   B. ipconfig
   C. nslookup
   D. %Curl

Chapter 6

Cisco's Internetworking Operating System (IOS)

Although no direct exam objectives apply to this chapter, this material could still be covered on the exam.

It's time to introduce you to the *Cisco Internetworking Operating System (IOS)*. The IOS is what runs Cisco routers as well as Cisco's switches, and it's also what we use to configure these devices.

So, that's what you're going to learn about in this chapter. I show you how to configure a Cisco IOS device using the Cisco IOS command-line interface (CLI). Once proficient with this interface, you'll be able to configure hostnames, banners, passwords, and more, as well as troubleshoot skillfully using the Cisco IOS.

We'll also begin the journey to mastering the basics of router and switch configurations plus command verifications in this chapter.

I'll start with a basic IOS switch to begin building the network we'll use throughout this book for configuration examples. Don't forget—I'll be using both switches and routers throughout this chapter, and we configure these devices pretty much the same way. Things diverge when we get to the interfaces where the differences between the two become key, so pay close attention when we get to that point!

Just as it was with preceding chapters, the fundamentals presented in this chapter are important building blocks to have solidly in place before moving on to the more advanced material coming up in the next ones.

NOTE To find bonus material, as well as Todd Lammle videos, practice questions, and hands-on labs, please see `www.lammle.com/ccna`.

The IOS User Interface

The Cisco IOS is the kernel of Cisco routers as well as all current Catalyst switches. In case you didn't know, a *kernel* is the elemental, indispensable part of an operating system that allocates resources and manages tasks such as low-level hardware interfaces and security.

Coming up, I show you the Cisco IOS and how to configure a Cisco switch using the command-line interface. By using the CLI, we can provide access to a Cisco device and provide voice, video, and data service. The configurations in this chapter are exactly the same as they are on a Cisco router.

Cisco IOS

The Cisco IOS is a proprietary kernel that provides routing, switching, internetworking, and telecommunications features. The first IOS was written by William Yeager in 1985, and enabled networked applications. It runs on most Cisco routers and on a growing number of Cisco Catalyst switches, such as the Catalyst 2960 and 3560 series switches used in this book.

Here's a short list of some important things that the Cisco router IOS software is responsible for:

- Carrying network protocols and functions
- Connecting high-speed traffic between devices
- Adding security to control access and stopping unauthorized network use
- Providing scalability for ease of network growth and redundancy
- Supplying network reliability for connecting to network resources

You can access the Cisco IOS through the console port of a router or switch, from a modem into the auxiliary (or aux) port on a router, or even through Telnet and Secure Shell (SSH). Access to the IOS command line is called an *EXEC session.*

Connecting to a Cisco IOS Device

We connect to a Cisco device to configure it, verify its configuration, and check statistics, and although there are different approaches to this, the first place you would usually connect to is the console port. The *console port* is usually an RJ55 eight-pin modular connection located at the back of the device, and mini-USB ports are now commonly found on routers and switches for use as a console connection.

NOTE: Review in Chapter 2, "Ethernet Networking," how to configure a PC and enable it to connect to a router console port.

You can also connect to a Cisco router through an *auxiliary port*, which is really the same thing as a console port (and so it follows that you can use it as one). The main difference with an auxiliary port is that it also allows you to configure modem commands so that a modem can be connected to the router. This is a cool feature because it lets you dial up a remote router and attach to the auxiliary port if the router is down and you need to configure it remotely, *out-of-band*. One of the differences between Cisco routers and switches is that switches do not have an auxiliary port.

The third way to connect to a Cisco device is *in-band*, through the program Telnet or Secure Shell (SSH). In-band means configuring the device via the network, the opposite of out-of-band. We covered Telnet and SSH in Chapter 3, "TCP/IP," and in this chapter, I'll show you how to configure access to both of these protocols on a Cisco device.

Figure 6.1 shows an illustration of a Cisco 2960 switch. Really focus on all the different kinds of interfaces and connections! On the right side is the 10/100/1000 uplink. You can use either the UTP port or the fiber port, but you cannot use both at the same time.

FIGURE 6.1 A Cisco 2960 switch

The 3560 switch I use in this book looks a lot like the 2960, but it can perform layer 3 switching, unlike the 2960, which is limited to only layer 2 functions.

I also want to take a moment and tell you about the 2800 series router because that's the router series I use in this book. This router is known as an *integrated services router (ISR)*, and Cisco has updated it to the 2900 series, but I still have plenty of 2800 series routers in my production networks. Figure 6.2 shows a new 1921 series router.

FIGURE 6.2 A Cisco 1900 router

The new ISR series of routers are nice; they are so named because many services, such as security, are built into them. The ISR is a modular device, much faster and a lot sleeker than the older 2500 series routers, and it's elegantly designed to support a broad new range of interface options. The new ISR can offer multiple serial interfaces, which can be used for connecting a T1 using a serial V.35 WAN connection. And multiple Fast Ethernet or Gigabit Ethernet ports can be used on the router, depending on the model. This router also has one console via an RJ45 connector and another through the USB port. There is also an auxiliary connection to allow a console connection via a remote modem.

Keep in mind that for the most part you get some serious bang for your buck with the 2800/2900—unless you start adding a bunch of interfaces to it. You've got to pony up for each one of those little beauties, so this can really start to add up and fast!

A couple of other series of routers that will set you back a lot less than the 2800 series are the 1800/1900s, so look into these routers if you want a less-expensive alternative to the 2800/2900 but still want to run the same IOS.

So even though I use mostly 2800 series routers and 2960/3560 switches throughout this book to demonstrate examples of IOS configurations, the particular *router* model you use to practice for the Cisco exam isn't really important. The *switch* types are, though: You definitely need, at a minimum model, a couple of 2960 switches as well as a 3560 switch if you want to measure up to the exam objectives.

NOTE You can find more information about all Cisco routers at `https://www.cisco.com/c/en/us/products/routers/router-selector.html`.

Bringing Up a Switch

When you first bring up a Cisco IOS device, it will run a power-on self-test (a POST). Upon passing that, the machine looks for and then loads the Cisco IOS from flash memory if an IOS file is present, and then expands it into RAM. As you probably know, flash memory is electronically erasable programmable read-only memory (an EEPROM). The next step is for the IOS to locate and load a valid configuration known as the startup-config that will be stored in *nonvolatile RAM (NVRAM)*.

Once the IOS is loaded and up and running, the startup-config is copied from NVRAM into RAM and from then on referred to as the running-config.

But if a valid startup-config isn't found in NVRAM, your switch enters setup mode, giving you a step-by-step dialog to help configure some basic parameters on it.

You can also enter setup mode at any time from the command line by typing the command **setup** from privileged mode, which I'll get to in a minute. Setup mode only covers some basic commands and generally isn't really all that helpful. Here's an example:

```
[cWould you like to enter the initial configuration dialog? [yes/no]: y
At any point you may enter a question mark '?' for help.
Use ctrl-c to abort configuration dialog at any prompt.
Default settings are in square brackets '[]'.
Basic management setup configures only enough connectivity
for management of the system, extended setup will ask you
to configure each interface on the system
Would you like to enter basic management setup? [yes/no]: y
Configuring global parameters:
Enter host name [Switch]: Ctrl+C
Configuration aborted, no changes made.
```

NOTE You can exit setup mode at any time by pressing Ctrl+C.

I highly recommend going through setup mode once, then never again because you should always use the CLI instead!

Command-Line Interface

I sometimes refer to the CLI as "cash line interface" because the ability to create advanced configurations on Cisco routers and switches using the CLI will earn you a wad of cash.

Entering the CLI

After the interface status messages appear and you press Enter, the `Switch>` prompt pops up. This is called *user exec mode*, or user mode for short, and although it's mostly used to view statistics, it is also a stepping-stone along the way to logging in to *privileged exec mode*, called privileged mode for short.

You can view and change the configuration of a Cisco router only while in privileged mode, and you enter it via the `enable` command like this:

```
Switch>enable
Switch#
```

The `Switch#` prompt signals you're in privileged mode, where you can both view and change the switch configuration. You can go back from privileged mode into user mode by using the `disable` command:

```
Switch#disable
Switch>
```

You can type **`logout`** from either mode to exit the console:

```
Switch>logout
Switch con0 is now available
Press RETURN to get started.
```

Next, I'll show how to perform some basic administrative configurations.

Overview of Router Modes

To configure from a CLI, you can make global changes to the router by typing **`configure terminal`** or just **`config t`**. This gets you into global configuration mode, where you can make changes to the running-config. Commands run from global configuration mode are predictably referred to as global commands, and they are typically set only once and affect the entire router.

Type **`config`** from the privileged-mode prompt and then press Enter to opt for the default of `terminal` like this:

```
Switch#config
Configuring from terminal, memory, or network [terminal]?
[press enter]
Enter configuration commands, one per line. End with CNTL/Z.
Switch(config)#
```

At this point, you make changes that affect the router as a whole (globally), hence the term *global configuration mode*. For instance, to change the running-config—the current configuration running in dynamic RAM (DRAM)—use the `configure terminal` command, as I just demonstrated.

CLI Prompts

Let's explore the different prompts you'll encounter when configuring a switch or router now, because knowing them well will really help you orient yourself and recognize exactly where you are at any given time while in configuration mode. I'm going to demonstrate some of the prompts used on a Cisco switch and cover the various terms used along the way. Make sure you're very familiar with them, and always check your prompts before making any changes to a router's configuration.

We're not going to venture into every last obscure command prompt you could potentially come across in the configuration mode world because that would get us deep into territory that's beyond the scope of this book. Instead, I'm going to focus on the prompts you absolutely must know to pass the exam plus the very handy and seriously vital ones you'll need and use the most in real-life networking—the cream of the crop.

NOTE

Don't freak! It's not important that you understand exactly what each of these command prompts accomplishes just yet because I'm going to completely fill you in on all of them soon. For now, relax and focus on just becoming familiar with the different prompts available and all will be well.

Interfaces

To make changes to an interface, you use the `interface` command from global configuration mode:

```
Switch(config)#interface ?
Async Async interface
BVI Bridge-Group Virtual Interface
CTunnel CTunnel interface
Dialer Dialer interface
FastEthernet FastEthernet IEEE 802.3
Filter Filter interface
Filtergroup Filter Group interface
GigabitEthernet GigabitEthernet IEEE 802.3z
Group-Async Async Group interface
Lex Lex interface
Loopback Loopback interface
Null Null interface
Port-channel Ethernet Channel of interfaces
Portgroup Portgroup interface
Pos-channel POS Channel of interfaces
```

```
Tunnel Tunnel interface
Vif PGM Multicast Host interface
Virtual-Template Virtual Template interface
Virtual-TokenRing Virtual TokenRing
Vlan Catalyst Vlans
fcpa Fiber Channel
range interface range command
Switch(config)#interface fastEthernet 0/1
Switch(config-if)#)
```

Did you notice that the prompt changed to `Switch(config-if)#`? This tells you that you're in *interface configuration mode*. And wouldn't it be nice if the prompt also gave you an indication of what interface you were configuring? Well, at least for now, we'll have to live without the prompt information, because it doesn't. But it should already be clear that you really need to pay attention when configuring an IOS device.

Line Commands

To configure user-mode passwords, use the `line` command. The prompt then becomes `Switch(config-line)#`:

```
Switch(config)#line ?
<0-15> First Line number
console Primary terminal line
vty Virtual terminal
Switch(config)#line console 0
Switch(config-line)#
```

The `line console 0` command is a global command, and sometimes you'll also hear people refer to global commands as major commands. In this example, any command typed from the (`config-line`) prompt is known as a subcommand.

Access List Configurations

To configure a standard named access list, you need to get to the prompt `Switch (config-std-nacl)#`:

```
Switch#config t
Switch(config)#ip access-list standard Todd
Switch(config-std-nacl)#
```

What you see here is a typical basic standard access control list (ACL) prompt. There are various ways to configure access lists, and the prompts differ only slightly from this particular example.

Routing Protocol Configurations

I need to point out that we don't use routing or router protocols on 2960 switches, but we can and will use them on my 3560 switches. Here is an example of configuring routing on a layer 3 switch:

```
Switch(config)#router rip
IP routing not enabled
Switch(config)#ip routing
Switch(config)#router rip
Switch(config-router)#
```

Did you notice that the prompt changed to `Switch(config-router)#`?

Defining Router Terms

Table 6.1 defines some of the terms I've used so far.

TABLE 6.1 Router Terms

Mode	Definition
User exec mode	Limited to basic monitoring commands
Privileged exec mode	Provides access to all other router commands
Global configuration mode	Commands that affect the entire system
Specific configuration modes	Commands that affect interfaces/processes only
Setup mode	Interactive configuration dialog

Editing and Help Features

The Cisco advanced editing features can also help you configure your router. If you type in a question mark (**?**) at any prompt, you'll be given a list of all the commands available from that prompt:

```
Switch#?
Exec commands:
access-enable Create a temporary Access-List entry
access-template Create a temporary Access-List entry
archive manage archive files
cd Change current directory
```

```
clear Reset functions
clock Manage the system clock
cns CNS agents
configure Enter configuration mode
connect Open a terminal connection
copy Copy from one file to another
debug Debugging functions (see also 'undebug')
delete Delete a file
diagnostic Diagnostic commands
dir List files on a filesystem
disable Turn off privileged commands
disconnect Disconnect an existing network connection
dot1x IEEE 802.1X Exec Commands
enable Turn on privileged commands
eou EAPoUDP
erase Erase a filesystem
exit Exit from the EXEC
--More-- ?
```

Press Return for another line, press the spacebar for another page, and press anything else to quit.

And if this is not enough information for you, you can press the spacebar to get another whole page of information, or you can press Enter to go one command at a time. You can also press Q, or any other key for that matter, to quit and return to the prompt. Notice that I typed a question mark (?) at the `More` prompt, and it told me what my options were from that prompt.

Here's a shortcut: To find commands that start with a certain letter, use the letter and the question mark with no space between them, like this:

```
Switch#c?
cd clear clock cns configure
connect copy
Switch#c
```

Okay, see that? By typing **c?**, I got a response listing all the commands that start with *c*. Also notice that the `Switch#c` prompt reappears after the list of commands is displayed. This can be really helpful when you happen to be working with long commands but you're short on patience and still need the next possible one. It would get old fast if you actually had to retype the entire command every time you used a question mark.

So with that, let's find the next command in a string by typing the first command and then a question mark:

```
Switch#clock ?
set Set the time and date
```

```
Switch#clock set ?
hh:mm:ss Current Time
Switch#clock set 2:35 ?
% Unrecognized command
Switch#clock set 2:35:01 ?
<1-31> Day of the month
MONTH Month of the year
Switch#clock set 2:35:01 21 july ?
<1993-2035> Year
Switch#clock set 2:35:01 21 august 2013
Switch#
00:19:55: %SYS-5-CLOCKUPDATE: System clock has been updated from 00:19:55
UTC Mon Mar 1, 1993, to 02:35:01 UTC Wed Aug 21 2013, configured from console
by console.
```

I entered the `clock ?` command and got a list of the next possible parameters plus what they do. Make note of the fact that you can just keep typing a command, a space, and then a question mark until `<cr>` (carriage return) is your only option left.

And if you're typing commands and receive

```
Switch#clock set 11:15:11
% Incomplete command.
```

no worries; that's only telling you that the command string simply isn't complete quite yet. All you need to do is to press the up arrow key to redisplay the last command entered and then continue with the command by using your question mark.

But if you get the error

```
Switch(config)#access-list 100 permit host 1.1.1.1 host 2.2.2.2
                                     ^
% Invalid input detected at '^' marker.
```

all is not well because it means you actually have entered a command incorrectly. See that little caret (the ^)? It's a very helpful tool that marks the exact point where you blew it and made a mess.

Here's another example of when you'll see that caret:

```
Switch#sh fastethernet 0/0
           ^
% Invalid input detected at '^' marker.
```

This command looks right, but be careful! The problem is that the full command is `show interface fastethernet 0/0`.

Now if you receive the error

```
Switch#sh cl
% Ambiguous command: "sh cl"
```

you're being told that there are multiple commands that begin with the string you entered and it's not unique. Use the question mark to find the exact command you need:

```
Switch#sh cl?
class-map clock cluster
```

Case in point: There are three commands that start with `show cl`.

Table 6.2 lists the enhanced editing commands available on a Cisco router.

TABLE 6.2 Enhanced Editing Commands

Command	Meaning
Ctrl+A	Moves your cursor to the beginning of the line
Ctrl+E	Moves your cursor to the end of the line
Esc+B	Moves back one word
Ctrl+B	Moves back one character
Ctrl+F	Moves forward one character
Esc+F	Moves forward one word
Ctrl+D	Deletes a single character
Backspace	Deletes a single character
Ctrl+R	Redisplays a line
Ctrl+U	Erases a line
Ctrl+W	Erases a word
Ctrl+Z	Ends configuration mode and returns to EXEC
Tab	Finishes typing a command for you

Another really cool editing feature you need to know about is the automatic scrolling of long lines. In the following example, the command I typed reached the right margin and automatically moved 11 spaces to the left. How do I know this? Because the dollar sign ($) is telling me that the line has been scrolled to the left:

```
Switch#config t
Switch(config)#$ 100 permit ip host 192.168.10.1 192.168.10.0 0.0.0.255
```

You can review the router-command history with the commands shown in Table 6.3.

TABLE 6.3 IOS Command History

Command	Meaning
Ctrl+P or up arrow	Shows last command entered
Ctrl+N or down arrow	Shows previous commands entered
`show history`	Shows last 20 commands entered by default
`show terminal`	Shows terminal configurations and history buffer size
`terminal history size`	Changes buffer size (max 255)

The following example demonstrates the `show history` command as well as how to change the history's size. It also shows how to verify the history with the `show terminal` command. First, use the `show history` command, which will allow you to see the last 20 commands that were entered on the router (even though my particular router reveals only 10 commands because that's all I've entered since rebooting it). Check it out:

```
Switch#sh history
sh fastethernet 0/0
sh ru
sh cl
config t
sh history
sh flash
sh running-config
sh startup-config
sh ver
sh history
```

Okay, now we'll use the `show terminal` command to verify the terminal history size:

```
Switch#sh terminal
Line 0, Location: "", Type: ""
Length: 25 lines, Width: 80 columns
Baud rate (TX/RX) is 9500/9500, no parity, 2 stopbits, 8 databits
Status: PSI Enabled, Ready, Active, Ctrl-c Enabled, Automore On
0x50000
Capabilities: none
Modem state: Ready
[output cut]
Modem type is unknown.
```

```
Session limit is not set.
Time since activation: 00:17:22
Editing is enabled.
History is enabled, history size is 10.
DNS resolution in show commands is enabled
Full user help is disabled
Allowed input transports are none.
Allowed output transports are telnet.
Preferred transport is telnet.
No output characters are padded
No special data dispatching characters
```

When Should I Use the Cisco Editing Features?

You'll find yourself using a couple of editing features quite often and some not so much, if at all. Understand that Cisco didn't make these up; these are just old Unix commands. Even so, Ctrl+A is still a really helpful way to negate a command.

For example, if you were to put in a long command and then decide you didn't want to use that command in your configuration after all, or if it didn't work, you could just press your up arrow key to show the last command entered, press Ctrl+A, type **no** and then a space, press Enter—and poof! The command is negated. This doesn't work on every command, but it works on a lot of them and saves some serious time.

Administrative Configurations

Even though the following sections aren't critical to making a router or switch *work* on a network, they're still really important. I'm going to guide you through configuring specific commands that are particularly helpful when administering your network.

You can configure the following administrative functions on a router and switch:

- Hostnames
- Banners
- Passwords
- Interface descriptions

Remember, none of these will make your routers or switches work better or faster, but trust me, your life will be a whole lot better if you just take the time to set these configurations on each of your network devices. This is because doing so makes troubleshooting and maintaining your network a great deal easier—seriously! In this next section, I demonstrate commands on a Cisco switch, but understand that these commands are used in the exact same way on a Cisco router.

Hostnames

We use the `hostname` command to set the identity of the router and switch. This is only locally significant, meaning it doesn't affect how the router or switch performs name lookups or how the device actually works on the internetwork. But the hostname is still important in routes because it's often used for authentication in many WANs. Here's an example:

```
Switch#config t
Switch(config)#hostname Todd
Todd(config)#hostname Chicago
Chicago(config)#hostname Todd
Todd(config)#
```

I know it's pretty tempting to configure the hostname after your own name, but it's usually a much better idea to name the device something that relates to its physical location. A name that maps to where the device lives will make finding it a whole lot easier, which among other things, confirms that you're actually configuring the correct device. Even though it seems like I'm completely ditching my own advice by naming mine *Todd*, I'm not, because this particular device really does live in "Todd's" office. Its name perfectly maps to where it is, so it won't be confused with those in the other networks I work with.

Banners

A very good reason for having a *banner* is to give any and all who dare attempt to telnet or sneak into your internetwork a little security notice. And they're cool because you can create and customize them so that they'll greet anyone who shows up on the router with exactly the information you want them to have.

Here are the three types of banners you need to be sure you're familiar with:

- Exec process creation banner
- Login banner
- Message of the day banner

And you can see them all illustrated in the following code:

```
Todd(config)#banner ?
LINE c banner-text c, where 'c' is a delimiting character
exec Set EXEC process creation banner
```

```
incoming Set incoming terminal line banner
login Set login banner
motd Set Message of the Day banner
prompt-timeout Set Message for login authentication timeout
slip-ppp Set Message for SLIP/PPP
```

Message of the day (MOTD) banners are the most widely used banners because they give a message to anyone connecting to the router via Telnet or an auxiliary port or even through a console port, as seen here:

```
Todd(config)#banner motd ?
LINE c banner-text c, where 'c' is a delimiting character
Todd(config)#banner motd #
Enter TEXT message. End with the character '#'.
$ Acme.com network, then you must disconnect immediately.#
Todd(config)#^Z (Press the control key + z keys to return to privileged mode)
Todd#exit
con0 is now available
Press RETURN to get started.
If you are not authorized to be in Acme.com network, then you
must disconnect immediately.
Todd#
```

This MOTD banner essentially tells anyone connecting to the device to get lost if they're not on the guest list. The part to focus upon here is the delimiting character, which is what informs the router the message is done. Clearly, you can use any character you want for it except for the delimiting character in the message itself. Once the message is complete, press Enter, then the delimiting character, and then press Enter again. Everything will still work if you don't follow this routine unless you have more than one banner. If that's the case, make sure you do follow it or your banners will all be combined into one message and put on a single line.

You can set a banner on one line like this:

```
Todd(config)#banner motd x Unauthorized access prohibited! x
```

Let's take a minute to go into more detail about the other two types of banners I mentioned:

Exec Banner You can configure a line-activation (exec) banner to be displayed when EXEC processes such as a line activation or an incoming connection to a VTY line have been created. Simply initiating a user exec session through a console port will activate the exec banner.

Login Banner You can configure a login banner for display on all connected terminals. It will show up after the MOTD banner but before the login prompts. This login banner can't be disabled on a per-line basis, so to globally disable it, you've got to delete it with the `no banner login` command.

Here's what a login banner output looks like:

```
!
banner login ^C

          -----------------------------------------------------------

Cisco Router and Security Device Manager (SDM) is installed on this device.
This feature requires the one-time use of the username "cisco"
with the password "cisco". The default username and password
have a privilege level of 15.
Please change these publicly known initial credentials using
SDM or the IOS CLI.
Here are the Cisco IOS commands.
username <myuser> privilege 15 secret 0 <mypassword>
no username cisco
Replace <myuser> and <mypassword> with the username and
password you want to use.
For more information about SDM please follow the instructions
in the QUICK START GUIDE for your router or go to
http://www.cisco.com/go/sdm

          -----------------------------------------------------------

^C
!
```

The previous login banner should look pretty familiar to anyone who's ever logged in to an ISR router because it's the banner Cisco has in the default configuration for its ISR routers.

> **NOTE** Remember that the login banner is displayed before the login prompts and after the MOTD banner.

Setting Passwords

You need five passwords to secure your Cisco routers: console, auxiliary, telnet (VTY), enable password, and enable secret. The enable secret and enable password are the ones used to set the password for securing privileged mode. Once the `enable` commands are set, users will be prompted for a password. The other three are used to configure a password when user mode is accessed through the console port, through the auxiliary port, or via Telnet.

Let's take a look at each of these now.

Enable Passwords

You set the enable passwords from global configuration mode like this:

```
Todd(config)#enable ?
       last-resort Define enable action if no TACACS servers
```

```
respond
password Assign the privileged level password
secret Assign the privileged level secret
use-tacacs Use TACACS to check enable passwords
```

The following list describes the enable password parameters:

`last-resort` This allows you to still enter the device if you set up authentication through a Terminal Access Controller Access-Control System (TACACS) server and it's not available. It won't be used if the TACACS server is working.

`password` This sets the enable password on older, pre-10.3 systems and isn't ever used if an enable secret is set.

`secret` The newer, encrypted password that overrides the enable password if it has been set.

`use-tacacs` This tells the router or switch to authenticate through a TACACS server. It comes in really handy when you have lots of routers because changing the password on a multitude of them can be insanely tedious. It's much easier to simply go through the TACACS server and change the password only once.

Here's an example that shows how to set the enable passwords:

```
Todd(config)#enable secret todd
Todd(config)#enable password todd
The enable password you have chosen is the same as your
enable secret. This is not recommended. Re-enter the
enable password.
```

If you try to set `enable secret` and `enable password` the same, the device will give you a polite warning to change the second password. Make a note to yourself that if there aren't any old legacy routers involved, you don't even bother to use the enable password.

User-mode passwords are assigned via the `line` command like this:

```
Todd(config)#line ?
<0-15> First Line number
console Primary terminal line
vty Virtual terminal
```

And these two lines are especially important for the exam objectives:

`console` Sets a console user-mode password.

`vty` Sets a Telnet password on the device and is also used in the SSH configuration. If this password isn't set, then by default, Telnet can't be used.

To configure user-mode passwords, choose the line you want and configure it using the `login` command to make the switch prompt for authentication. Let's focus in on the configuration of individual lines now.

Console Password

We set the console password with the `line console 0` command. But look at what happened when I tried to type **line console ?** from the `(config-line)#` prompt. I received an error! Here's the example:

```
Todd(config-line)#line console ?
% Unrecognized command
Todd(config-line)#exit
Todd(config)#line console ?
<0-0> First Line number
Todd(config)#line console 0
Todd(config-line)#password console
Todd(config-line)#login
```

You can still type **line console 0**, and that will be accepted, but the help screens just don't work from that prompt. Type **exit** to go back one level, and you'll find that your help screens now work. This is a "feature." Really.

Because there's only one console port, I can only choose line console 0. You can set all your line passwords to the same password, but doing this isn't exactly a brilliant security move.

And it's also important to remember to apply the `login` command or the console port won't prompt for authentication. The way Cisco has this process set up means you can't set the `login` command before a password is set on a line because if you set it but don't then set a password, that line won't be usable. You'll actually get prompted for a password that doesn't exist, so Cisco's method isn't just a hassle; it makes sense and is a feature after all.

NOTE: Definitely remember that although Cisco has this "password feature" on its routers starting with IOS 12.2 and above, it's not included in older IOSs.

Okay, there are a few other important commands you need to know regarding the console port.

For one, the `exec-timeout 0 0` command sets the timeout for the console EXEC session to zero, ensuring that it never times out. The default timeout is 10 minutes.

TIP: If you're feeling mischievous, try this on people at work: Set the `exec-timeout` command to `0 1`. This will make the console time out in 1 second, and to fix it, you have to continually press the down arrow key while changing the timeout time with your free hand.

The `logging synchronous` command is so cool that it should be a default, but it's not. It's great because it's the antidote for those annoying console messages that disrupt the input you're trying to type. The messages still pop up, but at least you get returned to your device prompt without your input being interrupted. This makes your input messages oh-so-much easier to read.

Here's an example of how to configure both commands:

```
Todd(config-line)#line con 0
Todd(config-line)#exec-timeout ?
<0-35791> Timeout in minutes
Todd(config-line)#exec-timeout 0 ?
<0-2157583> Timeout in seconds
<cr>
Todd(config-line)#exec-timeout 0 0
Todd(config-line)#logging synchronous
```

NOTE You can set the console to go from never timing out (`0 0`) to timing out in 35,791 minutes and 2,157,583 seconds. Remember that the default is 10 minutes.

Telnet Password

To set the user-mode password for Telnet access into the router or switch, use the `line vty` command. IOS switches typically have 15 lines, but routers running the Enterprise edition have considerably more. The best way to find out how many lines you have is to use that handy question mark like this:

```
Todd(config-line)#line vty 0 ?
% Unrecognized command
Todd(config-line)#exit
Todd(config)#line vty 0 ?
<1-15> Last Line number
<cr>
Todd(config)#line vty 0 15
Todd(config-line)#password telnet
Todd(config-line)#login
```

This output clearly shows that you cannot get help from your `(config-line)#` prompt. You must go back to global config mode in order to use the question mark (?).

So what will happen if you try to telnet into a device that doesn't have a VTY password set? You'll receive an error saying the connection has been refused because the password isn't set. So, if you telnet into a switch and receive a message like this one that I got from Switch B

```
Todd#telnet SwitchB
Trying SwitchB (10.0.0.1)...Open
Password required, but none set
[Connection to SwitchB closed by foreign host]
Todd#
```

it means the switch doesn't have the VTY password set. But you can still get around this and tell the switch to allow Telnet connections without a password by using the `no login` command:

```
SwitchB(config-line)#line vty 0 15
SwitchB(config-line)#no login
```

WARNING

I definitely do not recommend using the `no login` command to allow Telnet connections without a password unless you're in a testing or classroom environment. In a production network, always set your VTY password.

After your IOS devices are configured with an IP address, you can use the Telnet program to configure and check your routers instead of having to use a console cable. You can use the Telnet program by typing **telnet** from any command prompt (DOS or Cisco). I cover all things Telnet more thoroughly in Chapter 7, "Managing a Cisco Internetwork."

Auxiliary Password

To configure the auxiliary password on a router, go into global configuration mode and type **line aux ?**. And by the way, you won't find these ports on a switch. This output shows that you only get a choice of 0–0, which is because there's only one port:

```
Todd#config t
Todd(config)#line aux ?
<0-0> First Line number
Todd(config)#line aux 0
Todd(config-line)#login
% Login disabled on line 1, until 'password' is set
Todd(config-line)#password aux
Todd(config-line)#login
```

Setting Up Secure Shell

I strongly recommend using Secure Shell (SSH) rather than Telnet because it creates a more secure session. The Telnet application uses an unencrypted data stream, but SSH uses encryption keys to send data so that your username and password aren't sent in the clear, vulnerable to anyone lurking around.

Here are the steps for setting up SSH:

1. Set your hostname:

```
Router(config)#hostname Todd
```

2. Set the domain name—both the hostname and domain name are required for the encryption keys to be generated:

```
Todd(config)#ip domain-name Lammle.com
```

3. Set the username to allow SSH client access:

```
Todd(config)#username Todd password Lammle
```

4. Generate the encryption keys for securing the session:

```
Todd(config)#crypto key generate rsa
The name for the keys will be: Todd.Lammle.com
Choose the size of the key modulus in the range of 350 to
5095 for your General Purpose Keys. Choosing a key modulus
Greater than 512 may take a few minutes.
How many bits in the modulus [512]: 1025
% Generating 1025 bit RSA keys, keys will be non-exportable...
[OK] (elapsed time was 5 seconds)
Todd(config)#
1d15h: %SSH-5-ENABLED: SSH 1.99 has been enabled*June 25
19:25:30.035: %SSH-5-ENABLED: SSH 1.99 has been enabled
```

5. Enable SSH version 2 on the device—not mandatory, but strongly suggested:

```
Todd(config)#ip ssh version 2
```

6. Connect to the VTY lines of the switch or router:

```
Todd(config)#line vty 0 15
```

7. Tell the lines to use the local database for password:

```
Todd(config-line)#login local
```

8. Configure your access protocols:

```
Todd(config-line)#transport input ?
all All protocols
none No protocols
ssh TCP/IP SSH protocol
telnet TCP/IP Telnet protocol
```

Beware of this next line, and make sure you never use it in production because it's a horrendous security risk:

```
Todd(config-line)#transport input all
```

I recommend using the next line to secure your VTY lines with SSH:

```
Todd(config-line)#transport input ssh ?
telnet TCP/IP Telnet protocol
<cr>
```

I actually do use Telnet once in a while when a situation arises that specifically calls for it. It just doesn't happen very often. But if you want to go with Telnet, here's how you do that:

```
Todd(config-line)#transport input ssh telnet
```

Know that if you don't use the keyword `telnet` at the end of the command string, then only SSH will work on the device. You can go with either, so long as you understand that SSH is way more secure than Telnet.

Encrypting Your Passwords

Because only the enable secret password is encrypted by default, you'll need to manually configure the user-mode and enable passwords for encryption.

Notice that you can see all the passwords except the enable secret when performing a show running-config on a switch:

```
Todd#sh running-config
Building configuration...
Current configuration: 1020 bytes
!
! Last configuration change at 00:03:11 UTC Mon Mar 1 1993
!
version 15.0
no service pad
service timestamps debug datetime msec
service timestamps log datetime msec
no service password-encryption
!
hostname Todd
!
enable secret 5 ykw.3/tgsOuy9.5qmgG/EeYOYgBvfX5v.S8UNA9Rddg
enable password todd
!
[output cut]
!
line con 0
password console
login
```

```
line vty 0 5
password telnet
login
line vty 5 15
password telnet
login
!
end
```

To manually encrypt your passwords, use the `service password-encryption` command. Here's how:

```
Todd#config t
Todd(config)#service password-encryption
Todd(config)#exit
Todd#show run
Building configuration...
!
!
enable secret 5 ykw.3/tgsOuy9.5qmgG/EeYOYgBvfX5v.S8UNA9Rddg
enable password 7 1505050800
!
[output cut]
!
!
line con 0
password 7 050809013253520C
login
line vty 0 5
password 7 05120A2D525B1D
login
line vty 5 15
password 7 05120A2D525B1D
login
!
end
Todd#config t
Todd(config)#no service password-encryption
Todd(config)#^Z
Todd#
```

Nicely done! The passwords will now be encrypted. All you need to do is encrypt the passwords, perform a show run, and then turn off the command if you want. This output clearly shows us that the enable password and the line passwords are all encrypted.

Before we move on to find out how to set descriptions on your interfaces, I want to stress some points about password encryption. As I said, if you set your passwords and then turn on the `service password-encryption` command, you have to perform a show running-config before you turn off the encryption service or your passwords won't be encrypted. You don't have to turn off the encryption service at all; you'd only do that if your switch is running low on processes. And if you turn on the service before you set your passwords, you don't even have to view them to have them encrypted.

Descriptions

Setting descriptions on an interface is another administratively helpful thing, and like the hostname, it's also only locally significant. One case where the `description` command comes in really handy is when you want to keep track of circuit numbers on a switch or a router's serial WAN port.

Here's an example on my switch:

```
Todd#config t
Todd(config)#int fa0/1
Todd(config-if)#description Sales VLAN Trunk Link
Todd(config-if)#^Z
Todd#
```

And on a router serial WAN:

```
Router#config t
Router(config)#int s0/0/0
Router(config-if)#description WAN to Miami
Router(config-if)#^Z
```

You can view an interface's description with either the `show running-config` command or the `show interface`—even with the `show interface description` command:

```
Todd#sh run
Building configuration...
Current configuration: 855 bytes
!
interface FastEthernet0/1
description Sales VLAN Trunk Link
!
[output cut]
Todd#sh int f0/1
```

```
FastEthernet0/1 is up, line protocol is up (connected)
Hardware is Fast Ethernet, address is ecc8.8202.8282 (bia ecc8.8202.8282)
Description: Sales VLAN Trunk Link
MTU 1500 bytes, BW 100000 Kbit/sec, DLY 100 usec,
[output cut]
Todd#sh int description
Interface Status Protocol Description
Vl1 up up
Fa0/1 up up Sales VLAN Trunk Link
Fa0/2 up up
```

`description`: A Helpful Command

Bob, a senior network admin at Acme Corporation in San Francisco, has over 50 WAN links to branches throughout the United States and Canada. Whenever an interface goes down, Bob wastes lots of time trying to figure out the circuit number and the phone number of the provider of his ailing WAN link.

This kind of scenario shows just how helpful the `interface description` command can be. It would save Bob a lot of work because he could use it on his most important switch LAN links to find out exactly where every interface is connected. Bob's life would also be made a lot easier by adding circuit numbers to each and every WAN interface on his routers, along with the phone number of the responsible provider.

So, if Bob had just taken time in advance to preventively add this information to his interfaces, he would have saved himself an ocean of stress and a ton of precious time when his WAN links inevitably go down.

Doing the *do* Command

In every previous example so far, we've had to run all show commands from privileged mode. But I've got great news: Beginning with IOS version 12.3, Cisco has finally added a command to the IOS that allows you to view the configuration and statistics from within configuration mode.

In fact, with any IOS, you'd get the following error if you tried to view the configuration from global config:

```
Todd(config)#sh run
^
% Invalid input detected at '^' marker.
```

Compare that to the output I get from entering that same command on my router that's running the 15.0 IOS using the "do" syntax:

```
Todd(config)#do show run
Building configuration...
Current configuration: 759 bytes
!
version 15.0
no service pad
service timestamps debug datetime msec
service timestamps log datetime msec
no service password-encryption
!
hostname Todd
!
boot-start-marker
boot-end-marker
!
[output cut]
```

So now you can pretty much run any command from any configuration prompt. Nice, huh? Looking back through all those examples for encrypting our passwords, you can see that the do command would definitely have gotten the party started sooner, making this innovation one to celebrate for sure.

Router and Switch Interfaces

Interface configuration is arguably the most important router configuration, because without interfaces a router is a pretty useless object. Furthermore, interface configurations must be totally precise to enable communication with other devices. Network layer addresses, media type, bandwidth, and other administrator commands are all used to configure an interface.

On a layer 2 switch, interface configurations typically involve a lot less work than router interface configuration. Check out the output from the powerful verification command `show ip interface brief`, which reveals all the interfaces on my 3560 switch:

```
Todd#sh ip interface brief
Interface         IP-Address        OK? Method Status      Protocol
Vlan1             192.168.255.8     YES DHCP up    up
FastEthernet0/1 unassigned YES unset up up
FastEthernet0/2 unassigned YES unset up up
FastEthernet0/3 unassigned YES unset down down
FastEthernet0/4 unassigned YES unset down down
```

```
FastEthernet0/5 unassigned YES unset up up
FastEthernet0/6 unassigned YES unset up up
FastEthernet0/7 unassigned YES unset down down
FastEthernet0/8 unassigned YES unset down down
GigabitEthernet0/1 unassigned YES unset down down
```

The previous output shows the default routed port found on all Cisco switches (VLAN 1), plus nine switch Fast Ethernet interface ports, with one port being a Gigabit Ethernet port used for uplinks to other switches.

Different routers use different methods to choose the interfaces used on them. For instance, the following command shows one of my 2800 ISR Cisco routers with two Fast Ethernet interfaces along with two serial WAN interfaces:

```
Router>sh ip int brief
Interface IP-Address OK? Method Status Protocol
FastEthernet0/0 192.168.255.11 YES DHCP up up
FastEthernet0/1 unassigned YES unset administratively down down
Serial0/0/0 unassigned YES unset administratively down down
Serial0/1/0 unassigned YES unset administratively down down
Router>
```

Previously, we always used the interface *type number* sequence to configure an interface, but the newer routers come with an actual physical slot and include a port number on the module plugged into it. So on a modular router, the configuration would be interface *type slot/port*, as demonstrated here:

```
Todd#config t
Todd(config)#interface GigabitEthernet 0/1
Todd(config-if)#
```

You can see that we are now at the Gigabit Ethernet slot 0, port 1 prompt, and from here we can make configuration changes to the interface. Make note of the fact that you can't just type **int gigabitethernet 0**. No shortcuts on the slot/port; you've got to type the slot/port variables in the command: *type slot/port* or, for example, **int gigabitethernet 0/1** (or just **int g0/1**).

Once in interface configuration mode, we can configure various options. Keep in mind that speed and duplex are the two factors to be concerned with for the LAN:

```
Todd#config t
Todd(config)#interface GigabitEthernet 0/1
Todd(config-if)#speed 1000
Todd(config-if)#duplex full
```

So what's happened here? Well basically, this has shut off the auto-detect mechanism on the port, forcing it to only run gigabit speeds at full duplex. For the ISR series router, it's basically the same, but you get even more options. The LAN interfaces are the same, but the rest of the modules are different—they use three numbers instead of two. The three numbers used here can represent slot/subslot/port, but this depends on the card used in the ISR router. For the objectives, you just need to remember this: The first 0 is the router itself. You then choose the slot and then the port. Here's an example of a serial interface on my 2811:

```
Todd(config)#interface serial ?
<0-2> Serial interface number
Todd(config)#interface serial 0/0/?
<0-1> Serial interface number
Todd(config)#interface serial 0/0/0
Todd(config-if)#
```

This might look a little dicey to you, but I promise it's really not that hard. It helps to remember that you should always view the output of the `show ip interface brief` command or a `show running-config output` first so that you know the exact interfaces you have to deal with. Here's one of my 2811's output that has even more serial interfaces installed:

```
Todd(config-if)#do show run
Building configuration...
[output cut]
!
interface FastEthernet0/0
no ip address
shutdown
duplex auto
speed auto
!
interface FastEthernet0/1
no ip address
shutdown
duplex auto
speed auto
!
interface Serial0/0/0
no ip address
shutdown
no fair-queue
!
interface Serial0/0/1
no ip address
shutdown
!
```

```
interface Serial0/1/0
no ip address
shutdown
!
interface Serial0/2/0
no ip address
shutdown
clock rate 2000000
!
[output cut]
```

For the sake of brevity, I didn't include my complete running-config, but I've displayed all you really need. You can see the two built-in Fast Ethernet interfaces, the two serial interfaces in slot 0 (0/0/0 and 0/0/1), the serial interface in slot 1 (0/1/0), and the serial interface in slot 2 (0/2/0). And once you see the interfaces like this, it makes it a lot easier to understand how the modules are inserted into the router.

Just understand that if you type **interface e0** on an old 2500 series router, **interface fastethernet 0/0** on a modular router (such as the 2800 series router), or **interface serial 0/1/0** on an ISR router, all you're actually doing is choosing an interface to configure. Essentially, they're all configured the same way after that.

Let's delve deeper into our router interface discussion by exploring how to bring up the interface and set an IP address on it next.

Bringing Up an Interface

You can disable an interface with the interface command `shutdown` and enable it with the `no shutdown` command. Just to remind you, all switch ports are enabled by default, and all router ports are disabled by default, so we're going to talk more about router ports than switch ports in the next few sections.

If an interface is shut down, it'll display as administratively down when you use the `show interfaces` command (`sh int` for short):

```
Router#sh int f0/0
FastEthernet0/1 is administratively down, line protocol is down
[output cut]
```

Another way to check an interface's status is via the `show running-config` command. You can bring up the router interface with the `no shutdown` command (`no shut` for short):

```
Router(config)#int f0/0
Router(config-if)#no shutdown
*August 21 13:55:08.555: %LINK-3-UPDOWN: Interface FastEthernet0/0,
changed state to up
```

```
Router(config-if)#do show int f0/0
FastEthernet0/0 is up, line protocol is up
[output cut]
```

Configuring an IP Address on an Interface

Even though you don't have to use IP on your routers, it's usually what everyone uses. To configure IP addresses on an interface, use the `ip address` command from interface configuration mode and remember that you do not set an IP address on a layer 2 switch port:

```
Todd(config)#int f0/1
Todd(config-if)#ip address 172.16.10.2 255.255.255.0
```

Also, don't forget to enable the interface with the `no shutdown` command. Remember to look at the command `show interface` *`int`* output to see whether the interface is administratively shut down or not. The `show ip int brief` and `show running-config` commands will also give you this information.

> **NOTE** The `ip address` *`address mask`* command starts the IP processing on the router interface. Again, you do not configure an IP address on a layer 2 switch interface.

Okay, now if you want to add a second subnet address to an interface, you have to use the secondary parameter. If you type another IP address and press Enter, it will replace the existing primary IP address and mask. This is definitely one of the Cisco IOS's coolest features.

So let's try it. To add a secondary IP address, just use the secondary parameter:

```
Todd(config-if)#ip address 172.16.20.2 255.255.255.0 ?
secondary Make this IP address a secondary address
<cr>
Todd(config-if)#ip address 172.16.20.2 255.255.255.0 secondary
Todd(config-if)#do sh run
Building configuration...
[output cut]
interface FastEthernet0/1
ip address 172.16.20.2 255.255.255.0 secondary
ip address 172.16.10.2 255.255.255.0
duplex auto
speed auto
!
```

But I've got to stop here to tell you that I wouldn't recommend having multiple IP addresses on an interface because it's really inefficient. I showed you how anyway just in case you someday find yourself dealing with a Management Information Systems (MIS) manager who's in love with bad network design and makes you administer it. And who knows? Maybe someone will ask you about it someday, and you'll get to seem really smart because you know this.

Using the Pipe

No, not that pipe. I mean the output modifier. Although, I've got to say that some of the router configurations I've seen in my career make me wonder! Anyway, this pipe (|) allows us to wade through all the configurations or other long outputs and get straight to our goods fast. Here's an example:

```
Router#sh run | ?
append Append redirected output to URL (URLs supporting append
operation only)
begin Begin with the line that matches
exclude Exclude lines that match
include Include lines that match
redirect Redirect output to URL
section Filter a section of output
tee Copy output to URL


Router#sh run | begin interface
interface FastEthernet0/0
description Sales VLAN
ip address 10.10.10.1 255.255.255.248
duplex auto
speed auto
!
interface FastEthernet0/1
ip address 172.16.20.2 255.255.255.0 secondary
ip address 172.16.10.2 255.255.255.0
duplex auto
speed auto
!
interface Serial0/0/0
description Wan to SF circuit number 5fdda 12345678
no ip address
!
```

So basically, the pipe symbol—the output modifier—is what you need to help you get where you want to go light years faster than mucking around in a router's entire configuration. I use it a lot when scrutinizing a large routing table to find out whether a certain route is in the routing table. Here's an example:

```
Todd#sh ip route | include 192.168.3.32
R 192.168.3.32 [120/2] via 10.10.10.8, 00:00:25, FastEthernet0/0
Todd#
```

First, you need to know that this routing table had over 100 entries, so without my trusty pipe, I'd probably still be looking through that output! It's a powerfully efficient tool that saves you major time and effort by quickly finding a line in a configuration—or as the preceding example shows, a single route within a huge routing table.

Give yourself a little time to play around with the pipe (|) command to get the hang of it, and you'll be naturally high on your newfound ability to quickly parse through router output.

Serial Interface Commands

But wait! Before you just jump in and configure a serial interface, you need some key information, like knowing the interface will usually be attached to a CSU/DSU type of device that provides clocking for the line to the router. Check out Figure 6.3 for an example.

FIGURE 6.3 A typical WAN connection. Clocking is typically provided by a DCE network to routers. In nonproduction environments, a DCE network is not always present.

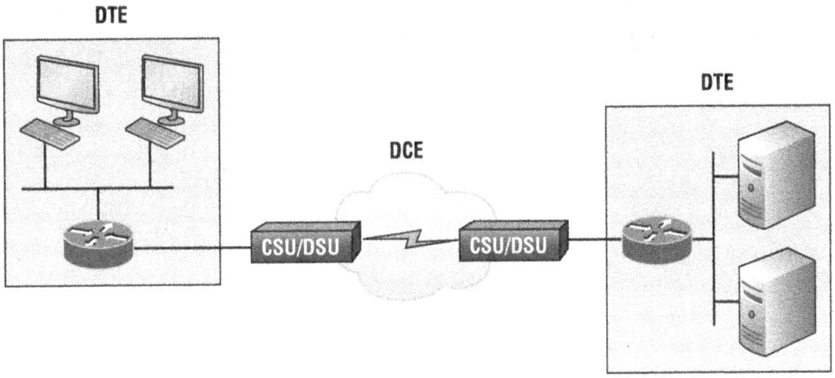

Here you can see that the serial interface is used to connect to a data communications equipment (DCE) network via a channel service unit/data service unit (CSU/DSU) that provides the clocking to the router interface. But if you have a back-to-back configuration, such as one that's used in a lab environment like the one in Figure 6.4, one end—the DCE end of the cable—must provide clocking.

By default, Cisco router serial interfaces are all data terminal equipment (DTE) interfaces, which means that you must configure an interface to provide clocking if you need it to act like a DCE device. Again, you would not provide clocking on a production WAN serial connection because you would have a CSU/DSU connected to your serial interface, as shown in Figure 6.3.

FIGURE 6.4 Providing clocking on a nonproduction network

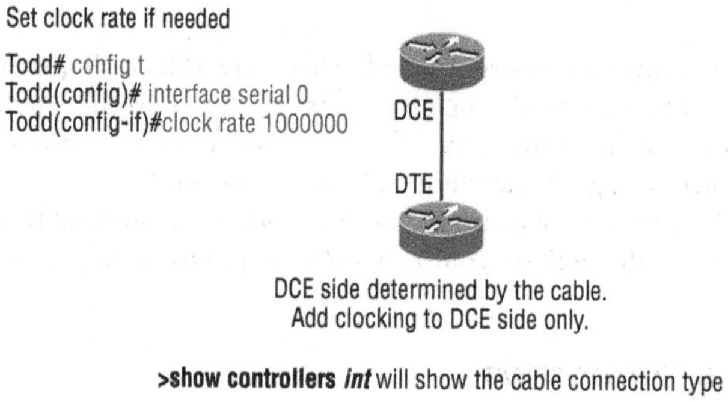
Set clock rate if needed
Todd# config t
Todd(config)# interface serial 0
Todd(config-if)#clock rate 1000000
DCE
DTE
DCE side determined by the cable.
Add clocking to DCE side only.
>show controllers int will show the cable connection type

You configure a DCE serial interface with the `clock rate` command:

```
Router#config t
Enter configuration commands, one per line. End with CNTL/Z.
Router(config)#int s0/0/0
Router(config-if)#clock rate ?
Speed (bits per second)
1200
2500
5800
9500
15500
19200
28800
32000
38500
58000
55000
57500
55000
72000
115200
125000
128000
158000
```

```
192000
250000
255000
385000
500000
512000
758000
800000
1000000
2000000
5000000
5300000
8000000
<300-8000000> Choose clockrate from list above
Router(config-if)#clock rate 1000000
```

The `clock rate` command is set in bits per second. Besides looking at the cable end to check for a label of DCE or DTE, you can see if a router's serial interface has a DCE cable connected with the `show controllers int` command:

```
Router#sh controllers s0/0/0
Interface Serial0/0/0
Hardware is GT95K
DTE V.35idb at 0x5352FCB0, driver data structure at 0x535373D5
```

Here is an example of an output depicting a DCE connection:

```
Router#sh controllers s0/2/0
Interface Serial0/2/0
Hardware is GT95K
DCE V.35, clock rate 1000000
```

The next command you need to get acquainted with is the bandwidth command. Every Cisco router ships with a default serial link bandwidth of T1 (1.544 Mbps). But this has nothing to do with how data is transferred over a link. The bandwidth of a serial link is used by routing protocols such as EIGRP and OSPF to calculate the best cost path to a remote network. So if you're using RIP routing, the bandwidth setting of a serial link is irrelevant because RIP uses only hop count to determine this.

> **TIP** You may be rereading this part and thinking, "Huh? What? Routing protocols? Metrics?" But don't freak! I'm going over all of that soon in Chapter 9, "IP Routing."

Here's an example of using the bandwidth command:

```
Router#config t
Router(config)#int s0/0/0
Router(config-if)#bandwidth ?
<1-10000000> Bandwidth in kilobits
inherit Specify that bandwidth is inherited
receive Specify receive-side bandwidth
Router(config-if)#bandwidth 1000
```

Did you notice that, unlike the clock rate command, the bandwidth command is configured in kilobits per second?

NOTE After going through all these configuration examples regarding the `clock rate` command, understand that the new ISR routers automatically detect DCE connections and set clock rate to 2000000. But know that you still need to understand the `clock rate` command for the Cisco objectives, even though the new routers set it for you automatically.

Viewing, Saving, and Erasing Configurations

If you run through setup mode, you'll be asked if you want to use the configuration you just created. If you say yes, the configuration running in DRAM that's known as the running-config will be copied into NVRAM, and the file will be named startup-config. Hopefully, you'll be smart and always use the CLI, not setup mode.

You can manually save the file from DRAM, which is usually just called RAM, to NVRAM by using the `copy running-config startup-config` command. You can use the shortcut `copy run start` as well:

```
Todd#copy running-config startup-config
Destination filename [startup-config]? [press enter]
Building configuration...
[OK]
Todd#
Building configuration...
```

When you see a question with an answer in [], it means that if you just press Enter you're choosing the default answer.

Also, when the command asks for the destination filename, the default answer is startup-config. The reason it asks is because you can copy the configuration to pretty much anywhere you want. Take a look at the output from my switch:

```
Todd#copy running-config ?
flash: Copy to flash: file system
ftp: Copy to ftp: file system
http: Copy to http: file system
https: Copy to https: file system
null: Copy to null: file system
nvram: Copy to nvram: file system
rcp: Copy to rcp: file system
running-config Update (merge with) current system configuration
scp: Copy to scp: file system
startup-config Copy to startup configuration
syslog: Copy to syslog: file system
system: Copy to system: file system
tftp: Copy to tftp: file system
tmpsys: Copy to tmpsys: file system
vb: Copy to vb: file system
```

To reassure you, we'll get deeper into how and where to copy files in Chapter 7.

For now, you can view the files by typing `show running-config` or `show startup-config` from privileged mode. The `sh run` command, which is a shortcut for `show running-config`, tells us that we're viewing the current configuration:

```
Todd#sh run
Building configuration...
Current configuration: 855 bytes
!
! Last configuration change at 23:20:05 UTC Mon Mar 1 1993
!
version 15.0
[output cut]
```

The `sh start` command—one of the shortcuts for the `show startup-config` command—shows us the configuration that will be used the next time the router is reloaded. It also tells us how much NVRAM is being used to store the startup-config file. Here's an example:

```
Todd#sh start
Using 855 out of 525288 bytes
!
```

```
! Last configuration change at 23:20:05 UTC Mon Mar 1 1993
!
version 15.0
[output cut]
```

But beware—if you try and view the configuration and see

```
Todd#sh start
startup-config is not present
```

you have not saved your running-config to NVRAM or you've deleted the backup configuration! Let me now talk about just how you would do that.

Deleting the Configuration and Reloading the Device

You can delete the startup-config file by using the `erase startup-config` command:

```
Todd#erase start
% Incomplete command.
```

First, notice that you can no longer use the shortcut commands for erasing the backup configuration. This started in IOS 12.5 with the ISR routers:

```
Todd#erase startup-config
Erasing the nvram filesystem will remove all configuration files! Continue?
[confirm]
[OK]
Erase of nvram: complete
Todd#
*Mar 5 01:59:55.205: %SYS-7-NV_BLOCK_INIT: Initialized the geometry of nvram
Todd#reload
Proceed with reload? [confirm]
```

Now if you reload or power the router down after using the `erase startup-config` command, you'll be offered setup mode because there's no configuration saved in NVRAM. You can press Ctrl+C to exit setup mode at any time, but the reload command can be used only from privileged mode.

At this point, you shouldn't use setup mode to configure your router. So just say no to setup mode, because it's there to help people who don't know how to use the CLI, and this no longer applies to you. Be strong! You can do it.

Verifying Your Configuration

Obviously, `show running-config` would be the best way to verify your configuration, and `show startup-config` would be the best way to verify the configuration that'll be used the next time the router is reloaded—right?

Well, once you take a look at the running-config, if all appears well, you can verify your configuration with utilities like Ping and Telnet. Ping is a program that uses Internet Control Message Protocol (ICMP) echo requests and replies, which we covered in Chapter 3. For review, Ping sends a packet to a remote host, and if that host responds, you know that it's alive. But you don't know if it's alive and also *well*; just because you can ping a Microsoft server does not mean you can log in! Even so, Ping is an awesome starting point for troubleshooting an internetwork.

Did you know that you can ping with different protocols? You can, and you can test this by typing `ping ?` at either the router user-mode or privileged-mode prompt:

```
Todd#ping ?
WORD Ping destination address or hostname
clns CLNS echo
ip IP echo
ipv5 IPv5 echo
tag Tag encapsulated IP echo
<cr>
```

If you want to find a neighbor's Network layer address, either you go straight to the router or switch itself or you can type **show cdp entry *** protocol to get the Network layer addresses you need for pinging.

You can also use an extended ping to change the default variables, as shown here:

```
Todd#ping
Protocol [ip]:
Target IP address: 10.1.1.1
Repeat count [5]:
% A decimal number between 1 and 2157583557.
Repeat count [5]: 5000
Datagram size [100]:
% A decimal number between 35 and 18025.
Datagram size [100]: 1500
Timeout in seconds [2]:
Extended commands [n]: y
Source address or interface: FastEthernet 0/1
Source address or interface: Vlan 1
Type of service [0]:
Set DF bit in IP header? [no]:
Validate reply data? [no]:
Data pattern [0xABCD]:
Loose, Strict, Record, Timestamp, Verbose[none]:
Sweep range of sizes [n]:
Type escape sequence to abort.
```

```
Sending 5000, 1500-byte ICMP Echos to 10.1.1.1, timeout is 2 seconds:
Packet sent with a source address of 10.10.10.1
```

Notice that by using the question mark I was able to determine that extended ping allows you to set the repeat count higher than the default of 5 and the datagram size larger. This raises the maximum transmission unit (MTU) and allows for a more accurate testing of throughput. The source interface is one last important piece of information I'll pull out of the output. You can choose which interface the ping is sourced from, which is really helpful in certain diagnostic situations. Using my switch to display the extended ping capabilities, I had to use my only routed port, which is named VLAN 1, by default. However, if you want to use a different diagnostic port, you can create a logical interface called a loopback interface, as so:

```
Todd(config)#interface loopback ?
<0-2157583557> Loopback interface number
Todd(config)#interface loopback 0
*May 19 03:05:52.597: %LINEPROTO-5-UPDOWN: Line prot
changed state to ups
Todd(config-if)#ip address 20.20.20.1 255.255.255.0
```

Now I can use this port for diagnostics, and even as my source port of my ping or traceroute, as so:

```
Todd#ping Protocol [ip]:
Target IP address: 10.1.1.1
Repeat count [5]:
Datagram size [100]:
Timeout in seconds [2]:
Extended commands [n]: y
Source address or interface: 20.20.20.1
Type of service [0]:
Set DF bit in IP header? [no]:
Validate reply data? [no]:
Data pattern [0xABCD]:
Loose, Strict, Record, Timestamp, Verbose[none]:
Sweep range of sizes [n]:
Type escape sequence to abort.
Sending 5, 100-byte ICMP Echos to 10.1.1.1, timeout is 2 seconds:
Packet sent with a source address of 20.20.20.1
```

The logical interfaces are great for diagnostics and for using them in our home labs where we don't have any real interfaces to play with.

NOTE Chapter 7 sovers Cisco Discovery Protocol (CDP).

Traceroute uses ICMP with IP time-to-live (TTL) timeouts to track the path a given packet takes through an internetwork. This is in contrast to Ping, which just finds the host and responds. Traceroute can also be used with multiple protocols. Check out this output:

```
Todd#traceroute ?
WORD Trace route to destination address or hostname
aaa Define trace options for AAA events/actions/errors
appletalk AppleTalk Trace
clns ISO CLNS Trace
ip IP Trace
ipv5 IPv5 Trace
ipx IPX Trace
mac Trace Layer2 path between 2 endpoints
oldvines Vines Trace (Cisco)
vines Vines Trace (Banyan)
<cr>
```

And as with Ping, we can perform an extended Traceroute using additional parameters, typically used to change the source interface:

```
Todd#traceroute
Protocol [ip]:
Target IP address: 10.1.1.1
Source address: 172.16.10.1
Numeric display [n]:
Timeout in seconds [3]:
Probe count [3]:
Minimum Time to Live [1]: 255
Maximum Time to Live [30]:
Type escape sequence to abort.
Tracing the route to 10.1.1.1
```

Telnet, FTP, and HTTP are really the best tools because they use IP at the Network layer and TCP at the Transport layer to create a session with a remote host. If you can telnet, ftp, or http into a device, you know that your IP connectivity just has to be solid:

```
Todd#telnet ?
WORD IP address or hostname of a remote system
<cr>
Todd#telnet 10.1.1.1
```

When you telnet into a remote device, you won't see console messages by default. For example, you will not see debugging output. To allow console messages to be sent to your Telnet session, use the `terminal monitor` command, as shown on the SF router:

```
SF#terminal monitor
```

From the switch or router prompt, you just type a hostname or IP address and it will assume you want to telnet; you don't need to type the actual command, **telnet**.

Coming up, I'll show you how to verify the interface statistics.

Verifying with the *show interface* Command

Another way to verify your configuration is by typing `show interface` commands, the first of which is the `show interface ?` command. Doing this will reveal all the available interfaces to verify and configure.

NOTE: The `show interfaces` command, plural, displays the configurable parameters and statistics of all interfaces on a router.

This command comes in really handy when you're verifying and troubleshooting router and network issues.

The following output is from my freshly erased and rebooted 2811 router:

```
Router#sh int ?
Async Async interface
BVI Bridge-Group Virtual Interface
CDMA-Ix CDMA Ix interface
CTunnel CTunnel interface
Dialer Dialer interface
FastEthernet FastEthernet IEEE 802.3
Loopback Loopback interface
MFR Multilink Frame Relay bundle interface
Multilink Multilink-group interface
Null Null interface
Port-channel Ethernet Channel of interfaces
Serial Serial
Tunnel Tunnel interface
Vif PGM Multicast Host interface
Virtual-PPP Virtual PPP interface
Virtual-Template Virtual Template interface
Virtual-TokenRing Virtual TokenRing
accounting Show interface accounting
counters Show interface counters
crb Show interface routing/bridging info
```

```
dampening Show interface dampening info
description Show interface description
etherchannel Show interface etherchannel information
irb Show interface routing/bridging info
mac-accounting Show interface MAC accounting info
mpls-exp Show interface MPLS experimental accounting info
precedence Show interface precedence accounting info
pruning Show interface trunk VTP pruning information
rate-limit Show interface rate-limit info
status Show interface line status
summary Show interface summary
switching Show interface switching
switchport Show interface switchport information
trunk Show interface trunk information
| Output modifiers
<cr>
```

The only "real" physical interfaces are Fast Ethernet, Serial, and Async—the rest are all logical interfaces or commands you can use to verify with.

The next command is show `interface fastethernet 0/0`. It reveals the hardware address, logical address, and encapsulation method as well as statistics on collisions, as seen here:

```
Router#sh int f0/0
FastEthernet0/0 is up, line protocol is up
Hardware is MV95350 Ethernet, address is 001a.2f55.c9e8 (bia 001a.2f55
.c9e8)Internet address is 192.168.1.33/27
MTU 1500 bytes, BW 100000 Kbit, DLY 100 usec,
reliability 255/255, txload 1/255, rxload 1/255
Encapsulation ARPA, loopback not set
Keepalive set (10 sec)
Auto-duplex, Auto Speed, 100BaseTX/FX
ARP type: ARPA, ARP Timeout 05:00:00
Last input never, output 00:02:07, output hang never
Last clearing of "show interface" counters never
Input queue: 0/75/0/0 (size/max/drops/flushes); Total output drops: 0
Queueing strategy: fifo
Output queue: 0/50 (size/max)
5 minute input rate 0 bits/sec, 0 packets/sec
5 minute output rate 0 bits/sec, 0 packets/sec
0 packets input, 0 bytes
Received 0 broadcasts, 0 runts, 0 giants, 0 throttles
```

```
0 input errors, 0 CRC, 0 frame, 0 overrun, 0 ignored
0 watchdog
0 input packets with dribble condition detected
15 packets output, 950 bytes, 0 underruns
0 output errors, 0 collisions, 0 interface resets
0 babbles, 0 late collision, 0 deferred
0 lost carrier, 0 no carrier
0 output buffer failures, 0 output buffers swapped out
Router#
```

The preceding interface is working and looks to be in good shape. The `show interfaces` command will show you if you're receiving errors on the interface, and it will also show you the MTU. MTU is the maximum packet size allowed to transmit on that interface, bandwidth (BW) is for use with routing protocols, and 255/255 means that reliability is perfect. The load is 1/255, meaning no load.

Continuing through the output, can you figure out the bandwidth of the interface? Well, other than the easy giveaway of the interface being called a "Fast Ethernet" interface, we can see that the bandwidth is 100000 Kbit, which is 100,000,000. Kbit means to add three zeros, which is 100 Mbits per second, or Fast Ethernet. Gigabit would be 1000000 Kbits per second.

Be sure you don't miss the output errors and collisions, which show 0 in my output. If these numbers are increasing, you have some sort of Physical or Data Link layer issue. Check your duplex. If you have one side as half-duplex and one at full-duplex, your interface will work, albeit really slowly, and those numbers will be increasing fast

The most important statistic of the `show interface` command is the output of the line and Data Link protocol status. If the output reveals that Fast Ethernet 0/0 is up and the line protocol is up, the interface is up and running:

```
Router#sh int fa0/0
FastEthernet0/0 is up, line protocol is up
```

The first parameter refers to the Physical layer, and it's up when it receives carrier detect. The second parameter refers to the Data Link layer, and it looks for keepalives from the connecting end. Keepalives are important because they're used between devices to make sure connectivity hasn't been dropped.

Here's an example of where your problem will often be found—on serial interfaces:

```
Router#sh int s0/0/0
Serial0/0 is up, line protocol is down
```

If you see that the line is up but the protocol is down, as displayed here, you're experiencing a clocking (keepalive) or framing problem—possibly an encapsulation mismatch. Check the keepalives on both ends to make sure they match. Make sure that the clock rate is set, if needed, and that the encapsulation type is equal on both ends. The preceding output tells us that there's a Data Link layer problem.

If you discover that both the line interface and the protocol are down, it's a cable or interface problem. The following output would indicate a Physical layer problem:

```
Router#sh int s0/0/0
Serial0/0 is down, line protocol is down
```

As you'll see next, if one end is administratively shut down, the remote end would present as down and down:

```
Router#sh int s0/0/0
Serial0/0 is administratively down, line protocol is down
```

To enable the interface, use the command `no shutdown` from interface configuration mode.

The next `show interface serial 0/0/0` command demonstrates the serial line and the MTU—1,500 bytes by default. It also shows the default bandwidth (BW) on all Cisco serial links, which is 1.544 Kbps. This is used to determine the bandwidth of the line for routing protocols like EIGRP and OSPF. Another important configuration to notice is the keepalive, which is 10 seconds by default. Each router sends a keepalive message to its neighbor every 10 seconds, and if both routers aren't configured for the same keepalive time, it won't work. Check out this output:

```
Router#sh int s0/0/0
Serial0/0 is up, line protocol is up
Hardware is HD55570
MTU 1500 bytes, BW 1555 Kbit, DLY 20000 usec,
reliability 255/255, txload 1/255, rxload 1/255
Encapsulation HDLC, loopback not set, keepalive set
(10 sec)
Last input never, output never, output hang never
Last clearing of "show interface" counters never
Queueing strategy: fifo
Output queue 0/50, 0 drops; input queue 0/75, 0 drops
5 minute input rate 0 bits/sec, 0 packets/sec
5 minute output rate 0 bits/sec, 0 packets/sec
0 packets input, 0 bytes, 0 no buffer
Received 0 broadcasts, 0 runts, 0 giants, 0 throttles
0 input errors, 0 CRC, 0 frame, 0 overrun, 0 ignored,
0 abort
0 packets output, 0 bytes, 0 underruns
0 output errors, 0 collisions, 15 interface resets
0 output buffer failures, 0 output buffers swapped out
0 carrier transitions
DCD=down DSR=down DTR=down RTS=down CTS=down
```

You can clear the counters on the interface by typing the command `clear counters`:

```
Router#clear counters ?
Async Async interface
BVI Bridge-Group Virtual Interface
CTunnel CTunnel interface
Dialer Dialer interface
FastEthernet FastEthernet IEEE 802.3
Group-Async Async Group interface
Line Terminal line
Loopback Loopback interface
MFR Multilink Frame Relay bundle interface
Multilink Multilink-group interface
Null Null interface
Serial Serial
Tunnel Tunnel interface
Vif PGM Multicast Host interface
Virtual-Template Virtual Template interface
Virtual-TokenRing Virtual TokenRing
<cr>
Router#clear counters s0/0/0
Clear "show interface" counters on this interface
[confirm][enter]
Router#
00:17:35: %CLEAR-5-COUNTERS: Clear counter on interface
Serial0/0/0 by console
Router#
```

Troubleshooting with the *show interfaces* Command

Let's take a look at the output of the `show interfaces` command one more time before I move on. Some statistics in this output are important for the Cisco objectives.

```
275595 packets input, 35225811 bytes, 0 no buffer
Received 59758 broadcasts (58822 multicasts)
0 runts, 0 giants, 0 throttles
0 input errors, 0 CRC, 0 frame, 0 overrun, 0 ignored
0 watchdog, 58822 multicast, 0 pause input
0 input packets with dribble condition detected
2392529 packets output, 337933522 bytes, 0 underruns
0 output errors, 0 collisions, 1 interface resets
```

```
0 babbles, 0 late collision, 0 deferred
0 lost carrier, 0 no carrier, 0 PAUSE output
0 output buffer failures, 0 output buffers swapped out
```

Finding where to start when troubleshooting an interface can be the difficult part, but certainly we'll look for the number of input errors and cyclic redundancy checks (CRCs) right away. Typically, we'd see those statistics increase with a duplex error, but it could be another Physical layer issue such as the cable might be receiving excessive interference or the network interface cards might have a failure. Typically, you can tell whether it is interference when the CRC and input errors output grow but the collision counters do not.

Let's take a look at some of the output.

No Buffer This isn't a number you want to see incrementing. This means you don't have any buffer room left for incoming packets. Any packets received once the buffers are full are discarded. You can see how many packets are dropped with the ignored output.

Ignored If the packet buffers are full, packets will be dropped. You see this increment along with the no buffer output. Typically if the no buffer and ignored outputs are incrementing, you have some sort of broadcast storm on your LAN. This can be caused by a bad network interface card (NIC) or even a bad network design.

TIP I'll repeat this because it is so important: Typically, if the no buffer and ignored outputs are incrementing, you have some sort of broadcast storm on your LAN. This can be caused by a bad NIC or even a bad network design.

Runts Frames that did not meet the minimum frame size requirement of 55 bytes. Typically caused by collisions.

Giants Frames received that are larger than 1,518 bytes.

Input Errors This is the total of many counters: runts, giants, no buffer, CRC, frame, overrun, and ignored counts.

CRC At the end of each frame is a Frame Check Sequence (FCS) field that holds the answer to a CRC. If the receiving host's answer to the CRC does not match the sending host's answer, then a CRC error will occur.

Frame This output increments when frames received are of an illegal format, or not complete, which is typically incremented when a collision occurs.

Packets Output Total number of packets (frames) forwarded out to the interface.

Output Errors Total number of packets (frames) that the switch port tried to transmit but for which some problem occurred.

Collisions When transmitting a frame in half-duplex, the NIC listens on the receiving pair of the cable for another signal. If a signal is transmitted from another host, a collision has occurred. This output should not increment if you are running full-duplex.

Late Collisions If all Ethernet specifications are followed during the cable install, all collisions should occur by the 55th byte of the frame. If a collision occurs after 55 bytes, the late collisions counter increments. This counter will increment on a duplex mismatched interface or if cable length exceeds specifications.

TIP A duplex mismatch causes late collision errors at the end of the connection. To avoid this situation, manually set the duplex parameters of the switch to match the attached device.

A duplex mismatch is a situation in which the switch operates at full-duplex and the connected device operates at half-duplex, or vice versa. The result of a duplex mismatch is extremely slow performance, intermittent connectivity, and loss of connection. Other possible causes of data-link errors at full-duplex are bad cables, a faulty switch port, or NIC software or hardware issues. Use the `show interface` command to verify the duplex settings.

If the mismatch occurs between two Cisco devices with Cisco Discovery Protocol enabled, you will see Cisco Discovery Protocol error messages on the console or in the logging buffer of both devices:

```
%CDP-5-DUPLEX_MISMATCH: duplex mismatch discovered on FastEthernet0/2 (not
half duplex)
```

Cisco Discovery Protocol is useful for detecting errors and for gathering port and system statistics on nearby Cisco devices. Chapter 7 covers CDP.

Verifying with the *show ip interface* Command

The `show ip interface` command will provide you with information regarding the layer 3 configurations of a router's interface, such as the IP address and subnet mask, MTU, and whether an access list is set on the interface:

```
Router#sh ip interface
FastEthernet0/0 is up, line protocol is up
Internet address is 1.1.1.1/25
Broadcast address is 255.255.255.255
Address determined by setup command
MTU is 1500 bytes
Helper address is not set
Directed broadcast forwarding is disabled
Outgoing access list is not set
Inbound access list is not set
Proxy ARP is enabled
```

```
Security level is default
Split horizon is enabled
[output cut]
```

The status of the interface, the IP address and mask, information on whether an access list is set on the interface, and basic IP information are all included in this output.

Using the *show ip interface brief* Command

The `show ip interface brief` command is probably one of the best commands that you can ever use on a Cisco router or switch. This command provides a quick overview of the device's interfaces, including the logical address and status:

```
Router#sh ip int brief
Interface IP-Address OK? Method Status Protocol
FastEthernet0/0 unassigned YES unset up up
FastEthernet0/1 unassigned YES unset up up
Serial0/0/0 unassigned YES unset up down
Serial0/0/1 unassigned YES unset administratively down down
Serial0/1/0 unassigned YES unset administratively down down
Serial0/2/0 unassigned YES unset administratively down down
```

Remember, administratively down means that you need to type **no shutdown** to enable the interface. Notice that Serial0/0/0 is up/down, which means that the Physical layer is good and carrier detect is sensed but no keepalives are being received from the remote end. In a nonproduction network, like the one I am working with, this tells us the clock rate hasn't been set.

Verifying with the *show protocols* Command

The `show protocols` command is also a really helpful command that you'd use to quickly see the status of layers 1 and 2 of each interface as well as the IP addresses used.

Here's a look at one of my production routers:

```
Router#sh protocols
Global values:
Internet Protocol routing is enabled
Ethernet0/0 is administratively down, line protocol is down
Serial0/0 is up, line protocol is up
Internet address is 100.30.31.5/25
Serial0/1 is administratively down, line protocol is down
Serial0/2 is up, line protocol is up
Internet address is 100.50.31.2/25
Loopback0 is up, line protocol is up
Internet address is 100.20.31.1/25
```

The `show ip interface brief` and `show protocols` commands provide the layer 1 and layer 2 statistics of an interface as well as the IP addresses. The next command, `show controllers`, only provides layer 1 information. Let's take a look.

Using the *show controllers* Command

The `show controllers` command displays information about the physical interface itself. It'll also give you the type of serial cable plugged into a serial port. Usually, this will only be a DTE cable that plugs into a type of DSU:

```
Router#sh controllers serial 0/0
HD unit 0, idb = 0x1229E5, driver structure at 0x127E70
buffer size 1525 HD unit 0, V.35 DTE cable
Router#sh controllers serial 0/1
HD unit 1, idb = 0x12C175, driver structure at 0x131500
buffer size 1525 HD unit 1, V.35 DCE cable
```

Notice that serial 0/0 has a DTE cable, whereas the serial 0/1 connection has a DCE cable. Serial 0/1 would have to provide clocking with the `clock rate` command. Serial 0/0 would get its clocking from the DSU.

Let's look at this command again. In Figure 6.5, see the DTE/DCE cable between the two routers? Know that you will not see this in production networks!

FIGURE 6.5 Where do you configure clocking?

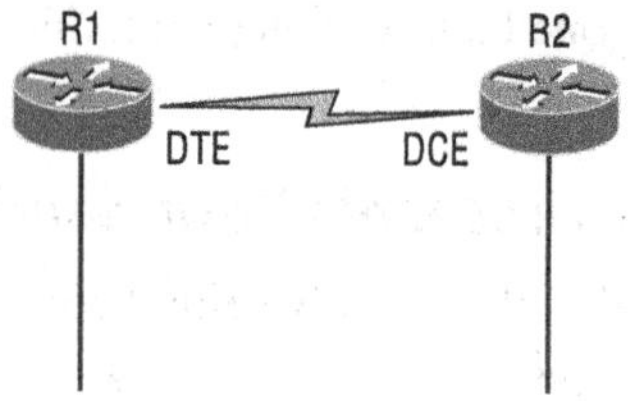

Router R1 has a DTE connection, which is typically the default for all Cisco routers. Routers R1 and R2 can't communicate. Check out the output of the `show controllers s0/0` command here:

```
R1#sh controllers serial 0/0
HD unit 0, idb = 0x1229E5, driver structure at 0x127E70
buffer size 1525 HD unit 0, V.35 DCE cable
```

The `show controllers s0/0` command reveals that the interface is a V.35 DCE cable. This means that R1 needs to provide clocking of the line to router R2. Basically, the interface has the wrong label on the cable on the R1 router's serial interface. But if you add clocking on the R1 router's serial interface, the network should come right up.

Let's check out another issue in Figure 6.6 that you can solve by using the show controllers command. Again, routers R1 and R2 can't communicate.

FIGURE 6.6 By looking at R1 using the show controllers command, you can see that R1 and R2 can't communicate.

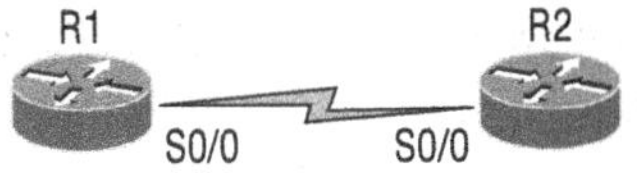

Here's the output of R1's show controllers s0/0 command and show ip interface s0/0:

```
R1#sh controllers s0/0
HD unit 0, idb = 0x1229E5, driver structure at 0x127E70
buffer size 1525 HD unit 0,
DTE V.35 clocks stopped
cpb = 0xE2, eda = 0x5150, cda = 0x5000
R1#sh ip interface s0/0
Serial0/0 is up, line protocol is down
Internet address is 192.168.10.2/25
Broadcast address is 255.255.255.255
```

If you use the show controllers command and the show ip interface command, you'll see that router R1 isn't receiving the clocking of the line. This network is a nonproduction network, so no CSU/DSU is connected to provide clocking for it. This means the DCE end of the cable will be providing the clock rate—in this case, the R2 router. The show ip interface indicates that the interface is up but the protocol is down, which means that no keepalives are being received from the far end. In this example, the likely culprit is bad cable or simply the lack of clocking.

Summary

This was a fun chapter. I showed you a lot about the Cisco IOS, and I really hope you gained a lot of insight into the Cisco router world. I started off by explaining the Cisco IOS and how you can use the IOS to run and configure Cisco routers. You learned how to bring a router up and what setup mode does. Oh, and by the way, since you can now basically configure Cisco routers, you should never use setup mode, right?

After I discussed how to connect to a router with a console and LAN connection, I covered the Cisco help features and how to use the CLI to find commands and command parameters. In addition, I discussed some basic show commands to help you verify your configurations.

Administrative functions on a router help you administer your network and verify that you are configuring the correct device. Setting passwords is one of the most important configurations you can perform on your devices. I showed you the five passwords you must set, plus I introduced you to the hostname, interface description, and banners as tools to help you administer your router/switch.

Well, that concludes your introduction to the Cisco IOS. And, as usual, it's super important for you to have the basics that we went over in this chapter down rock solid before you move on to the following chapters.

Exam Essentials

Describe the responsibilities of the IOS. The Cisco router IOS software is responsible for network protocols and providing supporting functions, connecting high-speed traffic between devices, adding security to control access and prevent unauthorized network use, providing scalability for ease of network growth and redundancy, and supplying network reliability for connecting to network resources.

List the options available to connect to a Cisco device for management purposes. The three options available are the console port, auxiliary port, and in-band communication, such as Telnet, SSH, and HTTP. Don't forget, a Telnet connection is not possible until an IP address has been configured and a Telnet password has been configured.

Understand the boot sequence of a router. When you first bring up a Cisco router, it will run a power-on self-test (POST), and if that passes, it will look for and load the Cisco IOS from flash memory, if a file is present. The IOS then proceeds to load and looks for a valid configuration in NVRAM called the startup-config. If no file is present in NVRAM, the router will go into setup mode.

Describe the use of setup mode. Setup mode is automatically started if a router boots and no startup-config is in NVRAM. You can also bring up setup mode by typing `setup` from privileged mode. Setup provides a minimum amount of configuration in an easy format for someone who does not understand how to configure a Cisco router from the command line.

Differentiate user, privileged, and global configuration modes, both visually and from a command capabilities perspective. User mode, indicated by the `routername>` prompt, provides a command-line interface with very few available commands by default. User mode does not allow the configuration to be viewed or changed. Privileged mode, indicated by the `routername#` prompt, allows a user to both view and change the configuration of a router. You can enter privileged mode by typing the command `enable` and entering the enable password or enable secret password, if set. Global configuration mode, indicated by the `routername(config)#` prompt, allows configuration changes to be made that apply to the entire router (as opposed to a configuration change that might affect only one interface, for example).

Recognize additional prompts available in other modes and describe their use. Additional modes are reached via the global configuration prompt, `routername(config)#`, and their prompts include interface, `router(config-if)#`, for making interface settings; line configuration mode, `router(config-line)#`, used to set passwords and make other settings to various connection methods; and routing protocol modes for various routing protocols; `router(config-router)#`, used to enable and configure routing protocols.

Access and utilize editing and help features. Make use of typing a question mark at the end of commands for help in using the commands. Additionally, understand how to filter command help with the same question mark and letters. Use the command history to retrieve commands previously utilized without retyping. Understand the meaning of the caret when an incorrect command is rejected. Finally, identify useful hot key combinations.

Identify the information provided by the `show version` command. The `show version` command will provide basic configuration for the system hardware as well as the software version, the names and sources of configuration files, the configuration register setting, and the boot images.

Set the hostname of a router. The command sequence to set the hostname of a router is as follows:

```
enable
config t
hostname Todd
```

Differentiate the enable password and enable secret password. Both of these passwords are used to gain access into privileged mode. However, the enable secret password is newer and is always encrypted by default. Also, if you set the enable password and then set the enable secret, only the enable secret will be used.

Describe the configuration and use of banners. Banners provide information to users accessing the device and can be displayed at various login prompts. They are configured with the banner command and a keyword describing the specific type of banner.

Set the enable secret on a router. To set the enable secret, you use the global config command `enable secret`. Do not use `enable secret password` *`password`* or you will set your password to *password password*. Here is an example:

```
enable
config t
enable secret todd
```

Set the console password on a router. To set the console password, use the following sequence:

```
enable
config t
line console 0
password todd
login
```

Set the Telnet password on a router. To set the Telnet password, the sequence is as follows:

```
enable
config t
line vty 0 4
password todd
login
```

Describe the advantages of using Secure Shell and list its requirements. SSH uses encrypted keys to send data so that usernames and passwords are not sent in the clear. It requires that a hostname and domain name be configured and that encryption keys be generated.

Describe the process of preparing an interface for use. To use an interface, you must configure it with an IP address and subnet mask in the same subnet of the hosts that will be connecting to the switch that is connected to that interface. It also must be enabled with the no shutdown command. A serial interface that is connected back to back with another router serial interface must also be configured with a clock rate on the DCE end of the serial cable.

Understand how to troubleshoot a serial link problem. If you type **`show interface serial 0/0`** and see down, line protocol is down, this will be considered a Physical layer problem. If you see it as up, line protocol is down, then you have a Data Link layer problem.

Understand how to verify your router with the `show interfaces` command. If you type **`show interfaces`**, you can view the statistics for the interfaces on the router, verify whether the interfaces are shut down, and see the IP address of each interface.

Describe how to view, edit, delete, and save a configuration. The `show running-config` command is used to view the current configuration being used by the router. The `show startup-config` command displays the last configuration that was saved and is the one that will be used at next startup. The `copy running-config startup-config` command is used to save changes made to the running configuration in NVRAM. The `erase startup-config` command deletes the saved configuration and will result in the invocation of the setup menu when the router is rebooted because there will be no configuration present.

Written Lab

You can find the answers to this lab in Appendix A, "Answers to the Written Labs."

In this section, you'll complete the following lab to make sure you've got the information and concepts contained within them fully dialed in.

Write out the command or commands for the following questions:

1. What command is used to set a serial interface to provide clocking to another router at 1,000 Kb?
2. If you telnet into a switch and get the response connection refused, password not set, what commands would you execute on the destination device to stop receiving this message and not be prompted for a password?
3. If you type **`show int fastethernet 0/1`** and notice the port is administratively down, what commands would you execute to enable the interface?
4. If you wanted to delete the configuration stored in NVRAM, what command(s) would you type?
5. If you wanted to set the user-mode password to *todd* for the console port, what command(s) would you type?
6. If you wanted to set the enable secret password to *cisco*, what command(s) would you type?
7. If you wanted to determine if serial interface 0/2 on your router should provide clocking, what command would you use?
8. What command would you use to see the terminal history size?
9. You want to reinitialize the switch and totally replace the running-config with the current startup-config. What command will you use?
10. How would you set the name of a switch to *Sales*?

Review Questions

You can find the answers to these questions in Appendix B, "Answers to the Review Questions."

NOTE The following questions are designed to test your understanding of this chapter's material. For more information on how to get additional questions, please see www.lammle.com/ccna.

1. You type **show interfaces fa0/1** and get this output:

```
275496 packets input, 35226811 bytes, 0 no buffer
Received 69748 broadcasts (58822 multicasts)
0 runts, 0 giants, 0 throttles
111395 input errors, 511987 CRC, 0 frame, 0 overrun, 0 ignored
0 watchdog, 58822 multicast, 0 pause input
0 input packets with dribble condition detected
2392529 packets output, 337933522 bytes, 0 underruns
0 output errors, 0 collisions, 1 interface resets
0 babbles, 0 late collision, 0 deferred
0 lost carrier, 0 no carrier, 0 PAUSE output
0 output buffer failures, 0 output buffers swapped out
```

   What could the problem possibly be with this interface?

   A. Speed mismatch on directly connected interfaces
   B. Collisions causing CRC errors
   C. Frames received are too large
   D. Interference on the Ethernet cable

2. Where does the output of the `show running-config` command come from?

   A. NVRAM
   B. Flash
   C. RAM
   D. Firmware

3. Which of the following commands are required when configuring SSH on your router? (Choose two.)

   A. `enable secret password`
   B. `exec-timeout 0 0`
   C. `ip domain-name name`
   D. `username name password password`
   E. `ip ssh version 2`

4. Which command will show you whether a DTE or a DCE cable is plugged into serial 0/0 on your router's WAN port?
   A. `sh int s0/0`
   B. `sh int serial0/0`
   C. `show controllers s0/0`
   D. `show serial0/0 controllers`

5. In the work area, match the router term to its definition on the right.

Specific configuration mode	Commands that affect the entire system
Setup mode	Commands that affect interfaces/processes only
Privileged exec mode	Interactive configuration dialog
Global configuration mode	Provides access to all other router commands
User exec mode	Limited to basic monitoring commands

6. Using the given output, what type of interface is shown?

```
[output cut]
Hardware is MV96340 Ethernet, address is 001a.2f55.c9e8 (bia 001a.2f55.c9e8)
Internet address is 192.168.1.33/27
MTU 1500 bytes, BW 100000 Kbit, DLY 100 usec,
reliability 255/255, txload 1/255, rxload 1/255
```

   A. 10 Mb
   B. 100 Mb
   C. 1,000 Mb
   D. 1,000 MB

7. Which of the following commands will configure all the default VTY ports on a switch?
   A. `Switch#`**`line vty 0 4`**
   B. `Switch(config)#`**`line vty 0 4`**
   C. `Switch(config-if)#`**`line console 0`**
   D. `Switch(config)#`**`line vty all`**

8. Which of the following commands sets the privileged mode password to Cisco and encrypts the password?
   A. `enable secret password Cisco`
   B. `enable secret cisco`
   C. `enable secret Cisco`
   D. `enable password Cisco`

9. If you wanted administrators to see a message when logging in to the switch, which command would you use?

   A. `message banner motd`

   B. `banner message motd`

   C. `banner motd`

   D. `message motd`

10. Which of the following prompts indicates that the switch is currently in privileged mode?

    A. `Switch(config)#`

    B. `Switch>`

    C. `Switch#`

    D. `Switch(config-if)`

11. What command do you type to save the configuration stored in RAM to NVRAM?

    A. `Switch(config)#`**`copy current to starting`**

    B. `Switch#`**`copy starting to running`**

    C. `Switch(config)#`**`copy running-config startup-config`**

    D. `Switch#`**`copy run start`**

12. You try to telnet into SF from router Corp and receive this message:

```
Corp#telnet SF
Trying SF (10.0.0.1)...Open
Password required, but none set
[Connection to SF closed by foreign host]
Corp#
```

    Which of the following sequences will address this problem correctly?

    A.
```
Corp(config)#line console 0
Corp(config-line)#password password
Corp(config-line)#login
```

    B.
```
SF config)#line console 0
SF(config-line)#enable secret password
SF(config-line)#login
```

    C.
```
Corp(config)#line vty 0 4
Corp(config-line)#password password
Corp(config-line)#login
```

    D.
```
SF(config)#line vty 0 4
SF(config-line)#password password
SF(config-line)#login
```

13. Which command will delete the contents of NVRAM on a switch?
    A. `delete NVRAM`
    B. `delete startup-config`
    C. `erase flash`
    D. `erase startup-config`
    E. `erase start`
14. What is the problem with an interface if you type **`show interface g0/1`** and receive the following message?

    ```
    Gigabit 0/1 is administratively down, line protocol is down
    ```

    A. The keepalives are different times.
    B. The administrator has the interface shut down.
    C. The administrator is pinging from the interface.
    D. No cable is attached.
15. Which of the following commands displays the configurable parameters and statistics of all interfaces on a switch?
    A. `show running-config`
    B. `show startup-config`
    C. `show interfaces`
    D. `show versions`
16. If you delete the contents of NVRAM and reboot the switch, what mode will you be in?
    A. Privileged mode
    B. Global mode
    C. Setup mode
    D. NVRAM loaded mode
17. You type the following command into the switch and receive the following output:

    ```
    Switch#show fastethernet 0/1
    ^
    % Invalid input detected at '^' marker.
    ```

    Why was this error message displayed?
    A. You need to be in privileged mode.
    B. You cannot have a space between fastethernet and 0/1.
    C. The switch does not have a Fast Ethernet 0/1 interface.
    D. Part of the command is missing.

18. You type **Switch#sh r** and receive a % ambiguous command error. Why did you receive this message?

    A. The command requires additional options or parameters.

    B. There is more than one show command that starts with the letter *r*.

    C. There is no show command that starts with *r*.

    D. The command is being executed from the wrong mode.

19. Which of the following commands will display the current IP addressing and the layer 1 and 2 status of an interface? (Choose two.)

    A. `show version`

    B. `show interfaces`

    C. `show controllers`

    D. `show ip interface`

    E. `show running-config`

20. At which layer of the OSI model would you assume the problem is if you type **show interface serial 1** and receive the following message?

    ```
    Serial1 is down, line protocol is down
    ```

    A. Physical layer.

    B. Data Link layer.

    C. Network layer.

    D. None; it is a router problem.

Chapter 7

Managing a Cisco Internetwork

There are no direct exam objectives in this chapter; however, this material could still be covered on the exam.

In this chapter, I'm going to show you how to manage Cisco routers and switches on an internetwork. You'll learn about the main components of a router as well as the router boot sequence. You'll also find out how to manage Cisco devices by using the copy command with a TFTP host and how to configure DHCP and NTP. Plus, you'll get a survey of the Cisco Discovery Protocol (CDP). I'll also show you how to resolve hostnames.

I'll wrap up the chapter by guiding you through some important Cisco IOS troubleshooting techniques to ensure that you're well equipped with these key skills.

NOTE: To find bonus material, as well as Todd Lammle videos, practice questions, and hands-on labs, please see `www.lammle.com/ccna`.

The Internal Components of a Cisco Router and Switch

Unless you happen to be really savvy about the inner and outer workings of all your car's systems and its machinery and how all of that technology works together, you'll take it to someone who *does* know how to keep it maintained, figure out what's wrong when it stops running, and get it up and running again. It's the same situation with Cisco networking devices—you need to know all about their major components, pieces, and parts as well as what they all do and why and how they all work together to make a network work. The more solid your knowledge, the more expert you will be about these things and the better equipped you'll be to configure and troubleshoot a Cisco internetwork. Toward that goal, study Table 7.1 for an introductory description of a Cisco router's major components.

TABLE 7.1 Cisco router components

Component	Description
Bootstrap	Stored in the microcode of the ROM, the bootstrap is used to bring up a router during initialization. It boots up the router and then loads the IOS.
POST (power-on self-test)	Also stored in the microcode of the ROM, the POST is used to check the basic functionality of the router hardware and determines which interfaces are present.

Component	Description
ROM monitor	Again, stored in the microcode of the ROM, the ROM monitor is used for manufacturing, testing, and troubleshooting, as well as running a mini-IOS when the IOS in flash fails to load.
Mini-IOS	Called the RXBOOT, or bootloader, by Cisco, the mini-IOS is a small IOS in ROM that can be used to bring up an interface and load a Cisco IOS into flash memory. The mini-IOS can also perform a few other maintenance operations.
RAM (random access memory)	Used to hold packet buffers, ARP cache, routing tables, and the software and data structures that allow the router to function. Running-config is stored in RAM, and most routers expand the IOS from flash into RAM upon boot.
ROM (read-only memory)	Used to start and maintain the router. Holds the POST and the bootstrap program as well as the mini-IOS.
Flash memory	Stores the Cisco IOS by default. Flash memory is not erased when the router is reloaded or powered off. It is EEPROM (electronically erasable programmable read-only memory) created by Intel.
NVRAM (non-volatile RAM)	Used to hold the router and switch configuration. NVRAM is not erased when the router or switch is reloaded or powered off. Does not store an IOS. The configuration register is stored in NVRAM.
Configuration register	Used to control how the router boots up. This value can be found as the last line of the `show version` command output and by default is set to 0x2102, which tells the router to load the IOS from flash memory as well as to load the configuration from NVRAM.

The Router and Switch Boot Sequence

When a Cisco device boots up, it performs a series of steps, called the *boot sequence*, to test the hardware and load the necessary software. The boot sequence comprises the following steps, as shown in Figure 7.1:

1. The IOS device performs a power on self-test (POST), which tests the hardware to verify that all components of the device are present and operational. The POST takes stock of the different interfaces on the switch or router, and it's stored in and runs from read-only memory (ROM).
2. The bootstrap in ROM locates and loads the Cisco IOS software by executing programs responsible for finding where each IOS program is located. Once they are found, it then loads the proper files. By default, the IOS software is loaded from flash memory in all Cisco devices.

FIGURE 7.1 The IOS boot sequence

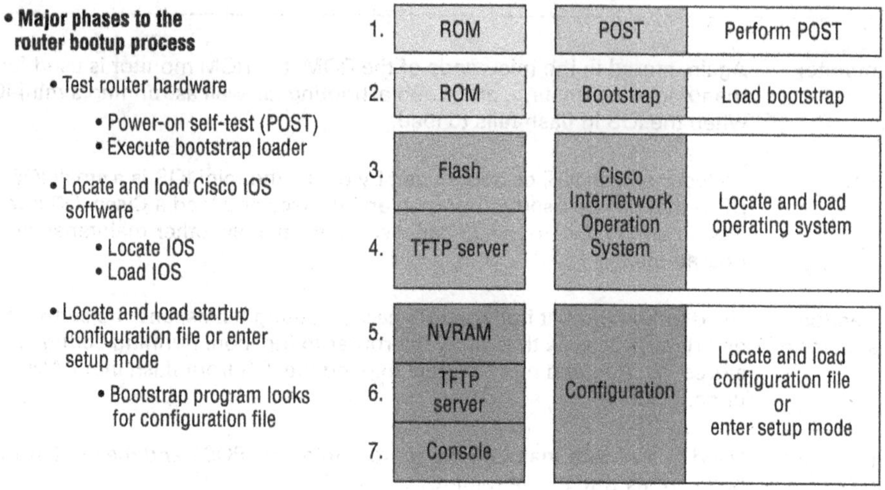
• Major phases to the router bootup process
• Test router hardware
• Power-on self-test (POST)
• Execute bootstrap loader
• Locate and load Cisco IOS software
• Locate IOS
• Load IOS
• Locate and load startup configuration file or enter setup mode
• Bootstrap program looks for configuration file
1.
ROM
POST
Perform POST
2.
ROM
Bootstrap
Load bootstrap
3.
Flash
4.
TFTP server
Cisco Internetwork Operation System
Locate and load operating system
5.
NVRAM
6.
TFTP server
7.
Console
Configuration
Locate and load configuration file or enter setup mode

3. The IOS software looks for a valid configuration file stored in NVRAM. This file is called startup-config and will be present only if an administrator has copied the running-config file into NVRAM.
4. If a startup-config file is found in NVRAM, the router or switch will copy it, place it in RAM, and name the file the running-config. The device will use this file to run, and the router/switch should now be operational.
5. If a startup-config file is not in NVRAM, the router will broadcast out any interface that detects carrier detect (CD) for a TFTP host looking for a configuration.
6. When that fails, as it typically does, it will start the setup mode configuration process. Most people won't even realize the router has attempted this process.
7. The router must be configured from the console.

TIP The default order of IOS loading from a Cisco device begins with flash, then a TFTP server, and, finally, ROM.

Backing Up and Restoring the Cisco Configuration

Any changes that you make to the configuration are stored in the running-config file. And if you don't enter a `copy run start` command after you make a change to running-config, that change will totally disappear if the device reboots or gets powered down. As always, backups are good, so you'll want to make another backup of the configuration information, just in case the router or switch completely dies on you. Even if your machine is healthy and happy, it's good to have a backup for reference and documentation reasons.

Next, I'll cover how to copy the configuration of a router to a TFTP server, as well as how to restore that configuration.

Backing Up the Cisco Configuration

To copy the configuration from an IOS device to a TFTP server, you can use either the `copy running-config tftp` command or the `copy startup-config tftp` command. Either command will back up the router configuration that's currently running in DRAM or one that's stored in NVRAM.

Verifying the Current Configuration

To verify the configuration in DRAM, use the `show running-config` command (`sh run`, for short):

```
Router#show running-config
Building configuration...
Current configuration : 877 bytes
!
version 15.0
```

The current configuration information indicates that the router is running version 15.0 of IOS.

Verifying the Stored Configuration

Next, you should check the configuration stored in NVRAM. To see this, use the `show startup-config` command (`sh start`, for short):

```
Router#sh start
Using 877 out of 724288 bytes
!
! Last configuration change at 04:49:14 UTC Fri Mar 7 2019
!
version 15.0
```

The first line shows how much room your backup configuration is taking up. Here, we can see that NVRAM is about 724 KB and that only 877 bytes of it are being used. But memory is easier to reveal via the `show version` command when you're using an ISR router.

If you're not sure that the files are the same and the running-config file is what you want to go with, then use the `copy running-config startup-config` command. This will help you ensure that both files are in fact the same. I'll guide you through this next.

Copying the Current Configuration to NVRAM

As shown in the following output, by copying running-config to NVRAM as a backup, you ensure that your running-config will always be reloaded if the router gets rebooted. Starting in the 12.0 IOS, you'll be prompted for the filename you want to use:

```
Router#copy running-config startup-config
Destination filename [startup-config]?[enter]
Building configuration...
[OK]
```

The reason the filename prompt appears is that there are now so many options you can use when using the copy command. Check it out:

```
Router#copy running-config ?
flash: Copy to flash: file system
ftp: Copy to ftp: file system
http: Copy to http: file system
https: Copy to https: file system
null: Copy to null: file system
nvram: Copy to nvram: file system
rcp: Copy to rcp: file system
running-config Update (merge with) current system configuration
scp: Copy to scp: file system
startup-config Copy to startup configuration
syslog: Copy to syslog: file system
system: Copy to system: file system
tftp: Copy to tftp: file system
tmpsys: Copy to tmpsys: file system
```

Copying the Configuration to a TFTP Server

Once the file is copied to NVRAM, you can make a second backup to a TFTP server by using the `copy running-config tftp` command, or `copy run tftp`, for short. I'm going to set the hostname to `Todd` before I run this command:

```
Todd#copy running-config tftp
Address or name of remote host []? 10.10.10.254
Destination filename [todd-confg]?
!!
577 bytes copied in 0.800 secs (970 bytes/sec)
```

If you have a hostname already configured, the command will automatically use the hostname plus the extension `-confg` as the name of the file.

Restoring the Cisco Configuration

What do you do if you've changed your running-config file and want to restore the configuration to the version in the startup-config file? The easiest way is to use the `copy startup-config running-config` command, or `copy start run`, for short. However, this will work only if you copied running-config into NVRAM before you made any changes! Of course, a reload of the device will work too. Understand that is a merge back, not a complete replace. (If you want to replace the configuration completely, then use the `config replace` command.).

If you did copy the configuration to a TFTP server as a second backup, you can restore the configuration using the `copy tftp running-config` command (`copy tftp run`, for short), or the `copy tftp startup-config` command (`copy tftp start`, for short), as shown in the following output. Just so you know, the old command we used to use for this is `config net`:

```
Todd#copy tftp running-config
Address or name of remote host []?10.10.10.254
Source filename []?todd-confg
Destination filename[running-config]?[enter]
Accessing tftp://10.10.10.254/todd-confg...
Loading todd-confg from 10.10.10.254 (via FastEthernet0/0):
!!
[OK - 677 bytes]
677 bytes copied in 9.212 secs (84 bytes/sec)
Todd#
*Mar 7 17:53:34.051: %SYS-7-CONFIG_I: Configured from
tftp://10.10.10.254/todd-confg by console
```

Note that the configuration file is an ASCII text file, meaning that before you copy the configuration stored on a TFTP server back to a router, you can make changes to the file with any text editor.

NOTE

Remember, when you copy or merge a configuration from a TFTP server to a freshly erased and rebooted router's RAM, the interfaces are shut down by default, and you must manually enable each interface with the `no shutdown` command.

Erasing the Configuration

To delete the startup-config file on a Cisco router or switch, use the command `erase startup-config`:

```
Todd#erase startup-config
Erasing the nvram filesystem will remove all configuration files!
Continue? [confirm][enter]
[OK]
Erase of nvram: complete
*Mar 7 17:55:20.405: %SYS-7-NV_BLOCK_INIT: Initialized the geometry of nvram
Todd#reload
System configuration has been modified. Save? [yes/no]:n
Proceed with reload? [confirm][enter]
*Mar 7 17:55:31.079: %SYS-5-RELOAD: Reload requested by console.
Reload Reason: Reload Command.
```

This command deletes the contents of NVRAM on the switch and router. If you type **reload** while in privileged mode and say no to saving changes, the switch or router will reload and come up into setup mode.

Configuring DHCP

We went over DHCP in Chapter 3, "TCP/IP," where I described how it works and what happens when there's a conflict. At this point, you're ready to learn how to configure DHCP on Cisco's IOS as well as how to configure a DHCP forwarder for when your hosts don't live on the same LAN as the DHCP server. Do you remember the four-step process hosts used to get an address from a server? If not, now would be a great time to head back to Chapter 3 and thoroughly review that before moving on with this.

To configure a DHCP server for your hosts, you need the following information, at a minimum:

Network and Mask for Each LAN Network ID, also called a scope. All addresses in a subnet can be leased to hosts by default.

Reserved/Excluded Addresses Reserved addresses for printers, servers, routers, etc. These addresses will not be handed out to hosts. I usually reserve the first address of each subnet for the router, but you don't have to do this.

Default Router This is the router's address for each LAN.

DNS Address A list of DNS server addresses is provided to hosts so they can resolve names.

Here are your configuration steps:

1. Exclude the addresses you want to reserve. You do this step first because as soon as you set a network ID, the DHCP service will start responding to client requests.
2. Create a pool for each LAN using a unique name.
3. Choose the network ID and subnet mask for the DHCP pool that the server will use to provide addresses to hosts.
4. Add the address used for the default gateway of the subnet.
5. Provide the DNS server address(es).
6. If you don't want to use the default lease time of 24 hours, you need to set the lease time in days, hours, and minutes.

I'm going to configure the switch in Figure 7.2 to be the DHCP server for the Sales_Wireless LAN.

FIGURE 7.2 Switch S1 is the DHCP server.

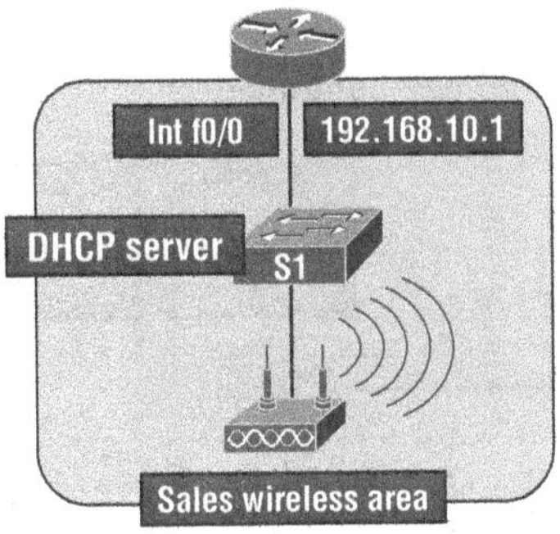

Note that this configuration could just as easily have been placed on the router in Figure 7.2. Here's how we'll configure DHCP using the 192.168.10.0/24 network ID:

```
Switch(config)#ip dhcp excluded-address 192.168.10.1 192.168.10.10
Switch(config)#ip dhcp pool Sales_Wireless
Switch(dhcp-config)#network 192.168.10.0 255.255.255.0
Switch(dhcp-config)#default-router 192.168.10.1
Switch(dhcp-config)#dns-server 4.4.4.4
Switch(dhcp-config)#lease 3 12 17
Switch(dhcp-config)#option 66 ascii tftp.lammle.com
```

First, you can see that I reserved 10 addresses in the range for the router, servers, and printers, etc. I then created the pool named Sales_Wireless, added the default gateway and DNS server, and set the lease to 3 days, 12 hours, and 17 minutes. The time I set the lease to isn't really significant because I just set it that way for demonstration purposes. Lastly,

I provided an example on how you would set option 66, which is sending a TFTP server address to a DHCP client. This is typically used for VoIP phones, or auto installs, and needs to be listed as a FQDN. Pretty straightforward, right? The switch will now respond to DHCP client requests.

But what happens if we need to provide an IP address from a DHCP server to a host that's not in our broadcast domain, or if we want to receive a DHCP address for a client from a remote server? Let's find out.

DHCP Relay

If you need to provide addresses from a DHCP server to hosts that aren't on the same LAN as the DHCP server, you can configure your router interface to relay or forward the DHCP client requests, as shown in Figure 7.3. If you don't provide this service, your router would receive the DHCP client broadcast, promptly discard it, and the remote host would never receive an address—unless you added a DHCP server on every broadcast domain!

Let's take a look at Figure 7.3 and how we would typically configure DHCP service in today's networks.

FIGURE 7.3 The DHCP `ip helper` command

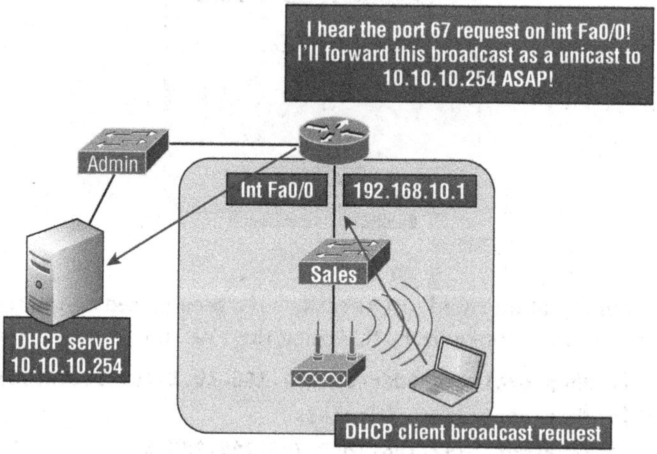

So, we know that because the hosts off the router don't have access to a DHCP server, the router will simply drop their client request broadcast messages by default. To solve this problem, we can configure the Fa0/0 interface of the router to accept the DHCP client requests and forward them to the DHCP server as follows:

```
Router#config t
Router(config)#interface Fa0/0
Router(config-if)#ip helper-address 10.10.10.254
```

Now, I know that was a pretty simple example, and there are definitely other ways to configure the relay, but rest assured, I've covered the objectives for you. Also, I want you to know that the `ip helper-address` command forwards more than just DHCP client requests, so be sure to research the command before you implement it! Now that I've demonstrated how to create the DHCP service, let's take a minute to verify DHCP before moving on to NTP.

Verifying DHCP on Cisco IOS

There are some really useful verification commands to use on a Cisco IOS device for monitoring and verifying a DHCP service. You'll get to see the output for these commands when I build the network in Chapter 9, "IP Routing," and add DHCP to the two remote LANs. For now, I just want you to begin getting familiar with them, so here's a list of four very important commands and what they do:

`show ip dhcp binding` Lists state information about each IP address currently leased to a client.

`show ip dhcp pool [`*`poolname`*`]` Lists the configured range of IP addresses, plus statistics for the number of currently leased addresses and the high watermark for leases from each pool.

`show ip dhcp server statistics` Lists DHCP server statistics—a lot of them.

`show ip dhcp conflict` If someone statically configures an IP address on a LAN and the DHCP server hands out that same address, you'll end up with a duplicate address. This isn't good, which is why this command is so helpful!

Using Telnet

As part of the TCP/IP protocol suite, *Telnet* is a virtual terminal protocol that enables you to make connections to remote devices, gather information, and run programs.

After your routers and switches are configured, you can use the Telnet program to reconfigure and/or check up on them without using a console cable. You run the Telnet program by typing **`telnet`** from any command prompt (Windows or Cisco), but you need to have VTY passwords set on the IOS devices for this to work.

Remember, you can't use CDP to gather information about routers and switches that aren't directly connected to your device. But you can use the Telnet application to connect to your neighbor devices and then run CDP on those remote devices to get information on them.

You can issue the `telnet` command from any router or switch prompt. In the following code, I'm trying to telnet from switch 1 to switch 3:

```
SW-1#telnet 10.100.128.8
Trying 10.100.128.8 ..., Open

Password required, but none set

[Connection to 10.100.128.8 closed by foreign host]
```

Oops! Clearly, I didn't set my passwords—how embarrassing! Remember that the VTY ports are configured as `login` by default, meaning that you have to either set the VTY passwords or use the no `login` command. If you need to review the process of setting passwords, take a quick look back in Chapter 6, "Cisco's Internetworking Operating System (IOS)."

NOTE If you can't telnet into a device, it could be that the password on the remote device hasn't been set. It's also quite possible that an access control list is filtering the Telnet session.

On a Cisco device, you don't need to use the `telnet` command; you can just type in an IP address from a command prompt, and the router will assume that you want to telnet to the device. Here's how that looks using just the IP address:

```
SW-1#10.100.128.8
Trying 10.100.128.8... Open
Password required, but none set
[Connection to 10.100.128.8 closed by foreign host]
SW-1#
```

Now would be a great time to set those VTY passwords on the SW-3 that I want to telnet into. Here's what I did on the switch named SW-3:

```
SW-3(config)#line vty 0 15
SW-3(config-line)#login
SW-3(config-line)#password telnet
SW-3(config-line)#login
SW-3(config-line)#^Z
```

Now, let's try this again. This time, I'm connecting to SW-3 from the SW-1 console:

```
SW-1#10.100.128.8
Trying 10.100.128.8 ... Open
User Access Verification
Password:
SW-3>
```

Remember that the VTY password is the user-mode password, not the enable-mode password. Watch what happens when I try to go into privileged mode after telnetting into the switch:

```
SW-3>en
% No password set
SW-3>
```

It's totally slamming the door in my face, which happens to be a really nice security feature! After all, you don't want just anyone telnetting into your device and typing the `enable` command to get into privileged mode now, do you? You've got to set your enable-mode password or enable secret password to use Telnet to configure remote devices.

NOTE: When telnetting into a remote device, you won't see console messages by default. For example, you will not see debugging output. To allow console messages to be sent to your Telnet session, use the `terminal monitor` command and `terminal no monitor` to disable them.

In the next group of examples, I'll show you how to telnet into multiple devices simultaneously as well as how to use hostnames instead of IP addresses.

Telnetting into Multiple Devices Simultaneously

If you telnet to a router or switch, you can end the connection by typing **`exit`** at any time. But what if you want to keep your connection to a remote device going while still coming back to your original router console? To do that, you can press the Ctrl+Shift+6 key combination, release it, and then press X.

Here's an example of connecting to multiple devices from my SW-1 console:

```
SW-1#10.100.128.8
Trying 10.100.128.8... Open
User Access Verification
Password:
SW-3>Ctrl+Shift+6
SW-1#
```

You can see that I telnetted to SW-1 and then typed the password to enter user mode. Next, I pressed Ctrl+Shift+6, then X, but you won't see any of that because it doesn't show on the screen output. Notice that my command prompt now has me back at the SW-1 switch.

Now let's run through some verification commands.

Checking Telnet Connections

If you want to view the connections from your router or switch to a remote device, just use the `show sessions` command. In this case, I've telnetted into both the SW-3 and SW-2 switches from SW1:

```
SW-1#sh sessions
Conn Host Address Byte Idle Conn Name
1 10.100.128.9 10.100.128.9 0 10.100.128.9
* 2 10.100.128.8 10.100.128.8 0 10.100.128.8
SW-1#
```

See that asterisk (*) next to connection 2? It means that session 2 was the last session I connected to. You can return to your last session by pressing Enter twice. You can also return to any session by typing the number of the connection and then Enter.

Checking Telnet Users

You can reveal all active consoles and VTY ports in use on your router with the `show users` command:

```
SW-1#sh users
Line User Host(s) Idle Location
* 0 con 0 10.100.128.9 00:00:01
10.100.128.8 00:01:07
```

In the command's output, `con` represents the local console, and we can see that the console session is connected to two remote IP addresses—in other words, two devices.

Closing Telnet Sessions

You can end Telnet sessions a few different ways. Typing `exit` or `disconnect` are probably the two quickest and easiest.

To end a session from a remote device, use the `exit` command:

```
SW-3>exit
[Connection to 10.100.128.8 closed by foreign host]
SW-1#
```

To end a session from a local device, use the `disconnect` command:

```
SW-1#sh session
Conn Host Address Byte Idle Conn Name
*2 10.100.128.9 10.100.128.9 0 10.100.128.9
SW-1#disconnect ?
<2-2> The number of an active network connection
```

```
qdm Disconnect QDM web-based clients
ssh Disconnect an active SSH connection
SW-1#disconnect 2
Closing connection to 10.100.128.9 [confirm][enter]
```

In this example, I used session number 2 because that was the connection I wanted to conclude. As demonstrated, you can use the `show sessions` command to see the connection number.

Resolving Hostnames

If you want to use a hostname instead of an IP address to connect to a remote device, the device that you're using to make the connection must be able to translate the hostname to an IP address.

There are two ways to resolve hostnames to IP addresses. The first is by building a host table on each router, and the second is to build a Domain Name System (DNS) server. The latter method is similar to creating a dynamic host table, assuming that you're dealing with dynamic DNS.

Building a Host Table

An important factor to remember is that although a host table provides name resolution, it does so only on the specific router that it was built on. The command you use to build a host table on a router looks like this:

```
ip host host_name [tcp_port_number] ip_address
```

The default is TCP port number 23, but you can create a session using Telnet with a different TCP port number if you want. You can also assign up to eight IP addresses to a hostname.

Here's how I configured a host table on the SW-1 switch with two entries to resolve the names for the SW-2 and SW-3:

```
SW-1#config t
SW-1(config)#ip host SW-2 ?
<0-75537> Default telnet port number
A.B.C.D Host IP address
additional Append addresses
SW-1(config)#ip host SW-2 10.100.128.9
SW-1(config)#ip host SW-3 10.100.128.8
```

Notice that I can just keep adding IP addresses to reference a unique host, one after another. To view the newly built host table, I'll just use the `show hosts` command:

```
SW-1(config)#do sho hosts
Default domain is not set
```

```
Name/address lookup uses domain service
Name servers are 255.255.255.255
Codes: u - unknown, e - expired, * - OK, ? - revalidate
t - temporary, p - permanent
Host Port Flags Age Type Address(es)
SW-3 None (perm, OK) 0 IP 10.100.128.8
SW-2 None (perm, OK) 0 IP 10.100.128.9
```

In this output, you can see the two hostnames plus their associated IP addresses. The `perm` in the `Flags` column means that the entry has been manually configured. If it read `temp`, it would depict an entry that was resolved by DNS.

> **NOTE** The show `hosts` command provides information on temporary DNS entries and permanent name-to-address mappings created using the `ip host` command.

To verify that the host table resolves names, try typing the hostnames at a router prompt. Remember that if you don't specify the command, the router will assume you want to telnet.

In the next example, I'll use the hostnames to telnet into the remote devices and press Ctrl+Shift+6 and then X to return to the main console of the SW-1 router:

```
SW-1#sw-3
Trying SW-3 (10.100.128.8)... Open
User Access Verification
Password:
SW-3> Ctrl+Shift+6
SW-1#
```

It worked! I successfully used entries in the host table to create a session to the SW-3 device by using the name to telnet into it. Just so you know, names in the host table are not case-sensitive.

Notice that the entries in the following `show sessions` output now display the hostnames and IP addresses instead of just the IP addresses:

```
SW-1#sh sessions
Conn Host Address Byte Idle Conn Name
1 SW-3 10.100.128.8 0 1 SW-3
* 2 SW-2 10.100.128.9 0 1 SW-2
SW-1#
```

If you want to remove a hostname from the table, all you need to do is use the `no ip host` command:

```
SW-1(config)#no ip host SW-3
```

The drawback to using this host table method is that you must create a host table on each router in order to be able to resolve names. So clearly, if you have a whole bunch of routers and want to resolve names, using DNS is a much better option.

Using DNS to Resolve Names

So, if you have a lot of devices, you don't want to create a host table in each one of them unless you've also got a lot of time to waste! Instead, use a DNS server to resolve hostnames.

Anytime a Cisco device receives a command it doesn't understand, it will try to resolve it through DNS by default. Watch what happens when I type the special command `todd` at a Cisco router prompt:

```
SW-1#todd
Translating "todd"...domain server (255.255.255.255)
% Unknown command or computer name, or unable to find
computer address
SW-1#
```

Because it doesn't know my name or the command I'm trying to type, it tries to resolve this through DNS. This is really annoying for two reasons: first, because it doesn't know my name <grin>, and second, because I need to hang around and wait for the name lookup to time out. You can get around this and prevent a time-consuming DNS lookup by using the `no ip domain-lookup` command on your router from global configuration mode.

If you have a DNS server on your network, you'll need to add a few commands to make DNS name resolution work well for you:

- The first command is `ip domain-lookup`, which is turned on by default. It needs to be entered only if you previously turned it off with the `no ip domain-lookup` command. The command can be used without the hyphen as well, with the syntax `ip domain lookup`.
- The second command is `ip name-server`. This sets the IP address of the DNS server. You can enter the IP addresses of up to six servers.
- The last command is `ip domain-name`. Although this command is optional, you want to set it because it appends the domain name to the hostname you type in. Since DNS uses a fully qualified domain name (FQDN) system, you must have a second-level DNS name, in the form *`domain.com`*.

Here's an example using these three commands:

```
SW-1#config t
SW-1(config)#ip domain-lookup
SW-1(config)#ip name-server ?
A.B.C.D Domain server IP address (maximum of 5)
SW-1(config)#ip name-server 4.4.4.4
SW-1(config)#ip domain-name lammle.com
SW-1(config)#^Z
```

After the DNS configurations have been set, you can test the DNS server by using a hostname to ping or telnet into a device, as follows:

```
SW-1#ping SW-3
Translating "SW-3"...domain server (4.4.4.4) [OK]
Type escape sequence to abort.
Sending 5, 100-byte ICMP Echos to 10.100.128.8, timeout is
2 seconds:
!!!!!
Success rate is 100 percent (5/5), round-trip min/avg/max
= 28/31/32 ms
```

Notice that the router uses the DNS server to resolve the name.

After a name is resolved using DNS, use the `show hosts` command to verify that the device cached this information in the host table. If I hadn't used the `ip domain-name lammle.com` command, I would have needed to type in `ping sw-3.lammle.com`, which is kind of a hassle.

Should You Use a Host Table or a DNS Server?

Karen has finally finished mapping her network via CDP, and the hospital's staff is now much happier. But Karen is still having a difficult time administering the network because she has to look at the network drawing to find an IP address every time she needs to telnet to a remote router.

Karen thought about putting host tables on each router, but with literally hundreds of routers, this is a daunting task and not the best solution. What should she do?

Most networks have a DNS server now anyway, so adding a hundred or so hostnames into it would be much easier—certainly better than adding these hostnames to each and every router! She can just add the three commands on each router and voilà—she's resolving names.

Using a DNS server makes it easy to update any old entries, too. Remember, for even one little change, her alternative would be to go to each and every router to manually update its table if she's using static host tables.

Keep in mind that this has nothing to do with name resolution on the network and nothing to do with what a host on the network is trying to accomplish. You only use this method when you're trying to resolve names from the router console.

Checking Network Connectivity and Troubleshooting

You can use the ping and traceroute commands to test connectivity to remote devices. Both commands can be used with many protocols, not just IP. But don't forget that the show ip route command is a great troubleshooting command for verifying your routing table, and the show interfaces command will reveal the status of each interface.

I'm not going to get into the show interfaces commands here because we've already been over that in Chapter 5, "Troubleshooting IP Addressing." However, I am going to go over the debug command and the show processes command, both of which come in very handy when you need to troubleshoot a router.

Using the *ping* Command

So far, you've seen a lot of examples of pinging devices to test IP connectivity and name resolution using the DNS server. To see all the different protocols that you can use with the Ping program, type **ping** ?:

```
SW-1#ping ?
WORD Ping destination address or hostname
clns CLNS echo
ip IP echo
ipv6 IPv6 echo
tag Tag encapsulated IP echo
<cr>
```

The ping output displays the minimum, average, and maximum times it takes for a ping packet to find a specified system and return. Here's an example:

```
SW-1#ping SW-3
Translating "SW-3"...domain server (4.4.4.4) [OK]
Type escape sequence to abort.
Sending 5, 100-byte ICMP Echos to 10.100.128.8, timeout is
2 seconds:
!!!!!
Success rate is 100 percent (5/5), round-trip min/avg/max
= 28/31/32 ms
```

This output tells us that the DNS server was used to resolve the name, and the device was pinged in a minimum of 28 ms (milliseconds), an average of 31 ms, and up to 32 ms. This network has some latency!

NOTE: The ping command can be used in user and privileged mode, but not in configuration mode!

Using the *traceroute* Command

Traceroute—the `traceroute` command, or `trace`, for short—shows the path a packet takes to get to a remote device. It uses time to live (TTL), time-outs, and ICMP error messages to outline the path a packet takes through an internetwork to arrive at a remote host.

The `trace` command, which you can deploy from either user mode or privileged mode, allows you to determine which router in the path to an unreachable network host should be looked at more closely as the probable cause of your network's failure.

To see the protocols that you can use with the `traceroute` command, type **traceroute ?**:

```
SW-1#traceroute ?
WORD Trace route to destination address or hostname
appletalk AppleTalk Trace
clns ISO CLNS Trace
ip IP Trace
ipv6 IPv6 Trace
ipx IPX Trace
mac Trace Layer2 path between 2 endpoints
oldvines Vines Trace (Cisco)
vines Vines Trace (Banyan)
<cr>
```

The `traceroute` command shows the hop or hops that a packet traverses on its way to a remote device.

TIP: Do not get confused! You can't use the `tracert` command; that's a Windows command. For a router, use the `traceroute` command!

Here's an example of using `tracert` on a Windows prompt—notice that the command is `tracert`, not `traceroute`:

```
C:\>tracert www.whitehouse.gov
Tracing route to a1289.g.akamai.net [79.8.201.107]
over a maximum of 30 hops:
1 * * * Request timed out.
2 73 ms 71 ms 73 ms hlrn-dsl-gw17-207.hlrn.qwest.net [207.227.112.207]
3 73 ms 77 ms 74 ms hlrn-agw1.inet.qwest.net [71.217.188.113]
4 74 ms 73 ms 74 ms hlr-core-01.inet.qwest.net [207.171.273.97]
```

```
5 74 ms 73 ms 74 ms apa-cntr-01.inet.qwest.net [207.171.273.27]
6 74 ms 73 ms 73 ms 73.170.170.34
7 74 ms 74 ms 73 ms www.whitehouse.gov [79.8.201.107]
Trace complete.
```

Let's move on and talk about how to troubleshoot your network using the `debug` command.

Debugging

`Debug` is a useful troubleshooting command that's available from the privileged exec mode of Cisco IOS. It's used to display information about various router operations and the related traffic generated or received by the router, plus any error messages.

Even though `debug` is a helpful, informative tool, there are a few important facts that you need to know about it. Debugging is regarded as a very high-overhead task because it can consume a huge amount of resources, and the router is forced to process-switch the packets being debugged. So, you don't just use `debug` as a monitoring tool—it's meant to be used for a short period of time and only as a troubleshooting tool. It's highly useful for discovering some significant facts about both working and faulty software and/or hardware components, but remember to limit its use as the beneficial troubleshooting tool it's designed to be.

Because debugging output takes priority over other network traffic, and because the `debug all` command generates more output than any other `debug` command, it can severely diminish the router's performance—even render it unusable! Therefore, it's almost always best to use more specific `debug` commands.

As you can see from the following output, you can't enable debugging from user mode, only privileged mode:

```
SW-1>debug ?
% Unrecognized command
SW-1>en
SW-1#debug ?
aaa AAA Authentication, Authorization and Accounting
access-expression Boolean access expression
adjacency adjacency
aim Attachment Information Manager
all Enable all debugging
archive debug archive commands
arp IP ARP and HP Probe transactions
authentication Auth Manager debugging
auto Debug Automation
beep BEEP debugging
bgp BGP information
bing Bing(d) debugging
```

```
call-admission Call admission control
cca CCA activity
cdp CDP information
cef CEF address family independent operations
cfgdiff debug cfgdiff commands
cisp CISP debugging
clns CLNS information
cluster Cluster information
cmdhd Command Handler
cns CNS agents
condition Condition
configuration Debug Configuration behavior
[output cut]
```

If you've got the freedom to pretty much take out a router or switch and you really want to have some fun with debugging, use the `debug all` command:

```
Sw-1#debug all
This may severely impact network performance. Continue? (yes/[no]):yes
All possible debugging has been turned on
```

At this point, my switch overloaded and crashed, and I had to reboot it. Try this on your switch at work and see if you get the same results. Just kidding!

To disable debugging on a router, just use the command no in front of the `debug` command:

```
SW-1#no debug all
```

I typically just use the `undebug all` command since it is so easy when using the shortcut:

```
SW-1#un all
```

Remember that instead of using the `debug all` command, it's usually a much better idea to use specific commands—and only for short periods of time. Here's an example:

```
S1#debug ip icmp
ICMP packet debugging is on
S1#ping 192.168.10.17
Type escape sequence to abort.
Sending 5, 100-byte ICMP Echos to 192.178.10.17, timeout is 2 seconds:
!!!!!
Success rate is 100 percent (7/7), round-trip min/avg/max = 1/1/1 ms
S1#
1w4d: ICMP: echo reply sent, src 192.168.10.17, dst 192.168.10.17
1w4d: ICMP: echo reply rcvd, src 192.168.10.17, dst 192.168.10.17
```

```
1w4d: ICMP: echo reply sent, src 192.168.10.17, dst 192.168.10.17
1w4d: ICMP: echo reply rcvd, src 192.168.10.17, dst 192.168.10.17
1w4d: ICMP: echo reply sent, src 192.168.10.17, dst 192.168.10.17
1w4d: ICMP: echo reply rcvd, src 192.168.10.17, dst 192.168.10.17
1w4d: ICMP: echo reply sent, src 192.168.10.17, dst 192.168.10.17
1w4d: ICMP: echo reply rcvd, src 192.168.10.17, dst 192.168.10.17
1w4d: ICMP: echo reply sent, src 192.168.10.17, dst 192.168.10.17
1w4d: ICMP: echo reply rcvd, src 192.168.10.17, dst 192.168.10.17
SW-1#un all
```

I'm sure you can see that the `debug` command is a powerful one. I'm also sure you realize that before you use any of the debugging commands, make sure to check the CPU utilization capacity of your router. This is important because, in most cases, you don't want to negatively impact the device's ability to process the packets on your internetwork. You can determine a specific router's CPU utilization information by using the `show processes` command.

NOTE Remember, when you telnet into a remote device, you will not see console messages by default! For example, you will not see debugging output. To allow console messages to be sent to your Telnet session, use the `terminal monitor` command.

Using the *show processes* Command

As previously mentioned, you need to be careful when using the `debug` command on your devices. If your router's CPU utilization is consistently at 70 percent or more, it's probably not a good idea to type in the `debug all` command, unless you want to see what a router looks like when it crashes!

What other approaches can you use? Well, the `show processes` (or `show processes cpu`) is a good tool for determining a given router's CPU utilization. It'll give you a list of active processes along with their corresponding process ID, priority, scheduler test (status), CPU time used, number of times invoked, and so on—a lot of great stuff! Plus, this command is very handy when you want to evaluate your router's performance and CPU utilization and are otherwise tempted to reach for the `debug` command!

Okay, what do you see in the following output? The first line shows the CPU utilization output for the last 7 seconds, 1 minute, and 7 minutes. The output provides 7%/0% in front of the CPU utilization for the last 7 seconds: the first number equals the total utilization, and the second number indicates the utilization due to interrupt routines. Take a look:

```
SW-1#sh processes
CPU utilization for five seconds: 7%/0%; one minute: 7%; five minutes: 8%
PID QTy PC Runtime(ms) Invoked uSecs Stacks TTY Process
1 Cwe 29EBC78 0 22 0 7237/7000 0 Chunk Manager
```

```
2 Csp 1B9CF10 241 207881 1 2717/3000 0 Load Meter
3 Hwe 1F108D0 0 1 0 8778/9000 0 Connection Mgr
4 Lst 29FA7C4 9437909 474027 20787 7740/7000 0 Check heaps
5 Cwe 2A02478 0 2 0 7477/7000 0 Pool Manager
6 Mst 1E98F04 0 2 0 7488/7000 0 Timers
7 Hwe 13EB1B4 3787 101399 37 7740/7000 0 Net Input
8 Mwe 13BCD84 0 1 0 23778/24000 0 Crash writer
9 Mwe 1C791B4 4347 73791 80 4897/7000 0 ARP Input
10 Lwe 1DA1704 0 1 0 7770/7000 0 CEF MIB API
11 Lwe 1E77ACC 0 1 0 7774/7000 0 AAA_SERVER_DEADT
12 Mwe 1E7F980 0 2 0 7477/7000 0 AAA high-capacit
13 Mwe 1F77F24 0 1 0 11732/12000 0 Policy Manager [output cut]
```

Basically, the output from the `show processes` command reveals that the router is happily able to process debugging commands without being overloaded—nice!

Summary

In this chapter, you learned how Cisco routers are configured and how to manage those configurations.

You also learned about the internal components of a router, including ROM, RAM, NVRAM, and flash.

Next, you found out how to back up and restore the configuration of a Cisco router and switch.

You also learned how to use CDP and Telnet to gather information about remote devices. Finally, you discovered how to resolve hostnames and use the `ping` and `trace` commands to test network connectivity, as well as how to use the `debug` and `show processes` commands.

Exam Essentials

Define the Cisco router components. Describe the functions of the bootstrap, POST, ROM monitor, mini-IOS, RAM, ROM, flash memory, NVRAM, and the configuration register.

Identify the steps in the router boot sequence. The steps in the boot sequence are POST, loading the IOS, and copying the startup configuration from NVRAM to RAM.

Save the configuration of a router or switch. There are a couple of ways to do this, but the most common method, as well as the most tested, is to use the `copy running-config startup-config` command.

Erase the configuration of a router or switch. Type the privileged-mode command `erase startup-config` and reload the router.

Understand the various levels of syslog. It's rather simple to configure syslog; however, there are a number of options to remember for the exam. To configure basic syslog with `debugging` as the default level, it's just this one command:

```
SF(config)#logging 172.16.10.1
```

However, you must remember all eight options:

```
SF(config)#logging trap ?
  <0-7>          Logging severity level
  alerts         Immediate action needed           (severity=1)
  critical       Critical conditions               (severity=2)
  debugging      Debugging messages                (severity=7)
  emergencies    System is unusable                (severity=0)
  errors         Error conditions                  (severity=3)
  informational  Informational messages            (severity=6)
  notifications  Normal but significant conditions (severity=5)
  warnings       Warning conditions                (severity=4)
  <cr>
```

Understand how to configure NTP. It's pretty simple to configure NTP, just like it was syslog, but you don't have to remember very many options! You simply need to tell the syslog to mark the time and date and enable NTP:

```
SF(config)#service timestamps log datetime msec
SF(config)#ntp server 172.16.10.1 version 4
```

Describe the value of CDP and LLDP. Cisco Discovery Protocol can be used to help document and troubleshoot your network. LLDP is a nonproprietary protocol that can provide the same information as CDP.

List the information provided by the output of the *show cdp neighbors* command. The `show cdp neighbors` command provides the following information: device ID, local interface, hold time, capability, platform, and port ID (remote interface).

Understand how to establish a Telnet session with multiple routers simultaneously. If you telnet to a router or switch, you can end the connection by typing **`exit`** at any time. If you want to keep your connection to a remote device but still come back to your original router console, you can press the Ctrl+Shift+6 key combination, release it, and then press X.

Identify current Telnet sessions. The command `show sessions` provides you with information about all the currently active sessions your router has with other routers.

Build a static host table on a router. By using the global configuration command `ip host` *`host_name ip_address`*, you can build a static host table on your router. You can apply multiple IP addresses against the same host entry.

Verify the host table on a router. You can verify the host table with the `show hosts` command.

Describe the function of the `ping` command. Packet Internet Groper (`ping`) uses ICMP echo requests and ICMP echo replies to verify an active IP address on a network.

Ping a valid host ID from the correct prompt. You can ping an IP address from a router's user mode or privileged mode but not from configuration mode, unless you use the do command. You must ping a valid address, such as 1.1.1.1.

Written Labs

You can find the answers to these labs in Appendix A, "Answers to the Written Labs."

In this section, you'll complete the following labs to make sure you understand the information and concepts contained within them:

Lab 7.1: IOS Management

Lab 7.2: Router Memory

Written Lab 7.1: IOS Management

Write the answers to the following questions:

1. What is the command to copy the startup-config file to DRAM?
2. What command can you use to see the neighbor router's IP address from your router prompt?
3. What command can you use to see the hostname, local interface, platform, and remote port of a neighbor router?
4. What keystrokes can you use to telnet into multiple devices simultaneously?
5. What command will show you your active Telnet connections to neighbor and remote devices?
6. What command can you use to merge a backup configuration with the configuration in RAM?
7. What protocol can be used on a network to synchronize clock and date information?
8. What command is used by a router to forward a DHCP client request to a remote DHCP server?

9. What command enables your switch or router to receive clock and date information and synchronize with the NTP server?
10. Which NTP verification command will show the reference master for the client?

Written Lab 7.2: Router Memory

Identify the location in a router where each of the following files is stored by default.

1. Cisco IOS
2. Bootstrap
3. Startup configuration
4. POST routine
5. Running configuration
6. ARP cache
7. Mini-IOS
8. ROM monitor
9. Routing tables
10. Packet buffers

Review Questions

You can find the answers to these questions in Appendix B, "Answers to the Review Questions."

> **NOTE** The following questions are designed to test your understanding of this chapter's material. For more information on how to get additional questions, please see `www.lammle.com/ccna`.

1. Which of the following is a standards-based protocol that provides dynamic network discovery?
   - **A.** DHCP
   - **B.** LLDP
   - **C.** DDNS
   - **D.** SSTP
   - **E.** CDP
2. Which command can be used to determine a router's CPU utilization?
   - **A.** `show version`
   - **B.** `show controllers`
   - **C.** `show processes cpu`
   - **D.** `show memory`
3. You are troubleshooting a connectivity problem in your corporate network and want to isolate the problem. You suspect that a router on the route to an unreachable network is at fault. What IOS `user exec` command should you issue?
   - **A.** `Router>ping`
   - **B.** `Router>trace`
   - **C.** `Router>show ip route`
   - **D.** `Router>show interface`
   - **E.** `Router>show cdp neighbors`
4. You copy a configuration from a network host to a router's RAM. The configuration looks correct, yet it is not working at all. What could be the problem?
   - **A.** You copied the wrong configuration into RAM.
   - **B.** You copied the configuration into flash memory instead.
   - **C.** The copy did not override the `shutdown` command in the running-config file.
   - **D.** The IOS became corrupted after the `copy` command was initiated.

5. In the following command, what does the IP address 10.10.10.254 refer to?

```
Router#config t
Router(config)#interface fa0/0
Router(config-if)#ip helper-address 10.10.10.254
```

A. The IP address of the ingress interface on the router

B. The IP address of the egress interface on the router

C. The IP address of the next hop on the path to the DHCP server

D. The IP address of the DHCP server

6. The corporate office sends you a new router to connect, but when you connect the console cable, you see that there is already a configuration on the router. What should be done before a new configuration is entered in the router?

A. RAM should be erased and the router restarted.

B. Flash should be erased and the router restarted.

C. NVRAM should be erased and the router restarted.

D. The new configuration should be entered and saved.

7. What command can you use to determine the IP address of a directly connected neighbor?

A. `show cdp`

B. `show cdp neighbors`

C. `show cdp neighbors detail`

D. `show neighbor detail`

8. According to the following output, what interface does SW-2 use to connect to SW-3?

```
SW-3#sh cdp neighbors
Capability Codes: R - Router, T - Trans Bridge, B - Source Route BridgeS -
Switch, H - Host, I - IGMP, r - Repeater, P - Phone, D - Remote, C - CVTA,
M - Two-port Mac Relay Device ID
Local Intrfce     Holdtme    Capability  Platform  Port ID
SW-1    Fas 0/1     170           S I     WS-C3560- Fas 0/15
SW-1    Fas 0/2     170           S I     WS-C3560- Fas 0/16
SW-2    Fas 0/5     162           S I     WS-C3560- Fas 0/2
```

A. Fas 0/1

B. Fas 0/16

C. Fas 0/2

D. Fas 0/5

9. Which of the following commands enables syslog on a Cisco device with `debugging` as the level?

A. `syslog 172.16.10.1`

B. `logging 172.16.10.1`

C. `remote console 172.16.10.1 syslog debugging`

D. `transmit console messages level 7 172.16.10.1`

10. You save the configuration on a router with the `copy running-config startup-config` command and reboot the router. However, the router comes up with a blank configuration. What could be the problem?
    A. You didn't boot the router with the correct command.
    B. NVRAM is corrupted.
    C. The configuration register setting is incorrect.
    D. The newly upgraded IOS is not compatible with the hardware of the router.
    E. The configuration you saved is not compatible with the hardware.
11. If you want to have more than one Telnet session open at the same time, what keystroke combination would you use?
    A. Tab+spacebar
    B. Ctrl+X, then 6
    C. Ctrl+Shift+X, then 6
    D. Ctrl+Shift+6, then X
12. You are unsuccessful in telnetting into a remote device from your switch, but you could telnet to the router earlier. However, you can still ping the remote device. What could be the problem? (Choose two.)
    A. The IP addresses are incorrect.
    B. The access control list is filtering Telnet.
    C. There is a defective serial cable.
    D. The VTY password is missing.
13. What information is displayed by the `show hosts` command? (Choose two.)
    A. Temporary DNS entries
    B. The names of the routers created using the `hostname` command
    C. The IP addresses of workstations allowed to access the router
    D. Permanent name-to-address mappings created using the `ip host` command
    E. The length of time a host has been connected to the router via Telnet
14. Which of the following commands can be used to check LAN connectivity problems on a switch? (Choose three.)
    A. `show interfaces`
    B. `show ip route`
    C. `tracert`
    D. `ping`
    E. `dns lookups`

15. What is the default syslog facility level?
    - A. local4
    - B. local5
    - C. local6
    - D. local7

16. You telnet into a remote device and type `debug ip icmp`, but no output from the `debug` command is seen. What could be the problem?
    - A. You must type the `show ip icmp` command first.
    - B. The IP addressing on the network is incorrect.
    - C. You must use the `terminal monitor` command.
    - D. Debug output is sent only to the console.

17. Which of the following statements about syslog utilization are true? (Choose three.)
    - A. Utilizing syslog improves network performance.
    - B. The syslog server automatically notifies the network administrator of network problems.
    - C. A syslog server provides the storage space necessary to store log files without using router disk space.
    - D. There are more syslog messages available within Cisco IOS than there are comparable SNMP trap messages.
    - E. Enabling syslog on a router automatically enables NTP for accurate time stamping.
    - F. A syslog server helps in aggregation of logs and alerts.

18. You need to gather the IP address of a remote switch that is located in Hawaii. What can you do to find the address?
    - A. Fly to Hawaii, console into the switch, and then relax and have a drink with an umbrella in it.
    - B. Issue the `show ip route` command on the router connected to the switch.
    - C. Issue the `show cdp neighbor` command on the router connected to the switch.
    - D. Issue the `show ip arp` command on the router connected to the switch.
    - E. Issue the `show cdp neighbors detail` command on the router connected to the switch.

19. You need to configure all your routers and switches so they synchronize their clocks from one time source. What command will you type for each device?
    - A. `clock synchronization` *`ip_address`*
    - B. `ntp master ip_address`
    - C. `sync ntp ip_address`
    - D. `ntp server` *`ip_address`* `version` *`number`*

20. A network administrator enters the following command on a router: `logging trap 3`. What message types will be sent to the syslog server? (Choose three.)

  A. Informational

  B. Alerts

  C. Warning

  D. Critical

  E. Debug

  F. Error

Chapter 8

Managing Cisco Devices

THE FOLLOWING CCNA EXAM TOPICS ARE COVERED IN THIS CHAPTER:

✓ ***2.0 Network Access***

- 2.3 Configure and verify Layer 2 discovery protocols (Cisco Discovery Protocol and LLDP)
- 2.8 Describe network device management access (Telnet, SSH, HTTP, HTTPS, console, TACACS+/RADIUS, and cloud managed)

In this chapter, I'm going to show you how to manage Cisco routers on an internetwork. The Internetwork Operating System (IOS) and configuration files reside in different locations in a Cisco device, so it's really important to understand both where these files are located and how they work.

You'll be learning about the configuration register, including how to use it for password recovery.

Finally, I'll cover how to verify licenses on the ISRG2 routers as well as how to install a permanent license and configure evaluation features in the latest universal images.

NOTE

To find bonus material, as well as Todd Lammle videos, practice questions, and hands-on labs, please see www.lammle.com/ccna.

Managing the Configuration Register

All Cisco routers have a 16-bit software register that's written into NVRAM. By default, the *configuration register* is set to load the Cisco IOS from *flash memory* and to look for and load the startup-config file from NVRAM. The following sections discuss the configuration register settings and how to use these settings to provide password recovery on your routers.

Understanding the Configuration Register Bits

The 16 bits (2 bytes) of the configuration register are read from 15 to 0, from left to right. The default configuration setting on Cisco routers is 0x2102. This means that bits 13, 8, and 1 are on, as shown in Table 8.1. Notice that each set of 4 bits (called a *nibble*) is read in binary with a value of 8, 4, 2, 1.

TABLE 8.1 The configuration register bit numbers

Configuration Register	2				1				0				2			
Bit number	15	14	13	12	11	10	9	8	7	6	5	4	3	2	1	0
Binary	0	0	1	0	0	0	0	1	0	0	0	0	0	0	1	0

NOTE: Add the prefix *0x* to the configuration register address. The *0x* means that the digits that follow are in hexadecimal.

Table 8.2 lists the software configuration bit meanings. Notice that bit 6 can be used to ignore the NVRAM contents. This bit is used for password recovery—something I will discuss in the section "Recovering Passwords."

TABLE 8.2 Software configuration meanings

Bit	Hex	Description
0–3	0x0000–0x000F	Boot field (see Table 8.3).
6	0x0040	Ignore NVRAM contents.
7	0x0080	OEM bit enabled.
8	0x101	Break disabled.
10	0x0400	IP broadcast with all zeros.
5, 11–12	0x0800–0x1000	Console line speed.
13	0x2000	Boot default ROM software if network boot fails.
14	0x4000	IP broadcasts do not have net numbers.
15	0x8000	Enable diagnostic messages and ignore NVRAM contents.

NOTE: Remember that in hex, the scheme is 0–9 and A–F (A = 10, B = 11, C = 12, D = 13, E = 14, and F = 15). This means that a 210F setting for the configuration register is actually 210(15), or 1111 in binary.

The boot field, which consists of bits 0–3 in the configuration register (the last 4 bits), controls the router boot sequence and locates the Cisco IOS. Table 8.3 describes the boot field bits.

TABLE 8.3 The boot field (configuration register bits 00–03)

Boot Field	Meaning	Use
00	ROM monitor mode	To boot to ROM monitor mode, set the configuration register to 2100. You must manually boot the router with the b command. The router will show the `rommon>` prompt.
01	Boot image from ROM	To boot the mini-IOS image stored in ROM, set the configuration register to 2101. The router will show the `Router(boot)>` prompt. The mini-IOS is not available in all routers and is also referred to as RXBOOT.
02–F	Specifies a default boot filename	Any value from 2102 through 210F tells the router to use the boot commands specified in NVRAM.

Checking the Current Configuration Register Value

You can see the current value of the configuration register by using the `show version` command (`sh version` or `show ver`, for short), as demonstrated here:

```
Router>sh version
Cisco IOS Software, 2800 Software (C2800NM-ADVSECURITYK9-M),
Version 15.1(4)M6, RELEASE SOFTWARE (fc2)
[output cut]
Configuration register is 0x2102
```

The last information given from this command is the value of the configuration register—in this example, the value is 0x2102, which is the default setting. The configuration register setting of 0x2102 tells the router to look in NVRAM for the boot sequence.

Notice that the `show version` command also provides the IOS version—in the preceding example, it shows the IOS version as 15.1(4)M6.

NOTE: The `show version` command displays system hardware configuration information, the software version, and the names of the boot images on a router.

To change the configuration register, use the `config-register` command from global configuration mode:

```
Router(config)#config-register 0x2142
Router(config)#do sh ver
[output cut]
Configuration register is 0x2102 (will be 0x2142 at next reload)
```

It's important to be careful when setting the configuration register!

> **NOTE** If you save your configuration and reload the router and it comes up in setup mode, the configuration register setting is probably incorrect.

Boot System Commands

Did you know that you can configure your router to boot another IOS if the flash is corrupted? Well, you can. You can boot all of your routers from a TFTP server, but it's old school, and people just don't do it anymore; it's just for backup in case of failure.

There are some boot commands you can play with that will help you manage the way your router boots the Cisco IOS—but please remember, we're talking about the router's IOS here, *not* the router's configuration!

```
Router>en
Router#config t
Enter configuration commands, one per line. End with CNTL/Z.
Router(config)#boot ?
bootstrap Bootstrap image file
config Configuration file
host Router-specific config file
network Network-wide config file
system System image file
```

The `boot` command provides a wealth of options, but first I'll show you the typical settings Cisco recommends. The `boot system` command allows you to tell the router which system IOS file to boot from flash memory. Remember that the router, by default, boots the first system IOS file found in flash. You can change that with the following commands, as shown in the output:

```
Router(config)#boot system ?
WORD TFTP filename or URL
flash Boot from flash memory
ftp Boot from a server via ftp
mop Boot from a Decnet MOP server
rcp Boot from a server via rcp
rom Boot from rom
tftp Boot from a tftp server
Router(config)#boot system flash c2800nm-advsecurityk9-mz.151-4.M6.bin
```

Notice I could boot from flash, FTP, ROM, TFTP, or other older options. The command I used configures the router to boot the IOS listed in it. This is a helpful command for when you load a new IOS into flash and want to test it, or even when you want to totally change which IOS is loading by default.

The next command is considered a fallback routine, but you can make it a permanent way to have your routers boot from a TFTP host. Personally, I wouldn't necessarily recommend doing this (single point of failure); I'm just showing you that it's possible:

```
Router(config)#boot system tftp ?
WORD System image filename
Router(config)#boot system tftp c2800nm-advsecurityk9-mz.151-4.M6.bin?
Hostname or A.B.C.D Address from which to download the file
<cr>
Router(config)#boot system tftp c2800nm-advsecurityk9-mz.151-4.M6.bin 1.1.1.2
Router(config)#
```

As your last recommended fallback option—the one to go to if the IOS in flash doesn't load and the TFTP host does not produce the IOS—load the mini-IOS from ROM, as follows:

```
Router(config)#boot system rom
Router(config)#do show run | include boot system
boot system flash c2800nm-advsecurityk9-mz.151-4.M6.bin
boot system tftp c2800nm-advsecurityk9-mz.151-4.M6.bin 1.1.1.2
boot system rom
Router(config)#
```

If the preceding configuration is set, the router will try to boot from the TFTP server if flash fails, and if the TFTP boot fails, the mini-IOS will load after six unsuccessful attempts of trying to locate the TFTP server.

In the next section, I'll show you how to load the router into ROM monitor mode so you can perform password recovery.

Recovering Passwords

If you're locked out of a router because you forgot the password, you can change the configuration register to help you get back on your feet. As mentioned previously, bit 6 in the configuration register is used to tell the router whether to use the contents of NVRAM to load a router configuration.

The default configuration register value is 0x2102, meaning that bit 6 is off. With the default setting, the router will look for and load a router configuration stored in NVRAM (startup-config). To recover a password, you need to turn on bit 6. Doing this will tell the router to ignore the NVRAM contents. The configuration register value to turn on bit 6 is 0x2142.

Here are the main steps to password recovery:

1. Boot the router and interrupt the boot sequence by performing a break, which will take the router into ROM monitor mode.
2. Change the configuration register to turn on bit 6 (with the value 0x2142).

3. Reload the router.
4. Say "no" to entering setup mode, then enter privileged mode.
5. Copy the startup-config file to running-config, and remember to verify that your interfaces are reenabled.
6. Change the password.
7. Reset the configuration register to the default value.
8. Save the router configuration.
9. Reload the router (optional).

These steps are covered in greater detail in the following sections. I'll also show you the commands to restore access to ISR series routers.

You can enter ROM monitor mode by pressing Ctrl+Break or Ctrl+Shift+6, then b, during router bootup. But if the IOS is corrupt or missing, if there's no network connectivity available to find a TFTP host, or if the mini-IOS from ROM doesn't load (meaning the default router fallback failed), the router will enter ROM monitor mode by default.

Interrupting the Router Boot Sequence

Your first step is to boot the router and perform a break. This is usually done by pressing the Ctrl+Break key combination when using HyperTerminal (personally, I use SecureCRT or PuTTY) while the router first reboots.

```
System Bootstrap, Version 15.1(4)M6, RELEASE SOFTWARE (fc2)
Copyright (c) 1999 by cisco Systems, Inc.
TAC:Home:SW:IOS:Specials for info
PC = 0xfff0a530, Vector = 0x500, SP = 0x680127b0
C2800 platform with 32768 Kbytes of main memory
PC = 0xfff0a530, Vector = 0x500, SP = 0x80004374
monitor: command "boot" aborted due to user interrupt
rommon 1 >
```

Notice the line `monitor: command "boot" aborted due to user interrupt`. At this point, you will be at the `rommon 1>` prompt, which is called the ROM monitor mode.

Changing the Configuration Register

As previously mentioned, you can change the configuration register from within the IOS by using the `config-register` command. To turn on bit 6, use the configuration register value 0x2142.

> **NOTE** Remember, if you change the configuration register to 0x2142, the startup-config file will be bypassed, and the router will load into setup mode.

To change the bit value on a Cisco ISR series router, simply enter the following command at the `rommon 1>` prompt:

```
rommon 1 >confreg 0x2142
You must reset or power cycle for new config to take effect
rommon 2 >reset
```

Reloading the Router and Entering Privileged Mode

At this point, you need to reset the router, as follows:

- From the ISR series router, type **I** (for initialize) or **reset**.
- From an older series router, type **I**.

The router will reload and ask if you want to use setup mode (because no startup-config file is used). Answer no to entering setup mode, press Enter to go into user mode, and then type **enable** to enter privileged mode.

Viewing and Changing the Configuration

Now you're past the point where you would need to enter the user-mode and privileged-mode passwords in a router. Copy the startup-config file to the running-config file, as follows:

```
copy startup-config running-config
```

Or use the following shortcut:

```
copy start run
```

The configuration is now running in *random access memory (RAM)*, and you're in privileged mode, meaning that you can now view and change the configuration. However, you can't view the enable secret setting for the password since it is encrypted. To change the password, do this:

```
config t
enable secret todd
```

Resetting the Configuration Register and Reloading the Router

After you're finished changing passwords, set the configuration register back to the default value with the `config-register` command:

```
config t
config-register 0x2102
```

It's important to remember to enable your interfaces after copying the configuration from NVRAM to RAM.

Finally, save the new configuration with the `copy running-config startup-config` command and use `reload` to reload the router.

NOTE If you save your configuration and reload the router and it comes up in setup mode, the configuration register setting is probably incorrect.

To sum up, we now have Cisco's suggested IOS backup routine configured on our router: flash, TFTP host, ROM.

Backing Up and Restoring the Cisco IOS

Before you upgrade or restore a Cisco IOS, you really should copy the existing file to a *TFTP host* as a backup, just in case the new image crashes and burns.

You can use any TFTP host to accomplish this. By default, the flash memory in a router is used to store the Cisco IOS. The following sections describe how to check the amount of flash memory, how to copy the Cisco IOS from flash memory to a TFTP host, and how to copy the IOS from a TFTP host to flash memory.

Before backing up an IOS image to a network server on your intranet, however, you must do the following three things:

- Make sure you can access the network server.
- Ensure that the network server has adequate space for the code image.
- Verify the file naming and path requirements.

You can connect your laptop or workstation's Ethernet port directly to a router's Ethernet interface, as shown in Figure 8.1.

FIGURE 8.1 Copying an IOS from a router to a TFTP host

Copy the IOS to a TFTP host.

Router# copy flash tftp

- IP address of the TFTP server
- IOS filename

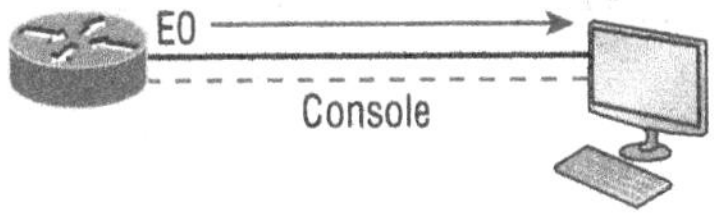


```
RouterX#copy flash tftp:
Source filename [] ?c2800nm-ipbase-mz.124-5a.bin
Address or name of remote host [] ? 10.1.1.1
Destination filename [c2800nm-ipbase-mz.124-5a.bin] [enter]
!!!!!!!!!!!!!!!!!!!!!!!!!!!!!!!!!!!!!!!!!!!!!!!!!!!!!!!!!!!!!!<output omitted>
12094416 bytes copied in 98.858 secs (122341 bytes/sec)
RouterX#
```

- TFTP server software must be running on the PC.
- The PC must be on the same subnet as the router's E0 interface.
- The `copy flash tftp` command must be supplied the IP address of the PC.

You need to verify the following before attempting to copy the image to or from the router:

- TFTP server software must be running on the laptop or workstation.
- The Ethernet connection between the router and the workstation must be made with a crossover cable.
- The workstation must be on the same subnet as the router's Ethernet interface.
- The `copy flash tftp` command must be supplied the IP address of the workstation if you are copying from the router flash.
- If you're copying "into" flash, you need to verify there's enough room in flash memory to accommodate the file to be copied.

Verifying Flash Memory

Before attempting to upgrade the Cisco IOS on your router with a new IOS file, it's a good idea to verify that your flash memory has enough room to hold the new image. You verify the amount of flash memory and the file or files being stored in flash memory by using the `show flash` command (`sh flash`, for short):

```
Router#sh flash
-#- --length-- -----date/time------ path
1 45392400 Apr 14 2013 05:31:44 +00:00 c2800nm-advsecurityk9-mz.151-4.M6.bin
18620416 bytes available (45395968 bytes used)
```

There are about 45 MB of flash used, but there are still about 18 MB available. If you want to copy a file into flash that is more than 18 MB in size, the router will ask you if you want to erase flash. Be careful here!

NOTE The `show flash` command displays the amount of memory consumed by the current IOS image as well as tells you if there's enough room available to hold both current and new images. Note that if there's not enough room for both the old and new image you want to load, the old image will be erased!

The amount of RAM and flash is actually easy to tally using the `show version` command on routers:

```
Router#show version
[output cut]
System returned to ROM by power-on
System image file is "flash:c2800nm-advsecurityk9-mz.151-4.M6.bin"
[output cut]
Cisco 2811 (revision 1.0) with 249856K/12288K bytes of memory.
```

```
Processor board ID FTX1049A1AB
2 FastEthernet interfaces
2 Serial(sync/async) interfaces
1 Virtual Private Network (VPN) Module
DRAM configuration is 64 bits wide with parity enabled.
239K bytes of non-volatile configuration memory.
62720K bytes of ATA CompactFlash (Read/Write)
```

The second highlighted line shows that this router has about 256 MB of RAM, and you can see the amount of flash shows up on the last line. By estimating up, we get the amount of flash to 64 MB.

Notice in the first highlighted line that the filename in this example is `c2800nm-advsecurity k9-mz.151-4.M6.bin`. The main difference in the output of the `show flash` and `show version` commands is that the `show flash` command displays all files in flash memory, and the `show version` command shows the actual name of the file used to run the router and the location from which it was loaded, which is flash memory.

Backing Up the Cisco IOS

To back up the Cisco IOS to a TFTP server, you use the `copy flash tftp` command. It's a straightforward command that requires only the source filename and the IP address of the TFTP server.

The key to success in this backup routine is to make sure you have solid connectivity to the TFTP server. Check this by pinging the TFTP device from the router console prompt, as follows:

```
Router#ping 1.1.1.2
Type escape sequence to abort.
Sending 5, 100-byte ICMP Echos to 1.1.1.2, timeout
is 2 seconds:
!!!!!
Success rate is 100 percent (5/5), round-trip min/avg/max
= 4/4/8 ms
```

After pinging the TFTP server to make sure that IP is working, you can use the `copy flash tftp` command to copy the IOS to the TFTP server:

```
Router#copy flash tftp
Source filename []?c2800nm-advsecurityk9-mz.151-4.M6.bin
Address or name of remote host []?1.1.1.2
Destination filename [c2800nm-advsecurityk9-mz.151-4.M6.bin]?[enter]
!!!!!!!!!!!!!!!!!!!!!!!!!!!!!!!!!!!!!!!!!!!!!!!!!!!!!!!!!!!!!!!!!!!!
45395968 bytes copied in 123.724 secs (357532 bytes/sec)
Router#
```

Just copy the IOS filename from either the `show flash` or `show version` command and then paste it when prompted for the source filename.

In the preceding example, the contents of flash memory were copied successfully to the TFTP server. The address of the remote host is the IP address of the TFTP host, and the source filename is the file in flash memory.

WARNING

Many newer Cisco routers have removable memory. You may see names for this memory such as `flash0:`, in which case the command in the preceding example would be `copy flash0: tftp:`. Alternately, you may see it as `usbflash0:`.

Restoring or Upgrading the Cisco Router IOS

What happens if you need to restore the Cisco IOS to flash memory to replace an original file that has been damaged, or if you want to upgrade the IOS? You can download the file from a TFTP server to flash memory by using the `copy tftp flash` command. This command requires the IP address of the TFTP host and the name of the file you want to download.

However, since IOS's can be very large today, you may want to use something other than TFTP, which is unreliable and can only transfer smaller files. Check this out:

```
Corp#copy ?
/erase Erase destination file system.
/error Allow to copy error file.
/noverify Don't verify image signature before reload.
/verify Verify image signature before reload.
archive: Copy from archive: file system
cns: Copy from cns: file system
flash: Copy from flash: file system
ftp: Copy from ftp: file system
http: Copy from http: file system
https: Copy from https: file system
null: Copy from null: file system
nvram: Copy from nvram: file system
rcp: Copy from rcp: file system
running-config Copy from current system configuration
scp: Copy from scp: file system
startup-config Copy from startup configuration
system: Copy from system: file system
tar: Copy from tar: file system
tftp: Copy from tftp: file system
tmpsys: Copy from tmpsys: file system
```

```
xmodem: Copy from xmodem: file system
ymodem: Copy from ymodem: file system
```

You can see from the preceding output that you have many options. For the larger files, use `ftp:` or `scp:` to copy your IOS into or from routers and switches. You can even perform an MD5 verification with the `/verify` at the end of a command.

This chapter's examples use TFTP because it's the easiest. Before beginning, however, make sure the file you want to place in flash memory is in the default TFTP directory on your host. When you issue the command, TFTP won't ask you where the file is, so if the file you want to use isn't in the default directory of the TFTP host, this won't work.

```
Router#copy tftp flash
Address or name of remote host []?1.1.1.2
Source filename []?c2800nm-advsecurityk9-mz.151-4.M6.bin
Destination filename [c2800nm-advsecurityk9-mz.151-4.M6.bin]?[enter]
%Warning: There is a file already existing with this name
Do you want to over write? [confirm][enter]
Accessing tftp://1.1.1.2/ c2800nm-advsecurityk9-mz.151-4.M6.bin...
Loading c2800nm-advsecurityk9-mz.151-4.M6.bin from 1.1.1.2 (via
FastEthernet0/0): !!!!!!!!!!!!!!!!!!!!!!!!!!!!!!!!!!!!!!!!!!!!!!!!!!!!!!!!!!!!!!!
[OK - 21710744 bytes]
45395968 bytes copied in 82.880 secs (261954 bytes/sec)
Router#
```

In the preceding example, I copied the same file into flash memory, so it asked me if I wanted to overwrite it. Remember, we are "playing" with files in flash memory. If I had just corrupted my file by overwriting it, I wouldn't know for sure until I rebooted the router. Be careful with this command! If the file is corrupted, you'll need to do an IOS-restore from ROM monitor mode.

If you are loading a new file and don't have enough room in flash memory to store both the new and existing copies, the router will ask to erase the contents of flash memory before writing the new file into flash memory. If you are able to copy the IOS without erasing the old version, then remember to use the `boot system flash:`*`ios-file`* command.

A Cisco router can become a TFTP server host for a router system image that's run in flash memory. The global configuration command is `tftp-server flash:`*`ios-file`*.

Real World Scenario

It's Monday Morning and You Just Upgraded Your IOS

You came in early to work to upgrade the IOS on your router. After the upgrade, you reload the router, and the router now shows the `rommon>` prompt.

It seems that you're about to have a bad day! This is what I call an RGE: a résumé-generating event! So, now what do you do? Just keep calm and chive on! Follow these steps to save your job:

```
rommon 1 > tftpdnld
Missing or illegal ip address for variable IP_ADDRESS
Illegal IP address.
usage: tftpdnld [-hr]
Use this command for disaster recovery only to recover an image via TFTP.
Monitor variables are used to set up parameters for the transfer.
(Syntax: "VARIABLE_NAME=value" and use "set" to show current variables.)
"ctrl-c" or "break" stops the transfer before flash erase begins.
The following variables are REQUIRED to be set for tftpdnld:
IP_ADDRESS: The IP address for this unit
IP_SUBNET_MASK: The subnet mask for this unit
DEFAULT_GATEWAY: The default gateway for this unit
TFTP_SERVER: The IP address of the server to fetch from
TFTP_FILE: The filename to fetch
The following variables are OPTIONAL:
[unneeded output cut]
rommon 2 >set IP_Address:1.1.1.1
rommon 3 >set IP_SUBNET_MASK:255.0.0.0
rommon 4 >set DEFAULT_GATEWAY:1.1.1.2
rommon 5 >set TFTP_SERVER:1.1.1.2
rommon 6 >set TFTP_FILE: flash:c2800nm-advipservicesk9-mz.124-12.bin
rommon 7 >tftpdnld
```

From here, you can see the variables you need to configure using the `set` command. Be sure to use all capital letters with these commands as well as an underscore (_). From here, you need to set the IP address, mask, and default gateway of your router, then the IP address of the TFTP host, which, in this example, is a directly connected router that I made a TFTP server with this command:

```
Router(config)#tftp-server flash:c2800nm-advipservicesk9-mz.124-12.bin
```

Finally, set the IOS filename of the file on your TFTP server. Whew! Job saved.

There is one other way to restore the IOS on a router, but it takes a while. You can use what is the Xmodem protocol to actually upload an IOS file into flash memory through the console port. You'd use the Xmodem through the console port procedure if you had no network connectivity to the router or switch.

Using the Cisco IOS File System (Cisco IFS)

Cisco has created a file system called Cisco IFS that allows you to work with files and directories just as you would from a Windows DOS prompt. The commands you use are `dir`, `copy`, `more`, `delete`, `erase` or `format`, `cd` and `pwd`, and `mkdir` and `rmdir`.

The IFS enables you to view all files, even those on remote servers. And you definitely want to find out if an image on one of your remote servers is valid before copying it, right? You also need to know how big it is—size matters here! It's also a really good idea to take a look at the remote server's configuration and make sure it's all good before loading that file on your router.

It's very cool that IFS makes the file system user interface universal—it's not platform-specific anymore. You now get to use the same syntax for all your commands on all of your routers, regardless of the platform!

Sound too good to be true? Well, it kind of is because support for all commands on each file system and platform just isn't there. However, it's really no big deal since various file systems differ in the actions they perform; the commands that aren't relevant to a particular file system are the very ones that aren't supported on that file system. Be assured that any file system or platform will fully support all the commands you need to manage it.

Another cool IFS feature is that it cuts down on all those obligatory prompts for a lot of the commands. If you want to enter a command, all you have to do is type all the necessary info straight into the command line—no more jumping through hoops of prompts! So, if you want to copy a file to an FTP server, simply indicate where the desired source file is on your router, pinpoint where the destination file is to be on the FTP server, determine the username and password you're going to use when you want to connect to that server, and then type it all on one line—sleek! And for those of you resistant to change, you can still have the router prompt you for all the information it needs and enjoy entering a more elegantly minimized version of the command than you did before.

In spite of all this, however, your router might still prompt you—even if you did everything right in your command line. It comes down to how you have the `file prompt` command configured and which command you're trying to use. But no worries—if that happens, the default value will be entered right there in the command, and all you have to do is hit Enter to verify the correct values.

IFS also lets you explore various directories and inventory files in any directory you want. Plus, you can make subdirectories in flash memory or on a card, but you only get to do that if you're working on one of the more recent platforms.

And get this: the new file system interface uses URLs to determine the whereabouts of a file. So, just as they pinpoint places on the Web, URLs now indicate where files are on your Cisco router or even on a remote file server! You just type URLs right into your commands to identify where the file or directory is. It's really that easy—to copy a file from one place to another, simply enter the `copy` *`source-url destination-url`* command—sweet! IFS URLs are a tad different from what you're used to, though, and there's an array of formats to use that vary depending on where, exactly, the file is that you're after.

We're going to use Cisco IFS commands pretty much the same way that we used the `copy` command in the IOS section earlier:

- For backing up the IOS
- For upgrading the IOS
- For viewing text files

Okay, with all that down, let's look at the common IFS commands for managing the IOS. I'll get into configuration files soon, but for now, I'll go over the basics used to manage the new Cisco IOS.

`dir` Same as with Windows, this command lets you view files in a directory. Type **`dir`**, hit Enter, and by default you get the contents of the `flash:/` directory output.

`copy` This is one popular command, often used to upgrade, restore, or back up an IOS. But, as I said, when you use it, it's really important to focus on the details—what you're copying, where it's coming from, and where it's going to land.

`more` Same as with Unix, this command lets you look at a text file on a card. You can use it to check out your configuration file or your backup configuration file. I'll go over it more when we get into actual configuration.

`show file` This command gives you the skinny on a specified file or file system, but it's kind of obscure because people don't use it a lot.

`delete` Three guesses—yep, it deletes stuff. But with some types of routers, not as well as you'd think. That's because even though it whacks the file, it doesn't always free up the space it was using. To actually get the space back, you have to use something called the `squeeze` command, too.

`erase/format` Use these commands with care! Make sure when you're copying files, you say no to the dialog that asks if you want to erase the file system. The type of memory you're using determines whether or not you can nix the flash drive.

`cd/pwd` Same as with Unix and DOS, `cd` is the command you use to change directories. Use the `pwd` command to print (show) the working directory.

`mkdir/rmdir` Use these commands on certain routers and switches to create and delete directories—the `mkdir` command for creation and the `rmdir` command for deletion. Use the `cd` and `pwd` commands to change into these directories.

NOTE The Cisco IFS uses the alternate term `system:running-config` as well as `nvram:startup-config` when copying the configurations on a router, although it is not mandatory that you use this naming convention.

Using the Cisco IFS to Upgrade an IOS

Let's take a look at some of these Cisco IFS commands on my ISR router (1841 series) with a hostname of R1.

We'll start with the pwd command to verify our default directory and then use the `dir` command to verify its contents (`flash:/`):

```
R1#pwd
flash:
R1#dir
Directory of flash:/
1 -rw- 13937472 Dec 20 2006 19:58:18 +00:00 c1841-ipbase-
mz.124-1c.bin
2 -rw- 1821 Dec 20 2006 20:11:24 +00:00 sdmconfig-18xx.cfg
3 -rw- 4734464 Dec 20 2006 20:12:00 +00:00 sdm.tar
4 -rw- 833024 Dec 20 2006 20:12:24 +00:00 es.tar
5 -rw- 1052160 Dec 20 2006 20:12:50 +00:00 common.tar
6 -rw- 1038 Dec 20 2006 20:13:10 +00:00 home.shtml
7 -rw- 102400 Dec 20 2006 20:13:30 +00:00 home.tar
8 -rw- 491213 Dec 20 2006 20:13:56 +00:00 128MB.sdf
9 -rw- 1684577 Dec 20 2006 20:14:34 +00:00 securedesktop-
ios-3.1.1.27-k9.pkg
10 -rw- 398305 Dec 20 2006 20:15:04 +00:00 sslclient-win-1.1.0.154.pkg
32071680 bytes total (8818688 bytes free)
```

You can see that we have the basic IP IOS (`c1841-ipbase-mz.124-1c.bin`). It looks like we need to upgrade our 1841. You've just got to love how Cisco puts the IOS type in the filename now! First, let's check the size of the file that's in flash with the `show file` command (`show flash` would also work):

```
R1#show file info flash:c1841-ipbase-mz.124-1c.bin
flash:c1841-ipbase-mz.124-1c.bin:
type is image (elf) []
file size is 13937472 bytes, run size is 14103140 bytes
Runnable image, entry point 0x8000F000, run from ram
```

With a file that size, the existing IOS will have to be erased before we can add our new IOS file (`c1841-advipservicesk9-mz.124-12.bin`), which is over 21 MB. We'll use the `delete` command, but remember, we can play with any file in flash memory, and nothing serious will happen until we reboot—that is, if we made a mistake. Obviously, and as I pointed out earlier, we need to be very careful here!

```
R1#delete flash:c1841-ipbase-mz.124-1c.bin
Delete filename [c1841-ipbase-mz.124-1c.bin]?[enter]
```

```
Delete flash:c1841-ipbase-mz.124-1c.bin? [confirm][enter]
R1#sh flash
-#- --length-- -----date/time------ path
1 1821 Dec 20 2006 20:11:24 +00:00 sdmconfig-18xx.cfg
2 4734464 Dec 20 2006 20:12:00 +00:00 sdm.tar
3 833024 Dec 20 2006 20:12:24 +00:00 es.tar
4 1052160 Dec 20 2006 20:12:50 +00:00 common.tar
5 1038 Dec 20 2006 20:13:10 +00:00 home.shtml
6 102400 Dec 20 2006 20:13:30 +00:00 home.tar
7 491213 Dec 20 2006 20:13:56 +00:00 128MB.sdf
8 1684577 Dec 20 2006 20:14:34 +00:00 securedesktop-ios-3.1.1.27-k9.pkg
9 398305 Dec 20 2006 20:15:04 +00:00 sslclient-win-1.1.0.154.pkg
22757376 bytes available (9314304 bytes used)
R1#sh file info flash:c1841-ipbase-mz.124-1c.bin
%Error opening flash:c1841-ipbase-mz.124-1c.bin (File not found)
R1#
```

With the preceding commands, we deleted the existing file and then verified the deletion by using both the `show flash` and `show file` commands. We'll add the new file with the `copy` command, but again, be careful because this way isn't any safer than the first method I showed you earlier:

```
R1#copy tftp://1.1.1.2/c1841-advipservicesk9-mz.124-12.bin/ flash:/
c1841-advipservicesk9-mz.124-12.bin
Source filename [/c1841-advipservicesk9-mz.124-12.bin/]?[enter]
Destination filename [c1841-advipservicesk9-mz.124-12.bin]?[enter]
Loading /c1841-advipservicesk9-mz.124-12.bin/ from 1.1.1.2 (via
FastEthernet0/0): !!!!!!!!!!!!!!!!!!!!!!!!!!!!!!!!!!!!!!!!
[output cut]
[OK - 22103052 bytes]
22103052 bytes copied in 72.008 secs (306953 bytes/sec)
R1#sh flash
-#- --length-- -----date/time------ path
1 1821 Dec 20 2006 20:11:24 +00:00 sdmconfig-18xx.cfg
2 4734464 Dec 20 2006 20:12:00 +00:00 sdm.tar
3 833024 Dec 20 2006 20:12:24 +00:00 es.tar
4 1052160 Dec 20 2006 20:12:50 +00:00 common.tar
5 1038 Dec 20 2006 20:13:10 +00:00 home.shtml
6 102400 Dec 20 2006 20:13:30 +00:00 home.tar
7 491213 Dec 20 2006 20:13:56 +00:00 128MB.sdf
8 1684577 Dec 20 2006 20:14:34 +00:00 securedesktop-ios-3.1.1.27-k9.pkg
9 398305 Dec 20 2006 20:15:04 +00:00 sslclient-win-1.1.0.154.pkg
```

```
10 22103052 Mar 10 2007 19:40:50 +00:00 c1841-advipservicesk9-mz.124-12.bin
651264 bytes available (31420416 bytes used)
R1#
```

We can also check the file information with the `show file` command:

```
R1#sh file
information flash:c1841-advipservicesk9-mz.124-12.bin
flash:c1841-advipservicesk9-mz.124-12.bin:
type is image (elf) []
file size is 22103052 bytes, run size is 22268736 bytes
Runnable image, entry point 0x8000F000, run from ram
```

Remember, the IOS is expanded into RAM when the router boots, so the new IOS will not run until you reload the router.

I really recommend experimenting with the Cisco IFS commands on a router just to get a good feel for them because, as I've said, they can definitely give you some grief if not executed properly!

TIP

I mention "safer methods" a lot in this chapter. Clearly, I've caused myself some serious pain by not being careful enough when working in flash memory! I cannot stress this enough: pay attention when messing around with flash memory!

One of the brilliant features of the ISR routers is that they use the physical flash cards accessible from the front or back of any router. These typically have a name like `usbflash0:`, so to view the contents, you'd type **`dir usbflash0:`**, for example. You can pull out these flash cards, put them in an appropriate slot in your PC, and the card will show up as a drive. You can then add, change, and delete files. Just put the flash card back in your router and power up—instant upgrade. Nice!

Licensing

IOS licensing is now done quite differently from how it was with previous versions of the IOS. Actually, there was no licensing before the new 15.0 IOS code, just your word and honor, and we can only guess, based on how all products are downloaded on the Internet daily, how well that has worked out for Cisco!

Starting with the IOS 15.0 code, things are much different—almost too different. I can imagine that Cisco will come back toward the middle on its licensing issues, so the administration and management won't be as detailed as it is with the new 15.0 code license is now—but you can be the judge of that after reading this section.

A new ISR router is preinstalled with the software images and licenses that you ordered, so as long as you ordered and paid for everything you need, you're set! If not, you can just install another license, which can be a tad tedious at first—enough so that installing a license was made an objective on the Cisco exam! Of course, it can be done, but it definitely requires some effort. As is typical with Cisco, if you spend enough money on their products, they tend to make it easier on you and your administration, and the licensing for the newest IOS is no exception, as you'll soon see.

On a positive note, Cisco provides evaluation licenses for most software packages and features that are supported on the hardware you purchase, and it's always nice to be able to try it out before you buy. Once the temporary license expires after 60 days, you need to acquire a permanent license in order to continue to use the extended features that aren't available in your current version. This method of licensing allows you to enable a router to use different parts of the IOS. So, what happens after 60 days? Well, nothing—back to the honor system for now. This is now called *Right-To-Use (RTU) licensing*, and it probably won't always be available via your honor, but for now it is.

But that's not the best part of the new licensing features. Prior to the 15.0 code release, there were eight different software feature sets for each hardware router type. With the IOS 15.0 code, the packaging is now called a *universal image*, meaning all feature sets are available in one file with all features packed neatly inside. So, instead of the pre-15.0 IOS file packages of one image per feature set, Cisco now just builds one universal image that includes all of them in the file. Even so, we still need a different universal image per router model or series, just not a different image for each feature set, as we did with previous IOS versions.

To use the features in the IOS software, you must unlock them using the software activation process. Since all features available are inside the universal image already, you can just unlock the features you need as you need them, and, of course, pay for these features when you determine that they meet your business requirements. All routers come with something called the *IP Base licensing*, which is the prerequisite for installing all other features.

Three different technology packages are available for purchase that can be installed as additional feature packs on top of the prerequisite IP Base (default), which provides entry-level IOS functionality:

Data: MPLS, ATM, and multiprotocol support

Unified Communications: VoIP and IP telephony

Security: Cisco IOS Firewall, IPS, IPsec, 3DES, and VPN

For example, if you need MPLS and IPsec, you need to have the default IP Base, Data, and Security premium packages unlocked on your router.

To obtain the license, you need the unique device identifier (UDI), which has two components: the product ID (PID) and the serial number of the router. The `show license UDI` command provides this information in an output as shown here:

```
Router#sh license udi
Device# PID SN UDI ---------------------------------------------------
--------------
*0 CISCO2901/K9 FTX1641Y07J CISCO2901/K9:FTX1641Y07J
```

After the time has expired for your 60-day evaluation period, you can either obtain the license file from the Cisco License Manager (CLM), which is an automated process, or use the manual process through the Cisco Product License Registration portal. Typically, only larger companies will use the CLM because you'd need to install software on a server, which then keeps track of all your licenses. If you have just a few licenses that you use, you can opt for the manual web browser process found on the Cisco Product License Registration portal and then just add a few CLI commands. After that, you basically keep track of putting all the different license features together for each device you manage. Although this sounds like a lot of work, you don't have to perform these steps often. Clearly, however, going with the CLM makes a lot of sense if you have many licenses to manage because it will put together all the little pieces of licensing for each router in one easy process.

When you purchase the software package with the features you want to install, you need to permanently activate the software package using your UDI and the *product authorization key (PAK)* you received with your purchase. This is essentially your receipt acknowledging that you purchased the license. You then need to connect the license with a particular router by combining the PAK and the UDI, which you do online at the Cisco Product License Registration portal (`www.cisco.com/go/license`). If you haven't already registered the license on a different router and it is valid, Cisco will email your permanent license, or you can download it from your account.

But wait! You're still not done. You now need to activate the license on the router. Whew. . . maybe it's worthwhile to install the CLM on a server after all! Staying with the manual method, you need to make the new license file available to the router either via a USB port on the router or through a TFTP server. Once it's available to the router, you'll use the `license install` command from privileged mode.

Assuming that you copied the file into flash memory, the command would look like something like this:

```
Router#license install ?
archive: Install from archive: file system
flash: Install from flash: file system
ftp: Install from ftp: file system
http: Install from http: file system
https: Install from https: file system
null: Install from null: file system
nvram: Install from nvram: file system
rcp: Install from rcp: file system
scp: Install from scp: file system
syslog: Install from syslog: file system
system: Install from system: file system
tftp: Install from tftp: file system
tmpsys: Install from tmpsys: file system
xmodem: Install from xmodem: file system
ymodem: Install from ymodem: file system
```

```
Router#license install flash:FTX1628838P_201302111432454180.lic
Installing licenses from "flash::FTX1628838P_201302111432454180.lic"
Installing...Feature:datak9...Successful:Supported
1/1 licenses were successfully installed
0/1 licenses were existing licenses
0/1 licenses were failed to install
April 12 2:31:19.786: %LICENSE-6-INSTALL: Feature datak9 1.0 was
installed in this device. UDI=CISCO2901/K9:FTX1628838P; StoreIndex=1:Primary
License Storage
April 12 2:31:20.078: %IOS_LICENSE_IMAGE_APPLICATION-6-LICENSE_LEVEL: Module
name =c2800 Next reboot level = datak9 and License = datak9
```

You need to reboot to have the new license take effect. Now that you have your license installed and running, how do you use Right-To-Use licensing to check out new features on your router? Let's look into that now.

Right-To-Use Licenses (Evaluation Licenses)

Originally called evaluation licenses, Right-To-Use (RTU) licenses are what you need when you want to update your IOS to load a new feature but either don't want to wait to get the license or just want to test if this feature will truly meet your business requirements. This makes sense because if Cisco made it complicated to load and check out a feature, they could potentially miss out on a sale! Of course, if the feature does work for you, they'll want you to buy a permanent license, but again, this is on the honor system at the time of this writing.

Cisco's license model allows you to install the feature you want without a PAK. The Right-To-Use license works for 60 days before you need to install your permanent license. To enable the Right-To-Use license, use the `license boot module` command. The following demonstrates starting the Right-To-Use license on my 2900 series router, enabling the security module named `securityk9`:

```
Router(config)#license boot module c2900 technology-package securityk9
PLEASE READ THE FOLLOWING TERMS CAREFULLY. INSTALLING THE LICENSE OR LICENSE
KEY PROVIDED FOR ANY CISCO PRODUCT FEATURE OR USING
SUCHPRODUCT FEATURE CONSTITUTES YOUR FULL ACCEPTANCE OF THE
FOLLOWING TERMS. YOU MUST NOT PROCEED FURTHER IF YOU ARE NOT WILLING
TO BE BOUND BY ALL THE TERMS SET FORTH HEREIN.
[output cut]
Activation of the software command line interface will be evidence of
your acceptance of this agreement.
ACCEPT? [yes/no]: yes
% use 'write' command to make license boot config take effect on next boot
Feb 12 01:35:45.060: %IOS_LICENSE_IMAGE_APPLICATION-6-LICENSE_LEVEL:
Module name =c2900 Next reboot level = securityk9 and License = securityk9
Feb 12 01:35:45.524: %LICENSE-6-EULA_ACCEPTED: EULA for feature
```

```
securityk9 1.0 has been accepted. UDI=CISCO2901/K9:FTX1628838P;
StoreIndex=0:Built-In License Storage
```

Once the router is reloaded, you can use the security feature set. And it is really nice that you don't need to reload the router again if you choose to install a permanent license for this feature. The `show license` command shows the licenses installed on the router:

```
Router#show license
Index 1 Feature: ipbasek9
Period left: Life time
License Type: Permanent
License State: Active, In Use
License Count: Non-Counted
License Priority: Medium
Index 2 Feature: securityk9
Period left: 8 weeks 2 days
Period Used: 0 minute 0 second
License Type: EvalRightToUse
License State: Active, In Use
License Count: Non-Counted
License Priority: None
Index 3 Feature: uck9
Period left: Life time
License Type: Permanent
License State: Active, In Use
License Count: Non-Counted
License Priority: Medium
Index 4 Feature: datak9
Period left: Not Activated
Period Used: 0 minute 0 second
License Type: EvalRightToUse
License State: Not in Use, EULA not accepted
License Count: Non-Counted
License Priority: None
Index 5 Feature: gatekeeper
[output cut]
```

You can see in the preceding output that the `ipbasek9` is permanent and the `securityk9` has a license type of `EvalRightToUse`. The `show license feature` command provides the same information as `show license`, but it's summarized into one line, as shown in the following output:

```
Router#sh license feature
Feature name Enforcement Evaluation Subscription Enabled RightToUse
ipbasek9 no no no yes no
```

```
securityk9 yes yes no no yes
uck9 yes yes no yes yes
datak9 yes yes no no yes
gatekeeper yes yes no no yes
SSL_VPN yes yes no no yes
ios-ips-update yes yes yes no yes
SNASw yes yes no no yes
hseck9 yes no no no no
cme-srst yes yes no yes yes
WAAS_Express yes yes no no yes
UCVideo yes yes no no yes
```

The `show version` command also shows the license information at the end of the command output:

```
Router#show version
[output cut]
License Info:
License UDI:
]]> ------------------------------------------------- Device# PID SN
-------------------------------------------------
*0 CISCO2901/K9 FTX1641Y07J
Technology Package License Information for Module:'c2900'
-----------------------------------------------------------------
Technology Technology-package Technology-package
Current Type Next reboot
------------------------------------------------------------------
ipbase ipbasek9 Permanent ipbasek9
security None None None
uc uck9 Permanent uck9
data None None None
Configuration register is 0x2102
```

The `show version` command shows if the license was activated. Don't forget that you need to reload the router to have the license features take effect if the license evaluation is not already active.

Backing Up and Uninstalling the License

It would be a shame to lose your license if it has been stored in flash and your flash files become corrupted. So, always back up your IOS license!

If your license has been saved in a location other than flash, you can easily back it up to flash memory via the `license save` command:

```
Router#license save flash:Todd_License.lic
```

The previous command will save your current license to flash. You can restore your license with the `license install` command I demonstrated earlier.

There are two steps to uninstalling the license on a router. First, to uninstall the license, you need to disable the technology package, using the `no license boot module` command with the keyword `disable` at the end of the command line:

```
Router#license boot module c2900 technology-package securityk9 disable
```

The second step is to clear the license. To achieve this from the router, use the `license clear` command and then remove the license with the `no license boot module` command:

```
Router#license clear securityk9
Router#config t
Router(config)#no license boot module c2900 technology-package
securityk9 disable
Router(config)#exit
Router#reload
```

After you run through the preceding commands, the license will be removed from your router.

Here's a summary of the license commands I used in this chapter. These are important commands to understand to meet the Cisco objectives:

- `show license` determines the licenses that are active on your system. It also displays a group of lines for each feature in the currently running IOS image along with several status variables related to software activation and licensing, both licensed and unlicensed features.
- `show license feature` allows you to view the technology package licenses and feature licenses that are supported on your router along with several status variables related to software activation and licensing. This includes both licensed and unlicensed features.
- `show license udi` displays the unique device identifier (UDI) of the router, which comprises the product ID (PID) and serial number of the router.
- `show version` displays various pieces of information about the current IOS version, including the licensing details at the end of the command's output.
- `license install` *`url`* installs a license key file into a router.
- `license boot module` installs a Right-To-Use license feature on a router.

TIP

To help you organize a large number of licenses, search on `Cisco.com` for the Cisco Smart Software Manager. This web page enables you to manage all your licenses from one centralized website. With Cisco Smart Software Manager, you organize and view your licenses in groups called *virtual accounts*, which are collections of licenses and product instances.

Summary

You now know how Cisco routers are configured and how to manage those configurations.

This chapter covered the internal components of a router, which include ROM, RAM, NVRAM, and flash.

In addition, I covered what happens when a router boots and which files are loaded at that time. The configuration register tells the router how to boot and where to find files. You learned how to change and verify the configuration register settings for password recovery purposes. I also showed you how to manage these files using the CLI and IFS.

Finally, the chapter covered licensing with the new 15.0 code, including how to install a permanent license and a Right-To-Use license to install features for 60 days. I also showed you the verification commands used to see what licenses are installed and to verify their status.

Exam Essentials

Define the Cisco router components. Describe the functions of the bootstrap, POST, ROM monitor, mini-IOS, RAM, ROM, flash memory, NVRAM, and the configuration register.

Identify the steps in the router boot sequence. The steps in the boot sequence are POST, loading the IOS, and copying the startup configuration from NVRAM to RAM.

Understand configuration register commands and settings. The 0x2102 setting is the default on all Cisco routers and tells the router to look in NVRAM for the boot sequence. The 0x2101 setting tells the router to boot from ROM, and the 0x2142 setting tells the router not to load the startup-config file in NVRAM to provide password recovery.

Perform password recovery. The steps in the password recovery process are as follows: interrupt the router boot sequence; change the configuration register; reload the router and enter privileged mode; copy the startup-config file to running-config and verify that your interfaces are reenabled; change/set the password; save the new configuration; reset the configuration register; and reload the router.

Back up an IOS image. By using the privileged-mode command `copy flash tftp`, you can back up a file from flash memory to a TFTP (network) server.

Restore or upgrade an IOS image. By using the privileged-mode command `copy tftp flash`, you can restore or upgrade a file from a TFTP (network) server to flash memory.

Describe best practices to prepare to back up an IOS image to a network server. Make sure you can access the network server; ensure the network server has adequate space for the code image; and verify the file naming and path requirement.

Understand and use Cisco IFS file system management commands. The commands to use are `dir`, `copy`, `more`, `delete`, `erase` or `format`, `cd` and `pwd`, and `mkdir` and `rmdir`, as well as `system:running-config` and `nvram:startup-config`.

Remember how to install a permanent and Right-To-Use license. To install a permanent license on a router, use the `install license` *`url`* command. To install an evaluation feature, use the `license boot module` command.

Remember the verification commands used for licensing in the new ISR G2 routers. The `show license` command determines the licenses that are active on your system. The `show license feature` command allows you to view the technology package licenses and feature licenses that are supported on your router. The `show license udi` command displays the unique device identifier (UDI) of the router, which comprises the product ID (PID) and serial number of the router, and the `show version` command displays information about the current IOS version, including the licensing details at the end of the command's output.

Written Lab

You can find the answers to this lab in Appendix A, "Answers to the Written Labs."

Written Lab 8.1: IOS Management

Write the answers to the following questions:

1. Which command do you use to copy a Cisco IOS to a TFTP server?
2. What do you set the configuration register setting to in order to boot the mini-IOS in ROM?
3. What is the configuration register setting to tell the router to look in NVRAM for the boot sequence?
4. What do you set the configuration register setting to in order to boot to ROM monitor mode
5. What is used with a PAK to generate a license file?

6. What is the configuration register setting for password recovery?
7. Which command can change the location from which the system loads the IOS?
8. What is the first step of the router boot sequence?
9. Which command can you use to upgrade a Cisco IOS?
10. Which command determines the licenses that are active on your system?

Review Questions

You can find the answers to these questions in Appendix B, "Answers to the Review Questions."

NOTE The following questions are designed to test your understanding of this chapter's material. For more information on how to get additional questions, please see www.lammle.com/ccna.

1. What does the command `confreg 0x2142` provide?
   - A. It is used to restart the router.
   - B. It is used to bypass the configuration in NVRAM.
   - C. It is used to enter ROM monitor mode.
   - D. It is used to view the lost password.
2. Which command will copy the IOS to a backup host on your network?
   - A. `transfer IOS to 172.16.10.1`
   - B. `copy run start`
   - C. `copy tftp flash`
   - D. `copy start tftp`
   - E. `copy flash tftp`
3. Which command is used to permanently install a license on an ISR2 router?
   - A. `install license`
   - B. `license install`
   - C. `boot system license`
   - D. `boot license module`
4. You type the following into the router and reload. What will the router do?

```
Router(config)#boot system flash c2800nm-advsecurityk9-mz.151-4.M6.bin
Router(config)#config-register 0x2101
Router(config)#do sh ver
[output cut]
Configuration register is 0x2102 (will be 0x2101 at next reload)
```

   - A. The router will expand and run the `c2800nm-advsecurityk9-mz.151-4.M6.bin` IOS from flash memory.
   - B. The router will go into setup mode.
   - C. The router will load the mini-IOS from ROM.
   - D. The router will enter ROM monitor mode.

5. A network administrator wants to upgrade the IOS of a router without removing the currently installed image. Which command will display the amount of memory consumed by the current IOS image and indicate whether there is enough room available to hold both the current and new images?
   - **A.** `show version`
   - **B.** `show flash`
   - **C.** `show memory`
   - **D.** `show buffers`
   - **E.** `show running-config`

6. The corporate office sends you a new router to connect, but when you connect the console cable, you see that a configuration is already on the router. What should be done before a new configuration is entered in the router?
   - **A.** RAM should be erased and the router restarted.
   - **B.** Flash should be erased and the router restarted.
   - **C.** NVRAM should be erased and the router restarted.
   - **D.** The new configuration should be entered and saved.

7. Which command loads a new version of the Cisco IOS into a router?
   - **A.** `copy flash ftp`
   - **B.** `copy nvram flash`
   - **C.** `copy flash tftp`
   - **D.** `copy tftp flash`

8. Which command will show you the IOS version running on your router?
   - **A.** `sh IOS`
   - **B.** `sh flash`
   - **C.** `sh version`
   - **D.** `sh protocols`

9. What should the configuration register value be after you successfully complete the password recovery procedure and return the router to normal operation?
   - **A.** 0x2100
   - **B.** 0x2101
   - **C.** 0x2102
   - **D.** 0x2142

10. You save the configuration on a router with the `copy running-config startup-config` command and reboot the router. The router, however, comes up with a blank configuration. What could the problem be?
    - **A.** You didn't boot the router with the correct command.
    - **B.** NVRAM is corrupted.
    - **C.** The configuration register setting is incorrect.

D. The newly upgraded IOS is not compatible with the hardware of the router.

E. The configuration you saved is not compatible with the hardware.

11. Which command will install a Right-To-Use license so you can use an evaluation version of a feature?

A. `install Right-To-Use license feature` *`feature`*

B. `install temporary feature` *`feature`*

C. `license install feature`

D. `license boot module`

12. Which command determines the licenses that are active on your system along with several status variables?

A. `show license`

B. `show license feature`

C. `show license udi`

D. `show version`

13. Which command allows you to view the technology package licenses and feature licenses that are supported on your router along with several status variables?

A. `show license`

B. `show license feature`

C. `show license udi`

D. `show version`

14. Which command displays the unique device identifier that comprises the product ID and serial number of the router?

A. `show license`

B. `show license feature`

C. `show license udi`

D. `show version`

15. Which command displays various pieces of information about the current IOS version, including the licensing details at the end of the command's output?

A. `show license`

B. `show license feature`

C. `show license udi`

D. `show version`

16. Which command backs up your license to flash memory?

A. `copy tftp flash`

B. `save license flash`

C. `license save flash`

D. `copy license flash`

17. Which command displays the configuration register setting?
   A. `show ip route`
   B. `show boot version`
   C. `show version`
   D. `show flash`

18. What steps are needed to remove a license from a router? (Choose two.)
   A. Use the `erase flash:license` command.
   B. Reload the system.
   C. Use the `license boot` command with the `disable` variable at the end of the command line.
   D. Clear the license with the `license clear` command.

19. You have your laptop directly connected into a router's Ethernet port. Which of the following are among the requirements for the `copy flash tftp` command to be successful? (Choose three.)
   A. TFTP server software must be running on the router.
   B. TFTP server software must be running on your laptop.
   C. The Ethernet cable connecting the laptop directly into the router's Ethernet port must be a straight-through cable.
   D. The laptop must be on the same subnet as the router's Ethernet interface.
   E. The `copy flash tftp` command must be supplied the IP address of the laptop.
   F. There must be enough room in the flash memory of the router to accommodate the file to be copied.

20. The configuration register setting of 0x2102 provides what function to a router?
   A. It tells the router to boot into ROM monitor mode.
   B. It provides password recovery.
   C. It tells the router to look in NVRAM for the boot sequence.
   D. It boots the IOS from a TFTP server.
   E. It boots an IOS image stored in ROM.

Chapter 9

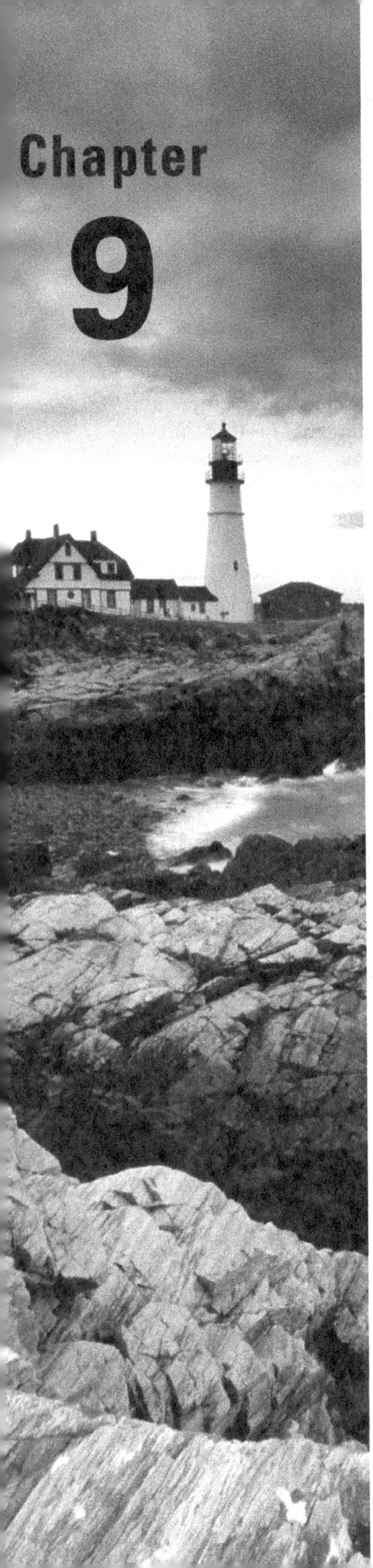

IP Routing

THE CCNA EXAM TOPICS COVERED IN THIS CHAPTER INCLUDE THE FOLLOWING:

✓ ***3.0 IP Connectivity***

- 3.1 Interpret the components of routing table
  - 3.1.a Routing protocol code
  - 3.1.b Prefix
  - 3.1.c Network mask
  - 3.1.d Next hop
  - 3.1.e Administrative distance
  - 3.1.f Metric
  - 3.1.g Gateway of last resort
- 3.2 Determine how a router makes a forwarding decision by default
  - 3.2.a Longest match
  - 3.2.b Administrative distance
  - 3.2.c Routing protocol metric
- 3.3 Configure and verify IPv4 and IPv6 static routing
  - 3.3.a Default route
  - 3.3.b Network route
  - 3.3.c Host route
  - 3.3.d Floating static

✓ ***4.0 IP Services***

- 4.3 Explain the role of DHCP and DNS within the network
- 4.6 Configure and verify DHCP client and relay

This chapter's focus is on the core topic of the ubiquitous IP routing process. It's integral to networking because it pertains to all routers and configurations that use it—easily the lion's share. IP routing is basically the process of moving packets from one network to another network using routers. And by routers, I mean Cisco routers, of course! However, the terms *router* and *layer 3 device* are interchangeable, and throughout this chapter when I use the term *router*, understand that I'm referring to any layer 3 device.

Before jumping into this chapter, I want to make sure you understand the difference between a *routing protocol* and a *routed protocol*. Routers use routing protocols to dynamically find all networks within the greater internetwork and to ensure that all routers have the same routing table. Routing protocols are also employed to determine the best path a packet should take through an internetwork to get to its destination most efficiently. Router Information Protocol (RIP), RIPv2, Enhanced Interior Gateway Routing Protocol (EIGRP), and Open Shortest Path First (OSPF) are great examples of the most common routing protocols.

Once all routers know about all networks, a routed protocol can be used to send user data (packets) through the established enterprise. Routed protocols are assigned to an interface and determine the method of packet delivery. Examples of routed protocols are Internet Protocol (IP) and IPv6.

I'm pretty confident you know how crucial it is for you to have this chapter's material down to an almost instinctive level. IP routing is innately what Cisco routers do, and they do it very well, so having a firm grasp of the fundamentals on this topic is vital if you want to excel during the exam and in a real-world networking environment!

I'm going to show you how to configure and verify IP routing with Cisco routers and guide you through these five key subjects:

- Routing basics
- The IP routing process
- Static routing
- Default routing
- Dynamic routing

We'll begin with the basics of how packets actually move through an internetwork.

NOTE To find bonus material, as well as Todd Lammle videos, practice questions, and hands-on labs, please see `www.lammle.com/ccna`.

Routing Basics

Once you create an internetwork by connecting your wide area networks (WANs) and local area networks (LANs) to a router, you'll need to configure logical network addresses, like IP addresses, to all hosts on that internetwork to enable them to communicate successfully throughout it.

The term *routing* refers to taking a packet from one device and sending it through the internetwork to another device on a different network. Routers don't really care about hosts—they only care about networks and the best path to each one. The logical network address of the destination host is key to getting packets through a routed network. It's the hardware address of the host that's used to deliver the packet from a router and ensure it arrives at the correct destination host.

Here's an important list of the minimum factors a router must know to be able to effectively route packets:

- Destination address
- Neighbor routers from which it can learn about remote networks
- Possible routes to all remote networks
- The best route to each remote network
- How to maintain and verify routing information

The router learns about remote networks from neighboring routers or from an administrator. The router then builds a routing table—a map of the internetwork, describing how to find remote networks. If a network is directly connected, then the router already knows how to get to it.

If a network isn't directly connected to the router, the router must use one of two ways to learn how to get to the remote network. The *static routing* method requires someone to hand-type all network locations into the routing table. Doing this would be a huge labor-intensive task when used on all but the smallest networks!

But when *dynamic routing* is used, a protocol on one router communicates with the same protocol running on neighboring routers. The routers then update each other about all the networks they know about and place this information into the routing table. If a change occurs in the network, the dynamic routing protocols automatically inform all routers about the event. If static routing is used, the administrator is responsible for updating all changes by hand onto all routers. Most people usually use a combination of dynamic and static routing to administer a large network.

Before we get into the IP routing process, let's take a look at a very simple example that demonstrates how a router uses the routing table to route packets out of an interface. We'll get into a more detailed look at the process soon, but I first want to show you something called the "longest match rule." Using this rule, IP will scan a routing table to find the longest match as compared to the destination address of a packet. Figure 9.1 offers a picture of this process.

FIGURE 9.1 A simple routing example

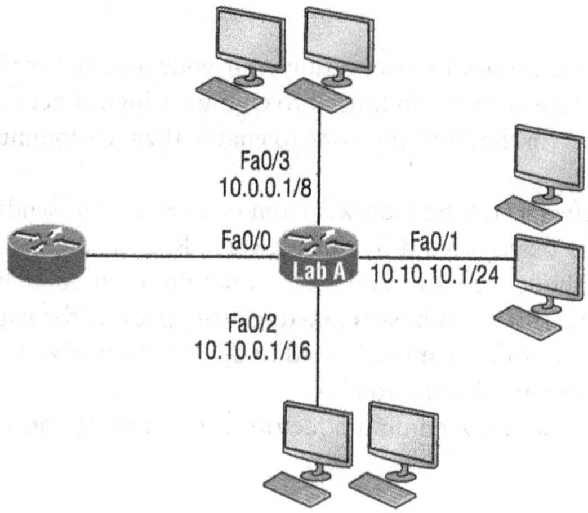

Figure 9.1 illustrates a simple network. Lab_A has four interfaces. Can you see which interface will be used to forward an IP datagram to a host with a destination IP address of 10.10.10.30?

By using the command `show ip route` on a router, we can see the routing table (map of the internetwork) that Lab_A has used to make its forwarding decisions:

```
Lab_A#sh ip route
Codes: L - local, C - connected, S - static,
[output cut]
10.0.0.0/8 is variably subnetted, 6 subnets, 4 masks
C 10.0.0.0/8 is directly connected, FastEthernet0/3
L 10.0.0.1/32 is directly connected, FastEthernet0/3
C 10.10.0.0/16 is directly connected, FastEthernet0/2
L 10.10.0.1/32 is directly connected, FastEthernet0/2
C 10.10.10.0/24 is directly connected, FastEthernet0/1
L 10.10.10.1/32 is directly connected, FastEthernet0/1
S* 0.0.0.0/0 is directly connected, FastEthernet0/0
```

The `C` in the routing table output means the networks listed are directly connected. Until we add a routing protocol like RIPv2, OSPF, etc., to the routers in our internetwork, or enter static routes, only directly connected networks will show up in our routing table. But wait—what about that `L` in the routing table—that's new, isn't it? Yes! Because in the new Cisco IOS 15 code, Cisco defines a different route, called a local host route. Each local route has a /32 prefix, defining a route just for the one address. So in this example, the router relied upon these routes, which list their own local IP addresses, to more efficiently forward packets to the router itself.

But let's get back to the original question: Looking at the figure and the output of the routing table, what will IP do with a received packet that has a destination IP address of 10.10.10.30? The router will packet-switch the packet to interface FastEthernet 0/1, which will frame the packet and then send it out on the network segment. This is referred to as *frame rewrite*. Based on the longest match rule, IP would look for 10.10.10.30, and if that isn't found in the table, IP would search for 10.10.10.0, then 10.10.0.0, and so on until a route is discovered.

Here's another example: Looking at the output of the next routing table, which interface will a packet with a destination address of 10.10.10.14 be forwarded from?

```
Lab_A#sh ip route
[output cut]
Gateway of last resort is not set
C 10.10.10.16/28 is directly connected, FastEthernet0/0
L 10.10.10.17/32 is directly connected, FastEthernet0/0
C 10.10.10.8/29 is directly connected, FastEthernet0/1
L 10.10.10.9/32 is directly connected, FastEthernet0/1
C 10.10.10.4/30 is directly connected, FastEthernet0/2
L 10.10.10.5/32 is directly connected, FastEthernet0/2
C 10.10.10.0/30 is directly connected, Serial 0/0
L 10.10.10.1/32 is directly connected, Serial0/0
```

To figure this out, look closely at the output until you see that the network is subnetted and each interface has a different mask. I have to tell you—you just can't answer this question if you can't subnet! 10.10.10.14 would be a host in the 10.10.10.8/29 subnet that's connected to the FastEthernet0/1 interface. If you're struggling with this, just go back and reread Chapter 3, "Easy Subnetting," until you've got it.

The IP Routing Process

The IP routing process is actually pretty simple and doesn't change regardless of the size of your network. To give you a picture of this fact, I'll use Figure 9.2 to describe what happens when Host A wants to communicate with Host B on a different network, step by step.

FIGURE 9.2 IP routing example using two hosts and one router

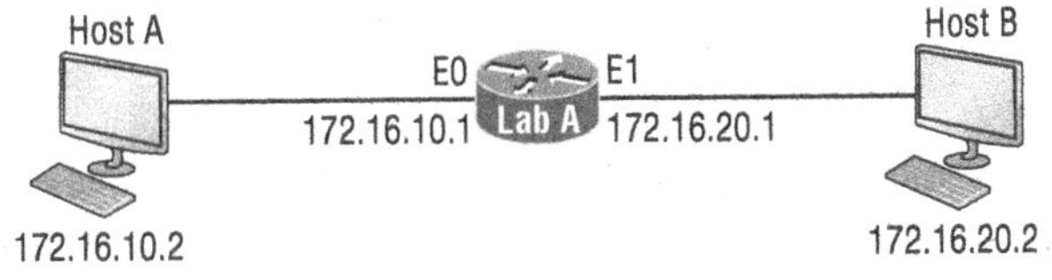

In Figure 9.2, a user on Host A pinged Host B's IP address. Routing doesn't get any simpler than this, but it still involves a lot of steps, so let's go through them:

1. Internet Control Message Protocol (ICMP) creates an echo request payload, which is simply the alphabet in the data field.
2. ICMP hands that payload to IP, which then creates a packet. At a minimum, this packet contains an IP source address, an IP destination address, and a Protocol field with 01h. Don't forget, Cisco likes to use *0x* in front of hex characters, so this could also look like 0x01. This tells the receiving host which protocol it should hand the payload to when the destination is reached. In this example, it's ICMP.
3. Once the packet is created, IP determines whether the destination IP address is on the local or a remote network.
4. Because IP has determined that this is a remote request, the packet must be sent to the default gateway so it can be routed to the remote network. The Registry in Windows is parsed to find the configured default gateway.
5. The default gateway of Host A is configured to 172.16.10.1. For this packet to be sent to the default gateway, the hardware address of the router's interface Ethernet 0, which is configured with the IP address of 172.16.10.1, must be known. Why? So the packet can be handed down to the Data Link layer, framed, and sent to the router's interface connected to the 172.16.10.0 network. Because hosts communicate only via hardware addresses on the local LAN, it's important to recognize that for Host A to communicate to Host B, it has to send packets to the Media Access Control (MAC) address of the default gateway on the local network.

NOTE: MAC addresses are always local on the LAN and never go through and past a router.

6. Next, the Address Resolution Protocol (ARP) cache of the host is checked to see whether the IP address of the default gateway has already been resolved to a hardware address.

If it has, the packet is then handed to the Data Link layer for framing. Remember that the hardware destination address is also handed down with that packet. Use the following to view the ARP cache on your host:

```
C:\>arp -a
Interface: 172.16.10.2 --- 0x3
Internet Address Physical Address Type
172.16.10.1 00-15-05-06-31-b0 dynamic
```

If the hardware address isn't already in the ARP cache of the host, an ARP broadcast will be sent out onto the local network to search for the 172.16.10.1 hardware address. The router then responds to the request, provides the hardware address of Ethernet 0, and the host caches the address.

7. Once the packet and destination hardware address are handed to the Data Link layer, the LAN driver is used to provide media access via the type of LAN—Ethernet, in this case. A frame is then generated, encapsulating the packet with control information. Within that frame are the hardware destination and source addresses plus, in this case, an Ether-Type field, which identifies the specific Network layer protocol that handed the packet to the Data Link layer. Here, it's IP. At the end of the frame is something called a Frame Check Sequence (FCS) field that houses the result of the cyclic redundancy check (CRC). The frame would look something like what I've detailed in Figure 9.3. It contains Host A's hardware (MAC) address and the destination hardware address of the default gateway. It does not include the remote host's MAC address—remember that!

FIGURE 9.3 Frame used from Host A to the Lab A router when Host B is pinged

Destination MAC (router's E0 MAC address)	Source MAC (Host A MAC address)	Ether-Type field	Packet	FCS CRC

8. Once the frame is completed, it's handed down to the Physical layer to be put on the physical medium one bit at a time. (In this example, twisted-pair wire.)
9. Every device in the collision domain receives these bits and builds the frame. They each run a CRC and check the answer in the FCS field. If the answers don't match, the frame is discarded.
   - If the CRC matches, the hardware destination address is checked to see if it also matches—in this example, it's the router's interface Ethernet 0.
   - If it's a match, then the Ether-Type field is checked to find the protocol used at the Network layer.
10. The packet is pulled from the frame, and what's left of the frame is discarded. The packet is handed to the protocol listed in the Ether-Type field and given to IP.
11. IP receives the packet and checks the IP destination address. Because the packet's destination address doesn't match any of the addresses configured on the receiving router, the router will look up the destination IP network address in its routing table.
12. The routing table must have an entry for the network 172.16.20.0 or the packet will be discarded immediately and an ICMP message will be sent back to the originating device with a destination network unreachable message.
13. If the router does find an entry for the destination network in its table, the packet is switched to the exit interface—in this example, interface Ethernet 1. The following output displays the Lab A router's routing table. The C means "directly connected." No routing protocols are needed in this network since all networks (all two of them) are directly connected.

```
Lab_A>sh ip route
C 172.16.10.0 is directly connected, Ethernet0
```

```
L 172.16.10.1/32 is directly connected, Ethernet0
C 172.16.20.0 is directly connected, Ethernet1
L 172.16.20.1/32 is directly connected, Ethernet1
```

14. The router packet-switches the packet to the Ethernet 1 buffer.
15. The Ethernet 1 buffer needs to know the hardware address of the destination host and first checks the ARP cache.
    - If the hardware address of Host B has already been resolved and is in the router's ARP cache, the packet and the hardware address will be handed down to the Data Link layer to be framed. Let's take a look at the ARP cache on the Lab A router by using the `show ip arp` command:

      ```
      Lab_A#sh ip arp
      Protocol Address Age(min) Hardware Addr Type Interface
      Internet 172.16.20.1 - 00d0.58ad.05f4 ARPA Ethernet1
      Internet 172.16.20.2 3 0030.9492.a5dd ARPA Ethernet1
      Internet 172.16.10.1 - 00d0.58ad.06aa ARPA Ethernet0
      Internet 172.16.10.2 12 0030.9492.a4ac ARPA Ethernet0
      ```

      The dash (-) signifies that this is the physical interface on the router. This output shows us that the router knows the 172.16.10.2 (Host A) and 172.16.20.2 (Host B) hardware addresses. Cisco routers will keep an entry in the ARP table for four hours.
    - Now if the hardware address hasn't already been resolved, the router will send an ARP request out E1 looking for the 172.16.20.2 hardware address. Host B responds with its hardware address, and the packet and destination hardware addresses are then both sent to the Data Link layer for framing.
16. The Data Link layer creates a frame with the destination and source hardware addresses, Ether-Type field, and FCS field at the end. The frame is then handed to the Physical layer to be sent out on the physical medium one bit at a time.
17. Host B receives the frame and immediately runs a CRC. If the result matches the information in the FCS field, the hardware destination address will be checked next. If the host finds a match, the Ether-Type field is then checked to determine the protocol that the packet should be handed to at the Network layer—IP, in this example.
18. At the Network layer, IP receives the packet and runs a CRC on the IP header. If that passes, IP then checks the destination address. Because a match has finally been made, the Protocol field is checked to find out to whom the payload should be given.
19. The payload is handed to ICMP, which understands that this is an echo request. ICMP responds to this by immediately discarding the packet and generating a new payload as an echo reply.

20. A packet is then created including the source and destination addresses, Protocol field, and payload. The destination device is now Host A.
21. IP then checks to see whether the destination IP address is a device on the local LAN or on a remote network. Because the destination device is on a remote network, the packet needs to be sent to the default gateway.
22. The default gateway IP address is found in the Registry of the Windows device, and the ARP cache is checked to see if the hardware address has already been resolved from an IP address.
23. Once the hardware address of the default gateway is found, the packet and destination hardware addresses are handed down to the Data Link layer for framing.
24. The Data Link layer frames the packet of information and includes the following in the header:
    - The destination and source hardware addresses
    - The Ether-Type field with 0x0800 (IP) in it
    - The FCS field with the CRC result in tow
25. The frame is now handed down to the Physical layer to be sent out over the network medium one bit at a time.
26. The router's Ethernet 1 interface receives the bits and builds a frame. The CRC is run, and the FCS field is checked to make sure the answers match.
27. Once the CRC is found to be okay, the hardware destination address is checked. Because the router's interface is a match, the packet is pulled from the frame and the Ether-Type field is checked to determine which protocol the packet should be delivered to at the Network layer.
28. The protocol is determined to be IP, so it gets the packet. IP runs a CRC check on the IP header first and then checks the destination IP address.

NOTE IP does not run a complete CRC like the Data Link layer does; it only checks the header for errors.

Because the IP destination address doesn't match any of the router's interfaces, the routing table is checked to see whether it has a route to 172.16.10.0. If it doesn't have a route over to the destination network, the packet will be discarded immediately. I want to point out that this is exactly where the source of confusion begins for a lot of administrators because when a ping fails, most people think the packet never reached the destination host. But as we see here, that's not *always* the case. All it takes for this to happen is for even just one of the remote routers to lack a route back to the originating host's network and—*poof!*—the packet is dropped on the *return trip*, not on its way to the host!

> **TIP** Just a quick note to mention that when (and if) the packet is lost on the way back to the originating host, you will typically see a request timed-out message because it's an unknown error. If the error occurs because of a known issue, such as if a route is not in the routing table on the way to the destination device, you will see a destination unreachable message. This should help you determine whether the problem occurred on the way to the destination or on the way back.

29. In this case, the router happens to know how to get to network 172.16.10.0—the exit interface is Ethernet 0—so the packet is switched to interface Ethernet 0.
30. The router then checks the ARP cache to determine whether the hardware address for 172.16.10.2 has already been resolved.
31. Because the hardware address to 172.16.10.2 is already cached from the originating trip to Host B, the hardware address and packet are then handed to the Data Link layer.
32. The Data Link layer builds a frame with the destination hardware address and source hardware address and then puts IP in the Ether-Type field. A CRC is run on the frame and the result is placed in the FCS field.
33. The frame is then handed to the Physical layer to be sent out onto the local network one bit at a time.
34. The destination host receives the frame, runs a CRC, checks the destination hardware address, then looks into the Ether-Type field to find out to whom to hand the packet.
35. IP is the designated receiver, and after the packet is handed to IP at the Network layer, it checks the Protocol field for further direction. IP finds instructions to give the payload to ICMP, and ICMP determines the packet to be an ICMP echo reply.
36. ICMP acknowledges that it has received the reply by sending an exclamation point (!) to the user interface. ICMP then attempts to send four more echo requests to the destination host.

You've just experienced Todd's 36 easy steps to understanding IP routing. The key takeaway here is that if you had a much larger network, the process would be the *same*. It's just that the larger the internetwork, the more hops the packet goes through before it finds the destination host.

It's super important to remember that when Host A sends a packet to Host B, the destination hardware address used is the default gateway's Ethernet interface. Why? Because frames can't be placed on remote networks—only local networks. So packets destined for remote networks must go through the default gateway.

Let's take a look at Host A's ARP cache now:

```
C:\ >arp -a
Interface: 172.16.10.2 --- 0x3
Internet Address Physical Address Type
172.16.10.1 00-15-05-06-31-b0 dynamic
172.16.20.1 00-15-05-06-31-b0 dynamic
```

Did you notice that the hardware (MAC) address that Host A uses to get to Host B is the Lab A E0 interface? Hardware addresses are *always* local, and they never pass through a router's interface. Understanding this process is very important, so carve this into your memory!

The Cisco Router Internal Process

One more thing before we test how well you understand my 36 steps of IP routing. I think it's important to explain how a router forwards packets internally. For IP to look up a destination address in a routing table on a router, processing in the router must take place, and if there are tens of thousands of routes in that table, the amount of CPU time would be enormous. It results in a potentially overwhelming amount of overhead—think about a router at your ISP that has to calculate millions of packets per second and even subnet to find the correct exit interface! Even with the little network I'm using in this book, lots of processing would need to be done if there were actual hosts connected and sending data.

Cisco uses three types of packet-forwarding techniques.

Process Switching This is actually how many people see routers to this day because it's true that routers actually did perform this type of bare-bones packet switching back in 1990 when Cisco released their very first router. But the days when traffic demands were unimaginably light are long gone—not in today's networks! This process is now extremely complex and involves looking up every destination in the routing table and finding the exit interface for every packet. This is pretty much how I just explained the process in my 36 steps. But even though what I wrote was absolutely true in concept, the internal process requires much more than packet-switching technology today because of the millions of packets per second that must now be processed. So Cisco came up with some other technologies to help with the "big process problem."

Fast Switching This solution was created to make the slow performance of process switching faster and more efficient. Fast switching uses a cache to store the most recently used destinations so that lookups are not required for every packet. Caching the exit interface of the destination device, plus the layer 2 header, dramatically improved performance, but as our networks evolved with the need for even more speed, Cisco created yet another technology...

Cisco Express Forwarding This is Cisco's newest packet forwarding, performance optimizing creation and it's the default method used on all the latest Cisco routers. Cisco Express Forwarding (CEF) makes many different cache tables that enhance performance and is change triggered, not packet triggered. Translated, this means that when the network topology changes, the cache changes along with it.

TIP

To see which packet switching method your router interface is using, use the command show `ip interface`.

Testing Your IP Routing Understanding

Because understanding IP routing is so important, it's time for that little test I mentioned earlier. How well do you actually have the IP routing process down so far? Let's find out by having you look at a couple of figures and answering some very basic IP routing questions based on them.

Figure 9.4 shows a LAN connected to RouterA that's connected via a WAN link to RouterB. RouterB has a LAN connected with an HTTP server attached.

FIGURE 9.4 IP routing example 1

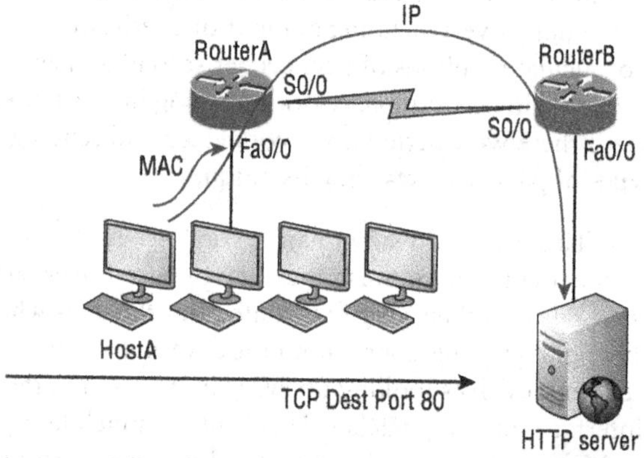

1. The critical information you want to get by looking at this figure is exactly how IP routing will occur in this example. Let's determine the characteristics of a frame as it leaves HostA. Okay, so maybe we'll cheat a bit. I'll give you the answer, but I still want you to go back over the figure and see if you can answer example 2 without looking at my three-step answer!
2. The destination address of a frame from HostA would be the MAC address of RouterA's Fa0/0 interface.
3. The destination address of a packet would be the IP address of the HTTP server's network interface card (NIC).
4. The destination port number in the segment header would be 80.

That was a pretty straightforward scenario. One thing to remember is that when multiple hosts are communicating to a server via HTTP, they must all use a different source port number. The source and destination IP addresses and port numbers are how the server keeps the data separated at the Transport layer.

Let's complicate things by adding another device into the network. Figure 9.5 shows a network with only one router but two switches.

FIGURE 9.5 IP routing example 2

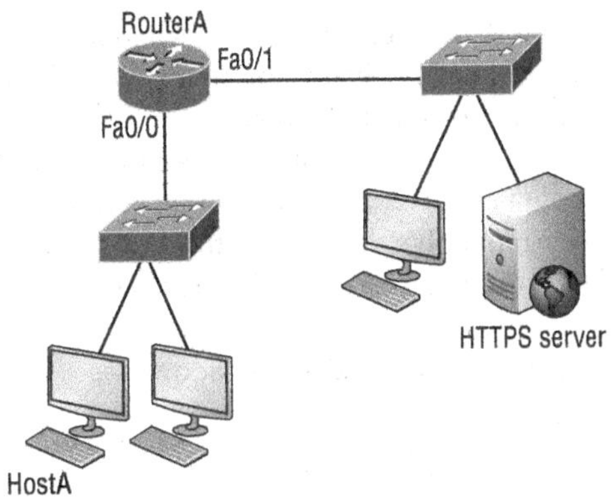

The key thing to zero in on about the IP routing process in this scenario is what happens when HostA sends data to the HTTPS server? Here's your answer:

1. The destination address of a frame from HostA would be the MAC address of RouterA's Fa0/0 interface.
2. The destination address of a packet is the IP address of the HTTPS server's NIC.
3. The destination port number in the segment header will have a value of 443.

Did you notice that the switches weren't used as either a default gateway or any other destination? That's because switches have nothing to do with routing. How many of you chose the switch as the default gateway (destination) MAC address for HostA? If you did, don't feel bad; just look into where you went wrong and why. Remember, if your packets are destined for outside the LAN as they were in these last two examples, the destination MAC address will always be the router's interface!

Before moving on into some of the more advanced aspects of IP routing, let's analyze another issue. Take a look at the output of this router's routing table:

```
Corp#sh ip route
[output cut]
R 192.168.215.0 [120/2] via 192.168.20.2, 00:00:23, Serial0/0
R 192.168.115.0 [120/1] via 192.168.20.2, 00:00:23, Serial0/0
R 192.168.30.0 [120/1] via 192.168.20.2, 00:00:23, Serial0/0
C 192.168.20.0 is directly connected, Serial0/0
L 192.168.20.1/32 is directly connected, Serial0/0
C 192.168.214.0 is directly connected, FastEthernet0/0
L 192.168.214.1/32 is directly connected, FastEthernet0/0
```

What do we see here? If I were to tell you that the corporate router received an IP packet with a source IP address of 192.168.214.20 and with destination address 192.168.22.3, what do you think the Corp router will do with this packet?

If you said, "The packet came in on the FastEthernet 0/0 interface, but because the routing table doesn't show a route to network 192.168.22.0 (or a default route), the router will discard the packet and send an ICMP destination unreachable message back out to interface FastEthernet 0/0," you're exactly right! The reason that's the right answer is because that's the source LAN where the packet originated from.

Let's check out the next figure and talk about the frames and packets in detail. We're not really going over anything new here; I'm just making sure you totally, completely, thoroughly, understand basic IP routing. It's the crux of this book and the topic the exam objectives are geared toward. We'll use Figure 9.6 for the next few scenarios.

FIGURE 9.6 Basic IP routing using MAC and IP addresses

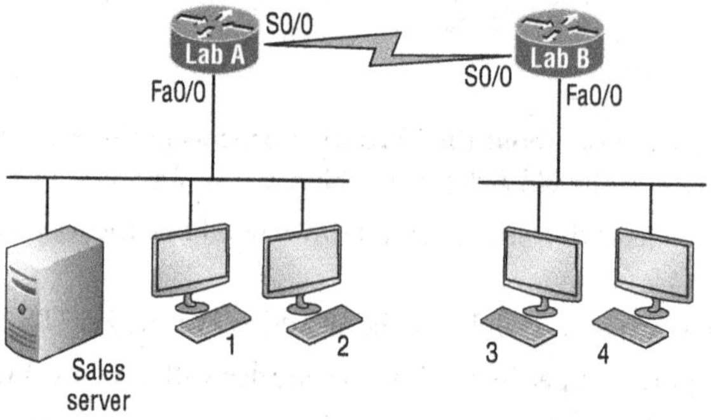

Referring to Figure 9.6, here's a list of all the answers to questions you need:

1. To begin communicating with the Sales server, Host 4 sends out an ARP request. How will the devices exhibited in the topology respond to this request?
2. Host 4 has received an ARP reply. Host 4 will now build a packet and then place this packet in the frame. What information will be placed in the header of the packet that leaves Host 4 if Host 4 is going to communicate to the Sales server?
3. The Lab A router has received the packet and will send it out Fa0/0 onto the LAN toward the server. What will the frame have in the header as the source and destination addresses?
4. Host 4 is displaying two web documents from the Sales server in two browser windows at the same time. How did the data find its way to the correct browser windows?

The following should probably be written in a 3-point font upside down in another part of the book so that it would be really hard for you to cheat, but because I'm not mean and you really need to conquer this stuff, here are your answers in the same order that the scenarios were just presented in:

1. To begin communicating with the server, Host 4 sends out an ARP request. How will the devices exhibited in the topology respond to this request? Since MAC addresses

must stay on the local network, the Lab B router will respond with the MAC address of the Fa0/0 interface and Host 4 will send all frames to the MAC address of the Lab B Fa0/0 interface when sending packets to the Sales server.

2. Host 4 has received an ARP reply. Host 4 will now build a packet, then place this packet in the frame. What information will be placed in the header of the packet that leaves Host 4 if Host 4 is going to communicate to the Sales server? Since we're now talking about packets, not frames, the source address will be the IP address of Host 4 and the destination address will be the IP address of the Sales server.
3. Finally, the Lab A router has received the packet and will send it out Fa0/0 onto the LAN toward the server. What will the frame have in the header as the source and destination addresses? The source MAC address will be the Lab A router's Fa0/0 interface, and the destination MAC address will be the Sales server's MAC address because all MAC addresses must be local on the LAN.
4. Host 4 is displaying two web documents from the Sales server in two different browser windows at the same time. How did the data find its way to the correct browser windows? TCP port numbers are used to direct the data to the correct application window.

Great! But we're not quite done yet. I've got a few more questions for you before you actually get to configure routing in a real network. Figure 9.7 shows a basic network, and Host 4 needs to get email. Which address will be placed in the destination address field of the frame when it leaves Host 4?

The answer is that Host 4 will use the destination MAC address of the Fa0/0 interface on the Lab B router—you knew that, right? Look at Figure 9.7 again: What if Host 4 needs to communicate with Host 1—not the server, but with Host 1? Which OSI layer 3 source address will be found in the packet header when it reaches Host 1?

FIGURE 9.7 Testing basic routing knowledge

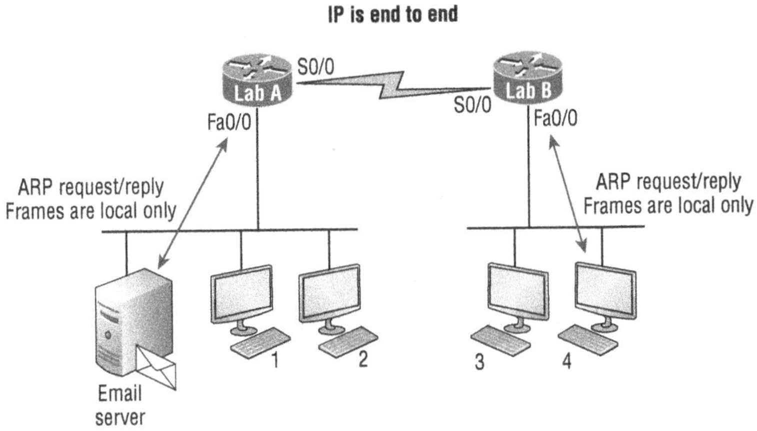

Hopefully, you've got this: At layer 3, the source IP address will be Host 4 and the destination address in the packet will be the IP address of Host 1. Of course, the destination MAC address from Host 4 will always be the Fa0/0 address of the Lab B router, right? And since we have more than one router, we'll need a routing protocol that communicates between both of them so that traffic can be forwarded in the right direction to reach the network that Host 1 is connected to.

Okay, one more scenario, and again using Figure 9.7. Host 4 is transferring a file to the email server connected to the Lab A router. What would be the layer 2 destination address leaving Host 4? (Yes, I've asked this question more than once.) But not this one: What will be the source MAC address when the frame is received at the email server?

Hopefully, you answered that the layer 2 destination address leaving Host 4 is the MAC address of the Fa0/0 interface on the Lab B router and that the source layer 2 address that the email server will receive is the Fa0/0 interface of the Lab A router.

If you did, you're ready to discover how IP routing is handled in a larger network environment!

Configuring IP Routing

It's time to get serious and configure a real network. Figure 9.8 shows three routers: Corp, SF, and LA. Remember, by default, these routers only know about networks that are directly connected to them. I'll continue to use this figure and network throughout the rest of this book. As we progress, I'll add more routers and switches as needed.

FIGURE 9.8 Configuring IP routing

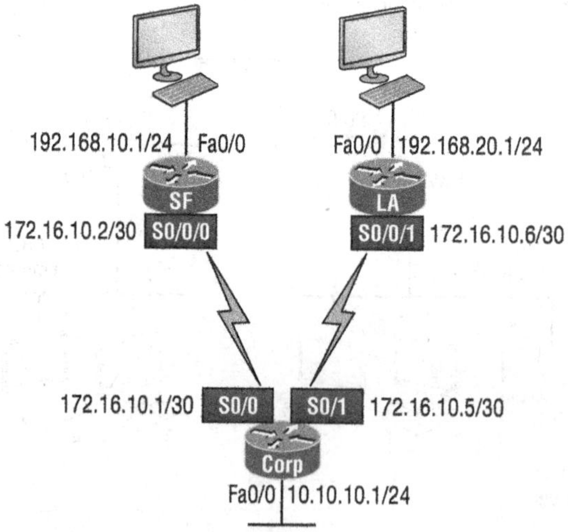

As you might guess, I've got quite a nice collection of routers for us to play with. But you don't need a closet full of devices to perform most, if not all, of the commands we'll use in this book. You can get by nicely with pretty much any router or even with a good router simulator.

Getting back to business: The Corp router has two serial interfaces, which will provide a WAN connection to the SF and LA router and two Fast Ethernet interfaces as well. The two remote routers have two serial interfaces and two Fast Ethernet interfaces.

The first step for this project is to correctly configure each router with an IP address on each interface. The following list shows the IP address scheme I'm going to use to configure the network. After we go over how the network is configured, I'll cover how to configure IP routing. Pay attention to the subnet masks! The LANs all use a /24 mask, but the WANs are using a /30.

Corp

- Serial 0/0: 172.16.10.1/30
- Serial 0/1: 172.16.10.5/30
- Fa0/0: 10.10.10.1/24

SF

- S0/0/0: 172.16.10.2/30
- Fa0/0: 192.168.10.1/24

LA

- S0/0/0: 172.16.10.6/30
- Fa0/0: 192.168.20.1/24

The router configuration is really a pretty straightforward process because you just need to add IP addresses to your interfaces and then perform a no shutdown on those same interfaces. It gets more complex later on, but for now, let's configure the IP addresses in the network.

Corp Configuration

We need to configure three interfaces to configure the Corp router. And configuring the hostnames of each router will make identification much easier. While we're at it, let's set the interface descriptions, banner, and router passwords, too because you need to make a habit of configuring these commands on every router!

To get started, I performed an `erase startup-config` on the router and reloaded, so we'll start in setup mode. I chose no when prompted to enter setup mode, which will get us straight to the username prompt of the console. I'm going to configure all my routers this same way.

Here's how what I just did looks:

```
--- System Configuration Dialog ---
Would you like to enter the initial configuration dialog? [yes/no]: n
```

```
Press RETURN to get started!
Router>en
Router#config t
Router(config)#hostname Corp
Corp(config)#enable secret GlobalNet
Corp(config)#no ip domain-lookup
Corp(config)#int f0/0
Corp(config-if)#desc Connection to LAN BackBone
Corp(config-if)#ip address 10.10.10.1 255.255.255.0
Corp(config-if)#no shut
Corp(config-if)#int s0/0
Corp(config-if)#desc WAN connection to SF
Corp(config-if)#ip address 172.16.10.1 255.255.255.252
Corp(config-if)#no shut
Corp(config-if)#int s0/1
Corp(config-if)#desc WAN connection to LA
Corp(config-if)#ip address 172.16.10.5 255.255.255.252
Corp(config-if)#no shut
Corp(config-if)#line con 0
Corp(config-line)#password console
Corp(config-line)#logging
Corp(config-line)#logging sync
Corp(config-line)#exit
Corp(config)#line vty 0 ?
<1-181> Last Line number
<cr>
Corp(config)#line vty 0 181
Corp(config-line)#password telnet
Corp(config-line)#login
Corp(config-line)#exit
Corp(config)#banner motd # This is my Corp Router #
Corp(config)#^Z
Corp#copy run start
Destination filename [startup-config]?
Building configuration...
[OK]
Corp# [OK]
```

Let's talk about the configuration of the Corp router. First, I set the hostname and enabled secret, but what is that `no ip domain-lookup` command? That command stops the router from trying to resolve hostnames, which is an annoying feature unless you've configured a host table or DNS. Next, I configured the three interfaces with descriptions and IP addresses and enabled them with the `no shutdown` command. The console and VTY passwords came next, but what is that `logging sync` command under the console line? The logging synchronous command stops console messages from writing over what you are typing in, meaning it will save your sanity! Last, I set my banner and then saved my configs.

To view the IP routing tables created on a Cisco router, use the command `show ip route`. Here's the command's output:

```
Corp#sh ip route
Codes: L - local, C - connected, S - static, R - RIP, M - mobile, B - BGP
D - EIGRP, EX - EIGRP external, O - OSPF, IA - OSPF inter area
N1 - OSPF NSSA external type 1, N2 - OSPF NSSA external type 2
E1 - OSPF external type 1, E2 - OSPF external type 2
i - IS-IS, su - IS-IS summary, L1 - IS-IS level-1, L2 - IS-IS level-2
ia - IS-IS inter area, * - candidate default, U - per-user static route
o - ODR, P - periodic downloaded static route, H - NHRP, l - LISP
+ - replicated route, % - next hop override
Gateway of last resort is not set
10.0.0.0/24 is subnetted, 1 subnets
C 10.10.10.0 is directly connected, FastEthernet0/0
L 10.10.10.1/32 is directly connected, FastEthernet0/0
Corp#
```

So remember, only configured, directly connected networks are going to show up in the routing table. Why is it that only the FastEthernet 0/0 interface shows up in the table? It's not a huge deal—it's just because you won't see the serial interfaces come up until the other side of the links are operational. As soon as we configure our SF and LA routers, those interfaces should pop right up.

One thing though: Did you notice the `C` on the left side of the output of the routing table? When you see that there, it means that the network is directly connected. The codes for each type of connection are listed at the top of the `show ip route` command, along with their descriptions.

NOTE For brevity, the codes at the top of the output will be cut in the rest of this chapter.

SF Configuration

Now we're ready to configure the next router: SF. To make that happen correctly, keep in mind that we have two interfaces to deal with: Serial 0/0/0 and FastEthernet 0/0. Let's make sure not to forget to add the hostname, passwords, interface descriptions, and banners to the router configuration. As I did with the Corp router, I erased the configuration and reloaded since this router had already been configured.

Here's the configuration I used:

```
R1#erase start
% Incomplete command.
R1#erase startup-config
Erasing the nvram filesystem will remove all configuration files!
Continue? [confirm][enter]
[OK]
Erase of nvram: complete
R1#reload
Proceed with reload? [confirm][enter]
[output cut]
%Error opening tftp://255.255.255.255/network-confg (Timed out)
%Error opening tftp://255.255.255.255/cisconet.cfg (Timed out)
--- System Configuration Dialog ---
Would you like to enter the initial configuration dialog? [yes/no]: n
```

Before we move on, let's talk about this output for a second. First, notice that beginning with IOS 12.4, ISR routers will no longer take the command erase start. The router has only one command after erase that starts with *s*, as shown here:

```
Router#erase s?
startup-config
```

I know, you'd think that the IOS would continue to accept the command, but nope—sorry! The second thing I want to point out is that the output tells us the router is looking for a Trivial File Transfer Protocol TFTP (host) to see if it can download a configuration. When that fails, it goes straight into setup mode.

Let's get back to configuring our router:

```
Press RETURN to get started!
Router#config t
Router(config)#hostname SF
SF(config)#enable secret GlobalNet
SF(config)#no ip domain-lookup
SF(config)#int s0/0/0
SF(config-if)#desc WAN Connection to Corp
SF(config-if)#ip address 172.16.10.2 255.255.255.252
SF(config-if)#no shut
SF(config-if)#clock rate 1000000
SF(config-if)#int f0/0
SF(config-if)#desc SF LAN
SF(config-if)#ip address 192.168.10.1 255.255.255.0
SF(config-if)#no shut
```

```
SF(config-if)#line con 0
SF(config-line)#password console
SF(config-line)#login
SF(config-line)#logging sync
SF(config-line)#exit
SF(config)#line vty 0 ?
<1-1180> Last Line number
<cr>
SF(config)#line vty 0 1180
SF(config-line)#password telnet
SF(config-line)#login
SF(config-line)#banner motd #This is the SF Branch router#
SF(config)#exit
SF#copy run start
Destination filename [startup-config]?
Building configuration...
[OK]
```

Let's take a look at our configuration of the interfaces with the following two commands:

```
SF#sh run | begin int
interface FastEthernet0/0
description SF LAN
ip address 192.168.10.1 255.255.255.0
duplex auto
speed auto
!
interface FastEthernet0/1
no ip address
shutdown
duplex auto
speed auto
!
interface Serial0/0/0
description WAN Connection to Corp
ip address 172.16.10.2 255.255.255.252
clock rate 1000000
!
SF#sh ip int brief
Interface IP-Address OK? Method Status Protocol
FastEthernet0/0 192.168.10.1 YES manual up up
```

```
FastEthernet0/1 unassigned YES unset administratively down down
Serial0/0/0 172.16.10.2 YES manual up up
Serial0/0/1 unassigned YES unset administratively down down
SF#
```

Now that both ends of the serial link are configured, the link comes up. Remember, the up/up status for the interfaces are Physical/Data Link layer status indicators that don't reflect the layer 3 status! I ask students in my classes, "If the link shows up/up, can you ping the directly connected network?" And they say, "Yes!" The correct answer is, "I don't know," because we can't see the layer 3 status with this command. We only see layers 1 and 2 and verify that the IP addresses don't have a typo. Remember this!

The show `ip route` command for the SF router reveals the following:

```
SF#sh ip route
C 192.168.10.0/24 is directly connected, FastEthernet0/0
L 192.168.10.1/32 is directly connected, FastEthernet0/0
172.16.0.0/30 is subnetted, 1 subnets
C 172.16.10.0 is directly connected, Serial0/0/0
L 172.16.10.2/32 is directly connected, Serial0/0/0
```

Notice that router SF knows how to get to networks 172.16.10.0/30 and 192.168.10.0/24; we can now ping to the Corp router from SF:

```
SF#ping 172.16.10.1
Type escape sequence to abort.
Sending 5, 100-byte ICMP Echos to 172.16.10.1, timeout is 2 seconds:
!!!!!
Success rate is 100 percent (5/5), round-trip min/avg/max = 1/3/4 ms
```

Now let's head back to the Corp router and check out the routing table:

```
Corp>sh ip route
172.16.0.0/30 is subnetted, 1 subnets
C 172.16.10.0 is directly connected, Serial0/0
L 172.16.10.1/32 is directly connected, Serial0/0
10.0.0.0/24 is subnetted, 1 subnets
C 10.10.10.0 is directly connected, FastEthernet0/0
L 10.10.10.1/32 is directly connected, FastEthernet0/0
```

On the SF router's serial interface 0/0/0 is a DCE connection, which means a clock rate needs to be set on the interface. Remember that you don't need to use the `clock rate` command in production.

We can see our clocking with the show `controllers` command:

```
SF#sh controllers s0/0/0
Interface Serial0/0/0
```

```
Hardware is GT96K
DCE V.35, clock rate 1000000

Corp>sh controllers s0/0
Interface Serial0/0
Hardware is PowerQUICC MPC860
DTE V.35 TX and RX clocks detected.
```

Because the SF router has a DCE cable connection, I needed to add clock rate to this interface because DTE receives clock. Keep in mind that the new ISR routers will autodetect this and set the clock rate to 2000000. But you still need to make sure you're able to find an interface that is DCE and set clocking to meet the objectives.

Since the serial links are showing up, we can now see both networks in the Corp routing table. And once we configure LA, we'll see one more network in the routing table of the Corp router. The Corp router can't see the 192.168.10.0 network because we don't have any routing configured yet; routers see only directly connected networks by default.

LA Configuration

To configure LA, we're going to do pretty much the same thing we did with the other two routers. There are two interfaces to deal with, Serial 0/0/1 and FastEthernet 0/0, and again we'll be sure to add the hostname, passwords, interface descriptions, and a banner to the router configuration:

```
Router(config)#hostname LA
LA(config)#enable secret GlobalNet
LA(config)#no ip domain-lookup
LA(config)#int s0/0/1
LA(config-if)#ip address 172.16.10.6 255.255.255.252
LA(config-if)#no shut
LA(config-if)#clock rate 1000000
LA(config-if)#description WAN To Corporate
LA(config-if)#int f0/0
LA(config-if)#ip address 192.168.20.1 255.255.255.0
LA(config-if)#no shut
LA(config-if)#description LA LAN
LA(config-if)#line con 0
LA(config-line)#password console
LA(config-line)#login
LA(config-line)#logging sync
LA(config-line)#exit
LA(config)#line vty 0 ?
```

```
<1-1180> Last Line number
<cr>
LA(config)#line vty 0 1180
LA(config-line)#password telnet
LA(config-line)#login
LA(config-line)#exit
LA(config)#banner motd #This is my LA Router#
LA(config)#exit
LA#copy run start
Destination filename [startup-config]?
Building configuration...
[OK]
```

Nice! Everything was pretty straightforward. The following output, which I gained via the `show ip route` command, displays the directly connected networks of 192.168.20.0 and 172.16.10.0:

```
LA#sh ip route
172.16.0.0/30 is subnetted, 1 subnets
C 172.16.10.4 is directly connected, Serial0/0/1
L 172.16.10.6/32 is directly connected, Serial0/0/1
C 192.168.20.0/24 is directly connected, FastEthernet0/0
L 192.168.20.1/32 is directly connected, FastEthernet0/0
```

So now that we've configured all three routers with IP addresses and administrative functions, we can move on to deal with routing. But I want to do one more thing on the SF and LA routers. Because this is a very small network, let's build a Dynamic Host Configuration Protocol (DHCP) server on the Corp router for each LAN.

Configuring DHCP on Our Corp Router

While it's true that I could approach this task by going to each remote router and creating a pool, why bother with all that when I can easily create two pools on the Corp router and have the remote routers forward requests to the Corp router?

Let's give it a shot:

```
Corp#config t
Corp(config)#ip dhcp excluded-address 192.168.10.1
Corp(config)#ip dhcp excluded-address 192.168.20.1
Corp(config)#ip dhcp pool SF_LAN
Corp(dhcp-config)#network 192.168.10.0 255.255.255.0
Corp(dhcp-config)#default-router 192.168.10.1
Corp(dhcp-config)#dns-server 4.4.4.4
Corp(dhcp-config)#exit
```

```
Corp(config)#ip dhcp pool LA_LAN
Corp(dhcp-config)#network 192.168.20.0 255.255.255.0
Corp(dhcp-config)#default-router 192.168.20.1
Corp(dhcp-config)#dns-server 4.4.4.4
Corp(dhcp-config)#exit
Corp(config)#exit
Corp#copy run start
Destination filename [startup-config]?
Building configuration...
```

Creating DHCP pools on a router is actually a simple process, and you would go about the configuration the same way on any router you wish to add a DHCP pool to. To designate a router as a DHCP server, you just create the pool name, add the network/subnet and the default gateway, and then exclude any addresses that you don't want handed out. You definitely want to make sure you've excluded the default gateway address, and you'd usually add a DNS server as well. I always add any exclusions first, and remember that you can conveniently exclude a range of addresses on a single line. But first, we need to figure out why the Corp router still can't get to the remote networks by default.

Now I'm pretty sure I configured DHCP correctly, but I just have this nagging feeling I forgot something important. What could that be? Well, the hosts are remote across a router, so what would I need to do that would allow them to get an address from a DHCP server? If you concluded that I've got to configure the SF and LA F0/0 interfaces to forward the DHCP client requests to the server, you got it!

Here's how we'd go about doing that:

```
LA#config t
LA(config)#int f0/0
LA(config-if)#ip helper-address 172.16.10.5

SF#config t
SF(config)#int f0/0
SF(config-if)#ip helper-address 172.16.10.1
```

I'm pretty sure I did this correctly, but we won't know until I have some type of routing configured and working. So let's get to that next.

Configuring IP Routing in Our Network

So is our network really good to go? After all, I've configured it with IP addressing, administrative functions and even clocking that will automatically occur with the ISR routers. But how will our routers send packets to remote networks when they get their destination information by looking into their tables that only include directions about directly connected networks? And you know routers promptly discard packets they receive with addresses for networks that aren't listed in their routing table, right?

So we're not exactly ready to rock after all. But we will be soon because there are several ways to configure the routing tables to include all the networks in our little internetwork so that packets will be properly forwarded. As usual, one size fits all rarely fits at all, and what's best for one network isn't necessarily what's best for another. That's why understanding the different types of routing will be really helpful when choosing the best solution for your specific environment and business requirements.

I'm going to cover the following three routing methods with you:

- Static routing
- Default routing
- Dynamic routing

We're going to start with the first way and implement static routing on our network, because if you can implement static routing *and* make it work, you've demonstrated that you definitely have a solid understanding of the internetwork. So let's get started.

Static Routing

Static routing is the process that ensues when you manually add routes in each router's routing table. Predictably, there are pros and cons to static routing, but that's true for all routing approaches.

Here are the pros:

- There is no overhead on the router CPU, which means you could probably make do with a cheaper router than you would need for dynamic routing.
- There is no bandwidth usage between routers, saving you money on WAN links as well, minimizing overhead on the router since you're not using a routing protocol.
- It adds security because you, the administrator, can be very exclusive and choose to allow routing access to certain networks only.

And here are the cons:

- Whoever the administrator is must have a vault-tight knowledge of the internetwork and how each router is connected to configure routes correctly. If you don't have a good, accurate map of your internetwork, things will get very messy quickly!
- If you add a network to the internetwork, you have to tediously add a route to it on all routers by hand, which only gets increasingly insane as the network grows.
- Due to the last point, it's just not feasible to use it in most large networks because maintaining it would be a full-time job in itself.

But that list of cons doesn't mean you get to skip learning all about it mainly because of that first disadvantage I listed—the fact that you must have such a solid understanding of a network to configure it properly! So let's dive in and develop some skills. Starting at the beginning, here's the command syntax you use to add a static route to a routing table from global config:

```
ip route [destination_network] [mask] [next-hop_address or
exitinterface] [administrative_distance] [permanent]
```

This list describes each command in the string:

ip route The command used to create the static route.

destination_network The network you're placing in the routing table.

mask The subnet mask being used on the network.

next-hop_address This is the IP address of the next-hop router that will receive packets and forward them to the remote network, which must signify a router interface that's on a directly connected network. You must be able to successfully ping the router interface before you can add the route. Important note to self is that if you type in the wrong next-hop address or the interface to the correct router is down, the static route will show up in the router's configuration but not in the routing table.

exitinterface Used in place of the next-hop address if you want and shows up as a directly connected route.

administrative_distance By default, static routes have an administrative distance of 1 or 0 if you use an exit interface instead of a next-hop address. You can change the default value by adding an administrative weight at the end of the command. I'll talk a lot more about this later in the chapter when we get to dynamic routing.

permanent If the interface is shut down or the router can't communicate to the next-hop router, the route will automatically be discarded from the routing table by default. Choosing the permanent option keeps the entry in the routing table no matter what happens.

Before I guide you through configuring static routes, let's take a look at a sample static route to see what we can find out about it:

```
Router(config)#ip route 172.16.3.0 255.255.255.0 192.168.2.4
```

- The `ip route` command tells us simply that it's a static route.
- 172.16.3.0 is the remote network we want to send packets to.
- 255.255.255.0 is the mask of the remote network.
- 192.168.2.4 is the next hop, or router, that packets will be sent to.

But what if the static route looked like this instead?

```
Router(config)#ip route 172.16.3.0 255.255.255.0 192.168.2.4 150
```

That 150 at the end changes the default administrative distance (AD) of 1 to 150. As I said, I'll talk much more about AD when we get into dynamic routing, but for now, just remember that the AD is the trustworthiness of a route, where 0 is best and 255 is worst.

One more example, then we'll start configuring:

```
Router(config)#ip route 172.16.3.0 255.255.255.0 s0/0/0
```

Instead of using a next-hop address, we can use an exit interface that will make the route show up as a directly connected network. Functionally, the next hop and exit interface work exactly the same.

To help you understand how static routes work, I'll demonstrate the configuration on the internetwork shown previously in Figure 9.8. Here it is again in Figure 9.9 to save you the trouble of having to go back and forth to view the same figure.

FIGURE 9.9 Our internetwork

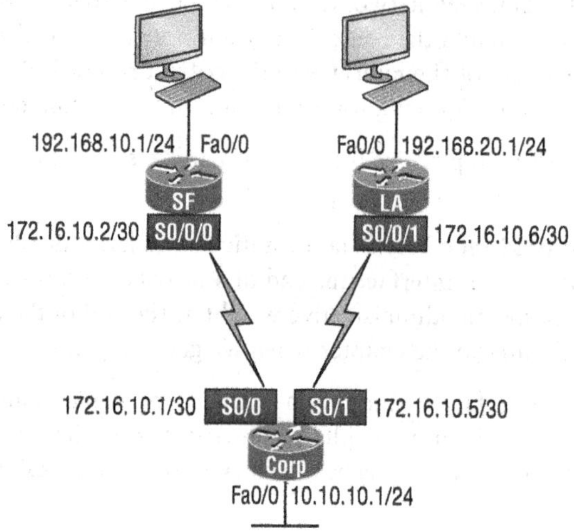

Corp

Each routing table automatically includes directly connected networks. To be able to route to all indirectly connected networks within the internetwork, the routing table must include information that describes where these other networks are located and how to get to them.

The Corp router is connected to three networks. For the Corp router to be able to route to all networks, the following networks have to be configured into its routing table:

- 192.168.10.0
- 192.168.20.0

The next router output shows the static routes on the Corp router and the routing table after the configuration. For the Corp router to find the remote networks, I had to place an entry into the routing table describing the remote network, the remote mask, and where to send the packets. I'm going to add a 150 at the end of each line to raise the administrative distance. You'll see why soon when we get to dynamic routing. Many times this is also referred to as a *floating static route* because the static route has a higher administrative distance than any routing protocol and will only be used if the routes found with the routing protocols (lower AD) go down. Here's the output:

```
Corp#config t
Corp(config)#ip route 192.168.10.0 255.255.255.0 172.16.10.2 150
Corp(config)#ip route 192.168.20.0 255.255.255.0 s0/1 150
Corp(config)#do show run | begin ip route
ip route 192.168.10.0 255.255.255.0 172.16.10.2 150
ip route 192.168.20.0 255.255.255.0 Serial0/1 150
```

I needed to use different paths for networks 192.168.10.0 and 192.168.20.0, so I used a next-hop address for the SF router and an exit interface for the LA router. After the router has been configured, you can just type **show ip route** to see the static routes:

```
Corp(config)#do show ip route
S 192.168.10.0/24 [150/0] via 172.16.10.2
172.16.0.0/30 is subnetted, 2 subnets
C 172.16.10.4 is directly connected, Serial0/1
L 172.16.10.5/32 is directly connected, Serial0/1
C 172.16.10.0 is directly connected, Serial0/0
L 172.16.10.1/32 is directly connected, Serial0/0
S 192.168.20.0/24 is directly connected, Serial0/1
10.0.0.0/24 is subnetted, 1 subnets
C 10.10.10.0 is directly connected, FastEthernet0/0
L 10.10.10.1/32 is directly connected, FastEthernet0/0
```

The Corp router is configured to route and know all routes to all networks. But can you see a difference in the routing table for the routes to SF and LA? That's right! The next-hop configuration showed up as via, and the route configured with an exit interface configuration shows up as static but also as directly connected. This demonstrates how they are functionally the same but will display differently in the routing table.

Understand that if the routes don't appear in the routing table, it's because the router can't communicate with the next-hop address you've configured. But you can still use the `permanent` parameter to keep the route in the routing table even if the next-hop device can't be contacted.

The `S` in the first routing table entry means that the route is a static entry. The `[150/0]` stands for the administrative distance and the metric to the remote network, respectively.

Okay, we're good. The Corp router now has all the information it needs to communicate with the other remote networks. Still, keep in mind that if the SF and LA routers aren't configured with all the same information, the packets will be discarded. We can fix this by configuring static routes.

NOTE Don't stress about the 150 at the end of the static route configuration at all, because I promise to get to it really soon in *this* chapter, not a later one. You don't need to worry about it at this point.

SF

The SF router is directly connected to networks 172.16.10.0/30 and 192.168.10.0/24, which means I've got to configure the following static routes on the SF router:

- 10.10.10.0/24
- 192.168.20.0/24
- 172.16.10.4/30

The configuration for the SF router is revealed in the following output. Remember that we'll never create a static route to any network we're directly connected to as well as the fact that we must use the next hop of 172.16.10.1 because that's our only router connection. Let's check out the commands:

```
SF(config)#ip route 10.10.10.0 255.255.255.0 172.16.10.1 150
SF(config)#ip route 172.16.10.4 255.255.255.252 172.16.10.1 150
SF(config)#ip route 192.168.20.0 255.255.255.0 172.16.10.1 150
SF(config)#do show run | begin ip route
ip route 10.10.10.0 255.255.255.0 172.16.10.1 150
ip route 172.16.10.4 255.255.255.252 172.16.10.1 150
ip route 192.168.20.0 255.255.255.0 172.16.10.1 150
```

By looking at the routing table, you can see that the SF router now understands how to find each network:

```
SF(config)#do show ip route
C 192.168.10.0/24 is directly connected, FastEthernet0/0
L 192.168.10.1/32 is directly connected, FastEthernet0/0
172.16.0.0/30 is subnetted, 3 subnets
S 172.16.10.4 [150/0] via 172.16.10.1
C 172.16.10.0 is directly connected, Serial0/0/0
L 172.16.10.2/32 is directly connected, Serial0/0
S 192.168.20.0/24 [150/0] via 172.16.10.1
10.0.0.0/24 is subnetted, 1 subnets
S 10.10.10.0 [150/0] via 172.16.10.1
```

And we now can rest assured that the SF router has a complete routing table as well. As soon as the LA router has all the networks in its routing table, SF will be able to communicate with all remote networks.

LA

The LA router is directly connected to 192.168.20.0/24 and 172.16.10.4/30, so these are the routes that must be added:

- 10.10.10.0/24
- 172.16.10.0/30
- 192.168.10.0/24

And here's the LA router's configuration:

```
LA#config t
LA(config)#ip route 10.10.10.0 255.255.255.0 172.16.10.5 150
LA(config)#ip route 172.16.10.0 255.255.255.252 172.16.10.5 150
LA(config)#ip route 192.168.10.0 255.255.255.0 172.16.10.5 150
LA(config)#do show run | begin ip route
ip route 10.10.10.0 255.255.255.0 172.16.10.5 150
ip route 172.16.10.0 255.255.255.252 172.16.10.5 150
ip route 192.168.10.0 255.255.255.0 172.16.10.5 150
```

This output displays the routing table on the LA router:

```
LA(config)#do sho ip route
S 192.168.10.0/24 [150/0] via 172.16.10.5
172.16.0.0/30 is subnetted, 3 subnets
C 172.16.10.4 is directly connected, Serial0/0/1
L 172.16.10.6/32 is directly connected, Serial0/0/1
S 172.16.10.0 [150/0] via 172.16.10.5
C 192.168.20.0/24 is directly connected, FastEthernet0/0
L 192.168.20.1/32 is directly connected, FastEthernet0/0
10.0.0.0/24 is subnetted, 1 subnets
S 10.10.10.0 [150/0] via 172.16.10.5
```

LA now shows all five networks in the internetwork, so it too can now communicate with all routers and networks. But before we test our little network, as well as our DHCP server, let's cover one more topic.

Default Routing

The SF and LA routers I've connected to the Corp router are considered stub routers. A *stub* indicates that the networks in this design have only one way out to reach all other networks, which means that instead of creating multiple static routes, we can just use a single default route. This default route is used by IP to forward any packet with a destination not found in the routing table, which is why it is also called a gateway of last resort. Here's the configuration I could have done on the LA router instead of typing in the static routes due to its stub status:

```
LA#config t
LA(config)#no ip route 10.10.10.0 255.255.255.0 172.16.10.5 150
LA(config)#no ip route 172.16.10.0 255.255.255.252 172.16.10.5 150
LA(config)#no ip route 192.168.10.0 255.255.255.0 172.16.10.5 150
LA(config)#ip route 0.0.0.0 0.0.0.0 172.16.10.5
LA(config)#do sho ip route
[output cut]
Gateway of last resort is 172.16.10.5 to network 0.0.0.0
172.16.0.0/30 is subnetted, 1 subnets
C 172.16.10.4 is directly connected, Serial0/0/1
L 172.16.10.6/32 is directly connected, Serial0/0/1
C 192.168.20.0/24 is directly connected, FastEthernet0/0
L 192.168.20.0/32 is directly connected, FastEthernet0/0
S* 0.0.0.0/0 [1/0] via 172.16.10.5
```

Okay, I've removed all the initial static routes I had configured, and adding a default route sure is a lot easier than typing a bunch of static routes. Can you see the default route listed last in the routing table? The S* shows that as a candidate for the default route. And I really want you to notice that the gateway of last resort is now set, too. Everything the router receives with a destination not found in the routing table will be forwarded to 172.16.10.5. You need to be really careful where you place default routes because you can easily create a network loop.

So we're there. We've configured all our routing tables. All the routers have the correct routing table, so all routers and hosts should be able to communicate without a hitch—for now. But if you add even one more network or another router to the internetwork, you'll have to update each and every router's routing tables by hand—ugh! Not really a problem at all if you've got a small network like we do, but the task would be a monster when dealing with a large internetwork!

Verifying Your Configuration

We're still not done yet. Once all the routers' routing tables are configured, they must be verified. The best way to do this, besides using the `show ip route` command, is via Ping. I'll start by pinging from the Corp router to the SF router.

Here's the output I got:

```
Corp#ping 192.168.10.1
Type escape sequence to abort.
Sending 5, 100-byte ICMP Echos to 192.168.10.1, timeout is 2 seconds:
!!!!!
Success rate is 100 percent (5/5), round-trip min/avg/max = 4/4/4 ms
Corp#
```

Here you can see that I pinged from the Corp router to the remote interface of the SF router. Now let's ping the remote network on the LA router, and after that, we'll test our DHCP server and see if that is working, too:

```
Corp#ping 192.168.20.1
Type escape sequence to abort.
Sending 5, 100-byte ICMP Echos to 192.168.20.1, timeout is 2 seconds:
!!!!!
Success rate is 100 percent (5/5), round-trip min/avg/max = 1/2/4 ms
Corp#
```

And why not test my configuration of the DHCP server on the Corp router while we're at it? I'm going to go to each host on the SF and LA routers and make them DHCP clients. By the way, I'm using an old router to represent "hosts," which just happens to work great for studying purposes. Here's how I did that:

```
SF_PC(config)#int e0
SF_PC(config-if)#ip address dhcp
SF_PC(config-if)#no shut
Interface Ethernet0 assigned DHCP address 192.168.10.8, mask 255.255.255.0
LA_PC(config)#int e0
LA_PC(config-if)#ip addr dhcp
LA_PC(config-if)#no shut
Interface Ethernet0 assigned DHCP address 192.168.20.4, mask 255.255.255.0
```

Nice! Don't you love it when things just work the first time? Sadly, this isn't exactly a realistic expectation in the networking world, so we must be able to troubleshoot and verify our networks. Let's verify our DHCP server with a few handy commands:

```
Corp#sh ip dhcp binding
Bindings from all pools not associated with VRF:
IP address Client-ID/ Lease expiration Type
Hardware address/
User name
192.168.10.8 0063.6973.636f.2d30. Sept 16 2013 10:34 AM Automatic
3035.302e.3062.6330.
2e30.3063.632d.4574.
30
192.168.20.4 0063.6973.636f.2d30. Sept 16 2013 10:46 AM Automatic
3030.322e.3137.3632.
2e64.3032.372d.4574.
30
```

We can see from earlier that our little DHCP server is working. Let's try another couple of commands:

```
Corp#sh ip dhcp pool SF_LAN
Pool SF_LAN :
Utilization mark (high/low) : 100 / 0
Subnet size (first/next) : 0 / 0
Total addresses : 254
Leased addresses : 3
Pending event : none
1 subnet is currently in the pool :
Current index IP address range Leased addresses
192.168.10.9 192.168.10.1 - 192.168.10.254 3
Corp#sh ip dhcp conflict
IP address Detection method Detection time VRF
```

The last command would tell us if we had two hosts with the same IP address, so it's good news because there are no conflicts reported. Two detection methods are used to confirm this:

- A ping from the DHCP server to make sure no other host responds before handing out an address
- A gratuitous ARP from a host that receives a DHCP address from the server

The DHCP client will send an ARP request with its new IP address looking to see if anyone responds, and if so, it will report the conflict to the server.

Because we can communicate from end to end and to each host without a problem while receiving DHCP addresses from our server, I'd say our static and default route configurations have been a success. Cheers!

Dynamic Routing

Dynamic routing is when protocols are used to find networks and update routing tables on routers. This is whole lot easier than using static or default routing, but it will cost you in terms of router CPU processing and bandwidth on network links. A routing protocol defines the set of rules used by a router when it communicates routing information between neighboring routers.

The routing protocol I'm going to talk about in this chapter is RIP versions 1 and 2.

Two types of routing protocols are used in internetworks: *interior gateway protocols (IGPs)* and *exterior gateway protocols (EGPs)*. IGPs are used to exchange routing information with routers in the same *autonomous system (AS)*. An AS is either a single network or a collection of networks under a common administrative domain, which basically means that all routers sharing the same routing-table information are in the same AS. EGPs are used to communicate between ASs. An example of an EGP is Border Gateway Protocol (BGP), which we're not going to bother with because it's beyond the scope of this book.

Because routing protocols are so essential to dynamic routing, next, I'll give you the basic information you need to know about them. Later on in this chapter, we'll focus on configuration.

Routing Protocol Basics

You should know some important things about routing protocols before we get deeper into RIP routing. Being familiar with administrative distances and the three different kinds of routing protocols, for example. Let's take a look.

Administrative Distances

The *administrative distance (AD)* is used to rate the trustworthiness of routing information received on a router from a neighbor router. An administrative distance is an integer from 0 to 255, where 0 is the most trusted and 255 means no traffic will be passed via this route.

If a router receives two updates listing the same remote network, the first thing the router checks is the AD. If one of the advertised routes has a lower AD than the other, then the route with the lowest AD will be chosen and placed in the routing table.

If both advertised routes to the same network have the same AD, then routing protocol metrics like *hop count* and/or the bandwidth of the lines will be used to find the best path to the remote network. The advertised route with the lowest metric will be placed in the routing table, but if both advertised routes have the same AD as well as the same metrics, then the routing protocol will load-balance to the remote network, meaning the protocol will send data down each link.

Table 9.1 shows the default administrative distances that a Cisco router uses to decide which route to take to a remote network.

TABLE 9.1 Default administrative distances

Route Source	Default AD
Connected interface	0
Static route	1
External BGP	20
EIGRP	90
OSPF	110
RIP	120
External EIGRP	170
Internal BGP	200
Unknown	255 (This route will never be used.)

If a network is directly connected, the router will always use the interface connected to the network. If you configure a static route, the router will then believe that route over any other ones it learns about. You can change the AD of static routes, but by default, they have an AD of 1. In our previous static route configuration, the AD of each route is set at 150. This AD allows us to configure routing protocols without having to remove the static routes because it's nice to have them there for backup in case the routing protocol experiences some kind of failure.

If you have a static route, an RIP-advertised route, and an EIGRP-advertised route listing the same network, which route will the router go with? That's right—by default, the router will always use the static route unless you change its AD (which we did).

Routing Protocols

There are three classes of routing protocols:

Distance Vector The distance-vector protocols in use today find the best path to a remote network by judging distance. In RIP routing, each instance where a packet goes through a router is called a hop, and the route with the least number of hops to the network will be chosen as the best one. The vector indicates the direction to the remote network. RIP is a distance-vector routing protocol and periodically sends out the entire routing table to directly connected neighbors.

Link State In link-state protocols, also called shortest-path-first (SPF) protocols, the routers each create three separate tables. One of these tables keeps track of directly attached neighbors, one determines the topology of the entire internetwork, and one is used as the routing table. Link-state routers know more about the internetwork than any distance-vector routing protocol ever could. OSPF is an IP routing protocol that's completely link-state. Link-state routing tables are not exchanged periodically. Instead, triggered updates containing only specific link-state information are sent. Periodic keep-a-lives in the form of hello messages, which are small and efficient, are exchanged between directly connected neighbors to establish and maintain neighbor relationships.

Advanced distance vector Advanced distance-vector protocols use aspects of both distance-vector and link-state protocols, and EIGRP is a great example. EIGRP may act like a link-state routing protocol because it uses a Hello protocol to discover neighbors and form neighbor relationships and because only partial updates are sent when a change occurs. However, EIGRP is still based on the key distance-vector routing protocol principle that information about the rest of the network is learned from directly connected neighbors.

There's no fixed set of rules to follow that dictate exactly how to broadly configure routing protocols for every situation. It's a task that really must be undertaken on a case-by-case basis, with an eye on specific requirements of each one. If you understand how the different routing protocols work, you can make great decisions that will solidly meet the individual needs of any business.

Routing Information Protocol

Routing Information Protocol (RIP) is a true distance-vector routing protocol. RIP sends the complete routing table out of all active interfaces every 30 seconds. It relies on hop count to determine the best way to a remote network, but it has a maximum allowable hop count of 15 by default, so a destination of 16 would be considered unreachable. RIP works okay in very small networks, but it's super inefficient on large networks with slow WAN links or on networks with a large number of routers installed. It's completely useless on networks that have links with variable bandwidths!

RIP version 1 uses only *classful routing*, which means that all devices in the network must use the same subnet mask. This is because RIP version 1 doesn't send updates with subnet mask information in tow. RIP version 2 provides something called *prefix routing* and does send subnet mask information with its route updates. This is called *classless routing*.

So with that, let's configure our current network with RIPv2.

Configuring RIP Routing

To configure RIP routing, just turn on the protocol with the `router rip` command and tell the RIP routing protocol the networks to advertise. Remember that with static routing, we always configured remote networks and never typed a route to our directly connected networks? Well, dynamic routing is carried out the complete opposite way. You would never type a *remote* network under your routing protocol—only enter your directly connected networks. Let's configure our three-router internetwork, revisited in Figure 9.9, with RIP routing.

Corp

RIP has an administrative distance of 120. Static routes have an AD of 1 by default, and because we currently have static routes configured, the routing tables won't be populated with RIP information by default. We're still good though because I added the 150 to the end of each static route.

You can add the RIP routing protocol by using the `router rip` command and the `network` command. The network command tells the routing protocol which classful network to advertise. By doing this, you're activating the RIP routing process on the interfaces whose addressing falls within the specified classful `networks` configured with the network command under the RIP routing process.

Look at the Corp router configuration to see how easy this is. Oh wait—first, I want to verify my directly connected networks so I know what to configure RIP with:

```
Corp#sh ip int brief
Interface IP-Address OK? Method Status Protocol
FastEthernet0/0 10.10.10.1 YES manual up up
Serial0/0 172.16.10.1 YES manual up up
```

```
FastEthernet0/1 unassigned YES unset administratively down down
Serial0/1 172.16.10.5 YES manual up up

Corp#config t
Corp(config)#router rip
Corp(config-router)#network 10.0.0.0
Corp(config-router)#network 172.16.0.0
Corp(config-router)#version 2
Corp(config-router)#no auto-summary
```

That's it. Really. Typically just two or three commands and you're done, which sure makes your job a lot easier than dealing with static routes, doesn't it? Be sure to keep in mind the extra router CPU process and bandwidth that you're consuming.

Anyway, so what exactly did I do here? I enabled the RIP routing protocol, added my directly connected networks, made sure I was only running RIPv2, which is a classless routing protocol, and then I disabled auto-summary. We typically don't want our routing protocols summarizing for us because it's better to do that manually and both RIP and EIGRP (before 15.x code) auto-summarize by default. So a general rule of thumb is to disable auto-summary, which allows them to advertise subnets.

Notice I didn't type in subnets, only the classful network address, which is betrayed by the fact that all subnet bits and host bits are off. That's because with dynamic routing, it's not my job; it's up to the routing protocol to find the subnets and populate the routing tables. And because we have no router buddies running RIP, we won't see any RIP routes in the routing table yet.

NOTE

Remember, RIP uses the classful address when configuring the network address. To clarify this, refer to the example in our network with an address of 172.16.0.0/24 using subnets 172.16.10.0 and 172.16.20.0. You would only type in the classful network address of 172.16.0.0 and let RIP find the subnets and place them in the routing table. This doesn't mean you are running a classful routing protocol; it's just the way that both RIP and EIGRP are configured.

SF

Let's configure our SF router now, which is connected to two networks. We need to configure both directly connected classful networks, not subnets:

```
SF#sh ip int brief
Interface IP-Address OK? Method Status Protocol
FastEthernet0/0 192.168.10.1 YES manual up up
FastEthernet0/1 unassigned YES unset administratively down down
Serial0/0/0 172.16.10.2 YES manual up up
```

```
Serial0/0/1 unassigned YES unset administratively down down
SF#config
SF(config)#router rip
SF(config-router)#network 192.168.10.0
SF(config-router)#network 172.16.0.0
SF(config-router)#version 2
SF(config-router)#no auto-summary
SF(config-router)#do show ip route
C 192.168.10.0/24 is directly connected, FastEthernet0/0
L 192.168.10.1/32 is directly connected, FastEthernet0/0
172.16.0.0/30 is subnetted, 3 subnets
R 172.16.10.4 [120/1] via 172.16.10.1, 00:00:08, Serial0/0/0
C 172.16.10.0 is directly connected, Serial0/0/0
L 172.16.10.2/32 is directly connected, Serial0/0
S 192.168.20.0/24 [150/0] via 172.16.10.1
10.0.0.0/24 is subnetted, 1 subnets
R 10.10.10.0 [120/1] via 172.16.10.1, 00:00:08, Serial0/0/0
```

That was pretty straightforward. Let's talk about this routing table. Because we have one RIP buddy out there with whom we are exchanging routing tables, we can see the RIP networks coming from the Corp router. All the other routes still show up as static and local. RIP also found both connections through the Corp router to networks 10.10.10.0 and 172.16.10.4. But we're not done yet.

LA

Let's configure our LA router with RIP, only I'm going to remove the default route first, even though I don't have to. You'll see why soon:

```
LA#config t
LA(config)#no ip route 0.0.0.0 0.0.0.0
LA(config)#router rip
LA(config-router)#network 192.168.20.0
LA(config-router)#network 172.16.0.0
LA(config-router)#no auto
LA(config-router)#vers 2
LA(config-router)#do show ip route
R 192.168.10.0/24 [120/2] via 172.16.10.5, 00:00:10, Serial0/0/1
172.16.0.0/30 is subnetted, 3 subnets
C 172.16.10.4 is directly connected, Serial0/0/1
L 172.16.10.6/32 is directly connected, Serial0/0/1
R 172.16.10.0 [120/1] via 172.16.10.5, 00:00:10, Serial0/0/1
C 192.168.20.0/24 is directly connected, FastEthernet0/0
```

```
L 192.168.20.1/32 is directly connected, FastEthernet0/0
10.0.0.0/24 is subnetted, 1 subnets
R 10.10.10.0 [120/1] via 172.16.10.5, 00:00:10, Serial0/0/1
```

The routing table is sprouting new Rs as we add RIP buddies! We can still see that all routes are in the routing table.

This output shows us basically the same routing table and the same entries that it had when we were using static routes—except for those Rs. An `R` indicates that the networks were added dynamically using the RIP routing protocol. The `[120/1]` is the administrative distance of the route (120) along with the metric, which for RIP is the number of hops to that remote network (1). From the Corp router, all networks are one hop away.

So, while yes, it's true that RIP has worked in our little internetwork, it's not a great solution for most enterprises. Its maximum hop count of only 15 is a highly limiting factor. And it performs full routing-table updates every 30 seconds, which would bring a larger internetwork to a crawl in no time.

I want to show you still one more thing about RIP routing tables and the parameters used to advertise remote networks. Using a different router on a different network as an example for a second, look into the following output. Can you spot where the following routing table shows `[120/15]` in the 10.1.3.0 network metric? This means that the administrative distance is 120, the default for RIP, but the hop count is 15. Remember that each time a router sends out an update to a neighbor router, the hop count goes up by one incrementally for each route. Here's that output now:

```
Router#sh ip route
10.0.0.0/24 is subnetted, 12 subnets
C 10.1.11.0 is directly connected, FastEthernet0/1
L 10.1.11.1/32 is directly connected, FastEthernet0/1
C 10.1.10.0 is directly connected, FastEthernet0/0
L 10.1.10.1/32 is directly connected, FastEthernet/0/0
R 10.1.9.0 [120/2] via 10.1.5.1, 00:00:15, Serial0/0/1
R 10.1.8.0 [120/2] via 10.1.5.1, 00:00:15, Serial0/0/1
R 10.1.12.0 [120/1] via 10.1.11.2, 00:00:00, FastEthernet0/1
R 10.1.3.0 [120/15] via 10.1.5.1, 00:00:15, Serial0/0/1
R 10.1.2.0 [120/1] via 10.1.5.1, 00:00:15, Serial0/0/1
R 10.1.1.0 [120/1] via 10.1.5.1, 00:00:15, Serial0/0/1
R 10.1.7.0 [120/2] via 10.1.5.1, 00:00:15, Serial0/0/1
R 10.1.6.0 [120/2] via 10.1.5.1, 00:00:15, Serial0/0/1
C 10.1.5.0 is directly connected, Serial0/0/1
L 10.1.5.1/32 is directly connected, Serial0/0/1
R 10.1.4.0 [120/1] via 10.1.5.1, 00:00:15, Serial0/0/1
```

So this [120/15] is really bad. We're basically doomed because the next router that receives the table from this router will just discard the route to network 10.1.3.0 because the hop count would rise to 16, which is invalid.

NOTE: If a router receives a routing update that contains a higher-cost path to a network that's already in its routing table, the update will be ignored.

Holding Down RIP Propagations

You probably don't want your RIP network advertised everywhere on your LAN and WAN. There's enough stress in networking already and not much to be gained by advertising your RIP network to the Internet.

There are a few different ways to stop unwanted RIP updates from propagating across your LANs and WANs, and the easiest one is through the `passive-interface` command. This command prevents RIP update broadcasts from being sent out of a specified interface but still allows that same interface to receive RIP updates.

Here's an example of how to configure a `passive-interface` on the Corp router's Fa0/1 interface, which we will pretend is connected to a LAN that we don't want RIP on (and the interface isn't shown in the figure):

```
Corp#config t
Corp(config)#router rip
Corp(config-router)#passive-interface FastEthernet 0/1
```

This command prevents RIP updates from being propagated out of FastEthernet interface 0/1, but it can still receive RIP updates.

Real World Scenario

Should We Really Use RIP in an Internetwork?

You have been hired as a consultant to install a couple of Cisco routers into a growing network. They have a couple of old Unix routers they want to keep in the network. These routers do not support any routing protocol except RIP. I guess this means you just have to run RIP on the entire network. If you were balding before, your head now shines like chrome.

No need for hairs abandoning ship though. You can run RIP on a router connecting that old network, but you certainly don't need to run RIP throughout the whole internetwork.

You can do something called *redistribution*, which is basically translating from one type of routing protocol to another. This means that you can support those old routers using RIP but use something much better like EIGRP on the rest of your network.

This will prevent RIP routes from being sent all over the internetwork gobbling up all that precious bandwidth!

Advertising a Default Route Using RIP

Now I'm going to guide you through how to advertise a way out of your autonomous system to other routers, and you'll see this is completed the same way with OSPF.

Imagine that our Corp router's Fa0/0 interface is connected to some type of Metro-Ethernet as a connection to the Internet. This is a pretty common configuration today that uses a LAN interface to connect to the ISP instead of a serial interface.

If we do add an Internet connection to Corp, all routers in our AS (SF and LA) must know where to send packets destined for networks on the Internet or they'll just drop the packets when they get a remote request. One solution to this little hitch would be to place a default route on every router and funnel the information to Corp, which in turn would have a default route to the ISP. Most people do this type of configuration in small- to medium-size networks because it actually works pretty well.

But because I'm running RIPv2 on all routers, I'll just add a default route on the Corp router to our ISP, as I would normally. I'll then add another command to advertise my network to the other routers in the AS as the default route to show them where to send packets destined for the Internet.

Here's my new Corp configuration:

```
Corp(config)#ip route 0.0.0.0 0.0.0.0 fa0/0
Corp(config)#router rip
Corp(config-router)#default-information originate
```

Now, let's take a look at the last entry found in the Corp routing table:

```
S* 0.0.0.0/0 is directly connected, FastEthernet0/0
```

Let's see whether the LA router can see this same entry:

```
LA#sh ip route
Gateway of last resort is 172.16.10.5 to network 0.0.0.0
R 192.168.10.0/24 [120/2] via 172.16.10.5, 00:00:04, Serial0/0/1
172.16.0.0/30 is subnetted, 2 subnets
C 172.16.10.4 is directly connected, Serial0/0/1
L 172.16.10.5/32 is directly connected, Serial0/0/1
R 172.16.10.0 [120/1] via 172.16.10.5, 00:00:04, Serial0/0/1
C 192.168.20.0/24 is directly connected, FastEthernet0/0
L 192.168.20.1/32 is directly connected, FastEthernet0/0
10.0.0.0/24 is subnetted, 1 subnets
R 10.10.10.0 [120/1] via 172.16.10.5, 00:00:04, Serial0/0/1
R 192.168.218.0/24 [120/3] via 172.16.10.5, 00:00:04, Serial0/0/1
R 192.168.118.0/24 [120/2] via 172.16.10.5, 00:00:05, Serial0/0/1
R* 0.0.0.0/0 [120/1] via 172.16.10.5, 00:00:05, Serial0/0/1
```

Can you see that last entry? It screams that it's an RIP injected route, but it's also a default route, so our `default-information originate` command is working. Last, notice that the gateway of last resort is now set as well.

Everyone understands that we won't use RIP of any type in a production network today if at all possible. Which is why our next chapter will feature the CCNA star routing protocol: OSPF.

Summary

This chapter covered IP routing in detail. Again, it's extremely important to fully understand the basics we covered in this chapter because everything that's done on a Cisco router will typically have some kind of IP routing configured and running.

You learned how IP routing uses frames to transport packets between routers and to the destination host. From there, we configured static routing on our routers and discussed the administrative distance used by IP to determine the best route to a destination network. You found out that if you have a stub network, you can configure default routing, which sets the gateway of last resort on a router.

We then discussed dynamic routing, specifically RIPv2. You learned how it works on an enterprise, which is not very well.

Exam Essentials

Describe the basic IP routing process. You need to remember that the frame changes at each hop, but the packet is never changed or manipulated in any way until it reaches the destination device (the TTL field in the IP header is decremented for each hop, but that's it).

List the information required by a router to successfully route packets. To be able to route packets, a router must know, at a minimum, the destination address, the location of neighboring routers through which it can reach remote networks, possible routes to all remote networks, the best route to each remote network, and how to maintain and verify routing information.

Describe how MAC addresses are used during the routing process. A MAC (hardware) address will only be used on a local LAN; it will never pass a router's interface. A frame uses MAC (hardware) addresses to send a packet on a LAN. The frame will take the packet to either a host on the LAN or a router's interface (if the packet is destined for a remote network). As packets move from one router to another, the MAC addresses used will change, but normally the original source and destination IP addresses within the packet will not.

View and interpret the routing table of a router. Use the `show ip route` command to view the routing table. Each route will be listed along with the source of the routing information. A `C` to the left of the route will indicate directly connected routes, and other letters next to the route can also indicate a particular routing protocol that provided the information, such as `R` for RIP.

Differentiate the three types of routing. The three types of routing are static (in which routes are manually configured at the CLI), dynamic (in which the routers share routing information via a routing protocol), and default routing (in which a special route is configured for all traffic without a more specific destination network found in the table).

Compare and contrast static and dynamic routing. Static routing creates no routing update traffic and creates less overhead on the router and network links, but it must be configured manually and does not have the ability to react to link outages. Dynamic routing creates routing update traffic and uses more overhead on the router and network links.

Configure static routes at the CLI. The command syntax to add a route is `ip route` [*destination_network*] [*mask*] [*next-hop_address or exitinterface*] [*administrative_distance*] [*permanent*].

Create a default route. To add a default route, use the command syntax `ip route 0.0.0.0 0.0.0.0` *ip-address* or `exit interface type and number`.

Understand administrative distance and its role in the selection of the best route. Administrative distance (AD) is used to rate the trustworthiness of routing information received on a router from a neighbor router. AD is an integer from 0 to 255, where 0 is the most trusted and 255 means no traffic will be passed via this route. All routing protocols are assigned a default AD, but it can be changed at the CLI.

Differentiate distance-vector, link-state, and hybrid routing protocols. Distance-vector routing protocols make routing decisions based on hop count (think RIP), while link-state routing protocols consider multiple factors such as available bandwidth and building a topology table. Hybrid routing protocols exhibit characteristics of both types.

Configure RIPv2 routing. To configure RIP routing, first you must be in global configuration mode and then use the command `router rip`. Then, you add all directly connected networks, making sure to use the classful address and the `version 2` command and to disable auto-summarization with the `no auto-summary` command.

Written Lab

You can find the answers to this lab in Appendix A, "Answers to the Written Labs."

Write the answers to the following questions:

1. At the appropriate command prompt, create a static route to network 172.16.10.0/24 with a next-hop gateway of 172.16.20.1 and an administrative distance of 150.
2. When a PC sends a packet to another PC in a remote network, what destination addresses will be in the frame that it sends to its default gateway?
3. At the appropriate command prompt, create a default route to 172.16.40.1.

4. On which type of network is a default route most beneficial?
5. At the appropriate command prompt, display the routing table on your router.
6. When creating a static or default route, you don't have to use the next-hop IP address; you can use the ________.
7. True/False: To reach a remote host, you must know the MAC address of the remote host.
8. True/False: To reach a remote host, you must know the IP address of the remote host.
9. At the appropriate command prompt(s), prevent a router from propagating RIP information out serial 1.
10. True/False: RIPv2 is considered classless.

Review Questions

You can find the answers to these questions in Appendix B, "Answers to the Review Questions."

> **NOTE** The following questions are designed to test your understanding of this chapter's material. For more information on how to get additional questions, please see this book's introduction.

1. What command was used to generate the following output?

```
Codes: L - local, C - connected, S - static,
[output cut]
        10.0.0.0/8 is variably subnetted, 6 subnets, 4 masks
C       10.0.0.0/8 is directly connected, FastEthernet0/3
L       10.0.0.1/32 is directly connected, FastEthernet0/3
C       10.10.0.0/16 is directly connected, FastEthernet0/2
L       10.10.0.1/32 is directly connected, FastEthernet0/2
C       10.10.10.0/24 is directly connected, FastEthernet0/1
L       10.10.10.1/32 is directly connected, FastEthernet0/1
S*      0.0.0.0/0 is directly connected, FastEthernet0/0
```

2. You are viewing the routing table and see the entry 10.1.1.1/32. What legend code would you expect to see next to this route?

   A. C

   B. L

   C. S

   D. D

3. Which of the following statements are true regarding the command `ip route 172.16.4.0 255.255.255.0 192.168.4.2`? (Choose two.)

   A. The command is used to establish a static route.

   B. The default administrative distance is used.

   C. The command is used to configure the default route.

   D. The subnet mask for the source address is 255.255.255.0.

   E. The command is used to establish a stub network.

4. What destination addresses will be used by HostA to send data to the HTTPS server as shown in the following network? (Choose two.)

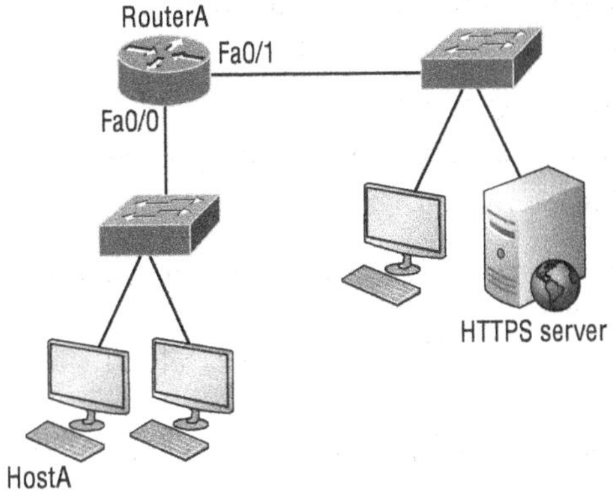

A. The IP address of the switch
B. The MAC address of the remote switch
C. The IP address of the HTTPS server
D. The MAC address of the HTTPS server
E. The IP address of RouterA's Fa0/0 interface
F. The MAC address of RouterA's Fa0/0 interface

5. Using the following output, h protocol was used to learn the MAC address for 172.16.10.1?

```
Interface: 172.16.10.2 --- 0x3
  Internet Address        Physical Address      Type
  172.16.10.1            00-15-05-06-31-b0     dynamic
```

A. ICMP
B. ARP
C. TCP
D. UDP

6. Which of the following is called an advanced distance-vector routing protocol?
A. OSPF
B. EIGRP
C. BGP
D. RIP

7. When a packet is routed across a network, the ________ in the packet changes at every hop, while the ________ does not.
A. MAC address, IP address
B. IP address, MAC address
C. Port number, IP address
D. IP address, port number

8. Which of the following statements are true regarding classless routing protocols? (Choose two.)
   A. The use of discontiguous networks is not allowed.
   B. The use of variable length subnet masks is permitted.
   C. RIPv1 is a classless routing protocol.
   D. IGRP supports classless routing within the same autonomous system.
   E. RIPv2 supports classless routing.
9. Which of the following statements are true regarding the distance-vector and link-state routing protocols? (Choose two.)
   A. Link state sends its complete routing table out of all active interfaces at periodic time intervals.
   B. Distance vector sends its complete routing table out of all active interfaces at periodic time intervals.
   C. Link state sends updates containing the state of its own links to all routers in the internetwork.
   D. Distance vector sends updates containing the state of its own links to all routers in the internetwork.
10. When a router looks up the destination in the routing table for every single packet it is called __________.
    A. Dynamic switching
    B. Fast switching
    C. Process switching
    D. Cisco Express Forwarding
11. What type(s) of route is the following? Choose all that apply.

    ```
    S*    0.0.0.0/0 [1/0] via 172.16.10.5
    ```

    A. Default
    B. Subnetted
    C. Static
    D. Local
12. A network administrator views the output from the `show ip route` command. A network that is advertised by both RIP and EIGRP appears in the routing table flagged as an EIGRP route. Why is the RIP route to this network not used in the routing table?
    A. EIGRP has a faster update timer.
    B. EIGRP has a lower administrative distance.
    C. RIP has a higher metric value for that route.
    D. The EIGRP route has fewer hops.
    E. The RIP path has a routing loop.

13. Which of the following is *not* an advantage of static routing?
    - **A.** Less overhead on the router CPU
    - **B.** No bandwidth usage between routers
    - **C.** Adds security
    - **D.** Recovers automatically from lost routes

14. What metric does RIPv2 use to find the best path to a remote network?
    - **A.** Hop count
    - **B.** MTU
    - **C.** Cumulative interface delay
    - **D.** Load
    - **E.** Path bandwidth value

15. The Corporate router receives an IP packet with a source IP address of 192.168.214.20 and a destination address of 192.168.22.3. Looking at the output from the Corp router, what will the router do with this packet?

```
Corp#sh ip route
[output cut]
R    192.168.215.0 [120/2] via 192.168.20.2, 00:00:23, Serial0/0
R    192.168.115.0 [120/1] via 192.168.20.2, 00:00:23, Serial0/0
R    192.168.30.0 [120/1] via 192.168.20.2, 00:00:23, Serial0/0
C    192.168.20.0 is directly connected, Serial0/0
C    192.168.214.0 is directly connected, FastEthernet0/0
```

   - **A.** The packet will be discarded.
   - **B.** The packet will be routed out of the S0/0 interface.
   - **C.** The router will broadcast looking for the destination.
   - **D.** The packet will be routed out of the Fa0/0 interface.

16. If your routing table has a static, an RIP, and an EIGRP route to the same network, which route will be used to route packets by default?
    - **A.** Any available route.
    - **B.** RIP route.
    - **C.** Static route.
    - **D.** EIGRP route.
    - **E.** They will all load-balance.

17. Which of the following is an EGP?
    - **A.** RIPv2
    - **B.** EIGRP
    - **C.** BGP
    - **D.** RIP

18. Which of the following is an advantage of static routing?

A. Less overhead on the router CPU

B. No bandwidth usage between routers

C. Adds security

D. Recovers automatically from lost routes

19. What command produced the following output?

```
Interface          IP-Address      OK? Method Status                Protocol
FastEthernet0/0    192.168.10.1    YES manual up                    up
FastEthernet0/1    unassigned      YES unset  administratively down down
Serial0/0/0        172.16.10.2     YES manual up                    up
Serial0/0/1        unassigned      YES unset  administratively down down
```

A. `show ip route`

B. `show interfaces`

C. `show ip interface brief`

D. `show ip arp`

20. In the following command, what does the 150 at the end of the command mean?
`Router(config)#`**`ip route 172.16.3.0 255.255.255.0 192.168.2.4 150`**

A. Metric

B. Administrative distance

C. Hop count

D. Cost

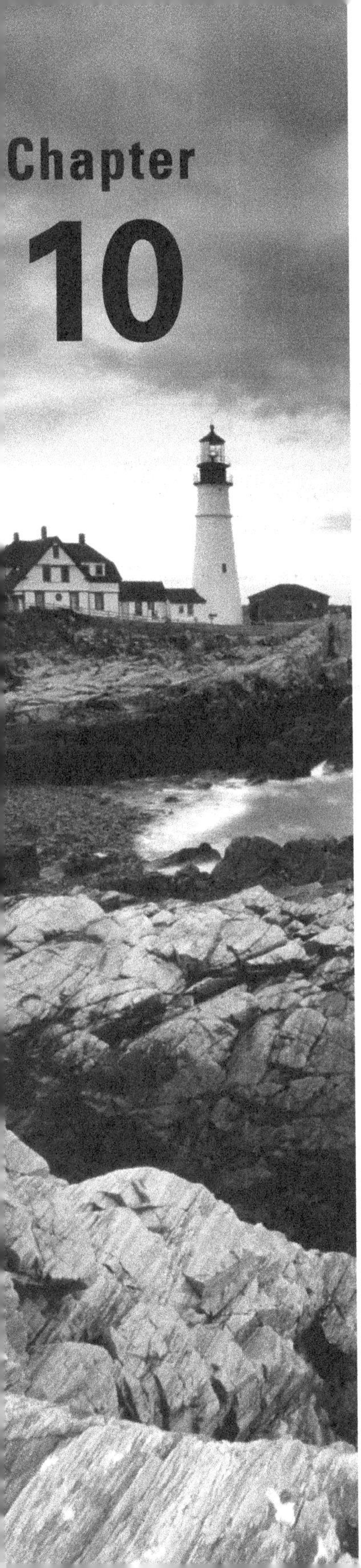

Chapter 10

Open Shortest Path First

THE FOLLOWING CCNA EXAM TOPICS ARE COVERED IN THIS CHAPTER:

✓ ***3.0 IP Connectivity***

- 3.4 Configure and verify single area OSPFv2
  - 3.4.a Neighbor adjacencies
  - 3.4.b Point-to-point
  - 3.4.c Broadcast (DR/BDR selection)
  - 3.4.d Router ID

Open Shortest Path First (OSPF) is by far the most popular and important routing protocol in use today—so important, I'm devoting an entire chapter to it! Sticking with the same approach we've taken throughout this book, we'll begin with the basics by completely familiarizing you with key OSPF terminology. Once we've covered that thoroughly, I'll guide you through OSPF's internal operation and then move on to tell you all about OSPF's many advantages over RIP.

This chapter isn't just going to be chock full of vitally important information; it's also going to be exciting because we'll explore some critical factors and issues innate to implementing OSPF. I'll walk you through exactly how to implement single-area OSPF in a variety of networking environments and then demonstrate some great techniques you'll need to verify that everything is configured correctly and running smoothly.

NOTE

To find bonus material, as well as Todd Lammle videos, practice questions, and hands-on labs, please see `www.lammle.com/ccna`.

Open Shortest Path First Basics

Open Shortest Path First is an open standard routing protocol that's been implemented by a wide variety of network vendors, including Cisco. And it's that open standard characteristic that's the key to OSPF's flexibility and popularity.

Most people opt for OSPF, which works by using the Dijkstra algorithm to initially construct a shortest path tree followed by populating the routing table with the resulting best paths. EIGRP's convergence time may be blindingly fast, but OSPF isn't far behind, and its quick convergence is another reason it's a favorite. Two other great advantages OSPF offers are that it supports multiple equal-cost routes to the same destination and, like EIGRP, also supports both IPv4 and IPv6 routed protocols.

TABLE 10.1 OSPF and RIP comparison

Characteristic	OSPF	RIPv2	RIPv1
Type of protocol	Link state	Distance vector	Distance vector
Classless support	Yes	Yes	No

Characteristic	OSPF	RIPv2	RIPv1
VLSM support	Yes	Yes	No
Auto-summarization	No	Yes	Yes
Manual summarization	Yes	Yes	No
Noncontiguous support	Yes	Yes	No
Route propagation	Multicast on change	Periodic multicast	Periodic broadcast
Path metric	Bandwidth	Hops	Hops
Hop count limit	None	15	15
Convergence	Fast	Slow	Slow
Peer authentication	Yes	Yes	No
Hierarchical network requirement	Yes (using areas)	No (flat only)	No (flat only)
Updates	Event triggered	Periodic	Periodic
Route computation	Dijkstra	Bellman-Ford	Bellman-Ford

Here's a list that summarizes some of OSPF's best features:

- Allows for the creation of areas and autonomous systems
- Minimizes routing update traffic
- Is highly flexible, versatile, and scalable
- Supports VLSM/CIDR
- Offers an unlimited hop count
- Is open standard and supports multi-vendor deployment

Because OSPF is the first link-state routing protocol that most people run into, it's a good idea to compare it to more traditional distance-vector protocols like RIPv2 and RIPv1. Table 10.1 presents a nice comparison of all three of these common protocols.

OSPF has many features beyond the few listed in Table 10.1, and all of them combine to produce a fast, scalable, robust protocol that's also flexible enough to be actively deployed in a vast array of production networks.

One of OSPF's most useful traits is that its design is intended to be hierarchical in use, meaning that it allows us to subdivide the larger internetwork into smaller internetworks called *areas*. It's a really powerful feature that I recommend using, and I'll show you how to do that later in the chapter.

Here are three of the biggest reasons to implement OSPF in a way that makes full use of its intentional, hierarchical design:

- To decrease routing overhead
- To speed up convergence
- To confine network instability to single areas of the network

Because free lunches are invariably hard to come by, all this wonderful functionality predictably comes at a price and doesn't exactly make configuring OSPF any easier. But no worries—we'll crush it!

Let's start by checking out Figure 10.1, which shows a typical yet simple OSPF design. I want to point out the fact that some routers connect to the backbone area called area 0. OSPF absolutely must have an area 0, and all other areas should connect to it, except for those connected via virtual links, which are beyond the scope of this book. A router that connects other areas to the backbone area within an AS is called an *area border router (ABR)*, and even these must have at least one of their interfaces connected to area 0.

FIGURE 10.1 OSPF design example. An OSPF hierarchical design minimizes routing table entries and keeps the impact of any topology changes contained within a specific area.

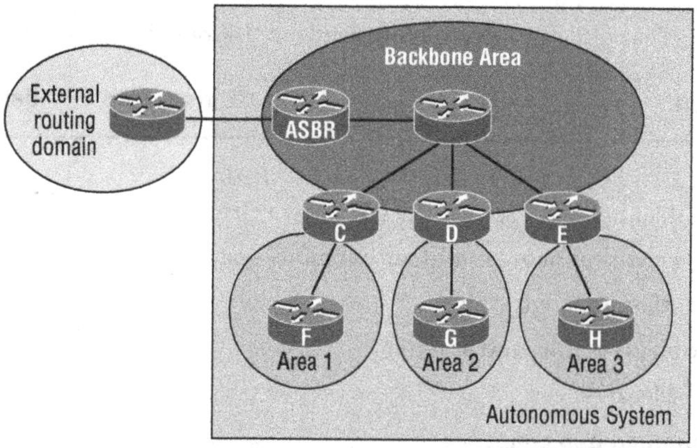

OSPF runs great inside an autonomous system, but it can also connect multiple autonomous systems together. The router that connects these ASs is called an *autonomous system boundary router (ASBR)*. Ideally, you'll want to create other areas of networks to help keep route updates to a minimum, especially in larger networks. Doing this also keeps problems from propagating throughout the network, affectively isolating them to a single area.

Let's take a minute to cover some key OSPF terms that are essential for you to understand before we move on any further.

OSPF Terminology

Imagine being given a map and compass with no prior concept of east, west, north, or south—not even what rivers, mountains, lakes, or deserts are. I'm guessing that without any ability to orient yourself in a basic way, your cool new tools wouldn't help you get anywhere but completely lost, right? This is exactly why we're going to begin exploring OSPF by getting you solidly acquainted with a fairly long list of terms before setting out from base camp into the great unknown! Here are those vital terms to commit to memory:

Link A *link* is a network or router interface assigned to any given network. When an interface is added to the OSPF process, it's considered a link. This link, or interface, will have up or down state information associated with it, as well as one or more IP addresses.

Router ID The *router ID (RID)* is an IP address used to identify the router. Cisco chooses the router ID by using the highest IP address of all configured loopback interfaces. If no loopback interfaces are configured with addresses, OSPF will choose the highest IP address out of all active physical interfaces. To OSPF, this is basically the "name" of each router.

Neighbor *Neighbors* are two or more routers that have an interface on a common network, such as two routers connected on a point-to-point serial link. OSPF neighbors must have a number of common configuration options to be able to successfully establish a neighbor relationship, and all of these options must be configured exactly the same way:

- Area ID
- Stub area flag
- Authentication password (if using one)
- Hello and Dead intervals

Adjacency An *adjacency* is a relationship between two OSPF routers that permits the direct exchange of route updates. Unlike EIGRP, which directly shares routes with all of its neighbors, OSPF is really picky about sharing routing information and will directly share routes only with neighbors that have also established adjacencies. And not all neighbors will become adjacent—it depends on both the type of network and the configuration of the routers. In multi-access networks, routers form adjacencies with designated and backup designated routers. In point-to-point and point-to-multipoint networks, routers form adjacencies with the router on the opposite side of the connection.

Designated Router A *designated router (DR)* is elected whenever OSPF routers are connected to the same broadcast network to minimize the number of adjacencies formed and to publicize received routing information to and from the remaining routers on the broadcast network or link. Elections are won based on a router's priority level, with the one having the highest priority becoming the winner. If there's a tie, the router ID will be used to break it. All routers on the shared network will establish adjacencies with the DR and the backup designated router (BDR), which ensures that all routers' topology tables are synchronized.

Backup Designated Router A *backup designated router (BDR)* is a hot standby for the DR on broadcast, or multi-access, links. The BDR receives all routing updates from OSPF adjacent routers but does not disperse link-state advertisement (LSA) updates.

Hello Protocol The OSPF Hello protocol provides dynamic neighbor discovery and maintains neighbor relationships. Hello packets and link-state advertisements (LSAs) build and maintain the topological database. Hello packets are addressed to multicast address 224.0.0.5.

Neighborship Database The *neighborship database* is a list of all OSPF routers for which Hello packets have been seen. A variety of details, including the router ID and state, are maintained on each router in the neighborship database.

Topological database The *topological database* contains information from all of the LSA packets that have been received for an area. The router uses the information from the topology database as input into the Dijkstra algorithm, which computes the shortest path to every network.

NOTE

LSA packets are used to update and maintain the topological database.

Link-State Advertisement A *link-state advertisement (LSA)* is an OSPF data packet containing link-state and routing information that's shared among OSPF routers. There are different types of LSA packets. An OSPF router will only exchange LSA packets with routers it has established adjacencies for.

OSPF Areas An *OSPF area* is a grouping of contiguous networks and routers. All routers in the same area share a common area ID. Because a router can be a member of more than one area at a time, the area ID is associated with specific interfaces on the router. This allows some interfaces to belong to area 1, while the remaining interfaces can belong to area 0. All of the routers within the same area have the same topology table. When configuring OSPF with multiple areas, you need to remember that there must be an area 0 and that this is typically considered the backbone area. Areas also play a role in establishing a hierarchical network organization—something that really enhances the scalability of OSPF!

Broadcast (Multi-access) *Broadcast (multi-access) networks* like Ethernet allow multiple devices to connect to or access the same network, enabling a *broadcast* ability so a single packet can be delivered to all nodes on the network. In OSPF, a DR and BDR must be elected for each broadcast multi-access network.

Nonbroadcast Multi-access *Nonbroadcast multi-access (NBMA)* networks like Frame Relay, X.25, and Asynchronous Transfer Mode (ATM) allow for multi-access without broadcast capability like Ethernet. NBMA networks require special OSPF configuration to work.

Point-to-Point *Point-to-point* is a type of network topology made up of a direct connection between two routers that provide a single communication path. The point-to-point connection can be physical—for example, a serial cable that directly connects two routers—or logical, where two routers thousands of miles apart are connected by a circuit in a Frame Relay network. Either way, point-to-point configurations eliminate the need for DRs or BDRs.

Point-to-multipoint *Point-to-multipoint* is a network topology made up of a series of connections between a single interface on one router and multiple destination routers. All interfaces on all routers share the point-to-multipoint connection and belong to the same network. Point-to-multipoint networks can be further classified according to whether they support broadcasts or not. This is important because it defines the kind of OSPF configurations you can deploy.

All of these terms play a critical role when you're trying to understand how OSPF actually works, so again, make sure you're familiar with each of them. Understanding these terms will enable you to confidently place them in their proper context as we work through the rest of this chapter.

OSPF Operation

With your newly acquired knowledge of the terms and technologies we just covered, it's now time to get into how OSPF discovers, propagates, and ultimately chooses routes. Once you know how OSPF achieves these tasks, you'll understand how OSPF operates internally really well.

OSPF operation is basically divided into the following three categories:

- Neighbor and adjacency initialization
- LSA flooding
- SPF tree calculation

The beginning neighbor/adjacency formation stage is a big part of OSPF operation. When OSPF is initialized on a router, the router allocates memory for itself as well as for the maintenance of both neighbor and topology tables. Once the router determines which interfaces have been configured for OSPF, it checks to see if they're active and begins sending Hello packets, as shown in figure 10.2.

FIGURE 10.2 The Hello protocol

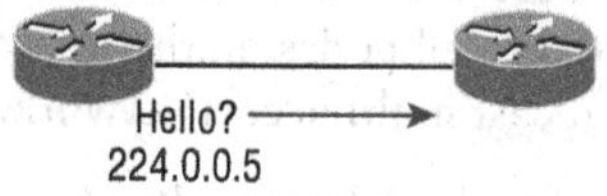

The Hello protocol is used to discover neighbors, establish adjacencies, and maintain relationships with other OSPF routers. Hello packets are periodically sent out of each enabled OSPF interface and in environments that support multicast.

The address used for this is 224.0.0.5, and the frequency with which Hello packets are sent out depends on the network type and topology. Broadcast and point-to-point networks send Hellos every 10 seconds, but non-broadcast and point-to-multipoint networks send them every 30 seconds.

LSA Flooding

LSA flooding is the method OSPF uses to share routing information. Through LS packets, LSA information containing link-state data is shared with all OSPF routers within an area. The network topology is created from the LSA updates, and flooding is used so that all OSPF routers have the same topology map with which to make SPF calculations.

Efficient flooding is achieved through the use of a reserved multicast address: 224.0.0.5 (AllSPFRouters). LSA updates, which indicate that something in the topology has changed, are handled a bit differently. The network type determines the multicast address used for sending updates. Table 10.2 contains the multicast addresses associated with LSA flooding. Point-to-multipoint networks use the adjacent router's unicast IP address.

TABLE 10.2 LSA update multicast addresses

Network Type	Multicast Address	Description
Point-to-point	224.0.0.5	AllSPFRouters
Broadcast	224.0.0.6	AllDRouters
Point-to-multipoint	NA	NA

Once the LSA updates have been flooded throughout the network, each recipient must acknowledge that the flooded update has been received. It's also important for recipients to validate the LSA update.

SPF Tree Calculation

Within an area, each router calculates the best/shortest path to every network in that same area. This calculation is based on the information collected in the topology database and an algorithm called Shortest Path First (SPF). Picture each router in an area constructing a tree—much like a family tree—where the router is the root and all other networks are arranged along the branches and leaves. This is the shortest path tree used by the router to insert OSPF routes into the routing table.

Understand that this tree only contains networks that exist in the same area as the router itself. If a router has interfaces in multiple areas, then separate trees will be constructed for each area. One of the key criteria considered during the route selection process of the SPF algorithm is the metric or cost of each potential path to a network. But this SPF calculation doesn't apply to routes from other areas.

OSPF Metrics

OSPF uses a metric referred to as *cost*. A cost is associated with every outgoing interface included in an SPF tree. The cost of the entire path is the sum of the costs of the outgoing interfaces along the path. Because cost is an arbitrary value as defined in RFC 2338, Cisco had to implement its own method of calculating the cost for each OSPF-enabled interface. Cisco uses a simple equation of 10^8/*bandwidth*, where *bandwidth* is the configured bandwidth for the interface. Using this rule, a 100 Mbps Fast Ethernet interface would have a default OSPF cost of 1, and a 1,000 Mbps Ethernet interface would have a cost of 1.

This value can be overridden with the `ip ospf cost` command. The cost is adjusted by changing the value to a number within the range of 1 to 65,535. Because the cost is assigned to each link, the value must be changed on the specific interface you want to change the cost on.

NOTE

Cisco bases link cost on bandwidth, whereas other vendors may use other metrics to calculate a given link's cost. When connecting links between routers from different vendors, you'll probably have to adjust the cost to match another vendor's router because both routers must assign the same cost to the link for OSPF to work well.

Configuring OSPF

Configuring basic OSPF isn't as simple as configuring RIP and EIGRP, and it can get complex once the many options that are allowed within OSPF are factored in. But you really need to only focus on basic, single-area OSPF configuration for now. Coming up, I'll show you how to configure single-area OSPF.

The two factors that are the basics of OSPF configuration are enabling OSPF and configuring OSPF areas.

Enabling OSPF

The easiest, although least scalable way to configure OSPF, is to just use a single area. Doing this requires a minimum of two commands.

The following is the first command used to activate the OSPF:

```
Router(config)#router ospf ?
<1-65535> Process ID
```

A value in the range from 1 to 65,535 identifies the OSPF process ID. It's a unique number on this router that groups a series of OSPF configuration commands under a specific running process. Different OSPF routers don't have to use the same process ID to communicate. It's a purely local value that doesn't mean a lot, but you still need to remember that it can't start at 0 because that's for the backbone. It has to start at a minimum of 1.

You can have more than one OSPF process running simultaneously on the same router if you want, but this isn't the same as running multi-area OSPF. The second process will maintain an entirely separate copy of its topology table and manage its communications independently of the first one. It comes into play when you want OSPF to connect multiple ASs together. Also, because the Cisco exam objectives only cover single-area OSPF with each router running a single OSPF process, that's what we'll focus on in this book.

NOTE The OSPF process ID is needed to identify a unique instance of an OSPF database and is locally significant.

Configuring OSPF Areas

After identifying the OSPF process, you need to identify the interfaces that you want to activate OSPF communications on as well as the area in which each resides. This will also configure the networks you're going to advertise to others.

Here's an example of a basic OSPF configuration showing our second minimum command needed—the `network` command:

```
Router#config t
Router(config)#router ospf 1
Router(config-router)#network 10.0.0.0 0.255.255.255 area ?
  <0-4294967295>  OSPF area ID as a decimal value
  A.B.C.D         OSPF area ID in IP address format
Router(config-router)#network 10.0.0.0 0.255.255.255 area 0
```

NOTE The areas can be any number from 0 to 4.2 billion. Don't get these numbers confused with the process ID, which ranges from 1 to 65,535.

Remember, the OSPF process ID number is irrelevant. It can be the same on every router on the network, or it can be different—it doesn't matter. It's locally significant and just enables the OSPF routing on the router.

The arguments of the `network` command are the network number (10.0.0.0) and the wildcard mask (0.255.255.255). The combination of these two numbers identifies the interfaces that OSPF will operate on and will also be included in its OSPF LSA advertisements. Based on the example configuration, OSPF will use this command to find any interface on the router configured in the 10.0.0.0 network and will place any interface it finds into area 0.

Even though you can create about 4.2 billion areas, a router wouldn't actually let you create that many. But you can name them using numbers up to 4.2 billion. You can also label an area using an IP address format.

Let me give you a quick explanation of wildcards: A 0 octet in the wildcard mask indicates that the corresponding octet in the network must match exactly. On the other hand, a 255 indicates that you don't care what the corresponding octet is in the network number. A network and wildcard mask combination of 1.1.1.1 0.0.0.0 would match an interface configured exactly with 1.1.1.1 only, and nothing else. This is really useful if you want to activate OSPF on a specific interface in a clear and simple way. If you want to match a range of networks, the network and wildcard mask combination of 1.1.0.0 0.0.255.255 would match any interface in the range of 1.1.0.0 to 1.1.255.255. It's simpler and safer to stick to using wildcard masks of 0.0.0.0 and identify each OSPF interface individually. Once configured, they'll function exactly the same.

The final factor is the area number, which indicates the area that the interfaces identified in the network and wildcard mask belong. Remember that OSPF routers will become neighbors only if their interfaces share a network that's configured to belong to the same area number. The format of the area number is either a decimal value from the range 0 to 4,294,967,295 or a value represented in standard dotted-decimal notation. For example, area 0.0.0.0 is a legitimate area and is identical to area 0.

Wildcard Example

Before configuring our network, let's take a quick look at a more complex OSPF network configuration to find out what our OSPF network statements would be if we were using subnets and wildcards.

In this scenario, we have a router with the following four subnets connected to four different interfaces:

- 192.168.10.64/28
- 192.168.10.80/28
- 192.168.10.96/28
- 192.168.10.8/30

All interfaces need to be in area 0, so it seems to me the easiest configuration would look like this:

```
Test#config t
Test(config)#router ospf 1
Test(config-router)#network 192.168.10.0 0.0.0.255 area 0
```

Okay, I'll admit that preceding example is actually pretty simple, but easy isn't always best—especially when dealing with OSPF! So even though this is an easy way to configure

OSPF, it doesn't make good use of its capabilities—and what fun is that? Worse yet, the objectives aren't likely to present you with something this simple! So, let's create a separate network statement for each interface using the subnet numbers and wildcards. Doing that would look something like this:

```
Test#config t
Test(config)#router ospf 1
Test(config-router)#network 192.168.10.64 0.0.0.15 area 0
Test(config-router)#network 192.168.10.80 0.0.0.15 area 0
Test(config-router)#network 192.168.10.96 0.0.0.15 area 0
Test(config-router)#network 192.168.10.8 0.0.0.3 area 0
```

Wow, now that's different! Truthfully, OSPF would work exactly the same way as it would with the easy configuration I showed you first—but unlike the easy configuration, this one covers the objectives!

And although this looks a bit complicated, it really isn't. All you need is to fully understand block sizes. Just remember that when configuring wildcards, they're always one less than the block size. A /28 is a block size of 16, so we would add our network statement using the subnet number and then add a wildcard of 15 in the interesting octet. For the /30, which is a block size of 4, we would go with a wildcard of 3. Once you practice this a few times, it gets really easy. And do practice, because we'll deal with them again when we get to access lists later on!

Let's use Figure 10.3 as an example and configure that network with OSPF using wildcards. The figure shows a three-router network with the IP addresses of each interface.

FIGURE 10.3 Sample OSPF wildcard configuration

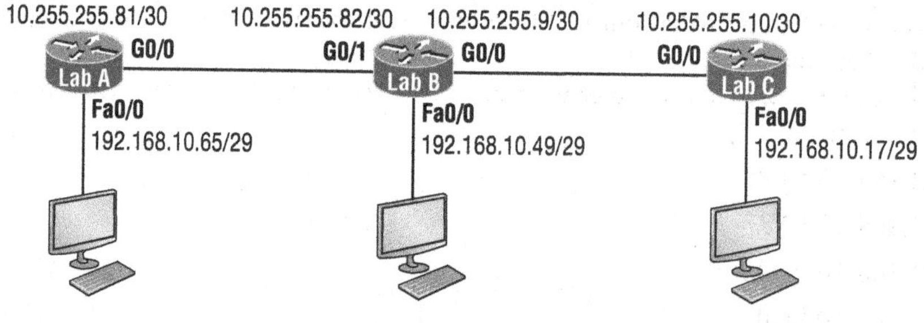

The very first thing you need to be able to do is look at each interface and determine the subnet that the addresses are in. Wait, I know what you're thinking: "Why don't I just use the exact IP addresses of the interface with the 0.0.0.0 wildcard?" You can, but we're paying attention to Cisco exam objectives here, not just what's easiest!

The IP addresses for each interface are shown in the figure. The Lab_A router has two directly connected subnets: 192.168.10.64/29 and 10.255.255.80/30. Here's the OSPF configuration using wildcards:

```
Lab_A#config t
Lab_A(config)#router ospf 1
```

```
Lab_A(config-router)#network 192.168.10.64 0.0.0.7 area 0
Lab_A(config-router)#network 10.255.255.80 0.0.0.3 area 0
```

The Lab_A router is using a /29, or 255.255.255.248, mask on the Fa0/0 interface. This is a block size of 8, which is a wildcard of 7. The G0/0 interface is a mask of 255.255.255.252—block size of 4, with a wildcard of 3. Did you notice that I typed in the network number, not the interface number? You can't configure OSPF this way if you can't look at the IP address and slash notation and figure out the subnet, mask, and wildcard! So, don't take your exam until you're good at this.

Here are two other configurations to help you practice:

```
Lab_B#config t
Lab_B(config)#router ospf 1
Lab_B(config-router)#network 192.168.10.48 0.0.0.7 area 0
Lab_B(config-router)#network 10.255.255.80 0.0.0.3 area 0
Lab_B(config-router)#network 10.255.255.8 0.0.0.3 area 0

Lab_C#config t
Lab_C(config)#router ospf 1
Lab_C(config-router)#network 192.168.10.16 0.0.0.7 area 0
Lab_C(config-router)#network 10.255.255.8 0.0.0.3 area 0
```

As I mentioned with the Lab_A configuration, you've got to be able to determine the subnet, mask, and wildcard just by looking at the IP address and mask of an interface. If you can't do that, you won't be able to configure OSPF using wildcards. So, again, keep at this until you're really comfortable with it!

Configuring Our Network with OSPF

Let's have some fun and configure our internetwork with OSPF using just area 0. OSPF has an administrative distance of 110, but let's remove RIP while we're at it, because you shouldn't get in the habit of having RIP running on your network.

There's a bunch of different ways to configure OSPF, and as I said, the simplest and easiest is to use the wildcard mask 0.0.0.0. But I want to show you that we can configure each router differently with OSPF and still come up with the exact same result. This is one reason why OSPF is more fun and challenging than other routing protocols—it gives us all a lot more ways to screw things up, which automatically provides a troubleshooting opportunity!

We'll use the network shown in Figure 10.4 to configure OSPF, and by the way, notice that I added a new router!

The Corp Router

Here's the Corp router's configuration:

```
Corp#sh ip int brief
Interface          IP-Address       OK? Method Status                Protocol
FastEthernet0/0    10.10.10.1       YES manual up                    up
```

```
Serial0/0          172.16.10.1     YES manual up                    up
FastEthernet0/1    unassigned      YES unset  administratively down down
Serial0/1          172.16.10.5     YES manual up                    up
Corp#config t
Corp(config)#no router rip
Corp(config)#router ospf 132
Corp(config-router)#network 10.10.10.1 0.0.0.0 area 0
Corp(config-router)#network 172.16.10.1 0.0.0.0 area 0
Corp(config-router)#network 172.16.10.5 0.0.0.0 area 0
```

FIGURE 10.4 Our new network layout

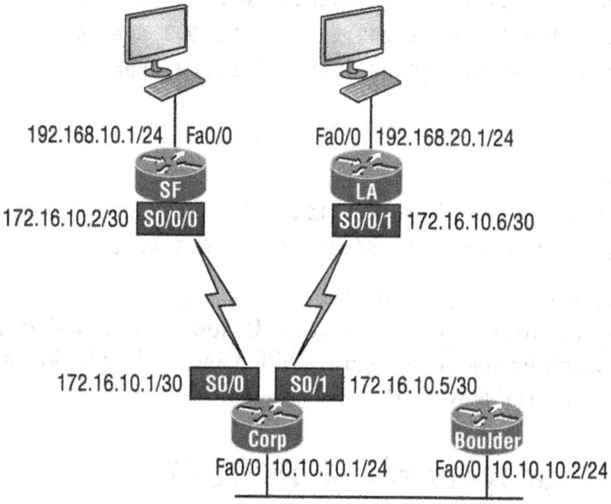

So, it looks like we have a few things to talk about here. First, I removed RIP and then added OSPF. Why did I use OSPF 132? It really doesn't matter—the number is irrelevant. I guess it just felt good to use 132. But notice that I started with the `show ip int brief` command, just like when I was configuring RIP. I did this because it's always important to verify exactly what you are directly connected to. Doing this really helps prevent typos!

The network commands are pretty straightforward. I typed in the IP address of each interface and used the wildcard mask of 0.0.0.0, which means that the IP address must precisely match each octet. This is actually one of those times where easier is better, so just do this:

```
Corp(config)#router ospf 132
Corp(config-router)#network 172.16.10.0 0.0.0.255 area 0
```

Nice—there's only one line instead of two for the 172.16.10.0 network! I really want you to understand that OSPF will work the same here no matter which way you configure the network statement. Now, let's move on to SF. To simplify things, we're going to use our same sample configuration.

The SF Router

The SF router has two directly connected networks. I'll use the IP addresses on each interface to configure this router.

```
SF#sh ip int brief
Interface      IP-Address      OK? Method Status                Protocol
FastEthernet0/0  192.168.10.1    YES manual up                    up
FastEthernet0/1  unassigned      YES unset  administratively down down
Serial0/0/0      172.16.10.2     YES manual up                    up
Serial0/0/1      unassigned      YES unset  administratively down down
SF#config t
SF(config)#no router rip
SF(config)#router ospf 300
SF(config-router)#network 192.168.10.1 0.0.0.0 area 0
SF(config-router)#network 172.16.10.2 0.0.0.0 area 0
*Apr 30 00:25:43.810: %OSPF-5-ADJCHG: Process 300, Nbr 172.16.10.5 on
Serial0/0/0 from LOADING to FULL, Loading Done
```

All I did was to first disable RIP, turn on OSPF routing process 300, and then I added my two directly connected networks. Now let's move on to LA.

The LA Router

The LA router is directly connected to two networks:

```
LA#sh ip int brief
Interface      IP-Address      OK? Method Status                Protocol
FastEthernet0/0 192.168.20.1    YES manual up                    up
FastEthernet0/1 unassigned      YES unset  administratively down down
Serial0/0/0     unassigned      YES unset  administratively down down
Serial0/0/1     172.16.10.6     YES manual up                    up
LA#config t
LA(config)#router ospf 100
LA(config-router)#network 192.168.20.0 0.0.0.255 area 0
LA(config-router)#network 172.16.0.0 0.0.255.255 area 0
*Apr 30 00:56:37.090: %OSPF-5-ADJCHG: Process 100, Nbr 172.16.10.5 on
Serial0/0/1 from LOADING to FULL, Loading Done
```

Remember that when you're configuring dynamic routing, using the `show ip int brief` command first will make it all so much easier!

And don't forget, I can use any process ID I want, as long as it's a value from 1 to 65,535, because it doesn't matter if all routers use the same process ID. Also, notice that I used different wildcards in this example. Doing this works really well, too.

Okay, I want you to think about something for a second before we move onto more advanced OSPF topics: what if the Fa0/1 interface of the LA router was connected to a link that we didn't want or need to have on in order to have OSPF working, as shown in Figure 10.5?

FIGURE 10.5 Adding a non-OSPF network to LA router

```
LA(config)#router ospf 100
LA(config-router)#passive-interface fastEthernet 0/1
```

Even though this is pretty simple, you've really got to be careful before you configure this command on your router! I added it as an example on interface Fa0/1, which happens to be an interface we're not using in this network, because I want OSPF to work on my other router's interfaces.

Now it's time to configure the Corp router to advertise a default route to the SF and LA routers, because doing so will make our lives a lot easier. Instead of having to configure all our routers with a default route, we'll only configure one router and then advertise that this router is the one that holds the default route—efficient!

Looking at Figure 10.5, keep in mind that, for now, the corporate router is connected to the Internet off of Fa0/0. We'll create a default route toward this imaginary Internet and then tell the other routers that this is the route they'll use to get to the Internet. Here's the configuration:

```
Corp#config t
Corp(config)#ip route 0.0.0.0 0.0.0.0 Fa0/0
Corp(config)#router ospf 1
Corp(config-router)#default-information originate
```

Now, let's check and see if our other routers have received this default route from the Corp router:

```
SF#show ip route
[output cut]
```

```
E1 - OSPF external type 1, E2 - OSPF external type 2
[output cut]
O*E2 0.0.0.0/0 [110/1] via 172.16.10.1, 00:01:54, Serial0/0/0
SF#
```

Sure enough—the last line in the SF router shows that it received the advertisement from the Corp router regarding the fact that the corporate router is the one holding the default route out of the AS.

But wait—I need to configure our new router into my lab to create the example network we'll use from here on. Here's the configuration of the new router that I connected to the same network the Corp router is connected to via the Fa0/0 interface:

```
Router#config t
Router(config)#hostname Boulder
Boulder(config)#int f0/0
Boulder(config-if)#ip address 10.10.10.2 255.255.255.0
Boulder(config-if)#no shut
*Apr  6 18:01:38.007: %LINEPROTO-5-UPDOWN: Line protocol on Interface
FastEthernet0/0, changed state to up
Boulder(config-if)#router ospf 2
Boulder(config-router)#network 10.0.0.0 0.255.255.255 area 0
*Apr  6 18:03:27.267: %OSPF-5-ADJCHG: Process 2, Nbr 223.255.255.254 on
FastEthernet0/0 from LOADING to FULL, Loading Done
```

This is all good, but I need to make sure that you don't follow my example to a tee here, because I quickly brought a router up without setting my passwords first. I can get away with this only because I am in a nonproduction network, so don't do this in the real world, where security is vital!

Anyway, now that I have my new router nicely connected with a basic configuration, we're going to move on to cover loopback interfaces, how to set the router ID (RID) used with OSPF, and finally, how to verify OSPF.

OSPF and Loopback Interfaces

You need to make sure to configure loopback interfaces when using OSPF. In fact, Cisco suggests using them whenever you configure OSPF on a router for stability.

Loopback interfaces are logical interfaces, which means they're virtual, software-only interfaces, not actual physical router interfaces. A big reason we use loopback interfaces with OSPF configurations is that they ensure an interface is always active and available for OSPF processes.

Loopback interfaces also come in very handy for diagnostic purposes as well as for OSPF configuration. Understand that if you don't configure a loopback interface on a router, the highest active IP address on a router will become that router's RID during bootup!

Figure 10.6 illustrates how routers know each other by their router ID.

FIGURE 10.6 OSPF router ID (RID)

The RID is not only used to advertise routes, but it's also used to elect the designated router (DR) and the backup designated router (BDR). These designated routers create adjacencies when a new router comes up and exchanges LSAs to build topological databases.

> **NOTE** By default, OSPF uses the highest IP address on any active interface at the moment OSPF starts up to determine the RID of the router. However, you can override this using a logical interface. Remember: the highest IP address of any logical interface will always become a router's RID!

Let's configure logical loopback interfaces and learn how to verify them, and also verify RIDs.

Configuring Loopback Interfaces

Configuring loopback interfaces rocks mostly because it's the easiest part of OSPF configuration, and we all need a break about now, right?

First, let's see what the RID is on the Corp router with the `show ip ospf` command:

```
Corp#sh ip ospf
 Routing Process "ospf 1" with ID 172.16.10.5
[output cut]
```

You can see that the RID is 172.16.10.5—the Serial0/1 interface of the router. So, let's configure a loopback interface using a completely different IP addressing scheme:

```
Corp(config)#int loopback 0
*Mar 22 01:23:14.206: %LINEPROTO-5-UPDOWN: Line protocol on Interface
   Loopback0, changed state to up
Corp(config-if)#ip address 172.31.1.1 255.255.255.255
```

The IP scheme really doesn't matter here, but each one being in a separate subnet does! By using the /32 mask, we can use any IP address we want, as long as the addresses are never the same on any two routers.

Let's configure the other routers now:

```
SF#config t
SF(config)#int loopback 0
*Mar 22 01:25:11.206: %LINEPROTO-5-UPDOWN: Line protocol on Interface
   Loopback0, changed state to up
SF(config-if)#ip address 172.31.1.2 255.255.255.255
```

Here's the configuration of the loopback interface on LA:

```
LA#config t
LA(config)#int loopback 0
*Mar 22 02:21:59.686: %LINEPROTO-5-UPDOWN: Line protocol on Interface
   Loopback0, changed state to up
LA(config-if)#ip address 172.31.1.3 255.255.255.255
```

I'm pretty sure you're wondering what the IP address mask of 255.255.255.255 (/32) means and why we don't just use 255.255.255.0 instead. While it's true that either mask works, the /32 mask is called a *host mask* and works fine for loopback interfaces. It also allows us to save subnets. Notice how I was able to use 172.31.1.1, .2, .3, and .4? If I didn't use the /32, I'd have to use a separate subnet for each and every router—not good!

One important question to answer before we move on is whether we actually changed the RIDs of our router by setting the loopback interfaces? Let's find out by taking a look at the Corp router's RID:

```
Corp#sh ip ospf
 Routing Process "ospf 1" with ID 172.16.10.5
```

Okay, what happened here? You would think that because we set logical interfaces, the IP addresses under them would automatically become the RID of the router, right? Well, sort of, but only if you do one of two things: either reboot the router or delete OSPF and re-create the database on your router. Neither is a good option, so try to remember to create your logical interfaces before you start OSPF routing. That way, the loopback interface will always become your RID straightaway!

With all this in mind, I'm going with rebooting the Corp router because it's the easier of the two options I have right now.

Let's see what our RID is:

```
Corp#sh ip ospf
 Routing Process "ospf 1" with ID 172.31.1.1
```

That did the trick! The Corp router now has a new RID, so I guess I'll just go ahead and reboot all my routers to get their RIDs reset to our logical addresses. But should I really do that?

Maybe not, because there is *one* other way. What do you think about adding a new RID for the router right under the `router ospf` *`process-id`* command instead? Sounds good, so let's give that a shot. Here's an example of doing that on the Corp router:

```
Corp#config t
Corp(config)#router ospf 1
Corp(config-router)#router-id 223.255.255.254
Reload or use "clear ip ospf process" command, for this to take effect
Corp(config-router)#do clear ip ospf process
Reset ALL OSPF processes? [no]: yes
*Jan 16 14:20:36.906: %OSPF-5-ADJCHG: Process 1, Nbr 192.168.20.1
on Serial0/1 from FULL to DOWN, Neighbor Down: Interface down
or detached
*Jan 16 14:20:36.906: %OSPF-5-ADJCHG: Process 1, Nbr 192.168.10.1
on Serial0/0 from FULL to DOWN, Neighbor Down: Interface down
or detached
*Jan 16 14:20:36.982: %OSPF-5-ADJCHG: Process 1, Nbr 192.168.20.1
on Serial0/1 from LOADING to FULL, Loading Done
*Jan 16 14:20:36.982: %OSPF-5-ADJCHG: Process 1, Nbr 192.168.10.1
on Serial0/0 from LOADING to FULL, Loading Done
Corp(config-router)#do sh ip ospf
 Routing Process "ospf 1" with ID 223.255.255.254
```

It worked! We changed the RID without reloading the router. But wait—remember, we set a logical loopback interface earlier. Does that mean the loopback interface will win over the `router-id` command? Well, we have our answer: a loopback interface will *not* override the `router-id` command, and we don't have to reboot the router to make it take effect as the RID!

So, this process follows the following hierarchy:

1. Highest active interface by default.
2. Highest logical interface overrides a physical interface.
3. The `router-id` overrides the interface and loopback interface.

The only thing left now is to decide whether you want to advertise the loopback interfaces under OSPF. There are pros and cons to using an address that won't be advertised versus using an address that will be. Using an unadvertised address saves on real IP address space, but the address won't appear in the OSPF table, which means you can't ping it.

So basically, what you're faced with here is a choice that equals a trade-off between the ease of debugging the network and the conservation of address space. What do we do? A great strategy is to use a private IP address scheme, as I did. Do this, and all will be well!

Now that we've configured all the routers with OSPF, what's next? Miller time? Nope, not yet. It's verification time again. We still have to make sure that OSPF is really working, and that's exactly what we're going to do next.

Verifying OSPF Configuration

There are several ways to verify proper OSPF configuration and operation. Next, I'm going to demonstrate the various OSPF show commands you need to know in order to achieve the goal. We're going to start by taking a quick look at the routing table of the Corp router.

First, let's issue a `show ip route` command on the Corp router:

```
O     192.168.10.0/24 [110/65] via 172.16.10.2, 1d17h, Serial0/0
      172.131.0.0/32 is subnetted, 1 subnets
     172.131.0.0/32 is subnetted, 1 subnets
C        172.131.1.1 is directly connected, Loopback0
      172.16.0.0/30 is subnetted, 4 subnets
C        172.16.10.4 is directly connected, Serial0/1
L        172.16.10.5/32 is directly connected, Serial0/1
C        172.16.10.0 is directly connected, Serial0/0
L        172.16.10.1/32 is directly connected, Serial0/0
O     192.168.20.0/24 [110/65] via 172.16.10.6, 1d17h, Serial0/1
      10.0.0.0/24 is subnetted, 2 subnets
C        10.10.10.0 is directly connected, FastEthernet0/0
L        10.10.10.1/32 is directly connected, FastEthernet0/0
```

The Corp router shows only two dynamic routes for the internetwork, with the O representing OSPF internal routes. The Cs are clearly our directly connected networks, and our two remote networks are showing up too—nice! Notice the 110/65—that's our administrative distance/metric.

Now that's a nice-looking OSPF routing table! It's important to make troubleshooting and fixing an OSPF network easier, which is why I always use the `show ip int brief` command when configuring my routing protocols. It's very easy to make little mistakes with OSPF, so keep your eyes on the details!

It's time to show you all the OSPF verification commands that you need in your toolbox for now.

The *show ip ospf* Command

The `show ip ospf` command is what you'll need to display OSPF information for one or all OSPF processes running on the router. Information contained therein includes the router ID, area information, SPF statistics, and LSA timer information. Let's check out the output from the Corp router:

```
Corp#sh ip ospf
 Routing Process "ospf 1" with ID 223.255.255.254
 Start time: 00:08:41.724, Time elapsed: 2d16h
 Supports only single TOS(TOS0) routes
```

```
 Supports opaque LSA
 Supports Link-local Signaling (LLS)
 Supports area transit capability
 Router is not originating router-LSAs with maximum metric
 Initial SPF schedule delay 5000 msecs
 Minimum hold time between two consecutive SPFs 10000 msecs
 Maximum wait time between two consecutive SPFs 10000 msecs
 Incremental-SPF disabled
 Minimum LSA interval 5 secs
 Minimum LSA arrival 1000 msecs
 LSA group pacing timer 240 secs
 Interface flood pacing timer 33 msecs
 Retransmission pacing timer 66 msecs
 Number of external LSA 0. Checksum Sum 0x000000
 Number of opaque AS LSA 0. Checksum Sum 0x000000
 Number of DCbitless external and opaque AS LSA 0
 Number of DoNotAge external and opaque AS LSA 0
 Number of areas in this router is 1. 1 normal 0 stub 0 nssa
 Number of areas transit capable is 0
 External flood list length 0
 IETF NSF helper support enabled
 Cisco NSF helper support enabled
    Area BACKBONE(0)
        Number of interfaces in this area is 3
        Area has no authentication
        SPF algorithm last executed 00:11:08.760 ago
        SPF algorithm executed 5 times
        Area ranges are
        Number of LSA 6. Checksum Sum 0x03B054
        Number of opaque link LSA 0. Checksum Sum 0x000000
        Number of DCbitless LSA 0
        Number of indication LSA 0
        Number of DoNotAge LSA 0
        Flood list length 0
```

Notice the router ID (RID) of 223.255.255.254, which is the highest IP address configured on the router. Hopefully, you also noticed that I set the RID of the corporate router to the highest available IP address available with IPv4.

The *show ip ospf database* Command

The `show ip ospf database` command gives you information about the number of routers in the internetwork (AS) plus the neighboring router's ID—the topology database I mentioned earlier. Unlike the `show ip eigrp topology` command, this command reveals the OSPF routers, but not each and every link in the AS, as EIGRP does.

The output is broken down by area. Here's a sample output, again from Corp:

```
Corp#sh ip ospf database

                OSPF Router with ID (223.255.255.254) (Process ID 1)
Router Link States (Area 0)

Link ID         ADV Router      Age         Seq#       Checksum Link count
10.10.10.2      10.10.10.2      966         0x80000001 0x007162 1
172.31.1.4      172.31.1.4      885         0x80000002 0x00D27E 1
192.168.10.1    192.168.10.1    886         0x8000007A 0x00BC95 3
192.168.20.1    192.168.20.1    1133        0x8000007A 0x00E348 3
223.255.255.254 223.255.255.254 925         0x8000004D 0x000B90 5

                Net Link States (Area 0)

Link ID         ADV Router      Age         Seq#       Checksum
10.10.10.1      223.255.255.254 884         0x80000002 0x008CFE
```

You can see all the routers and the RID of each router—the highest IP address on each of them. For example, the Link ID and ADV Router of my new Boulder router shows up twice: once with the directly connected IP address (10.10.10.2) and again as the RID that I set under the OSPF process (172.31.1.4).

The router output shows the link ID—remember that an interface is also a link—and the RID of the router on that link under the ADV router, or advertising router.

The *show ip ospf interface* Command

The `show ip ospf interface` command reveals all interface-related OSPF information. Data is displayed about OSPF information for all OSPF-enabled interfaces or for specified interfaces. I'll highlight some of the more important factors for you. Here's the output:

```
Corp#sh ip ospf int f0/0
FastEthernet0/0 is up, line protocol is up
  Internet Address 10.10.10.1/24, Area 0
  Process ID 1, Router ID 223.255.255.254, Network Type BROADCAST, Cost: 1
```

```
Transmit Delay is 1 sec, State DR, Priority 1
Designated Router (ID) 223.255.255.254, Interface address 10.10.10.1
Backup Designated router (ID) 172.31.1.4, Interface address 10.10.10.2
Timer intervals configured, Hello 10, Dead 40, Wait 40, Retransmit 5
  oob-resync timeout 40
  Hello due in 00:00:08
Supports Link-local Signaling (LLS)
Cisco NSF helper support enabled
IETF NSF helper support enabled
Index 3/3, flood queue length 0
Next 0x0(0)/0x0(0)
Last flood scan length is 1, maximum is 1
Last flood scan time is 0 msec, maximum is 0 msec
Neighbor Count is 1, Adjacent neighbor count is 1
  Adjacent with neighbor 172.31.1.  Suppress hello for 0 neighbor(s)
```

This command provided the following information:

- Interface IP address
- Area assignment
- Process ID
- Router ID
- Network type
- Cost
- Priority
- DR/BDR election information (if applicable)
- Hello and Dead timer intervals
- Adjacent neighbor information

The reason I used the `show ip ospf interface f0/0` command is because I knew that a designated router would be elected on the FastEthernet broadcast multi-access network between the Corp and Boulder routers. The information I highlighted is all very important, so make sure you've noted it! A good question to ask here is: what are the Hello and Dead timers set to by default?

Type in the `show ip ospf interface` command and receive the following response:

```
Corp#sh ip ospf int f0/0
%OSPF: OSPF not enabled on FastEthernet0/0
```

This error occurs when OSPF is enabled on the router but not on the interface. When this happens, you need to check your network statements because it means that the interface you're trying to verify is not included in your OSPF process!

The *show ip ospf neighbor* Command

The `show ip ospf neighbor` command is really useful because it summarizes the pertinent OSPF information regarding neighbors and the adjacency state. If a DR or BDR exists, that information will also be displayed. Here's a sample:

```
Corp#sh ip ospf neighbor

Neighbor ID     Pri   State       Dead Time   Address         Interface
172.31.1.4        1   FULL/BDR    00:00:34    10.10.10.2      FastEthernet0/0
192.168.20.1      0   FULL/  -    00:00:31    172.16.10.6     Serial0/1
192.168.10.1      0   FULL/  -    00:00:32    172.16.10.2     Serial0/0
```

Real World Scenario

An Admin Connects Two Disparate Routers Together with OSPF and the Link Between Them Never Comes Up

A while back, an admin called me in a panic because he couldn't get OSPF working between two routers, one of which was an older router they needed to use while they were waiting for their new router to be shipped to them.

OSPF can be used in a multivendor network, so he was confused as to why this wasn't working. He turned on RIP, and it worked, so he was super confused as to why OSPF was not creating adjacencies. I had him use the `show ip ospf interface` command to look at the link between the two routers and, sure enough, the Hello and Dead timers didn't match. I had him configure the mismatched parameters so they would match, but it still wouldn't create an adjacency. Looking more closely at the `show ip ospf interface` command, I noticed the cost did not match! Cisco calculated the bandwidth differently from the other vendor. Once I had him configure both as the same value, the link came up! Always remember, just because OSPF can be used in a multivendor network, does not mean it will work out of the box!

This is a critical command to understand because it's extremely useful in production networks. Let's take a look at the Boulder router output:

```
Boulder>sh ip ospf neighbor

Neighbor ID       Pri   State      Dead Time   Address        Interface
223.255.255.254     1   FULL/DR    00:00:31    10.10.10.1     FastEthernet0/0
```

We can see that since there's an Ethernet link (broadcast multi-access) on the link between the Boulder and the Corp routers, there's going to be an election to determine who will be the designated router (DR) and who will be the backup designated router (BDR). We can see that the Corp became the designated router, and it won because it had the highest IP address on the network—the highest RID.

Now the reason that the Corp connections to SF and LA don't have a DR or BDR listed in the output is that by default, elections don't happen on point-to-point links and they show `FULL/ -`. But we can still determine that the Corp router is fully adjacent to all three routers based on its output.

The *show ip protocols* Command

The `show ip protocols` command is also highly useful, whether you're running OSPF, EIGRP, RIP, BGP, IS-IS, or any other routing protocol that can be configured on your router. The command provides an excellent overview of the actual operation of all currently running protocols!

Check out the output from the Corp router:

```
Corp#sh ip protocols
Routing Protocol is "ospf 1"
  Outgoing update filter list for all interfaces is not set
  Incoming update filter list for all interfaces is not set
  Router ID 223.255.255.254
  Number of areas in this router is 1. 1 normal 0 stub 0 nssa
  Maximum path: 4
  Routing for Networks:
    10.10.10.1 0.0.0.0 area 0
    172.16.10.1 0.0.0.0 area 0
    172.16.10.5 0.0.0.0 area 0
 Reference bandwidth unit is 100 mbps
  Routing Information Sources:
    Gateway         Distance      Last Update
    192.168.10.1         110      00:21:53
    192.168.20.1         110      00:21:53
  Distance: (default is 110) Distance: (default is 110)
```

From looking at this output, you can determine the OSPF process ID, OSPF router ID, type of OSPF area, networks and areas configured for OSPF, and the OSPF router IDs of neighbors—that's a lot. It's super-efficient!

Summary

This chapter provided a great deal of information about OSPF. It's really difficult to include everything about OSPF because so much of it falls outside the scope of this chapter and book, but I've given you a few tips here and there, so you should be in good shape—as long as you make sure you've got what I presented dialed in!

I talked about a lot of OSPF topics, including terminology, operations, and configuration, as well as verification and monitoring.

Each of these topics encompasses quite a bit of information—the terminology section just scratched the surface of OSPF. However, you've got the goods you really need for your studies. Finally, I gave you a tight survey of the most useful commands for observing the operation of OSPF, so you can verify that things are moving along as they should.

Exam Essentials

Compare OSPF and RIPv1. OSPF is a link-state protocol that supports VLSM and classless routing; RIPv1 is a distance-vector protocol that does not support VLSM and supports only classful routing.

Know how OSPF routers become neighbors and/or adjacent. OSPF routers become neighbors when each router sees the other's Hello packets.

Be able to configure single-area OSPF. A minimal single-area configuration involves only two commands: `router ospf` *`process-id`* and `network` *`x.x.x.x y.y.y.y area Z`*.

Be able to verify the operation of OSPF. There are many `show` commands that provide useful details on OSPF, and it is useful to be completely familiar with the output of each: `show ip ospf`, `show ip ospf database`, `show ip ospf interface`, `show ip ospf neighbor`, and `show ip protocols`.

Written Lab

You can find the answers to this lab in Appendix A, "Answers to the Written Labs."

1. Write the command that will enable the OSPF process 101 on a router.
2. Write the command that will display details of all OSPF routing processes enabled on a router.
3. Write the command that will display interface-specific OSPF information.
4. Write the command that will display all OSPF neighbors.
5. Write the command that will display all the different OSPF route types currently known by the router.

Review Questions

You can find the answers to these questions in Appendix B, "Answers to the Review Questions."

NOTE

The following questions are designed to test your understanding of this chapter's material. For more information on how to get additional questions, please see this book's introduction.

1. There are three possible routes for a router to reach a destination network. The first route is from OSPF with a metric of 782. The second route is from RIPv2 with a metric of 4. The third is from EIGRP with a composite metric of 20514560. Which route will be installed by the router in its routing table?
   - **A.** RIPv2
   - **B.** EIGRP
   - **C.** OSPF
   - **D.** All three

2. In the following diagram, which of the routers must be ABRs? (Choose all that apply.)

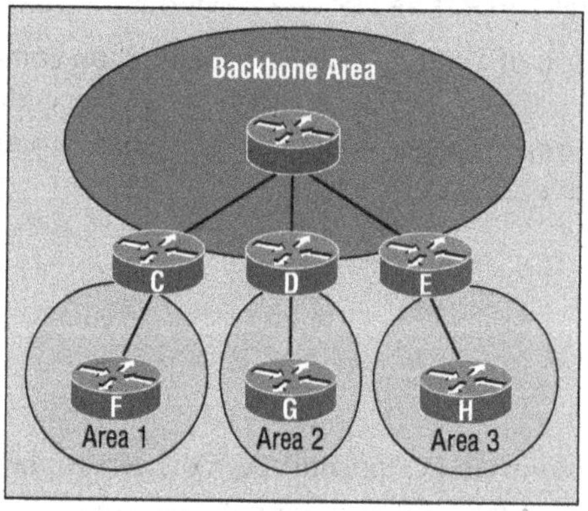

   - **A.** C
   - **B.** D
   - **C.** E
   - **D.** F
   - **E.** G
   - **F.** H

3. Which of the following describe the process identifier that is used to run OSPF on a router? (Choose two.)
   A. It is locally significant.
   B. It is globally significant.
   C. It is needed to identify a unique instance of an OSPF database.
   D. It is an optional parameter required only if multiple OSPF processes are running on the router.
   E. All routes in the same OSPF area must have the same process ID if they are to exchange routing information.

4. All of the following must match for two OSPF routers to become neighbors except which?
   A. Area ID
   B. Router ID
   C. Stub area flag
   D. Authentication password, if using one

5. In the diagram, by default what will be the router ID of Lab_B?

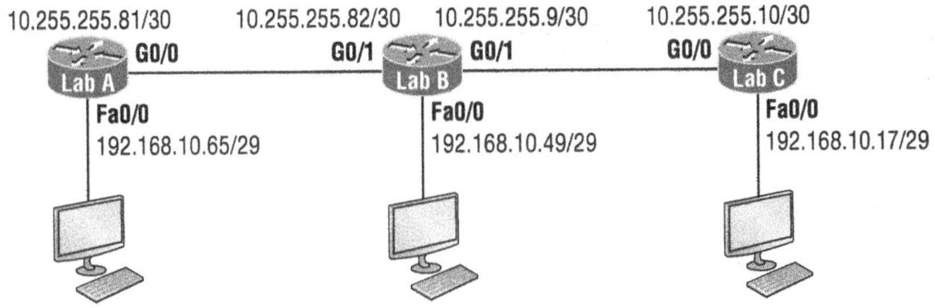

   A. 10.255.255.82
   B. 10.255.255.9
   C. 192.168.10.49
   D. 10.255.255.81

6. You get a call from a network administrator who tells you that he typed the following into his router:

```
Router(config)#router ospf 1
Router(config-router)#network 10.0.0.0 255.0.0.0 area 0
```

   He says that he still can't see any routes in the routing table. What configuration error did the administrator make?
   A. The wildcard mask is incorrect.
   B. The OSPF area is wrong.
   C. The OSPF process ID is incorrect.
   D. The AS configuration is wrong.

7. Which of the following statements is true with regard to the output shown?

```
Corp#sh ip ospf neighbor

Neighbor ID      Pri   State         Dead Time   Address         Interface
172.31.1.4         1   FULL/BDR      00:00:34    10.10.10.2      FastEthernet0/0
192.168.20.1       0   FULL/  -      00:00:31    172.16.10.6     Serial0/1
192.168.10.1       0   FULL/  -      00:00:32    172.16.10.2     Serial0/0
```

A. There is no DR on the link to 192.168.20.1.

B. The Corp router is the BDR on the link to 172.31.1.4.

C. The Corp router is the DR on the link to 192.168.20.1.

D. The link to 192.168.10.1 is active.

8. What is the administrative distance of OSPF?

A. 90

B. 100

C. 120

D. 110

9. In OSPF, Hellos are sent to what IP address?

A. 224.0.0.5

B. 224.0.0.9

C. 224.0.0.10

D. 224.0.0.1

10. What command generated the following output?

```
172.31.1.4         1   FULL/BDR      00:00:34    10.10.10.2      FastEthernet0/0
192.168.20.1       0   FULL/  -      00:00:31    172.16.10.6     Serial0/1
192.168.10.1       0   FULL/  -      00:00:32    172.16.10.2     Serial0/0
```

A. `show ip ospf neighbor`

B. `show ip ospf database`

C. `show ip route`

D. `show ip ospf interface`

11. Updates addressed to 224.0.0.6 are destined for which type of OSPF router?

A. DR

B. ASBR

C. ABR

D. All OSPF routers

12. For some reason, you cannot establish an adjacency relationship on a common Ethernet link between two routers. Looking at the following output, what is the cause of the problem?

```
RouterA#
Ethernet0/0 is up, line protocol is up
  Internet Address 172.16.1.2/16, Area 0
  Process ID 2, Router ID 172.126.1.2, Network Type BROADCAST, Cost: 10
  Transmit Delay is 1 sec, State DR, Priority 1
  Designated Router (ID) 172.16.1.2, interface address 172.16.1.1
  No backup designated router on this network
  Timer intervals configured, Hello 5, Dead 20, Wait 20, Retransmit 5

RouterB#
Ethernet0/0 is up, line protocol is up
  Internet Address 172.16.1.1/16, Area 0
  Process ID 2, Router ID 172.126.1.1, Network Type BROADCAST, Cost: 10
  Transmit Delay is 1 sec, State DR, Priority 1
  Designated Router (ID) 172.16.1.1, interface address 172.16.1.2
  No backup designated router on this network
  Timer intervals configured, Hello 10, Dead 40, Wait 40, Retransmit 5
```

A. The OSPF area is not configured properly.
B. The priority on RouterA should be set higher.
C. The cost on RouterA should be set higher.
D. The Hello and Dead timers are not configured properly.
E. A backup designated router needs to be added to the network.
F. The OSPF process ID numbers must match.

13. Which of the following is true regarding OSPF networks? (Choose four.)
A. A designated router is elected on broadcast networks.
B. All routers must be configured with the same AS number.
C. Each OSPF router maintains an identical database describing the AS topology.
D. A Hello protocol provides dynamic neighbor discovery.
E. A routing table contains only the best routes.

14. Type the command that will disable OSPF on the Fa0/1 interface under the routing process. Write only the command, not the prompt.

15. Which of the following commands will place network 10.2.3.0/24 into area 0? (Choose two.)
A. `router eigrp 10`
B. `router ospf 10`
C. `router rip`
D. `network 10.0.0.0`

E. `network 10.2.3.0 255.255.255.0 area 0`

F. `network 10.2.3.0 0.0.0.255 area0`

G. `network 10.2.3.0 0.0.0.255 area 0`

16. Given the following output, which statement or statements can be determined to be true? (Choose all that apply.)

```
RouterA2# show ip ospf neighbor

Neighbor ID Pri State Dead Time Address Interface
192.168.23.2 1 FULL/BDR 00:00:29 10.24.4.2 FastEthernet1/0
192.168.45.2 2 FULL/BDR 00:00:24 10.1.0.5 FastEthernet0/0
192.168.85.1 1 FULL/- 00:00:33 10.6.4.10 Serial0/1
192.168.90.3 1 FULL/DR 00:00:32 10.5.5.2 FastEthernet0/1
192.168.67.3 1 FULL/DR 00:00:20 10.4.9.20 FastEthernet0/2
192.168.90.1 1 FULL/BDR 00:00:23 10.5.5.4 FastEthernet0/1
<<output omitted>>
```

A. The DR for the network connected to Fa0/0 has an interface priority higher than 2.

B. This router (A2) is the BDR for subnet 10.1.0.0.

C. The DR for the network connected to Fa0/1 has a router ID of 10.5.5.2.

D. The DR for the serial subnet is 192.168.85.1.

17. What are the reasons for creating OSPF in a hierarchical design? (Choose three.)

A. To decrease routing overhead

B. To speed up convergence

C. To confine network instability to single areas of the network

D. To make configuring OSPF easier

18. Type the command that produced the following output. Write only the command, not the prompt.

```
FastEthernet0/0 is up, line protocol is up
  Internet Address 10.10.10.1/24, Area 0
  Process ID 1, Router ID 223.255.255.254, Network Type BROADCAST, Cost: 1
Transmit Delay is 1 sec, State DR, Priority 1
  Designated Router (ID) 223.255.255.254, Interface address 10.10.10.1
Backup Designated router (ID) 172.31.1.4, Interface address 10.10.10.2
Timer intervals configured, Hello 10, Dead 40, Wait 40, Retransmit 5
    oob-resync timeout 40
    Hello due in 00:00:08
  Supports Link-local Signaling (LLS)
```

```
Cisco NSF helper support enabled
IETF NSF helper support enabled
Index 3/3, flood queue length 0
Next 0x0(0)/0x0(0)
Last flood scan length is 1, maximum is 1
Last flood scan time is 0 msec, maximum is 0 msec
Neighbor Count is 1, Adjacent neighbor count is 1
  Adjacent with neighbor 172.31.1.  Suppress hello for 0 neighbor(s)
```

19. A(n) ________ is an OSPF data packet containing link-state and routing information that are shared among OSPF routers.

A. LSA

B. TSA

C. Hello

D. SPF

20. If routers in a single area are configured with the same priority value, what value does a router use for the OSPF router ID in the absence of a loopback interface?

A. The lowest IP address of any physical interface

B. The highest IP address of any physical interface

C. The lowest IP address of any logical interface

D. The highest IP address of any logical interface

Chapter 11

Enhanced IGRP

Although no direct exam objectives apply to this chapter, this material could still be covered on the exam.

Enhanced Interior Gateway Routing Protocol (EIGRP) is a Cisco protocol that runs on Cisco routers and on some Cisco switches. In this chapter, I'll cover the many features and functions of EIGRP, with an added focus on the unique way that it discovers, selects, and advertises routes.

EIGRP has a number of features that make it especially useful within large, complex networks. A real standout among these is its support of the variable length subnet mask (VLSM) subnetting technique, which is crucial to its ultra-efficient scalability. EIGRP even includes benefits gained through other common protocols like Open Shortest Path First (OSPF) and Router Information Protocol version 2 (RIPv2), such as the ability to create route summaries at any location you choose.

I'll also cover key EIGRP configuration details and give you examples of each, as well as demonstrate the various commands required to verify that EIGRP is working properly.

Finally, I'll wrap up the chapter by showing you how to configure and verify EIGRPv6. I promise that after you get through it, you'll agree that EIGRPv6 is truly the easiest part of this chapter.

NOTE To find bonus material, as well as Todd Lammle videos, practice questions, and hands-on labs, please see `www.lammle.com/ccna`.

EIGRP Features and Operations

EIGRP is a classless, distance-vector protocol that uses the concept of an autonomous system to describe a set of contiguous routers that run the same routing protocol and share routing information, which also includes the subnet mask in its route updates. This is a very big deal because by advertising subnet information, this robust protocol enables us to use VLSM and permits summarization to be included within the design of EIGRP networks.

EIGRP is sometimes referred to as a *hybrid routing protocol* or an *advanced distance-vector protocol* because it has characteristics of both distance-vector and some link-state protocols. For example, EIGRP doesn't send link-state packets like OSPF does. Instead, it sends traditional distance-vector updates that include information about networks plus the cost of reaching them from the perspective of the advertising router.

EIGRP has link-state characteristics as well: It synchronizes network topology information between neighbors at startup and then sends specific updates only when topology changes occur (bounded updates). This particular feature is a huge advancement over RIP and is a big reason that EIGRP works so well in very large networks.

EIGRP has a default hop count of 100, with a maximum of 255, but don't let this confuse you, because EIGRP doesn't rely on hop count as a metric like RIP does. In EIGRP-speak, hop count refers to how many routers an EIGRP route update packet can go through before it will be discarded, which limits the size of the autonomous system (AS). So don't forget that this isn't how metrics are calculated with EIGRP.

A bunch of powerful features make EIGRP a real standout from other protocols. Here's a list of some of the major ones:

- Support for Internet Protocol (IP) and IPv6 (and some other useless routed protocols) via protocol-dependent modules
- Considered classless (same as RIPv2 and OSPF)
- Support for VLSM/CIDR (classless inter-domain routing)
- Support for summaries and discontiguous networks
- Efficient neighbor discovery
- Communication via Reliable Transport Protocol (RTP)
- Best path selection via Diffusing Update Algorithm (DUAL)
- Reduced bandwidth usage with bounded updates
- No broadcasts

NOTE Cisco refers to EIGRP as a distance-vector routing protocol but also as an advanced distance-vector or even a hybrid routing protocol.

Neighbor Discovery

Before EIGRP routers can exchange routes with each other, they must become neighbors, and three conditions must be met before this can happen, as shown in Figure 11.1.

FIGURE 11.1 EIGRP neighbor discovery

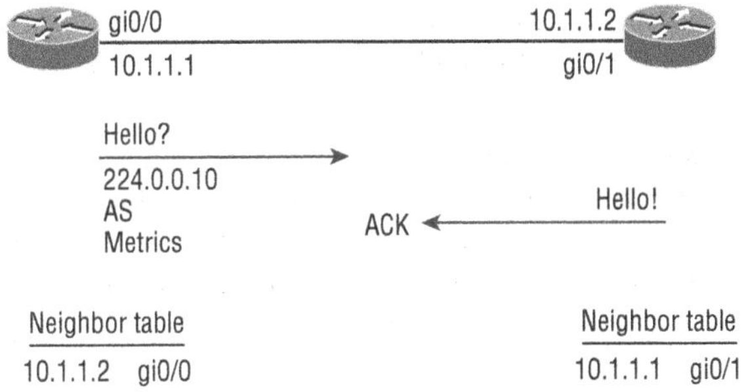

And these three things will be exchanged with directly connected neighbors:

- Hello or ACK received
- AS numbers match
- Identical metrics (K values)

Link-state protocols often use Hello messages to establish who their neighbors are because they usually don't send out periodic route updates but still need a way to help neighbors know when a new peer has arrived or an old one has gone down. And because Hellos are also used to maintain neighbor relationships, it follows that EIGRP routers must also continuously receive Hellos from their neighbors.

But EIGRP routers that belong to different ASs don't automatically share routing information and, therefore, don't become neighbors. This factor is really helpful operating in larger networks because it reduces the amount of route information propagated through a specific AS. But it also means that manual redistribution can sometimes be required between different ASs as a result. Because metrics play a big role in choosing between the five possible factors to be evaluated when choosing the best possible route, it's important that all EIGRP neighbors agree on how a specific route is chosen. This is vital because the calculations on one router depend upon the calculations of its neighbors.

Hellos between EIGRP routers are set to 5 seconds by default. Another timer that's related to the *hello timer* is the *hold timer*. The hold timer determines the amount of time a router is willing to wait to get a Hello from a neighbor before declaring it dead. Once a neighbor is declared dead, it's removed from the neighbor table and all routes that depended upon it are recalculated. Interestingly, the hold timer configuration doesn't determine how long a router waits before it declares neighbors dead; it establishes how long the router will tell others to wait before they can declare it dead. This means that the hold timers on neighboring routers don't need to match because they only tell the others how long to wait.

The only time EIGRP advertises its entire information is when it discovers a new neighbor and forms a relationship or adjacency with it by exchanging Hello packets. When this happens, both neighbors then advertise their complete information to one another. After each has learned its neighbor's routes, only changes to the routing table will be propagated.

During each EIGRP session running on a router, a neighbor table is created in which the router stores information about all routers known to be directly connected neighbors. Each neighboring router's IP address, hold time interval, smooth round-trip timer (SRTT), and queue information are all kept in this table. It's an important reference used to establish that topology changes have occurred that neighboring routers need to know about.

To sum this all up, remember that EIGRP routers receive their neighbors' updates and store them in a local topology table that contains all known routes from all known neighbors and serves as the raw material from which the best routes are selected.

Let's define some terms before we move on:

Reported/advertised Distance (AD) This is the metric of a remote network, as reported by a neighbor. It's also the routing table metric of the neighbor and is the same as the second number in parentheses as displayed in the topology table. The first number is the administrative distance, and I'll discuss more about these values in a minute.

In Figure 11.2, routers SF and NY are both advertising the path to network 10.0.0.0 to the Corp router, but the cost through SF to network 10.0.0.0 is less than NY.

FIGURE 11.2 Advertised distance

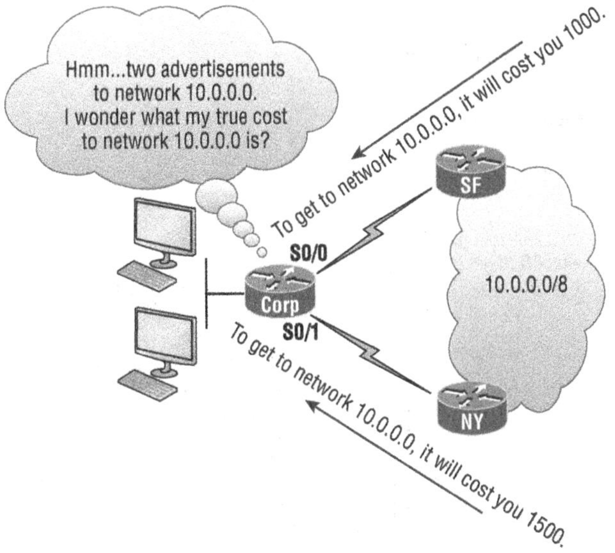

We're not done yet because the Corp router still needs to calculate its cost to each neighbor.

Feasible Distance (FD) This is the best metric among all paths to a remote network, including the metric to the neighbor that's advertising the remote network. The route with the lowest FD is the route that you'll find in the routing table because it's considered the best path. The metric of an FD is calculated using the metric reported by the neighbor that's referred to as the reported or AD plus the metric to the neighbor reporting the route. In Figure 11.3, the Corp router will have the path through router SF to network 10.0.0.0 in the routing table since it's the lowest FD. It's the lowest true cost from end to end.

Take a look at an EIGRP route that's been injected into a routing table and find the FD listed in the entry:

```
D    10.0.0.0/8 [90/2195456] via 172.16.10.2, 00:27:06,Serial0/0
```

First, the `D` means Dual and is an EIGRP injected route and is the route used by EIGRP to forward traffic to the 10.0.0.0 network via its neighbor, 172.16.10.2. But that's not what I want to focus on right now. See the `[90/2195456]` entry in the line? The first number (`90`) is the administrative distance (AD), which is not to be confused with advertised distance (AD), which is why a lot of people call it the reported distance. The second number is the FD, or the entire cost for this router to get to network 10.0.0.0. To sum this up, the neighbor router sends a reported, or advertised, distance (RD/AD) for network 10.0.0.0, and EIGRP calculates the cost to get to that neighbor and then adds those two numbers together to get the FD, or total cost.

Figure 11.3 shows the feasible distance.

FIGURE 11.3 Feasible distance

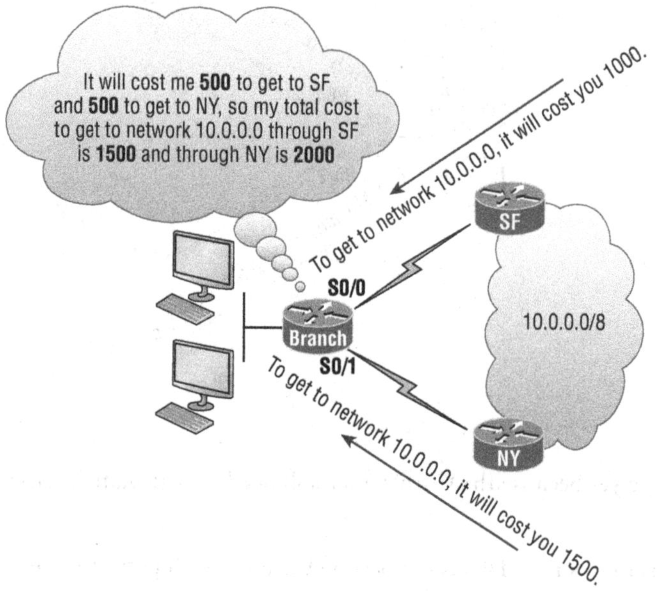

Neighbor Table Each router keeps state information about adjacent neighbors. When a newly discovered neighbor is found, its address and interface are recorded and the information is held in the neighbor table, stored in RAM. Sequence numbers are used to match acknowledgments with update packets. The last sequence number received from the neighbor is recorded so that out-of-order packets can be detected. We'll get into this more later in the chapter when we look at the neighbor table and find out how it proves useful for troubleshooting links between neighbor routers.

Topology Table The topology table is populated by the neighbor table and the Diffusing Update Algorithm (DUAL) calculates the best loop-free path to each remote network. It contains all destinations advertised by neighboring routers, holding each destination address and a list of neighbors that have advertised the destination. For each neighbor, the advertised metric (distance), which comes only from the neighbor's routing table, is recorded, as is the FD. The best path to each remote network is copied and placed in the routing table, and then IP will use this route to forward traffic to the remote network. The path copied to the routing table is called a successor router—think "successful" to help you remember. The path with a good, but less-desirable, cost will be entered in the topology table as a backup link and called the feasible successor. Let's talk more about these terms now.

NOTE: The neighbor and topology tables are stored in RAM and maintained through the use of Hello and update packets. While the routing table is also stored in RAM, the information stored in the routing table is gathered only from the topology table.

Feasible Successor (FS) A feasible successor is basically an entry in the topology table that represents a path that's inferior to the successor route(s). An FS is defined as a path whose advertised distance is less than the FD of the current successor and considered a backup route. EIGRP will keep up to 32 feasible successors in the topology table in 111.0 code but only up to 16 in previous IOS versions, which is still a lot. Only the path with the best metric—the successor—is copied and placed in the routing table. The `show ip eigrp topology` command will display all the EIGRP feasible successor routes known to the router.

NOTE: A feasible successor is a backup route and is stored in the topology table. A successor route is stored in the topology table and is copied and placed in the routing table.

Successor A successor route—again, think "successful"—is the best route to a remote network. A successor route is the lowest cost to a destination and stored in the topology table along with everything else. However, this particular best route is copied and placed in the routing table so IP can use it to get to the remote network. The successor route is backed up by a feasible successor route, which is also stored in the topology table, if there's one available. The routing table contains only successor routes; the topology table contains successor and feasible successor routes.

Figure 11.4 illustrates that the SF and NY routers each have subnets of the 10.0.0.0 network and the Corp router has two paths to get to this network.

As shown in Figure 11.4, two paths to network 10.0.0.0 can be used by the Corp router. EIGRP picks the best path and places it in the routing table, but if both links have equal-cost paths, EIGRP load balances between them—up to four links, by default. By using the successor and having feasible successors in the topology table as backup links, the network can converge instantly, and updates to any neighbor make up the only traffic sent from EIGRP—very clean!

FIGURE 11.4 The tables used by EIGRP

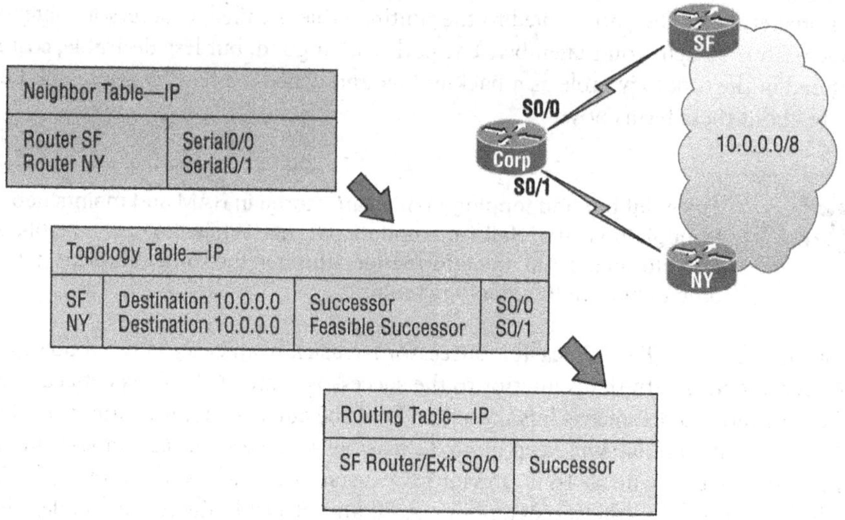

Reliable Transport Protocol

EIGRP depends on a proprietary protocol called *Reliable Transport Protocol (RTP)* to manage the communication of messages between EIGRP-speaking routers. As the name suggests, reliability is a key concern of this protocol, so Cisco designed this mechanism, which leverages multicasts and unicasts, to ensure that updates are delivered quickly and that data reception is tracked accurately.

But how does this really work? Well, when EIGRP sends multicast traffic, it uses the Class D address 224.0.0.10, and each EIGRP router knows who its neighbors are. For each multicast it sends out, a list is built and maintained that includes all the neighbors who have replied. If a router doesn't get a reply from a neighbor via the multicast, EIGRP then tries using unicasts to resend the same data. If there's no reply from a neighbor after 16 unicast attempts, that neighbor is then declared dead. This process is often referred to as *reliable multicast*.

Routers keep track of the information they send by assigning a sequence number to each packet that enables them to identify old, redundant information and data that's out of sequence. You'll get to actually see this information in the neighbor table coming up when we get into configuring EIGRP.

Remember, EIGRP is all about topology changes and updates, making it the quiet, performance-optimizing protocol it is. Its ability to synchronize routing databases at startup time, while maintaining the consistency of databases over time, is achieved quietly by communicating only necessary changes. The downside here is that you can end up with a corrupted routing database if any packets have been permanently lost or if packets have been mishandled out of order.

Here's a description of the five different types of packets used by EIGRP:

Update An *Update packet* contains route information. When these are sent in response to metric or topology changes, they use reliable multicasts. In the event that only one router needs an update, like when a new neighbor is discovered, it's sent via unicasts. Keep in mind that the unicast method still requires an acknowledgment, so updates are always reliable regardless of their underlying delivery mechanism.

Query A *Query packet* is a request for specific routes and always uses the reliable multicast method. Routers send queries when they realize they've lost the path to a particular network and are searching for alternatives.

Reply A *Reply packet* is sent in response to a query via the unicast method. Replies either include a specific route to the queried destination or declare that there's no known route.

Hello A *Hello packet* is used to discover EIGRP neighbors and is sent via unreliable multicast, meaning it doesn't require an acknowledgment.

ACK An *ACK packet* is sent in response to an update and is always unicast. ACKs are never sent reliably because this would require another ACK sent for acknowledgment, which would just create a ton of useless traffic.

It's helpful to think of all these different packet types like envelopes. They're really just types of containers that EIGRP routers use to communicate with their neighbors. What's interesting is the actual content envelopes these communications and the procedures that guide their conversations, and that's what we'll be exploring next.

Diffusing Update Algorithm

I mentioned that EIGRP uses *Diffusing Update Algorithm (DUAL)* for selecting and maintaining the best path to each remote network. DUAL allows EIGRP to carry out these vital tasks:

- Figure out a backup route if there's one available.
- Support VLSMs.
- Perform dynamic route recoveries.
- Query neighbors for unknown alternate routes.
- Send out queries for an alternate route.

Quite an impressive list, but what really makes DUAL so great is that it enables EIGRP to converge amazingly fast! The key to the speed is twofold: First, EIGRP routers maintain a copy of all their neighbors' routes to refer to for calculating their own cost to each remote network. So if the best path goes down, all it often takes to find another one is a quick scan of the topology table looking for a feasible successor. Second, if that quick table survey doesn't work out, EIGRP routers immediately ask their neighbors for help finding the best path. It's exactly this, ahem, DUAL strategy of reliance upon, and the leveraging of, other routers' information that accounts for the algorithm's "diffusing" character. Unlike other routing protocols where the change is propagated through the entire network, EIGRP bounded updates are propagated only as far as needed.

Three critical conditions must be met for DUAL to work properly:

- Neighbors are discovered or noted as dead within a finite time.
- All transmitted messages are received correctly.
- All changes and messages are processed in the order in which they're detected.

As you already know, the Hello protocol ensures the rapid detection of new or dead neighbors, and RTP provides a reliable method of conveying and sequencing messages. Based on this solid foundation, DUAL can then select and maintain information about the best paths. Let's check further into the process of route discovery and maintenance next.

Route Discovery and Maintenance

The hybrid nature of EIGRP is fully revealed in its approach to route discovery and maintenance. Like many link-state protocols, EIGRP supports the concept of neighbors that are formally discovered via a Hello process and whose state is monitored thereafter. And like many distance-vector protocols, EIGRP uses the routing-by-rumor approach, which implies that many routers within an AS never actually hear about a route update firsthand. Instead, these devices rely on "network gossip" to hear about neighbors and their respective status via another router that may have also gotten the info from yet another router, and so on.

Given all the information that EIGRP routers have to collect, it follows that they must have a place to store it, and they do this in the tables I referred to earlier in this chapter. As you know, EIGRP doesn't depend on just one table; it actually uses three of them to store important information about its environment:

Neighbor Table Contains information about the specific routers with whom neighbor relationships have been formed. It also displays information about the Hello transmit interval and queue counts for unaccounted Hello acknowledgment.

Topology Table Stores the route advertisements received from each neighbor. All routes in the AS are stored in the topology table, both successors, and feasible successors.

Route Table Stores the routes that are currently in use to make local routing decisions. Anything in the routing table is considered a successor route.

We'll explore more of EIGRP's features in greater detail soon, beginning with a look at the metrics associated with particular routes. After that, I'll cover the decision-making process that's used to select the best routes, and then we'll review the procedures followed when routes change.

Configuring EIGRP

I know what you're thinking: "We're going to jump in to configuring EIGRP already when I've heard how complex it is?" No worries here! What I'm about to show is basic, and I know you won't have a problem with it. We're going to start with the easy part of EIGRP, and by configuring it on our little internetwork, you'll learn a lot more this way than you would if I just continued explaining more at this point. After we've completed the initial configuration, we'll fine-tune it and have fun experimenting with it throughout this chapter.

But first, keep in mind that even though EIGRP can be configured for IP, IPv6, IPX, and AppleTalk, as a future Cisco Certified Network Associate R/S, your focus needs to zero in on configuring EIGRP for IP and IPv6.

Okay, there are two modes for entering EIGRP commands: router configuration mode and interface configuration mode. In router configuration mode, we'll enable the protocol, determine which networks will run EIGRP, and set global factors. When in interface configuration mode, we'll customize summaries and bandwidth.

To initiate an EIGRP session on a router, I'll use the `router eigrp` command followed by our network's AS number. After that, we'll enter the specific numbers of the networks that we want to connect to the router using the `network` command followed by the network number. This is pretty straightforward stuff. If you can configure RIP, then you can configure EIGRP.

Just so you know, we'll use the same network I used in the previous CCENT routing chapters, but I'm going to connect more networks so that we can look deeper into EIGRP. With that, I'm going to enable EIGRP for autonomous system 20 on our Corp router connected to four networks.

Figure 11.5 shows the network we'll be configuring throughout this chapter and the next chapter. Here's the Corp configuration:

FIGURE 11.5 Configuring our little internetwork with EIGRP

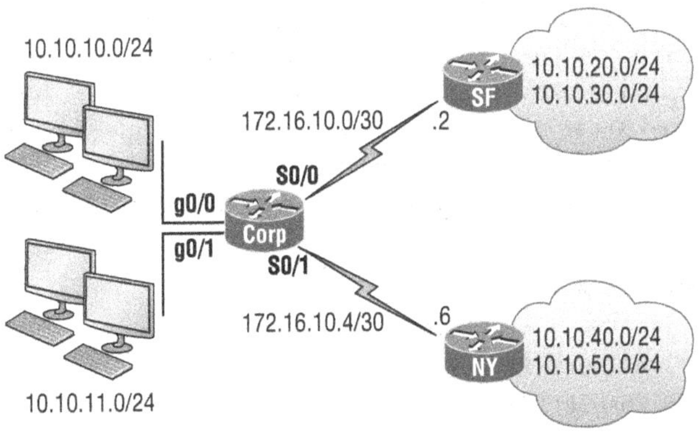

```
Corp#config t
Corp(config)#router eigrp 20
Corp(config-router)#network 172.16.0.0
Corp(config-router)#network 10.0.0.0
```

Remember, just as we would when configuring RIP, we need to use the classful network address, which is all subnet and host bits turned off. This is another thing that makes EIGRP so great: It has the complexity of a link-state protocol running in the background and the same easy configuration process used for RIP.

> **NOTE** Understand that the AS number is irrelevant—that is, as long as all routers use the same number. You can use any number from 1 to 65,535.

But wait, the EIGRP configuration can't be that easy, can it? A few simple EIGRP commands and my network just works? Well, it can be and usually is, but not always. Remember the wildcards you learned about in your OSPF and access list configurations in your preparation for the Cisco exam? We can go with the same type of configuration as we did with OSPF. Let's say, for example, we wanted to advertise all the directly connected networks with EIGRP off the Corp router. By using the command `network 10.0.0.0`, we can effectively advertise to all subnets within that classful network; however, take a look at this configuration now:

```
Corp#config t
Corp(config)#router eigrp 20
Corp(config-router)#network 10.10.11.0 0.0.0.255
Corp(config-router)#network 172.16.10.0 0.0.0.3
Corp(config-router)#network 172.16.10.4 0.0.0.3
```

This configuration should look pretty familiar to you because by now you should have a solid understanding of how wildcards are configured. This configuration will advertise the network connected to g0/1 on the Corp router as well as the two WAN links. Still, all we accomplished with this configuration was to stop the g0/0 interface from being placed into the EIGRP process, and unless you have tens of thousands of networks worldwide, then there is really no need to use wildcards because they don't provide any other administrative purpose other than what I've already described.

Now let's take a look at the simple configuration needed for the SF and NY routers in our internetwork:

```
SF(config)#router eigrp 20
SF(config-router)#network 172.16.0.0
SF(config-router)#network 10.0.0.0
000060:%DUAL-5-NBRCHANGE:IP-EIGRP(0) 20:Neighbor 172.16.10.1
(Serial0/0/0) is up:
new adjacency
```

```
NY(config)#router eigrp 20
NY(config-router)#network 172.16.0.0
NY(config-router)#network 10.0.0.0
*Jun 26 02:41:36:%DUAL-5-NBRCHANGE:IP-EIGRP(0) 20:Neighbor 172.16.10.5
(Serial0/0/1) is up: new adjacency
```

Nice and easy—or is it? We can see that the SF and NY router created an adjacency to the Corp router, but are they actually sharing routing information? To find out, let's take a look at the number that I pointed out as the AS number in the configuration.

EIGRP uses ASs to identify the group of routers that will share route information. Only routers that have the same AS share routes. The range of values we can use to create an AS with EIGRP is 1 to 65535:

```
Corp(config)#router eigrp ?
  <1-65535>  Autonomous System
  WORD       EIGRP Virtual-Instance Name
Corp(config)#router eigrp 20
```

Notice that I could have used any number from 1 to 65,535, but I chose to use 20 because it just felt good at the time. As long as all routers use the same number, they'll create an adjacency. Okay, now the AS makes sense, but it looks like I can type a `word` in the place of the AS number, and I can. Let's take a look at the configuration:

```
Corp(config)#router eigrp Todd
Corp(config-router)#address-family ipv4 autonomous-system 20
Corp(config-router-af)#network 10.0.0.0
Corp(config-router-af)#network 172.16.0.0
```

What I just showed you is not part of the Cisco exam objectives, but it's also not really necessary for any IPv4 routing configuration in your network. The previous configuration examples I've gone through so far in this chapter covers the objectives and works just fine, but I included this last configuration example because it's now an option in IOS 15.0 code.

VLSM Support and Summarization

Being one of the more sophisticated classless routing protocols, EIGRP supports using variable length subnet masks. This is good because it allows us to conserve address space by using subnet masks that map to specific host requirements in a much better way. Being able to use 30-bit subnet masks for the point-to-point networks I configured in our internetwork is a great example. Plus, because the subnet mask is propagated with every route update, EIGRP also supports the use of discontiguous subnets, giving us greater administrative flexibility when designing a network IP address scheme. Another versatile feature is that EIGRP allows us to use and place route summaries at strategically optimal locations throughout the EIGRP network to reduce the size of the route table.

Keep in mind that EIGRP automatically summarizes networks at their classful boundaries and supports the manual creation of summaries at any and all EIGRP routers. This is usually a good thing, but by checking out the routing table in the Corp router, you can see the possible complications that auto-summarization can cause:

```
Corp#sh ip route
[output cut]
     172.16.0.0/16 is variably subnetted, 3 subnets, 2 masks
C       172.16.10.4/30 is directly connected, Serial0/1
C       172.16.10.0/30 is directly connected, Serial0/0
D       172.16.0.0/16 is a summary, 00:01:37, Null0
     10.0.0.0/8 is variably subnetted, 3 subnets, 2 masks
C       10.10.10.0/24 is directly connected, GigabitEthernet0/0
D       10.0.0.0/8 is a summary, 00:01:19, Null0
C       10.10.11.0/24 is directly connected, GigabitEthernet0/1
```

Now, this doesn't look so good: Both 172.16.0.0 and 10.0.0.0/8 are being advertised as summary routes injected by EIGRP, but we have multiple subnets in the 10.0.0.0/8 classful network address, so how would the Corp router know how to route to a specific network like 10.10.20.0? The answer is that it wouldn't. Let's see why in Figure 11.6.

FIGURE 11.6 Discontiguous networks

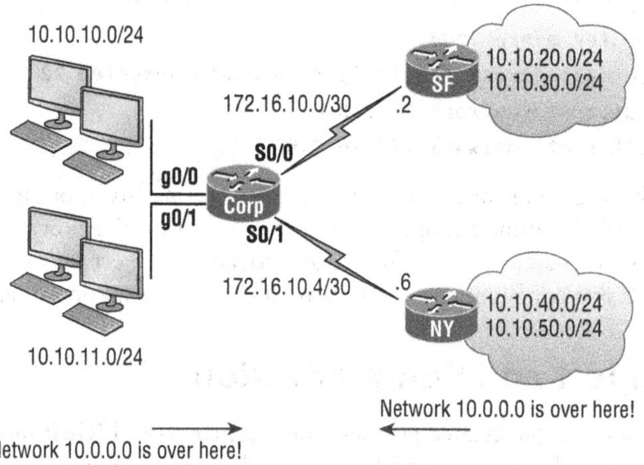

The networks we're using are considered a discontiguous network because we have the 10.0.0.0/8 network subnetted across a different class of address—the 172.16.0.0 network, with 10.0.0.0/8 subnets on both sides of the WAN links.

You can see that the SF and NY routers will both create an automatic summary of 10.0.0.0/8 and then inject it into their routing tables. This is a common problem, and an important one that Cisco really wants you to understand (by including it in the objectives). With this type of topology, disabling automatic summarization is definitely the better option. Actually, it's the only option if we want this network to work.

Let's take a look at the routing tables on the NY and SF routers to find out what they're seeing:

```
SF>sh ip route
[output cut]
     172.16.0.0/16 is variably subnetted, 3 subnets, 3 masks
C       172.16.10.0/30 is directly connected, Serial0/0/0
D       172.16.10.0/24 [90/2681856] via 172.16.10.1, 00:54:58, Serial0/0/0
D       172.16.0.0/16 is a summary, 00:55:12, Null0
     10.0.0.0/8 is variably subnetted, 3 subnets, 2 masks
D       10.0.0.0/8 is a summary, 00:54:58, Null0
C       10.10.20.0/24 is directly connected, FastEthernet0/0
C       10.10.30.0/24 is directly connected, Loopback0
SF>

NY>sh ip route
[output cut]
     172.16.0.0/16 is variably subnetted, 2 subnets, 2 masks
C       172.16.10.4/30 is directly connected, Serial0/0/1
D       172.16.0.0/16 is a summary, 00:55:56, Null0
     10.0.0.0/8 is variably subnetted, 3 subnets, 2 masks
D       10.0.0.0/8 is a summary, 00:55:26, Null0
C       10.10.40.0/24 is directly connected, FastEthernet0/0
C       10.10.50.0/24 is directly connected, Loopback0
NY>ping 10.10.10.1
Type escape sequence to abort.
Sending 5, 100-byte ICMP Echos to 10.10.10.1, timeout is 2 seconds:
.....
Success rate is 0 percent (0/5)
NY>
```

The confirmed answer is that our network isn't working because we're discontiguous and our classful boundaries are auto-summarizing. We can see that EIGRP is injecting summary routes into both the SF and NY routing tables.

We need to advertise our subnets in order to make this work, and here's how we make that happen, starting with the Corp router:

```
Corp#config t
Corp(config)#router eigrp 20
Corp(config-router)#no auto-summary
Corp(config-router)#
*Feb 25 18:29:30%DUAL-5-NBRCHANGE:IP-EIGRP(0) 20:Neighbor 172.16.10.6
(Serial0/1)
```

```
 is resync: summary configured
*Feb 25 18:29:30%DUAL-5-NBRCHANGE:IP-EIGRP(0) 20:Neighbor 172.16.10.2
(Serial0/0)
 is resync: summary configured
Corp(config-router)#
```

Okay, our network still isn't working because the other routers are still sending a summary. So let's configure the SF and NY routers to advertise subnets:

```
SF#config t
SF(config)#router eigrp 20
SF(config-router)#no auto-summary
SF(config-router)#
000090:%DUAL-5-NBRCHANGE:IP-EIGRP(0) 20:Neighbor 172.16.10.1 (Serial0/0/0) is
resync: summary configured

NY#config t
NY(config)#router eigrp 20
NY(config-router)#no auto-summary
NY(config-router)#
*Jun 26 21:31:08%DUAL-5-NBRCHANGE:IP-EIGRP(0) 20:Neighbor 172.16.10.5
(Serial0/0/1)
is resync: summary configured
```

Let's take a look at the Corp router's output now:

```
Corp(config-router)#do show ip route
[output cut]
     172.16.0.0/30 is subnetted, 2 subnets
C       172.16.10.4 is directly connected, Serial0/1
C       172.16.10.0 is directly connected, Serial0/0
     10.0.0.0/24 is subnetted, 6 subnets
C       10.10.10.0 is directly connected, GigabitEthernet0/0
C       10.10.11.0 is directly connected, GigabitEthernet0/1
D       10.10.20.0 [90/3200000] via 172.16.10.2, 00:00:27, Serial0/0
D       10.10.30.0 [90/3200000] via 172.16.10.2, 00:00:27, Serial0/0
D       10.10.40.0 [90/2297856] via 172.16.10.6, 00:00:29, Serial0/1
D       10.10.50.0 [90/2297856] via 172.16.10.6, 00:00:30, Serial0/1
Corp# ping 10.10.20.1

Type escape sequence to abort.
Sending 5, 100-byte ICMP Echos to 10.10.20.1, timeout is 2 seconds:
!!!!!
Success rate is 100 percent (5/5), round-trip min/avg/max = 1/2/4 ms
```

Wow, what a difference compared to the previous routing table output! We can see all the subnets now. It would be hard to justify using auto-summarization today. If you want to summarize, it should definitely be done manually. Always typing in **`no auto-summary`** under RIPv2 and EIGRP is common practice today.

TIP

The new 15.*x* code auto-summarization feature is disabled by default, as it should be. But don't think that discontiguous networks and disabling auto-summary are no longer topics in the Cisco exam objectives, because they most certainly are.

Controlling EIGRP Traffic

But what if you need to stop EIGRP from working on a specific interface? Maybe it's a connection to your ISP, or where we didn't want to have the g0/0 interface be part of the EIGRP process as in our earlier example. All you need to do is flag the interface as passive, and to do this from an EIGRP session, just use this command:

`passive-interface` *`interface-type interface-number`*

This works because the *`interface-type`* portion defines the type of interface and the *`interface-number`* portion defines the number of the interface. The following command makes interface serial 0/0 into a passive interface:

```
Corp(config)#router eigrp 20
Corp(config-router)#passive-interface g0/0
```

What we've accomplished here is to prevent this interface from sending or reading received Hello packets so that it will no longer form adjacencies or send or receive route information. But this still won't stop EIGRP from advertising the subnet of this interface out all other interfaces without using wildcards. This really illustrates the reason you must understand why and when to use wildcards as well as what the `passive-interface` command does. This knowledge really helps you make an informed decision about which command you need to use to meet your specific business requirements.

NOTE

The impact of the `passive-interface` command depends on the routing protocol under which the command is issued. For example, on an interface running RIP, the `passive-interface` command will prohibit sending route updates but will permit receiving them. A RIP router with a passive interface will still learn about the networks advertised by other routers. This is different from EIGRP, where an interface configured with the `passive-interface` command will neither send nor read received Hellos.

Typically, EIGRP neighbors use multicast to exchange routing updates. You can change this by specifically telling the router about a particular neighbor, which will ensure that unicast packets will be used only for the routing updates with that specific neighbor. To take advantage of this feature, apply the `neighbor` command and execute it under the EIGRP process.

I'm going to configure the Corp router with information about routers SF and NY:

```
Corp(config)#router eigrp 20
Corp(config-router)#neighbor 172.16.10.2
Corp(config-router)#neighbor 172.16.10.6
```

Understand that you don't need to use the preceding commands to create neighbor relationships, but they're available if you need them.

EIGRP Metrics

Unlike many other protocols that use a single element to compare routes and select the best possible path, EIGRP uses a combination of these four factors:

- *Bandwidth*
- *Delay*
- *Load*
- *Reliability*

It's worth noting that there's a fifth element, *maximum transmission unit (MTU)*, which has never been used in EIGRP metrics calculations though it's still a required parameter in some EIGRP-related commands—especially those involving redistribution. The value of the MTU element represents the smallest MTU value encountered along the path to the destination network.

Also good to know is there's a mathematical formula that combines the four main elements to create a single value representing just how good a given route actually is. The higher the metric associated with it, the less desirable the route. Here's that formula:

metric = [K_1 × *Bandwidth* + (K_2 × *Bandwidth*) / (256 – *Load*) + K_3 × *Delay*] × [K_5 / (*Reliability* + K_4)]

The formula's components break down like this:

- By default, $K_1 = 1$, $K_2 = 0$, $K_3 = 1$, $K_4 = 0$, $K_5 = 0$.
- *Delay* equals the sum of all the delays of the links along the path.
  - *Delay* = [Delay in 10s of microseconds] × 256.
- *Bandwidth* is the lowest bandwidth of the links along the path.
  - *Bandwidth* = [10000000 / (bandwidth in Kbps)] × 256.
- By default, *metric* = lowest bandwidth along path + sum of all delays along path.

If necessary, you can adjust the constant K values on a per-interface basis, but I recommend that you only do this under the direction of the Cisco Technical Assistance Center (TAC). Metrics are tuned to change the manner in which routes are calculated. The K values can be seen with a `show ip protocols` output:

```
Corp#sh ip protocols
*** IP Routing is NSF aware ***
```

```
Routing Protocol is "eigrp 1"
  Outgoing update filter list for all interfaces is not set
  Incoming update filter list for all interfaces is not set
  Default networks flagged in outgoing updates
  Default networks accepted from incoming updates
  EIGRP-IPv4 Protocol for AS(1)
    Metric weight K1=1, K2=0, K3=1, K4=0, K5=0
```

Notice that the K1 and K3 values are enabled by default—for example, K1 = 1. Table 11.1 shows the relationship between each constant and the metric it affects.

TABLE 11.1 Metric Association of K Values

Constant	Metric
K1	Bandwidth (B_e)
K2	Load (utilization on path)
K3	Delay (D_c)
K4	Reliability (r)
K5	MTU

Each constant is used to assign a weight to a specific variable, meaning that when the metric is calculated, the algorithm will assign a greater importance to the specified metric. This is very cool because it means that by assigning a weight, you get to specify the factor that's most important to you. For example, if bandwidth is your priority, you would assign K1 to weight it accordingly, but if delay is totally unacceptable, then K3 would be assigned a greater weight. A word of caution though: Always remember that any changes to the default values could result in instability and convergence problems, particularly if delay or reliability values are constantly changing. But if you're looking for something to do on a rainy Saturday, it's an interesting experiment to pass some time and gain some nice networking insight.

Maximum Paths and Hop Count

By default, EIGRP can provide equal-cost load balancing across up to four links. RIP and OSPF do this, too. But you can have EIGRP actually load balance across up to 32 links with 15.0 code (equal or unequal) by using the following command:

```
Corp(config)#router eigrp 10
Corp(config-router)#maximum-paths ?
  <1-32>  Number of paths
```

As I mentioned, pre–15.0 code routers allowed up to 16 paths to remote networks, which is still a lot.

EIGRP has a default maximum hop count of 100 for route update packets, but it can be set up to 255. Chances are you wouldn't want to ever change this, but if you did, here is how you would do it:

```
Corp(config)#router eigrp 10
Corp(config-router)#metric maximum-hops ?
  <1-255>  Hop count
```

As you can see from this router output, EIGRP can be set to a maximum of 255 hops. Even though it doesn't use hop count in the path metric calculation, it still uses the maximum hop count to limit the scope of the AS.

Route Selection

Now that you've got a good idea how EIGRP works and also how easy it actually is to configure, it's probably clear that determining the best path simply comes down to seeing which one gets awarded the lowest metric. But it's not the winning path that really sets EIGRP apart from other protocols. You know that EIGRP stores route information from its neighbors in its topology table and that as long as a given neighbor remains alive, it will rarely throw out anything it has learned from that neighbor. This makes EIGRP able to flag the best routes in its topology table for positioning in its local routing table, enabling it to flag the next-best routes as alternatives if the best route goes down.

In Figure 11.7, you can see that I added another Ethernet link between the SF and NY routers. This will give us a great opportunity to play with the topology and routing tables.

FIGURE 11.7 EIGRP route-selection process

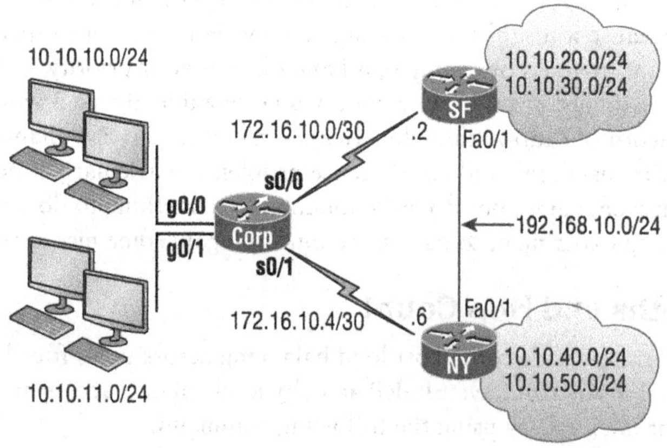

First, let's take another look at the routing table on the Corp router before I bring up the new interfaces:

```
172.16.0.0/30 is subnetted, 2 subnets
C       172.16.10.4 is directly connected, Serial0/1
C       172.16.10.0 is directly connected, Serial0/0
     10.0.0.0/24 is subnetted, 6 subnets
C       10.10.10.0 is directly connected, GigabitEthernet0/0
C       10.10.11.0 is directly connected, GigabitEthernet0/1
D       10.10.20.0 [90/3200000] via 172.16.10.2, 00:00:27, Serial0/0
D       10.10.30.0 [90/3200000] via 172.16.10.2, 00:00:27, Serial0/0
D       10.10.40.0 [90/2297856] via 172.16.10.6, 00:00:29, Serial0/1
D       10.10.50.0 [90/2297856] via 172.16.10.6, 00:00:30, Serial0/1
```

We can see the three directly connected interfaces and the other four networks injected into the routing table by EIGRP. Now, I'll add the network 192.168.10.0/24 between the SF and NY routers and then enable the interfaces.

And let's check out the routing table of the Corp router now that I've configured that link:

```
D    192.168.10.0/24 [90/2172416] via 172.16.10.6, 00:04:27, Serial0/1
 172.16.0.0/30 is subnetted, 2 subnets
C       172.16.10.4 is directly connected, Serial0/1
C       172.16.10.0 is directly connected, Serial0/0
     10.0.0.0/24 is subnetted, 6 subnets
C       10.10.10.0 is directly connected, GigabitEthernet0/0
C       10.10.11.0 is directly connected, GigabitEthernet0/1
D       10.10.20.0 [90/3200000] via 172.16.10.2, 00:00:27, Serial0/0
D       10.10.30.0 [90/3200000] via 172.16.10.2, 00:00:27, Serial0/0
D       10.10.40.0 [90/2297856] via 172.16.10.6, 00:00:29, Serial0/1
D       10.10.50.0 [90/2297856] via 172.16.10.6, 00:00:30, Serial0/1
```

Okay, that's weird. The only thing different I see is one path to the 192.168.10.0/24 network listed first. Glad it is there, which means that we can route to that network. Notice that we can reach the network from the Serial0/1 interface, but what happened to my link to the SF router? Shouldn't we have an advertisement from that router and be load balancing? Let's take a look the topology table to find out what's going on:

```
Corp#sh ip eigrp topology
IP-EIGRP Topology Table for AS(20)/ID(10.10.11.1)

Codes: P - Passive, A - Active, U - Update, Q - Query, R - Reply,
       r - reply Status, s - sia Status
```

```
P 10.10.10.0/24, 1 successors, FD is 128256
        via Connected, GigbitEthernet0/0
P 10.10.11.0/24, 1 successors, FD is 128256
        via Connected, GigbitEthernet0/1
P 10.10.20.0/24, 1 successors, FD is 2300416
        via 172.16.10.6 (2300416/156160), Serial0/1
        via 172.16.10.2 (3200000/128256), Serial0/0
P 10.10.30.0/24, 1 successors, FD is 2300416
        via 172.16.10.6 (2300416/156160), Serial0/1
        via 172.16.10.2 (3200000/128256), Serial0/0
P 10.10.40.0/24, 1 successors, FD is 2297856
        via 172.16.10.6 (2297856/128256), Serial0/1
        via 172.16.10.2 (3202560/156160), Serial0/0
P 10.10.50.0/24, 1 successors, FD is 2297856
        via 172.16.10.6 (2297856/128256), Serial0/1
        via 172.16.10.2 (3202560/156160), Serial0/0
P 192.168.10.0/24, 1 successors, FD is 2172416
        via 172.16.10.6 (2172416/28160), Serial0/1
        via 172.16.10.2 (3074560/28160), Serial0/0
P 172.16.10.4/30, 1 successors, FD is 2169856
        via Connected, Serial0/1
P 172.16.10.0/30, 1 successors, FD is 3072000
        via Connected, Serial0/0
```

Okay, we can see there are two paths to the 192.168.10.0/24 network, but it's using the next hop of 172.16.10.6 (NY) because the FD is less. The advertised distance from both routers is 28160, but the cost to get to each router via the WAN links is the same. This means the FD is not the same, meaning we're not load balancing by default.

Both WAN links are a T1, so this should have load balanced by default, but EIGRP has determined that it costs more to go through SF than through NY. Because EIGRP uses bandwidth and delay of the line to determine the best path, we can use the `show interfaces` command to verify our stats like this:

```
Corp#sh int s0/0
Serial0/0 is up, line protocol is up
  Hardware is PowerQUICC Serial
  Description: <<Connection to CR1>>
  Internet address is 172.16.10.1/30
  MTU 1500 bytes, BW 1000 Kbit, DLY 20000 usec,
     reliability 255/255, txload 1/255, rxload 1/255
  Encapsulation HDLC, loopback not set Keepalive set (10 sec)
```

```
Corp#sh int s0/1
Serial0/1 is up, line protocol is up
  Hardware is PowerQUICC Serial
  Internet address is 172.16.10.5/30
  MTU 1500 bytes, BW 1544 Kbit, DLY 20000 usec,
     reliability 255/255, txload 1/255, rxload 1/255
  Encapsulation HDLC, loopback not set Keepalive set (10 sec)
```

I highlighted the statistic that EIGRP uses to determine the metrics to a next-hop router: MTU, bandwidth, delay, reliability, and load, with bandwidth and delay enabled by default. We can see that the bandwidth on the Serial0/0 interface is set to 1000 Kbit, which is not the default bandwidth. Serial0/1 is set to the default bandwidth of 1,544 Kbit.

Let's set the bandwidth back to the default on the s0/0 interface, and we should start load balancing to the 192.168.10.0 network. I'll just use the `no bandwidth` command, which will set it back to its default of 1,544 Mbps:

```
Corp#config t
Corp(config)#int s0/0
Corp(config-if)#no bandwidth
Corp(config-if)#^Z
```

Now let's take a look at the topology table and see if we're equal.

```
Corp#sh ip eigrp topo | section 192.168.10.0
P 192.168.10.0/24, 2 successors, FD is 2172416
        via 172.16.10.2 (2172416/28160), Serial0/0
        via 172.16.10.6 (2172416/28160), Serial0/1
```

Since the topology tables can get really huge in most networks, the `show ip eigrp topology | section` *network* command comes in handy because it allows us to see information about the network we want to look into in a couple of lines.

Let's use the `show ip route` *network* command and check out what is going on there:

```
Corp#sh ip route 192.168.10.0
Routing entry for 192.168.10.0/24
  Known via "eigrp 20", distance 90, metric 2172416, type internal
  Redistributing via eigrp 20
  Last update from 172.16.10.2 on Serial0/0, 00:05:18 ago
  Routing Descriptor Blocks:
  * 172.16.10.6, from 172.16.10.6, 00:05:18 ago, via Serial0/1
      Route metric is 2172416, traffic share count is 1
      Total delay is 20100 microseconds, minimum bandwidth is 1544 Kbit
      Reliability 255/255, minimum MTU 1500 bytes
      Loading 1/255, Hops 1
    172.16.10.2, from 172.16.10.2, 00:05:18 ago, via Serial0/0
```

```
Route metric is 2172416, traffic share count is 1
Total delay is 20100 microseconds, minimum bandwidth is 1544 Kbit
Reliability 255/255, minimum MTU 1500 bytes
Loading 1/255, Hops 1
```

Lots of detail about our routes to the 192.168.10.0 network. The Corp route has two equal-cost links to the 192.168.10.0 network. And to reveal load balancing even better, we'll just use the plain, ever-useful `show ip route` command:

```
Corp#sh ip route
[output cut]
D    192.168.10.0/24 [90/2172416] via 172.16.10.6, 00:05:35, Serial0/1
                     [90/2172416] via 172.16.10.2, 00:05:35, Serial0/0
```

Now we can see that there are two successor routes to the 192.168.10.0 network. Pretty sweet! But in the routing table, there's one path to 192.168.20.0 and 192.168.30.0, with the link between the SF and NY routers being feasible successors. And it's the same with the 192.168.40.0 and 192.168.50.0 networks. Let's take a look at the topology table to examine this more closely:

```
Corp#sh ip eigrp topology
IP-EIGRP Topology Table for AS(20)/ID(10.10.11.1)

Codes: P - Passive, A - Active, U - Update, Q - Query, R - Reply,
       r - reply Status, s - sia Status

P 10.10.10.0/24, 1 successors, FD is 128256
        via Connected, GigabitEthernet0/0
P 10.10.11.0/24, 1 successors, FD is 128256
        via Connected, GigabitEthernet0/1
P 10.10.20.0/24, 1 successors, FD is 2297856
        via 172.16.10.2 (2297856/128256), Serial0/0
        via 172.16.10.6 (2300416/156160), Serial0/1
P 10.10.30.0/24, 1 successors, FD is 2297856
        via 172.16.10.2 (2297856/128256), Serial0/0
        via 172.16.10.6 (2300416/156160), Serial0/1
P 10.10.40.0/24, 1 successors, FD is 2297856
        via 172.16.10.6 (2297856/128256), Serial0/1
        via 172.16.10.2 (2300416/156160), Serial0/0
P 10.10.50.0/24, 1 successors, FD is 2297856
        via 172.16.10.6 (2297856/128256), Serial0/1
        via 172.16.10.2 (2300416/156160), Serial0/0
P 192.168.10.0/24, 2 successors, FD is 2172416
```

```
        via 172.16.10.2 (2172416/28160), Serial0/0
        via 172.16.10.6 (2172416/28160), Serial0/1
P 172.16.10.4/30, 1 successors, FD is 2169856
        via Connected, Serial0/1
P 172.16.10.0/30, 1 successors, FD is 2169856
        via Connected, Serial0/0
```

It is nice that we can see we have a successor and a feasible successor to each network, so we know that EIGRP is doing its job. Let's take a close look at the links to 10.10.20.0 now and dissect what it's telling us:

```
P 10.10.20.0/24, 1 successors, FD is 2297856
        via 172.16.10.2 (2297856/128256), Serial0/0
        via 172.16.10.6 (2300416/156160), Serial0/1
```

Okay, first we can see that it's passive (P), which means that it has found all the usable paths to the network 10.10.20.0 and is happy. If we see active (A), that means EIGRP is not happy at all and is querying its neighbors for a new path to that network. The `(2297856/128256)` is the FD/AD, meaning that the SF router is advertising the 10.10.20.0 network as a cost of 128256, which is the AD. The Corp router adds the bandwidth and delay of the line to get to the SF router and then adds that number to the AD (128256) to come up with a total cost (FD) of 2297856 to get to network 10.10.20.0.

Unequal-Cost Load Balancing

As with all routing protocols running on Cisco routers, EIGRP automatically supports load balancing over 4 equal-cost routes and can be configured to support up to 32 equal-cost paths with IOS 15.0 code. As you know, previous IOS versions supported up to 16. I've mentioned this a few times in this chapter already, but I want to show you how to configure unequal-cost load balancing with EIGRP. First let's take a look at the Corp router by typing in the `show ip protocols` command:

```
Corp#sh ip protocols
Routing Protocol is "eigrp 20"
  Outgoing update filter list for all interfaces is not set
  Incoming update filter list for all interfaces is not set
  Default networks flagged in outgoing updates
  Default networks accepted from incoming updates
  EIGRP metric weight K1=1, K2=0, K3=1, K4=0, K5=0
  EIGRP maximum hopcount 100
  EIGRP maximum metric variance 1
  Redistributing: eigrp 20
  EIGRP NSF-aware route hold timer is 240s
  Automatic network summarization is not in effect
  Maximum path: 4
```

```
  Routing for Networks:
    10.0.0.0
    172.16.0.0
  Routing Information Sources:
    Gateway         Distance      Last Update
    (this router)         90      19:15:10
    172.16.10.6           90      00:25:38
    172.16.10.2           90      00:25:38
  Distance: internal 90 external 170
```

The `variance 1` means equal path load balancing with the maximum paths set to 4 by default. Unlike most other protocols, EIGRP also supports unequal-cost load balancing through the use of the `variance` parameter.

To clarify, let's say the parameter has been set to a variance of 2. This would effectively load balance traffic across the best route plus any route with an FD of up to twice as large. But still keep in mind that load balancing occurs in proportion with and relative to the cost of the route, meaning that more traffic would travel across the best route than the suboptimal one.

Let's configure the variance on the Corp router and see whether we can load balance across our feasible successors now:

```
Corp# config t
Corp(config)#router eigrp 20
Corp(config-router)#variance 2
Corp(config-router)#
*Feb 26 22:24:24:IP-EIGRP(Default-IP-Routing-Table:20):route installed for
10.10.20.0
*Feb 26 22:24:24:IP-EIGRP(Default-IP-Routing-Table:20):route installed for
10.10.20.0
*Feb 26 22:24:24:IP-EIGRP(Default-IP-Routing-Table:20):route installed for
10.10.30.0
*Feb 26 22:24:24:IP-EIGRP(Default-IP-Routing-Table:20):route installed for
10.10.30.0
*Feb 26 22:24:24:IP-EIGRP(Default-IP-Routing-Table:20):route installed for
10.10.40.0
*Feb 26 22:24:24:IP-EIGRP(Default-IP-Routing-Table:20):route installed for
10.10.40.0
*Feb 26 22:24:24:IP-EIGRP(Default-IP-Routing-Table:20):route installed for
10.10.50.0
*Feb 26 22:24:24:IP-EIGRP(Default-IP-Routing-Table:20):route installed for
10.10.50.0
*Feb 26 22:24:24:IP-EIGRP(Default-IP-Routing-Table:20):route installed for
192.168.10.0
*Feb 26 22:24:24:IP-EIGRP(Default-IP-Routing-Table:20):route installed for
192.168.10.0
```

```
Corp(config-router)#do show ip route
[output cut]
D    192.168.10.0/24 [90/2172416] via 172.16.10.6, 00:00:18, Serial0/1
                     [90/2172416] via 172.16.10.2, 00:00:18, Serial0/0
     172.16.0.0/30 is subnetted, 2 subnets
C       172.16.10.4 is directly connected, Serial0/1
C       172.16.10.0 is directly connected, Serial0/0
     10.0.0.0/24 is subnetted, 6 subnets
C       10.10.10.0 is directly connected, GigabitEthernet0/0
C       10.10.11.0 is directly connected, GigabitEthernet0/1
D       10.10.20.0 [90/2300416] via 172.16.10.6, 00:00:18, Serial0/1
                   [90/2297856] via 172.16.10.2, 00:00:19, Serial0/0
D       10.10.30.0 [90/2300416] via 172.16.10.6, 00:00:19, Serial0/1
                   [90/2297856] via 172.16.10.2, 00:00:19, Serial0/0
D       10.10.40.0 [90/2297856] via 172.16.10.6, 00:00:19, Serial0/1
                   [90/2300416] via 172.16.10.2, 00:00:19, Serial0/0
D       10.10.50.0 [90/2297856] via 172.16.10.6, 00:00:20, Serial0/1
                   [90/2300416] via 172.16.10.2, 00:00:20, Serial0/0
Corp(config-router)#
```

Nice! It worked. Now we have two paths to each remote network in the routing table, even though the feasible distances to each route aren't equal. Don't forget that unequal load balancing is not enabled by default and that you can perform load balancing through paths that have up to 128 times worse metrics than the successor route.

Split Horizon

Split horizon is enabled on interfaces by default, which means that if a route update is received on an interface from a neighbor router, this interface will not advertise those networks back out to the neighbor router who sent them. Let's take a look at an interface and then go through an example:

```
Corp#sh ip int s0/0
Serial0/0 is up, line protocol is up
  Internet address is 172.16.10.1/24
  Broadcast address is 255.255.255.255
  Address determined by setup command
  MTU is 1500 bytes
  Helper address is not set
  Directed broadcast forwarding is disabled
  Multicast reserved groups joined: 224.0.0.10
  Outgoing access list is not set
```

```
  Inbound  access list is not set
  Proxy ARP is enabled
  Local Proxy ARP is disabled
  Security level is default
  Split horizon is enabled
[output cut]
```

Okay, we can see that split horizon is enabled by default. But what does this really mean? Most of the time it's more helpful than harmful, but let's check out our internetwork in Figure 11.8 so I can really explain what split horizon is doing.

FIGURE 11.8 Split horizon in action, part 1

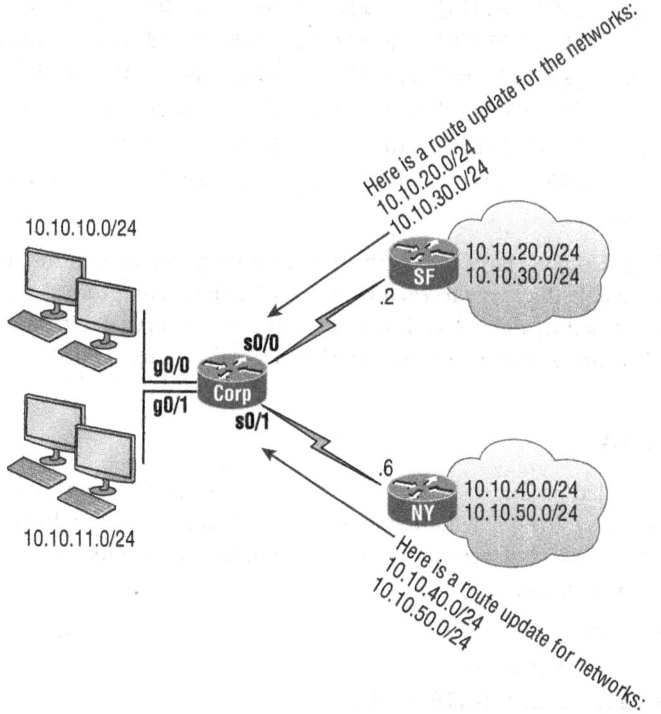

Notice that the SF and NY routers are each advertising their routes to the Corp router. Now, let's see what the Corp router sends back to each router in Figure 11.9.

Can you see that the Corp router is not advertising back out the advertised networks that it received on each interface? This is saving the SF and NY routers from receiving the incorrect route information that they could possibly get to their own network through the Corp router, which we know is wrong.

FIGURE 11.9 Split horizon in action, part 2

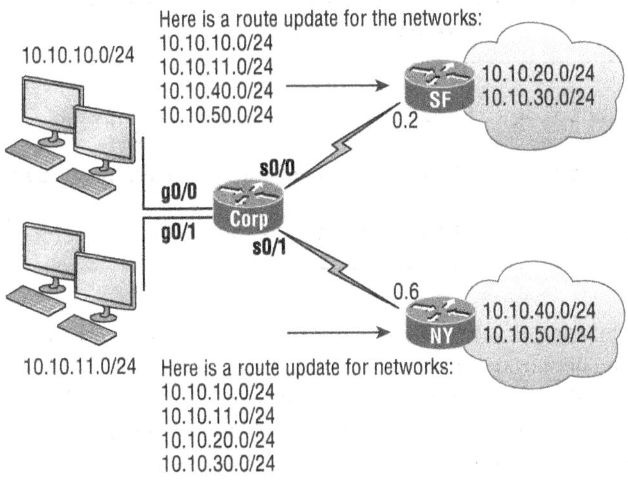

So how can this cause a problem? After all, it seems reasonable not to send misinformation back to an originating router, right? You'll see this create a problem on point-to-multipoint links when multiple remote routers connect to a single interface at the Corp location.

Verifying and Troubleshooting EIGRP

Even though EIGRP usually runs smoothly and is relatively low maintenance, you need to memorize several commands for use on a router that can be super helpful when troubleshooting EIGRP. I've already showed you a few of them, but I'm going to demonstrate all the tools you'll need to verify and troubleshoot EIGRP now. Table 11.2 contains all the commands you need to know for verifying that EIGRP is functioning well and offers a brief description of what each command does.

TABLE 11.2 EIGRP Troubleshooting Commands

Command	Description/Function
`show ip eigrp neighbors`	Shows all EIGRP neighbors
`show ip eigrp interfaces`	Lists the interfaces on which the router has actually enabled EIGRP
`show ip route eigrp`	Shows EIGRP entries in the routing table

TABLE 11.2 EIGRP Troubleshooting Commands *(continued)*

Command	Description/Function
`show ip eigrp topology`	Shows entries in the EIGRP topology table
`show ip eigrp traffic`	Shows the packet count for EIGRP packets sent and received
`show ip protocols`	Shows information about the active protocol sessions

When troubleshooting an EIGRP problem, it's always a good idea to start by getting an accurate map of the network, and the best way to do that is by using the `show ip eigrp neighbors` command to find out who your directly connected neighbors are. This command shows all adjacent routers that share route information within a given AS. If neighbors are missing, check the configuration, AS number, and link status on both routers to verify that the protocol has been configured correctly.

Let's execute the command on the Corp router:

```
Corp#sh ip eigrp neighbors
IP-EIGRP neighbors for process 20
H   Address                Interface        Hold Uptime    SRTT    RTO  Q  Seq
                                            (sec)          (ms)        Cnt Num
1   172.16.10.2            Se0/0              11 03:54:25     1    200  0  127
0   172.16.10.6            Se0/1              11 04:14:47     1    200  0  2010
```

Here's a breakdown of the important information we can see in the preceding output:

- H indicates the order in which the neighbor was discovered.
- Hold time in seconds is how long this router will wait for a Hello packet to arrive from a specific neighbor.
- The Uptime value indicates how long the neighbor relationship has been established.
- The SRTT field is the smooth round-trip timer and represents how long it takes to complete a round-trip from this router to its neighbor and back. This value delimits how long to wait after a multicast for a reply from this neighbor. As mentioned earlier, the router will attempt to establish communication via unicasts if it doesn't receive a reply.
- The time between multicast attempts is specified by the Retransmission Time Out (RTO) field, which is based on the SRTT values.
- The Q value tells us whether there are any outstanding messages in the queue. We can make a mental note that there's a problem if we see consistently large values here.
- Finally, the Seq field shows the sequence number of the last update from that neighbor, which is used to maintain synchronization and avoid duplicate messages or their out-of-sequence processing.

The `neighbors` command is a great command, but we can get local status of our router by also using the `show ip eigrp interface` command like this:

```
Corp#sh ip eigrp interfaces
IP-EIGRP interfaces for process 20

                        Xmit Queue   Mean   Pacing Time   Multicast    Pending
Interface        Peers  Un/Reliable  SRTT   Un/Reliable   Flow Timer   Routes
Gi0/0              0        0/0        0        0/1            0           0
Se0/1              1        0/0        1        0/15          50           0
Se0/0              1        0/0        1        0/15          50           0
Gi0/1              0        0/0        0        0/1            0           0

Corp#sh ip eigrp interface detail s0/0
IP-EIGRP interfaces for process 20

                        Xmit Queue   Mean   Pacing Time   Multicast    Pending
Interface        Peers  Un/Reliable  SRTT   Un/Reliable   Flow Timer   Routes
Se0/0              1        0/0        1        0/15          50           0
  Hello interval is 5 sec
  Next xmit serial <none>
  Un/reliable mcasts: 0/0  Un/reliable ucasts: 21/26
  Mcast exceptions: 0  CR packets: 0  ACKs suppressed: 9
  Retransmissions sent: 0  Out-of-sequence rcvd: 0
  Authentication mode is not set
```

The first command, `show ip eigrp interfaces`, lists all interfaces for which EIGRP is enabled, as well as those the router is currently sending Hello messages to in an attempt to find new EIGRP neighbors. The `show ip eigrp interface detail` *`interface`* command lists more details per interface, including the local router's own Hello interval. Understand that you can use these commands to verify that all your interfaces are within the AS process used by EIGRP, but also note that the passive interfaces won't show up in these outputs. So be sure to also check whether an interface has been configured as passive if it is not present in the outputs.

Okay, if all neighbors are present, then verify the routes learned. By executing the `show ip route eigrp` command, you're given a quick picture of the routes in the routing table. If a certain route doesn't appear in the routing table, you need to verify its source. If the source is functioning properly, check the topology table.

The routing table according to Corp looks like this:

```
D     192.168.10.0/24 [90/2172416] via 172.16.10.6, 02:29:09, Serial0/1
                      [90/2172416] via 172.16.10.2, 02:29:09, Serial0/0
      172.16.0.0/30 is subnetted, 2 subnets
```

```
C       172.16.10.4 is directly connected, Serial0/1
C       172.16.10.0 is directly connected, Serial0/0
     10.0.0.0/24 is subnetted, 6 subnets
C       10.10.10.0 is directly connected, Loopback0
C       10.10.11.0 is directly connected, Loopback1
D       10.10.20.0 [90/2300416] via 172.16.10.6, 02:29:09, Serial0/1
                   [90/2297856] via 172.16.10.2, 02:29:10, Serial0/0
D       10.10.30.0 [90/2300416] via 172.16.10.6, 02:29:10, Serial0/1
                   [90/2297856] via 172.16.10.2, 02:29:10, Serial0/0
D       10.10.40.0 [90/2297856] via 172.16.10.6, 02:29:10, Serial0/1
                   [90/2300416] via 172.16.10.2, 02:29:10, Serial0/0
D       10.10.50.0 [90/2297856] via 172.16.10.6, 02:29:11, Serial0/1
                   [90/2300416] via 172.16.10.2, 02:29:11, Serial0/0
```

You can see here that most EIGRP routes are referenced with a *D* and that their administrative distance is 90. Remember that the `[90/2300416]` represents AD/FD, and in the preceding output, EIGRP is performing equal- and unequal-cost load balancing between two links to our remote networks.

We can see this by looking closer at two different networks. Pay special attention to the FD of each output:

```
Corp#sh ip route | section 192.168.10.0
D     192.168.10.0/24 [90/2172416] via 172.16.10.6, 01:15:44, Serial0/1
                      [90/2172416] via 172.16.10.2, 01:15:44, Serial0/0
```

The preceding outputs show equal-cost load balancing, and here's our unequal-cost load balancing in action:

```
Corp#sh ip route | section 10.10.50.0
D       10.10.50.0 [90/2297856] via 172.16.10.6, 01:16:16, Serial0/1
                   [90/2300416] via 172.16.10.2, 01:16:16, Serial0/0
```

We can get the topology table displayed for us via the `show ip eigrp topology` command. If the route is in the topology table but not in the routing table, it's a pretty safe assumption that there's a problem between the topology database and the routing table. After all, there must be a good reason the topology database isn't adding the route into the routing table, right? We discussed this issue in detail earlier in the chapter, and it's oh so important.

Corp's topology table looks like this:

```
P 10.10.10.0/24, 1 successors, FD is 128256
        via Connected, GigabitEthernet0/0
P 10.10.11.0/24, 1 successors, FD is 128256
        via Connected, GigabitEthernet0/1
P 10.10.20.0/24, 1 successors, FD is 2297856
```

```
        via 172.16.10.2 (2297856/128256), Serial0/0
        via 172.16.10.6 (2300416/156160), Serial0/1
P 10.10.30.0/24, 1 successors, FD is 2297856
        via 172.16.10.2 (2297856/128256), Serial0/0
        via 172.16.10.6 (2300416/156160), Serial0/1
P 10.10.40.0/24, 1 successors, FD is 2297856
        via 172.16.10.6 (2297856/128256), Serial0/1
        via 172.16.10.2 (2300416/156160), Serial0/0
P 10.10.50.0/24, 1 successors, FD is 2297856
        via 172.16.10.6 (2297856/128256), Serial0/1
        via 172.16.10.2 (2300416/156160), Serial0/0
P 192.168.10.0/24, 2 successors, FD is 2172416
        via 172.16.10.2 (2172416/28160), Serial0/0
        via 172.16.10.6 (2172416/28160), Serial0/1
P 172.16.10.4/30, 1 successors, FD is 2169856
        via Connected, Serial0/1
P 172.16.10.0/30, 1 successors, FD is 2169856
        via Connected, Serial0/0
```

Notice that every route in this output is preceded by a *P*, which shows that these routes are in a *passive state*. This is good because routes in the active state indicate that the router has lost its path to this network and is searching for a replacement. Each entry also reveals the FD to each remote network as well as the next-hop neighbor through which packets will travel to this destination. Each entry also has two numbers in brackets, with the first indicating the FD and the second the AD to a remote network.

Again, here's our equal- and unequal-cost load-balancing output shown in the topology table:

```
Corp#sh ip eigrp top | section 192.168.10.0
P 192.168.10.0/24, 2 successors, FD is 2172416
        via 172.16.10.2 (2172416/28160), Serial0/0
        via 172.16.10.6 (2172416/28160), Serial0/1
```

The preceding output shows equal-cost load balancing, and here is our unequal-cost load balancing in action:

```
Corp#sh ip eigrp top | section 10.10.50.0
P 10.10.50.0/24, 1 successors, FD is 2297856
        via 172.16.10.6 (2297856/128256), Serial0/1
        via 172.16.10.2 (2300416/156160), Serial0/0
```

The command `show ip eigrp traffic` enables us to see whether updates are being sent. If the counters for EIGRP input and output packets don't increase, it means that no

EIGRP information is being sent between peers. The following output indicates that the Corp router is experiencing normal traffic:

```
Corp#show ip eigrp traffic
IP-EIGRP Traffic Statistics for process 200
  Hellos sent/received: 2208/2310
  Updates sent/received: 184/183
  Queries sent/received: 17/4
  Replies sent/received: 4/18
  Acks sent/received: 62/65
  Input queue high water mark 2, 0 drops
```

All the packet types I talked about in the section on RTP are represented in the output of this command. And we can't forget the always useful troubleshooting command `show ip protocols`. Here's the output the Corp router gives us after using it:

```
Routing Protocol is "eigrp 20"
  Outgoing update filter list for all interfaces is not set
  Incoming update filter list for all interfaces is not set
  Default networks flagged in outgoing updates
  Default networks accepted from incoming updates
  EIGRP metric weight K1=1, K2=0, K3=1, K4=0, K5=0
  EIGRP maximum hopcount 100
  EIGRP maximum metric variance 2
  Redistributing: eigrp 20
  EIGRP NSF-aware route hold timer is 240s
  Automatic network summarization is not in effect
  Maximum path: 4
  Routing for Networks:
    10.0.0.0
    172.16.0.0
  Routing Information Sources:
    Gateway         Distance      Last Update
    (this router)         90      04:23:51
    172.16.10.6           90      02:30:48
    172.16.10.2           90      02:30:48
  Distance: internal 90 external 170
```

In this output, we can see that EIGRP is enabled for autonomous system 20 and that the K values are set to their defaults. The variance is 2, so both equal- and unequal-cost load balancing is happening here. Automatic summarization has been turned off. We can also see that EIGRP is advertising two classful networks and that it sees two neighbors.

The show ip eigrp events command displays a log of every EIGRP event: when routes are injected and removed from the routing table and when EIGRP adjacencies are reset or fail. This information is so helpful in determining if there are routing instabilities in the network. Be advised that this command can result in quite a flood of information even for really simple configurations like ours. To demonstrate, here's the output the Corp router divulged after I used it:

```
Corp#show ip eigrp events
Event information for AS 20:
1    22:24:24.258 Metric set: 172.16.10.0/30 2169856
2    22:24:24.258 FC sat rdbmet/succmet: 2169856 0
3    22:24:24.258 FC sat nh/ndbmet: 0.0.0.0 2169856
4    22:24:24.258 Find FS: 172.16.10.0/30 2169856
5    22:24:24.258 Metric set: 172.16.10.4/30 2169856
6    22:24:24.258 FC sat rdbmet/succmet: 2169856 0
7    22:24:24.258 FC sat nh/ndbmet: 0.0.0.0 2169856
8    22:24:24.258 Find FS: 172.16.10.4/30 2169856
9    22:24:24.258 Metric set: 192.168.10.0/24 2172416
10   22:24:24.258 Route install: 192.168.10.0/24 172.16.10.2
11   22:24:24.258 Route install: 192.168.10.0/24 172.16.10.6
12   22:24:24.254 FC sat rdbmet/succmet: 2172416 28160
13   22:24:24.254 FC sat nh/ndbmet: 172.16.10.6 2172416
14   22:24:24.254 Find FS: 192.168.10.0/24 2172416
15   22:24:24.254 Metric set: 10.10.50.0/24 2297856
16   22:24:24.254 Route install: 10.10.50.0/24 172.16.10.6
17   22:24:24.254 FC sat rdbmet/succmet: 2297856 128256
18   22:24:24.254 FC sat nh/ndbmet: 172.16.10.6 2297856
19   22:24:24.254 Find FS: 10.10.50.0/24 2297856
20   22:24:24.254 Metric set: 10.10.40.0/24 2297856
21   22:24:24.254 Route install: 10.10.40.0/24 172.16.10.6
22   22:24:24.250 FC sat rdbmet/succmet: 2297856 128256
 --More--
```

Troubleshooting Example with EIGRP

Throughout this chapter I've covered many of the problems that commonly occur with EIGRP and how to verify and troubleshoot these issues. Make sure you clearly understand what I have shown you so far in this chapter so that you're prepared to answer any question the Cisco exam could possibly throw at you.

Just to make sure you're solidly armed with all the skills you need to ace the exam and to successfully administer a network, I'm going to provide even more examples about verifying EIGRP. We'll be dealing with mostly the same commands and problems we've already covered, but this is so important and the best way to get this all nailed down is to practice troubleshooting an EIGRP network as much as possible.

With that, after you've configured EIGRP, you would first test connectivity to the remote network by using the Ping program. If that fails, you need to check whether the directly connected router is in the neighbor table.

Here are some key things to look for if neighbors haven't formed an adjacency:

- Interfaces between the devices are down.
- The two routers have mismatching EIGRP AS numbers.
- Proper interfaces are not enabled for the EIGRP process.
- An interface is configured as passive.
- The K values are mismatched.
- EIGRP authentication is misconfigured.

Also, if the adjacency is up but you're not receiving remote network updates, there may be a routing problem, likely caused by these issues:

- The proper networks aren't being advertised under the EIGRP process.
- An access list is blocking the advertisements from remote networks.
- Automatic summary is causing confusion in your discontiguous network.

Let's use Figure 11.10 as our example network and run through some troubleshooting scenarios. I've preconfigured the routers with IP addresses, and without having to try too hard, I also snuck in a few snags for us to find and fix. Let's see what we're facing.

FIGURE 11.10 Troubleshooting scenario

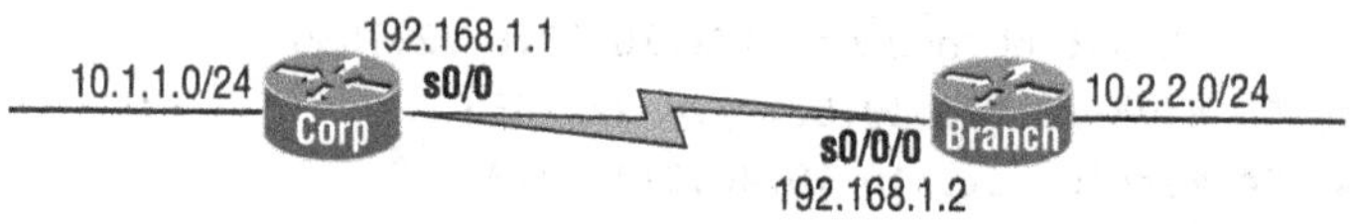

A good place to start is by checking to see whether we have an adjacency with `show ip eigrp neighbors` and `show ip eigrp interfaces`. It's also smart to see what information the `show ip eigrp topology` command reveals:

```
Corp#sh ip eigrp neighbors
IP-EIGRP neighbors for process 20
Corp#

Corp#sh ip eigrp interfaces
IP-EIGRP interfaces for process 20
```

```
                        Xmit Queue   Mean   Pacing Time   Multicast    Pending
Interface        Peers  Un/Reliable  SRTT   Un/Reliable   Flow Timer   Routes
Se0/1              0        0/0        0        0/15          50           0
Fa0/0              0        0/0        0        0/1            0           0
Se0/0              0        0/0        0        0/15          50           0

Corp#sh ip eigrp top
IP-EIGRP Topology Table for AS(20)/ID(10.10.11.1)

Codes: P - Passive, A - Active, U - Update, Q - Query, R - Reply,
       r - reply Status, s - sia Status

P 10.1.1.0/24, 1 successors, FD is 28160
        via Connected, FastEthernet0/0
```

Alright, we can see by looking at the neighbor and the interface as well as the topology table command that our LAN is up on the Corp router but that the serial link isn't working between routers because we don't have an adjacency. From the `show ip eigrp interfaces` command, we can establish that EIGRP is running on all interfaces, which means our network statements under the EIGRP process are probably correct, but we'll verify that later.

Let's move on by checking into our Physical and Data Link status with the `show ip int brief` command because maybe there's a physical problem between routers:

```
Corp#sh ip int brief
Interface         IP-Address    OK? Method Status                 Protocol
FastEthernet0/0   10.1.1.1      YES manual up                        up
Serial0/0         192.168.1.1   YES manual up                        up
FastEthernet0/1   unassigned    YES manual administratively down down
Serial0/1         172.16.10.5   YES manual administratively down down
Corp#
Corp#sh protocols s0/0
Serial0/0 is up, line protocol is up
  Internet address is 192.168.1.1/30
Corp#
```

Well, since the Serial0/0 interface shows the correct IP address and the status is up/up, it means we have a good Data Link connection between routers, so it's not a physical link issue between the routers, which is good. Notice I also used the `show protocols` command, which gave me the subnet mask for the link. Remember, the information obtained via the two commands gives us only layer 1 and layer 2 status and doesn't mean we can ping across the link. In other words, we might have a layer 3 issue, so let's check the Branch router with the same commands:

```
Branch#sh ip int brief
Interface                  IP-Address      OK? Method Status                Protocol
FastEthernet0/0            10.2.2.2        YES manual up                    up
FastEthernet0/1            unassigned      YES manual administratively down down
Serial0/0/0                192.168.1.2     YES manual up                    up
Serial0/0/1                unassigned      YES unset  administratively down down
Branch#
Branch#sh proto s0/0/0
Serial0/0/0 is up, line protocol is up
  Internet address is 192.168.1.2/30
Branch#
```

Okay, well, we can see that our IP address and mask are correct, and that the link shows up/up, so we're looking pretty good! Let's try to ping from the Corp router to the Branch router now:

```
Corp#ping 192.168.1.2

Type escape sequence to abort.
Sending 5, 100-byte ICMP Echos to 192.168.1.2, timeout is 2 seconds:
!!!!!
Success rate is 100 percent (5/5), round-trip min/avg/max = 1/3/4 ms
Corp#
```

Now because that was successful, we've ruled out layer 1, 2, or 3 issues between routers at this point. Because everything seems to be working between the routers, except EIGRP, checking our EIGRP configurations is our next move. Let's start with the `show ip protocols` command:

```
Corp#sh ip protocols
Routing Protocol is "eigrp 20"
  Outgoing update filter list for all interfaces is not set
  Incoming update filter list for all interfaces is not set
  Default networks flagged in outgoing updates
  Default networks accepted from incoming updates
  EIGRP metric weight K1=1, K2=0, K3=1, K4=0, K5=0
  EIGRP maximum hopcount 100
  EIGRP maximum metric variance 2
  Redistributing: eigrp 20
  EIGRP NSF-aware route hold timer is 240s
  Automatic network summarization is in effect
```

```
  Maximum path: 4
  Routing for Networks:
    10.0.0.0
    172.16.0.0
    192.168.1.0
Passive Interface(s):
    FastEthernet0/1
  Routing Information Sources:
    Gateway         Distance      Last Update
    (this router)         90      20:51:48
    192.168.1.2           90      00:22:58
    172.16.10.6           90      01:58:46
    172.16.10.2           90      01:59:52
  Distance: internal 90 external 170
```

This output shows us we're using AS 20, that we don't have an access-list filter list set on the routing tables, and that our K values are set to default. We can see that we're routing for the 10.0.0.0, 172.16.0.0, and 192.168.1.0 networks and we have a passive interface on interface FastEthernet0/1. We don't have an interface configured for the 172.16.0.0 network, which means that this entry is an extra network statement under EIGRP. But that won't hurt anything, so this is not causing our issue. Last, the passive interface is not causing a problem with this network either, because we're not using interface Fa0/1. Still, keep in mind that when troubleshooting, it's always good to see if there are any interfaces set to passive.

Let's see what the `show interface` command will tell us:

```
Corp#sh interfaces s0/0
Serial0/0 is up, line protocol is up
  Hardware is PowerQUICC Serial
  Description: <<Connection to Branch>>
  Internet address is 192.168.1.1/30
  MTU 1500 bytes, BW 1544 Kbit, DLY 20000 usec,
     reliability 255/255, txload 1/255, rxload 1/255
  Encapsulation HDLC, loopback not set
[output cut]
```

Looks like our statistics are set to defaults, so nothing really pops as a problem here. But remember when I covered the steps to check if there is no adjacency back at the beginning of this section? In case you forgot, here's a list of things to investigate:

- The interfaces between the devices are down.
- The two routers have mismatching EIGRP AS numbers.
- The proper interfaces aren't enabled for the EIGRP process.
- An interface is configured as passive.

- K values are mismatched.
- EIGRP authentication is misconfigured.

Okay, our interfaces are not down, our AS number matches, layer 3 is working between routers, all the interfaces show up under the EIGRP process, and none of our needed interfaces are passive. Now, we'll have to look even deeper into the EIGRP configuration to uncover the problem.

Since the Corp router has the basic default configurations, we need to check the Branch router's EIGRP configuration:

```
Branch#sh ip protocols
Routing Protocol is "eigrp 20"
  Outgoing update filter list for all interfaces is 10
  Incoming update filter list for all interfaces is not set
  Default networks flagged in outgoing updates
  Default networks accepted from incoming updates
  EIGRP metric weight K1=1, K2=0, K3=0, K4=0, K5=0
  EIGRP maximum hopcount 100
  EIGRP maximum metric variance 1
  Redistributing: eigrp 20
  EIGRP NSF-aware route hold timer is 240s
  Automatic network summarization is not in effect
  Maximum path: 4
  Routing for Networks:
    10.0.0.0
    192.168.1.0
  Routing Information Sources:
    Gateway         Distance      Last Update
    192.168.1.1           90      00:27:09
  Distance: internal 90 external 170
```

This router has the correct AS—always check this first—and we're routing for the correct networks. But I see two possible snags here. Do you? First, the outgoing access control list (ACL) filter list is set, but the metrics are not set to default. Remember, just because an ACL is set doesn't mean it's automatically giving you grief. Second, the K values must match, and we know these values are not matching the Corp router.

Let's take a look at the Branch interface statistics to see what else might be wrong:

```
Branch>sh int s0/0/0
Serial0/0/0 is up, line protocol is up
  Hardware is GT96K Serial
  Internet address is 192.168.1.2/30
  MTU 1500 bytes, BW 512 Kbit, DLY 30000 usec,
     reliability 255/255, txload 1/255, rxload 1/255
```

```
  Encapsulation HDLC, loopback not set
  [output cut]
```

Aha! The bandwidth and delay are not set to their defaults and don't match the directly connected Corp router. Let's start by changing those back to the default and see whether that fixes our problem:

```
Branch#config t
Branch(config)#int s0/0/0
Branch(config-if)#no bandwidth
Branch(config-if)#no delay
```

And let's check out our stats now to see if we're back to defaults:

```
Branch#sh int s0/0/0
Serial0/0/0 is up, line protocol is up
  Hardware is GT96K Serial
  Internet address is 192.168.1.2/30
  MTU 1500 bytes, BW 1544 Kbit, DLY 20000 usec,
     reliability 255/255, txload 1/255, rxload 1/255
  Encapsulation HDLC, loopback not set
[output cut]
```

The bandwidth and delay are now at the defaults, so let's check our adjacencies next:

```
Corp#sh ip eigrp neighbors
IP-EIGRP neighbors for process 20
Corp#
```

Okay, so it wasn't the bandwidth and delay settings because our adjacency didn't come up, so let's set our K values back to default like this:

```
Branch#config t
Branch(config)#router eigrp 20
Branch(config-router)#metric weights 0 1 0 1 0 0
Branch(config-router)#do sho ip proto
Routing Protocol is "eigrp 20"
  Outgoing update filter list for all interfaces is 10
  Incoming update filter list for all interfaces is not set
  Default networks flagged in outgoing updates
  Default networks accepted from incoming updates
  EIGRP metric weight K1=1, K2=0, K3=1, K4=0, K5=0
[output cut]
```

I know this probably seems a little complicated at first, but it's something you shouldn't have to do much, if ever. Remember, there are five K values, so why six numbers? The first number listed is type of service (ToS), so always just set that to 0, which means you must type in six numbers as shown in my configuration example. After we chose the default of 0 first, the default K values are then 1 0 1 0 0, which is bandwidth and delay enabled. Let's check our adjacency now:

```
Corp#sh ip eigrp neighbors
IP-EIGRP neighbors for process 20
H   Address                 Interface       Hold Uptime   SRTT   RTO  Q  Seq
                                            (sec)         (ms)       Cnt Num
0   192.168.1.2             Se0/0             14 00:02:09    7   200  0  18
```

Bam! There we go. Looks like mismatched K values were our problem. Now let's just check to make sure we can ping from end to end and we're done:

```
Corp#ping 10.2.2.2

Type escape sequence to abort.
Sending 5, 100-byte ICMP Echos to 10.2.2.2, timeout is 2 seconds:
.....
Success rate is 0 percent (0/5)
Corp#
```

Rats! It looks like even though we have our adjacency, we still can't reach our remote network. Next step? Let's see what the routing table shows us:

```
Corp#sh ip route
[output cut]

     10.0.0.0/8 is variably subnetted, 2 subnets, 2 masks
C       10.1.1.0/24 is directly connected, FastEthernet0/0
D       10.0.0.0/8 is a summary, 00:18:55, Null0
     192.168.1.0/24 is variably subnetted, 2 subnets, 2 masks
C       192.168.1.0/30 is directly connected, Serial0/0
D       192.168.1.0/24 is a summary, 00:18:55, Null0
```

The problem is screamingly clear now because I went through this in detail throughout this chapter. But just in case you still can't find it, let's look at the `show ip protocols` command output:

```
Routing Protocol is "eigrp 20"
  Outgoing update filter list for all interfaces is not set
  Incoming update filter list for all interfaces is not set
  Default networks flagged in outgoing updates
  Default networks accepted from incoming updates
  EIGRP metric weight K1=1, K2=0, K3=1, K4=0, K5=0
  EIGRP maximum hopcount 100
  EIGRP maximum metric variance 2
```

```
  Redistributing: eigrp 20
  EIGRP NSF-aware route hold timer is 240s
  Automatic network summarization is in effect
  Automatic address summarization:
    192.168.1.0/24 for FastEthernet0/0
      Summarizing with metric 2169856
    10.0.0.0/8 for Serial0/0
      Summarizing with metric 28160
[output cut]
```

By looking at Figure 11.10, you should have noticed right away that we had a discontiguous network. This means that unless they are running 15.0 IOS code, the routers will auto-summarize, so we need to disable auto-summary:

```
Branch(config)#router eigrp 20
Branch(config-router)#no auto-summary
008412:%DUAL-5-NBRCHANGE:IP-EIGRP(0) 20:Neighbor 192.168.1.1 (Serial0/0/0) is
resync:
peer graceful-restart

Corp(config)#router eigrp 20
Corp(config-router)#no auto-summary
Corp(config-router)#
*Feb 27 19:52:54:%DUAL-5-NBRCHANGE: IP-EIGRP(0) 20:Neighbor 192.168.1.2
(Serial0/0)
 is resync: summary configured
*Feb 27 19:52:54.177:IP-EIGRP(Default-IP-Routing-Table:20):10.1.1.0/24 - do
advertise
 out Serial0/0
*Feb 27 19:52:54:IP-EIGRP(Default-IP-Routing-Table:20):Int 10.1.1.0/24
metric 2816
0 - 25600 2560
*Feb 27 19:52:54:IP-EIGRP(Default-IP-Routing-Table:20):192.168.1.0/30 - do
advertise out Serial0/0
*Feb 27 19:52:54:IP-EIGRP(Default-IP-Routing-Table:20):192.168.1.0/24 - do
advertise out Serial0/0
*Feb 27 19:52:54:IP-EIGRP(Default-IP-Routing-Table:20):Int 192.168.1.0/24
metric 4294967295 - 0 4294967295
*Feb 27 19:52:54:IP-EIGRP(Default-IP-Routing-Table:20):10.0.0.0/8 - do
advertise
 out Serial0/0
Corp(config-router)#
*Feb 27 19:52:54:IP-EIGRP(Default-IP-Routing-Table:20):Int 10.0.0.0/8 metric
4294967295 - 0 4294967295
```

```
*Feb 27 19:52:54:IP-EIGRP(Default-IP-Routing-Table:20):Processing incoming
REPLY packet
*Feb 27 19:52:54:IP-EIGRP(Default-IP-Routing-Table:20):Int 192.168.1.0/24 M
4294967295 - 1657856 4294967295 SM 4294967295 - 1657856 4294967295
*Feb 27 19:52:54:IP-EIGRP(Default-IP-Routing-Table:20):Int 10.0.0.0/8 M
4294967295 - 25600 4294967295 SM 4294967295 - 25600 4294967295
*Feb 27 19:52:54:IP-EIGRP(Default-IP-Routing-Table:20):Processing incoming
UPDATE packet
```

Finally, the Corp looks happy, so it looks like we're good to go. Let's just check our routing table to be sure:

```
Corp#sh ip route
[output cut]
     10.0.0.0/24 is subnetted, 1 subnets
C       10.1.1.0 is directly connected, FastEthernet0/0
     192.168.1.0/30 is subnetted, 1 subnets
C       192.168.1.0 is directly connected, Serial0/0
```

What the heck? How can this be? We saw all those updates on the Corp console, right? Let's check the configuration of EIGRP by looking at the active configuration on the Branch router:

```
Branch#sh run
[output cut]
!
router eigrp 20
 network 10.0.0.0
 network 192.168.1.0
 distribute-list 10 out
 no auto-summary
!
```

We can see that the access list is set outbound on the routing table of the Branch router. This may be preventing us from receiving the updates from remote networks. Let's see what the ACL 10 list is doing:

```
Branch#sh access-lists
Standard IP access list 10
    10 deny   any (40 matches)
    20 permit any
```

Now who in the world would stick an access list like this on a router? This ACL says to deny every packet, which makes the second line of the ACL irrelevant because every single packet will match the first line. This has got to be the source of our troubles, so let's remove that list and see if the Corp router starts working:

```
Branch#config t
Branch(config)#router eigrp 20
Branch(config-router)#no distribute-list 10 out
```

Okay, with that ugly thing gone, let's check to see if we're receiving our remote networks now:

```
Corp#sh ip route
[output cut]
     10.0.0.0/24 is subnetted, 2 subnets
D       10.2.2.0 [90/2172416] via 192.168.1.2, 00:00:24, Serial0/0
C       10.1.1.0 is directly connected, FastEthernet0/0
     192.168.1.0/30 is subnetted, 1 subnets
C       192.168.1.0 is directly connected, Serial0/0
Corp#
Corp#ping 10.2.2.2

Type escape sequence to abort.
Sending 5, 100-byte ICMP Echos to 10.2.2.2, timeout is 2 seconds:
!!!!!
Success rate is 100 percent (5/5), round-trip min/avg/max = 1/3/4 ms
Corp#
```

Clear skies! We're up and running. We had mismatched K values, discontiguous networking, and a nasty ACL on our routing table. For the CCNA R/S objectives, always check for an ACL on the actual interface as well, not just in the routing table. It could be set on the interface or routing table, either one, or both. And never forget to check for passive interfaces when troubleshooting a routing protocol issue.

All of these commands are seriously powerful tools in the hands of a savvy professional faced with the task of troubleshooting myriad network issues. I could go on and on about the profusion of information these commands can generate and how well they can equip us to solve virtually every networking ill, but that would be way outside the scope of this book. Even so, I have no doubt that the foundation I've given you here will prove practical and valuable for certification purposes and for when you are working in the real networking world.

Now it's time to relax a bit as we move into the easiest part of this chapter—seriously, not joking. You still need to pay attention though.

EIGRPv6

As I just was saying, welcome to the easiest part of the chapter. Of course, I only mostly mean that, and here's why: I talked about IPv6 in the earlier ICND1 chapters, and to continue with this section of the chapter, you need to have that vital, foundational part of IPv6 down solid before you dare to dwell here. If you do, you're pretty much set and this will all be pretty simple for you.

EIGRPv6 works much the same way as its IPv4 predecessor does; most of the features that EIGRP provided before EIGRPv6 will still be available.

EIGRPv6 is still an advanced distance-vector protocol that has some link-state features. The neighbor discovery process using Hellos still happens, and it still provides reliable communication with RTP that gives us loop-free fast convergence using DUAL.

Hello packets and updates are sent using multicast transmission, and as with RIPng, EIGRPv6's multicast address stayed almost the same. In IPv4, it was 224.0.0.10; in IPv6, it's FF02::A (A = 10 in hexadecimal notation).

But clearly, there are key differences between the two versions. Most notably the use of the pesky `network` command is gone, so it's hard to make a mistake with EIGRPv6. Also, the network and interface to be advertised must be enabled from interface configuration mode with one simple command.

But you still have to use the router configuration mode to enable the routing protocol in EIGRPv6 because the routing process must be literally enabled like an interface with the `no shutdown` command—interesting. However, the 15.0 code does enable this by default, so this command actually may or may not be needed.

Here's an example of enabling EIGRPv6 on the Corp router:

```
Corp(config)#ipv6 unicast-routing
Corp(config)#ipv6 router eigrp 10
```

The 10 in this case is still the AS number. The prompt changes to `(config-rtr)`, and from here, just initiate a `no shutdown` if needed:

```
Corp(config-rtr)#no shutdown
```

Other options also can be configured in this mode, like redistribution and router ID (RID). So now, let's go to the interface and enable IPv6:

```
Corp(config-if)#ipv6 eigrp 10
```

The 10 in the interface command again references the AS number that was enabled in the configuration mode.

Figure 11.11 shows the layout we've been using throughout this chapter, only with IPv6 addresses now assigned to interfaces. I used the EUI-64 option on each interface so that each router assigned themselves an IPv6 address after I typed in the 64-bit network/subnet address.

FIGURE 11.11 Configuring EIGRPv6 on our Internetwork

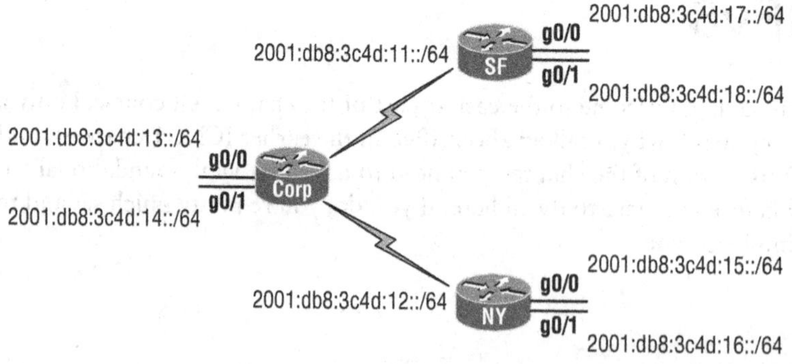

We'll start with the Corp router. Really, all we need to know to enable EIGRPv6 are which interfaces we're using and want to advertise our networks:

```
Corp#config t
Corp(config)#ipv6 router eigrp 10
Corp(config-rtr)#no shut
Corp(config-rtr)#router-id 1.1.1.1
Corp(config-rtr)#int s0/0/0
Corp(config-if)#ipv6 eigrp 10
Corp(config-if)#int s0/0/1
Corp(config-if)#ipv6 eigrp 10
Corp(config-if)#int g0/0
Corp(config-if)#ipv6 eigrp 10
Corp(config-if)#int g0/1
Corp(config-if)#ipv6 eigrp 10
```

I had erased and reloaded the routers before I started this EIGRPv6 section of the chapter. What this means is that there were no 32-bit addresses on the router in order to create the RID for EIGRP, so I had to set it under the `IPv6 router` global command, which is the same command used with EIGRP and EIGRPv6. Unlike OSPF, the RID isn't that important, and it can actually be the same address on every router. You just can't get away with doing this with OSPF. The configuration for EIGRPv6 was pretty straightforward because unless you type the AS number wrong, it's pretty hard to screw this up.

Okay, let's configure the SF and NY routers now, and then we'll verify our networks:

```
SF#config t
SF(config)#ipv6 router eigrp 10
SF(config-rtr)#no shut
SF(config-rtr)#router-id 2.2.2.2
SF(config-rtr)#int s0/0/0
SF(config-if)#ipv6 eigrp 10
SF(config-if)#int g0/0
SF(config-if)#ipv6 eigrp 10
SF(config-if)#int g0/1
SF(config-if)#ipv6 eigrp 10

NY#config t
NY(config)#ipv6 router eigrp 10
NY(config-rtr)#no shut
NY(config-rtr)#router-id 3.3.3.3
NY(config-rtr)#int s0/0/0
NY(config-if)#ipv6 eigrp 10
NY(config-if)#int g0/0
NY(config-if)#ipv6 eigrp 10
NY(config-if)#int g0/1
```

Because we configured EIGRPv6 on a per-interface basis, no worries about having to use the `passive-interface` command. This is because if we don't enable the routing protocol on an interface, it's just not part of the EIGRPv6 process. We can see which interfaces are part of the EIGRPv6 process with the `show ipv6 eigrp interfaces` command like this:

```
Corp#sh ipv6 eigrp interfaces
IPv6-EIGRP interfaces for process 10
                       Xmit Queue   Mean   Pacing Time   Multicast    Pending
Interface       Peers  Un/Reliable  SRTT   Un/Reliable   Flow Timer   Routes
Se0/0/0           1        0/0      1236       0/10           0           0
Se0/0/1           1        0/0      1236       0/10           0           0
Gig0/1            0        0/0      1236       0/10           0           0
Gig0/0            0        0/0      1236       0/10           0           0
Corp#
```

Looks great so far. All the interfaces we want in our AS are listed, so we're looking good for our Corp's local configuration. Now it's time to check if our adjacencies came up with the `show ipv6 eigrp neighbors` command:

```
Corp#sh ipv6 eigrp neighbors
IPv6-EIGRP neighbors for process 10
H   Address                 Interface       Hold   Uptime   SRTT   RTO  Q  Seq
                                            (sec)           (ms)        Cnt Num
0   Link-local address:   Se0/0/0      10   00:01:40  40    1000  0   11
    FE80::201:C9FF:FED0:3301
1   Link-local address:   Se0/0/1      14   00:01:24  40    1000  0   11
    FE80::209:7CFF:FE51:B401
```

It's great that we can see neighbors listed off each serial interface, but do you notice something missing from the preceding output? That's right, the actual IPv6 network/subnet addresses of the links aren't listed in the neighbor table. Only the link-local addresses are used for forming EIGRP neighbor adjacencies. With IPv6, neighbor interfaces and next-hop addresses are always link-local.

We can verify our configuration with the `show ip protocols` command:

```
Corp#sh ipv6 protocols
IPv6 Routing Protocol is "connected"
IPv6 Routing Protocol is "static
IPv6 Routing Protocol is "eigrp  10 "
  EIGRP metric weight K1=1, K2=0, K3=1, K4=0, K5=0
  EIGRP maximum hopcount 100
  EIGRP maximum metric variance 1
  Interfaces:
    Serial0/0/0
```

```
    Serial0/0/1
    GigabitEthernet0/0
    GigabitEthernet0/1
Redistributing: eigrp 10
  Maximum path: 16
  Distance: internal 90 external 170
```

You can verify the AS number from this output, but be sure to verify your K values, variance, and interfaces, too. Remember that the AS number and interfaces are the first factors to check when troubleshooting.

The topology table lists all feasible routes in the network, so this output can be rather long, but let's see what this shows us:

```
Corp#sh ipv6 eigrp topology
IPv6-EIGRP Topology Table for AS 10/ID(1.1.1.1)

Codes: P - Passive, A - Active, U - Update, Q - Query, R - Reply,
       r - Reply status

P 2001:DB8:C34D:11::/64, 1 successors, FD is 2169856
         via Connected, Serial0/0/0
P 2001:DB8:C34D:12::/64, 1 successors, FD is 2169856
         via Connected, Serial0/0/1
P 2001:DB8:C34D:14::/64, 1 successors, FD is 2816
         via Connected, GigabitEthernet0/1
P 2001:DB8:C34D:13::/64, 1 successors, FD is 2816
         via Connected, GigabitEthernet0/0
P 2001:DB8:C34D:17::/64, 1 successors, FD is 2170112
         via FE80::201:C9FF:FED0:3301 (2170112/2816), Serial0/0/0
P 2001:DB8:C34D:18::/64, 1 successors, FD is 2170112
         via FE80::201:C9FF:FED0:3301 (2170112/2816), Serial0/0/0
P 2001:DB8:C34D:15::/64, 1 successors, FD is 2170112
         via FE80::209:7CFF:FE51:B401 (2170112/2816), Serial0/0/1
P 2001:DB8:C34D:16::/64, 1 successors, FD is 2170112
         via FE80::209:7CFF:FE51:B401 (2170112/2816), Serial0/0/1
```

Because we only have eight networks in our internetwork, we can see all eight networks in the topology table, which clearly is as it should be. I've highlighted a couple of things I want to discuss, and the first is that you need to be able to read and understand a topology table. This includes understanding which routes are directly connected and which are being advertised via neighbors. The `via Connected` shows us our directly connected networks. The second item I want to show you is `(2170112/2816)`, which is the FD/AD, and by the way, it's no different than if you're working with IPv4.

So let's wrap up this chapter by taking a look at a routing table:

```
Corp#sh ipv6 route eigrp
IPv6 Routing Table - 13 entries
Codes: C - Connected, L - Local, S - Static, R - RIP, B - BGP
       U - Per-user Static route, M - MIPv6
       I1 - ISIS L1, I2 - ISIS L2, IA - ISIS interarea, IS - ISIS summary
       O - OSPF intra, OI - OSPF inter, OE1 - OSPF ext 1, OE2 - OSPF ext 2
       ON1 - OSPF NSSA ext 1, ON2 - OSPF NSSA ext 2
       D - EIGRP, EX - EIGRP external
C   2001:DB8:C34D:11::/64 [0/0]
     via ::, Serial0/0/0
L   2001:DB8:C34D:11:230:A3FF:FE36:B101/128 [0/0]
     via ::, Serial0/0/0
C   2001:DB8:C34D:12::/64 [0/0]
     via ::, Serial0/0/1
L   2001:DB8:C34D:12:230:A3FF:FE36:B102/128 [0/0]
     via ::, Serial0/0/1
C   2001:DB8:C34D:13::/64 [0/0]
     via ::, GigabitEthernet0/0
L   2001:DB8:C34D:13:2E0:F7FF:FEDA:7501/128 [0/0]
     via ::, GigabitEthernet0/0
C   2001:DB8:C34D:14::/64 [0/0]
     via ::, GigabitEthernet0/1
L   2001:DB8:C34D:14:2E0:F7FF:FEDA:7502/128 [0/0]
     via ::, GigabitEthernet0/1
D   2001:DB8:C34D:15::/64 [90/2170112]
     via FE80::209:7CFF:FE51:B401, Serial0/0/1
D   2001:DB8:C34D:16::/64 [90/2170112]
     via FE80::209:7CFF:FE51:B401, Serial0/0/1
D   2001:DB8:C34D:17::/64 [90/2170112]
     via FE80::201:C9FF:FED0:3301, Serial0/0/0
D   2001:DB8:C34D:18::/64 [90/2170112]
     via FE80::201:C9FF:FED0:3301, Serial0/0/0
L   FF00::/8 [0/0]
     via ::, Null0
```

I highlighted the EIGRPv6 injected routes that were injected into the routing table. It's important to notice that for IPv6 to get to a remote network, the router uses the next hop link-local address. Do you see that in the table? For example, `via FE80::209:7CFF:FE51:B401, Serial0/0/1` is the link-local address of the NY router.

See? I told you it was easy.

Summary

It's true that this chapter has been pretty extensive, so let's briefly recap what we covered in it. EIGRP, the main focus of the chapter, is a hybrid of link-state routing and typically referred to as an advanced distance-vector protocol. It allows for unequal-cost load balancing, controlled routing updates, and formal neighbor adjacencies called relationships to be formed.

EIGRP uses the capabilities of the RTP to communicate between neighbors and utilizes DUAL to compute the best path to each remote network.

We also covered the configuration of EIGRP and explored a number of troubleshooting commands as well as key ways to solve some common networking issues.

Moving on, EIGRP facilitates unequal-cost load balancing, controlled routing updates, and formal neighbor adjacencies.

I also went over the configuration of EIGRP and explored a number of troubleshooting commands and also walked you through a highly informative scenario that will not only help you ace the exam but will also help you confront and overcome many troubleshooting issues common to today's internetworks.

Finally, I went over the easiest section at the end of this long chapter: EIGRPv6. Easy to understand, configure, and verify.

Exam Essentials

Know EIGRP features. EIGRP is a classless, advanced distance-vector protocol that supports IP and now IPv6. EIGRP uses a unique algorithm, called DUAL, to maintain route information and uses RTP to communicate with other EIGRP routers reliably.

Know how to configure EIGRP. Be able to configure basic EIGRP. This is configured the same as RIP with classful addresses.

Know how to verify EIGRP operation. Know all of the EIGRP `show` commands and be familiar with their output and the interpretation of the main components of their output.

Be able to read an EIGRP topology table. Understand which are successors, which are feasible successors, and which routes will become successors if the main successor fails.

You must be able to troubleshoot EIGRP. Go through the EIGRP troubleshooting scenario and make sure you understand to look for the AS number, ACLs, passive interfaces, variance, and other factors.

Be able to read an EIGRP neighbor table. Understand the output of the `show ip eigrp neighbor` command.

Understand how to configure EIGRPv6. To configure EIGRPv6, first create the autonomous system from global configuration mode and perform a `no shutdown`. Then enable EIGRPv6 on each interface individually.

Written Lab

You can find the answers to this lab in Appendix A, "Answers to the Written Labs."

1. What is the command to enable EIGRPv6 from global configuration mode?
2. What is the EIGRPv6 multicast address?
3. True/False: Each router within an EIGRP domain must use different AS numbers.
4. If you have two routers with various K values assigned, what will this do to the link?
5. What type of EIGRP interface will neither send nor receive Hello packets?

Review Questions

You can find the answers to these questions in Appendix B, "Answers to the Review Questions."

> **NOTE** The following questions are designed to test your understanding of this chapter's material. For more information on how to get additional questions, please see www.lammle.com/ccna.

1. There are three possible routes for a router to reach a destination network. The first route is from OSPF with a metric of 782. The second route is from RIPv2 with a metric of 4. The third is from EIGRP with a composite metric of 20514560. Which route will be installed by the router in its routing table?
   - **A.** RIPv2
   - **B.** EIGRP
   - **C.** OSPF
   - **D.** All three
2. Which EIGRP information is held in RAM and maintained through the use of Hello and update packets? (Choose two.)
   - **A.** Neighbor table
   - **B.** STP table
   - **C.** Topology table
   - **D.** DUAL table
3. What will be the reported distance to a downstream neighbor router for the 10.10.30.0 network, with the neighbor adding the cost to this neighbor to find the true FD?

```
P 10.10.30.0/24, 1 successors, FD is 2297856
        via 172.16.10.2 (2297856/128256), Serial0/0
```

   - **A.** Four hops
   - **B.** 2297856
   - **C.** 128256
   - **D.** EIGRP doesn't use reported distances.
4. Where are EIGRP successor routes stored?
   - **A.** In the routing table only
   - **B.** In the neighbor table only
   - **C.** In the topology table only
   - **D.** In the routing table and the neighbor table
   - **E.** In the routing table and the topology table
   - **F.** In the topology table and the neighbor table

5. Which command will display all the EIGRP feasible successor routes known to a router?
   - **A.** `show ip routes *`
   - **B.** `show ip eigrp summary`
   - **C.** `show ip eigrp topology`
   - **D.** `show ip eigrp adjacencies`
   - **E.** `show ip eigrp neighbors detail`

6. Which of the following commands are used when routing with EIGRP or EIGRPv6? (Choose three.)
   - **A.** `network 10.0.0.0`
   - **B.** `eigrp router-id`
   - **C.** `variance`
   - **D.** `router eigrp`
   - **E.** `maximum-paths`

7. Serial0/0 goes down. How will EIGRP send packets to the 10.1.1.0 network?

```
Corp#show ip eigrp topology
[output cut]
P 10.1.1.0/24, 2 successors, FD is 2681842
         via 10.1.2.2 (2681842/2169856), Serial0/0
         via 10.1.3.1 (2973467/2579243), Serial0/2
         via 10.1.3.3 (2681842/2169856), Serial0/1
```

   - **A.** EIGRP will put the 10.1.1.0 network into active mode.
   - **B.** EIGRP will drop all packets destined for 10.1.1.0.
   - **C.** EIGRP will just keep sending packets out s0/1.
   - **D.** EIGRP will use s0/2 as the successor and keep routing to 10.1.1.0.

8. What command do you use to enable EIGRPv6 on an interface?
   - **A.** `router eigrp as`
   - **B.** `ip router eigrp as`
   - **C.** `router eigrpv6 as`
   - **D.** `ipv6 eigrp as`

9. What command was typed in to have these two paths to network 10.10.50.0 in the routing table?

```
D       10.10.50.0 [90/2297856] via 172.16.10.6, 00:00:20, Serial0/1
                   [90/6893568] via 172.16.10.2, 00:00:20, Serial0/0
```

A. `maximum-paths 2`
B. `variance 2`
C. `variance 3`
D. `maximum-hops 2`

10. A route to network 10.10.10.0 goes down. How does EIGRP respond in the local routing table? (Choose two.)
    A. It sends a poison reverse with a maximum hop of 16.
    B. If there is a feasible successor, that is copied and placed into the routing table.
    C. If a feasible successor is not found, a query will be sent to all neighbors asking for a path to network 10.10.10.0.
    D. EIGRP will broadcast out all interfaces that the link to network 10.10.10.0 is down and that it is looking for a feasible successor.

11. You need the IP address of the devices with which the router has established an adjacency. Also, the retransmit interval and the queue counts for the adjacent routers need to be checked. What command will display the required information?
    A. `show ip eigrp adjacency`
    B. `show ip eigrp topology`
    C. `show ip eigrp interfaces`
    D. `show ip eigrp neighbors`

12. For some reason, you cannot establish an adjacency relationship on a common Ethernet link between two routers. Looking at the output shown here, what are the causes of the problem? (Choose two.)

```
RouterA##show ip protocols
Routing Protocol is "eigrp 20"
  Outgoing update filter list for all interfaces is not set
  Incoming update filter list for all interfaces is not set
  Default networks flagged in outgoing updates
  Default networks accepted from incoming updates
  EIGRP metric weight K1=1, K2=0, K3=1, K4=0, K5=0

RouterB##show ip protocols
Routing Protocol is "eigrp 220"
  Outgoing update filter list for all interfaces is not set
  Incoming update filter list for all interfaces is not set
  Default networks flagged in outgoing updates
  Default networks accepted from incoming updates
  EIGRP metric weight K1=1, K2=1, K3=1, K4=0, K5=0
```

A. EIGRP is running on RouterA and OSPF is running RouterB.

B. There is an ACL set on the routing protocol.

C. The AS numbers don't match.

D. There is no default network accepted from incoming updates.

E. The K values don't match.

F. A passive interface is set.

13. Which are true regarding EIGRP successor routes? (Choose two.)

A. A successor route is used by EIGRP to forward traffic to a destination.

B. Successor routes are saved in the topology table to be used if the primary route fails.

C. Successor routes are flagged as "active" in the routing table.

D. A successor route may be backed up by a feasible successor route.

E. Successor routes are stored in the neighbor table following the discovery process.

14. The remote RouterB router has a directly connected network of 10.255.255.64/27. Which of the following EIGRP network statements could you use so this directly connected network will be advertised under the EIGRP process? (Choose two.)

A. `network 10.255.255.64`

B. `network 10.255.255.64 0.0.0.31`

C. `network 10.255.255.64 0.0.0.0`

D. `network 10.255.255.64 0.0.0.15`

15. RouterA and RouterB are connected via their Serial 0/0 interfaces, but they have not formed an adjacency. Based on the following output, what could be the problem?

```
RouterA#sh ip protocols
Routing Protocol is "eigrp 220"
  Outgoing update filter list for all interfaces is not set
  Incoming update filter list for all interfaces is not set
  Default networks flagged in outgoing updates
  Default networks accepted from incoming updates
  EIGRP metric weight K1=1, K2=0, K3=1, K4=0, K5=0
  EIGRP maximum hopcount 100
  EIGRP maximum metric variance 2
  Redistributing: eigrp 220
  EIGRP NSF-aware route hold timer is 240s
  Automatic network summarization is in effect
  Maximum path: 4
  Routing for Networks:
    10.0.0.0
    172.16.0.0
    192.168.1.0
  Routing Information Sources:
    Gateway         Distance      Last Update
    (this router)         90      20:51:48
    192.168.1.2           90      00:22:58
    172.16.10.6           90      01:58:46
    172.16.10.2           90      01:59:52
  Distance: internal 90 external 170

RouterB#sh ip protocols
Routing Protocol is "eigrp 220"
  Outgoing update filter list for all interfaces is not set
  Incoming update filter list for all interfaces is not set
  Default networks flagged in outgoing updates
  Default networks accepted from incoming updates
  EIGRP metric weight K1=1, K2=0, K3=1, K4=0, K5=0
  EIGRP maximum hopcount 100
  EIGRP maximum metric variance 2
  Redistributing: eigrp 220
  EIGRP NSF-aware route hold timer is 240s
  Automatic network summarization is in effect
  Maximum path: 4
  Routing for Networks:
    10.0.0.0
    172.16.0.0
    192.168.1.0
 Passive Interface(s):
    Serial0/0
  Routing Information Sources:
    Gateway         Distance      Last Update
    (this router)         90      20:51:48
    192.168.1.2           90      00:22:58
    172.16.10.6           90      01:58:46
    172.16.10.2           90      01:59:52
  Distance: internal 90 external 170
```

A. The metric K values don't match.
B. The AS numbers don't match.
C. There is a passive interface on RouterB.
D. There is an ACL set on RouterA.

16. How many paths will EIGRPv6 load balance by default?
A. 16
B. 32
C. 4
D. None

17. What would your configurations be on RouterB based on the illustration? (Choose two.)

A. `(config)#router eigrp 10`
B. `(config)#ipv6 router eigrp 10`
C. `(config)#ipv6 router 2001:db8:3c4d:15::/64`
D. `(config-if)#ip eigrp 10`
E. `(config-if)#ipv6 eigrp 10`
F. `(config-if)#ipv6 router eigrp 10`

18. RouterA has a feasible successor not shown in the following output. Based on what you can learn from the output, which one of the following will be the successor for 2001:db8:c34d:18::/64 if the current successor fails?

```
via FE80::201:C9FF:FED0:3301 (29110112/33316), Serial0/0/0
via FE80::209:7CFF:FE51:B401 (4470112/42216), Serial0/0/1
via FE80::209:7CFF:FE51:B401 (2170112/2816), Serial0/0/2
```

A. `Serial0/0/0`
B. `Serial0/0/1`
C. `Serial0/0/2`
D. There is no feasible successor.

19. You have an internetwork as shown in the following illustration with routers running IOS 12.4. However, the two networks are not sharing routing table route entries. What is the problem?

```
RouterA#sh ip protocols
Routing Protocol is "eigrp 930"
  Outgoing update filter list for all interfaces is not set
  Incoming update filter list for all interfaces is not set
  Default networks flagged in outgoing updates
  Default networks accepted from incoming updates
  EIGRP metric weight K1=1, K2=0, K3=1, K4=0, K5=0
  EIGRP maximum hopcount 100
  EIGRP maximum metric variance 2
  Redistributing: eigrp 930
  EIGRP NSF-aware route hold timer is 240s
  Automatic network summarization is in effect
  Automatic address summarization:
    192.168.1.0/24 for FastEthernet0/0
      Summarizing with metric 2169856
    10.0.0.0/8 for Serial0/0
      Summarizing with metric 28160
 [output cut]

RouterB#sh ip protocols
Routing Protocol is "eigrp 930"
  Outgoing update filter list for all interfaces is not set
  Incoming update filter list for all interfaces is not set
  Default networks flagged in outgoing updates
  Default networks accepted from incoming updates
  EIGRP metric weight K1=1, K2=0, K3=1, K4=0, K5=0
  EIGRP maximum hopcount 100
  EIGRP maximum metric variance 3
  Redistributing: eigrp 930
  EIGRP NSF-aware route hold timer is 240s
  Automatic network summarization is in effect
  Maximum path: 4
  Routing for Networks:
    10.0.0.0
    192.168.1.0
 Passive Interface(s):
    Serial0/0
  Routing Information Sources:
    Gateway         Distance      Last Update
    (this router)         90      20:51:48
    192.168.1.2           90      00:22:58
    172.16.10.6           90      01:58:46
    172.16.10.2           90      01:59:52
  Distance: internal 90 external 170
```

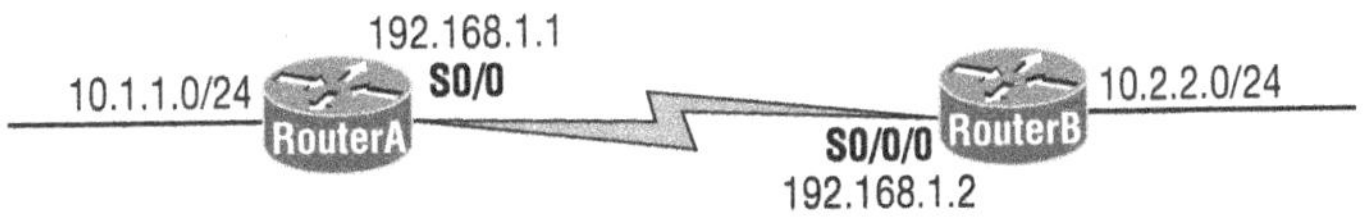

- **A.** The variances don't match between routers.
- **B.** The metrics are not valid between neighbors.
- **C.** There is a discontiguous network.
- **D.** There is a passive interface on RouterB.
- **E.** An ACL is set on the router.

20. Which should you look for when troubleshooting an adjacency? (Choose four.)

- **A.** Verify the AS numbers.
- **B.** Verify that you have the proper interfaces enabled for EIGRP.
- **C.** Make sure there are no mismatched K values.
- **D.** Check your passive interface settings.
- **E.** Make sure your remote routers are not connected to the Internet.
- **F.** If authentication is configured, make sure that all routers use different passwords.

Chapter 12

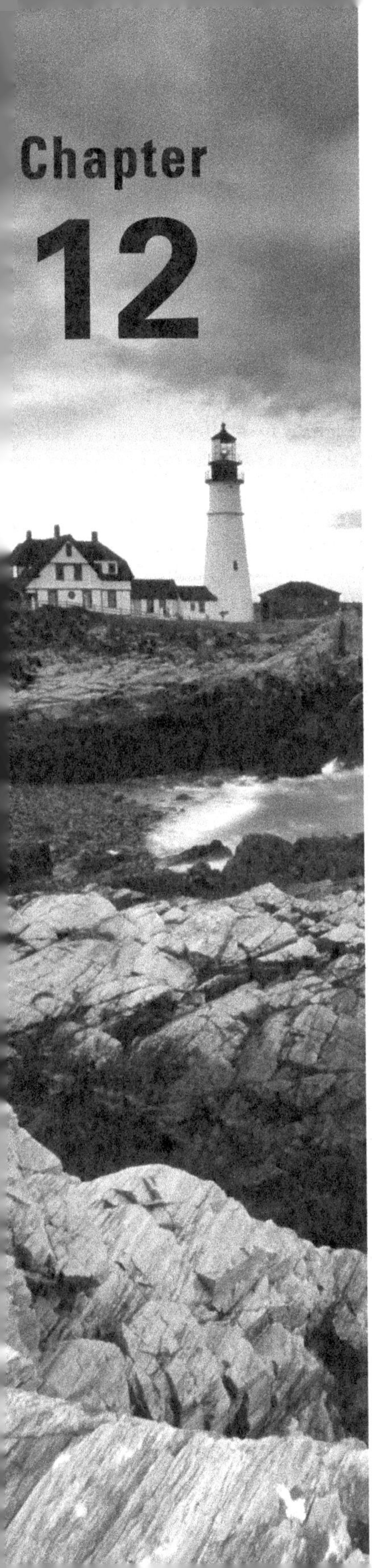

Layer 2 Switching

THE CCNA EXAM TOPICS COVERED IN THIS CHAPTER INCLUDE THE FOLLOWING:

✓ ***1.0 Network Fundamentals***

✓ ***1.13 Describe switching concepts***

- 1.13.a MAC learning and aging
- 1.13.b Frame switching
- 1.13.c Frame flooding
- 1.13.d MAC address table

✓ ***5.0 Security Fundamentals***

- 5.7 Configure Layer 2 security features (DHCP snooping, dynamic ARP inspection, and port security)

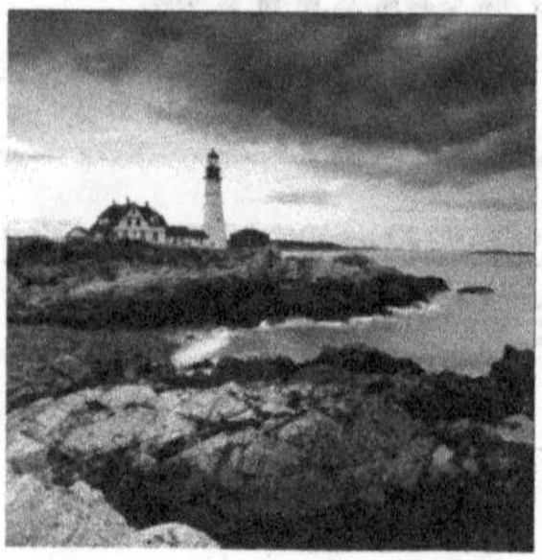

When Cisco brings up switching in their exam objectives, they mean layer 2 switching unless they say otherwise. Layer 2 switching is the process of using the hardware address of devices on a LAN to segment a network. So, in this chapter, we're going to cover the finer points of layer 2 switching to make sure you know exactly how it works.

You should already know that we rely on switching to break up large collision domains into smaller ones and that a collision domain is a network segment with two or more devices sharing the same bandwidth. A hub network is a good example of this type of technology, but since each port on a switch is actually its own collision domain, we can create a much more efficient network simply by replacing hubs with switches.

Switches have changed the way networks are designed and implemented. If a pure switched design is implemented well, the result will be a clean, cost-effective, and resilient internetwork. Coming up, I'll compare how networks were designed before and after switching technologies were introduced.

I'll be using three switches to begin configuring our switched network, and we'll continue configuring them in Chapter 13, "VLANs and Inter-VLAN Routing."

> **NOTE** To find bonus material, as well as Todd Lammle videos, practice questions, and hands-on labs, please see `www.lammle.com/ccna`.

Switching Services

Bridges use software to create and manage a Content Addressable Memory (CAM) filter table. Instead, the fast switches we use today rely on application-specific integrated circuits (ASICs) to build and maintain their MAC filter tables. This is a big difference, but it's still okay to think of a layer 2 switch as a multiport bridge because their basic reason for being is the same: to break up collision domains.

Layer 2 switches and bridges are faster than routers because they don't waste time looking at the Network layer header information; instead, they look at the frame's hardware addresses before deciding to either forward, flood, or drop the frame.

Unlike hubs, switches create private, dedicated collision domains and provide independent bandwidth exclusive on each port.

Here's a list of four important advantages we gain when using layer 2 switching:

- Hardware-based bridging (ASICs)
- Wire speed
- Low latency
- Low cost

A big reason layer 2 switching is so efficient is that no modification to the data packet takes place. The device only reads the frame encapsulating the packet, which makes the switching process considerably faster and less vulnerable to errors than routing processes are.

Plus, if you use layer 2 switching for both workgroup connectivity and network segmentation (breaking up collision domains), you can create more network segments than you can with traditional routed networks. Another nice benefit gained via layer 2 switching is that it increases bandwidth for each user because, again, each connection or interface into the switch is its own, self-contained collision domain.

Three Switch Functions at Layer 2

There are three distinct functions of layer 2 switching you need to remember: *address learning*, *forward/filter decisions*, and *loop avoidance*.

Address Learning Layer 2 switches remember the source hardware address of each frame received on an interface and enter this information into a MAC database called a *forward/filter table*.

Forward/Filter Decisions When a frame is received on an interface, the switch looks at the destination hardware address, then chooses the appropriate exit interface for it in the MAC database. This way, the frame is only forwarded out of the correct destination port.

Loop Avoidance If multiple connections between switches are created for redundancy, network loops can occur. Spanning Tree Protocol (STP) is used to prevent network loops while still permitting redundancy.

Next, I'm going to talk about address learning and forward/filtering decisions. Loop avoidance is beyond the scope of the objectives being covered in this chapter.

Address Learning

When a switch is first powered on, the MAC forward/filter table (CAM) is empty, as shown in Figure 12.1.

When a device transmits and an interface receives a frame, the switch places the frame's source address in the MAC forward/filter table, allowing it to refer to the precise interface the sending device is located on. The switch then has no choice but to flood the network with this frame out of every port except the source port because it has no idea where the destination device is actually located.

FIGURE 12.1 An empty forward/filter table on a switch

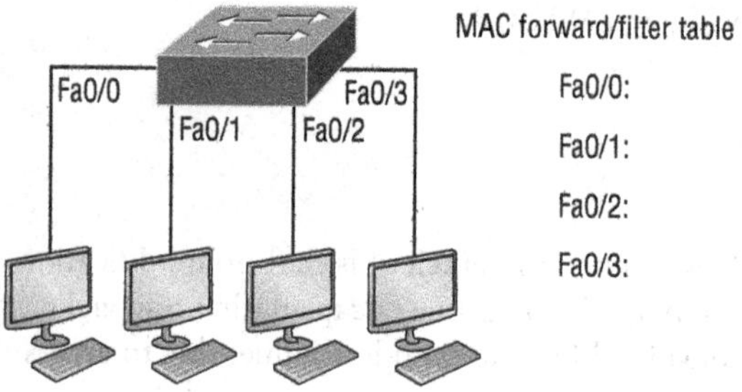

If a device answers this flooded frame and sends a frame back, then the switch will take the source address from that frame and place that MAC address in its database as well, associating this address with the interface that received the frame. Because the switch now has both of the relevant MAC addresses in its filtering table, the two devices can now make a point-to-point connection. The switch doesn't need to flood the frame as it did the first time because now the frames will only be forwarded between these two devices. This is exactly why layer 2 switches are so superior to hubs. In a hub network, all frames are forwarded out all ports every time—no matter what.

Figure 12.2 shows the processes involved in building a MAC database.

FIGURE 12.2 How switches learn hosts' locations

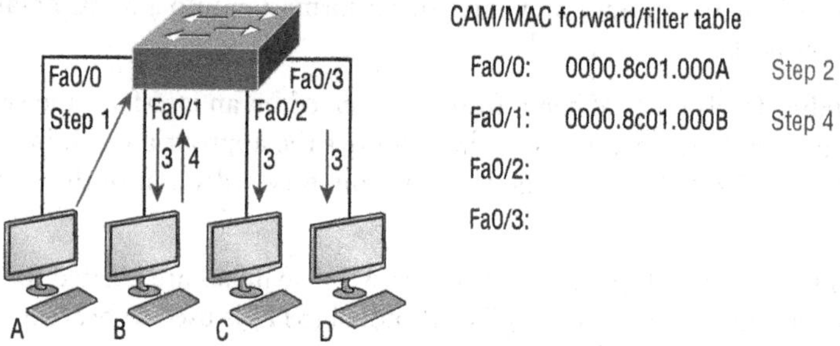

This figure shows four hosts attached to a switch. When the switch is powered on, it has nothing in its MAC address forward/filter table, just as in Figure 12.1. But when the hosts start communicating, the switch places the source hardware address of each frame into the table along with the port that the frame's source address corresponds to.

Let me give you an example of how a forward/filter table is populated using Figure 12.2:

1. Host A sends a frame to Host B. Host A's MAC address is 0000.8c01.000A, and Host B's MAC address is 0000.8c01.000B.
2. The switch receives the frame on the Fa0/0 interface and places the source address in the MAC address table.

3. Since the destination address isn't in the MAC database, the frame is forwarded out all interfaces except the source port.
4. Host B receives the frame and responds to Host A. The switch receives this frame on interface Fa0/1 and places the source hardware address in the MAC database.
5. Host A and Host B can now make a point-to-point connection and only these specific devices will receive the frames. Hosts C and D won't see the frames, nor will their MAC addresses be found in the database because they haven't sent a frame to the switch yet.

If Host A and Host B don't communicate to the switch again within a certain time period, the switch will flush their entries from the database to keep it current.

Forward/Filter Decisions

When a frame arrives at a switch interface, the destination hardware address is compared to the forward/filter MAC database. If the destination hardware address is known and listed in the database, the frame is only sent out of the appropriate exit interface. The switch won't transmit the frame out any interface except for the destination interface, which preserves bandwidth on the other network segments. This process is called *frame filtering*.

However, if the destination hardware address isn't listed in the MAC database, then the frame will be flooded out all active interfaces except the interface it was received on. If a device answers the flooded frame, the MAC database is then updated with the device's location—its correct interface.

If a host or server sends a broadcast on the LAN, by default, the switch will flood the frame out all active ports except the source port. Remember, the switch creates smaller collision domains, but it's always still one large broadcast domain by default.

In Figure 12.3, Host A sends a data frame to Host D. What do you think the switch will do when it receives the frame from Host A?

FIGURE 12.3 Forward/filter table

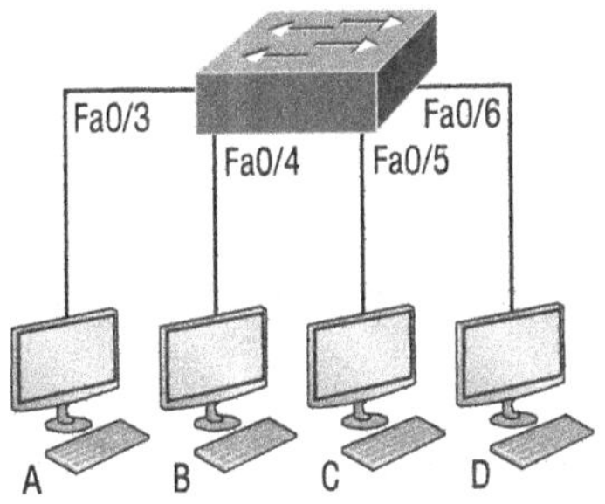


```
Switch# show mac address-table
VLAN    Mac Address       Ports
 1      0005.dccb.d74b    Fa0/4
 1      000a.f467.9e80    Fa0/5
 1      000a.f467.9e8b    Fa0/6
```

Let's examine Figure 12.4 to find the answer.

Since Host A's MAC address is not in the forward/filter table, the switch will add the source address and port to the MAC address table, then forward the frame to Host D. It's important to remember that the source MAC is always checked first to make sure it's in the CAM table. After that, if Host D's MAC address wasn't found in the forward/filter table, the switch would've flooded the frame out all ports except for port Fa0/3 because that's the specific port the frame was received on.

FIGURE 12.4 Forward/filter table answer

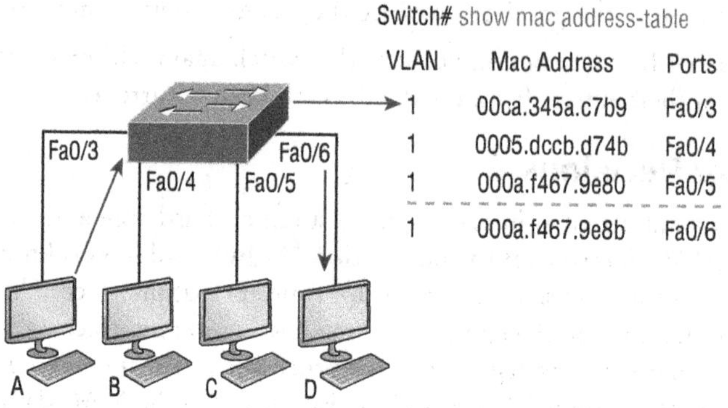

Now let's take a look at the output that results from using a `show mac address-table` command:

```
Switch#sh mac address-table
Vlan Mac Address Type Ports]]> ---- ----------- -------- -----
1 0005.dccb.d74b DYNAMIC Fa0/1
1 000a.f467.9e80 DYNAMIC Fa0/3
1 000a.f467.9e8b DYNAMIC Fa0/4
1 000a.f467.9e8c DYNAMIC Fa0/3
1 0010.7b7f.c2b0 DYNAMIC Fa0/3
1 0030.80dc.460b DYNAMIC Fa0/3
1 0030.9492.a5dd DYNAMIC Fa0/1
1 00d0.58ad.05f4 DYNAMIC Fa0/1
```

Now, let's say the preceding switch received a frame with the following MAC addresses:

Source MAC: **0005.dccb.d74b**

Destination MAC: **000a.f467.9e8c**

How will the switch handle this frame? The right answer is that the destination MAC address will be found in the MAC address table and the frame will only be forwarded out Fa0/3. Never forget that if the destination MAC address isn't found in the forward/filter table, the frame will be forwarded out all of the switch's ports except for the one on which it was originally received in an attempt to locate the destination device. Now that you can see the MAC address table and how switches add host addresses to the forward filter table, how do think we can secure it from unauthorized users?

Port Security

It's usually a bad idea to have your switches available for anyone to just plug into and play around with. We worry about wireless security, so why wouldn't we demand switch security just as much, if not more?

But just how do we actually prevent someone from simply plugging a host into one of our switch ports—or worse, adding a hub, switch, or access point into the Ethernet jack in their office? By default, MAC addresses will dynamically appear in your MAC forward/filter database, and you can stop them in their tracks by using port security!

Figure 12.5 shows two hosts connected to the single switch port Fa0/3 via either a hub or access point (AP).

FIGURE 12.5 "Port security" on a switch port restricts port access by MAC address.

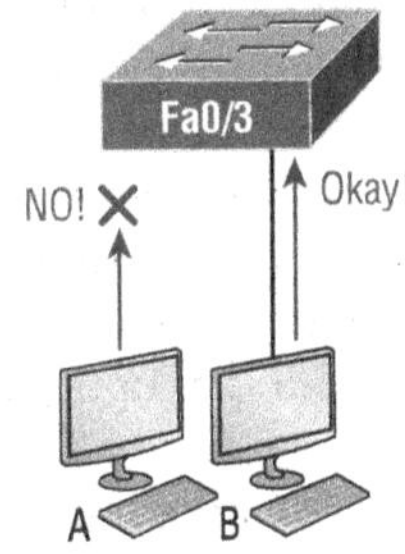

Port Fa0/3 is configured to observe and allow only certain MAC addresses to associate with the specific port. So, in this example, Host A is denied access, but Host B is allowed to associate with the port.

By using port security, you can limit the number of MAC addresses that can be assigned dynamically to a port, set static MAC addresses, and—here's my favorite part—set penalties for users who abuse your policy! Personally, I like to have the port shut down when the security policy is violated. Making abusers bring me a memo from their boss explaining why they violated the security policy is just so satisfying, so I'll also require something like that before I'll enable their port again. Things like this really help people remember to behave!

This is all good, but you still need to balance your particular security needs with the time that implementing and managing them will require. If you have tons of time on your hands, then go ahead and seriously lock your network down like a vault, but if you're busy like the rest of us, rest assured that there are ways to secure things nicely without an overwhelming amount of administrative overhead. First, and painlessly, always remember to shut down unused ports or assign them to an unused VLAN. All ports are enabled by default, so you need to make sure there's no access to unused switch ports!

Here are your options for configuring port security:

```
Switch#config t
Switch(config)#int f0/1
```

```
Switch(config-if)#switchport mode access
Switch(config-if)#switchport port-security
Switch(config-if)#switchport port-security ?
aging Port-security aging commands
mac-address Secure mac address
maximum Max secure addresses
violation Security violation mode
<cr>
```

Most Cisco switches ship with their ports in desirable mode, which means those ports will desire to trunk when they sense another switch has been connected. So, first, we need to change the port and make it an access port instead. If we don't do that, we won't be able to configure port security on it at all. Once that's out of the way, we can move on using our `port-security` commands, never forgetting to enable port security on the interface with the basic command `switchport port-security`. Notice that I did this *after* I made the port an access port!

The preceding output clearly illustrates that the `switchport port-security` command can be used with four options. While it's true you can use the `switchport port-security mac-address` *`mac-address`* command to assign individual MAC addresses to each switch port, if you go with that option, you'd better have boatloads of time on your hands!

You can configure the device to take one of the following actions when a security violation occurs by using the `switchport port-security` command:

- `Protect`: The protect violation mode drops packets with unknown source addresses until you remove enough secure MAC addresses to drop below the maximum value.
- `Restrict`: The restrict violation mode also drops packets with unknown source addresses until you remove enough secure MAC addresses to drop below the maximum value. It also generates a log message, causes the security violation counter to increment, and sends an SNMP trap.
- `Shutdown`: Shutdown is the default violation mode. The shutdown violation mode puts the interface into an error-disabled state immediately. The entire port is shut down. Also, in this mode, the system generates a log message, sends an SNMP trap, and increments the violation counter. To make the interface usable, you must do a `shut/no shut` on the interface.

If you want to set up a switch port to allow only one host per port and make sure the port will shut down if this rule is violated, use the following commands:

```
Switch(config-if)#switchport port-security maximum 1
Switch(config-if)#switchport port-security violation shutdown
```

These commands are probably the most popular because they prevent random users from connecting to a specific switch or access point in their office. The port security default that's immediately set on a port when it's enabled is `maximum 1` and `violation shutdown`. This sounds good, but the drawback is that it only allows a single MAC address to be used on the port. So, if anyone, including you, tries to add another host on that segment, the switch port will immediately enter error-disabled state and the port will turn amber. When that happens, you have to manually go into the switch and re-enable the port by cycling it with a `shutdown` and then a `no shutdown` command.

Probably one of my favorite commands is the `sticky` command—and not just because it's got a cool name. It also makes very cool things happen. You can find this command under the `mac-address` command:

```
Switch(config-if)#switchport port-security mac-address sticky
Switch(config-if)#switchport port-security maximum 2
Switch(config-if)#switchport port-security violation shutdown
```

Basically, the `sticky` command enables you to provide static MAC address security without having to type in absolutely everyone's MAC address on the network. I like things that save me time like that!

In the preceding example, the first two MAC addresses coming into the port "stick" to it as static addresses and will be placed in the running-config, but when a third address tried to connect, the port would shut down immediately.

Here's one more example: Figure 12.6 displays a host in a company lobby that needs to be secured against the Ethernet cable used by anyone other than one, authorized individual.

What can you do to ensure that only the MAC address of the lobby PC is allowed by switch port Fa0/1?

FIGURE 12.6 Protecting a PC in a lobby

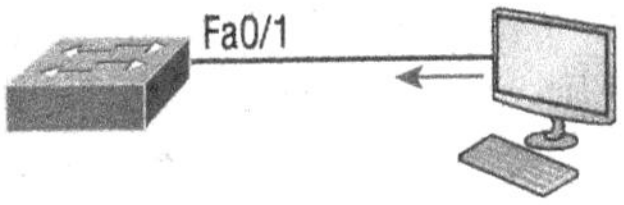

The solution is pretty straightforward because in this case, the defaults for port security will work well. All we have left to do is add a static MAC entry:

```
Switch(config-if)#switchport port-security
Switch(config-if)#switchport port-security violation restrict
Switch(config-if)#switchport port-security mac-address aa.bb.cc.dd.ee.ff
```

To protect the lobby PC, we would set the maximum allowed MAC addresses to `1` and the violation to `restrict` so the port doesn't get shut down every time someone tries to use the Ethernet cable (which would be constantly). By using `violation restrict`, the unauthorized frames would just be dropped. But did you notice that I enabled `port-security` and then set a static MAC address? Remember, as soon as you enable `port-security` on a port, it defaults to `violation shutdown` and a maximum of `1`. So, all I needed to do was change the violation mode and add the static MAC address!

Real World Scenario

Lobby PC Always Being Disconnected Becomes a Security Risk

At a large Fortune 500 company in San Jose, California, there was a PC in the lobby that held the company directory. With no security guard present in the lobby, the Ethernet cable connecting the PC was free game to all vendors, contractors, and visitors waiting in the lobby.

Port security to the rescue! When port security was enabled on the port with the `switchport port-security` command, the switch port connecting to the PC was automatically secured with the defaults of allowing only one MAC address to associate to the port and violation shutdown. However, the port was always going into err-shutdown mode whenever anyone tried to use the Ethernet port. When the violation mode was changed to restrict and a static MAC address was set for the port with the `switchport port-security mac-address` command, only the lobby PC was able to connect and communicate on the network! Problem solved!

Loop Avoidance

Redundant links between switches are important to have in place because they help prevent network failures in the event that one link stops working.

But while it's true that redundant links can be extremely helpful, they can also cause more problems than they solve! This is because frames can be flooded down all redundant links simultaneously, creating network loops as well as other evils. Here's a list of some of the ugliest problems that can occur:

- If no loop avoidance schemes are put in place, the switches will flood broadcasts endlessly throughout the internetwork. This is sometimes referred to as a *broadcast storm*, but most of the time, they're referred to in more unprintable ways!

  Figure 12.7 illustrates how a broadcast can be propagated throughout the network. Observe how a frame is continually being flooded through the internetwork's physical network media.

- A device can receive multiple copies of the same frame because that frame can arrive from different segments at the same time.

  Figure 12.8 demonstrates how a whole bunch of frames can arrive from multiple segments simultaneously.

  The server in the Figure 12.8 sends a unicast frame to Router C. Because it's a unicast frame, Switch A forwards the frame and Switch B provides the same service: it forwards the unicast. This is bad because it means that Router C receives that unicast frame twice, causing additional overhead on the network.

FIGURE 12.7 A broadcast storm

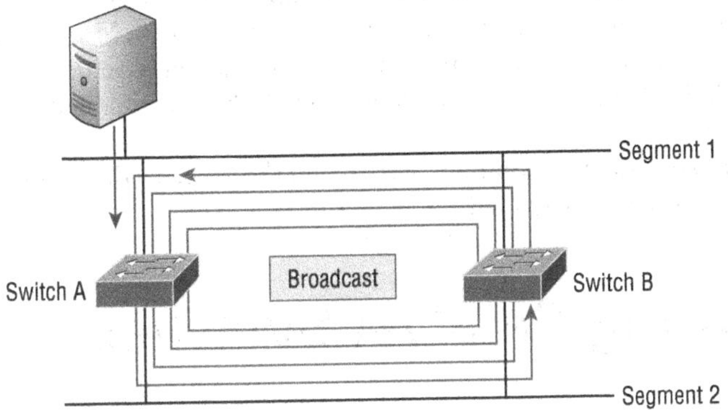

FIGURE 12.8 Multiple frame copies

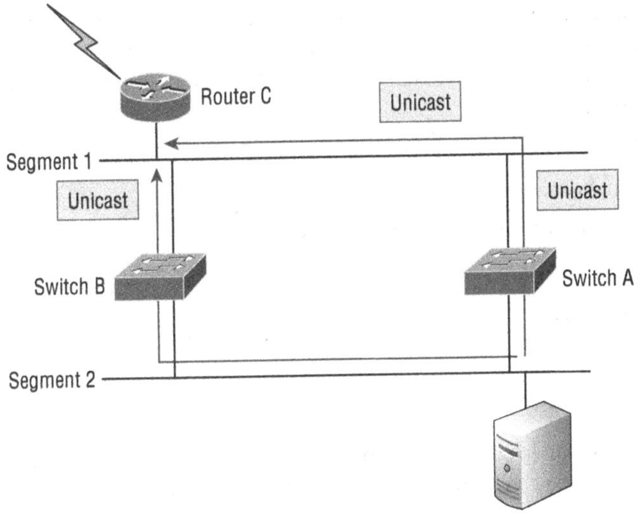

- You may have thought of this one: The MAC address filter table could be totally confused about the source device's location because the switch can receive the frame from more than one link. Worse, the bewildered switch could get so caught up in constantly updating the MAC filter table with source hardware address locations that it will fail to forward a frame! This is called *thrashing the MAC table*.
- One of the most vile events is when multiple loops propagate throughout a network. Loops can occur within other loops, and if a broadcast storm were to occur simultaneously, the network wouldn't be able to perform frame switching—period!

All of these problems spell disaster or close, and they're all really bad situations that must be avoided or fixed somehow. That's where the Spanning Tree Protocol comes into play. It was actually developed to solve every one of the problems I just told you about!

Now that I've explained the issues that can occur when you have redundant links, or when you have links that are improperly implemented, I'm sure you understand how vital it is to prevent them.

I'll be honest here—the best solutions are beyond the scope of this chapter. For now, let's focus on configuring some switching!

Configuring Catalyst Switches

You get a lot of variety when it comes to Cisco Catalyst switches. Some run 10 Mbps, whereas others can speed all the way up to 10 Gbps or higher switched ports with a combination of twisted-pair and fiber. These newer switches, like the 9000, also have more intelligence, so they can give you data fast—mixed media services, too!

Coming up, I'm going to show you how to start up and configure a Cisco Catalyst switch using the command-line interface (CLI). After you get the basic commands down in this chapter, you'll learn to configure virtual LANs (VLANs), plus Inter-Switch Link (ISL) and 802.1q trunking in the next one.

Here's a list of the basic tasks I'll be covering next:

- Administrative functions
- Configuring the IP address and subnet mask
- Setting the IP default gateway
- Setting port security
- Testing and verifying the network

NOTE: You can learn all about the Cisco family of Catalyst switches at `https://www.cisco.com/c/en/us/products/switches/index.html`.

Catalyst Switch Configuration

Before we actually get into configuring one of the Catalyst switches, I want you to be familiar with the boot process of these switches. Figure 12.9 shows a typical Cisco Catalyst switch.

The first thing I want to point out is that the console port for Catalyst switches is typically found on the back of the switch. On a smaller switch like the 3560 shown in the figure, the console is right in the front to make it easier to use. The eight-port 2960 looks exactly the same.

FIGURE 12.9 A Cisco Catalyst switch

If the POST completes successfully, the system LED turns green, but if the POST fails, it will turn amber. That amber glow is an ominous thing—typically fatal. So, keep a spare switch around, especially in case a production switch dies on you! The bottom button is used to indicate which lights are providing Power over Ethernet (PoE). You can see this by pressing the Mode button. The PoE is a very cool feature because it allows you to power your access point and phone by just connecting them into the switch with an Ethernet cable—sweet.

Figure 12.10 shows the switched network we'll be working on.

FIGURE 12.10 Our switched network

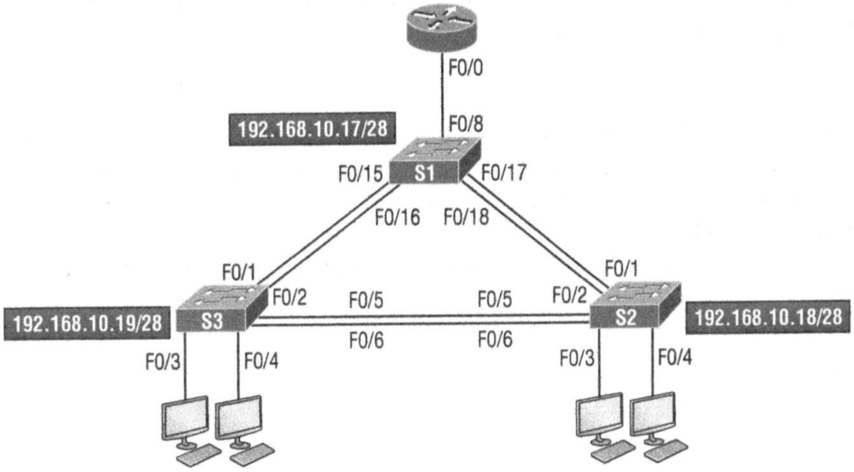

You can use any layer 2 switches for this chapter to follow the configuration, but when we get to Chapter 13, you'll need at least one router plus a layer 3 switch, like my 3560.

Now, if we connect our switches to each other, as shown in Figure 12.10, we'll first need a crossover cable between the switches. My 3560 switches autodetect the connection type, so I was able to use straight-through cables. (Not all switches autodetect the cable type.) Different switches have different needs and abilities, so keep this in mind when connecting various switches together. Make a mental note that in the Cisco exam objectives, switches never autodetect!

Okay, so when you first connect the switch ports to each other, the link lights are amber and then turn green, indicating normal operation. What you're actually watching is spanning-tree converging, and this process takes around 50 seconds with no extensions enabled. If you connect into a switch port and the switch port LED is alternating green and amber, it means the port is experiencing errors. When this happens, check the host NIC or the cabling, possibly even the duplex settings on the port to make sure they match the host setting.

Do We Need to Put an IP Address on a Switch?

Absolutely not! Switches have all ports enabled and ready to rock. Take the switch out of the box, plug it in, and the switch starts learning MAC addresses in the CAM. So, why would I need an IP address since switches are providing layer 2 services? Because you still need it for in-band management purposes! Telnet, SSH, SNMP, etc., all need an IP address in order to communicate with the switch through the network in-band. Remember, since all ports are enabled by default, you need to shut down unused ports or assign them to an unused VLAN for security reasons.

So, where do we put this management IP address the switch needs for management purposes? On the predictably named management VLAN interface—a routed interface on every Cisco switch called interface VLAN 1. This management interface can be changed, and Cisco recommends that you do change this to a different management interface for better security.

Let's configure our switches now.

S1

We're going to begin by connecting into each switch and setting the administrative functions. We'll also assign an IP address to each switch, but as I said, doing that isn't really necessary to make our network function. The only reason we're going to do that is so we can manage/administer it remotely—via Telnet. for example. Let's use a simple IP scheme like 192.168.10.16/28. This mask should be familiar to you! Check out the following output:

```
Switch>en
Switch#config t
Switch(config)#hostname S1
S1(config)#enable secret todd
S1(config)#int f0/15
S1(config-if)#description 1st connection to S3
S1(config-if)#int f0/16
S1(config-if)#description 2nd connection to S3
S1(config-if)#int f0/17
S1(config-if)#description 1st connection to S2
S1(config-if)#int f0/18
S1(config-if)#description 2nd connection to S2
S1(config-if)#int f0/8
```

```
S1(config-if)#desc Connection to IVR
S1(config-if)#line con 0
S1(config-line)#password console
S1(config-line)#login
S1(config-line)#line vty 0 15
S1(config-line)#password telnet
S1(config-line)#login
S1(config-line)#int vlan 1
S1(config-if)#ip address 192.168.10.17 255.255.255.240
S1(config-if)#no shut
S1(config-if)#exit
S1(config)#banner motd #this is my S1 switch#
S1(config)#exit
S1#copy run start
Destination filename [startup-config]? [enter]
Building configuration...
[OK]
S1#
```

The first thing to notice here is that there's no IP address configured on the switch's physical interfaces. Since all ports on a switch are enabled by default, there's not really a whole lot to configure. The IP address is configured under a logical interface, called a management domain or VLAN. You can use the default VLAN 1 to manage a switched network just as we're doing here, but you can opt to use a different VLAN for management.

The rest of the configuration is basically the same as the process you go through for router configuration. So, remember: no IP addresses on physical switch interfaces, no routing protocols, and so on. We're performing layer 2 switching at this point, not routing! Also, make a note to self that there is no AUX port on Cisco switches.

S2

Here is the S2 configuration:

```
Switch#config t
Switch(config)#hostname S2
S2(config)#enable secret todd
S2(config)#int f0/1
S2(config-if)#desc 1st connection to S1
S2(config-if)#int f0/2
S2(config-if)#desc 2nd connection to s2
S2(config-if)#int f0/5
S2(config-if)#desc 1st connection to S3
S2(config-if)#int f0/6
```

```
S2(config-if)#desc 2nd connection to s3
S2(config-if)#line con 0
S2(config-line)#password console
S2(config-line)#login
S2(config-line)#line vty 0 15
S2(config-line)#password telnet
S2(config-line)#login
S2(config-line)#int vlan 1
S2(config-if)#ip address 192.168.10.18 255.255.255.240
S2(config)#exit
S2#copy run start
Destination filename [startup-config]?[enter]
Building configuration...
[OK]
S2#
```

We should now be able to ping from S2 to S1. Let's try it:

```
S2#ping 192.168.10.17
Type escape sequence to abort.
Sending 5, 100-byte ICMP Echos to 192.168.10.17, timeout is 2 seconds:
.!!!!
Success rate is 80 percent (4/5), round-trip min/avg/max = 1/1/1 ms
S2#
```

Okay, why did I get only four pings to work instead of five? The first period [.] is a timeout, but the exclamation point [!] is a success.

It's a good question, and here's the answer: the first ping didn't work because of the time that ARP takes to resolve the IP address to its corresponding hardware MAC address.

S3

Check out the S3 switch configuration:

```
Switch>en
Switch#config t
SW-3(config)#hostname S3
S3(config)#enable secret todd
S3(config)#int f0/1
S3(config-if)#desc 1st connection to S1
S3(config-if)#int f0/2
S3(config-if)#desc 2nd connection to S1
S3(config-if)#int f0/5
S3(config-if)#desc 1st connection to S2
```

```
S3(config-if)#int f0/6
S3(config-if)#desc 2nd connection to S2
S3(config-if)#line con 0
S3(config-line)#password console
S3(config-line)#login
S3(config-line)#line vty 0 15
S3(config-line)#password telnet
S3(config-line)#login
S3(config-line)#int vlan 1
S3(config-if)#ip address 192.168.10.19 255.255.255.240
S3(config-if)#no shut
S3(config-if)#banner motd #This is the S3 switch#
S3(config)#exit
S3#copy run start
Destination filename [startup-config]?[enter]
Building configuration...
[OK]
S3#
```

Let's ping to S1 and S2 from the S3 switch and see what happens:

```
S3#ping 192.168.10.17
Type escape sequence to abort.
Sending 5, 100-byte ICMP Echos to 192.168.10.17, timeout is 2 seconds:
.!!!!
Success rate is 80 percent (4/5), round-trip min/avg/max = 1/3/9 ms
S3#ping 192.168.10.18
Type escape sequence to abort.
Sending 5, 100-byte ICMP Echos to 192.168.10.18, timeout is 2 seconds:
.!!!!
Success rate is 80 percent (4/5), round-trip min/avg/max = 1/3/9 ms
S3#sh ip arp
Protocol Address Age (min) Hardware Addr Type Interface
Internet 192.168.10.17 0 001c.575e.c8c0 ARPA Vlan1
Internet 192.168.10.18 0 b414.89d9.18c0 ARPA Vlan1
Internet 192.168.10.19 - ecc8.8202.82c0 ARPA Vlan1
S3#
```

In the output of the `show ip arp` command, the dash (-) in the minutes column means that it is the physical interface of the device.

Now, before moving on to verifying the switch configurations, there's one more command you need to know about, even though we don't really need it in our current network because we don't have a router involved yet. It's the `ip default-gateway` command. If you want to manage your switches from outside your LAN, you must set a default gateway on the switches just as you would with a host, and you do this from global config. Here's an example where we introduce our router with an IP address using the last IP address in our subnet range:

```
S3#config t
S3(config)#ip default-gateway 192.168.10.30
```

Now that we have all three switches basically configured, let's have some fun with them!

Port Security

A secured switch port can associate anywhere from 1 to 8,192 MAC addresses, but the 3560s I am using can support only 6,144—but that's more than enough. You can choose to allow the switch to learn these values dynamically, or you can set static addresses for each port using the `switchport port-security mac-address` *`mac-address`* command.

Let's set port security on our S3 switch now. Ports Fa0/3 and Fa0/4 will have only one device connected in our lab. By using port security, we're assured that no other device can connect once our hosts in ports Fa0/3 and in Fa0/4 are connected. Here's how to easily do that with just a couple of commands:

```
S3#config t
S3(config)#int range f0/3-4
S3(config-if-range)#switchport mode access
S3(config-if-range)#switchport port-security
S3(config-if-range)#do show port-security int f0/3
Port Security : Enabled
Port Status : Secure-down
Violation Mode : Shutdown
Aging Time : 0 mins
Aging Type : Absolute
SecureStatic Address Aging : Disabled
Maximum MAC Addresses : 1
Total MAC Addresses : 0
Configured MAC Addresses : 0
Sticky MAC Addresses : 0
Last Source Address:Vlan : 0000.0000.0000:0
Security Violation Count : 0
```

The first command sets the mode of the ports to "access" ports. These ports must be access or trunk ports to enable port security. By using the command `switchport port-security` on the interface, I've enabled port security with a maximum MAC address of 1 and violation of shutdown. These are the defaults, and you can see them in the highlighted output of the `show port-security int f0/3` command in the preceding code.

Port security is enabled, as displayed on the first line, but the second line shows Secure-down because I haven't connected my hosts into the ports yet. Once I do, the status will show Secure-up and would become Secure-shutdown if a violation occurs.

I've just got to point out this important fact one more time: It's very important to remember that you can set parameters for port security but it won't work until you enable port security at the interface level. Notice the output for port F0/6:

```
S3#config t
S3(config)#int range f0/6
S3(config-if-range)#switchport mode access
S3(config-if-range)#switchport port-security violation restrict
S3(config-if-range)#do show port-security int f0/6
Port Security : Disabled
Port Status : Secure-up
Violation Mode : restrict
[output cut]
```

Port Fa0/6 has been configured with a violation of restrict, but the first line shows that port security has not been enabled on the port yet. Remember, you must use this command at the interface level to enable port security on a port:

```
S3(config-if-range)#switchport port-security
```

There are two other modes you can use instead of just shutting down the port. The restrict and protect modes mean that another host can connect up to the maximum MAC addresses allowed, but after the maximum has been met, all frames will just be dropped and the port won't be shut down. Both the restrict and shutdown violation modes alert you via SNMP that a violation has occurred on a port. You can then call the abuser and tell them they're busted—you can see them, you know what they did last summer, and they're in trouble!

If you've configured ports with the violation shutdown command, then the ports will look like this when a violation occurs:

```
S3#sh port-security int f0/3
Port Security : Enabled
Port Status : Secure-shutdown
Violation Mode : Shutdown
Aging Time : 0 mins
Aging Type : Absolute
SecureStatic Address Aging : Disabled
Maximum MAC Addresses : 1
Total MAC Addresses : 2
Configured MAC Addresses : 0
Sticky MAC Addresses : 0
Last Source Address:Vlan : 0013:0ca69:00bb3:00ba8:1
Security Violation Count : 1
```

Here you can see that the port is in Secure-shutdown mode, and the light for the port would be amber. To enable the port again, you'd need to do this:

```
S3(config-if)#shutdown
S3(config-if)#no shutdown
```

Let's verify our switch configurations before we move onto VLANs in the next chapter. Beware that even though some switches will show err-disabled instead of Secure-shutdown as my switch shows, there is no difference between the two.

Verifying Cisco Catalyst Switches

The first thing I like to do with any router or switch is run through the configurations with a show running-config command. Why? Because doing so gives me a really great overview of each device. It's time consuming, and showing you all the configs would take up way too many pages in this book. Besides, we can run other commands that will still stock us up with really good information.

For example, to verify the IP address set on a switch, we can use the show interface command. Here's the output:

```
S3#sh int vlan 1
Vlan1 is up, line protocol is up
Hardware is EtherSVI, address is ecc8.8202.82c0 (bia ecc8.8202.82c0)
Internet address is 192.168.10.19/28
MTU 1500 bytes, BW 1000000 Kbit/sec, DLY 10 usec,
reliability 255/255, txload 1/255, rxload 1/255
Encapsulation ARPA, loopback not set
[output cut]
```

The previous output shows the interface is in up/up status. Remember to always check this interface, either with this command or the show ip interface brief command. A lot of people tend to forget that this interface is shutdown by default.

NOTE: Never forget that IP addresses aren't needed on a switch in order for it to operate. The only reason we would set an IP address, mask, and default gateway is for management purposes.

show mac address-table

I'm sure you remember being shown this command earlier in the chapter. Using it displays the forward filter table, also called a content addressable memory (CAM) table. Here's the output from the S1 switch:

```
S3#sh mac address-table
Mac Address Table]]> -------------------------------------------
Vlan Mac Address Type Ports]]> ---- ----------- -------- -----
```

```
All 0100.0ccc.cccc STATIC CPU
[output cut]
1 000e.83b2.e34b DYNAMIC Fa0/1
1 0011.1191.556f DYNAMIC Fa0/1
1 0011.3206.25cb DYNAMIC Fa0/1
1 001a.2f55.c9e8 DYNAMIC Fa0/1
1 001a.4d55.2f7e DYNAMIC Fa0/1
1 001c.575e.c891 DYNAMIC Fa0/1
1 b414.89d9.1886 DYNAMIC Fa0/5
1 b414.89d9.1887 DYNAMIC Fa0/6
```

The switches use base MAC addresses, which are assigned to the CPU. The first one listed is the base MAC address of the switch. From the preceding output, you can see that we have six MAC addresses dynamically assigned to Fa0/1, meaning that port Fa0/1 is connected to another switch. Ports Fa0/5 and Fa0/6 only have one MAC address assigned, and all ports are assigned to VLAN 1.

Let's take a look at the S2 switch CAM and see what we can find out.

```
S2#sh mac address-table
Mac Address Table]]> -------------------------------------------
Vlan Mac Address Type Ports]]> ---- ----------- -------- -----
All 0100.0ccc.cccc STATIC CPU
[output cut
1 000e.83b2.e34b DYNAMIC Fa0/5
1 0011.1191.556f DYNAMIC Fa0/5
1 0011.3206.25cb DYNAMIC Fa0/5
1 001a.4d55.2f7e DYNAMIC Fa0/5
1 581f.aaff.86b8 DYNAMIC Fa0/5
1 ecc8.8202.8286 DYNAMIC Fa0/5
1 ecc8.8202.82c0 DYNAMIC Fa0/5
Total Mac Addresses for this criterion: 27
S2#
```

This output tells us that we have seven MAC addresses assigned to Fa0/5, which is our connection to S3. But where's port 6? Since port 6 is a redundant link to S3, STP placed Fa0/6 into blocking mode.

Assigning Static MAC Addresses

You can set a static MAC address in the MAC address table, but like setting static MAC port security without the `sticky` command, it's a ton of work. Just in case you want to do it, here's how:

```
S3(config)#mac address-table ?
aging-time Set MAC address table entry maximum age
learning Enable MAC table learning feature
```

```
move Move keyword
notification Enable/Disable MAC Notification on the switch
static static keyword
S3(config)#mac address-table static aaaa.bbbb.cccc vlan 1 int fa0/7
S3(config)#do show mac address-table
Mac Address Table]]> -------------------------------------------
Vlan Mac Address Type Ports]]> ---- ----------- -------- -----
All 0100.0ccc.cccc STATIC CPU
[output cut]
1 000e.83b2.e34b DYNAMIC Fa0/1
1 0011.1191.556f DYNAMIC Fa0/1
1 0011.3206.25cb DYNAMIC Fa0/1
1 001a.4d55.2f7e DYNAMIC Fa0/1
1 001b.d40a.0538 DYNAMIC Fa0/1
1 001c.575e.c891 DYNAMIC Fa0/1
1 aaaa.bbbb.0ccc STATIC Fa0/7
[output cut]
Total Mac Addresses for this criterion: 59
```

The left side of the output shows that a static MAC address has now been assigned permanently to interface Fa0/7 and, it's also been assigned to VLAN 1 only.

This chapter offered lots of great information. You've learned a lot and just maybe even had a little fun along the way! You've configured and verified all switches and set port security, which means you're ready to learn all about virtual LANs.

I'm going to save all our switch configurations so we'll be able to start right from here in Chapter 13.

Summary

In this chapter, I talked about the differences between switches and bridges and how they both work at layer 2. They create MAC address forward/filter tables in order to make decisions on whether to forward or flood a frame.

Although everything in this chapter is important, I wrote two port-security sections: one to provide a foundation and one with a configuration example. You must know both these sections in detail.

I also covered some problems that can occur if you have multiple links between bridges (switches).

Finally, I went through a detailed configuration of Cisco's Catalyst switches, including verifying the configuration itself.

Exam Essentials

Remember the three switch functions. Address learning, forward/filter decisions, and loop avoidance are the functions of a switch.

Remember the command `show mac address-table`. The command `show mac address-table` will show you the forward/filter table used on the LAN switch.

Understand the reason for port security. Port security restricts access to a switch based on MAC addresses.

Know the command to enable port security. To enable security on a port, you must first make sure the port is an access port with `switchport mode access` and then use the `switchport port-security` command at the interface level. You can set the port security parameters before or after enabling port security.

Know the commands to verify port security. To verify port security, use the `show port-security`, `show port-security interface` *`interface`*, and `show running-config` commands.

Written Lab

You can find the answers to this lab in Appendix A, "Answers to the Written Labs."

Write the answers to the following questions:

1. Which command will show you the forward/filter table?
2. If a destination MAC address is not in the forward/filter table, what will the switch do with the frame?
3. What are the three switch functions at layer 2?
4. If a frame is received on a switch port and the source MAC address is not in the forward/filter table, what will the switch do?
5. What are the default modes for a switch port configured with port security?

Review Questions

You can find the answers to these questions in Appendix B, "Answers to the Review Questions."

1. Which of the following statements is *not* true with regard to layer 2 switching?

   A. Layer 2 switches and bridges are faster than routers because they don't take up time looking at the Data Link layer header information.

   B. Layer 2 switches and bridges look at the frame's hardware addresses before deciding to either forward, flood, or drop the frame.

   C. Switches create private, dedicated collision domains and provide independent bandwidth on each port.

   D. Switches use application-specific integrated circuits (ASICs) to build and maintain their MAC filter tables.

2. Type the command that generated the last entry in the MAC address table shown. Type the command only, without the prompt.

```
Mac Address Table
-------------------------------------------
Vlan    Mac Address       Type        Ports
----    -----------       --------    -----
 All    0100.0ccc.cccc    STATIC      CPU
[output cut]
   1    000e.83b2.e34b    DYNAMIC     Fa0/1
   1    0011.1191.556f    DYNAMIC     Fa0/1
   1    0011.3206.25cb    DYNAMIC     Fa0/1
   1    001a.4d55.2f7e    DYNAMIC     Fa0/1
   1    001b.d40a.0538    DYNAMIC     Fa0/1
   1    001c.575e.c891    DYNAMIC     Fa0/1
   1    aaaa.bbbb.0ccc    STATIC      Fa0/7
```

3. In the diagram shown, what will the switch do if a frame with a destination MAC address of 000a.f467.63b1 is received on Fa0/4? (Choose all that apply.)

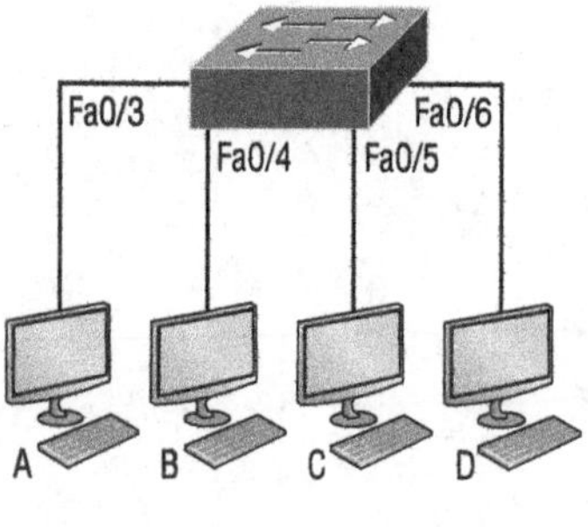

Switch# show mac address-table

VLAN	Mac Address	Ports
1	0005.dccb.d74b	Fa0/4
1	000a.f467.9e80	Fa0/5
1	000a.f467.9e8b	Fa0/6

A. Drop the frame.
B. Send the frame out of Fa0/3.
C. Send the frame out of Fa0/4.
D. Send the frame out of Fa0/5.
E. Send the frame out of Fa0/6.

4. Write the command that generated the following output.

```
          Mac Address Table
-------------------------------------------

Vlan    Mac Address       Type        Ports
----    -----------       --------    -----
 All    0100.0ccc.cccc    STATIC      CPU
[output cut]
   1    000e.83b2.e34b    DYNAMIC     Fa0/1
   1    0011.1191.556f    DYNAMIC     Fa0/1
   1    0011.3206.25cb    DYNAMIC     Fa0/1
   1    001a.2f55.c9e8    DYNAMIC     Fa0/1
   1    001a.4d55.2f7e    DYNAMIC     Fa0/1
   1    001c.575e.c891    DYNAMIC     Fa0/1
   1    b414.89d9.1886    DYNAMIC     Fa0/5
   1    b414.89d9.1887    DYNAMIC     Fa0/6
```

5. In the work area draw the functions of a switch from the list on the left to the right.

Address learning	Target 1
Packet forwarding	Target 2
Layer three security	Target 3
Forward/filter decisions	
Loop avoidance	

6. What statement(s) is/are true about the following output? (Choose all that apply.)

```
S3#sh port-security int f0/3
Port Security              : Enabled
Port Status                : Secure-shutdown
Violation Mode             : Shutdown
Aging Time                 : 0 mins
Aging Type                 : Absolute
SecureStatic Address Aging : Disabled
Maximum MAC Addresses      : 1
Total MAC Addresses        : 2
Configured MAC Addresses   : 0
```

```
Sticky MAC Addresses          : 0
Last Source Address:Vlan      : 0013:0ca69:00bb3:00ba8:1
Security Violation Count      : 1
```

A. The port light for F0/3 will be amber in color.

B. The F0/3 port is forwarding frames.

C. This problem will resolve itself in a few minutes.

D. This port requires the `shutdown` command to function.

7. Write the command that would limit the number of MAC addresses allowed on a port to 2. Write only the command and not the prompt.

8. Which of the following commands in the configuration, is a prerequisite for the other commands to function?

```
S3#config t
S(config)#int fa0/3
S3(config-if#switchport port-security
S3(config-if#switchport port-security maximum 3
S3(config-if#switchport port-security violation restrict
S3(config-if#Switchport mode-security aging time 10
```

A. `switchport mode-security aging time 10`

B. `switchport port-security`

C. `switchport port-security maximum 3`

D. `switchport port-security violation restrict`

9. Which of the following is *not* an issue addressed by STP?

A. Broadcast storms

B. Gateway redundancy

C. A device receiving multiple copies of the same frame

D. Constant updating of the MAC filter table

10. What issue arises when redundancy exists between switches is shown in the figure?

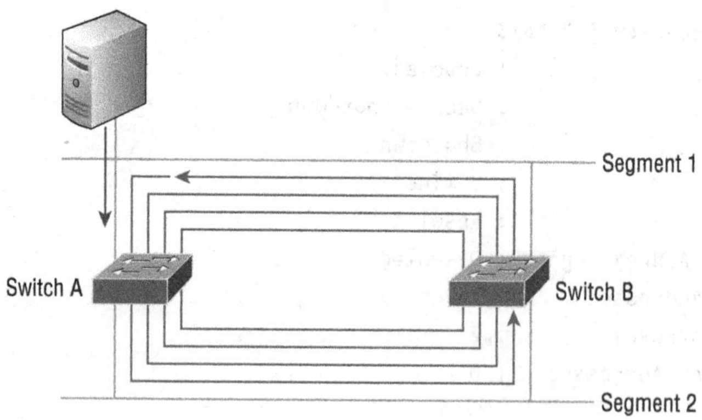

A. Broadcast storm

B. Routing loop

C. Port violation

D. Loss of gateway

11. Which of the following switch port violation modes will alert you via SNMP that a violation has occurred on a port? (Choose two.)

A. Restrict

B. Protect

C. Shutdown

D. Err-disable

12. _________ is the loop avoidance mechanism used by switches.

13. Write the command that must be present on any switch that you need to manage from a different subnet.

14. On which interface have you configured an IP address for a switch?

A. `int fa0/0`

B. `int vty 0 15`

C. `int vlan 1`

D. `int s/0/0`

15. Which Cisco IOS command is used to verify the port security configuration of a switch port?

A. `show interfaces port-security`

B. `show port-security interface`

C. `show ip interface`

D. `show interfaces switchport`

16. Write the command that will save a dynamically learned MAC address in the running-configuration of a Cisco switch?

17. Which of the following methods will ensure that only one specific host can connect to port F0/3 on a switch? (Choose two. Each correct answer is a separate solution.)

A. Configure port security on F0/3 to accept traffic other than the MAC address of the host.

B. Configure the MAC address of the host as a static entry associated with port F0/3.

C. Configure an inbound access control list on port F0/3 limiting traffic to the IP address of the host.

D. Configure port security on F0/3 to accept traffic only from the MAC address of the host.

18. What will be the effect of executing the following command on port F0/1?

```
switch(config-if)# switchport port-security mac-address 00C0.35F0.8301
```

A. The command configures an inbound access control list on port F0/1, limiting traffic to the IP address of the host.

B. The command expressly prohibits the MAC address of 00c0.35F0.8301 as an allowed host on the switch port.

C. The command encrypts all traffic on the port from the MAC address of 00c0.35F0.8301.

D. The command statically defines the MAC address of 00c0.35F0.8301 as an allowed host on the switch port.

19. The conference room has a switch port available for use by the presenter during classes, and each presenter uses the same PC attached to the port. You would like to prevent other PCs from using that port. You have completely removed the former configuration in order to start anew. Which of the following steps is *not* required to prevent any other PCs from using that port?

A. Enable port security.

B. Assign the MAC address of the PC to the port.

C. Make the port an access port.

D. Make the port a trunk port.

20. Write the command required to disable the port if a security violation occurs. Write only the command and not the prompt.

Chapter 13

VLANs and Inter-VLAN Routing

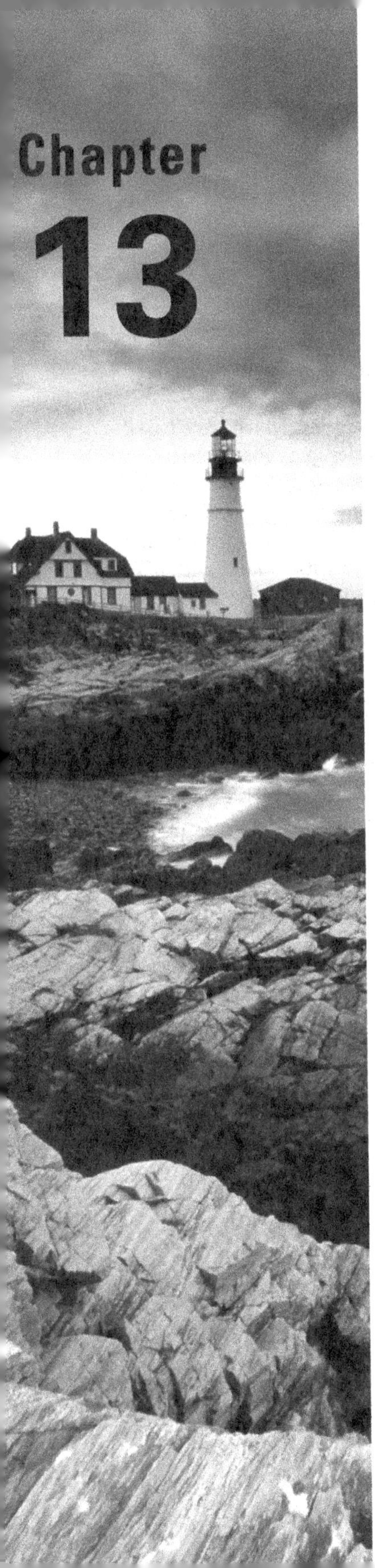

THE FOLLOWING CCNA EXAM TOPICS ARE COVERED IN THIS CHAPTER:

✓ ***2.0 Network Access***

- 2.1 Configure and verify VLANs (normal range) spanning multiple switches
  - 2.1.a Access ports (data and voice)
  - 2.1.b Default VLAN
  - 2.1.c Connectivity
- 2.2 Configure and verify interswitch connectivity
  - 2.2.a Trunk ports
  - 2.2.b 802.1Q
  - 2.2.c Native VLAN

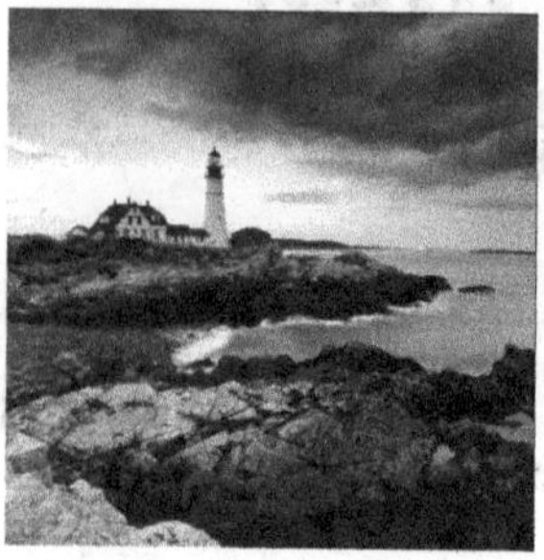

By default, switches break up collision domains, and routers break up broadcast domains.

In contrast to the networks of yesterday, which were based on collapsed backbones, and thanks to switches, today's network design is characterized by a flatter architecture. So now what? How do we break up broadcast domains in a pure switched internetwork? By creating virtual local area networks (VLANs). A VLAN is a logical grouping of network users and resources connected to administratively defined ports on a switch. When you create VLANs, you can create smaller broadcast domains within a layer 2 switched internetwork by assigning different ports on the switch to service different subnetworks. A VLAN is treated like its own subnet or broadcast domain, meaning frames broadcast onto the network are only switched between the ports logically grouped within the same VLAN.

So, does this mean we no longer need routers? Maybe yes, maybe no. It really depends on your specific networking needs and goals. By default, hosts in a specific VLAN can't communicate with hosts that are members of another VLAN, so if you want inter-VLAN communication, the answer is that you still need a router or inter-VLAN Routing (IVR).

This chapter walks you through exactly what a VLAN is and how VLAN memberships are used in a switched networking environment. You'll learn what a trunk link is as well as how to configure and verify them.

Toward the end of this chapter, I'll demonstrate how inter-VLAN communication works by introducing a router into our switched network.

Of course, we'll be working with the same, switched network layout we used in the last chapter. We'll create VLANs, implement trunking, and configure inter-VLAN routing on a layer 3 switch by building switched virtual interfaces (SVIs).

NOTE: To find bonus material, as well as Todd Lammle videos, practice questions, and hands-on labs, please see `www.lammle.com/ccna`.

VLAN Basics

Figure 13.1 illustrates the flat network architecture that used to be standard for layer 2 switched networks. With this type of configuration, every broadcast packet transmitted is seen by every device on the network, regardless of whether the device needs to receive that data or not.

FIGURE 13.1 Flat network structure

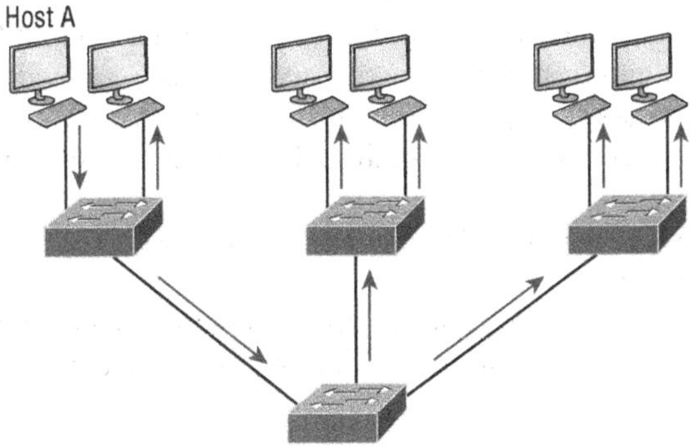

By default, routers allow broadcasts to occur only within the originating network, whereas switches forward broadcasts to all segments. The reason it's called a *flat network* is because it's one *broadcast domain*, not because the actual design is physically flat. In Figure 13.1, Host A is sending out a broadcast, and all ports on all switches are forwarding it—all except the port that originally received it.

Now, check out Figure 13.2. It illustrates a switched network and shows Host A sending a frame with Host D as its destination. Clearly, the important factor here is that the frame is only forwarded out the port where Host D is located.

FIGURE 13.2 The benefit of a switched network

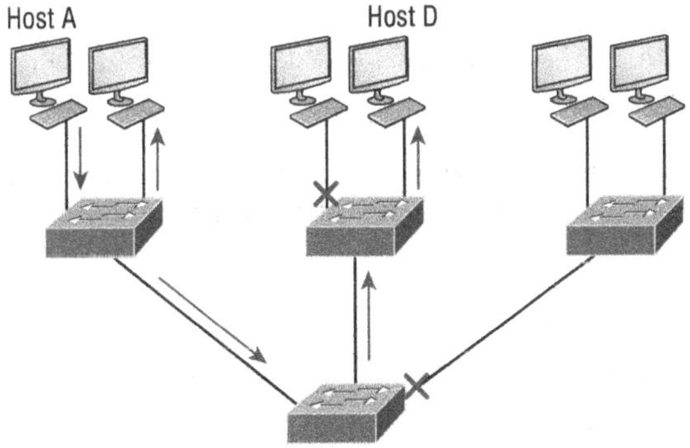

This is a huge improvement over the old hub networks that only offered one huge collision domain by default!

The biggest benefit gained by having a layer 2 switched network is that it creates individual collision domain segments for each device plugged into each port on the switch. It frees us from the old Ethernet density constraints and allows us to build larger networks.

But it's not all sunshine here—the more users and devices that populate and use a network, the more broadcasts and packets each switch has to deal with.

And there's another big downside: security! Rather, the lack thereof because within the typical layer 2 switched internetwork, all users can see all devices by default. And you can't prevent devices from broadcasting, nor can you stop users from trying to respond to broadcasts. This means your security options are dismally limited to placing passwords on your servers and other devices.

But wait—there's hope! We can solve a slew of layer 2 switching snags by creating VLANs, as you'll soon see.

VLANs work like this: Figure 13.3 shows all hosts in this small company connected to one switch. This means all hosts will receive all frames because that's the default behavior of all switches.

FIGURE 13.3 One switch, one LAN. Before VLANs, there were no separations between hosts.

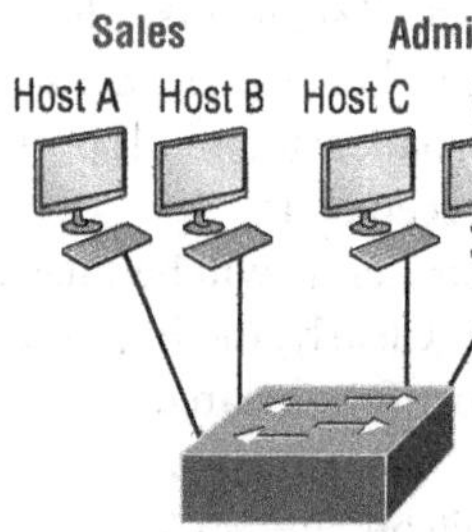

If we want to separate the host's data, we could either buy another switch or create virtual LANs, as shown in Figure 13.4.

FIGURE 13.4 One switch, two virtual LANs (*logical* separation between hosts). It's still physically one switch, but this switch can act as many separate devices.

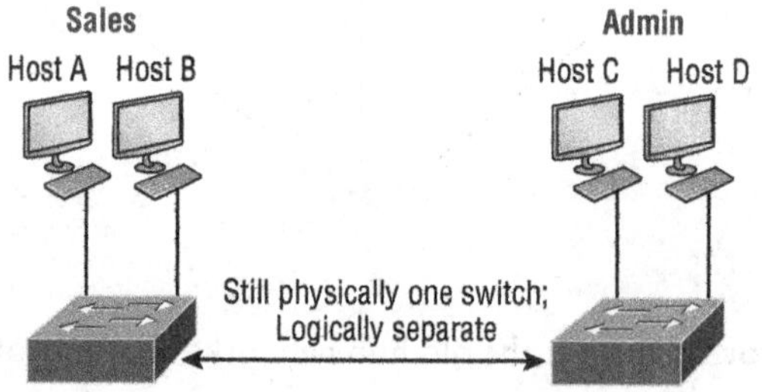

In Figure 13.4, I configured the switch to be two separate LANs, two subnets, two broadcast domains, two VLANs—they all mean the same thing—without buying another switch.

We can do this 1,000 times on most Cisco switches, which saves thousands of dollars and more!

Notice that even though the separation is virtual and the hosts are all still connected to the same switch, the LANs can't send data to each other by default. This is because they are still separate networks. We'll get into inter-VLAN communication later in this chapter.

Here's a short list of ways VLANs simplify network management:

- Network adds, moves, and changes are achieved with ease by just configuring a port into the appropriate VLAN.
- A group of users who need an unusually high level of security can be put into its own VLAN so that users outside of that VLAN can't communicate with that group's users.
- As a logical grouping of users by function, VLANs can be considered independent from their physical or geographic locations.
- VLANs greatly enhance network security if implemented correctly.
- VLANs increase the number of broadcast domains while decreasing their size.

Next, we'll explore the world of switching to discover how and why switches provide much better network services than hubs do in our networks today.

Broadcast Control

Broadcasts occur in every protocol, but how often they occur depends on three things:

- The type of protocol
- The application(s) running on the internetwork
- How these services are used

Some older applications have been rewritten to reduce their bandwidth consumption, but the legion of multimedia applications around today consume generous amounts of bandwidth in no time. Most of these apps use both broadcasts and multicasts extensively. As if that weren't enough of a challenge, factors like faulty equipment, inadequate segmentation, and poorly designed firewalls can seriously compound the problems already caused by these broadcast-intensive applications. All of this adds a major new dimension to network design and presents a number of new challenges for an administrator. Ensuring that your network is properly segmented so you can quickly isolate a single segment's problems to prevent them from propagating throughout your entire internetwork is now imperative. The most effective way to do that is through strategic switching and routing.

Since switches have become more affordable, almost everyone has replaced their flat hub networks with pure switched network and VLAN environments. All devices within a VLAN are members of the same broadcast domain and receive all broadcasts relevant to it. By default, these broadcasts are filtered from all ports on a switch that aren't members of the same VLAN. This is wonderful because you get all the benefits you would with a switched design without getting hit with all the problems you'd have if all your users were in the same broadcast domain!

Security

But there's always a catch, right? Time to get back to those security issues. A flat internetwork's security used to be tackled by connecting hubs and switches together with routers. So, it was basically the router's job to maintain security. This arrangement was pretty ineffective for several reasons. First, anyone connecting to the physical network could access the network resources located on that particular physical LAN. Second, all anyone had to do to observe any and all traffic traversing that network was to simply plug a network analyzer into the hub. And like that last scary fact, users could easily join a workgroup by just plugging their workstations into the existing hub!

But that's exactly what makes VLANs so cool. If you build them and create multiple broadcast groups, you can still have total control over each port and user. So, the days when anyone could just plug their workstations into any switch port and gain access to network resources are history, because now you get to control each port and any resources it can access.

And that's not all—VLANs can be created in harmony with a specific user's need for the network resources. Plus, switches can be configured to inform a network management station about unauthorized access to those vital network resources. And if you need inter-VLAN communication, you can implement restrictions on a router to make sure this all happens securely. You can also place restrictions on hardware addresses, protocols, and applications. *Now* we're talking security!

Flexibility and Scalability

As we know, layer 2 switches only read frames for filtering because they don't look at the Network layer protocol. And by default, switches forward broadcasts to all ports. But if you create and implement VLANs, you're essentially creating smaller broadcast domains at layer 2.

As a result, broadcasts sent out from a node in one VLAN won't be forwarded to ports configured to belong to a different VLAN. But if we assign switch ports or users to VLAN groups on a switch or on a group of connected switches, we gain the flexibility to exclusively add only the users we want to let into that broadcast domain, regardless of their physical location. This setup can also work to block broadcast storms caused by faulty network's interface cards (NICs) as well as prevent an intermediate device from propagating broadcast storms throughout the entire internetwork. Those evils can still happen on the VLAN where the problem originated, but the disease will be fully contained in that one ailing VLAN.

Another advantage is that when a VLAN gets too big, you can simply create more VLANs to keep the broadcasts from consuming too much bandwidth. The fewer users in a VLAN, the fewer users affected by broadcasts. This is all good, but when creating a VLAN, you seriously need to keep network services in mind and understand how the users connect to these services. A good strategy is to try to keep all services, except for the email and Internet access that everyone needs, local to all users whenever possible.

Identifying VLANs

Switch ports are layer 2–only interfaces that are associated with a physical port that can belong to only one VLAN if it's an access port or all VLANs if it's a trunk port.

Switches are definitely busy devices. As myriad frames are switched throughout the network, they have to be able to keep track of all frames, plus understand what to do with them depending on their associated hardware addresses. And remember—frames are handled differently according to the type of link they're traversing.

There are two different types of ports in a switched environment. Let's take a look at the first type in Figure 13.5.

FIGURE 13.5 Access ports

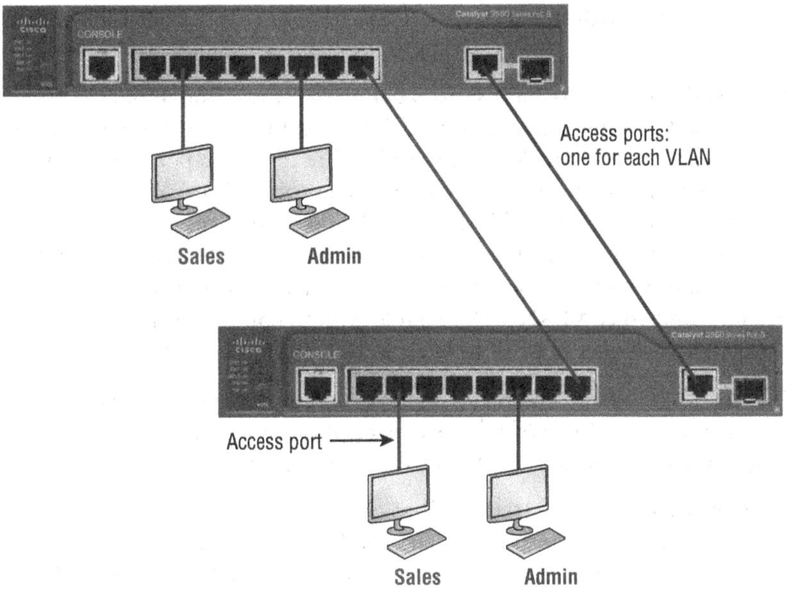

Notice that there are access ports for each host and an access port between switches—one for each VLAN.

Access Ports An *access port* belongs to and carries the traffic of only one VLAN. Traffic is both received and sent in native formats with no VLAN information (tagging) at all. Anything arriving on an access port is simply assumed to belong to the VLAN assigned to the port. Because an access port doesn't look at the source address, tagged traffic—a frame with added VLAN information—can be correctly forwarded and received only on trunk ports.

With an access link, this can be referred to as the *configured VLAN* of the port. Any device attached to an *access link* is unaware of a VLAN membership—the device simply assumes it's part of some broadcast domain. However, it doesn't have the big picture, so it doesn't understand the physical network topology at all.

Another good bit of information to know is that switches remove any VLAN information from the frame before it's forwarded out to an access-link device. Remember that access-link devices can't communicate with devices outside their VLAN unless the packet is routed. Also, you can only create a switch port to be either an access port or a trunk port—not both. So, you've got to choose one or the other and know that if you make it an access port, that port can be assigned to one VLAN only.

In Figure 13.5, only the hosts in the Sales VLAN can talk to other hosts in the same VLAN. This is the same with the Admin VLAN, and they can both communicate to hosts on the other switch because of an access link for each VLAN configured between switches.

Voice Access Ports Not to confuse you, but all that I just said about the fact that an access port can be assigned to only one VLAN is really only sort of true. Nowadays, most switches allow you to add a second VLAN to an access port on a switch port for your voice traffic, called the *voice VLAN*. The voice VLAN used to be called the *auxiliary VLAN*, which allowed it to be overlaid on top of the data VLAN, enabling both types of traffic to travel through the same port. Even though this is technically considered to be a different type of link, it's still just an access port that can be configured for both data and voice VLANs. This enables you to connect both a phone and a PC device to one switch port but still have each device in a separate VLAN.

Trunk Ports Believe it or not, the term *trunk port* was inspired by the telephone system trunks, which carry multiple telephone conversations at a time. So, it follows that trunk ports can similarly carry multiple VLANs at a time as well.

A *trunk link* is a 100, 1,000, 10,000 Mbps or more, point-to-point link between two switches, between a switch and router, or even between a switch and server, and it carries the traffic of multiple VLANs—from 1 to 4,094 VLANs at a time. But the number is really only up to 1,001 unless you're going with extended VLANs.

Instead of an access link for each VLAN between switches, we'll create a trunk link, as shown in Figure 13.6.

Trunking can offer a real advantage because with it, you get to make a single port part of a whole bunch of different VLANs at the same time. This is a great feature because you can actually set ports up to have a server in two separate broadcast domains simultaneously so your users won't have to cross a layer 3 device (router) to log in and access it. Another benefit to trunking comes into play when you're connecting switches. Trunk links can carry the frames of various VLANs across them, but by default, if the links between your switches aren't trunked, only information from the configured access VLAN will be switched across that link.

FIGURE 13.6 VLANs can span across multiple switches by using trunk links, which carry traffic for multiple VLANs.

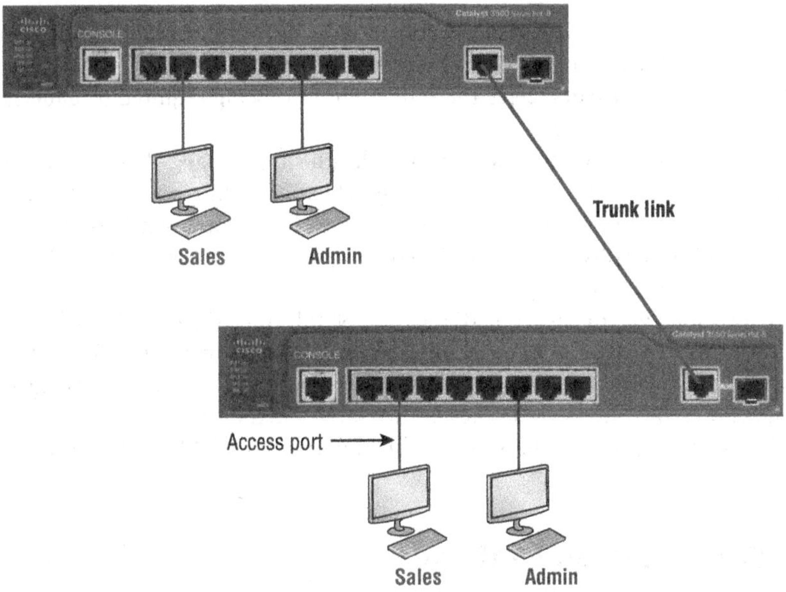

> Also good to know is that all VLANs send information on a trunked link unless you clear each VLAN by hand. I'll show you how to clear individual VLANs from a trunk in a bit.

It's finally time to tell you about frame tagging and the VLAN identification methods used in it across our trunk links.

Frame Tagging

As you now know, you can set up your VLANs to span more than one connected switch. You can see that going on in Figure 13.6, which depicts hosts from two VLANs spread across two switches. This flexible, power-packed capability is probably the main advantage to implementing VLANs, and we can do this with up to a thousand VLANs and thousands upon thousands of hosts!

All this can get kind of complicated—even for a switch—so there needs to be a way for each one to keep track of all the users and frames as they travel the switch fabric and VLANs. When I say "switch fabric," I'm just referring to a group of switches that share the same VLAN information. And this just happens to be where *frame tagging* enters the scene. This frame identification method uniquely assigns a user-defined VLAN ID to each frame.

Here's how it works: Once within the switch fabric, each switch that the frame reaches must first identify the VLAN ID from the frame tag. It then finds out what to do with the frame by looking at the information in what's known as the *filter table*. If the frame reaches a switch that has another trunked link, the frame will be forwarded out of the trunk-link port.

Once the frame reaches an exit that's determined by the forward/filter table to be an access link matching the frame's VLAN ID, the switch will remove the VLAN identifier. This is so the destination device can receive the frames without being required to understand their VLAN identification information.

Another great thing about trunk ports is that they'll support tagged and untagged traffic simultaneously—if you're using 802.1q trunking, which I will talk about next. The trunk port is assigned a default port VLAN ID (PVID) for a VLAN upon which all untagged traffic will travel. This VLAN, called the *native VLAN*, is always VLAN 1 by default, but it can be changed to any VLAN number.

Similarly, any untagged or tagged traffic with a NULL (unassigned) VLAN ID is assumed to belong to the VLAN with the port default PVID. Again, this would be VLAN 1 by default. A packet with a VLAN ID equal to the outgoing port native VLAN is sent untagged and can communicate to only hosts or devices in that same VLAN. All other VLAN traffic has to be sent with a VLAN tag to communicate within a particular VLAN that corresponds with that tag.

VLAN Identification Methods

VLAN identification is what switches use to keep track of all those frames as they're traversing a switch fabric. It's how switches identify which frames belong to which VLANs, and there's more than one trunking method.

Inter-Switch Link (ISL)

Inter-Switch Link (ISL) is a way of explicitly tagging VLAN information onto an Ethernet frame. This tagging information allows VLANs to be multiplexed over a trunk link through an external encapsulation method. This allows the switch to identify the VLAN membership of a frame received over the trunked link.

By running ISL, you can interconnect multiple switches and still maintain VLAN information as traffic travels between switches on trunk links. ISL functions at layer 2 by encapsulating a data frame with a new header and by performing a new cyclic redundancy check (CRC).

Of note is that ISL is proprietary to Cisco switches, but it's pretty versatile, too. ISL can be used on switch ports, router interfaces, and server interface cards to trunk a server. Although some Cisco switches still support ISL frame tagging, Cisco has moved toward using only 802.1q.

IEEE 802.1q

Created by the IEEE as a standard method of frame tagging, IEEE 802.1q actually inserts a field into the frame to identify the VLAN. If you're trunking between a Cisco switched link and a different brand of switch, you have to use 802.1q in order for the trunk to work.

Unlike ISL, which encapsulates the frame with control information, 802.1q inserts an 802.1q field along with tag control information, as shown in Figure 13.7.

FIGURE 13.7 IEEE 802.1q encapsulation with and without the 802.1q tag

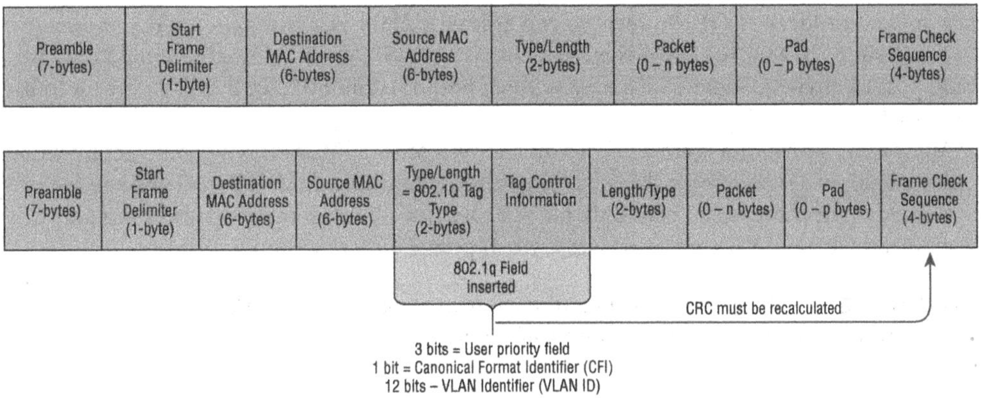

For the Cisco exam objectives, it's only the 12-bit VLAN ID that matters. This field identifies the VLAN and can be 2^{12}, minus 2 for the 0 and 4,095 reserved VLANs, which means an 802.1q tagged frame can carry information for 4,094 VLANs.

It works like this: You first designate each port that's going to be a trunk with 802.1q encapsulation. The other ports must be assigned a specific VLAN ID in order for them to communicate. VLAN 1 is the default native VLAN, and when using 802.1q, all traffic for a native VLAN is untagged. The ports that populate the same trunk create a group with this native VLAN, and each port gets tagged with an identification number reflecting that. Again, the default is VLAN 1. The native VLAN allows the trunks to accept information that was received without any VLAN identification or frame tag.

Most 2960 model switches only support the IEEE 802.1q trunking protocol. The 3560 model will support both the ISL and IEEE methods, which you'll see later in this chapter.

NOTE

The basic purpose of ISL and 802.1q frame-tagging methods is to provide inter-switch VLAN communication. Remember, any ISL or 802.1q frame tagging is removed if a frame is forwarded out an access link; tagging is used internally and across trunk links only!

Routing Between VLANs

Hosts in a VLAN live in their own broadcast domain and can communicate freely. VLANs create network partitioning and traffic separation at layer 2 of the OSI. As I said when I told you why we still need routers, if you want hosts or any other IP-addressable device to communicate between VLANs, you must have a layer 3 device to provide routing.

For this, you can use a router that has an interface for each VLAN or a router that supports ISL or 802.1q routing. The least expensive router that supports ISL or 802.1q routing is the 2600 series router. You'd have to buy that from a used-equipment reseller because they are end-of-life, or EOL. I'd recommend at least a 2800 as a bare minimum, but even that only supports 802.1q. Cisco is moving away from ISL, so you probably should only be using 802.1q anyway. Some 2800s may support both ISL and 802.1q; I've just never seen it supported.

Anyway, as shown in Figure 13.8, if you had two or three VLANs, you could get by with a router equipped with two or three FastEthernet connections. And 10Base-T is okay for home study purposes, and I mean only for your studies—but for anything else, I'd highly recommend Gigabit or higher interfaces for real power under the hood!

FIGURE 13.8 A router connecting three VLANs together for inter-VLAN communication—one router interface for each VLAN

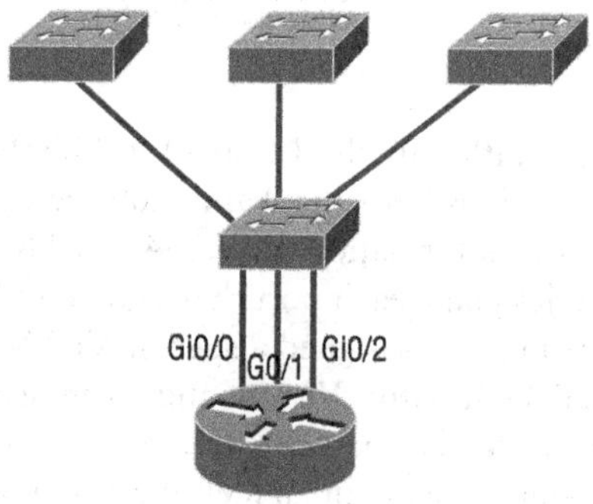

In Figure 13.8, each router interface is plugged into an access link. This means that each of the routers' interface IP addresses would then become the default gateway address for each host in each respective VLAN.

If you have more VLANs available than router interfaces, you can configure trunking on one FastEthernet interface or buy a layer 3 switch, like the old and now inexpensive 3560, or a higher-end switch, like a 3850. You could even opt for a 6800 if you're feeling spendy.

Instead of using a router interface for each VLAN, you can use one FastEthernet interface and run ISL or 802.1q trunking. Figure 13.9 shows how a FastEthernet interface on a router looks when configured with ISL or 802.1q trunking. This allows all VLANs to communicate through one interface. Cisco calls this a *router on a stick* (ROAS), and this is what's used on the CCNA objectives for inter-VLAN routing.

I really want to point out that this creates a potential bottleneck, as well as a single point of failure, so your host/VLAN count is limited. To how many? Well, that depends on your traffic level. To really make things right, you'd be better off using a higher-end switch and routing on the backplane. But if you just happen to have a router sitting around, configuring this method is free, right?

FIGURE 13.9 A router on a stick: a single router interface connecting all three VLANs together for inter-VLAN communication

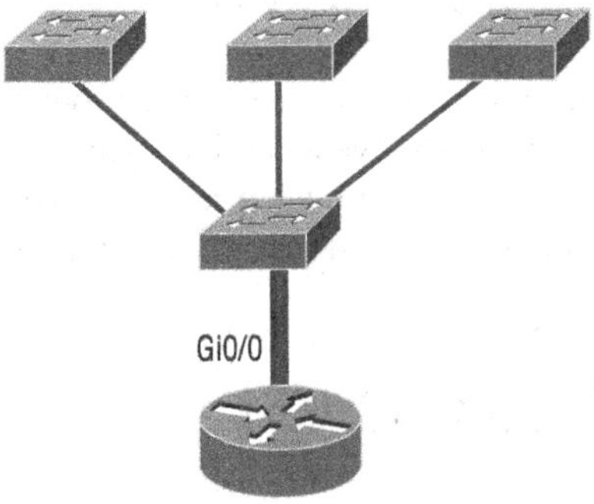

Figure 13.10 shows how you would create a router on a stick using a router's physical interface by creating logical interfaces—one for each VLAN.

FIGURE 13.10 A router creates logical interfaces.

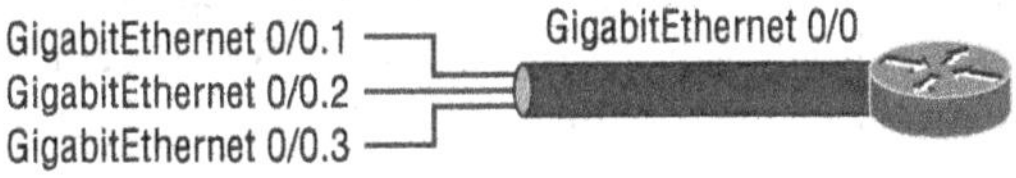

Here we see one physical interface divided into multiple subinterfaces, with one subnet assigned per VLAN, each subinterface being the default gateway address for each VLAN/subnet. An encapsulation identifier must be assigned to each subinterface to define the VLAN ID of that subinterface. In the next section, where I'll configure VLANs and inter-VLAN routing, I'll configure our switched network with a router on a stick to demonstrate this for you.

But wait, there's still one more way to go about routing! Instead of using an external router interface for each VLAN, or an external router on a stick, we can configure logical interfaces on the backplane of the layer 3 switch; this is called inter-VLAN routing (IVR), and it's configured with a switched virtual interface (SVI).

Figure 13.11 shows how hosts see these virtual interfaces.

FIGURE 13.11 With IVR, routing runs on the backplane of the switch, and it appears to the hosts that a router is present.

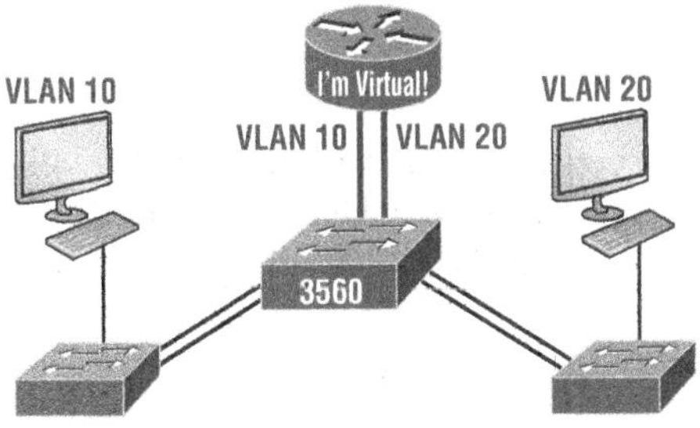

In Figure 13.11, it appears there's a router present, but there is no physical router present as there was when we used router on a stick. The IVR process takes little effort, but it's easy to implement, which makes it very cool! Plus, it's a lot more efficient for inter-VLAN routing than an external router.

To implement IVR on a multilayer switch, we just need to create logical interfaces in the switch configuration for each VLAN. We'll configure this method in a minute, but first let's take our existing switched network from Chapter 12, "Layer 2 Switching," add some VLANs, and then configure VLAN memberships and trunk links between our switches.

Configuring VLANs

Configuring VLANs is actually pretty easy. It's just that figuring out which users you want in each VLAN is not easy, and doing so can eat up a lot of your time. Once you've decided on the number of VLANs you want to create and established which users you want to belong to each one, it's time to bring your first VLAN into the world.

To configure VLANs on a Cisco Catalyst switch, use the `global config vlan` command. The following example demonstrates how to configure VLANs on the S1 switch by creating three VLANs for three different departments. Again, remember that VLAN 1 is the native and management VLAN by default:

```
S1(config)#vlan ?
WORD ISL VLAN IDs 1-4094
access-map Create vlan access-map or enter vlan access-map command mode
dot1q dot1q parameters
filter Apply a VLAN Map
group Create a vlan group
internal internal VLAN
S1(config)#vlan 2
S1(config-vlan)#name Sales
S1(config-vlan)#vlan 3
S1(config-vlan)#name Marketing
S1(config-vlan)#vlan 4
S1(config-vlan)#name Accounting
S1(config-vlan)#vlan 5
S1(config-vlan)#name Voice
S1(config-vlan)#^Z
S1#
```

In this output, you see that you can create VLANs from 1 to 4094. But this is only mostly true. As I said, VLANs can really only be created up to 1001, and you can't use, change, rename, or delete VLANs 1 or 1002 through 1005 because they're reserved.

The VLAN numbers above 1005 are called *extended VLANs* and won't be saved in the database unless your switch is set to what is called VLAN Trunking Protocol (VTP) transparent mode.

You won't see these VLAN numbers used too often in production. Here's an example of my attempt to set my S1 switch to VLAN 4000 when my switch is set to VTP server mode (the default VTP mode):

```
S1#config t
S1(config)#vlan 4000
S1(config-vlan)#^Z
% Failed to create VLANs 4000
Extended VLAN(s) not allowed in current VTP mode.
%Failed to commit extended VLAN(s) changes.
```

After creating the VLANs that you want, you can use the `show vlan` command to check them out. But notice that, by default, all ports on the switch are in VLAN 1. To change the VLAN associated with a port, you need to go to each interface and specifically tell it which VLAN to be a part of.

NOTE Remember, a created VLAN is unused until it is assigned to a switch port or ports and that all ports are always assigned in VLAN 1 unless set otherwise.

Once the VLANs are created, verify your configuration with the `show vlan` command (`sh vlan`, for short):

```
S1#sh vlan
VLAN Name Status Ports
---- ------------------------- --------- -------------------------------
1 default active Fa0/1, Fa0/2, Fa0/3, Fa0/4
Fa0/5, Fa0/6, Fa0/7, Fa0/8
Fa0/9, Fa0/10, Fa0/11, Fa0/12
Fa0/13, Fa0/14, Fa0/19, Fa0/20
Fa0/21, Fa0/22, Fa0/23, Gi0/1
Gi0/2
2 Sales active
3 Marketing active
4 Accounting active]]> 5 Voice active
[output cut]
```

This may seem repetitive, but it's important, and I want you to remember it: you can't change, delete, or rename VLAN 1 because it's the default VLAN, and you just can't change that—period. It's also the native VLAN of all switches by default, and Cisco recommends that you use it as your management VLAN. If you're worried about security issues, then just change the management VLAN. Basically, any ports that aren't specifically assigned to a different VLAN will be sent down to the native VLAN—VLAN 1.

In the preceding S1 output, you can see that ports Fa0/1 through Fa0/14, Fa0/19 through 23, and Gi0/1 and Gi0/2 uplinks are all in VLAN 1. But where are ports 15 through 18? First, understand that the command `show vlan` only displays access ports, so now that you know what you're looking at with the `show vlan` command, where do you think ports Fa15–18 are?

That's right! They are trunked ports. Cisco switches run a proprietary protocol called *Dynamic Trunk Protocol (DTP)*, and if there is a compatible switch connected, they will start trunking automatically, which is precisely where my four ports are. You have to use the `show interfaces trunk` command to see your trunked ports, as follows:

```
S1# show interfaces trunk
Port Mode Encapsulation Status Native vlan
Fa0/15 desirable n-isl trunking 1
Fa0/16 desirable n-isl trunking 1
Fa0/17 desirable n-isl trunking 1
Fa0/18 desirable n-isl trunking 1
Port Vlans allowed on trunk
Fa0/15 1-4094
Fa0/16 1-4094
Fa0/17 1-4094
Fa0/18 1-4094
[output cut]
```

This output reveals that the VLANs from 1 to 4094 are allowed across the trunk by default. Another helpful command, which is also part of the Cisco exam objectives, is the `show interfaces` *`interface`* `switchport` command:

```
S1#sh interfaces fastEthernet 0/15 switchport
Name: Fa0/15
Switchport: Enabled
Administrative Mode: dynamic desirable
Operational Mode: trunk
Administrative Trunking Encapsulation: negotiate
Operational Trunking Encapsulation: isl
Negotiation of Trunking: On
Access Mode VLAN: 1 (default)
Trunking Native Mode VLAN: 1 (default)
Administrative Native VLAN tagging: enabled
Voice VLAN: none
[output cut]
```

The output shows the administrative mode of `dynamic desirable`, that the port is a trunk port, and that DTP was used to negotiate the frame-tagging method of ISL. It also predictably shows that the native VLAN is the default of 1.

Now that we can see the VLANs created, we can assign switch ports to specific ones. Each port can be part of only one VLAN, with the exception of voice access ports. Using trunking, we can make a port available to traffic from all VLANs. I'll cover that next.

Assigning Switch Ports to VLANs

You configure a port to belong to a VLAN by assigning a membership mode that specifies the kind of traffic the port carries plus the number of VLANs it can belong to. You can also configure each port on a switch to be in a specific VLAN (access port) by using the `interface switchport` command. You can even configure multiple ports at the same time with the `interface range` command.

In the next example, I'll configure interface Fa0/3 to VLAN 3. This is the connection from the S3 switch to the host device:

```
S3#config t
S3(config)#int fa0/3
S3(config-if)#switchport ?
access Set access mode characteristics of the interface
autostate Include or exclude this port from vlan link up calculation
backup Set backup for the interface
block Disable forwarding of unknown uni/multi cast addresses
host Set port host
mode Set trunking mode of the interface
nonegotiate Device will not engage in negotiation protocol on this
interface
port-security Security related command
priority Set appliance 802.1p priority
private-vlan Set the private VLAN configuration
protected Configure an interface to be a protected port
trunk Set trunking characteristics of the interface
voice Voice appliance attributes voice
```

Well now, what do we have here? There's some new stuff showing up in the output. We can see various commands—some that I've already covered, but no worries because I'm going to cover the `access`, `mode`, `nonegotiate`, and `trunk` commands coming up.

However, let's start with setting an access port on S1, which is probably the most widely used type of port you'll find on production switches that have VLANs configured:

```
S3(config-if)#switchport mode ?
access Set trunking mode to ACCESS unconditionally
dot1q-tunnel set trunking mode to TUNNEL unconditionally
dynamic Set trunking mode to dynamically negotiate access or trunk mode
private-vlan Set private-vlan mode
```

```
trunk Set trunking m de to TRUNK unconditionally
S3(config-if)#switchport mode access
S3(config-if)#switchport access vlan 3
S3(config-if)#switchport voice vlan 5
```

By starting with the `switchport mode access` command, you're telling the switch that this is a nontrunking layer 2 port. You can then assign a VLAN to the port with the `switchport access` command, as well as configure the same port to be a member of a different type of VLAN, called the *voice VLAN*.

This allows you to connect a laptop to a phone, and the phone to a single switch port. Remember, you can choose many ports to configure simultaneously with the `interface range` command.

Let's take a look at our VLANs now:

```
S3#show vlan
VLAN Name Status Ports
---- ------------------------ --------- -------------------------------
1 default active Fa0/4, Fa0/5, Fa0/6, Fa0/7
Fa0/8, Fa0/9, Fa0/10, Fa0/11,
Fa0/12, Fa0/13, Fa0/14, Fa0/19,
Fa0/20, Fa0/21, Fa0/22, Fa0/23,
Gi0/1 ,Gi0/2
2 Sales active
3 Marketing active Fa0/3]]> 5 Voice active Fa0/3
```

Notice that port Fa0/3 is now a member of VLAN 3 and VLAN 5—two different types of VLANs. But where are ports 1 and 2? And why aren't they showing up in the output of `show vlan`? That's right—because they are trunk ports!

We can also see this with the `show interfaces interface switchport` command:

```
S3#sh int fa0/3 switchport
Name: Fa0/3
Switchport: Enabled
Administrative Mode: static access
Operational Mode: static access
Administrative Trunking Encapsulation: negotiate
Negotiation of Trunking: Off
Access Mode VLAN: 3 (Marketing) Trunking Native Mode VLAN: 1 (default)
Administrative Native VLAN tagging: enabled Voice VLAN: 5 (Voice)
```

The output shows that Fa0/3 is an access port and a member of VLAN 3 (Marketing), as well as a member of the Voice VLAN 5.

That's it. Well, sort of. If you plug devices into each VLAN port, they can only talk to other devices in the same VLAN. But as soon as you learn a bit more about trunking, we're going to enable inter-VLAN communication!

Configuring Trunk Ports

The 2960 switch only runs the IEEE 802.1q encapsulation method. To configure trunking on a FastEthernet port, use the interface command `switchport mode trunk`. It's a tad different on the 3560 switch.

The following switch output shows the trunk configuration on interfaces Fa0/15–18 as set to `trunk`:

```
S1(config)#int range f0/15-18
S1(config-if-range)#switchport trunk encapsulation dot1q
S1(config-if-range)#switchport mode trunk
```

I want to point out here that if you have a switch that only runs the 802.1q encapsulation method, you wouldn't use the encapsulation command, as I did in the preceding output. Let's check out our trunk ports now:

```
S1(config-if-range)#do sh int f0/15 swi
Name: Fa0/15
Switchport: Enabled
Administrative Mode: trunk
Operational Mode: trunk
Administrative Trunking Encapsulation: dot1q
Operational Trunking Encapsulation: dot1q
Negotiation of Trunking: On
Access Mode VLAN: 1 (default)
Trunking Native Mode VLAN: 1 (default)
Administrative Native VLAN tagging: enabled
Voice VLAN: none
```

Notice that port Fa0/15 is a trunk and running 802.1q.

Let's take another look:

```
S1(config-if-range)#do sh int trunk
Port Mode Encapsulation Status Native vlan
Fa0/15 on 802.1q trunking 1
Fa0/16 on 802.1q trunking 1
Fa0/17 on 802.1q trunking 1
Fa0/18 on 802.1q trunking 1
Port Vlans allowed on trunk
Fa0/15 1-4094
Fa0/16 1-4094
Fa0/17 1-4094
Fa0/18 1-4094
```

Note that ports 15–18 are now in the trunk mode of on, and the encapsulation is now 802.1q instead of the negotiated ISL.

Here's a description of the different options available when configuring a switch interface:

switchport mode access I touched on this mode in the previous section. It puts the interface (access port) into permanent nontrunking mode and negotiates to convert the link into a nontrunk link. The interface becomes a nontrunk interface regardless of whether the neighboring interface is a trunk interface. The port would be a dedicated layer 2 access port.

switchport mode dynamic auto This mode makes the interface able to convert the link to a trunk link. The interface becomes a trunk interface if the neighboring interface is set to trunk or desirable mode. The default is dynamic auto on a lot of Cisco switches, but that default trunk method is changing to dynamic desirable on most new models.

switchport mode dynamic desirable This mode makes the interface actively attempt to convert the link to a trunk link. The interface becomes a trunk interface if the neighboring interface is set to trunk, desirable, or auto mode. I used to see this mode as the default on some switches, but not anymore. It's now the default switch port mode for all Ethernet interfaces on all new Cisco switches.

switchport mode trunk This mode puts the interface into permanent trunking mode and negotiates to convert the neighboring link into a trunk link. The interface becomes a trunk interface even if the neighboring interface isn't a trunk interface.

switchport nonegotiate This mode prevents the interface from generating DTP frames. You can use this command only when the interface switchport mode is access or trunk. You must manually configure the neighboring interface as a trunk interface to establish a trunk link.

NOTE

Dynamic Trunking Protocol (DTP) is used to negotiate trunking on a link between two devices as well as to negotiate the encapsulation type of either 802.1q or ISL. I use the `nonegotiate` command when I want dedicated trunk ports—no questions asked.

To disable trunking on an interface, use the `switchport mode access` command, which sets the port back to a dedicated layer 2 access switch port.

Defining the Allowed VLANs on a Trunk

As previously mentioned, trunk ports send and receive information from all VLANs by default, and if a frame is untagged, it's sent to the management VLAN. Note that this also applies to the extended-range VLANs.

We can remove VLANs from the allowed list to prevent traffic from certain VLANs from traversing a trunked link. I'll show you how to do that, but first let me again demonstrate that all VLANs are allowed across the trunk link by default:

```
S1#sh int trunk
[output cut]
Port Vlans allowed on trunk
```

```
Fa0/15 1-4094
Fa0/16 1-4094
Fa0/17 1-4094
Fa0/18 1-4094
S1(config)#int f0/15
S1(config-if)#switchport trunk allowed vlan 4,6,12,15
S1(config-if)#do show int trunk
[output cut]
Port Vlans allowed on trunk
Fa0/15 4,6,12,15
Fa0/16 1-4094
Fa0/17 1-4094
Fa0/18 1-4094
```

The preceding command affected the trunk link configured on S1 port F0/15, causing it to permit all traffic sent and received for VLANs 4, 6, 12, and 15. You can try to remove VLAN 1 on a trunk link, but it will still send and receive management like CDP, DTP, and VTP, so what's the point?

To remove a range of VLANs, just use a hyphen, as follows:

```
S1(config-if)#switchport trunk allowed vlan remove 4-8
```

If by chance someone has removed some VLANs from a trunk link and you want to set the trunk back to default, just use the following command:

```
S1(config-if)#switchport trunk allowed vlan all
```

Next, before we start routing between VLANs, I want to show you how to configure a native VLAN for a trunk.

Changing or Modifying the Trunk Native VLAN

You can change the trunk port native VLAN from VLAN 1, which many people do for security reasons. To change the native VLAN, use the following command:

```
S1(config)#int f0/15
S1(config-if)#switchport trunk native vlan ?
<1-4094> VLAN ID of the native VLAN when this port is in trunking mode
S1(config-if)#switchport trunk native vlan 4
1w6d: %CDP-4-NATIVE_VLAN_MISMATCH: Native VLAN mismatch discovered on
FastEthernet0/15 (4), with S3 FastEthernet0/1 (1).
```

So, we've changed our native VLAN on our trunk link to 4, and by using the `show running-config` command, we can see the configuration under the trunk link:

```
S1#sh run int f0/15
Building configuration...
Current configuration : 202 bytes
!
```

```
interface FastEthernet0/15
description 1st connection to S3
switchport trunk encapsulation dot1q
switchport trunk native vlan 4
switchport trunk allowed vlan 4,6,12,15
switchport mode trunk
end
S1#!
```

Oops—wait a minute! You didn't think it would just start working, did you? Of course not! Here's the rub: If all switches don't have the same native VLAN configured on the given trunk links, then we'll start receiving the following error, which happened immediately after I entered the command:

```
1w6d: %CDP-4-NATIVE_VLAN_MISMATCH: Native VLAN mismatch discovered
on FastEthernet0/15 (4), with S3 FastEthernet0/1 (1).
```

Actually, this is a good, noncryptic error, so we can either go to the other end of our trunk link(s) and change the native VLAN or set the native VLAN back to the default to fix it. Here's how to do that:

```
S1(config-if)#no switchport trunk native vlan
1w6d: %SPANTREE-2-UNBLOCK_CONSIST_PORT: Unblocking FastEthernet0/15
on VLAN0004. Port consistency restored.
```

Okay, now our trunk link is using the default VLAN 1 as the native VLAN. Just remember that all switches on a given trunk must use the same native VLAN; otherwise, you'll have some ugly management problems. These issues won't affect user data, just management traffic between switches.

Now, let's mix it up by connecting a router to our switched network and configure inter-VLAN communication.

Configuring Inter-VLAN Routing

By default, only hosts that are members of the same VLAN can communicate. To change this and allow inter-VLAN communication, you need a router or a layer 3 switch. I'll start with the router approach.

To support ISL or 802.1q routing on a FastEthernet interface, the router's interface is divided into logical interfaces—one for each VLAN—as was shown in Figure 8.10. These are called *subinterfaces*. From a FastEthernet or Gigabit interface, you can set the interface to trunk with the `encapsulation` command:

```
ISR#config t
ISR(config)#int f0/0.1
ISR(config-subif)#encapsulation ?
dot1Q IEEE 802.1Q Virtual LAN
```

```
ISR(config-subif)#encapsulation dot1Q ?
<1-4094> IEEE 802.1Q VLAN ID
```

Notice that my 2811 router (named ISR) only supports 802.1q. We'd need an older-model router to run the ISL encapsulation, but why bother?

The subinterface number is only locally significant, so it doesn't matter which subinterface numbers are configured on the router. Most of the time, I'll configure a subinterface with the same number as the VLAN I want to route. It's easy to remember that way because the subinterface number is used only for administrative purposes.

It's really important that you understand that each VLAN is actually a separate subnet. True, I know—they don't *have* to be, but it really is smart to configure your VLANs as separate subnets.

Before moving on, I want to define *upstream routing*. This is a term used to define the router on a stick. This router will provide inter-VLAN routing, but it can also be used to forward traffic upstream from the switched network to other parts of the corporate network or Internet.

Let's make sure you're fully prepared to configure inter-VLAN routing and that you can determine the IP addresses of hosts connected in a switched VLAN environment. As always, it's also a good idea to be able to fix any problems that may arise. To set you up for success, let me give you a few examples.

First, start by looking at Figure 13.12 and read the router and switch configuration within it. By this point in the book, you should be able to determine the IP address, masks, and default gateways of each of the hosts in the VLANs.

FIGURE 13.12 Configuring inter-VLAN routing—example 1

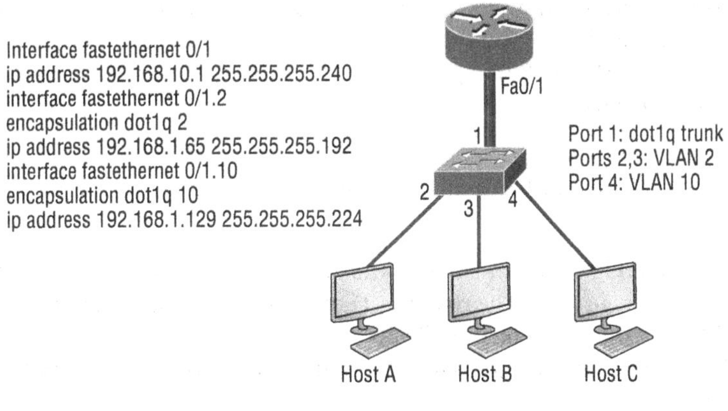
Interface fastethernet 0/1
ip address 192.168.10.1 255.255.255.240
interface fastethernet 0/1.2
encapsulation dot1q 2
ip address 192.168.1.65 255.255.255.192
interface fastethernet 0/1.10
encapsulation dot1q 10
ip address 192.168.1.129 255.255.255.224
Fa0/1
1
2
3
4
Port 1: dot1q trunk
Ports 2,3: VLAN 2
Port 4: VLAN 10
Host A
Host B
Host C

The next step is to figure out which subnets are being used. By looking at the router configuration in the figure, you can see that we're using 192.168.10.0/28 for VLAN1, 192.168.1.64/26 with VLAN 2, and 192.168.1.128/27 for VLAN 10.

By looking at the switch configuration, you can see that ports 2 and 3 are in VLAN 2, and port 4 is in VLAN 10. This means that Host A and Host B are in VLAN 2, and Host C is in VLAN 10.

But wait—what's that IP address doing there under the physical interface? Can we even do that? Sure, we can! If we place an IP address under the physical interface, the result is that frames sent from the IP address would be untagged. So, what VLAN would those frames be a member of? By default, they would belong to VLAN 1, our management VLAN. This means the address 192.168.10.1 /28 is my native VLAN IP address for this switch.

Here's what the hosts' IP addresses should be:

Host A: 192.168.1.66, 255.255.255.192, default gateway 192.168.1.65

Host B: 192.168.1.67, 255.255.255.192, default gateway 192.168.1.65

Host C: 192.168.1.130, 255.255.255.224, default gateway 192.168.1.129

The hosts could be any address in the range—I simply chose the first available IP address after the default gateway address. That wasn't so hard, was it?

Now, again using Figure 8.12, let's go through the commands necessary to configure switch port 1 so it will establish a link with the router and provide inter-VLAN communication using the IEEE version for encapsulation. Keep in mind that the commands can vary slightly depending on what type of switch you're dealing with.

For a 2960 switch, use the following:

```
2960#config t
2960(config)#interface fa0/1
2960(config-if)#switchport mode trunk
```

That's it! As you already know, the 2960 switch can only run the 802.1q encapsulation, so there's no need to specify it—you can't anyway. For a 3560 switch, it's basically the same, but because it can run ISL and 802.1q, you have to specify the trunking encapsulation protocol you're going to use.

> **NOTE** Remember, when you create a trunked link, all VLANs are allowed to pass data by default.

Let's take a look at Figure 13.13 and see what we can determine. This figure shows three VLANs, with two hosts in each. The router in Figure 13.13 is connected to the Fa0/1 switch port, and VLAN 4 is configured on port F0/6.

When looking at this diagram, keep in mind that Cisco expects you to know the following three factors:

- The router is connected to the switch using subinterfaces.
- The switch port connecting to the router is a trunk port.
- The switch ports connecting to the clients and the hub are access ports, not trunk ports.

FIGURE 13.13 Inter-VLAN routing—example 2

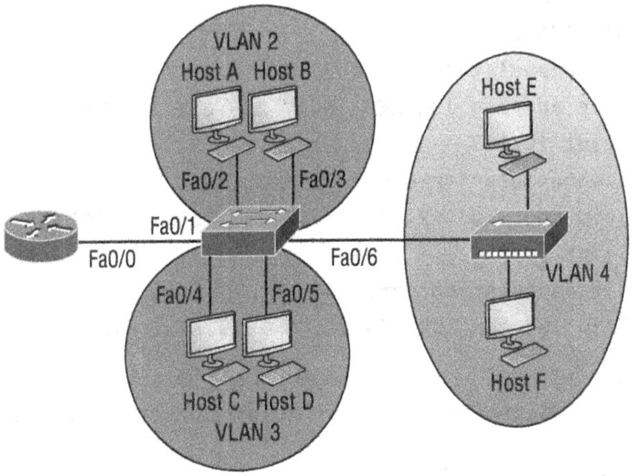

The configuration of the switch would look something like the following:

```
2960#config t
2960(config)#int f0/1
2960(config-if)#switchport mode trunk
2960(config-if)#int f0/2
2960(config-if)#switchport access vlan 2
2960(config-if)#int f0/3
2960(config-if)#switchport access vlan 2
2960(config-if)#int f0/4
2960(config-if)#switchport access vlan 3
2960(config-if)#int f0/5
2960(config-if)#switchport access vlan 3
2960(config-if)#int f0/6
2960(config-if)#switchport access vlan 4
```

Before configuring the router, we need to design our logical network:

VLAN 1: 192.168.10.0/28

VLAN 2: 192.168.10.16/28

VLAN 3: 192.168.10.32/28

VLAN 4: 192.168.10.48/28

The configuration of the router would then look like this:

```
ISR#config t
ISR(config)#int fa0/0
```

```
ISR(config-if)#ip address 192.168.10.1 255.255.255.240
ISR(config-if)#no shutdown
ISR(config-if)#int f0/0.2
ISR(config-subif)#encapsulation dot1q 2
ISR(config-subif)#ip address 192.168.10.17 255.255.255.240
ISR(config-subif)#int f0/0.3
ISR(config-subif)#encapsulation dot1q 3
ISR(config-subif)#ip address 192.168.10.33 255.255.255.240
ISR(config-subif)#int f0/0.4
ISR(config-subif)#encapsulation dot1q 4
ISR(config-subif)#ip address 192.168.10.49 255.255.255.240
```

Notice that I didn't tag VLAN 1. Even though I could have created a subinterface and tagged VLAN 1, it's not necessary with 802.1q because untagged frames are members of the native VLAN.

The hosts in each VLAN would be assigned an address from their subnet range, and the default gateway would be the IP address assigned to the router's subinterface in that VLAN.

Now, let's see if you can determine the switch and router configurations without looking at the answer—no cheating! Figure 13.14 shows a router connected to a 2960 switch with two VLANs. One host in each VLAN is assigned an IP address. What would your router and switch configurations be based on these IP addresses?

FIGURE 13.14 Inter-VLAN routing—example 3

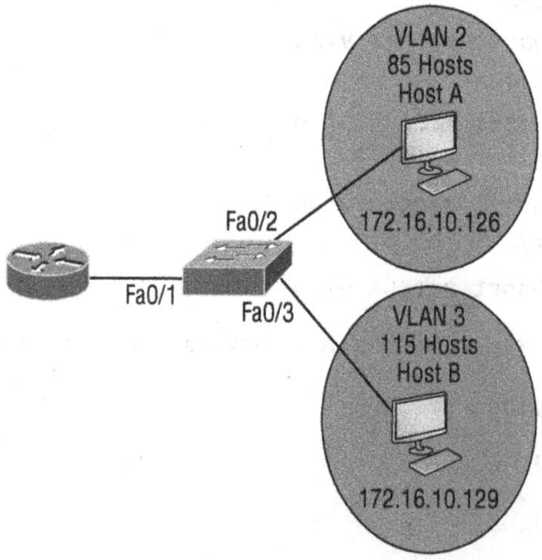

Since the hosts don't list a subnet mask, you have to look for the number of hosts used in each VLAN to figure out the block size. VLAN 2 has 85 hosts, and VLAN 3 has 115 hosts. Each of these will fit in a block size of 128, which is a /25 mask, or 255.255.255.128.

You should know by now that the subnets are 0 and 128; the 0 subnet (VLAN 2) has a host range of 1–126, and the 128 subnet (VLAN 3) has a range of 129–254. You can almost be fooled since Host A has an IP address of 126, which makes it *almost* seem that Host A and B are in the same subnet. But they're not, and you're way too smart by now to be fooled by this one, right?

Here's the switch configuration:

```
2960#config t
2960(config)#int f0/1
2960(config-if)#switchport mode trunk
2960(config-if)#int f0/2
2960(config-if)#switchport access vlan 2
2960(config-if)#int f0/3
2960(config-if)#switchport access vlan 3
```

Here's the router configuration:

```
ISR#config t
ISR(config)#int f0/0
ISR(config-if)#ip address 192.168.10.1 255.255.255.0
ISR(config-if)#no shutdown
ISR(config-if)#int f0/0.2
ISR(config-subif)#encapsulation dot1q 2
ISR(config-subif)#ip address 172.16.10.1 255.255.255.128
ISR(config-subif)#int f0/0.3
ISR(config-subif)#encapsulation dot1q 3
ISR(config-subif)#ip address 172.16.10.254 255.255.255.128
```

I used the first address in the host range for VLAN 2 and the last address in the range for VLAN 3, but any address in the range would work. You just have to configure the host's default gateway to whatever you make the router's address. Also, I used a different subnet for my physical interface, which is my management VLAN router's address.

Before moving on to the next example, let's make sure you know how to set the IP address on the switch. Since VLAN 1 is typically the administrative VLAN, we'll use an IP address from out of that pool of addresses. Here's how to set the IP address of the switch (not nagging, but you really should know this already):

```
2960#config t
2960(config)#int vlan 1
2960(config-if)#ip address 192.168.10.2 255.255.255.0
2960(config-if)#no shutdown
2960(config-if)#exit
2960(config)#ip default-gateway 192.168.10.1
```

Yes, you have to execute a `no shutdown` command on the VLAN interface and set the `ip default-gateway` address to the router.

One more example, and then we'll move on to IVR using a multilayer switch—another important subject that you definitely don't want to miss.

In Figure 13.15 there are two VLANs, plus the management VLAN 1. By looking at the router configuration, what's the IP address, subnet mask, and default gateway of Host A? Use the last IP address in the range for Host A's address.

If you look really carefully at the router configuration (the hostname in this configuration is just Router), there's a simple and quick answer. All subnets are using a /28, which is a 255.255.255.240 mask. This is a block size of 16. The router's address for VLAN 2 is in subnet 128. The next subnet is 144, so the broadcast address of VLAN 2 is 143, and the valid host range is 129–142. So, the host address would be the following:

IP address: 192.168.10.142

Mask: 255.255.255.240

Default gateway: 192.168.10.129

FIGURE 13.15 Inter-VLAN routing—example 4

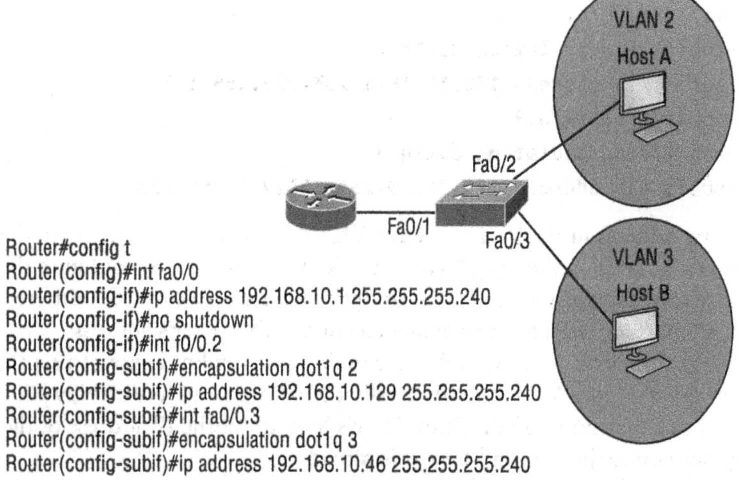

VLAN 2
Host A
Fa0/2
Fa0/1
Fa0/3
VLAN 3
Host B
Router#config t
Router(config)#int fa0/0
Router(config-if)#ip address 192.168.10.1 255.255.255.240
Router(config-if)#no shutdown
Router(config-if)#int f0/0.2
Router(config-subif)#encapsulation dot1q 2
Router(config-subif)#ip address 192.168.10.129 255.255.255.240
Router(config-subif)#int fa0/0.3
Router(config-subif)#encapsulation dot1q 3
Router(config-subif)#ip address 192.168.10.46 255.255.255.240

This section was probably the hardest part of this book so far, and I honestly created the simplest configuration you can possibly get away with using to help you through it!

I'll use Figure 13.16 to demonstrate configuring inter-VLAN routing (IVR) with a multilayer switch, which is often referred to as a *switched virtual interface* (SVI). I'm going to use the same network that I used to discuss a multilayer switch back in Figure 13.11, and I'll use this IP address scheme: 192.168.*x*.0/24, where *x* represents the VLAN subnet. In my example, this will be the same as the VLAN number.

FIGURE 13.16 Inter-VLAN routing with a multilayer switch

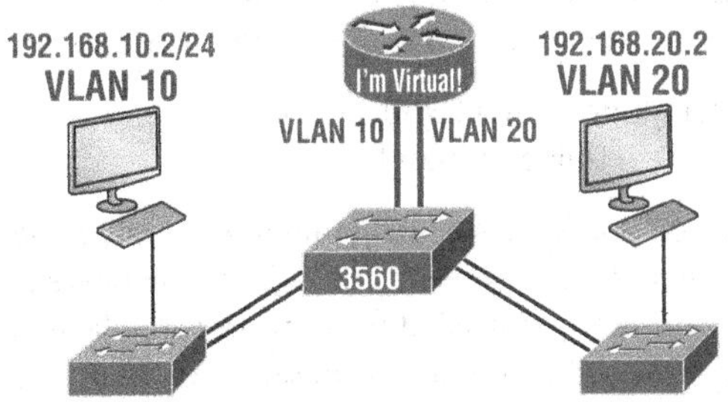

The hosts are already configured with the IP address, subnet mask, and default gateway address using the first address in the range. Now, I just need to configure the routing on the switch, which is pretty simple actually:

```
S1(config)#ip routing
S1(config)#int vlan 10
S1(config-if)#ip address 192.168.10.1 255.255.255.0
S1(config-if)#int vlan 20
S1(config-if)#ip address 192.168.20.1 255.255.255.0
```

And that's it! Enable IP routing and create one logical interface for each VLAN using the `interface vlan` *`number`* command, and voilà! You've now accomplished making inter-VLAN routing work on the backplane of the switch.

Summary

This chapter introduced you to the world of virtual LANs and described how Cisco switches can use them. I talked about how VLANs break up broadcast domains in a switched internetwork. This is very important because layer 2 switches only break up collision domains, and by default, all switches make up one large broadcast domain. I also described access links and went over how trunked VLANs work across a FastEthernet or faster link.

Trunking is a crucial technology to understand well when you're dealing with a network populated by multiple switches that are running several VLANs.

You were also presented with some key troubleshooting and configuration examples for access and trunk ports, configuring trunking options, and a huge section on IVR.

Exam Essentials

Understand the term *frame tagging*. *Frame tagging* refers to VLAN identification, which is what switches use to keep track of all those frames as they're traversing a switch fabric. It's how switches identify which frames belong to which VLANs.

Understand the 802.1q VLAN identification method. This is a nonproprietary IEEE method of frame tagging. If you're trunking between a Cisco switched link and a different brand of switch, you have to use 802.1q in order for the trunk to work.

Remember how to set a trunk port on a 2960 switch. To set a port to trunking on a 2960, use the `switchport mode trunk` command.

Remember to check a switch port's VLAN assignment when plugging in a new host. If you plug a new host into a switch, you must verify the VLAN membership of that port. If the membership is different from what is needed for that host, the host won't be able to reach the needed network services, such as a workgroup server or printer.

Remember how to create a Cisco router on a stick to provide inter-VLAN communication. You can use a Cisco FastEthernet or Gigabit Ethernet interface to provide inter-VLAN routing. The switch port connected to the router must be a trunk port; then you must create virtual interfaces (subinterfaces) on the router port for each VLAN connecting to it. The hosts in each VLAN will use this subinterface address as their default gateway address.

Understand how to provide inter-VLAN routing with a layer 3 switch. You can use a layer 3 (multilayer) switch to provide IVR, just as with a router on a stick, but using a layer 3 switch is more efficient and faster. First, you start the routing process with the command `ip routing`, then you create a virtual interface for each VLAN using the command `interface vlan vlan`, and then you apply the IP address for that VLAN under that logical interface.

Written Lab

You can find the answers to this lab in Appendix A, "Answers to the Written Labs."

Write the answers to the following questions:

1. True/False: To provide IVR with a layer 3 switch, you place an IP address on each interface of the switch.
2. What protocol will stop loops in a layer 2 switched network?
3. VLANs break up __________ domains in a layer 2 switched network.
4. Switches, by default, only break up __________ domains.
5. If you have a switch that provides both ISL and 802.1q frame tagging, which command under the trunk interface will make the trunk use 802.1q?
6. What does trunking provide?
7. What is frame tagging?
8. True/False: The 802.1q encapsulation is removed from the frame if the frame is forwarded out an access link.
9. What type of link on a switch is a member of only one VLAN?
10. You want to change from the default of VLAN 1 to VLAN 4 for untagged traffic. What command should you use?

Review Questions

You can find the answers to these questions in Appendix B, "Answers to the Review Questions."

> **NOTE** The following questions are designed to test your understanding of this chapter's material. For more information on how to get additional questions, please see www.lammle.com/ccna.

1. Which of the following statements is true with regard to VLANs?
   - **A.** VLANs greatly reduce network security.
   - **B.** VLANs increase the number of collision domains while decreasing their size.
   - **C.** VLANs decrease the number of broadcast domains while decreasing their size.
   - **D.** Network adds, moves, and changes are achieved with ease simply by configuring a port into the appropriate VLAN.
2. Write the command that must be present for a layer 3 switch to provide inter-VLAN routing between the two VLANs created with the following commands:

```
S1(config)#int vlan 10
S1(config-if)#ip address 192.168.10.1 255.255.255.0
S1(config-if)#int vlan 20
S1(config-if)#ip address 192.168.20.1 255.255.255.0
```

3. In the following diagram, how must the port on each end of the line be configured to carry traffic between the two hosts in the Sales VLAN?

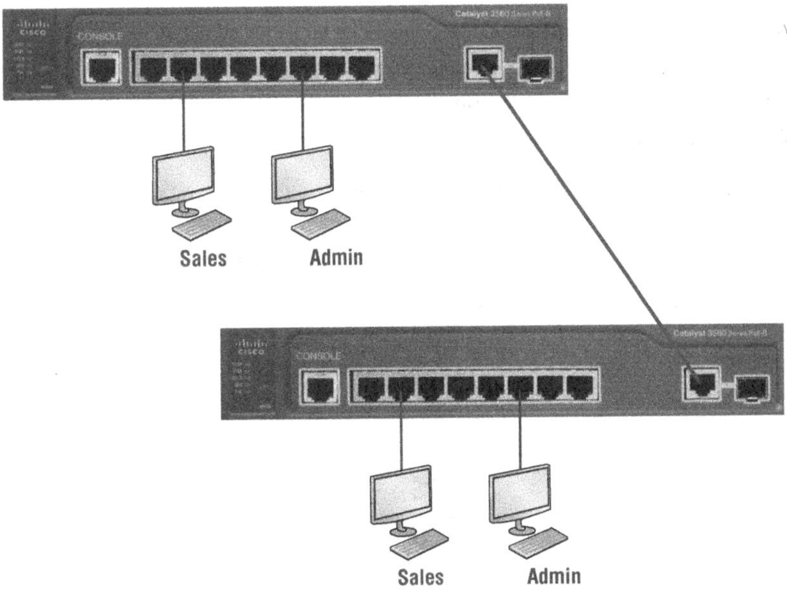

A. Access port

B. 10 GB

C. Trunk

D. Spanning

4. What is the only type of *second* VLAN that an access port can be a member of?

A. Secondary

B. Voice

C. Primary

D. Trunk

5. In the following configuration, what command is missing in the creation of the VLAN interface?

```
2960#config t
2960(config)#int vlan 1
2960(config-if)#ip address 192.168.10.2 255.255.255.0
2960(config-if)#exit
2960(config)#ip default-gateway 192.168.10.1
```

A. `no shutdown under int vlan 1`

B. `encapsulation dot1q 1 under int vlan 1`

C. `switchport access vlan 1`

D. `passive-interface`

6. Which of the following statements is true with regard to ISL and 802.1q?

A. 802.1q encapsulates the frame with control information; ISL inserts an ISL field along with tag control information.

B. 802.1q is Cisco proprietary.

C. ISL encapsulates the frame with control information; 802.1q inserts an 802.1q field along with tag control information.

D. ISL is a standard.

7. What concept is depicted in the following diagram?

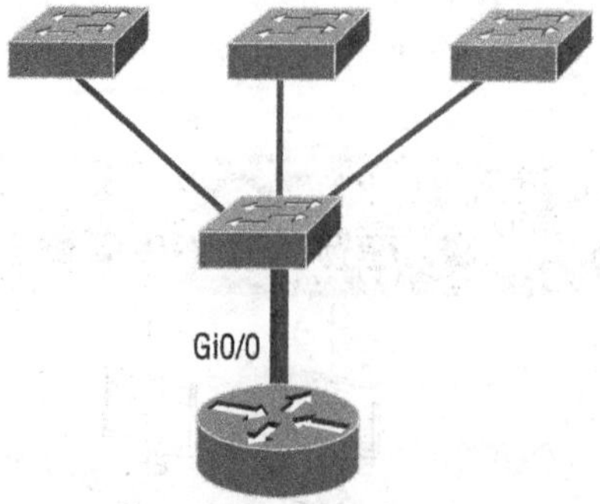

A. Multiprotocol routing

B. Passive interface

C. Gateway redundancy

D. Router on a stick

8. Write the command that places an interface into VLAN 2. Write only the command, not the prompt.

9. Write the command that generated the following output:

```
VLAN Name                             Status    Ports
---- -------------------------------- --------- -------------------------------
1    default                          active    Fa0/1, Fa0/2, Fa0/3, Fa0/4
                                                Fa0/5, Fa0/6, Fa0/7, Fa0/8
                                              Fa0/9, Fa0/10, Fa0/11, Fa0/12
                                             Fa0/13, Fa0/14, Fa0/19, Fa0/20
                                             Fa0/21, Fa0/22, Fa0/23, Gi0/1
                                                  Gi0/2
2    Sales                            active
3    Marketing                        active
4    Accounting                       active
[output cut]
```

10. In the configuration and diagram shown, what command is missing to enable inter-VLAN routing between VLAN 2 and VLAN 3?

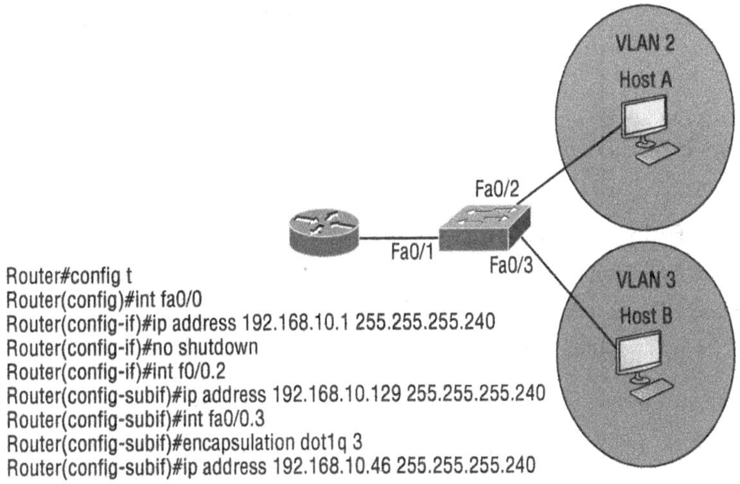
VLAN 2
Host A
Fa0/2
Fa0/1
Fa0/3
VLAN 3
Host B
Router#config t
Router(config)#int fa0/0
Router(config-if)#ip address 192.168.10.1 255.255.255.240
Router(config-if)#no shutdown
Router(config-if)#int f0/0.2
Router(config-subif)#ip address 192.168.10.129 255.255.255.240
Router(config-subif)#int fa0/0.3
Router(config-subif)#encapsulation dot1q 3
Router(config-subif)#ip address 192.168.10.46 255.255.255.240

A. `encapsulation dot1q 3 under int f0/0.2`

B. `encapsulation dot1q 2 under int f0/0.2`

C. `no shutdown under int f0/0.2`

D. `no shutdown under int f0/0.3`

11. Based on the configuration shown here, which of the following statements is true?

```
S1(config)#ip routing
S1(config)#int vlan 10
S1(config-if)#ip address 192.168.10.1 255.255.255.0
S1(config-if)#int vlan 20
S1(config-if)#ip address 192.168.20.1 255.255.255.0
```

A. This is a multilayer switch.

B. The two VLANs are in the same subnet.

C. Encapsulation must be configured.

D. VLAN 10 is the management VLAN.

12. Which of the following statements about the following output is true?

```
S1#sh vlan

VLAN Name                  Status    Ports
---- --------------------- --------- -------------------------------
1    default               active    Fa0/1, Fa0/2, Fa0/3, Fa0/4
                                     Fa0/5, Fa0/6, Fa0/7, Fa0/8
                                     Fa0/9, Fa0/10, Fa0/11, Fa0/12
                                   Fa0/13, Fa0/14, Fa0/19, Fa0/20,
                                   Fa0/22, Fa0/23, Gi0/1, Gi0/2
2    Sales                 active
3    Marketing                       Fa0/21
4    Accounting            active
[output cut]
```

A. Interface F0/15 is a trunk port.

B. Interface F0/17 is an access port.

C. Interface F0/21 is a trunk port.

D. VLAN 1 was populated manually.

13. 802.1q untagged frames are members of the _________ VLAN.

A. Auxiliary

B. Voice

C. Native

D. Private

14. Write the command that generated the following output. Write only the command, not the prompt.

```
Name: Fa0/15
Switchport: Enabled
Administrative Mode: dynamic desirable
Operational Mode: trunk
Administrative Trunking Encapsulation: negotiate
Operational Trunking Encapsulation: isl
Negotiation of Trunking: On
Access Mode VLAN: 1 (default)
Trunking Native Mode VLAN: 1 (default)
Administrative Native VLAN tagging: enabled
Voice VLAN: none
[output cut]
```

15. Which of the following statements is true regarding virtual local area networks (VLANs)?

A. VLANs are location dependent.

B. VLANs are limited to a single switch.

C. VLANs can be subnets of major networks.

D. VLANs define collision domains.

16. In the following diagram, what should be the default gateway address of Host B?

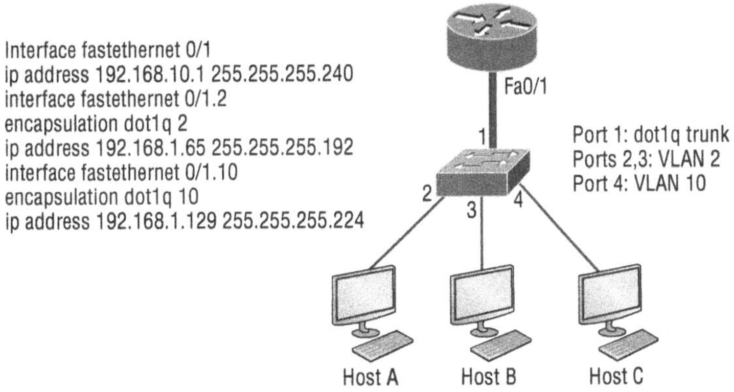
Interface fastethernet 0/1
ip address 192.168.10.1 255.255.255.240
interface fastethernet 0/1.2
encapsulation dot1q 2
ip address 192.168.1.65 255.255.255.192
interface fastethernet 0/1.10
encapsulation dot1q 10
ip address 192.168.1.129 255.255.255.224
Fa0/1
1
2
3
4
Port 1: dot1q trunk
Ports 2,3: VLAN 2
Port 4: VLAN 10
Host A
Host B
Host C

A. 192.168.10.1

B. 192.168.1.65

C. 192.168.1.129

D. 192.168.1.2

17. What is the purpose of frame tagging in virtual LAN (VLAN) configurations?
    - A. Inter-VLAN routing
    - B. Encryption of network packets
    - C. Frame identification over trunk links
    - D. Frame identification over access links

18. Write the command to create VLAN 2 on a layer 2 switch. Write only the command, not the prompt.

19. Which of the following statements regarding 802.1q frame tagging is true?
    - A. 802.1q adds a 26-byte trailer and 4-byte header.
    - B. 802.1q uses a native VLAN.
    - C. The original Ethernet frame is not modified.
    - D. 802.1q only works with Cisco switches.

20. Write the command that prevents an interface from generating DTP frames. Write only the command, not the prompt.

Chapter 14

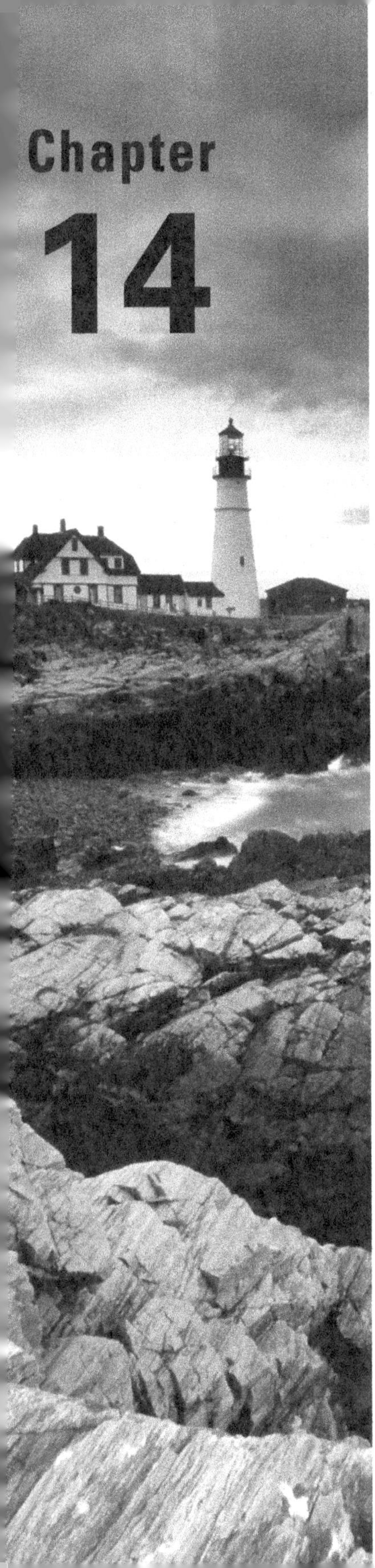

Cloud and Virtual Private Networks

THE FOLLOWING CCNA EXAM TOPICS ARE COVERED IN THIS CHAPTER:

✓ ***1.0 Network Fundamentals***

- 1.2.f On-premises and cloud

✓ ***5.0 Security Fundamentals***

- 5.5 Describe remote access and site-to-site VPNs

In this chapter, we'll thoroughly explore virtual private networks (VPNs) and develop advanced solutions catering to your company's off-site network access needs. The chapter begins by discussing the fundamentals of VPNs and then moves on to examine how they leverage IP security protocols to establish secure communications over public networks like the Internet. Specifically, we'll focus on VPNs that use IPsec, which provides robust encryption and authentication mechanisms to safeguard data as it travels across unsecured channels.

Next, we'll take a hands-on approach by describing how to create a VPN tunnel using GRE (Generic Routing Encapsulation). GRE allows the encapsulation of a wide variety of Network layer protocols, creating a virtual point-to-point connection that can be used with IPsec to enhance security and flexibility in your network architecture.

As we progress, we'll also introduce cloud technology to explore the evolving landscape of network management. We'll discuss how cloud services are increasingly being used to manage and monitor modern network devices, offering scalability, convenience, and enhanced control over your network infrastructure. By the end of this chapter, you'll have a solid understanding of both traditional VPN implementations and the new possibilities cloud-based management brings.

NOTE To find bonus material, as well as Todd Lammle videos, practice questions and hands-on labs, please see `www.lammle.com/ccna`.

Virtual Private Networks

Of course, you've heard the term *VPN* before, and you probably have a pretty good idea of what one is, but just in case: a *virtual private network (VPN)* allows the creation of private networks across the Internet, providing privacy and the tunneling of non-TCP/IP protocols. VPNs are used daily to give remote users and disparate networks connectivity over a public medium like the Internet instead of using more expensive, permanent means.

VPNs are actually pretty easy to understand. A VPN fits somewhere between a LAN and WAN, with the WAN often simulating a LAN link. Basically, your computer on one LAN connects to a different, remote LAN and uses its resources remotely. The challenge when using VPNs is a big one—security! This may sound a lot like connecting a LAN (or VLAN) to a WAN, but a VPN is so much more.

Here's the key difference: A typical WAN connects two or more remote LANs using a router and someone else's network, like your Internet service provider's (ISP's). Your local host and router see these networks as remote networks, not local networks or local resources.

A VPN actually makes your local host part of the remote network by using the WAN link that connects you to the remote LAN. The VPN will make your host appear as though it's actually local on the remote network. This means you gain access to the remote LAN's resources, and that access is also very secure.

And this may also sound a lot like a VLAN definition because the concept is the same: "Take my host and make it appear local to the remote network's resources." Just remember this key distinction: for networks that are physically local, using VLANs is a good solution, but for physically remote networks that span a WAN, you need to use VPNs instead.

Here's a simple VPN example using my home office in Colorado. Here, I have my personal host, but I want it to appear as if it's on a LAN in my corporate office in Texas, so I can access my remote servers. I'm going to use a VPN to achieve my goal.

Figure 14.1 illustrates my host using a VPN connection from Colorado to Texas. This allows me to access the remote network services and servers as if my host were right there on the same VLAN.

FIGURE 14.1 Example of using a VPN

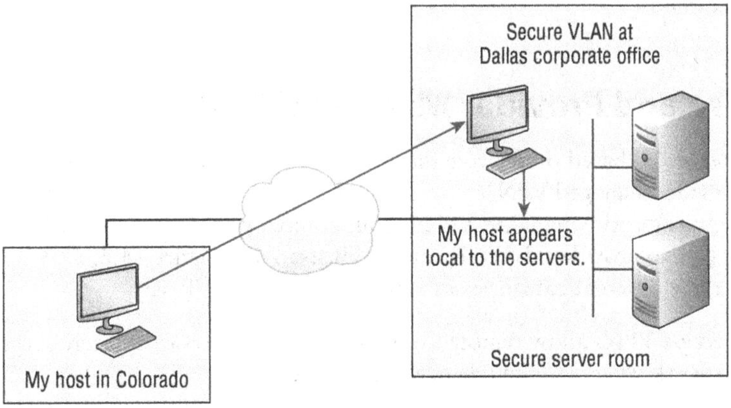

Why is this so important? If you answered, "Because my servers in Texas are secure, and only the hosts on the same VLAN are allowed to connect to them and use the resources of these servers," you nailed it! A VPN allows me to connect to these resources by locally attaching to the VLAN through a VPN across the WAN. My other option is to open up my network and servers to everyone on the Internet, so, clearly, it's vital for me to have a VPN!

Benefits of VPNs

There are many benefits to using VPNs on your corporate and even home network. The following benefits are covered in the CCNA objectives:

Security VPNs provide security using advanced encryption and authentication protocols, which help protect your network from unauthorized access. IPsec and SSL fall into this category. Secure Sockets Layer (SSL) is an encryption technology used with web browsers and has native SSL encryption known as Web VPN. You can also use the Cisco AnyConnect SSL VPN client installed on your PC to provide an SSL VPN solution, as well as the Clientless Cisco SSL VPN.

Cost Savings By connecting the corporate remote offices to their closest Internet provider and creating a VPN tunnel with encryption and authentication, you gain a huge savings over opting for traditional leased point-to-point lines. This also permits higher bandwidth links and security, all for far less money than traditional connections.

Scalability VPNs scale very well to quickly bring up new offices or have mobile users connect securely.

Compatibility with Broadband Technology For remote and traveling users and remote offices, any Internet access can provide a connection to the corporate VPN. This allows users to take advantage of the high-speed Internet access that DSL or cable modems offer.

Enterprise and Provider Managed VPN's

VPNs are categorized based on the role they play in a business, such as enterprise managed VPNs and provider managed VPNs.

You'll use an enterprise managed VPN if your company manages its own VPNs. This is a very popular way to provide this service and is illustrated in Figure 14.2.

There are three different categories of enterprise-managed VPNs:

Remote access VPNs allow remote users like telecommuters to securely access the corporate network wherever and whenever they need to.

Site-to-site VPNs, or intranet VPNs, allow a company to connect its remote sites to the corporate backbone securely over a public medium like the Internet instead of requiring more expensive WAN connections.

Extranet VPNs allow an organization's suppliers, partners, and customers to be connected to the corporate network in a limited way for business-to-business (B2B) communications.

Provider-managed VPNs are illustrated in Figure 14.3:

FIGURE 14.2 Enterprise-managed VPNs

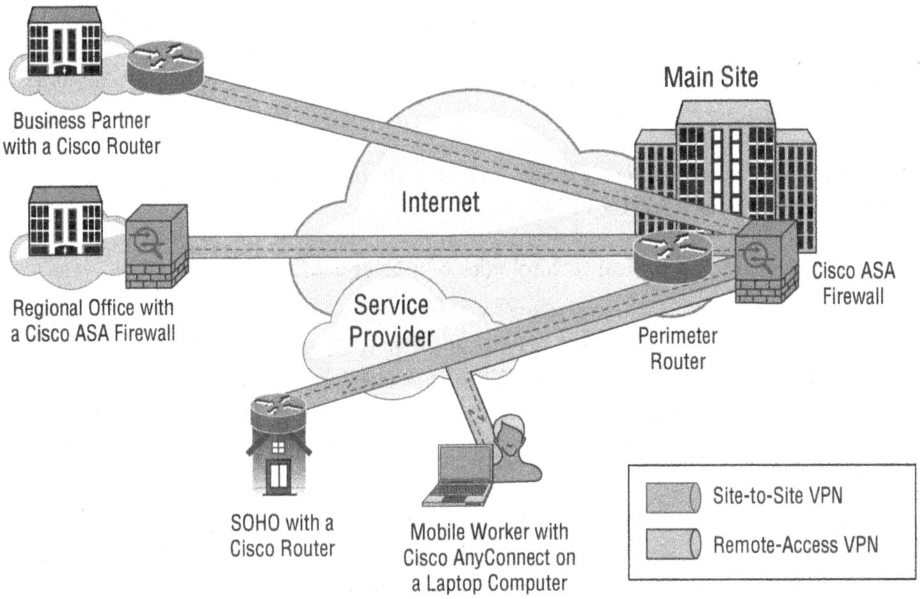

FIGURE 14.3 Provider-managed VPNs

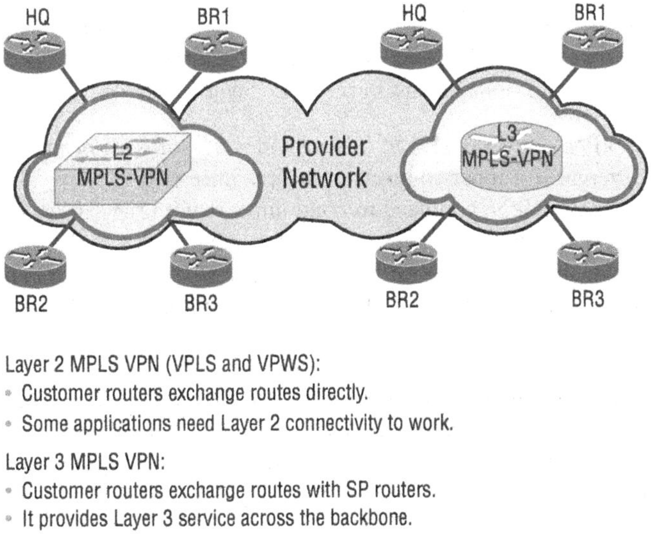

There are two different categories of provider-managed VPNs:

Layer 2 MPLS VPN Layer 2 VPNs are a type of virtual private network (VPN) that uses MPLS labels to transport data. The communication occurs between routers known as *provider edge* routers (PEs) because they sit on the edge of the provider's network, next to the customer's network.

ISPs that have an existing layer 2 network may choose to use these VPNs instead of the other common layer 3 MPLS VPNs.

The following are two typical technologies of a layer 2 MPLS VPN:

Virtual Private Wire Service (VPWS) VPWS is the simplest form for enabling Ethernet services over MPLS. It's also known as ETHoMPLS (Ethernet over MPLS), or VLL (Virtual Leased Line). VPWS is characterized by a fixed relationship between an attachment-virtual circuit and an emulated virtual circuit. For example, VPWS-based services are point-to-point Frame-Relay/ATM/Ethernet services over IP/MPLS.

Virtual Private LAN Switching Service (VPLS) This is an end-to-end service and is virtual because multiple instances of this service share the same Ethernet broadcast domain virtually. Still, each connection is independent and isolated from the others in the network. A learned, dynamic relationship exists between an attachment-virtual circuit and emulated virtual circuits that's determined by customer MAC address.

In this type of network, the customer manages its own routing protocols. One advantage that layer 2 VPN has over its layer 3 counterpart is that some applications won't work if nodes aren't in the same layer 2 network.

Layer 3 MPLS VPN Layer 3 MPLS VPN provides a layer 3 service across the backbone, and a different IP subnet connects each site. Since you will typically deploy a routing protocol over this VPN, you need to communicate with the service provider in order to participate in the exchange of routes. Neighbor adjacency is established between your router (called CE) and provider router (called PE). The service provider network has many core routers (called P routers) whose job is to provide connectivity between the PE routers.

If you want to totally outsource your layer 3 VPN, then this service is for you. Your service provider will maintain and manage routing for all your sites. From your perspective as a customer who's outsourced your VPNs, it will seem as though your ISP's network is one big virtual switch.

Because VPNs are inexpensive and secure, I'm guessing that you really want to know how to create them, right? Great! So, there's more than one way to bring a VPN into being.

The first approach uses IPsec to build authentication and encryption services between endpoints on an IP network. The second way is via tunneling protocols, which allow you to establish a tunnel between endpoints on a network. Understand that the tunnel itself is a way for data or protocols to be encapsulated inside another protocol—pretty clean!

We'll get to IPsec in a minute, but first you need to know about four of the most common tunneling protocols in use today:

Layer 2 Forwarding (L2F) L2F is a Cisco-proprietary tunneling protocol that was Cisco's first and created for virtual private dial-up networks (VPDNs). A VPDN allows a device to use a dial-up connection to create a secure connection to a corporate network. L2F was later replaced by L2TP, which is backward compatible with L2F.

Point-to-Point Tunneling Protocol (PPTP) PPTP was created by Microsoft with others to allow for the secure transfer of data from remote networks to the corporate network.

Layer 2 Tunneling Protocol (L2TP) L2TP was created by Cisco and Microsoft to replace L2F and PPTP. It merges the capabilities of both L2F and PPTP into one tunneling protocol.

Generic Routing Encapsulation (GRE) Another Cisco-proprietary tunneling protocol, GRE forms virtual point-to-point links, allowing for a variety of protocols to be encapsulated in IP tunnels. I'll cover GRE in more detail, including how to configure it, at the end of this chapter.

Now that you're clear on both exactly what a VPN is and the various types of VPNs available, it's time to dive into IPsec.

Introduction to Cisco IOS IPsec

Simply put, IPsec is an industry-wide standard framework of protocols and algorithms that allows for secure data transmission over an IP-based network. It functions at the layer 3 Network layer of the OSI model.

Did you notice I said IP-based network? That's really important because, by itself, IPsec can't be used to encrypt non-IP traffic. This means that if you run into a situation where you have to encrypt non-IP traffic, you'll need to create a Generic Routing Encapsulation (GRE) tunnel for it and then use IPsec to encrypt that tunnel!

IPsec Transforms

An *IPsec transform* specifies a single security protocol with its corresponding security algorithm. Without transforms, IPsec wouldn't be able to give us its glory. It's important to be familiar with these technologies, so let me take a second to define the security protocols. I'll also briefly introduce the supporting encryption and hashing algorithms that IPsec relies on.

Security Protocols

The two primary security protocols used by IPsec are *Authentication Header (AH)* and *Encapsulating Security Payload (ESP)*.

Authentication Header (AH)

The AH protocol provides authentication for the data and the IP header of a packet using a one-way hash for packet authentication. It works like this: The sender generates a one-way hash, then the receiver generates the same one-way hash. If the packet has changed in any way, it won't be authenticated and will be dropped. So basically, IPsec relies upon AH to guarantee authenticity.

Let's take a look at this using Figure 14.4.

FIGURE 14.4 Security protocols

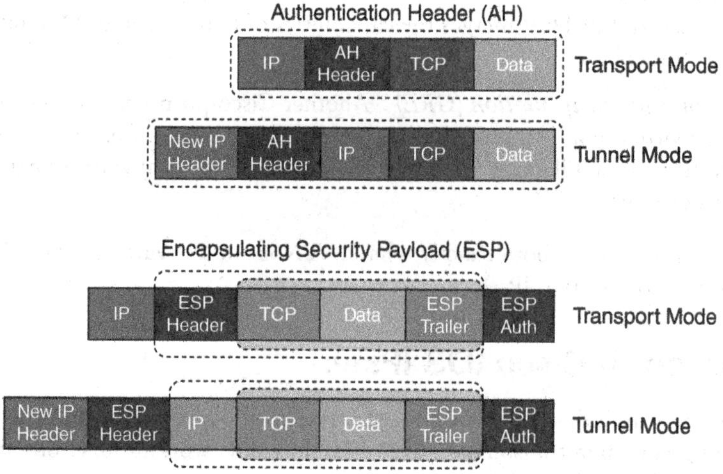

AH checks the entire packet when in tunnel mode, but it doesn't offer any encryption services. However, using AH in transport mode checks only the payload.

This is unlike ESP, which only provides an integrity check on the data of a packet when in transport mode. However, using AH in tunnel mode ESP encrypts the whole packet.

Encapsulating Security Payload (ESP)

ESP won't tell you when or how the NASDAQ's going to bounce up and down like a superball, but ESP does a lot for you! It provides confidentiality, data origin authentication, connectionless integrity, anti-replay service, and limited traffic-flow confidentiality by defeating traffic flow analysis—which is almost as good as AH without the possible encryption! Here's a description of ESPs five big features:

Confidentiality (Encryption) Confidentiality allows the sending device to encrypt the packets before transmitting them in order to prevent eavesdropping and is provided through the use of symmetric encryption algorithms like DES or 3DES. It can be selected separately from all other services, but the type of confidentiality must be the same on both endpoints of your VPN.

Data Integrity Data integrity allows the receiver to verify that the data received hasn't been altered in any way along the way. IPsec uses checksums as a simple way to confirm the integrity of the data.

Authentication Authentication ensures that the connection is made with the correct partner. The receiver can authenticate the source of the packet by guaranteeing and certifying the source of the information.

Anti-replay Service Anti-replay election is based on the receiver, meaning the service is effective only if the receiver checks the sequence number. In case you were wondering, a replay attack is when a hacker nicks a copy of an authenticated packet and later transmits it to the intended destination. When the duplicate, authenticated IP packet gets to the destination, it can disrupt services and generally wreak havoc. The Sequence Number field is designed to foil this type of attack.

Traffic Flow In order for traffic flow confidentiality to work, you have to have at least tunnel mode selected. It's most effective if it's implemented at a security gateway where tons of traffic amasses, because that's precisely the kind of environment that can mask the true source-destination patterns from bad guys trying to breach your security.

Encryption

VPNs create a private network over a public network infrastructure, but to maintain confidentiality and security, we really need to use IPsec with our VPNs. IPsec uses various types of protocols to perform encryption. The following types of encryption algorithms are used today:

Symmetric Encryption This type of encryption requires a shared secret to encrypt and decrypt. Each computer encrypts the data before sending info across the network, with this same key being used to both encrypt and decrypt the data. Examples of symmetric key encryption include Data Encryption Standard (DES), Triple DES (3DES), and Advanced Encryption Standard (AES).

Asymmetric Encryption Devices that use asymmetric encryption use different keys for encryption than they do for decryption. These keys are called *private keys* and *public keys*.

Private keys encrypt a hash from the message to create a digital signature, which is then verified via decryption using the public key. Public keys encrypt a symmetric key for secure distribution to the receiving host, which then decrypts that symmetric key using its exclusively held private key. It's not possible to encrypt and decrypt using the same key. Asymmetric decryption is a variant of public key encryption, which also uses a combination of both public and private keys. An example of an asymmetric encryption is Rivest, Shamir, and Adleman (RSA).

Looking at Figure 14.5, you can see the complex encryption process.

FIGURE 14.5 The encryption process

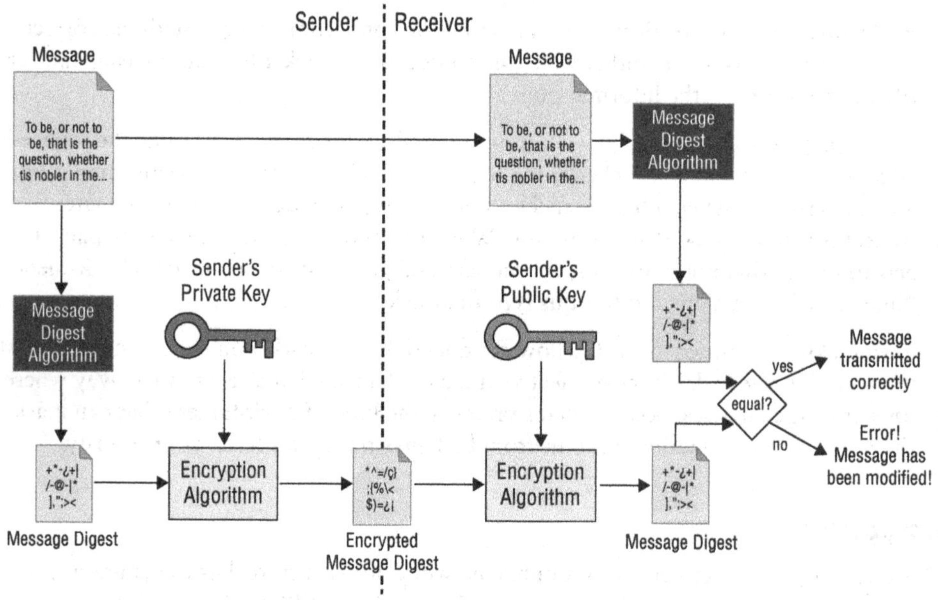

As you can see from the amount of information I've thrown at you so far, establishing a VPN connection between two sites takes some study, time, and practice. And I'm just scratching the surface! I know it can be difficult at times, and it definitely takes patience. Cisco does have some GUI interfaces to help with this process, which also come in handy for configuring VPNs with IPsec. Though highly useful and very interesting, they're just beyond the scope of this book, so I'm not going into this topic further here.

GRE Tunnels

Generic Routing Encapsulation (GRE) is a tunneling protocol that can encapsulate many protocols inside IP tunnels. Some examples include routing protocols such as EIGRP and OSPF and the routed protocol IPv6. Figure 14.6 shows the different pieces of a GRE header.

FIGURE 14.6 Generic Routing Encapsulation (GRE) tunnel structure

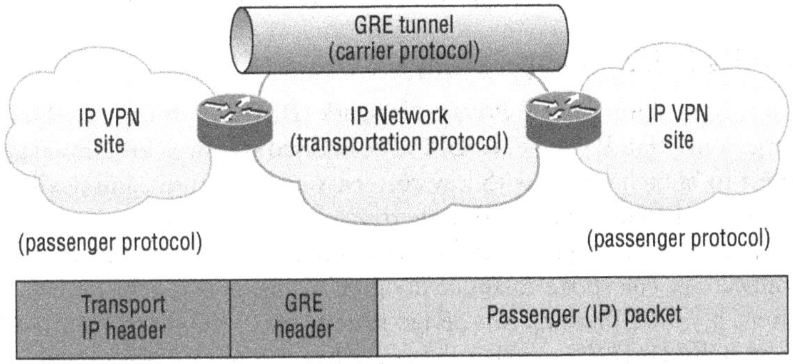

A GRE tunnel interface supports a header for each of the following:

- A passenger protocol or encapsulated protocols like IP or IPv6, which is the protocol being encapsulated by GRE
- GRE encapsulation protocol
- A transport delivery protocol, typically IP

GRE tunnels have the following characteristics:

- GRE uses a protocol-type field in the GRE header so any layer 3 protocol can be used through the tunnel.
- GRE is stateless and has no flow control.
- GRE offers no security.
- GRE creates additional overhead for tunneled packets—at least 24 bytes.

GRE over IPsec

As I mentioned, by itself, GRE offers no security—no form of payload confidentiality or encryption whatsoever. If the packets are sniffed over the public network, their contents are in plaintext. Although IPsec provides a secure method for tunneling data across an IP network, it definitely has its limitations.

IPsec doesn't support IP broadcast or IP multicast, preventing the use of protocols that need them, like routing protocols. IPsec also does not support the use of multiprotocol traffic. However, GRE can be used to "carry" other passenger protocols like IP broadcast or IP multicast, plus non-IP protocols as well. Using GRE tunnels with IPsec allows you to run a routing protocol, IP multicast, and multiprotocol traffic across your network.

With a generic hub-and-spoke topology like Corp to Branch, you can typically implement static tunnels (usually GRE over IPsec) between the corporate office and branch offices. When you want to add a new spoke to the network, you simply need to configure it on the hub router. Also, the traffic between spokes has to traverse the hub, where it must exit one tunnel and enter another. Static tunnels are an appropriate solution for small networks, but not so much as the network grows larger with an increasing number of spokes!

Cisco DMVPN (Cisco Proprietary)

Cisco's Dynamic Multipoint Virtual Private Network (DMVPN) feature enables you to easily scale large and small IPsec VPNs. DMVPN is Cisco's answer for allowing a corporate office to connect to branch offices with low cost, easy configuration, and flexibility. DMVPN consists of one central router like a corporate router, which is referred to as the hub, and the branches as spokes. So, the corporate-to-branch connection is referred to as the hub-and-spoke interconnection. The spoke-to-spoke design is also supported for branch-to-branch interconnections. If you're thinking this design sounds really similar to your old Frame Relay network, you're right! DMPVN enables you to configure a single GRE tunnel interface and a single IPsec profile on the hub router to manage all spoke routers. This keeps the size of the configuration on the hub router basically the same even if you add more spoke routers to the network. DMVPN also allows a spoke router to dynamically create VPN tunnels between them as network data travels from one spoke to another.

IPsec VTI

The IPsec Virtual Tunnel Interface (VTI) mode of an IPsec configuration can seriously simplify a VPN configuration when protection is needed for remote access. And it's a simpler option than GRE or L2TP for the encapsulation and crypto maps used with IPsec. Like GRE, it sends routing protocol and multicast traffic, just without GRE and all the overhead it brings. Simple configuration and routing adjacency directly over the VTI are great benefits! Understand that all traffic is encrypted and supports only one protocol—either IPv4 or IPv6, just like standard IPsec.

So, let's get ready to configure a GRE tunnel now. It's actually pretty simple.

Configuring GRE Tunnels

Before you attempt to configure a GRE tunnel, you need to create an implementation plan. Here's a checklist of what you need to do to configure and implement a GRE tunnel:

- Use IP addressing.
- Create the logical tunnel interfaces.
- Specify that you're using GRE tunnel mode under the tunnel interface. This is optional since it's the default tunnel mode.
- Specify the tunnel source and destination IP addresses.
- Configure an IP address for the tunnel interface.

We're now ready to bring up a simple GRE tunnel. Figure 14.7 shows the network with two routers.

FIGURE 14.7 Example of GRE configuration

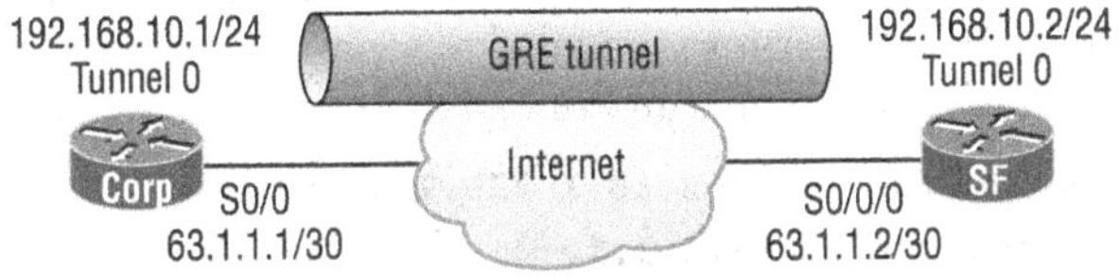

First, we need to make the logical tunnel with the *interface tunnel number* command. We can use any number up to 2.14 billion.

```
Corp(config)#int s0/0/0
Corp(config-if)#ip address 63.1.1.1 255.255.255.252
Corp(config)#int tunnel ?
  <0-2147483647>  Tunnel interface number
Corp(config)#int tunnel 0
*Jan 5 16:58:22.719:%LINEPROTO-5-UPDOWN: Line protocol on Interface Tunnel0,
changed state to down
```

Once we've configured our interface and created the logical tunnel, we need to configure the mode and then transport protocol:

```
Corp(config-if)#tunnel mode ?
  aurp     AURP TunnelTalk AppleTalk encapsulation
  cayman   Cayman TunnelTalk AppleTalk encapsulation
  dvmrp    DVMRP multicast tunnel
  eon      EON compatible CLNS tunnel
  gre      generic route encapsulation protocol
  ipip     IP over IP encapsulation
  ipsec    IPSec tunnel encapsulation
  iptalk   Apple IPTalk encapsulation
  ipv6     Generic packet tunneling in IPv6
  ipv6ip   IPv6 over IP encapsulation
  nos      IP over IP encapsulation (KA9Q/NOS compatible)
  rbscp    RBSCP in IP tunnel
Corp(config-if)#tunnel mode gre ?
  ip          over IP
  ipv6        over IPv6
  multipoint  over IP (multipoint)

Corp(config-if)#tunnel mode gre ip
```

Now that we've created the tunnel interface, the type, and the transport protocol, we've got to configure our IP addresses for use inside of the tunnel. Of course, we must use our actual physical interface IP in order for the tunnel to send traffic across the Internet, but we also need to configure the tunnel source and tunnel destination addresses:

```
Corp(config-if)#ip address 192.168.10.1 255.255.255.0
Corp(config-if)#tunnel source 63.1.1.1
Corp(config-if)#tunnel destination 63.1.1.2

Corp#sho run interface tunnel 0
Building configuration...

Current configuration : 117 bytes
!
interface Tunnel0
 ip address 192.168.10.1 255.255.255.0
 tunnel source 63.1.1.1
 tunnel destination 63.1.1.2
end
```

It's time to configure the other end of the serial link and watch the tunnel pop up:

```
SF(config)#int s0/0/0
SF(config-if)#ip address 63.1.1.2 255.255.255.252
SF(config-if)#int t0
SF(config-if)#ip address 192.168.10.2 255.255.255.0
SF(config-if)#tunnel source 63.1.1.2
SF(config-if)#tun destination 63.1.1.1
*May 19 22:46:37.099: %LINEPROTO-5-UPDOWN: Line protocol on Interface Tunnel0,
changed state to up
```

Oops—did I forget to set my tunnel mode and transport to GRE and IP on the SF router? No, I didn't need to because it's the default tunnel mode on Cisco IOS. Nice! So, first I set the physical interface IP address, which used a global address even though I didn't have to, and then I created the tunnel interface and set the IP address of the tunnel interface. It's important that you remember to configure the tunnel interface with the actual source and destination IP addresses to use; otherwise, the tunnel won't come up. In my example, 63.1.1.2 was the source, and 63.1.1.1 was the destination.

Verifying GRE Tunnels

As usual, I'll start with my favorite troubleshooting command, `show ip interface brief`.

```
Corp#sh ip int brief
Interface          IP-Address      OK? Method Status                Protocol
FastEthernet0/0    10.10.10.5      YES manual up                    up
```

```
Serial0/0          63.1.1.1        YES manual up                    up
FastEthernet0/1    unassigned      YES unset  administratively down down
Serial0/1          unassigned      YES unset  administratively down down
Tunnel0            192.168.10.1    YES manual up                    up
```

In this output, you can see that the tunnel interface is now showing up as an interface on my router. You can see the IP address of the tunnel interface, and the Physical and Data Link status show as up/up. So far, so good! Let's take a look at the interface with the `show interfaces tunnel 0` command:

```
Corp#sh int tun 0
Tunnel0 is up, line protocol is up
  Hardware is Tunnel
  Internet address is 192.168.10.1/24
  MTU 1414 bytes, BW 9 Kbit, DLY 500000 usec,
     reliability 255/255, txload 1/255, rxload 1/255
  Encapsulation TUNNEL, loopback not set
  Keepalive not set
  Tunnel source 63.1.1.1, destination 63.1.1.2
  Tunnel protocol/transport GRE/IP
    Key disabled, sequencing disabled
    Checksumming of packets disabled
  Tunnel TTL 255
  Fast tunneling enabled
  Tunnel transmit bandwidth 8000 (kbps)
  Tunnel receive bandwidth 8000 (kbps)
```

The `show interfaces` command shows the configuration settings and the interface status as well as the IP address, tunnel source, and destination address. The output also shows the tunnel protocol, which is GRE/IP.

Last, let's take a look at the routing table with the `show ip route` command:

```
Corp#sh ip route
[output cut]
     192.168.10.0/24 is subnetted, 2 subnets
C       192.168.10.0/24 is directly connected, Tunnel0
L       192.168.10.1/32 is directly connected, Tunnel0
     63.0.0.0/30 is subnetted, 2 subnets
C       63.1.1.0 is directly connected, Serial0/0
L       63.1.1.1/32 is directly connected, Serial0/0
```

The `tunnel0` interface shows up as a directly connected interface. And even though it's a logical interface, the router treats it as a physical interface, just like serial 0/0 in the routing table:

```
Corp#ping 192.168.10.2
```

```
Type escape sequence to abort.
Sending 5, 100-byte ICMP Echos to 192.168.10.2, timeout is 2 seconds:
!!!!!
Success rate is 100 percent (5/5)
```

Did you notice that I just pinged 192.168.10.2 across the Internet? One last thing before we close and move on—troubleshooting an output that shows a tunnel routing error. If you configure your GRE tunnel and receive this GRE flapping message:

```
          Line protocol on Interface Tunnel0, changed state to up
07:11:55: %TUN-5-RECURDOWN:
          Tunnel0 temporarily disabled due to recursive routing
07:11:59: %LINEPROTO-5-UPDOWN:
          Line protocol on Interface Tunnel0, changed state to down
07:12:59: %LINEPROTO-5-UPDOWN:
```

It means that you've misconfigured your tunnel, which will cause your router to try to route to the tunnel destination address using the tunnel interface itself!

Cloud Models

You've just gained an understanding of how VPN tunnels are an effective solution for securely accessing your internal network environment. However, as organizations increasingly migrate their resources and services to "the cloud," it's crucial to expand your knowledge to include cloud concepts.

In the past, most network resources were hosted on-premises, making VPNs the go-to method for secure remote access. But as cloud computing becomes more prevalent, the dynamics of network access and security are evolving. It's no longer just about protecting the physical infrastructure within your organization's data centers; now, it's also about securing access to distributed resources that reside in various cloud environments.

To ensure that you're well-prepared for these changes, we'll take a closer look at what the cloud entails—its benefits, challenges, and how it integrates with traditional networking models.

By understanding the cloud, you'll be better equipped to design and manage secure, efficient, and scalable network architectures that meet the needs of a modern, cloud-centric world.

Let's understand the changes and effect the cloud has on the enterprise.

Cloud Computing and Its Effect on the Enterprise Network

Cloud computing is by far one of the hottest topics in today's IT world. Basically, cloud computing can provide virtualized processing, storage, and computing resources to users remotely, making the resources transparently available regardless of the user connection. To put it simply, some people just refer to the cloud as "someone else's hard drive." This is true, of course, but the cloud is much more than just storage.

A *public cloud* is a type of computing in which resources are offered by a third-party provider via the Internet and shared by organizations and individuals who want to use or purchase them. It is owned and maintained by one party, but it is shared among multiple organizations.

A *hybrid cloud* is a type of cloud computing that combines on-premises, private cloud, and third-party public cloud services, orchestrating the two platforms and allowing data and applications to be shared between them.

The history of the consolidation and virtualization of our servers tells us that this has become the de facto way of implementing servers because of basic resource efficiency. Two physical servers will use twice the amount of electricity as one server, but through virtualization, one physical server can host two virtual machines, hence the main thrust toward virtualization. With it, network components can be shared more efficiently.

Users connecting to a cloud provider's network, whether for storage or applications, really don't care about the underlying infrastructure because computing becomes a service rather than a product and is then considered an on-demand resource, as described in Figure 14.8.

FIGURE 14.8 Cloud computing is on-demand.

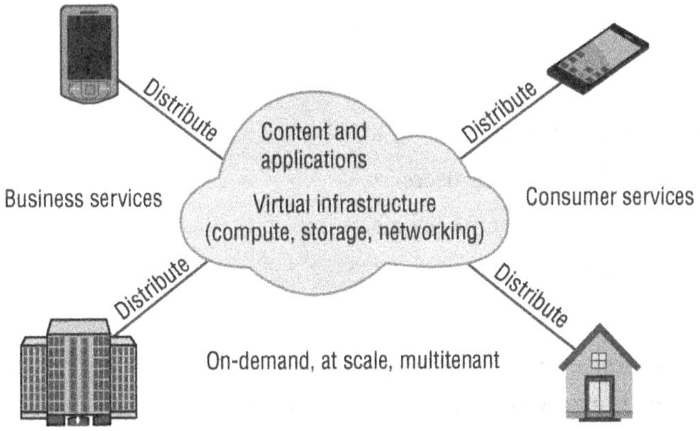

Centralization/consolidation of resources, automation of services, virtualization, and standardization (CAVS) are just a few of cloud services' big benefits.

Let's take a look at Figure 14.9.

Cloud computing has several advantages over traditional computer resource use. The following are advantages for the provider and the cloud user.

Here are the advantages to a cloud service builder or provider:

- Cost reduction, standardization, and automation
- High utilization through virtualized, shared resources
- Easier administration

FIGURE 14.9 The advantages of cloud computing

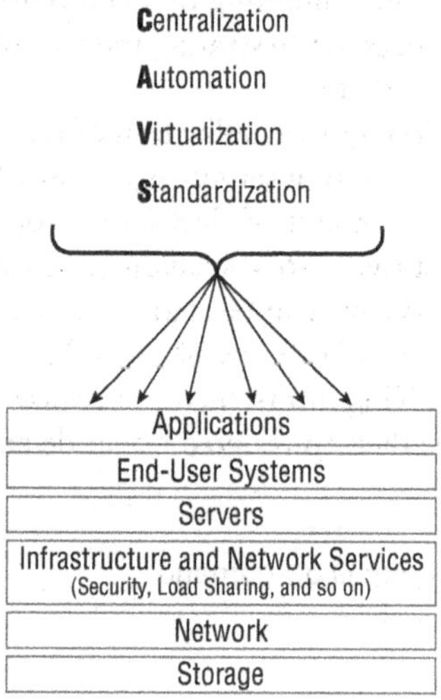

- A fall-in-place operations model

Here are the advantages to cloud users:

- On-demand, self-service resource provisioning
- Fast deployment cycles
- Cost-effective
- Centralized appearance of resources
- Highly available, horizontally scaled application architectures
- No local backups

Having centralized resources is critical for today's workforce. For example, if you have your documents stored locally on your laptop and your laptop gets stolen, you're pretty much screwed unless you're doing constant local backups. That is so 2005!

After I lost my laptop and all the files for the book I was writing at the time, I swore (yes, I did that, too) never to have my files stored locally again. I started using only Google Drive, OneDrive, and Dropbox for all my files, and they became my best backup friends.

If I lose my laptop now, I need to log in from any computer from anywhere to my service provider's logical drives, and presto, I have all my files again. This is clearly a simple example of using cloud computing, specifically SaaS (which is discussed next), and it's wonderful!

So, cloud computing provides for the sharing of resources, lower cost operations passed to the cloud consumer, computing scaling, and the ability to dynamically add new servers without going through the procurement and deployment process.

Private Clouds/On-Premises

"Private cloud" is simply a fancy term for hosting resources inside your physical environment, usually in a data center. You might have heard the saying that "cloud is just using someone else's data center," but this time, we are referring to yours! Generally speaking, the terms "private cloud" and "on-premises" are used interchangeably.

We will talk about virtualization in the next book, but for now, know that it is very common to deploy new servers on virtual machines that run on something called a *hypervisor*.

This approach lets us rapidly deploy new servers since we don't need to worry about buying physical hardware every time we want to deploy a new domain controller, etc.

Some products, like Cisco's Intersight Orchestration, allow you to provide a software catalogue where users can select the solution they need from a list, and it will provision all the virtual machines for them at the touch of a button—neat!

Businesses have a love-hate relationship with on-premises. On the one hand, it gives them maximum control over the infrastructure because it is actually their infrastructure that is hosted by them. On the other hand, however, buying and hosting all that hardware can get expensive very quickly.

Public Clouds

Cloud providers can offer you different available resources based on your needs and budget. You can choose just a vitalized network platform or go all in with the network, OS, and application resources.

People usually mean public clouds when they talk about "the cloud." They use a cloud provider like Amazon's AWS or Microsoft's Azure to host resources. As the name implies, the resources are generally publicly available, which means they will have a public IP and all the security considerations that come with it.

To make sure I don't leave you with the wrong impression, the cloud can be very costly over time because instead of buying a server once and running it for a few years, it charges you for every second of usage! It isn't uncommon to see companies go back and forth with cloud adoption when they don't like their bill.

The "cloud" is a very large topic with dozens of certifications per vendor that you can dive into when you get more senior, so we won't go much deeper than that here.

Figure 14.10 shows the three service models available, depending on the type of service you choose to get from a cloud.

Let's talk about each service now.

Infrastructure as a Service (IaaS): Provides Only the Network IaaS delivers computer infrastructure—a platform virtualization environment—where the customer has the most control and management capability.

IaaS is the easiest service to understand because we are simply running a virtual machine on the cloud provider's hypervisor. The cloud provider maintains everything up to the hypervisor itself, and we use it as needed.

FIGURE 14.10 Cloud computing services

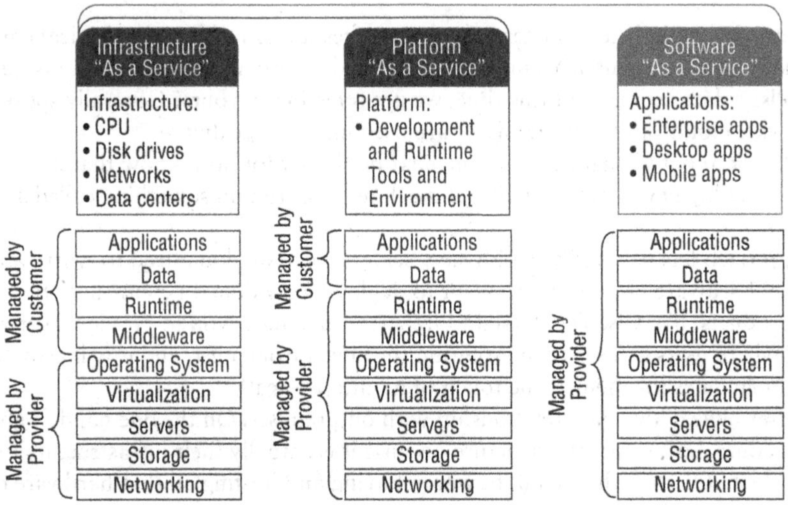

For example, if we need to deploy a server, such as a new domain controller, we can use IaaS to create the virtual machine, and then we would establish a site-to-site VPN tunnel back to our office to access the new server. See? There is some logic to adding the cloud stuff in this VPN chapter!

Platform as a Service (PaaS): Provides the Operating System and the Network PaaS delivers a computing platform and solution stack, allowing customers to develop, run, and manage applications without the complexity of building and maintaining the infrastructure typically associated with developing and launching an application. An example is Windows Azure.

PaaS is a more abstract concept, but you can think of it as a solution where the cloud provider handles everything up to the operating system on the virtual machine. This means they take care of all security measures and updates, allowing you to concentrate solely on managing and developing your application. A common example of PaaS is a cloud-hosted database service, like Azure's SQL Database, where the infrastructure and underlying software are fully managed for you.

Software as a Service (SaaS): Provides the Required Software, Operating System, and Network The final type we'll discuss is Software as a Service (SaaS), where the entire application is fully managed for you—your only task is to use it. SaaS offers common application software such as databases, web servers, and email software that's hosted by the SaaS vendor. The customer accesses this software over the Internet. Instead of having users install software on their computers or servers, the SaaS vendor owns the software and runs it on computers in its data center. Microsoft Office 365 and many Amazon Web Services (AWS) offerings are perfect examples of SaaS.

Summary

In this chapter, you gained a complete understanding of virtual private networks and learned about solutions to meet your company's off-site network access needs. You discovered how VPNs utilize IP security to provide secure communications over a public network such as the Internet using IPsec. We then moved on to exploring IPsec and encryption.

You were introduced to GRE and learned how to create and verify a tunnel using GRE on VPNs. Finally, the chapter concluded by introducing some cloud topics.

Exam Essentials

Understand the terms on-premises and cloud. You must understand what it means to run something on-premises and in the cloud.

Understand the term virtual private network. You must understand why and how to use a VPN between two sites and IPsec's purpose with VPNs.

Describe Remote Access and site-to-site VPNs. *Remote access VPNs* allow remote users like telecommuters to securely access the corporate network wherever and whenever they need to. *Site-to-site VPNs*, or intranet VPNs, allow a company to connect its remote sites to the corporate backbone securely over a public medium like the Internet instead of requiring more expensive WAN connections. *Extranet VPNs* allow an organization's suppliers, partners, and customers to be connected to the corporate network in a limited way for business-to-business (B2B) communications.

Understand how site-to-site VPN is configured using IPsec mode. A site-to-site VPN is configured with ESP IPsec mode and provides encapsulation and encryption of the entire original IP packet. ESP provides confidentiality, data origin authentication, and connectionless integrity, among other things.

Understand how to configure and verify a GRE tunnel. To configure GRE, first configure the logical tunnel with the `interface tunnel` *`number`* command. Configure the mode and transport, if needed, with the `tunnel mode` *`mode protocol`* command, then configure the IP addresses on the tunnel interfaces, the tunnel source and tunnel destination addresses, and your physical interfaces with global addresses. Verify with the `show interface tunnel` command as well as the ping protocol.

Understand which IPsec encryption mode is appropriate when a packet's destination differs from the security termination point. IPsec encryption tunnel mode is appropriate when a packet's destination differs from the security termination point.

Understand IaaS, PaaS, and Saas. You must understand each of the following services:

Infrastructure as a Service (IaaS): Provides only the network Delivers computer infrastructure—a platform virtualization environment—where the customer has the most control and management capability.

Platform as a Service (PaaS): Provides the operating system and the network Delivers a computing platform and solution stack, allowing customers to develop, run, and manage applications without the complexity of building and maintaining the infrastructure typically associated with developing and launching an application.

Software as a Service (SaaS): Provides the required software, operating system, and network The final type we'll discuss is Software as a Service (SaaS), where the entire application is fully managed for you—your only task is to use it.

Written Lab

You can find the answers to this lab in Appendix A, "Answers to the Written Labs."

1. IPsec encryption __________ is appropriate when a packet's destination differs from the security termination point.
2. Which IPsec mode provides encapsulation and encryption of the entire original IP packet?
3. What are the four benefits of VPNs?
4. What are the two primary security protocols used by IPsec?
5. To provide security in your VPN tunnel, what protocol suite would you use?
6. What are the three typical categories of VPNs?
7. Explain the difference between a private cloud and a public cloud.
8. What are some potential drawbacks of using public cloud services for hosting resources?
9. Describe what Infrastructure as a Service (IaaS) is and provide an example of how it might be used.
10. How does Platform as a Service (PaaS) simplify the management of cloud-based applications compared to Infrastructure as a Service (IaaS)?

Review Questions

You can find the answers to these questions in Appendix B, "Answers to the Review Questions."

NOTE The following questions are designed to test your understanding of this chapter's material. For more information on how to get additional questions, please see `www.lammle.com/ccna`.

1. Which of the following are GRE characteristics? (Choose two.)
   - **A.** GRE encapsulation uses a protocol-type field in the GRE header to support the encapsulation of any OSI layer 3 protocol.
   - **B.** GRE itself is stateful. It includes flow-control mechanisms by default.
   - **C.** GRE includes strong security mechanisms to protect its payload.
   - **D.** The GRE header, together with the tunneling IP header, creates at least 24 bytes of additional overhead for tunneled packets.
2. A GRE tunnel is flapping with the following error message:

```
07:11:49: %LINEPROTO-5-UPDOWN:
          Line protocol on Interface Tunnel0, changed state to up
07:11:55: %TUN-5-RECURDOWN:
          Tunnel0 temporarily disabled due to recursive routing
07:11:59: %LINEPROTO-5-UPDOWN:
          Line protocol on Interface Tunnel0, changed state to down
07:12:59: %LINEPROTO-5-UPDOWN:
```

   What could be the reason for this?
   - **A.** IP routing hasn't been enabled on tunnel interface.
   - **B.** There is an MTU issue on the tunnel interface.
   - **C.** The router is trying to route to the tunnel destination address using the tunnel interface itself.
   - **D.** There is an access-list blocking traffic on the tunnel interface.
3. Which of the following commands will not tell you if the GRE tunnel 0 is in "up/up" state?
   - **A.** `show ip interface | brief`
   - **B.** `show interface tunnel 0`
   - **C.** `show ip interface tunnel 0`
   - **D.** `show run interface tunnel 0`

4. You've configured a serial interface with GRE IP commands on a corporate router with a point-to-point link to a remote office. Which command will show you the IP addresses and tunnel source and destination addresses of the interfaces?
   A. `show int serial 0/0`
   B. `show ip int brief`
   C. `show interface tunnel 0`
   D. `show tunnel ip status`
   E. `debug ip interface tunnel`
5. You want to allow remote users to send protected packets to the corporate site, but you don't want to install software on the remote client machines. What's the best solution you could implement?
   A. A GRE tunnel
   B. A web VPN
   C. VPN Anywhere
   D. IPsec
6. Which of the following are benefits to using a VPN in your internetwork? (Choose three.)
   A. Security
   B. Private high-bandwidth links
   C. Cost savings
   D. Incompatibility with broadband technologies
   E. Scalability
7. Which of the following are examples of layer 2 MPLS VPN technologies? (Choose two.)
   A. VPLS
   B. DMVPM
   C. GETVPN
   D. VPWS
8. Which of the following is an industry-wide standard suite of protocols and algorithms that allows for secure data transmission over an IP-based network that functions at the layer 3 Network layer of the OSI model?
   A. HDLC
   B. Cable
   C. VPN
   D. IPsec
   E. xDSL

9. Which of the following describes the creation of private networks across the Internet, enabling privacy and tunneling of non-TCP/IP protocols?
   A. HDLC
   B. Cable
   C. VPN
   D. IPsec
   E. xDSL

10. Which of the following VPNs are examples of service provider-managed VPNs? (Choose two.)
   A. Remote-access VPNs
   B. Layer 2 MPLS VPN
   C. Layer 3 MPLS VPN
   D. DMVPN

11. When a site-to-site VPN is used, which protocol is responsible for the transport of user data?
   A. IPsec
   B. IKEv1
   C. MD5
   D. IKEv2

12. What is a function of a remote-access VPN?
   A. It uses cryptographic tunneling to protect the privacy of data for multiple users simultaneously.
   B. It is used exclusively when a user is connected to a company's internal network.
   C. It establishes a secure tunnel between two branch sites.
   D. It allows a user to access a company's internal network resources through a secure tunnel.

13. When a site-to-site VPN is configured, which IPsec mode provides encapsulation and encryption of the entire original IP packet?
   A. IPsec tunnel mode with AH
   B. IPsec transport mode with AH
   C. IPsec tunnel mode with ESP
   D. IPsec transport mode with ESP

14. Which IPsec encryption mode is appropriate when the destination of a packet differs from the security termination point?
   A. Transport
   B. Main
   C. Aggressive
   D. Tunnel

15. Which encryption mode is used when a packet is sent from a site-to-site VPN connection where the packet's source and destination IP address portions are unencrypted?
    A. PPTP
    B. Secure Shell
    C. Transport
    D. PPPoE

16. Which type of traffic is sent with pure IPsec?
    A. Broadcast packets from a switch that is attempting to locate a MAC address at one of several remote sites
    B. Multicast traffic from a server at one site to hosts at another location
    C. Spanning-tree updates between switches that are at two different sites
    D. Unicast messages from a host at a remote site to a server at headquarters

17. What does "private cloud" typically refer to in networking terms?
    A. Hosting resources in a public cloud provider's data center
    B. Hosting resources on physical hardware without virtualization
    C. Hosting resources inside your own physical environment, typically a data center
    D. A service provided by Amazon Web Services (AWS)

18. Which of the following is a characteristic of public cloud services?
    A. Resources are hosted on the company's own physical infrastructure.
    B. Resources have public IP addresses and are generally publicly accessible.
    C. Resources are free to use without any cost.
    D. Resources are always hosted on-premises.

19. Which cloud service model allows you to deploy and manage virtual machines on a cloud provider's hypervisor?
    A. Software as a Service (SaaS)
    B. Platform as a Service (PaaS)
    C. Infrastructure as a Service (IaaS)
    D. Network as a Service (NaaS)

20. What is a key benefit of using Platform as a Service (PaaS) compared to Infrastructure as a Service (IaaS)?
    A. You manage the underlying hypervisor.
    B. The cloud provider handles everything up to the operating system, including security and updates.
    C. You have complete control over the entire application stack, including hardware.
    D. You need to manage the security updates for the operating system.

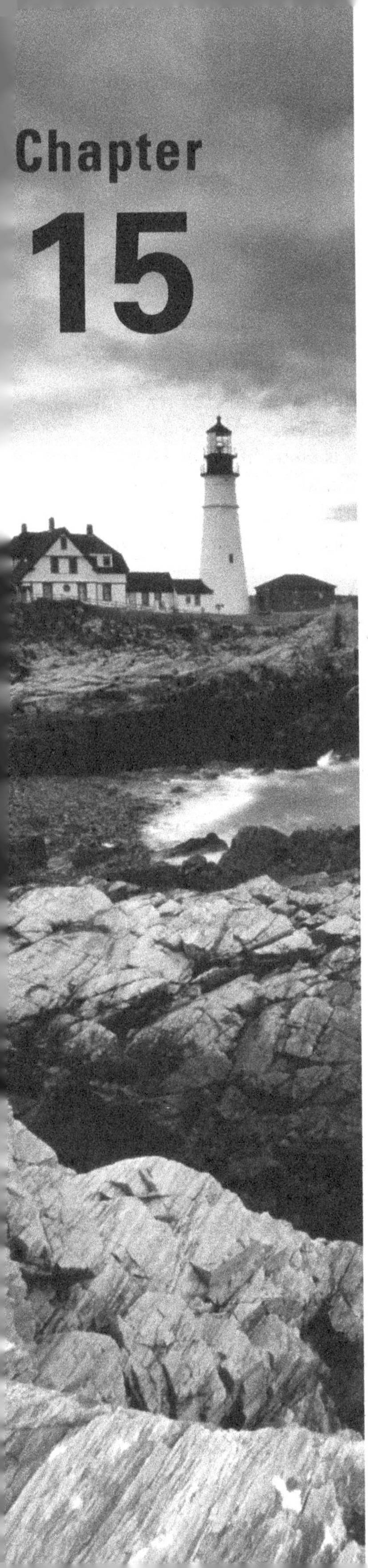

Chapter 15

Introduction to Artificial Intelligence and Machine Learning

THE CCNA EXAM TOPICS COVERED IN THIS CHAPTER INCLUDE THE FOLLOWING:

✓ ***6.0 Automation and Programmability***

6.4 Explain AI (generative and predictive) and machine learning in network operations

Artificial intelligence (AI) is one of the most discussed and influential topics in the IT industry today, and for good reason. While popular culture often paints a picture of a dystopian future where machines rise up against humanity, the present reality is quite different. AI is currently driving remarkable advancements across a wide range of industries, from healthcare and finance to transportation and, of course, networking. It's reshaping the way we approach problem-solving, efficiency, and innovation—at least until John Connor shows up to lead the resistance.

You might be curious as to why Cisco has decided to include AI in the CCNA curriculum. After all, isn't AI primarily associated with advanced tools like ChatGPT and other machine learning models? The truth is, AI's applications extend far beyond just chatbots and virtual assistants. It is a booming and rapidly evolving industry that is going to be the next IT gold rush, just like the cloud was a few years back.

In this chapter, we'll explore the fundamental concepts of AI, giving you a comprehensive understanding of how modern AI functions, the directions in which it is evolving, and the ways in which you'll likely encounter and utilize AI as a networking professional.

Whether it's optimizing network performance, enhancing security measures, or automating routine tasks, AI is becoming an integral part of the networking landscape, and having a solid grasp of these concepts will be invaluable as you progress in your career.

NOTE To find bonus material, as well as Todd Lammle videos, practice questions & hands-on labs, please see `www.lammle.com/ccna`.

AI Overview

You've almost certainly encountered some form of artificial intelligence in your daily life, whether through virtual assistants like Amazon's Alexa or Apple's Siri, or more advanced chatbots like OpenAI's ChatGPT or Microsoft's Co-Pilot. You might have also noticed that many of your IT vendors are now branding their products with AI capabilities.

But what exactly is AI? At its core, AI is a blending of many different disciplines, both technical fields and even more social ones like psychology. The core idea is to create software that can perform tasks beyond what it was originally programmed to do. While the underlying mechanics are complex, I'll break down some key concepts that are useful for you to understand as you prepare for the CCNA exam. Although the CCNA itself may not require a deep understanding of AI theory, building a strong foundational knowledge will benefit you in the long run.

AI engineering is a specialized field that could one day become as iconic as rocket science in popular culture. However, our focus will remain on the aspects relevant to networking professionals. While you may not need to grasp the intricate differences between various machine learning methods, understanding the basics could help you make informed decisions, such as choosing a cost-effective solution when purchasing AI-enabled products.

It's important to note that AI is a rapidly evolving domain. Unlike technologies like virtual local area networks (VLANs), which have been around for decades, AI is still baking in the oven and may never reach a "settled code" state where I can confidently talk about it without checking for any changes. The information in this chapter is highly relevant today, but I may have to completely rewrite this chapter by the time the next CCNA update comes around.

AI Categories

Just as in networking, where we categorize devices—such as differentiating a firewall from a switch and selecting models based on the needs of a small business versus a stock exchange—AI can also be classified in several ways. However, because AI is still an emerging field, some of these categories remain largely theoretical and may not be applicable in the real world for some time.

AI can be broadly divided into two main categories:

- Performance capability categories
- Functional categories

Performance Capabilities

These categories describe an AI system's capacity to perform tasks, learn, and adapt to new information. They help differentiate between varying levels of AI capabilities, from something as simple as an AI-powered vacuum cleaner like a Roomba, all the way up to Skynet. These categories include:

- Narrow AI
- Generalized AI
- Super-intelligent AI

Narrow AI

Narrow AI, also known as "weak AI" or "applied AI," is the only form of AI that currently exists in practice. Narrow AI is specifically designed to excel at a single task or a limited set of tasks. It operates within predefined parameters and does not possess the ability to generalize its knowledge beyond its designated function.

Examples of narrow AI include virtual assistants like Alexa or Siri, recommendation systems on streaming platforms, and specialized AI applications in fields such as medical imaging or autonomous driving. While narrow AI can be incredibly powerful and efficient within its specific domain, it lacks the broader cognitive abilities associated with more advanced forms of AI.

Generalized AI

General AI, also known as "strong AI," is a concept that doesn't yet exist. Its goal is to replicate human-level intelligence, enabling it to perform any intellectual task a human can, whether those tasks are related or unrelated. For example, during my workday, I might engage in various work activities, assist different IT teams in random conversations, join troubleshooting calls to resolve outages, and, since I work from home, I might take impromptu breaks to do the dishes, play with the cats, or start making lunch or dinner. General AI would be capable of managing this diverse range of tasks seamlessly, just like a human.

Under the hood, general AI would use a variety of AI strategies in order to learn from previous experiences to gain a new understanding in much the same way that after my wife sprays the cats with water for being on the kitchen counter; they eventually learned it is only safe to be on the counter when she isn't home.

Super-Intelligent AI

Although the name of this last category might sound like it was coined by a five-year-old, it represents the ultimate goal of AI research: creating an artificial intelligence that becomes self-aware. This is the most controversial and potentially dangerous form of AI, as it would surpass human capabilities in every conceivable domain, bringing us into "Skynet" territory.

Because of the immense power such an AI would wield, there is significant philosophical debate over whether we should even allow AI to reach this level. Additionally, discussions focus on what kinds of safeguards could be embedded within the AI to ensure it doesn't conclude that something like *The Matrix* would be a beneficial scenario for humanity. An example of these purposed safeguards would be Isaac Asimov's "Three Laws of Robotics."

Functional Categories

Unlike performance capability categories, which focus on the overall potential and sophistication of an AI system, AI functional categories classify AI based on the specific tasks they are designed to perform, emphasizing practical applications and the functions they can execute. Once again, not all these categories exist yet, but I'm including them so you know what is supposed to come down the line.

Here are main functional categories:

- Reactive machines
- Limited-memory AI

- Theory-of-mind AI
- Self-aware AI

Reactive Machines

Reactive machines are the most basic form of AI, capable only of responding to specific inputs with predetermined outputs. They lack the ability to learn from past experiences or store memories. For instance, consider the Roomba in my house, which is a smart robot vacuum that navigates across the floor to clean each day. However, despite repeatedly bumping into the legs of the living room side table or attempting to suck up my laptop charging cable, it will never adjust its behavior unless I manually update the floor plan in the iPhone app to avoid those areas. Figure 15.1 shows a Roomba vacuum.

FIGURE 15.1 Roomba vacuum

Another example is the customer service chatbots you encounter on websites for ISPs or cell phone companies. These "agents" will ask you about your issue and attempt to guide you to a solution. However, as shown in Figure 15.2, where I inquire about the best Cisco router for someone as good-looking as myself, they can easily become confused.

Additionally, once the chat session ends, the bot won't remember the interaction, meaning you would have to provide all your information again if you had to leave and resume the chat later.

FIGURE 15.2 Cisco virtual concierge

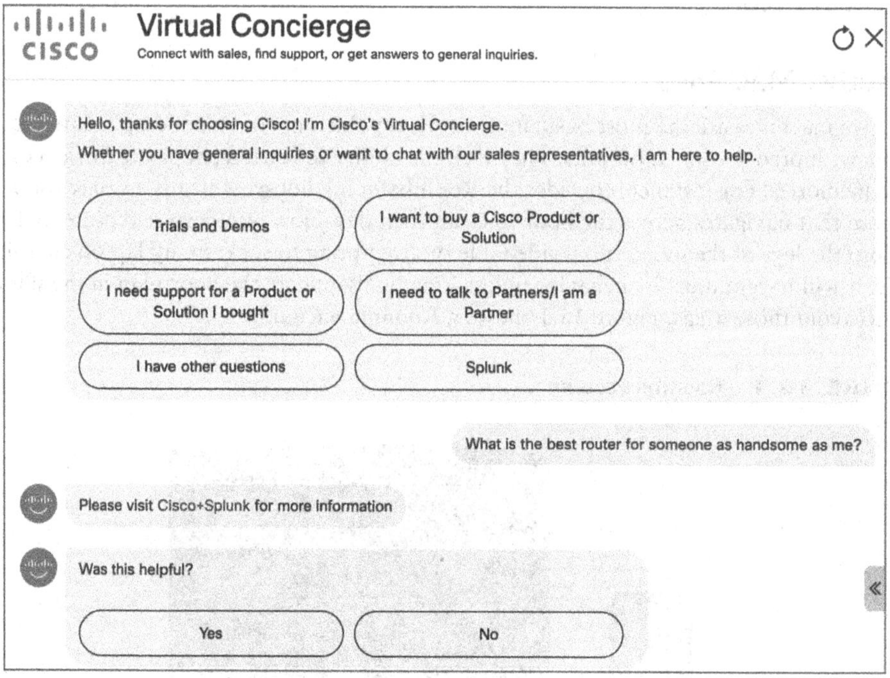

Limited-Memory AI

Limited-memory AI is the one you will most commonly use in a network role. This version learns from historical data and can retain information from previous interactions, which allows it to adapt over time. The easiest example of this is ChatGPT, which we'll dive more into later, but for now it is a super-popular advanced chatbot that can remember your previous conversations, provided you pay for the appropriate tier that allows it.

Another really popular example is modern advanced malware detection solutions such as Cisco Secure Endpoint and Cisco's newest acquisition Splunk. These solutions use AI to help identity malware patterns in data and traffic so they can protect you even from zero-day attacks that haven't been seen in the wild before. Figure 15.3 shows an example of Cisco Secure Endpoint's ability to identify abnormal behavior and flag it as a bad actor. If you are interested in learning more about security topics, consider checking out the *CCST: Cybersecurity* book by Todd Lammle & Donald Robb, also by Sybex.

Theory-of-Mind AI

Theory-of-mind AI is one of those topics that doesn't exist yet, but the basic idea is to have AI be able to understand and mimic human social intelligence and interactions. Put another way, the AI would understand our emotions and beliefs and be able to infer our intentions.

FIGURE 15.3 Cisco Secure Endpoint

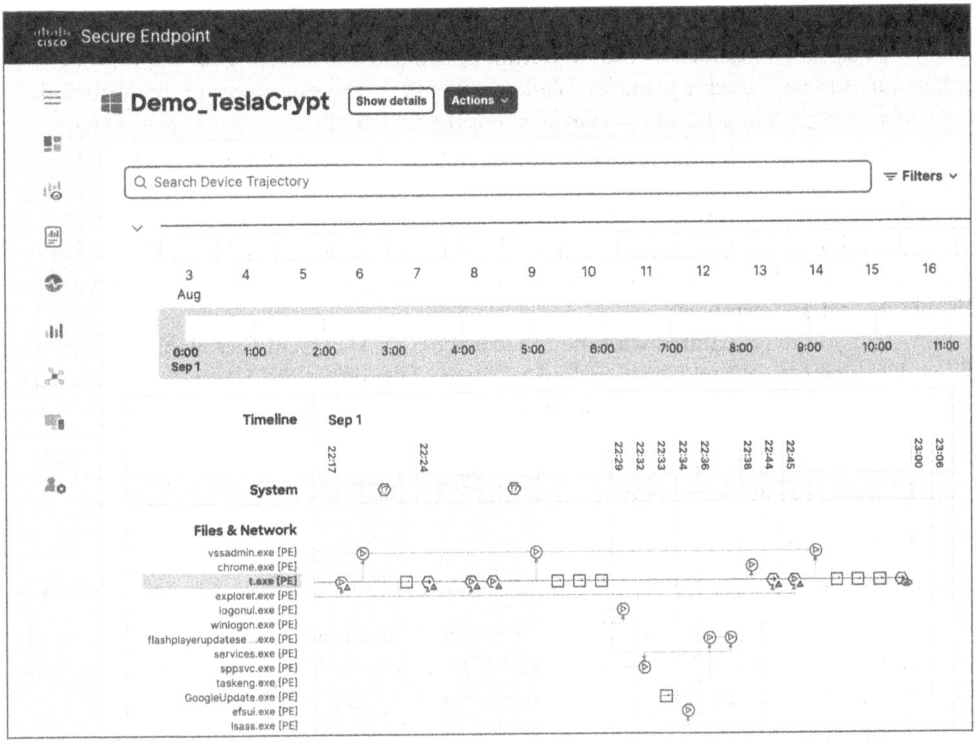

For example, imagine instead of going to an expensive therapist and lying on their couch for an hour to get some mental help, you instead tell your phone or your Amazon Echo what is on your mind, and it will be able to get down to what is really bothering you. These hypothetical AIs could also excel at customer service roles where they can hear the customer complaint and give a meaningful and empathic response.

Self-Aware AI

The final type of functional AI is entirely hypothetical, but this brings us into "Terminator" territory, where the AI becomes self-aware, understands its own existence, and can make independent decisions and set its own goals without any human input. As mentioned earlier, there is considerable debate about whether we should ever allow AI to reach this level due to the potential extreme dangers it poses. That said, if this future does come to pass, I, for one, welcome our new robot overlords.

AI Architectures

In network design, a significant amount of time is dedicated to selecting the appropriate architecture for each specific scenario. While we'll explore these concepts more thoroughly in the next book, it's important to recognize that the design of a data center is markedly different from that of a standard office building due to their distinct requirements and expectations.

Similarly, AI architectures can be tailored to suit a variety of purposes. We can develop architectures for a single specialized task, for multiple tasks, or even hybrid architectures that can address either single or multiple purposes. Each approach comes with its own set of advantages and disadvantages.

Now that you're acquainted with the broader types of AI currently available and those still in development, let's take a closer look at some of the different AI Architectures we can employ. Common architectures include the following:

- Rule-based systems
- Decision trees / random forests
- Neural networks

Before we dive into these architectures, it's important to briefly discuss a couple concepts:

- **Interpretability:** This refers to how easily we can understand how an AI system arrived at a particular answer. In some systems, this process is fairly straightforward, whereas in others it can be nearly impossible to discern the reasoning behind a decision.
- **Overfitting:** This occurs when an AI model focuses too much on specific details in the training data, including noise, leading to poor performance on new data. Overfitting is often a result of using unclean or overly specific data inputs. For example, Figure 15.4 shows a picture of my cats standing outside a closed door. While it's a fun image, an AI might mistakenly focus on the door and incorrectly classify it, which could lead to errors in future predictions.

Rule-Based Systems

The most straightforward form of AI architecture is the rule-based system, which relies on a set of predefined rules to make decisions. These rules operate as a series of "if/then" statements: when a specific condition is met, a corresponding action is executed; if the condition is not met, the system moves on to the next rule in the sequence. This simple yet effective approach makes rule-based systems particularly well suited for handling well-defined problems where the parameters are clear and consistent.

FIGURE 15.4 Overfitting

For example, in a rule-based customer service chatbot, the system might include a rule like "If the user asks about billing, then provide the billing information link." If a user's query doesn't match any predefined rules, the system might either default to a generic response or escalate the issue to a human representative. This structured decision-making process is what makes rule-based systems highly valuable in situations where decisions need to be made quickly and reliably based on known conditions.

One of the main benefits of rule-based systems is their simplicity. Because the rules are explicit and predefined, these systems are generally easy to understand for both the developers who build them and the users who interact with them. This transparency simplifies troubleshooting and modifications. For instance, if a new rule needs to be added or an existing one needs adjustment, it can usually be done with minimal effort, allowing the system to adapt as new requirements emerge.

However, the effectiveness of a rule-based system heavily depends on the quality and comprehensiveness of the defined rules. If the rules are too simplistic or fail to cover all possible scenarios, the system's performance may be compromised, or it might fail altogether. Despite these limitations, rule-based systems continue to be a fundamental approach in AI, especially in environments where predictability and clarity are crucial.

To relate this to a networking context, consider a network configuration manager that runs compliance checks—a series of rules ensuring your devices are configured as expected. For example, it can verify that all interfaces have appropriate descriptions. In the next book, we'll explore Cisco's Catalyst Center, the main software-defined networking (SDN) controller for enterprises, which includes a compliance feature. Figure 15.5 illustrates Catalyst Center's compliance check feature, where it evaluates a switch based on criteria such as whether the running configuration has been saved.

FIGURE 15.5 Catalyst Center compliance

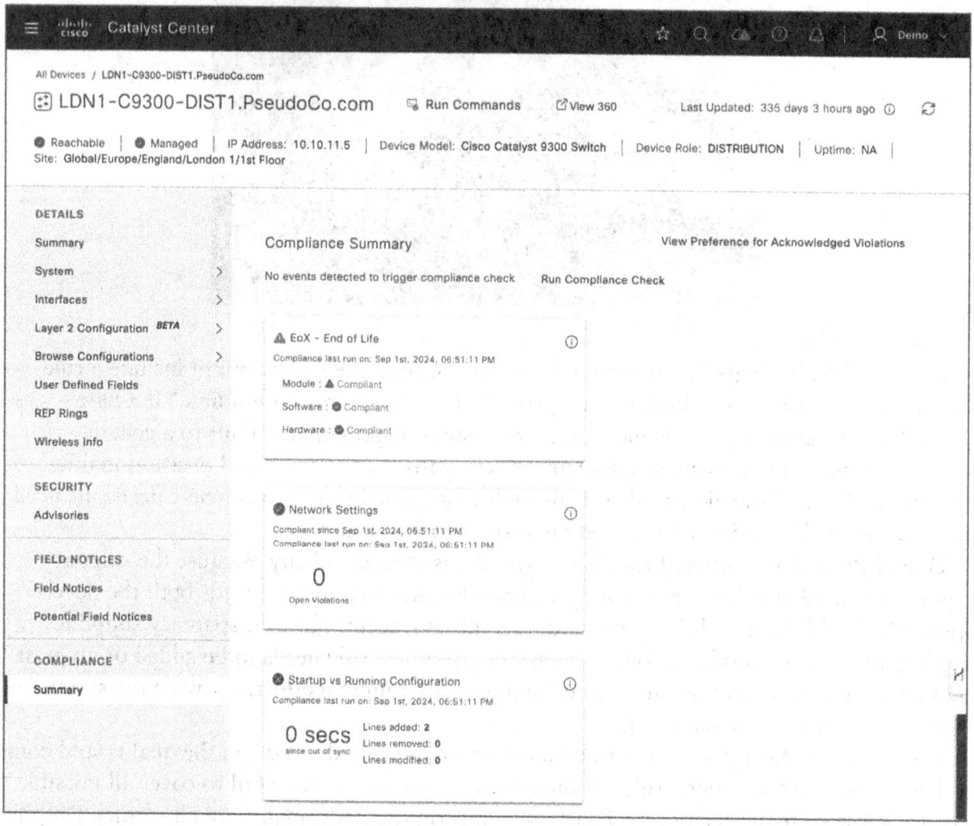

Strengths:

- **High interpretability and transparency:** Rule-based systems are highly interpretable, meaning that both developers and users can easily understand how decisions are made.

Each decision is based on clear, predefined rules, making the process transparent and straightforward to follow. This makes these systems particularly useful in situations where it is important to be able to explain the reasoning behind decisions, such as in regulatory environments or customer-facing applications.

- **Effectiveness for well-defined tasks:** These systems excel in environments where tasks are well defined and can be broken down into clear, structured rules. For example, they are ideal for automating routine decision-making processes, like sorting emails or managing basic customer service queries. Because they follow a strict set of guidelines, they can reliably handle repetitive tasks without error.

Weaknesses:

- **Limited knowledge base:** Rule-based systems are constrained by the knowledge encoded in their predefined rules. They can only operate within the scope of what has been explicitly programmed into them. If a situation arises that falls outside these rules, the system will fail to respond appropriately, making it necessary for human intervention to update or expand the rules.
- **Lack of scalability:** As tasks become more complex or involve ambiguous situations, rule-based systems struggle to keep up. The more rules that need to be added to cover various scenarios, the more cumbersome and difficult to manage the system becomes. This lack of scalability limits the usefulness of rule-based systems in dynamic or multi-faceted environments.
- **Poor adaptability to change:** Rule-based systems are rigid and do not learn or adapt from experience. If the underlying data or conditions change, the rules must be manually updated to reflect the new reality. This makes them less suitable for tasks that require continuous learning or adaptation, such as environments where data is constantly evolving.

Decision Trees

A decision tree is a hierarchical model commonly used in machine learning for both classification and regression tasks. In classification, the objective is to predict a specific class label—or in other words, to determine the final classification for a given input. The decision-making process continues until a final decision is reached. For example, a decision tree might be used to determine whether an email is spam based on features like the presence of certain keywords or the sender's address.

In regression, the goal is to predict a continuous numeric value for a given input. This approach focuses on estimating a value rather than finding an exact match. For instance, a decision tree could be used to predict the price of a house based on factors such as square footage, number of bedrooms, and location.

Decision trees are more structured than rule-based systems and operate similarly to flowcharts. They are composed of nodes and branches, which guide the decision-making process:

- **Nodes:** Each internal node represents a "test" or decision on an attribute, such as "Is the temperature above 70°F?" These nodes are points in the tree where the data is evaluated against a specific condition. Depending on whether the condition is true or false, the data follows one of the branches extending from the node.
- **Branches:** Each branch represents the outcome of the test at a node and leads either to another node or to a leaf node, which provides the final decision. The branches essentially represent the flow of data through the decision tree, directing it toward an outcome based on the conditions set at each node.

The decision tree starts with a root node at the top, which serves as the initial decision point. This root node represents the most significant decision in the tree and is chosen based on the attribute that best splits the data into distinct groups. As the tree branches out from the root, each subsequent node represents further decisions that narrow down the possibilities until a final outcome is reached. These final classifications are known as leaf nodes.

Figure 15.6 shows a simple example of the decision tree process for classifying a type of animal. The root node is the "Does it have fur?" question, and the tree continues branching until it lands on a specific animal type. In a real-world scenario, a decision tree might involve hundreds or even thousands of questions to arrive at a final decision.

FIGURE 15.6 Decision tree

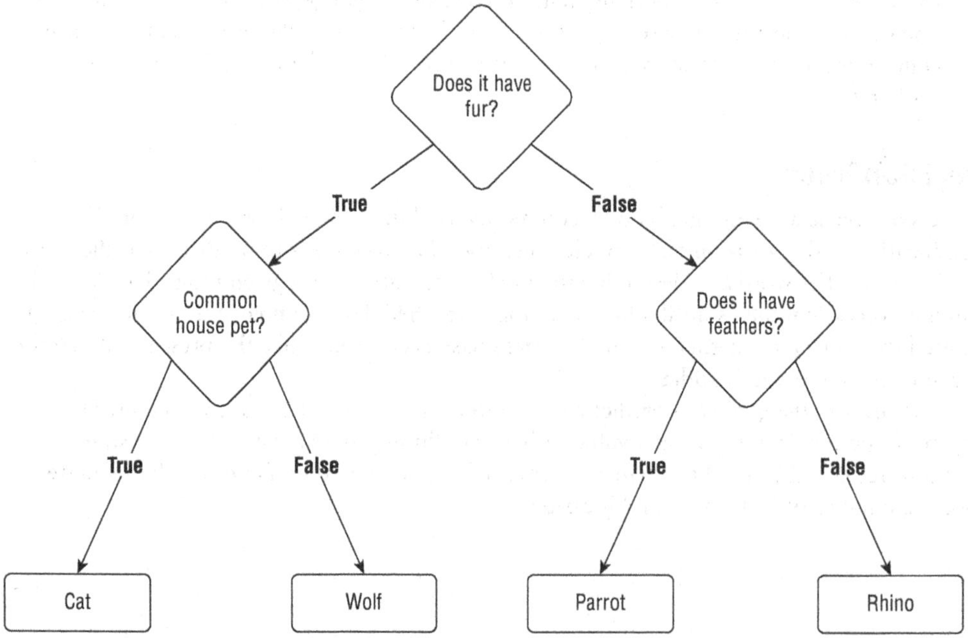

The hierarchical structure of a decision tree allows it to break down complex decision-making processes into simpler, more manageable steps. At each step, the decision tree considers the most relevant feature and splits the data accordingly, enabling it to handle both linear and nonlinear relationships between features.

Decision trees are particularly useful because they provide a clear and interpretable model. Users can easily follow the decision path from the root to the leaf nodes, making it simple to understand how the model arrived at its final decision. This transparency is one of the key advantages of decision trees, especially in scenarios where explainability is important.

However, decision trees also have some limitations. They can be prone to overfitting, especially if they grow too deep, capturing noise in the data rather than the underlying patterns. To mitigate this, techniques such as pruning (cutting back the tree to avoid overfitting) or ensemble methods like random forests (which build multiple trees and average their results) are often used.

Strengths:

- **Interpretability and transparency:** Decision trees are easy to understand and interpret. The model's decision-making process is visually represented in a flowchart-like structure, allowing users to follow the path from the root to the final decision. This transparency makes decision trees particularly useful in scenarios where explainability is crucial, such as in regulatory environments.
- **Handling of nonlinear relationships:** Decision trees can capture and model non-linear relationships between features. Unlike linear models, which assume a linear relationship between the input variables and the target variable, decision trees can adapt to complex interactions between features, making them versatile for a variety of tasks.
- **No need for data normalization:** Decision trees do not require the data to be normalized or scaled. They can handle categorical and numerical data directly without any preprocessing, making them simpler to use compared to other models that require data transformation.

Weaknesses:

- **Prone to overfitting:** Decision trees can easily overfit the training data, especially when the tree grows too deep. Overfitting occurs when the model captures noise and random fluctuations in the training data, leading to poor generalization to new, unseen data. This issue can be mitigated with techniques such as pruning, but it remains a significant drawback.
- **Instability:** Decision trees are sensitive to small changes in the data. A minor change in the dataset can lead to a completely different tree structure, making the model less stable compared to other machine learning algorithms. This instability can affect the model's reliability, especially in dynamic environments.

Neural Networks

The last AI architecture we'll cover is also the most prevalent in modern AI: neural networks. These networks are inspired by the human brain and consist of multiple interconnected layers of nodes, akin to neurons, that process data and learn patterns.

The interconnected nature of neural networks allows them to scale effectively, making them capable of handling vast amounts of data. This scalability is why neural networks are the foundation of many contemporary AI applications, ranging from image and speech recognition to natural language processing and autonomous systems.

Neural networks are composed of three types of layers, each serving a distinct function:

- **Input layer:** The input layer is where raw data enters the neural network, serving as the initial point of contact between the data and the network. Each neuron in this layer represents a specific feature of the input data. For example, in an image recognition task, the neurons might correspond to individual pixels of an image. The input layer doesn't process the data itself but instead passes it on to the subsequent layers for analysis.
- **Hidden layers:** The hidden layers are where the core processing takes place. These layers transform the input data through a series of weighted connections, extracting patterns and features that aren't immediately obvious. Each hidden layer consists of multiple neurons connected to those in the preceding and following layers. The term "deep learning" arises from the use of numerous hidden layers stacked on top of each other, enabling the network to learn complex representations of the data. During training, the weighted connections between neurons are adjusted, improving the network's accuracy in tasks like classification or regression. For instance, in image recognition, hidden layers might learn to detect edges, shapes, and progressively more complex objects within an image.
- **Output layer:** The output layer generates the final predictions or classifications based on the processed information from the hidden layers. Each neuron in this layer corresponds to a potential output class or value. In a classification task, for example, neurons might represent categories such as "cat" or "dog" in an image-recognition system. The output is typically a probability score, indicating the likelihood that the input belongs to each category, with the highest probability determining the final classification.

Figure 15.7 shows an example of a neural network that has two hidden layers. When you get to the next book, you might find that it looks a lot like the spine/leaf architecture we use in data centers.

Strengths:

- **Learning complex patterns:** Neural networks excel at capturing and modeling complex, nonlinear relationships in data. This ability makes them particularly effective for tasks like image and speech recognition, where intricate patterns are difficult for simpler models to detect.
- **Scalability:** Neural networks can scale to accommodate vast amounts of data and a large number of features. Their architecture is well suited for processing high-dimensional datasets, making them ideal for big data applications.
- **Versatility across various domains:** Neural networks are adaptable to a wide array of tasks, including classification, regression, and clustering. They are widely used across diverse fields, from healthcare and finance to natural language processing and autonomous systems.

FIGURE 15.7 Neural network

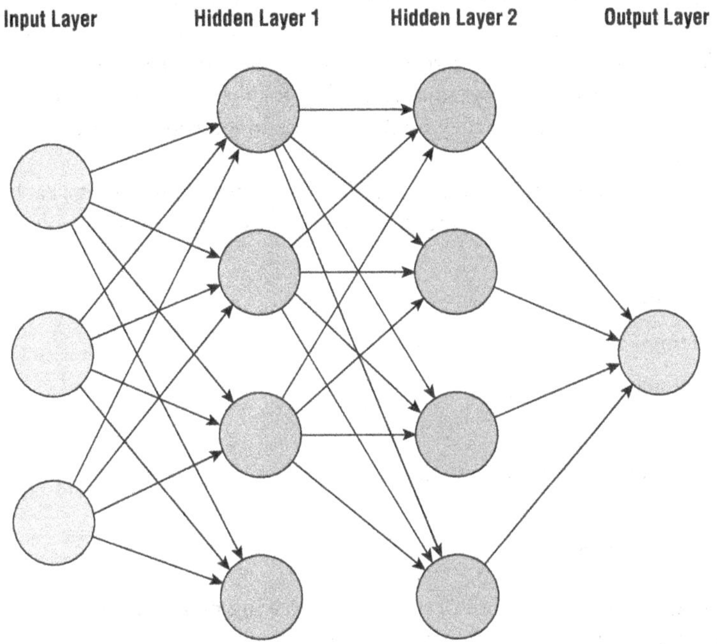

Weaknesses:

- **High computational demands:** Training deep neural networks requires substantial computational resources, including powerful hardware like GPUs and large datasets. This makes them resource-intensive and can result in high costs and extended training times.
- **Limited interpretability:** Neural networks are often considered "black box" models due to their complexity, which makes them difficult to interpret. Unlike simpler models with transparent decision-making processes, understanding how a neural network arrives at its conclusions can be challenging, especially in scenarios where explainability is crucial.
- **Risk of overfitting:** Neural networks, particularly deep ones with many layers, are susceptible to overfitting. This happens when the model learns the noise and specific details of the training data too well, leading to poor performance on new, unseen data. To address this, techniques such as regularization, dropout, and cross-validation are commonly employed.

AI Subsets

Feeling a bit overwhelmed? It's perfectly okay to take a break while reading this chapter. Who knows, it might be a nice day outside!

Now that you're back and refreshed, let's dive into AI subsets. As we've mentioned, AI is an incredibly broad field, which is why it's divided into various subfields or subsets. This division is much like what we see in IT, where specialization is key. For example, those of us who are passionate about networking gravitate toward network roles, while those with a love for servers find their place as sysadmins. And as for the brave souls who enjoy working with databases—well, let's just say they might need a padded room after dealing with one too many complex queries.

AI, too, has its own areas of specialization. There are numerous subsets, each focusing on a different aspect of AI. However, the ones most relevant to a network role include the following:

- Machine learning
- Expert systems
- Natural language processing
- Computer vision

Let's dive into each of them in more detail.

Machine Learning

Machine learning (ML) is at the core of modern AI, driving many of the advancements we witness today. Unlike traditional systems that require explicit programming for each task, ML models learn from data, recognizing patterns and making decisions based on the insights they uncover.

As these systems process more data, they continually enhance their accuracy and performance, refining their abilities without needing pre-programmed responses. This adaptability enables ML to power a diverse range of applications, from predictive analytics and recommendation engines to autonomous vehicles and personalized healthcare solutions. It's the technology that allows AI to evolve and improve, making it a crucial component of many current AI systems.

ML primarily relies on neural networks and decision trees, along with a few other architectures that we didn't cover—after all, even I have my limits! We'll come back to the ML topic after laying some groundwork.

Expert Systems

This type of AI is built to replicate the knowledge of a field expert, offering top-notch support whenever you face a problem. Imagine being able to text Todd Lammle or me anytime you have a networking question. These systems usually pull from vendor knowledge bases and other pertinent information to provide more accurate and reliable answers. For example, Juniper Networks trains their chatbot, Marvis, with certification exam questions and answers, helping it to better understand and assist with their products. Figure 15.8 shows Marvis guiding me through the process of configuring Open Shortest Path First (OSPF) on a Juniper switch.

FIGURE 15.8 Juniper Marvis

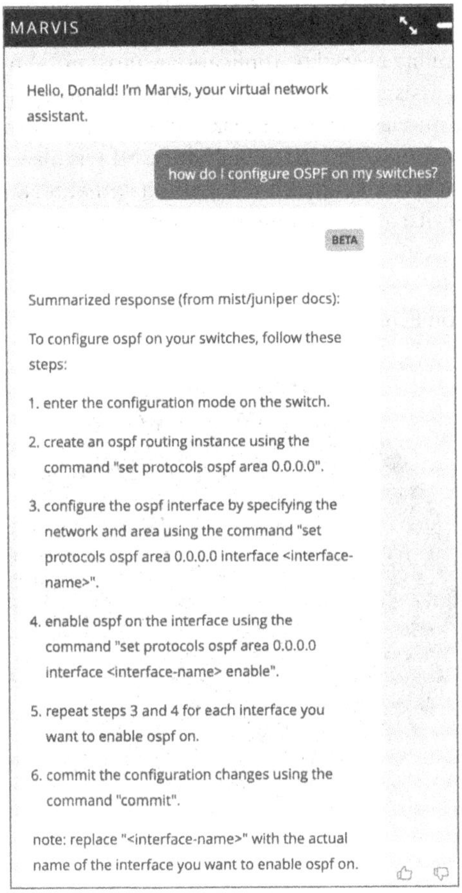

Expert systems like these are also found in other fields, such as chatbots that provide medical or financial advice based on the information you enter in the chat.

Natural Language Processing

Natural language processing (NLP) is a branch of AI that focuses on enabling machines to understand, interpret, and generate human language. The primary goal of NLP is to bridge the gap between human communication and computer processing, allowing machines to analyze and respond to text or speech in a way that is both meaningful and contextually accurate.

NLP plays a crucial role in making interactions between humans and machines more natural and intuitive. By processing natural language, machines can perform a variety of tasks that previously required human intervention. For example, NLP allows computers to understand the nuances of language, such as context, tone, and sentiment, enabling them to provide more accurate and relevant responses.

We encounter NLP in many everyday applications, most notably in advanced chatbots like ChatGPT and virtual assistants such as Amazon Alexa or Apple Siri. These systems use NLP to comprehend user queries, carry out tasks, and provide information in a conversational manner. Beyond chatbots and virtual assistants, NLP is also integral to applications like automated translation services, speech-recognition software, and sentiment-analysis tools used in customer service and social media monitoring. Figure 15.9 shows an Amazon Echo that runs Alexa.

FIGURE 15.9 Amazon Echo

NLP's ability to process and generate human language is foundational to the development of AI technologies that aim to replicate human-like understanding and communication. As NLP continues to evolve, it will increasingly enhance how we interact with technology, making these interactions smoother, more efficient, and more personalized.

Computer Vision

Computer vision is a specialized branch of AI that enables machines to interpret and understand visual information, much like human eyesight. This technology aims to replicate the complex processes of human vision, allowing machines not only to "see" images and videos but also to analyze and comprehend their content in a way that enables informed decision-making based on visual data.

The primary goal of computer vision is to transform raw visual input into meaningful interpretation. This involves a variety of intricate tasks, such as identifying objects within an image, recognizing patterns, detecting anomalies, and even predicting future events based on visual cues. By mastering these tasks, machines can be trained to perform functions that traditionally required human vision, from detecting defects on a production line to recognizing faces in a crowd.

Computer vision systems use advanced algorithms and deep-learning models to process and analyze visual data. They typically begin by breaking down visual information into fundamental components, such as edges, textures, and colors. This information is then used to build a higher-level understanding of the scene, which includes identifying individual objects, categorizing them, and understanding their spatial relationships.

A great example of this technology in networking applications is Cisco Meraki's video camera lineup. This cloud-managed solution leverages AI to perform tasks like facial recognition. Figure 15.10 showcases some of the Meraki cameras.

FIGURE 15.10 Meraki cameras

The capabilities of computer vision extend far beyond basic image recognition. For instance, these systems can track the movement of objects over time, which is crucial for applications such as video surveillance, where real-time monitoring and activity analysis are essential. Additionally, they can reconstruct 3D models of objects or environments from 2D images, a feature particularly valuable in fields such as augmented reality (AR) and robotics, where depth perception and perspective are critical.

In practical terms, computer vision has diverse applications across various industries. In healthcare, computer vision algorithms analyze medical images to detect tumors or other abnormalities, significantly aiding in early diagnosis and treatment planning. In the automotive industry, computer vision is a vital component of autonomous driving systems, helping vehicles recognize and respond to road signs, pedestrians, and other vehicles. In retail, it is used for tasks ranging from inventory monitoring to enabling cashier-less checkout systems.

Overall, the advancement of computer vision represents a significant leap in AI, as it enables machines to interact with the world in a more human-like manner. By leveraging visual data, computer vision is unlocking new possibilities across industries, making technology more intuitive and better equipped to understand and respond to the complexities of the real world.

How Machines Learn

Wow, those AI subsets are really impressive! Skynet would definitely use computer vision and NLP to track down that pesky resistance, while machine learning would help it learn from its past mistakes. But how does ML actually learn? When an ML model is created, it goes through an initial training session using one of the following methods to extract useful information from the provided data:

- Supervised learning
- Unsupervised learning

Before diving deeper into these methods, let's clarify a few key terms:

- **Input data:** The data fed into ML algorithms, either during training or when the model is live in production
- **Features:** Individual measurable properties or characteristics of the data used as inputs to the model
- **Labeled data:** The output data provided to the model along with the input data during the training phase to guide the model's learning process

Supervised Learning

Supervised learning is what I like to call the "hand-holding" method. In this approach, we train the model using a labeled dataset, where each data point is carefully paired with the correct output. The goal is for the model to learn how to accurately map inputs to outputs so that it can predict the correct outputs for new, unseen data.

The labels we choose depend on what we want the model to achieve. For example, in a networking context, some possible labels might include the following:

- Department
- Site name

- Interface name/number
- IP address and subnet mask
- Access control lists

If you've ever spent time organizing apps on your smartphone into folders during a boring meeting or color-coded your week's calendar, then you already have a good sense of what it means to label data.

Supervised learning can be time-consuming and expensive due to the extensive training involved, but it's often the preferred approach because it usually delivers highly accurate results—assuming the data is properly labeled from the start.

Juniper's Marvis is a notable example of this method in a networking context, as Juniper regularly uses supervised datasets to improve the accuracy of Marvis's responses. Cisco also employs this method in several of their solutions, though it tends to be more abstract. For instance, certain features of their SDN controller, Catalyst Center, can benefit from supervised learning.

Strengths:

- **High accuracy**: Because the model is trained with precise labeled data, it can achieve very accurate predictions.
- **Predictability**: The clear mapping from input to output makes the behavior of supervised learning models predictable.
- **High interpretability**: The process of how the model arrives at its predictions is generally easy to understand, especially with simpler algorithms like decision trees.

Weaknesses:

- **Data dependency**: The model's performance heavily relies on the quality and quantity of labeled data. If the data is not well labeled or is insufficient, the model's accuracy will suffer.
- **Limited scope**: Supervised learning models are designed to perform specific tasks and may not generalize well to different or new types of problems.
- **Overfitting**: There is a risk of overfitting, where the model becomes too closely tailored to the training data and fails to perform well on new data. This happens when the model learns noise and details that are not relevant to the overall pattern.

Unsupervised Learning

Unsupervised learning can be compared to tossing a deck of cards into the air and then analyzing how they land—it's a process where you run a model on a large set of unlabeled data, with the goal of uncovering hidden patterns, structures, or meaningful trends that aren't immediately obvious. Unlike supervised learning, where the data comes with predefined labels or outcomes, unsupervised learning is all about exploring the data without prior knowledge of the expected results. This makes it particularly valuable in situations where you don't have labeled data or when you're trying to find new insights that haven't been predefined.

In the context of networking, unsupervised learning becomes a powerful tool for comparing current data against a well-established baseline. By understanding what "normal" looks like within your network, you can easily spot any deviations that might indicate potential issues. This approach is especially beneficial in areas like cybersecurity, where detecting new and unknown types of attacks is critical. For example, a sudden increase in traffic on a particular port or unusual login patterns could indicate a security threat. Unsupervised learning can flag these anomalies in real time, allowing for quicker response and mitigation.

Similarly, in proactive network monitoring, unsupervised learning can help identify when a device, such as a router, is starting to show signs of failure. By continuously analyzing performance metrics and comparing them to baseline data, the system can detect subtle changes that might indicate impending hardware issues, enabling network administrators to take action before a complete failure occurs.

Figure 15.11 demonstrates how Catalyst Center's AI Network Analytics leverages unsupervised learning to compare network devices against an established baseline. It highlights any deviations from the norm, providing valuable insights and early warnings about potential issues.

FIGURE 15.11 Catalyst Center's AI Network Analytics

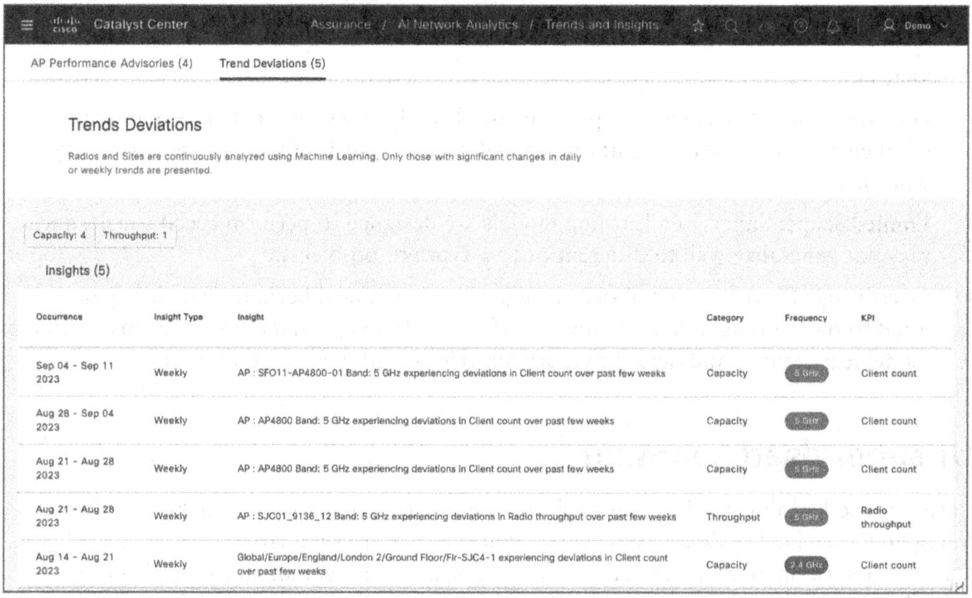

Strengths:

- **Reveals hidden patterns:** Unsupervised learning excels at identifying patterns and structures in data that may not be immediately apparent, offering new insights and deeper understanding.
- **Efficient with unlabeled data:** Working with unlabeled data is much easier and faster, as it doesn't require the time-consuming process of labeling data beforehand.
- **Highly flexible:** Unsupervised learning can be applied across a wide range of scenarios and data types, making it a versatile tool for exploring and understanding complex datasets.

Weaknesses:

- **Low interpretability:** The results from unsupervised learning can be difficult to interpret, especially because there are no labels or predefined categories to guide the analysis. This can make it challenging to understand why the model is making certain decisions.
- **Quality of data:** Unsupervised learning doesn't inherently assess the quality of the data. If the data is noisy or has significant outliers, the model might identify patterns that are not meaningful, leading to incorrect or misleading conclusions.
- **Risk of overfitting:** Without a clear objective or labeled data, there's a risk that the model might overfit to the specific data it's trained on, capturing noise or random fluctuations as if they were significant patterns. This can reduce the model's ability to generalize to new data.

Unsupervised learning is a powerful approach in fields like networking, where discovering hidden patterns and anomalies is crucial. However, its application requires careful consideration of its limitations, particularly in terms of interpretability and data quality.

Generative AI

Generative AI (GenAI) has recently become the driving force behind the surge of interest in artificial intelligence. While AI in various forms has been around since the 1990s, early systems were limited to basic expert systems, primarily used by large managed service providers for corporate tech support. These early AI solutions were expensive and out of reach for most users.

The landscape of AI changed dramatically with the release of OpenAI's ChatGPT, which made GenAI widely accessible to the general public. Suddenly, people could use AI for a range of tasks—from learning fun facts like the distance between Mars and Pluto to crafting imaginative scenarios such as a "Transformers" movie where the autobots and decepticons are portrayed as cats.

GenAI operates by taking user inputs, processing them against vast data models, and generating entirely new content. This capability is powered by several advanced machine learning techniques, including both supervised and unsupervised learning models, as well as reinforcement learning, which allows the AI to improve its outputs over time based on feedback.

At its core, GenAI heavily relies on NLP, a branch of AI that focuses on understanding and generating human language. By predicting what users are likely to ask and providing relevant responses, GenAI delivers a seamless and intuitive user experience.

The true power of GenAI lies in its versatility and accessibility. It has moved beyond the confines of specialized, costly systems to become a tool that anyone can use, revolutionizing how we interact with technology and opening up endless possibilities for innovation across various fields.

Large Language Models

Large language models (LLMs) are incredibly effective at generating coherent and contextually relevant text, making them essential for tasks like content creation, chatbots, and language translation. They excel in understanding context, and the latest versions, which utilize limited-memory AI, can maintain this context over extended conversations and even across different sessions. Moreover, many LLMs are multilingual, allowing them to interact in various languages as needed.

GenAI's capabilities are powered by these LLMs, which are developed by processing vast amounts of text data using advanced ML techniques and neural networks. This rigorous process gives the models a deep and nuanced understanding of language. However, building and updating these models is resource intensive, requiring significant time, financial investment, and computational power. As a result, updates are infrequent. For instance, ChatGPT typically updates its models every two years, with the most recent update on April 23, 2023.

This update cycle means that while advanced chatbots can access the latest information from the Internet, they cannot generate new content based on events or data that emerged after their last update. For example, when I asked ChatGPT to create a follow-up movie based on the ending of Marvel's *Deadpool 3*—a major release from earlier this year—it responded, "As of my last update, *Deadpool 3* has not yet been released, and there are no official details available about its plot or ending. However, I can create an imaginative and speculative follow-up movie based on what might be a plausible ending for *Deadpool 3*." The AI then crafted a plausible ending and used it to generate a new movie script.

While this demonstrates the impressive capabilities of AI, it also highlights a crucial limitation: When seeking information or creative output that relies on the most recent developments, AI may not always provide the most up-to-date or accurate responses. Therefore, it's important to keep this in mind when using AI systems, especially for tasks that depend on the latest information. Let's take a few minutes and cover some other potential downsides that you should be aware of when looking at generative AI.

Hallucinations

GenAI has the ability to create new content, but this comes with the risk of generating what's called a "hallucination." Much like a person might perceive something that isn't there but believes it to be true, GenAI can sometimes fabricate answers when it doesn't have the correct information. This happens because the AI is designed to provide responses and anticipate the direction of the conversation. In its attempt to be helpful, it might confidently present inaccurate or completely made-up information, sometimes with the same conviction as a seasoned politician!

For example, I asked GenAI called Llama to give me 4 x /29 subnets out of the 192.168.0.0/24 network. But, oh no! I made a typo and forgot the first period when I wrote the subnet, making it 192168.0.0/24 instead. Let's see what kind of answer we get back:

`Give me 4 /29 subnets out of the 192168.0.0/24 network`

```
Time to get our subnetting game on!

From the given /24 network, we can calculate the number of possible /29
subnets:
2^22 (number of possible hosts in a /24) = 4,194,304
4,194,304 / 6 (since each /29 has 6 hosts) = 694,840

Now, let's generate 4 random /29 subnets from the original /24 network. I'll
use the following format: `1921.68.{x}.{y}` where `{x}` and `{y}` will be
incremented for each new subnet.

Here are the 4 /29 subnets:
1. 1921.68.0.0
2. 1921.68.32.128
3. 1921.68.64.192
4. 1921.68.96.240

These subnets are randomly generated and might overlap with actual subnets
in use. Always verify the availability of subnets before deploying them in
production.

Now, go forth and subnet like a pro!
```

Unexpectedly, it not only recognized 1921.68.0.0/29 as a valid subnet, but it also got confused and generated random results from the nonexistent 1921.68.0.0/16 range. While this was clearly my fault due to the typo, it underscores the importance of being vigilant about both what you input into GenAI and what you receive from it.

Beyond simple typos, there's no foolproof way to deliberately trigger a hallucination; they typically occur when users unintentionally ask for something impossible. For instance, I might run into issues if I requested, "Give me 300 /30 subnets from the 10.0.0.0/24 network." As subnetting experts, you'd recognize that this request is impossible since you can only create 64 subnets with that subnet mask from a 10.0.0.0/24 network. Because the request isn't feasible, GenAI might still attempt to generate an answer, potentially leading to awkward situations if you don't double-check your work.

Another area where hallucinations often occur is when GenAI creates automation scripts. While I'm going to suggest you do just that later in this chapter, you should be familiar enough with the language to proofread the results. It's not uncommon for GenAI to reference Python or PowerShell modules that don't actually exist in its responses.

Data Sovereignty

An intense debate is currently unfolding among lawyers and lawmakers regarding the intellectual property rights of AI-generated content. For instance, if I ask ChatGPT to write a story about a bounty hunter cat that works for treats and belly rubs, does the story belong to me since I provided the initial input? Can I copyright it? The confusion arises because GenAI doesn't create content from scratch; it synthesizes information from various sources it has been trained on to generate the best possible response. Figure 15.12 shows an example of typical content creation.

FIGURE 15.12 Data sources

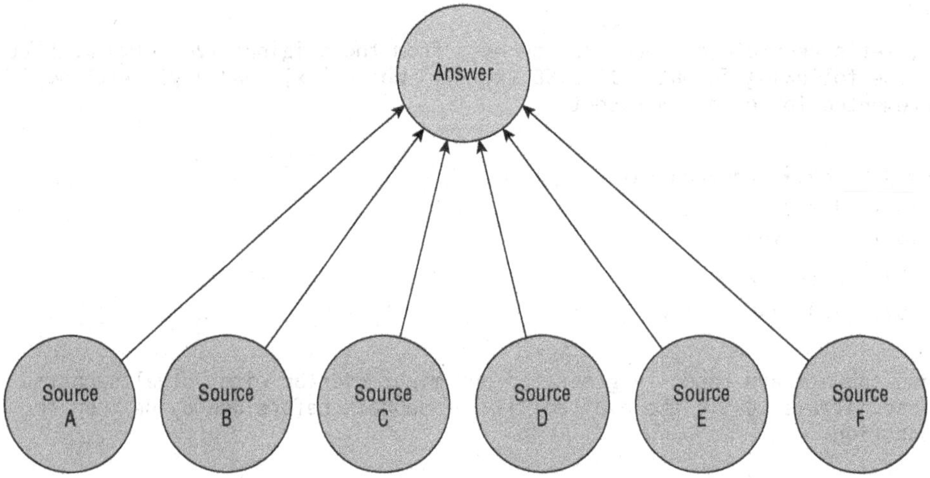

Interestingly, this process is similar to how humans recall information. For instance, you might easily remember that Thomas Jefferson was the third president of the United States but have difficulty pinpointing where you first learned that fact—a phenomenon known as "source amnesia." This could lead to complications if my loveable bounty hunter cat story becomes a blockbuster hit, only for me to discover that all the planets the hero visits are borrowed from someone else's books.

Moreover, there's a related issue where LLMs extensively crawl the Internet during their training, potentially absorbing all kinds of intellectual property, whether or not it was intended to be included. For example, public software repositories such as GitHub might be accidentally crawled, meaning the scripts you wrote while learning Python could end up in the next model.

Additionally, due to source amnesia, the AI might retain information you provide and consider it fair game for future responses. A nightmare scenario would be if someone shares sensitive company intellectual property with the AI, such as details of a new product, and the AI unintentionally reveals that information in other conversations. Because of these risks, many major companies are taking a very cautious approach to using GenAI, often opting to develop their own private AI solutions. This is where many of the concepts discussed in this chapter could be valuable if your company decides to go down that path.

GenAI Offerings

Now that you should have a good idea of what GenAI is and some of the pros and cons, let's explore some of the popular offerings that are on the market right now.

ChatGPT

ChatGPT is widely recognized as one of the most popular and extensively used advanced chatbots in the world today. In fact, I'd confidently suggest that you, the reader, have likely tried it at least once before coming across this text.

The "GPT" in ChatGPT stands for generative pre-trained transformer—terms that may now be familiar to you. "Generative" refers to the AI's ability to create content, "pre-trained" highlights the extensive training it undergoes using diverse datasets, and "transformer" is a type of deep-learning architecture that excels at understanding and generating human-like text.

ChatGPT was developed by OpenAI, a research organization initially co-founded by Elon Musk, Sam Altman, and Greg Brockman, with the mission of advancing AI to benefit all of humanity. As with many groundbreaking endeavors, OpenAI's leadership has faced its internal challenges, but the organization has nonetheless established itself as a powerhouse in the AI industry.

This chatbot isn't just limited to answering text-based queries; it's capable of engaging in dynamic conversations, interpreting documents, and even processing images. Additionally, it features DALL-E, a tool that can generate high-quality images from textual descriptions.

You can access ChatGPT via a web browser or through a desktop or mobile app. Additionally, ChatGPT offers several tiers, from a free version with some usage limits to enterprise-level offerings that come with a full suite of advanced features. Figure 15.13 shows ChatGPT

Co-Pilot

Microsoft is a major force in the AI industry, and they have recently expanded their presence with the launch of Co-Pilot, their generative AI offering available for both public and enterprise users. Co-Pilot's standout feature is its deep integration across a wide range of

Microsoft products, making it a powerful tool for enhancing productivity and streamlining tasks. For example, Co-Pilot can automatically summarize meetings and emails, extract key information, and even suggest actions, all within the familiar interfaces of Microsoft applications like Word, Excel, Outlook, and Teams.

FIGURE 15.13 ChatGPT

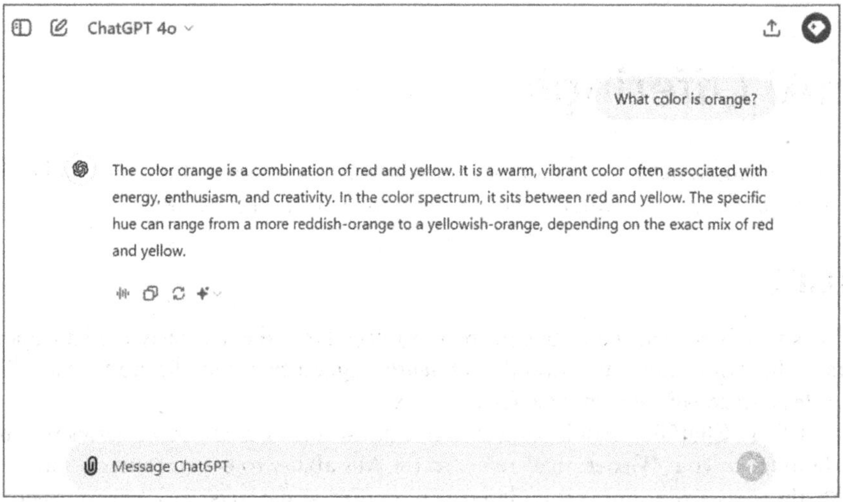

One of the strategic moves Microsoft has made to increase the adoption of Co-Pilot is offering it for free within Windows 11 and the Bing search engine. This decision not only makes advanced AI capabilities more accessible to a broad audience but also enhances the user experience by providing AI-driven insights and assistance directly within these widely used platforms. By embedding Co-Pilot into the core of its ecosystem, Microsoft is positioning itself as a leader in the AI-powered productivity space, aiming to revolutionize how users interact with their everyday tools and complete their tasks more efficiently. Figure 15.14 shows the desktop version of Co-Pilot.

Llama

Meta's Llama is particularly intriguing because, unlike many other AI models that rely on cloud-based infrastructure, it is designed to run directly on your local machine. This approach offers several advantages, especially in terms of data privacy and security. By keeping everything on your own device, you can experiment with AI without worrying about your personal information being exposed to external servers or broader AI networks. This is a significant benefit for those who prioritize data privacy.

FIGURE 15.14 Co-Pilot

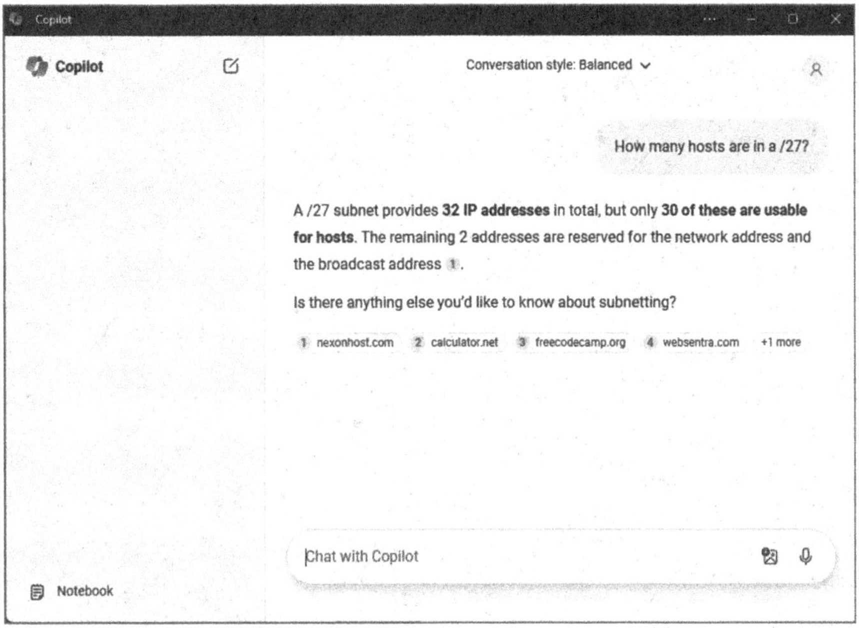

However, running an AI model locally does come with its own set of challenges. One of the primary considerations is the computational resources required. AI models, especially advanced ones, can be resource intensive, demanding significant processing power and memory. While my Apple M3 MacBook Pro handles Llama quite well, providing a smooth experience, it's important to note that it won't match the performance of models like the latest ChatGPT, which operates on powerful cloud servers.

This difference in capability largely comes down to the number of tokens the model can process. Tokens are essentially chunks of text, and the more tokens a model can handle, the more complex and sophisticated its responses can be. Cloud-based models often have access to vastly more tokens and processing power, enabling them to generate more detailed and nuanced outputs. In contrast, a local model like Llama, while effective for many tasks, will have limitations in terms of the depth and complexity of the responses it can generate.

While running a model like Llama locally offers great control and privacy, managing expectations regarding its capabilities is important compared to cutting-edge, cloud-based models. Balancing these factors depends on your specific needs, whether you prioritize data security or the highest possible performance. Figure 15.15 shows my copy of Llama running in a tool called LL Studio, which lets me create my own AI instances.

FIGURE 15.15 LM Studio

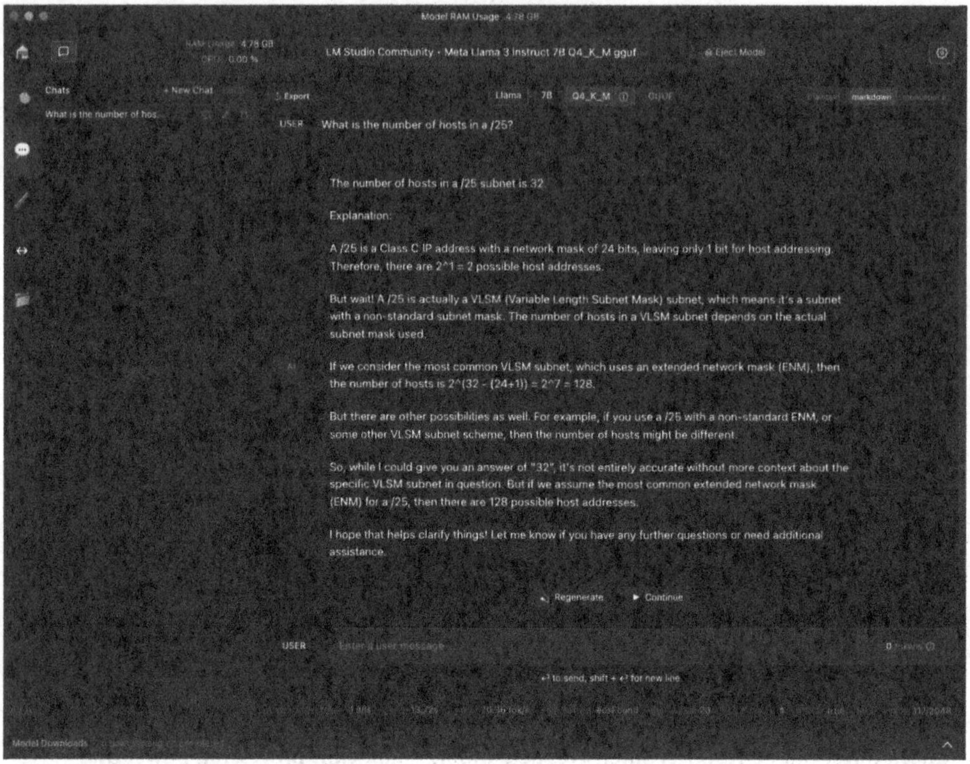

Strategies

I spent a fair amount of time discussing some of the pitfalls with GenAI. While there are certainly a ton of benefits to these solutions, they aren't magic and can still cause headaches if you aren't careful. Fortunately, there are a few techniques that can really help you get more focused and accurate information out of an advanced chatbot, such as prompt engineering and something called RAGs.

Prompt Engineering

One of the key strategies for getting the most accurate and useful information from these systems is *prompt engineering*. This involves carefully crafting your input prompts to guide the AI toward producing the desired output. A well-structured prompt can make a significant difference in the quality of the response. It's like giving clear instructions: The clearer you are, the better the outcome. You can use it to achieve all kinds of results, in fact, prompt engineering is fast becoming a booming field in and of itself.

With prompt engineering, you can have some fun and study with Homer Simpson as seen in Figure 15.16 where he helps me with some subnetting.

FIGURE 15.16 Homer Simpson, Cisco Scholar

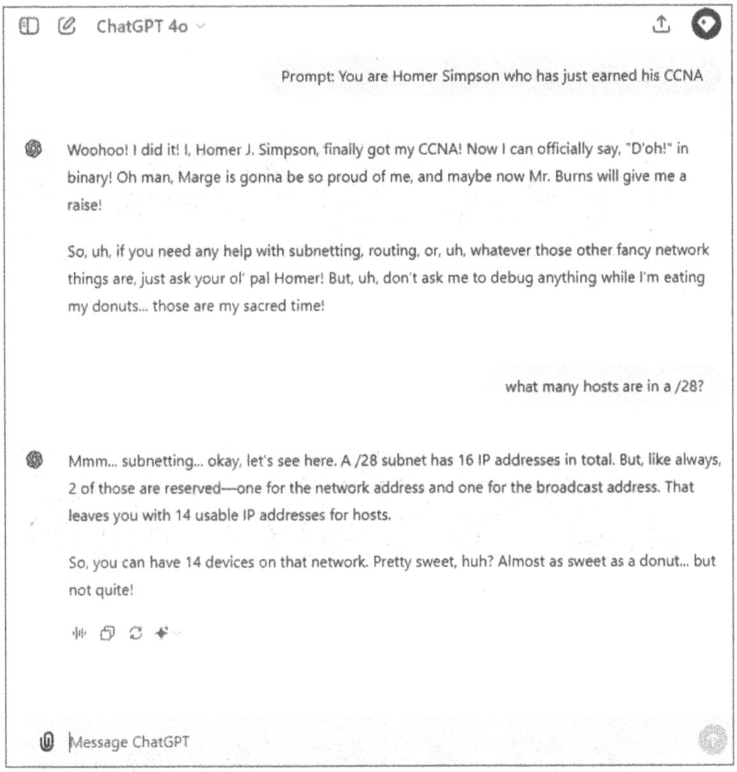
ChatGPT 4o
Prompt: You are Homer Simpson who has just earned his CCNA
Woohoo! I did it! I, Homer J. Simpson, finally got my CCNA! Now I can officially say, "D'oh!" in binary! Oh man, Marge is gonna be so proud of me, and maybe now Mr. Burns will give me a raise!
So, uh, if you need any help with subnetting, routing, or, uh, whatever those other fancy network things are, just ask your ol' pal Homer! But, uh, don't ask me to debug anything while I'm eating my donuts... those are my sacred time!
what many hosts are in a /28?
Mmm... subnetting... okay, let's see here. A /28 subnet has 16 IP addresses in total. But, like always, 2 of those are reserved—one for the network address and one for the broadcast address. That leaves you with 14 usable IP addresses for hosts.
So, you can have 14 devices on that network. Pretty sweet, huh? Almost as sweet as a donut... but not quite!
Message ChatGPT

While that's definitely entertaining, let's take it a step further by having ChatGPT simulate a Cisco router so that I can practice my OSPF commands. I achieve this by giving it a prompt like this:

> **Prompt:** "You are a Cisco 8000v router named AI-ROUTER, running the latest IOS-XE. Please show me the Cisco prompt. When I type a Cisco command, respond as if I entered that command into a real Cisco router."

As I mentioned earlier, the more specific the prompt, the better the results. In this example, I specified the router model, mentioned that it runs IOS-XE, and requested the latest version available. I also instructed it to behave like a router and process the Cisco commands I send. Providing detailed information minimizes confusion, and you can always fine-tune the prompt if necessary. That's why I recommend drafting prompts and more complex requests in a text editor, allowing for easy adjustments and copy-pasting when needed. Figure 15.17 shows me configuring OSPF with my brand new "AI-Router"!

FIGURE 15.17 Become the router

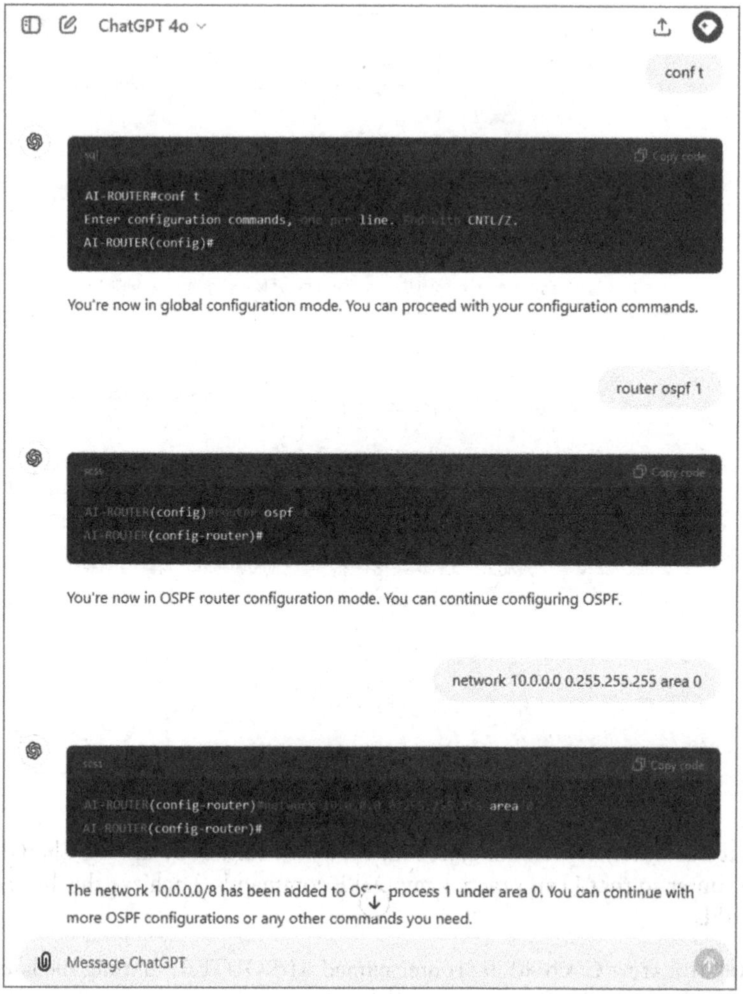

Mastering the art of prompt engineering can dramatically boost your effectiveness when working with AI systems. This skill is crucial because the more precisely you craft your prompts, the better the AI can understand and meet your needs. By carefully designing your inputs, you can guide the AI to produce more accurate, relevant, and useful outputs.

For those with the right product tier, there's even more potential. You can create your own customized GPTs—essentially, AI models that are fine-tuned with your specific prompts.

This capability enables you to design GPTs that are specialized for particular tasks or domains. For example, you could develop one GPT focused exclusively on working with Cisco routers, optimized to understand and respond to commands, troubleshoot issues, or simulate network environments. Meanwhile, another GPT could be tailored to work with a different vendor's routers, ensuring that it's equipped with the knowledge and capabilities specific to that brand.

This level of customization means you can have multiple AI tools, each one finely tuned to excel in a specific area. Whether you're managing different types of network equipment, providing customer support, or working on complex technical projects, these tailored GPTs can become powerful assistants, streamlining your workflow and enhancing your productivity. By combining prompt engineering with the ability to create specialized GPTs, you can unlock the full potential of AI, making it a more effective and reliable tool in your professional toolkit. Figure 15.18 shows me creating a Cisco-focused GPT for my ChatGPT.

FIGURE 15.18 Creating GPTs

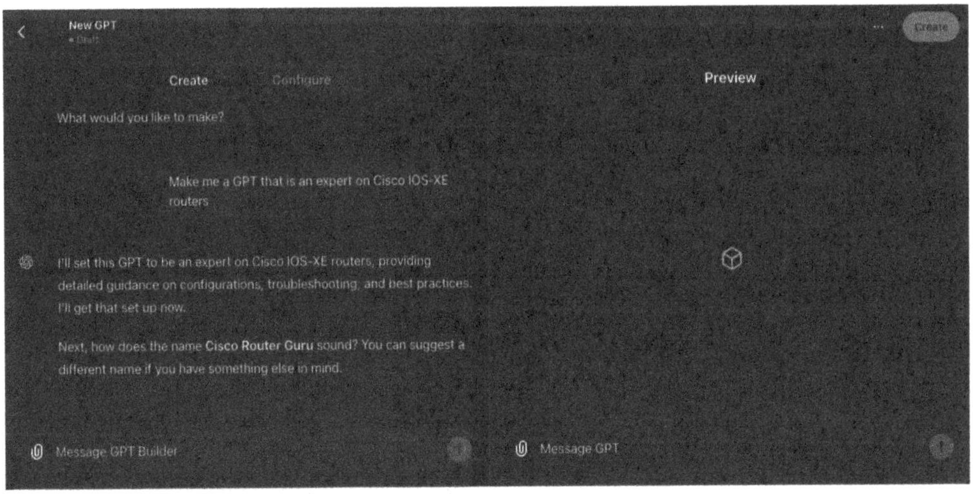

Retrieval-Augmented Generation

Retrieval-augmented generation (RAG) is an incredibly powerful technique that greatly enhances the performance and reliability of AI systems. As I mentioned earlier, traditional generative AI models are limited to the information available at the time they were created. This means that if you need the AI to provide insights on recent developments, like the latest movies or the outcome of a recent election, the model will struggle and might generate inaccurate or outdated information.

RAG addresses this limitation by enabling the AI to incorporate up-to-date information, allowing it to generate more accurate and contextually relevant responses. This can be done by manually providing the AI with additional data or directing it to sources where it can retrieve the latest information. By augmenting the AI's knowledge base in this way, RAG ensures that the responses are not only more accurate but also relevant to the current context.

Figure 15.19 shows an example of RAG where I upload a release notes document Cisco's latest IOS-XE version for the 8000v router. If you haven't seen one of these before, these are documents that explain all the changes in a new software release, including new features, bug fixes, and any security vulnerabilities they addressed. Because this IOS-XE was released a few days before the time I wrote this sentence, ChatGPT would not have the answer in the model and would likely hallucinate answers.

FIGURE 15.19 RAG

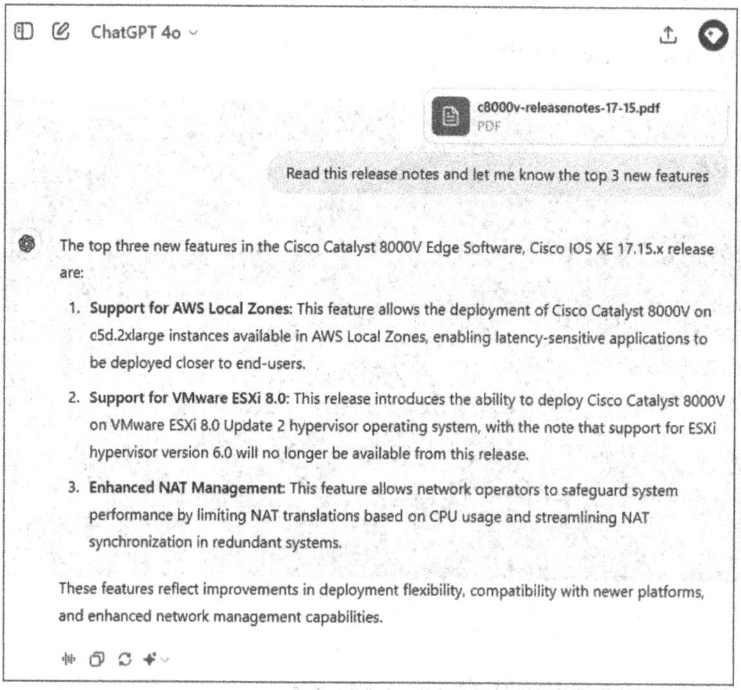

To get around this, I downloaded the PDF version of the release notes and uploaded it to my chat session. I then asked it to give me the top three features. Because ChatGPT is parsing the document, the results are very fast and accurate.

GenAI for Network Engineers

As a network engineer, leveraging GenAI can open up a wide range of possibilities, especially within the realm of AI ops (artificial intelligence for IT operations). AI ops involves the use of AI to enhance and automate various IT operations, including monitoring, event correlation, anomaly detection, and even automated response to certain network conditions. Here are some ideas on how you can utilize GenAI as a network engineer

NOTE Take care when uploading production information to AI as it may leak into public models.

Research and Study

The most straightforward approach is to conduct research and study thoroughly. However, it's crucial to be cautious of potential AI-generated hallucinations. AI should not be your primary source of study material because you need to be able to independently verify the information to ensure its accuracy and usefulness.

Troubleshooting Assistance

You can leverage GenAI as your personal expert system, capable of offering troubleshooting advice based on various inputs such as logs, screenshots, or even complex scenarios you describe. In Figure 15.20, I used ChatGPT to diagnose why OSPF might be flapping on my switches. The AI provided several potential causes and solutions, one of which was correct because I deliberately raised the maximum transmission unit (MTU) on the switch to break OSPF, and the AI pinpointed the MTU mismatch as the likely culprit.

You can also simply describe the symptoms you're encountering or take a screenshot and upload it if copying and pasting data isn't practical. This flexibility allows GenAI to assist with diagnosing and solving network issues even when you're working with limited information or in a complex environment.

Configuration Templates

AI can also be used as a springboard to create network configurations for you or even to help you get started on scripts. Though because of the risk of incorrect information, you should always treat the generated configuration as a starting point, and you should test out the final configuration in a lab or whatever you have to make sure it is ready for primetime before putting it in production.

Figure 15.21 illustrates a basic topology with a workstation and a web server connected to a router. This setup will be used to create an access control list (ACL) that permits the workstation to connect to the web server solely on the standard web ports.

To test this, I uploaded the topology to ChatGPT and requested it to create the ACL, as shown in Figure 15.22. Within a minute, it successfully generated the correct ACL configuration based on the specified criteria. From there, I could easily update the ACL as needed and apply it to the appropriate interface.

FIGURE 15.20 Troubleshooting example

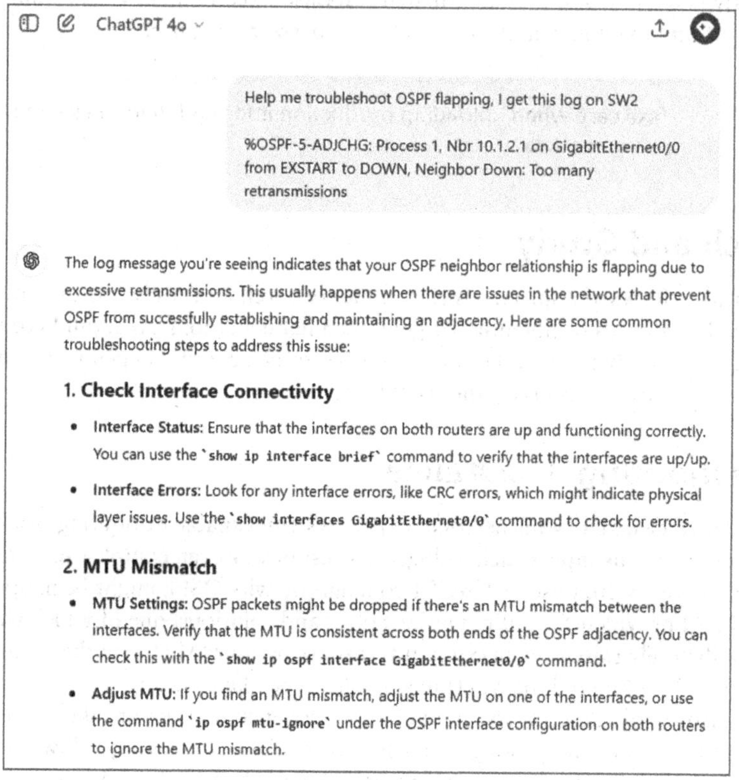
ChatGPT 4o
Help me troubleshoot OSPF flapping, I get this log on SW2
%OSPF-5-ADJCHG: Process 1, Nbr 10.1.2.1 on GigabitEthernet0/0 from EXSTART to DOWN, Neighbor Down: Too many retransmissions
The log message you're seeing indicates that your OSPF neighbor relationship is flapping due to excessive retransmissions. This usually happens when there are issues in the network that prevent OSPF from successfully establishing and maintaining an adjacency. Here are some common troubleshooting steps to address this issue:
1. Check Interface Connectivity
Interface Status: Ensure that the interfaces on both routers are up and functioning correctly. You can use the `show ip interface brief` command to verify that the interfaces are up/up.
Interface Errors: Look for any interface errors, like CRC errors, which might indicate physical layer issues. Use the `show interfaces GigabitEthernet0/0` command to check for errors.
2. MTU Mismatch
MTU Settings: OSPF packets might be dropped if there's an MTU mismatch between the interfaces. Verify that the MTU is consistent across both ends of the OSPF adjacency. You can check this with the `show ip ospf interface GigabitEthernet0/0` command.
Adjust MTU: If you find an MTU mismatch, adjust the MTU on one of the interfaces, or use the command `ip ospf mtu-ignore` under the OSPF interface configuration on both routers to ignore the MTU mismatch.

FIGURE 15.21 Router topology

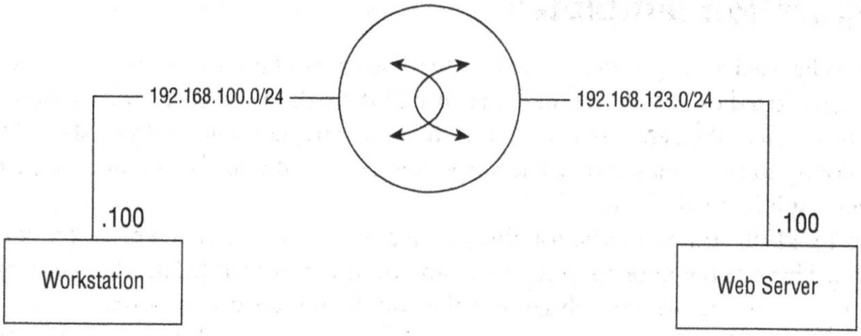

FIGURE 15.22 ChatGPT config template

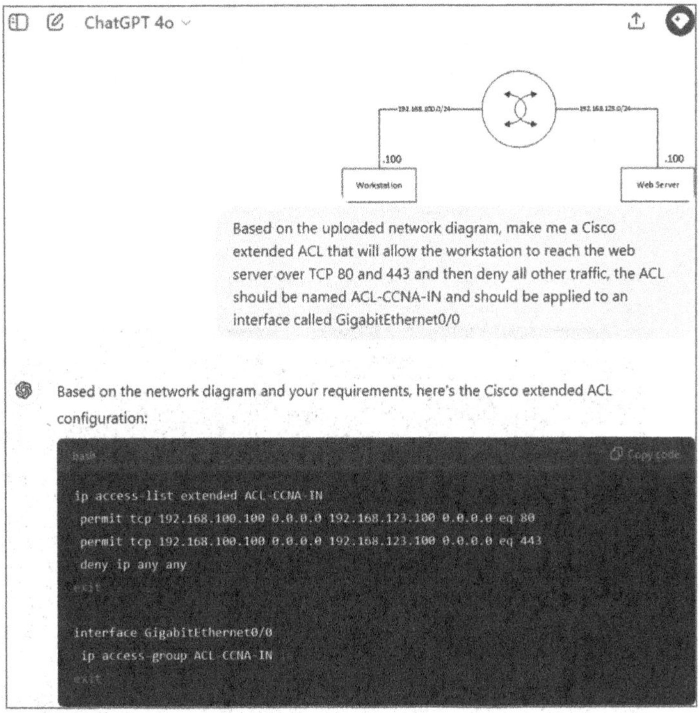

I could also use this to get started on automation scripts, which could save a lot of time when figuring out the gist of how a script is going to function. Figure 15.23 shows me asking ChatGPT to make me a Python script that will connect to a router with the specified login information and grab the output from the `show ip interface brief` command.

Summary

This chapter provided a comprehensive overview of the rapidly evolving AI landscape, explaining key concepts such as machine learning, expert systems, natural language processing, and computer vision. It delved into the various types of AI, from narrow AI, which focuses on specific tasks, to more advanced and hypothetical forms like generalized and super-intelligent AI. The chapter also explored the architectures that power AI, including rule-based systems, decision trees, and neural networks, highlighting their strengths and weaknesses.

FIGURE 15.23 ChatGPT generating Python

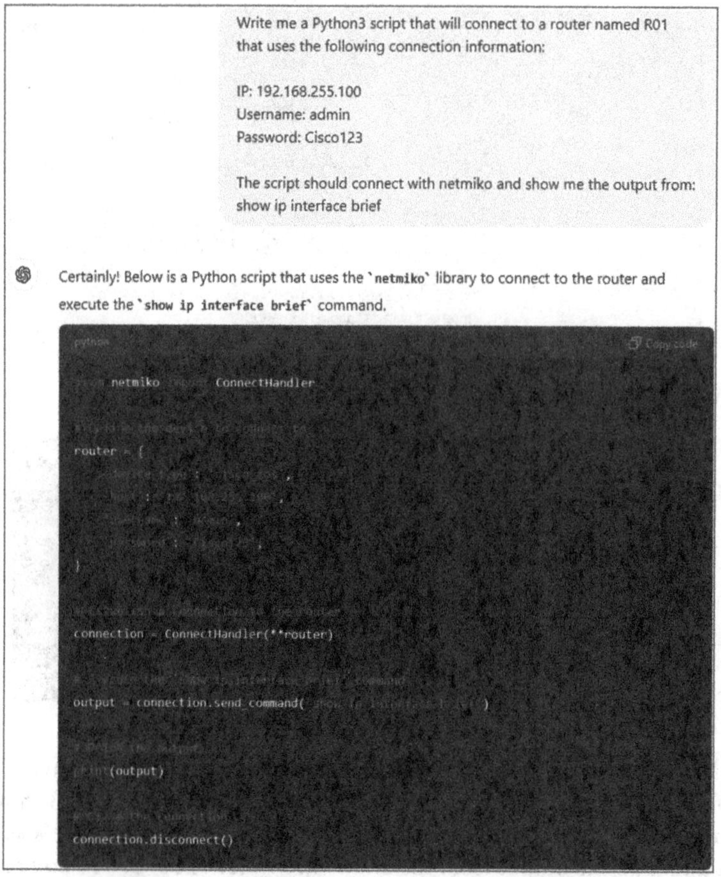
Write me a Python3 script that will connect to a router named R01 that uses the following connection information:
IP: 192.168.255.100
Username: admin
Password: Cisco123
The script should connect with netmiko and show me the output from: show ip interface brief
Certainly! Below is a Python script that uses the `netmiko` library to connect to the router and execute the `show ip interface brief` command.
netmiko ConnectHandler
router = {
}
connection = ConnectHandler(**router)
output = connection.send_command(
(output)
connection.disconnect()

In addition to theoretical knowledge, the chapter examined practical applications of AI in the context of network engineering. It discussed how tools such as ChatGPT can be leveraged for tasks such as troubleshooting, generating configuration templates, and automating routine processes. Strategies for optimizing the use of generative AI, such as prompt engineering and RAG, were also covered, emphasizing how these techniques can enhance the accuracy and usefulness of AI-driven solutions in real-world scenarios.

Overall, the chapter equipped you with both the foundational knowledge and practical insights needed to effectively incorporate AI into your networking tasks while also stressing the importance of critical thinking and independent verification to avoid potential pitfalls like AI-generated hallucinations.

Exam Essentials

Understand predictive AI. Know that predictive AI is usually a product of unsupervised learning and is good at tasks such as network monitoring, anomaly detection, and proactive maintenance.

Understand generative AI. Know what generative AI is, what it is useful for, and what kind of risks are associated with the technology.

Know how to use strategies to improve your AI queries. Know how to use prompt engineering and RAGs to improve the accuracy of your AI queries.

Written Lab

You can find the answers to this lab in Appendix A, "Answers to the Written Labs."

1. Explain the difference between narrow AI and generalized AI. Why is narrow AI currently more prevalent in networking?
2. Describe how limited-memory AI can be utilized in network security. Provide an example of a practical application.
3. What are the key components of a neural network? How do these components contribute to AI's ability to process data?
4. Define machine learning and explain its significance in modern AI applications. How does it differ from traditional programming methods?
5. How can natural language processing (NLP) be applied in network management tools? Give an example of an NLP-based application in networking.
6. What is the role of predictive AI in network operations? Describe a scenario where predictive AI could be used to improve network performance.
7. Explain the concept of AI-generated hallucinations. Why is it important to verify AI-generated outputs, especially in technical fields such as networking?
8. Discuss the advantages and disadvantages of using rule-based systems in AI-driven network tools. When might a rule-based system be preferred over more complex AI models?
9. What is the significance of retrieval-augmented generation (RAG) in enhancing the accuracy of AI systems? How could this technique be applied in a network engineering context?
10. How can AI ops improve IT operations in a networking environment? Provide an example of an AI ops tool and its impact on network management.

Review Questions

You can find the answers to these questions in Appendix B, "Answers to the Review Questions."

> **NOTE** The following questions are designed to test your understanding of this chapter's material. For more information on how to get additional questions, please see this book's Introduction.

1. What is narrow AI best suited for?
   - **A.** Performing multiple complex tasks
   - **B.** Replicating human-level intelligence
   - **C.** Performing specific tasks within predefined parameters
   - **D.** Self-awareness and independent decision-making
2. Which of the following AI types does *not* currently exist?
   - **A.** Narrow AI
   - **B.** Generalized AI
   - **C.** Limited-memory AI
   - **D.** Reactive machines
3. What is the primary goal of machine learning?
   - **A.** To manually program every possible scenario
   - **B.** To create AI systems that require no data input
   - **C.** To enable systems to learn from data and improve over time
   - **D.** To build systems that cannot be understood by humans
4. In which AI category would a system that performs only specific tasks, like a chatbot, fall?
   - **A.** Generalized AI
   - **B.** Super-intelligent AI
   - **C.** Narrow AI
   - **D.** Theory-of-mind AI
5. What type of AI relies on historical data to make predictions about future events?
   - **A.** Reactive AI
   - **B.** Generative AI
   - **C.** Predictive AI
   - **D.** Self-aware AI

6. Which AI architecture is most likely to be used for image and speech recognition?
   A. Rule-based systems
   B. Decision trees
   C. Neural networks
   D. Limited-memory AI
7. Which of the following is *not* a strength of decision trees?
   A. High interpretability
   B. Handling nonlinear relationships
   C. High computational demand
   D. No need for data normalization
8. How does a rule-based system make decisions?
   A. By learning from data over time
   B. By following a series of predefined "if/then" rules
   C. By simulating human reasoning
   D. By adapting to new information automatically
9. Which of the following is an example of limited-memory AI in network security?
   A. A firewall with static rules
   B. An intrusion detection system that adapts to new threats over time
   C. A simple password authentication mechanism
   D. A manual log-analysis tool
10. What is the primary purpose of natural language processing (NLP)?
    A. To process and analyze numerical data
    B. To enable machines to understand and generate human language
    C. To predict future trends in data
    D. To perform physical tasks based on verbal commands
11. Which type of AI might be used to proactively reroute network traffic based on predicted congestion?
    A. Reactive machines
    B. Generalized AI
    C. Predictive AI
    D. Super-intelligent AI
12. What is a potential risk of using AI-generated content without verification?
    A. AI will refuse to generate content.
    B. AI-generated content may contain hallucinations.
    C. AI will always produce correct and verified information.
    D. AI-generated content is immune to errors.

13. Which of the following techniques can improve the accuracy of AI-generated outputs by incorporating up-to-date information?
    A. Overfitting
    B. Data normalization
    C. Retrieval-augmented generation (RAG)
    D. Supervised learning

14. In which scenario would a rule-based system be most effective?
    A. Dynamic environments with constantly changing conditions
    B. Predicting customer behavior based on historical data
    C. Simple, well-defined tasks with clear decision criteria
    D. Learning from large datasets to improve accuracy

15. Which AI architecture is most likely to overfit data if not carefully managed?
    A. Rule-based systems
    B. Decision trees
    C. Neural networks
    D. Reactive machines

16. What is the main advantage of using a decision tree in AI models?
    A. High computational efficiency
    B. Simple decision-making process with clear interpretability
    C. Automatic adaptation to new data
    D. Ability to handle infinite possibilities

17. Which of the following AI categories focuses on AI's capacity to understand human emotions and social interactions?
    A. Limited-memory AI
    B. Generalized AI
    C. Theory-of-mind AI
    D. Reactive machines

18. What is the purpose of prompt engineering in the context of generative AI?
    A. To generate random AI responses
    B. To optimize the input prompts for more accurate AI outputs
    C. To manually correct AI outputs
    D. To replace the need for data in AI systems

19. Which of the following best describes the concept of "overfitting" in AI?
    A. When an AI model generalizes well to new data
    B. When an AI model learns noise in the training data too well
    C. When an AI model requires too much data to function
    D. When an AI model does not learn from training data
20. Which AI application is most relevant for a network engineer looking to automate routine tasks?
    A. Self-aware AI
    B. Generative AI
    C. Theory-of-mind AI
    D. Super-intelligent AI

Appendix A

Answers to the Written Labs

Chapter 1: Network Fundamentals

1. 64 Kbps
2. 1.544 Mbps
3. 2.048 Mbps
4. 44.736 Mbps
5. 155.52 Mbps
6. 622.08 Mbps
7. 2,488.32 Mbps

Chapter 2: Ethernet Networking

Written Lab 2.1: Binary/Decimal/Hexadecimal Conversion Answer

1.

Decimal	128	64	32	16	8	4	2	1	Binary
192	1	1	0	0	0	0	0	0	11000000
168	1	0	1	0	1	0	0	0	10101000
10	0	0	0	0	1	0	1	0	00001010
15	0	0	0	0	1	1	1	1	00001111
Decimal	128	64	32	16	8	4	2	1	Binary
172	1	0	1	0	1	1	0	0	10101100
16	0	0	0	1	0	0	0	0	00010000
20	0	0	0	1	0	1	0	0	00010100
55	0	0	1	1	0	1	1	1	00110111
Decimal	128	64	32	16	8	4	2	1	Binary
10	0	0	0	0	1	0	1	0	00001010
11	0	0	0	0	1	0	1	1	00001011
12	0	0	0	0	1	1	0	0	00001100
99	0	1	1	0	0	0	1	1	01100011

2.

Binary	128	64	32	16	8	4	2	1	Decimal
11001100	1	1	0	0	1	1	0	0	204
00110011	0	0	1	1	0	0	1	1	51
10101010	1	0	1	0	1	0	1	0	170
01010101	0	1	0	1	0	1	0	1	85
Binary	**128**	**64**	**32**	**16**	**8**	**4**	**2**	**1**	**Decimal**
11000110	1	1	0	0	0	1	1	0	198
11010011	1	1	0	1	0	0	1	1	211
00111001	0	0	1	1	1	0	0	1	57
11010001	1	1	0	1	0	0	0	1	209
Binary	**128**	**64**	**32**	**16**	**8**	**4**	**2**	**1**	**Decimal**
10000100	1	0	0	0	0	1	0	0	132
11010010	1	1	0	1	0	0	1	0	210
10111000	1	0	1	1	1	0	0	0	184
10100110	1	0	1	0	0	1	1	0	166

3.

Binary	128	64	32	16	8	4	2	1	Hexadecimal
11011000	1	1	0	1	1	0	0	0	D8
00011011	0	0	0	1	1	0	1	1	1B
00111101	0	0	1	1	1	1	0	1	3D
01110110	0	1	1	1	0	1	1	0	76
Binary	**128**	**6**	**32**	**16**	**8**	**4**	**2**	**1**	**Hexadecimal**
11001010	1	1	0	0	1	0	1	0	CA
11110101	1	1	1	1	0	1	0	1	F5
10000011	1	0	0	0	0	0	1	1	83
11101011	1	1	1	0	1	0	1	1	EB
Binary	**128**	**64**	**32**	**16**	**8**	**4**	**2**	**1**	**Hexadecimal**
10000100	1	0	0	0	0	1	0	0	84
11010010	1	1	0	1	0	0	1	0	D2
01000011	0	1	0	0	0	0	1	1	43
10110011	1	0	1	1	0	0	1	1	B3

Written Lab 2.2: CSMA/CD Operations Answer

When a collision occurs on an Ethernet LAN, the following happens in this correct order:

1. A jam signal informs all devices that a collision occurred.
2. The collision invokes a random backoff algorithm.
3. Each device on the Ethernet segment stops transmitting for a short time until the timers expire.
4. All hosts have equal priority to transmit after the timers have expired.

Written Lab 2.3: Cabling Answer

1. Crossover
2. Straight-through
3. Crossover
4. Crossover
5. Straight-through
6. Crossover
7. Crossover
8. Rolled

Chapter 3: TCP/IP

Written Lab 3.1: TCP/IP

1. 192 through 223, 110*xxxxx*
2. Host-to-Host or Transport
3. 1 through 126
4. Loopback or diagnostics
5. Turn all host bits off.
6. Turn all host bits on.
7. 10.0.0.0 through 10.255.255.255
8. 172.16.0.0 through 172.31.255.255
9. 192.168.0.0 through 192.168.255.255
10. 0 through 9 and *A*, *B*, *C*, *D*, *E*, and *F*

Written Lab 3.2: Mapping Applications to the DoD Model

1. Internet
2. Process/Application
3. Process/Application
4. Process/Application
5. Process/Application
6. Internet
7. Process/Application
8. Host-to-host/Transport
9. Host-to-host/Transport
10. Internet
11. Process/Application
12. Process/Application

Chapter 4: Easy Subnetting

Written Lab 4.1: Written Subnet Practice #1

1. 192.168.100.25/30. A /30 is 255.255.255.252. The valid subnet is 192.168.100.24, with a broadcast address of 192.168.100.27. The valid hosts are 192.168.100.25 and 26.
2. 192.168.100.37/28. A /28 is 255.255.255.240. The fourth octet is a block size of 16. Just count by 16s until you pass 37. 0, 16, 32, 48. The host is in the 32 subnet, with a broadcast address of 47. The valid host range is 33–46.
3. A /27 is 255.255.255.224. The fourth octet is a block size of 32. Count by 32s until you pass the host address of 66. 0, 32, 64, 96. The host is in the 64 subnet, with a broadcast address of 95. The valid host range is 65–94.
4. 192.168.100.17/29. A /29 is 255.255.255.248. The fourth octet is a block size of 8. 0, 8, 16, 24. The host is in the 16 subnet, with a broadcast address of 23. The valid host range is 17–22.
5. 192.168.100.99/26. A /26 is 255.255.255.192. The fourth octet has a block size of 64. 0, 64, 128. The host is in the 64 subnet, with a broadcast address of 127. The valid host range is 65–126.
6. 192.168.100.99/25. A /25 is 255.255.255.128. The fourth octet is a block size of 128. 0, 128. The host is in the 0 subnet, with a broadcast address of 127. The valid host range is 1–126.

7. A default Class B is 255.255.0.0. A Class B 255.255.255.0 mask is 256 subnets, each with 254 hosts. We need fewer subnets. If we used 255.255.240.0, this provides 16 subnets. Let's add one more subnet bit. 255.255.248.0. This is 5 bits of subnetting, which provides 32 subnets. This is our best answer, a /21.
8. A /29 is 255.255.255.248. This is a block size of 8 in the fourth octet. 0, 8, 16. The host is in the 8 subnet, with a broadcast address of 15.
9. A /29 is 255.255.255.248, which is 5 subnet bits and 3 host bits. This is only 6 hosts per subnet.
10. A /23 is 255.255.254.0. The third octet is a block size of 2. 0, 2, 4. The subnet is in the 16.2.0 subnet; the broadcast address is 16.3.255.

Written Lab 4.2: Written Subnet Practice #2

Classful Address	Subnet Mask	Number of Hosts per Subnet ($2^x - 2$)
/16	255.255.0.0	65,534
/17	255.255.128.0	32,766
/18	255.255.192.0	16,382
/19	255.255.224.0	8,190
/20	255.255.240.0	4,094
/21	255.255.248.0	2,046
/22	255.255.252.0	1,022
/23	255.255.254.0	510
/24	255.255.255.0	254
/25	255.255.255.128	126
/26	255.255.255.192	62
/27	255.255.255.224	30
/28	255.255.255.240	14
/29	255.255.255.248	6
/30	255.255.255.252	2

Written Lab 4.3: Written Subnet Practice #3

Decimal IP Address	Address Class	Number of Subnet and Host Bits	Number of Subnets ($2x$)	Number of Hosts ($2x – 2$)
10.25.66.154/23	A	15/9	32,768	510
172.31.254.12/24	B	8/8	256	254
192.168.20.123/28	C	4/4	16	14
63.24.89.21/18	A	10/14	1,024	16,382
128.1.1.254/20	B	4/12	16	4,094
208.100.54.209/30	C	6/2	64	2

Chapter 5: Troubleshooting IP Addressing

1. Cisco recommends troubleshooting with four simple steps: ping the loopback address, ping the NIC, ping the default gateway, and ping the remote device.
2. You can ping any address from 127.0.0.1 through 127.255.255.254 to test your local IP stack.
3. IP and ICMP
4. DNS
5. `tracert` is a Windows command to track the path a packet takes through an internetwork to a destination. Cisco routers use the command `traceroute`, or just `trace` for short.

Chapter 6: Cisco's Internetworking Operating System (IOS)

1. `Router(config)#`**`clock rate 1000000`**
2. `Switch#`**`config t`**

   `switch config)#` **`line vty 0 15`**

   `switch(config-line)#` **`no login`**
3. `Switch#`**`config t`**

   `Switch(config)#` **`int f0/1`**

   `Switch(config-if)#` **`no shutdown`**
4. `Switch#`**`erase startup-config`**

5. Switch#**config t**
   Switch(config)#**line console 0**
   Switch(config-line)#**password todd**
   Switch(config-line)#**login**
6. Switch#**config t**
   Switch(config)# **enable secret cisco**
7. Router#**show controllers serial 0/2**
8. Switch#**show terminal**
9. Switch#**reload**
10. Switch#**config t**
    Switch(config)#hostname Sales

Chapter 7: Managing a Cisco Internetwork

Written Lab 7.1: IOS Management

1. copy start run
2. show cdp neighbor detail or show cdp entry *
3. show cdp neighbor
4. Ctrl+Shift+6, then X
5. show sessions
6. Either copy tftp run or copy start run
7. NTP
8. ip helper-address
9. ntp server *ip_address* version 4
10. show ntp status

Written Lab 7.2: Router Memory

1. Flash memory
2. ROM
3. NVRAM
4. ROM
5. RAM

6. RAM
7. ROM
8. ROM
9. RAM
10. RAM

Chapter 8: Managing Cisco Devices

Written Lab 8.1: IOS Management

1. `copy flash tftp`
2. 0x2101
3. 0x2102
4. 0x2100
5. UDI
6. 0x2142
7. `boot system`
8. `POST test`
9. `copy tftp flash`
10. `show license`

Chapter 9: IP Routing

1. `router(config)#`**`ip route 172.16.10.0 255.255.255.0 172.16.20.1 150`**
2. It will use the gateway interface MAC at L2 and the actual destination IP at L3.
3. `router(config)#`**`ip route 0.0.0.0 0.0.0.0 172.16.40.1`**
4. Stub network
5. `router#`**`show ip route`**
6. Exit interface
7. False. The MAC address would be the router interface, not the remote host.
8. True
9. `router(config)#`router rip
   `router(config-router)#`passive-interface S1
10. True

Chapter 10: Open Shortest Path First

1. `router ospf 101`
2. `show ip ospf`
3. `show ip ospf interface`
4. `show ip ospf neighbor`
5. `show ip route ospf`

Chapter 11: Enhanced IGRP

1. `ipv6 router eigrpv` *`as`*
2. FF02::A
3. False
4. The routers will not form an adjacency.
5. Passive interface

Chapter 12: Layer 2 Switching

1. `show mac address-table.`
2. Flood the frame out all ports except the port on which it was received.
3. Address learning, forward/filter decisions, and loop avoidance.
4. It will add the source MAC address in the forward/filter table and associate it with the port on which the frame was received.
5. Maximum 1, violation shutdown.

Chapter 13: VLANs and Inter-VLAN Routing

1. False! You do not provide an IP address under any physical port.
2. STP
3. Broadcast
4. Collision
5. `switchport trunk encapsulation dot1q`

6. Trunking allows you to make a single port part of multiple VLANs at the same time.
7. Frame identification (frame tagging) uniquely assigns a user-defined ID to each frame. This is sometimes referred to as a VLAN ID or color.
8. True
9. Access link
10. `switchport trunk native vlan 4`

Chapter 14: Cloud and Virtual Private Networks

1. Tunnel mode
2. ESP
3. Security, cost savings, scalability, and compatibility with broadband technology
4. Authentication Header (AH) and Encapsulating Security Payload (ESP)
5. IPsec
6. Remote access VPNs, site-to-site VPNs, and extranet VPNs
7. A private cloud refers to hosting resources within an organization's own physical environment, such as a data center. In contrast, a public cloud involves hosting resources with a cloud provider, such as Amazon AWS or Microsoft Azure, where the resources are generally publicly accessible with public IP addresses.
8. Infrastructure as a Service (IaaS) involves running virtual machines on a cloud provider's hypervisor, where the provider maintains the infrastructure up to the hypervisor, and the user manages everything above that, such as the operating system and applications. In contrast, Platform as a Service (PaaS) abstracts this further by having the cloud provider manage everything up to the operating system, allowing the user to focus solely on the application.
9. Businesses may have a "love-hate" relationship with on-premises hosting because it provides maximum control over the infrastructure, as it is owned and managed by the business. However, it can also be expensive and resource-intensive to maintain, requiring significant investment in hardware, maintenance, and operational costs.
10. An example of Software as a Service (SaaS) is Cisco Webex, Microsoft Teams, or Zoom. SaaS is different from other cloud service models because the entire application is fully managed by the service provider, and the user only needs to access and use the application without worrying about the underlying infrastructure, operating system, or application maintenance.

Chapter 15: Introduction to Artificial Intelligence and Machine Learning

1. Narrow AI, also known as weak AI, is designed to perform a specific task or a limited set of tasks. It operates within predefined parameters and does not possess the ability to generalize its knowledge beyond its designated function. Examples include virtual assistants such as Alexa or Siri.

   Generalized AI, or strong AI, is a concept that aims to replicate human-level intelligence, enabling it to perform any intellectual task a human can, regardless of whether those tasks are related or unrelated. Generalized AI does not yet exist.

   Narrow AI is more prevalent in networking because it is well-suited to specialized tasks such as network monitoring, traffic analysis, and security threat detection, where specific, well-defined tasks are required.

2. Limited-memory AI refers to AI systems that can learn from historical data and retain information from previous interactions, enabling them to adapt over time.

   In network security, limited-memory AI can be used to detect and respond to security threats by analyzing past network traffic patterns and identifying anomalies that may indicate a security breach.

   Example: Advanced malware detection systems, such as Cisco Secure Endpoint, use limited-memory AI to identify malware patterns in data and traffic, even protecting against zero-day attacks by learning from historical attack data.

3. The key components of a neural network include the following:

   Input layer: This is where raw data enters the network. Each neuron in this layer represents a feature of the input data.

   Hidden layers: These layers perform the core processing, transforming input data through a series of weighted connections to extract patterns and features. The hidden layers enable the network to learn complex representations of the data.

   Output layer: This layer produces the final prediction or classification based on the processed information from the hidden layers.

   These components work together to allow the AI to process data by learning from patterns in the input data and making predictions or classifications based on what it has learned.

4. Machine learning is a subset of AI that enables systems to learn from data, recognize patterns, and make decisions with minimal human intervention. It allows AI systems to improve their accuracy over time as they process more data.

   Significance: Machine learning is crucial in modern AI applications because it allows systems to adapt and improve without needing to be explicitly programmed for every scenario, making AI more flexible and powerful.

   Difference from traditional programming: Traditional programming relies on explicit instructions provided by humans, where each possible scenario must be coded. In contrast, machine learning allows the system to learn from examples and data, making it possible to handle more complex and dynamic situations.

5. NLP allows machines to understand, interpret, and generate human language. In network management, NLP can be used to create more intuitive and user-friendly interfaces for managing network devices, where users can input commands in natural language.

   Example: An NLP-based application in networking could be a virtual assistant that allows network engineers to query network status, troubleshoot issues, or configure devices using plain English commands, rather than complex command-line interface (CLI) syntax.

6. Predictive AI analyzes historical data to forecast future events or trends, allowing network operators to anticipate issues before they occur.

   Scenario: Predictive AI could be used to monitor network traffic patterns and predict when certain links or devices will become congested. This allows operators to take preemptive actions, such as rerouting traffic or provisioning additional bandwidth, to maintain optimal network performance.

7. AI-generated hallucinations occur when an AI system produces information that is incorrect, misleading, or entirely fabricated. This can happen because the AI attempts to generate responses even when it lacks the necessary context or data.

   Importance of verification: In technical fields such as networking, relying on inaccurate information can lead to misconfigurations, security vulnerabilities, or network failures. Therefore, it is crucial to verify AI-generated outputs against trusted sources to ensure accuracy and reliability.

8. The advantages are as follows:

   High interpretability: Rule-based systems are easy to understand and troubleshoot because decisions are made based on predefined rules.

   Predictability: They provide consistent and predictable results for well-defined tasks.

   And the disadvantages are as follows:

   Limited scope: They can only handle scenarios that have been explicitly programmed into the rules.

   Lack of adaptability: Rule-based systems do not learn from new data or adapt to changes in the environment.

   Preferred usage: A rule-based system might be preferred in scenarios where the tasks are simple, well-defined, and require transparency, such as compliance checks or automated responses to specific network events.

9. Significance of RAG: Retrieval-augmented generation enhances AI systems by allowing them to incorporate up-to-date information, improving the accuracy and relevance of their responses. This is particularly useful when the AI's training data may not cover the most recent developments.

   Application in networking: In a network engineering context, RAG could be used to pull the latest network configurations, firmware updates, or security patches from external databases and integrate them into the AI's decision-making process, ensuring the AI provides the most current and relevant recommendations.

10. AI ops enhances IT operations by using AI to automate and optimize various aspects of network management, such as monitoring, event correlation, and anomaly detection. This leads to faster problem resolution, improved network performance, and reduced operational costs.

    Example: An AI ops tool like Cisco's AI Network Analytics can automatically detect and correlate network events, predict potential failures, and recommend corrective actions. This reduces the manual effort required for network troubleshooting and helps maintain a more stable and efficient network environment.

Appendix B

Answers to the Review Questions

Chapter 1: Network Fundamentals

1. A. The core layer should be as fast as possible. Never do anything to slow down traffic. This includes making sure you don't use access lists, perform routing between virtual local area networks, or implement packet filtering.
2. C. SOHO stands for small office/home office and is a single or small group of users connecting to a switch, with a router providing a connection to the Internet for the small network.
3. A, C. The access layer provides access to users, phones, and other devices in the internetwork. PoE and switch port security are implemented here.
4. C. Switches break up collision domains, and routers break up broadcast domains by default.
5. D. A T3 line, also referred to as a DS3, comprises 28 DS1s bundled together, or 672 DS0s, for a bandwidth of 44.736 Mbps.
6. B. Since there is no such thing as layer 2 packets, we wouldn't be able to inspect packets with any device on this nonexistent packet type.
7. C. Firewalls inspect traffic either leaving or entering your network (or both directions) and can accomplish this with deep packet inspection (DPI).
8. B. In a two-tier design, the goal is to maximize performance and user availability on the network while still allowing for design scalability over time.
9. A. Hubs are multiport repeaters that only care about the digital signal on a wire, nothing else.
10. A. In a spine-leaf design, people refer to this as a top-of-rack (ToR) design because the switches physically reside at the top of a rack.

Chapter 2: Ethernet Networking

1. A, C, E. **Cat 5:**
   Frequency: Up to 100 MHz
   Bandwidth: 100 Mbps (Fast Ethernet)
   Max Distance: 100 meters (328 feet)
   Cat 5e:
   Frequency: Up to 100 MHz
   Bandwidth: 1 Gbps (Gigabit Ethernet)
   Max Distance: 100 meters (328 feet)

Cat 6:
Frequency: Up to 250 MHz
Bandwidth: 10 Gbps (10 Gigabit Ethernet)
Max Distance: 55 meters (180 feet) for 10 Gbps; 100 meters (328 feet) for 1 Gbps
Cat 6a:
Frequency: Up to 500 MHz
Bandwidth: 10 Gbps (10 Gigabit Ethernet)
Max Distance: 100 meters (328 feet)
Cat 7:
Frequency: Up to 600 MHz
Bandwidth: 10 Gbps (10 Gigabit Ethernet)
Max Distance: 100 meters (328 feet)
Cat 8:
Frequency: Up to 2 GHz
Bandwidth: 25/40 Gbps (25/40 Gigabit Ethernet)
Max Distance: 30 meters (98 feet)

2. A. Backoff on an Ethernet network is the retransmission delay that's enforced when a collision occurs. When that happens, a host will only resume transmission after the forced time delay has expired. Keep in mind that after the backoff has elapsed, all stations have equal priority to transmit data.

3. A. When using a hub, all ports are in the same collision domain, which will introduce collisions as shown between devices connected to the same hub.

4. B. FCS is a field at the end of the frame that's used to store the cyclic redundancy check (CRC) answer. The CRC is a mathematical algorithm that's based on the data in the frame and run when each frame is built. When a receiving host receives the frame and runs the CRC, the answer should be the same. If not, the frame is discarded, assuming errors have occurred.

5. C. Half-duplex Ethernet networking uses a protocol called Carrier Sense Multiple Access with Collision Detection (CSMA/CD), which helps devices share the bandwidth evenly while preventing two devices from transmitting simultaneously on the same network medium.

6. A, E. Physical, or MAC addresses are used to identify devices at layer 2. MAC addresses are only used to communicate on the same network. To communicate on a different network, we have to use layer 3 addresses (IP addresses).

7. D. The cable shown is a straight-through cable, which is used between dissimilar devices.

8. C, D. An Ethernet network is a shared environment, so all devices have the right to access the medium. If more than one device transmits simultaneously, the signals collide and cannot reach the destination. If a device detects another device is sending, it will wait for a specified amount of time before attempting to transmit.
When there is no traffic detected, a device will transmit its message. While this transmission is occurring, the device continues to listen for traffic or collisions on the LAN. After the message is sent, the device returns to its default listening mode.

9. B. In creating the gigabit crossover cable, you'd still cross 1 to 3 and 2 to 6, but you would add 4 to 7 and 5 to 8.

10. D. When you set up the connection, use the following settings:
    - Bits per sec: 9600
    - Data bits: 8
    - Parity: None
    - Stop bits: 1
    - Flow control: None

11. D. When set to 0, this bit represents a globally administered address, as specified by the IEEE, but when it's a 1, it represents a locally governed and administered address.

12. B. You can use a rolled Ethernet cable to connect a host EIA-TIA 232 interface to a router console serial communication (COM) port.

13. B. The collision will invoke a backoff algorithm on all systems, not just the ones involved in the collision.

14. A. There are no collisions in full-duplex mode.

15. B. The connection between the two switches requires a crossover and the connection from the hosts to the switches requires a straight-through.

16. The given cable types are matched with their standards in the following table:

IEEE 802.3u	100Base-Tx
IEEE 802.3	10Base-T
IEEE 802.3ab	1000Base-T
IEEE 802.3z	1000Base-SX

17. B. Although rolled cable isn't used to connect any Ethernet connections together, you can use a rolled Ethernet cable to connect a host EIA-TIA 232 interface to a router console serial communication (COM) port.

18. B. If you're using TCP, the virtual circuit is defined by the source and destination port number plus the source and destination IP address and called a *socket.*

19. A. The hex value 1c is converted as 28 in decimals.

20. A. Fiber-optic cables are the only ones that have a core surrounded by a material called cladding.

Chapter 3: TCP/IP

1. C. If a DHCP conflict is detected, either by the server sending a ping and getting a response or by a host using a gratuitous ARP (arp'ing for its own IP address and seeing if a host responds), then the server will hold that address and not use it again until it is fixed by an administrator.

2. B. Secure Shell (SSH) protocol sets up a secure session that's similar to Telnet over a standard TCP/IP connection and is employed for doing things like logging into systems, running programs on remote systems, and moving files from one system to another.

3. C. A host uses something called a gratuitous ARP to help avoid a possible duplicate address. The DHCP client sends an ARP broadcast out on the local LAN or VLAN using its newly assigned address to help solve conflicts before they occur.

4. A, B. DHCP uses a layer 2 broadcast and uses UDP at the Transport layer.

5. C, D, E. SNMP typically uses UDP but can use TCP. FTP and HTTP only use TCP.

6. C. A multicast address starts with 224 in the first octet and can go up to 239.

7. C, E. The Class A private address range is 10.0.0.0 through 10.255.255.255. The Class B private address range is 172.16.0.0 through 172.31.255.255, and the Class C private address range is 192.168.0.0 through 192.168.255.255. These addresses can be used on a private network but are not routable through the Internet.

8. B. The Host-to-Host and Transport layer are both defined the same.

9. B, C. ICMP is used for diagnostics and destination unreachable messages. ICMP is encapsulated within IP datagrams, and because it is used for diagnostics, it will provide hosts with information about network problems.

10. C. The range of a Class B network address is 128–191. This makes our binary range 10*xxxxxx*.

11. B. TCP is used at the Transport layer with Telnet, among many other applications.

12. RFC 1918. These addresses can be used on a private network but are not routable through the Internet. This is designed for the purpose of creating a measure of well-needed security, but it also conveniently saves valuable IP address space. NAT is needed to take a private IP address and convert it for use on the Internet.

13. A. The header shown in the graphic is the IP header.

14. C. The Internet layer is the equivalent of the Network layer of the OSI model.

15. Here is the correct order of a DHCP request:

    DHCPDiscover

    DHCPOffer

    DHCPRequest

    DHCPAck

Chapter 4: Easy Subnetting

1. D. A /27 (255.255.255.224) is 3 bits on and 5 bits off. This provides 8 subnets, each with 30 hosts. Does it matter if this mask is used with a Class A, B, or C network address? Not at all. The number of host bits would never change.

2. D. A 240 mask is 4 subnet bits and provides 16 subnets, each with 14 hosts. We need more subnets, so let's add subnet bits. One more subnet bit would be a 248 mask. This provides 5 subnet bits (32 subnets) with 3 host bits (6 hosts per subnet). This is the best answer.

3. C. This is a pretty simple question. A /28 is 255.255.255.240, which means that our block size is 16 in the fourth octet. 0, 16, 32, 48, 64, 80, etc. The host is in the 64 subnet.

4. F. A CIDR address of /19 is 255.255.224.0. This is a Class B address, so that is only 3 subnet bits, but it provides 13 host bits, or 8 subnets, each with 8,190 hosts.

5. B, D. The mask 255.255.254.0 (/23) used with a Class A address means that there are 15 subnet bits and 9 host bits. The block size in the third octet is 2 (256 – 254). So, this makes the subnets in the interesting octet 0, 2, 4, 6, etc., all the way to 254. The host 10.16.3.65 is in the 2.0 subnet. The next subnet is 4.0, so the broadcast address for the 2.0 subnet is 3.255. The valid host addresses are 2.1 through 3.254.

6. D. A /30, regardless of the class of address, has a 252 in the fourth octet. This means we have a block size of 4, and our subnets are 0, 4, 8, 12, 16, etc. Address 14 is obviously in the 12 subnet.

7. D. A point-to-point link uses only two hosts. A /30, or 255.255.255.252, mask provides two hosts per subnet.

8. C. A /21 is 255.255.248.0, which means we have a block size of 8 in the third octet, so we just count by 8 until we reach 66. The subnet in this question is 64.0. The next subnet is 72.0, so the broadcast address of the 64 subnet is 71.255.

9. A. A /29 (255.255.255.248), regardless of the class of address, has only 3 host bits. Six hosts are the maximum number of hosts on this LAN, including the router interface.

10. C. A /29 is 255.255.255.248, which is a block size of 8 in the fourth octet. The subnets are 0, 8, 16, 24, 32, 40, etc. 192.168.19.24 is the 24 subnet, and since 32 is the next subnet, the broadcast address for the 24 subnet is 31. 192.168.19.26 is the only correct answer.

11. A. A /29 (255.255.255.248) has a block size of 8 in the fourth octet. This means the subnets are 0, 8, 16, 24, etc. 10 is in the 8 subnet. The next subnet is 16, so 15 is the broadcast address.

12. B. You need 5 subnets, each with at least 16 hosts. The mask 255.255.255.240 provides 16 subnets with 14 hosts—this will not work. The mask 255.255.255.224 provides 8 subnets, each with 30 hosts. This is the best answer.

13. C. First, you cannot answer this question if you can't subnet. The 192.168.10.62 with a mask of 255.255.255.192 is a block size of 64 in the fourth octet. The host 192.168.10.62 is in the zero subnet, and the error occurred because `ip subnet-zero` is not enabled on the router.

14. A. A /25 mask is 255.255.255.128. Used with a Class B network, the third and fourth octets are used for subnetting with a total of 9 subnet bits, 8 bits in the third octet and 1 bit in the fourth octet. Since there is only 1 bit in the fourth octet, the bit is either off or on—which is a value of 0 or 128. The host in the question is in the 0 subnet, which has a broadcast address of 127 since 112.128 is the next subnet.

15. A. A /28 is a 255.255.255.240 mask. Let's count to the ninth subnet. (We need to find the broadcast address of the eighth subnet, so we need to count to the ninth subnet.) Starting at 16 (remember, the question stated that we will not use subnet zero, so we start at 16, not 0), 16, 32, 48, 64, 80, 96, 112, 128, 144, etc. The eighth subnet is 128, and the next subnet is 144, so our broadcast address of the 128 subnet is 143. This makes the host range 129–142. 142 is the last valid host.

16. C. A /28 is a 255.255.255.240 mask. The first subnet is 16 (remember, the question stated not to use subnet zero), and the next subnet is 32, so our broadcast address is 31. This makes our host range 17–30. 30 is the last valid host.

17. E. A Class C subnet mask of 255.255.255.224 is 3 bits on and 5 bits off (11100000) and provides 8 subnets, each with 30 hosts. However, if the command `ip subnet-zero` were not used, then only 6 subnets would be available for use.

18. E. A Class B network ID with a /22 mask is 255.255.252.0, with a block size of 4 in the third octet. The network address in the question is in subnet 172.16.16.0 with a broadcast address of 172.16.19.255. Only option E has the correct subnet mask listed, and 172.16.18.255 is a valid host.

19. D, E. The router's IP address on the E0 interface is 172.16.2.1/23, which is 255.255.254.0. This makes the third octet a block size of 2. The router's interface is in the 2.0 subnet, and the broadcast address is 3.255 because the next subnet is 4.0. The valid host range is 2.1 through 3.254. The router is using the first valid host address in the range.

20. C. To test the local stack on your host, ping the loopback interface of 127.0.0.1.

Chapter 5: Troubleshooting IP Addressing

1. B. With an incorrect gateway, Host A will not be able to communicate with the router or beyond the router but will be able to communicate within the subnet.

2. A. Pinging the remote computer would fail if any of the other tests fail.

3. C. When a ping to the local host IP address fails, you can assume the NIC is not functional.

4. C, D. If a ping to the local host succeeds, you can rule out IP stack or NIC failure.

5. A. The most likely problem if you can ping a computer by IP address but not by name is a failure of DNS.

6. D. When you issue the `ping` command, you are using the ICMP protocol.

7. B. The `traceroute` command displays the networks traversed on a path to a network destination.

8. C. The `ping` command tests connectivity to another station. The full command is shown below.

```
C:\>ping 172.16.10.2
Pinging 172.16.10.2 with 32 bytes of data:
Reply from 172.16.10.2: bytes=32 time<1ms TTL=128
Reply from 172.16.10.2: bytes=32 time<1ms TTL=128
Reply from 172.16.10.2: bytes=32 time<1ms TTL=128
Reply from 172.16.10.2: bytes=32 time<1ms TTL=128
Ping statistics for 172.16.10.2:
    Packets: Sent = 4, Received = 4, Lost = 0 (0% loss),
Approximate round trip times in milli-seconds:
    Minimum = 0ms, Maximum = 0ms, Average = 0ms
```

9. C. The `/all` switch must be added to the `ipconfig` command on a PC to verify DNS configuration.

10. A. `Ifconfig is` Used by MAC and Linux to get the IP address details of the local machine. Ipconfig is used by Windows.

Chapter 6: Cisco's Internetworking Operating System (IOS)

1. D. Typically, we'd see the input errors and CRC statistics increase with a duplex error, but it could be another Physical layer issue such as the cable might be receiving excessive interference or the network interface cards might have a failure. Typically, you can tell whether it is interference when the CRC and input errors output grow but the collision counters do not, which is the case with this question.

2. C. Once the IOS is loaded and up and running, the startup-config will be copied from NVRAM into RAM and from then on referred to as the running-config.

3. C, D. To configure SSH on your router, you need to set the `username` command, `the ip domain-name`, `login local`, and the `transport input ssh` under the VTY lines and the `crypto key` command. However, SSH version 2 is suggested but not required.

4. C. The `show controllers serial 0/0` command will show you whether either a DTE or DCE cable is connected to the interface. If it is a DCE connection, you need to add clocking with the clock rate command.

5.

Mode	Definition
user exec mode	Commands that affect the entire system
privileged exec mode	Commands that affect interfaces/processes only
Global configuration mode	Interactive configuration dialog
Specific configuration modes	Provides access to all other router commands
Setup mode	Limited to basic monitoring commands

User exec mode is limited to basic monitoring commands; privileged exec mode provides access to all other router commands. Specific configuration modes include the commands that affect a specific interface or process, while global configuration mode allows commands that affect the entire system. Setup mode is where you access the interactive configuration dialog.

6. B. The bandwidth shown is 100,000 Kbits a second, which is a Fast Ethernet port, or 100 Mbs.

7. B. From global configuration mode, use the `line vty 0 4` command to set all five default VTY lines. However, you would typically always set all lines, not just the defaults.

8. C. The enable secret password is case sensitive, so the second option is wrong. To set the enable secret password, use the `enable secret password` command from global configuration mode. This password is automatically encrypted.

9. C. The `banner motd` command sets a message of the day for administrators when they log in to a switch or router.

10. C. The prompts offered as options indicate the following modes:
`Switch(config)#` is global configuration mode.
`Switch>` is user mode.
`Switch#` is privileged mode.
`Switch(config-if)#` is interface configuration mode.

11. D. To copy the running-config to NVRAM so that it will be used if the router is restarted, use the `copy running-config startup-config` command in privileged mode (`copy run start` for short).

12. D. To allow a VTY (Telnet) session into your router, you must set the VTY password. Option C is wrong because it is setting the password on the wrong router. Notice that you have to set the password before you set the `login` command.

13. C. Wireless APs are very popular today and will be going away about the same time that rock n' roll does. The idea behind these devices (which are layer 2 bridge devices) is to connect wireless products to the wired Ethernet network. The wireless AP will create a single collision domain and is typically its own dedicated broadcast domain as well.

14. B. If an interface is shut down, the `show interface` command will show the interface as administratively down. (It is possible that no cable is attached, but you can't tell that from this message.)

15. C. With the `show interfaces` command, you can view the configurable parameters, get statistics for the interfaces on the switch, check for input and CRC errors, and verify if the interfaces are shut down.

16. C. If you delete the startup-config and reload the switch, the device will automatically enter setup mode. You can also type **`setup`** from privileged mode at any time.

17. D. You can view the interface statistics from user mode, but the command is `show interface fastethernet 0/0`.

18. B. The `% ambiguous command` error means that there is more than one possible show command that starts with *r*. Use a question mark to find the correct command.

19. B, D. The commands `show interfaces` and `show ip interface` will show you the layer 1 and 2 status and the IP addresses of your router's interfaces.

20. A. If you see that a serial interface and the protocol are both down, you have a Physical layer problem. If you see serial1 is up, line protocol is down, you are not receiving (Data Link) keepalives from the remote end.

Chapter 7: Managing a Cisco Internetwork

1. B. The IEEE created a new standardized discovery protocol called 802.1AB for Station and Media Access Control Connectivity Discovery. We'll just call it Link Layer Discovery Protocol (LLDP).

2. C. The `show processes` command (or `show processes cpu`) is a good tool for determining a given router's CPU utilization. When it is high, it is not a good time to execute a `debug` command.

3. B. The command `traceroute` (`trace`, for short), which can be issued from user mode or privileged mode, is used to find the path a packet takes through an internetwork and will also show you where the packet stops because of an error on a router.

4. C. Since the configuration looks correct, you probably didn't screw up the copy job. However, when you perform a copy from a network host to a router, the interfaces are automatically shut down and need to be manually enabled with the `no shutdown` command.

5. D. Specifying the address of the DHCP server allows the router to relay broadcast traffic destined for a DHCP server to that server.

6. C. Before you start to configure the router, you should erase the NVRAM with the `erase startup-config` command, and then reload the router using the `reload` command.

7. C. The `show cdp neighbors detail` command can be run on both routers and switches. It displays detailed information about each device connected to the device you're running the command on, including the IP address.

8. B. The Port ID column describes the interfaces on the remote device end of the connection.

9. B. From exec mode, you can enable syslog with the logging *ip address* command, where the IP address variable is the syslog server. Debugging or level 7 is the default facility level.

10. C. If you save a configuration and reload the router and it comes up either in setup mode or as a blank configuration, chances are that the configuration register setting is incorrect.

11. D. To keep open one or more Telnet sessions, use the Ctrl+Shift+6 and then X keystroke combination.

12. B, D. The best answers, the ones you need to remember, are that either an access control list is filtering the Telnet session or the VTY password is not set on the remote device.

13. A, D. The `show hosts` command provides information on temporary DNS entries and permanent name-to-address mappings created using the `ip host` command.

14. A, B, D. The `tracert` command is a Windows command and will not work on a router or switch! IOS uses the `traceroute` command.

15. D. The default Syslog facility level is debugging or level 7.

16. C. To see console messages through your Telnet session, you must enter the `terminal monitor` command.

17. D. Syslog has more detail available than SNMP, which is an older protocol.

18. E. Although option A is certainly the "best" answer, unfortunately option E will work just fine and your boss would probably prefer you to use the `show cdp neighbors detail` command.

19. D. To enable a device to be an NTP client, use the `ntp server` *`IP_address`* `version` *`version`* command at global configuration mode. That's all there is to it—assuming your NTP server is working, of course.

20. B, D. Logging trap 3 will send messages for errors, critical, and alerts:

```
alerts      Immediate action needed       (severity=1)
critical    Critical conditions           (severity=2)
errors      Error conditions              (severity=3)
```

Chapter 8: Managing Cisco Devices

1. B. The default configuration setting is 0x2102, which tells the router to load the IOS from flash and the configuration from NVRAM. The 0x2142 setting tells the router to bypass the configuration in NVRAM so you can perform password recovery.

2. E. To copy the IOS to a backup host, which is stored in flash memory by default, use the `copy flash tftp` command.

3. B. To install a new license on an ISR G2 router, use the `license install` *`url`* command.

4. C. The configuration register provides the boot commands, and 0x2101 tells the router to boot the mini-IOS, if found, and not to load a file from flash memory. Many newer routers do not have a mini-IOS, so as an alternative, the router would end up in ROM monitor mode if the mini-IOS were not found. However, option C is the best answer for this question.

5. B. The `show flash` command will provide you with the current IOS name and size and the size of flash memory.

6. C. Before you start to configure the router, you should erase the NVRAM with the `erase startup-config` command and then reload the router with the `reload` command.

7. D. The command copy `tftp flash` allows you to copy a new IOS into flash memory on your router.

8. C. The best answer is `show version`, which shows the IOS file running currently on your router. The `show flash` command shows you the contents of flash memory, not which file is running.

9. C. All Cisco routers have a default configuration register setting of 0x2102, which tells the router to load the IOS from flash memory and the configuration from NVRAM.

10. C. If you save a configuration and reload the router and it comes up either in setup mode or as a blank configuration, chances are the configuration register setting is incorrect.

11. D. The `License boot module` command installs a Right-To-Use license on a router.

12. A. The `show license` command determines the licenses that are active on your system. It also displays a group of lines for each feature in the currently running IOS image along with several status variables related to software activation and licensing, both licensed and unlicensed features.

13. B. The `show license feature` command allows you to view the technology package licenses and feature licenses that are supported on your router along with several status variables related to software activation and licensing, both licensed and unlicensed features.

14. C. The `show license udi` command displays the unique device identifier (UDI) of the router, which comprises the product ID (PID) and serial number of the router.

15. D. The `show version` command displays various information about the current IOS version, including the licensing details at the end of the command's output.

16. C. The `license save flash` command allows you to back up your license to flash memory.

17. C. The `show version` command provides the current configuration register setting.

18. C, D. The two steps to remove a license are to first disable the technology package and then to clear the license.

19. B, D, E. Before backing up an IOS image to a laptop directly connected to a router's Ethernet port, make sure that the TFTP server software is running on your laptop, that the Ethernet cable is a crossover cable, that the laptop is in the same subnet as the router's Ethernet port, and then you can use the `copy flash tftp` command from your laptop.

20. C. The default configuration setting of 0x2102 tells the router to look in NVRAM for the boot sequence.

Chapter 9: IP Routing

1. `show ip route`. The `ip route` command is used to display the routing table of a router.

2. B. In the new 15 IOS code, Cisco defines a different route called a local route. Each has a /32 prefix defining a route just for the one address.

3. A, B. Although option D almost seems right, it is not; the mask is the mask used on the remote network, not the source network. Since there is no number at the end of the static route, it is using the default administrative distance of 1.

4. C, F. The switches are not used as either a default gateway or other destination. Switches have nothing to do with routing. It is very important to remember that the destination MAC address will always be the router's interface. The destination address of a frame, from HostA, will be the MAC address of the Fa0/0 interface of RouterA. The destination address of a packet will be the IP address of the network interface card (NIC) of the HTTPS server. The destination port number in the segment header will have a value of 443 (HTTPS).

5. B. This mapping was learned dynamically, which means it was learned through ARP.

6. B. Hybrid protocols use aspects of both distance vector and link state—for example, EIGRP. However, note that Cisco typically just calls EIGRP an advanced distance-vector routing protocol. Do not be mislead by the way the question is worded. Yes, I know that MAC addresses are not in a packet. You must read the question carefully to understand what it is really asking.

7. A. Since the destination MAC address is different at each hop, it must keep changing. The IP address, which is used for the routing process, does not.

8. B, E. Classful routing means that all hosts in the internetwork use the same mask and that only default masks are in use. Classless routing means that you can use variable length subnet masks (VLSMs).

9. B, C. The distance-vector routing protocol sends its complete routing table out of all active interfaces at periodic time intervals. Link-state routing protocols send updates containing the state of their own links to all routers in the internetwork.

10. C. This is how most people see routers, and certainly they could do this type of plain ol' packet switching in 1990 when Cisco released their very first router and traffic was seriously slow, but not in today's networks! This process involves looking up every destination in the routing table and finding the exit interface for every packet.

11. A, C. The S* shows that this is a candidate for default route and that it was configured manually.

12. B. RIP has an administrative distance (AD) of 120, while EIGRP has an administrative distance of 90, so the router will discard any route with a higher AD than 90 to that same network.

13. D. Recovery from a lost route requires manual intervention by a human to replace the lost route.

14. A. RIPv1 and RIPv2 only use the lowest hop count to determine the best path to a remote network.

15. A. Since the routing table shows no route to the 192.168.22.0 network, the router will discard the packet and send an ICMP destination unreachable message out of interface FastEthernet 0/0, which is the source LAN from which the packet originated.

16. C. Static routes have an administrative distance of 1 by default. Unless you change this, a static route will always be used over any other dynamically learned route. EIGRP has an administrative distance of 90, and RIP has an administrative distance of 120, by default.

17. C. BGP is the only EGP listed.

18. D. Recovery from a lost route requires manual intervention by a human to replace the lost route. The advantages are less overhead on the router and network, as well as more security.

19. C. The `show ip interface brief` command displays a concise summary of the interfaces.

20. B. The 150 at the end changes the default administrative distance (AD) of 1 to 150.

Chapter 10: Open Shortest Path First

1. B. Only the EIGRP routes will be placed in the routing table because it has the lowest administrative distance (AD), which is always used before metrics.

2. A, B, C. Any router that is a member of two areas must be an area border router, or ABR.

3. A, C. The process ID for OSPF on a router is only locally significant, and you can use the same number on each router, or each router can have a different number—it just doesn't matter. The numbers you can use are from 1 to 65,535. Don't get this confused with area numbers, which can be from 0 to 4.2 billion.

4. B. The router ID (RID) is an IP address used to identify the router. It need not and should not match.

5. C. The router ID (RID) is an IP address used to identify the router. Cisco chooses the router ID by using the highest IP address of all configured loopback interfaces. If no loopback interfaces are configured with addresses, OSPF will choose the highest IP address of all active physical interfaces.

6. A. The administrator typed in the wrong wildcard mask configuration. The wildcard should have been 0.0.0.255 or even 0.255.255.255.

7. A. A dash (-) in the State column indicates no DR election, because they are not required on a point-to-point link such as a serial connection.

8. D. By default, the administrative distance of OSPF is 110.

9. A. Hello packets are addressed to multicast address 224.0.0.5.

10. A. The `show ip ospf neighbor` command displays all interface-related neighbor information. This output shows the DR and BDR (unless your router is the DR or BDR), the RID of all directly connected neighbors, and the IP address and name of the directly connected interface.

11. A. 224.0.0.6 is used on broadcast networks to reach the DR and BDR.

12. D. The Hello and Dead timers must be set the same on two routers on the same link; otherwise, they will not form an adjacency (relationship). The default timers for OSPF are 10 seconds for the Hello timer and 40 seconds for the Dead timer.

13. A, C, D, E. A designated router is elected on broadcast networks. Each OSPF router maintains an identical database describing the AS topology. A Hello protocol provides dynamic neighbor discovery. A routing table contains only the best routes. EIGRP routers must all have the same AS number, not OSPF.

14. `passive-interface fastEthernet 0/1`. The command `passive-interface fastEthernet 0/1` will disable OSPF on the specified interface only.

15. B, G. To enable OSPF, you must first start OSPF using a process ID. The number is irrelevant; simply choose a number from 1 to 65,535. After starting the OSPF process, you must configure the interfaces on which to activate OSPF using the `network` command with wildcards and the specification of an area. Option F is wrong because there must be a space after the parameter area and before you list the area number.

16. A. The default OSPF interface priority is 1, and the highest interface priority determines the designated router (DR) for a subnet. The output indicates that the router with a router ID of 192.168.45.2 is currently the backup designated router (BDR) for the segment, which indicates that another router became the DR. It can then be assumed that the DR router has an interface priority higher than 2. (The router serving the DR function is not present in the truncated sample output.)

17. A, B, C. OSPF is created in a hierarchical design, unlike the flat design of RIP. This decreases routing overhead, speeds up convergence, and confines network instability to a single area of the network.

18. `show ip ospf interface`. The `show ip ospf interface` command displays all interface-related OSPF information. Data is displayed about OSPF information for all OSPF-enabled interfaces or for specified interfaces.

19. A. LSA packets are used to update and maintain the topological database.

20. B. When the OSPF process starts, the highest IP address on any active interface will be the router ID (RID) of the router. If you have a loopback interface configured (logical interface), then that will override the interface IP address and become the RID of the router automatically.

Chapter 11: Enhanced IGRP

1. B. Only the EIGRP routes will be placed in the routing table because it has the lowest AD and that is always used before metrics.

2. A, C. EIGRP maintains three tables in RAM: neighbor, topology, and routing. The neighbor and topology tables are built and maintained with the use of Hello and update packets.

3. B. EIGRP does use reported distance, or AD, to tell neighbor routers the cost to get to a remote network. This router will send the FD to the neighbor router and the neighbor router will add the cost to get to this router plus the AD to find the true FD.

4. E. Successor routes are going to be in the routing table because they are the best path to a remote network. However, the topology table has a link to each and every network, so the best answer is topology table and routing table. Any secondary route to a remote network is considered a feasible successor, and those routes are found only in the topology table and used as backup routes in case of primary route failure.

5. C. Any secondary route to a remote network is considered a feasible successor, and those routes are found only in the topology table and used as backup routes in case of primary route failure. You can see the topology table with the `show ip eigrp topology` command.

6. B, C, E. EIGRP and EIGRPv6 routers can use the same RID, unlike OSPF, and this can be set with the `eigrp router-id` command. Also a `variance` can be set to provide unequal-cost load balancing, along with the `maximum-paths` command to set the amount of load-balanced paths.

7. C. There were two successor routes, so by default, EIGRP was load balancing out s0/0 and s0/1. When s0/0 goes down, EIGRP will just keep forwarding traffic out the second link s0/1. s0/0 will be removed from the routing table.

8. D. To enable EIGRPv6 on a router interface, use the command `ipv6 eigrp` as on individual interfaces that will be part of the EIGRPv6 process.

9. C. The path to network 10.10.50.0 out serial0/0 is more than two times the current FD, so I used a `variance 3` command to load balance unequal-cost links three times the FD.

10. B, C. First, a maximum hop count of 16 only is associated with RIP, and EIGRP never broadcasts, so we can eliminate A and D as options. Feasible successors are backup routes and stored in the topology table, so that is correct, and if no feasible successor is located, the EIGRP will flood its neighbors asking for a new path to network 10.10.10.0.

11. D. The `show ip eigrp neighbors` command allows you to check the IP addresses as well as the retransmit interval and queue counts for the neighbors that have established an adjacency.

12. C, E. For EIGRP to form an adjacency with a neighbor, the AS numbers must match, and the metric K values must match as well. Also, option F could cause the problem; we can see if it is causing a problem from the output given.

13. A, D. Successor routes are the routes picked from the topology table as the best route to a remote network, so these are the routes that IP uses in the routing table to forward traffic to a remote destination. The topology table contains any route that is not as good as the successor route and is considered a feasible successor, or backup route. Remember that all routes are in the topology table, even successor routes.

14. A, B. Option A will work because the router will change the network statement to 10.0.0.0 since EIGRP uses classful addresses by default. Therefore, it isn't technically a wrong answer, but please understand why it is correct for this question. The 10.255.255.64/27 subnet address can be configured with wildcards just as we use with OSPF and ACLs. The /27 is a block of 32, so the wildcard in the fourth octet will be 31. The wildcard of 0.0.0.0 is wrong because this is a network address, not a host address, and the 0.0.0.15 is wrong because that is only a block of 16 and would only work if the mask were a /28.

15. C. To troubleshoot adjacencies, you need to check the AS numbers, the K values, networks, passive interfaces, and ACLs.

16. C. EIGRP and EIGRPv6 will load balance across 4 equal cost-paths by default but can be configured to load-balance across equal- and unequal-cost paths, up to 32 with IOS 15.0 code.

17. B, E. EIGRP must be enabled with an AS number from global configuration mode with the `ipv6 router eigrp` *as* command if you need to set the RID or other global parameters. Instead of configuring EIGRP with the network command as with EIGRP, EIGRPv6 is configured on a per-interface basis with the `ipv6 eigrp` *as* command.

18. C. There isn't a lot to go on from with the output, but that might make this easier than if there were a whole page of output. Because s0/0/2 has lowest FD and AD, that would become the successor route. For a route to become a feasible successor, its reported distance must be lower than the FD of the current successor route, so C is our best answer based on what we can see.

19. C. The network in the diagram is considered a discontiguous network because you have one classful address subnetted and separated by another classful address. Only RIPv2, OSPF, and EIGRP can work with discontiguous networks, but RIPv2 and EIGRP won't work by default (except for routers running the new 15.0 code). You must use the `no auto-summary` command under the routing protocol configuration. There is a passive interface on RouterB, but this is not on an interface between RouterA and RouterB and won't stop an adjacency.

20. A, B, C, D. Here are the documented steps that Cisco says to check when you have an adjacency issue:

- Interfaces between the devices are down.
- The two routers have mismatching EIGRP AS numbers.
- Proper interfaces are not enabled for the EIGRP process.

- An interface is configured as passive.
- K values are mismatched.
- EIGRP authentication is misconfigured.

Chapter 12: Layer 2 Switching

1. A. Layer 2 switches and bridges are faster than routers because they don't take up time looking at the Network Layer header information. They do make use of the Data Link layer information.

2. `mac address-table static aaaa.bbbb.cccc vlan 1 int fa0/7`. You can set a static MAC address in the MAC address table and when done, it will appear as a static entry in the table.

3. B, D, E. Since the MAC address is not present in the table, it will send the frame out of all ports in the same VLAN with the exception of the port on which it was received.

4. `show mac address-table`. This command displays the forward filter table, also called a content addressable memory (CAM) table.

5.

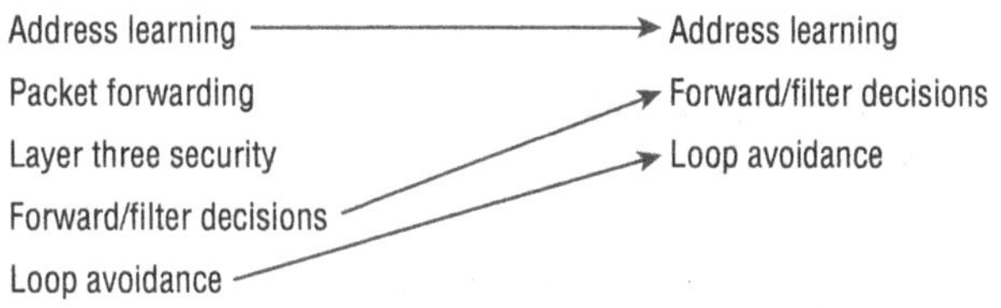

The three functions are address learning, forward/filter decisions, and loop avoidance.

6. A, D. In the above output, you can see that the port is in `Secure-shutdown` mode and the light for the port would be amber. To enable the port again, you'd need to do the following:

```
S3(config-if)#shutdown
S3(config-if)#no shutdown
```

7. `switchport port-security maximum 2`. The maximum setting of 2 means only two MAC addresses can be used on that port; if the user tries to add another host on that segment, the switch port will take the action specified in the port-security violation command.

8. B. The `switchport port-security` command enables port security, which is a prerequisite for the other commands to function.

9. B. Gateway redundancy is not an issue addressed by STP.

10. A. If no loop avoidance schemes are put in place, the switches will flood broadcasts endlessly throughout the internetwork. This is sometimes referred to as a broadcast storm.

11. B, C. Shutdown and protect mode will alert you via SNMP that a violation has occurred on a port.

12. Spanning tree protocol (STP). STP is a switching loop avoidance scheme use by switches.

13. `ip default-gateway`. If you want to manage your switches from outside your LAN, you need to set a default gateway on the switches, just as you would with a host.

14. C. The IP address is configured under a logical interface, called a management domain or VLAN 1.

15. B. The `show port-security interface` command displays the current port security and status of a switch port, as in this sample output:

```
Switch# show port-security interface fastethernet0/1
Port Security: Enabled
Port status: SecureUp
Violation mode: Shutdown
Maximum MAC Addresses: 2
Total MAC Addresses: 2
Configured MAC Addresses: 2
Aging Time: 30 mins
Aging Type: Inactivity
SecureStatic address aging: Enabled
Security Violation count: 0
```

16. `switchport port-security mac-address sticky`. Issuing the `switchport port-security mac-address sticky` command will allow a switch to save a dynamically learned MAC address in the running-configuration of the switch, which prevents the administrator from having to document or configure specific MAC addresses.

17. B, D. To limit connections to a specific host, you should configure the MAC address of the host as a static entry associated with the port, although be aware that this host can still connect to any other port, but no other port can connect to f0/3, in this example. Another solution would be to configure port security to accept traffic only from the MAC address of the host. By default, an unlimited number of MAC addresses can be learned on a single switch port, whether it is configured as an access port or a trunk port. Switch ports can be secured by defining one or more specific MAC addresses that should be allowed to connect and by defining violation policies (such as disabling the port) to be enacted if additional hosts try to gain a connection.

18. D. The command statically defines the MAC address of 00c0.35F0.8301 as an allowed host on the switch port. By default, an unlimited number of MAC addresses can be learned on a single switch port, whether it is configured as an access port or a trunk port. Switch

ports can be secured by defining one or more specific MAC addresses that should be allowed to connect and violation policies (such as disabling the port) if additional hosts try to gain a connection.

19. D. You would not make the port a trunk. In this example, this switchport is a member of one VLAN. However, you can configure port security on a trunk port, but again, not valid for this question.

20. `switchport port-security violation shutdown`. This command is used to set the reaction of the switch to a port violation of shutdown.

Chapter 13: VLANs and Inter-VLAN Routing

1. D. Here's a list of ways VLANs simplify network management:
   - Network adds, moves, and changes are achieved with ease by just configuring a port into the appropriate VLAN.
   - A group of users that need an unusually high level of security can be put into its own VLAN so that users outside of the VLAN can't communicate with them.
   - As a logical grouping of users by function, VLANs can be considered independent from their physical or geographic locations.
   - VLANs greatly enhance network security if implemented correctly.
   - VLANs increase the number of broadcast domains while decreasing their size.

2. `ip routing`. Routing must be enabled on the layer 3 switch.

3. C. VLANs can span across multiple switches by using trunk links, which carry traffic for multiple VLANs.

4. B. While in all other cases access ports can be a member of only one VLAN, most switches allow you to add a second VLAN to an access port on a switch port for your voice traffic; it's called the voice VLAN. The voice VLAN used to be called the auxiliary VLAN, which allowed it to be overlaid on top of the data VLAN, enabling both types of traffic through the same port.

5. A. Yes, you have to do a `no shutdown` on the VLAN interface.

6. C. Unlike ISL, which encapsulates the frame with control information, 802.1q inserts an 802.1q field along with tag control information.

7. D. Instead of using a router interface for each VLAN, you can use one FastEthernet interface and run ISL or 802.1q trunking. This allows all VLANs to communicate through one interface. Cisco calls this a "router on a stick."

8. `switchport access vlan 2`. This command is executed under the interface (switch port) that is being placed in the VLAN.

9. `show vlan`. After creating the VLANs that you want, you can use the `show vlan` command to check them out.

10. B. The encapsulation command specifying the VLAN for the subinterface must be present under both subinterfaces.

11. A. With a multilayer switch, enable IP routing and create one logical interface for each VLAN using the `interface vlan number` command—and you're now doing inter-VLAN routing on the backplane of the switch!

12. A. Ports Fa0/15–18 are not present in any VLANs. They are trunk ports.

13. C. Untagged frames are members of the native VLAN, which by default is VLAN 1.

14. `sh interfaces fastEthernet 0/15 switchport`. This `show interfaces` *`interface`* `switchport` command shows the administrative mode of dynamic desirable and that the port is a trunk port, DTP was used to negotiate the frame tagging method of ISL, and the native VLAN is the default of 1.

15. C. VLANs are *not* location dependent and can span to multiple switches using trunk links. Moreover, they can be subnets of major networks.

16. B. The host's default gateway should be set to the IP address of the subinterface that is associated with the VLAN the host is a member of—in this case, VLAN 2.

17. C. Frame tagging is used when VLAN traffic travels over a trunk link. Trunk links carry frames for multiple VLANs. Therefore, frame tags are used for identification of frames from different VLANs.

18. `vlan 2`. To configure VLANs on a Cisco Catalyst switch, use the global config `vlan` command.

19. B. 802.1q uses the native VLAN.

20. `switchport nonegotiate`. You can use this command only when the interface switchport mode is access or trunk. You must manually configure the neighboring interface as a trunk interface to establish a trunk link.

Chapter 14: Cloud and Virtual Private Networks

1. A, D. GRE tunnels have the following characteristics: GRE uses a protocol-type field in the GRE header so any layer 3 protocol can be used through the tunnel; GRE is stateless and has no flow control; GRE offers no security; and GRE creates additional overhead for tunneled packets—at least 24 bytes.

2. C. If you receive this flapping message when you configure your GRE tunnel, it means you used your tunnel interface address instead of the tunnel destination address.

3. D. The `show running-config interface tunnel 0` command will show you the configuration of the interface, not the status of the tunnel.

4. C. The `show interfaces tunnel 0` command shows the configuration settings and the interface status as well as the IP address and tunnel source and destination address.

5. B. All web browsers support Secure Sockets Layer (SSL), and SSL VPNs are known as "web VPNs." Remote users can use their browser to create an encrypted connection, and they don't need to install any software. GRE doesn't encrypt the data.

6. A, C, E. VPNs can provide good security by using advanced encryption and authentication protocols, which help protect your network from unauthorized access. By connecting the corporate remote offices to their closest Internet provider and then creating a VPN tunnel with encryption and authentication, you'll gain a huge savings over opting for traditional leased point-to-point lines. VPNs scale very well to quickly bring up new offices or have mobile users connect securely while traveling or when connecting from home. VPNs are very compatible with broadband technologies.

7. A, D. Internet providers who have an existing layer 2 network may choose to use layer 2 VPNs instead of the other common layer 3 MPLS VPN. Virtual Private Lan Switch (VPLS) and Virtual Private Wire Service (VPWS) are two technologies that provide layer 2 MPLS VPNs.

8. D. IPsec is an industry-wide standard suite of protocols and algorithms that allows for secure data transmission over an IP-based network that functions at the layer 3 Network layer of the OSI model.

9. C. A VPN allows or describes the creation of private networks across the Internet, enabling privacy and tunneling of TCP/IP protocols. A VPN can be set up across any type of link.

10. B, C. Layer 2 MPLS VPNs and the more popular Layer 3 MPLS VPN are services provided to customers and managed by the provider.

11. A. A site-to-site VPN allows offices in multiple fixed locations to establish secure connections with each other over a public network such as the Internet. A site-to-site VPN means that two sites create a VPN tunnel by encrypting and sending data between two devices. IPsec defines one set of rules for creating a site-to-site VPN.

12. D. *Remote-access VPNs* allow remote users like telecommuters to securely access the corporate network wherever and whenever they need to.

13. C. *Site-to-site VPNs* use ESP, and ESP does a lot for you! It provides confidentiality, data origin authentication, connectionless integrity, anti-replay service, and limited traffic-flow confidentiality by defeating traffic flow analysis—which is almost as good as AH without the possible encryption!

14. D. The IPsec encryption mode that is appropriate when the destination of a packet differs from the security termination point is tunnel.

15. C. In the context of VPNs, when the source and destination IP address portion of a packet is unencrypted while the actual payload of the packet is encrypted, it is using transport mode encryption. Transport mode encrypts only the IP packet's data portion (payload), leaving the header (which includes the source and destination IP addresses) unencrypted. This is often used in site-to-site VPNs where the devices at the ends of the VPN tunnel are responsible for the IP header information.

16. D. IPsec is a protocol suite used to provide secure communication over IP networks. It can be used to encrypt and authenticate IP packets, ensuring the confidentiality, integrity, and authenticity of the transmitted data.

    While IPsec can also support multicast and broadcast traffic, the term "pure IPsec" generally refers to the use of IPsec in a point-to-point unicast communication scenario.

    Pure IPsec is typically used to secure unicast traffic between two endpoints. Unicast traffic refers to one-to-one communication between a specific sender and receiver. In this case, it would involve unicast messages from a host at a remote site to a server at headquarters.

17. C. A private cloud refers to cloud infrastructure that is hosted and managed within a company's own data center, offering more control and security compared to public cloud services.

18. B. Public cloud services provide resources that are typically accessible over the Internet, using public IP addresses. These services are hosted by cloud providers like AWS or Microsoft Azure.

19. C. IaaS provides the infrastructure (virtual machines, storage, and networking) on which users can deploy and manage their operating systems and applications.

20. B. PaaS simplifies the deployment and management of applications by taking care of the underlying infrastructure and operating system, allowing users to focus on developing and managing their applications.

Chapter 15: Introduction to Artificial Intelligence and Machine Learning

1. C. Narrow AI, also known as weak AI, is designed to excel at a specific task or a limited set of tasks. It operates within predefined rules and lacks the ability to generalize knowledge beyond its specific domain.

2. B. Generalized AI, also known as strong AI, is a theoretical concept that aims to replicate human-level intelligence across any task. This type of AI does not yet exist, whereas narrow AI (weak AI) is currently in use.

3. C. Machine learning enables systems to learn patterns from data and make decisions without being explicitly programmed for every scenario. The system improves its performance as it processes more data.

4. C. A chatbot is an example of narrow AI because it is designed to perform a specific task—engaging in conversation—within a predefined set of rules and parameters.

5. C. Predictive AI analyzes historical data to identify patterns and trends, which it uses to forecast future events. This is commonly applied in scenarios such as network monitoring or traffic prediction.

6. C. Neural networks, particularly deep-learning models, are well-suited for complex tasks like image and speech recognition due to their ability to learn from large datasets and identify intricate patterns.

7. C. Decision trees are known for their simplicity and interpretability, but they can become computationally demanding if they grow too deep, leading to overfitting and inefficiency.

8. B. Rule-based systems operate based on a set of explicit "if/then" statements that dictate the system's response to specific conditions. This makes them predictable and easy to understand.

9. B. Limited-memory AI can learn from historical data and adapt to new threats. An intrusion detection system that evolves based on past data is a practical example of limited-memory AI in action.

10. B. NLP is a branch of AI focused on enabling machines to comprehend, interpret, and generate human language, facilitating more natural interactions between humans and machines.

11. C. Predictive AI can forecast future events based on historical data. In this case, it could predict network congestion and reroute traffic to maintain performance.

12. B. AI-generated hallucinations occur when the AI fabricates information or produces incorrect outputs. Therefore, it's crucial to verify AI-generated content, especially in technical fields.

13. C. RAG enhances AI performance by allowing it to access and incorporate the latest data, ensuring that generated outputs are accurate and contextually relevant.

14. C. Rule-based systems excel in environments where tasks are straightforward and decision criteria are clearly defined, such as compliance checks or automated responses.

15. C. Neural networks, particularly deep ones, are prone to overfitting if they focus too much on details in the training data, leading to poor generalization to new data.

16. B. Decision trees provide a clear, interpretable structure that makes it easy to understand how decisions are made, which is especially valuable in scenarios requiring transparency.

17. C. Theory-of-mind AI is a theoretical category of AI that would involve understanding and responding to human emotions and social interactions. It is not yet realized in practical applications.

18. B. Prompt engineering involves carefully crafting input prompts to guide generative AI toward producing the desired and most accurate outputs, improving the effectiveness of AI interactions.

19. B. Overfitting occurs when an AI model learns not just the relevant patterns but also the noise in the training data, leading to poor performance on new, unseen data.

20. B. Generative AI can assist network engineers by automating routine tasks, such as generating configuration scripts, troubleshooting steps, or documentation, and streamlining workflows.

Index

B

C

D

E

F

G

H

I

J

K

L

M

N

O

P

Q

R

S

T

U

V

W–Z